CEDAR CREST COLLEGE LIBRARY
ALLENTOWN, PA. 18104

D1253560

Wide Screen Movies

Wide Screen Movies

A History and Filmography of Wide Gauge Filmmaking

by
Robert E. Carr
and
R.M. Hayes

McFarland & Company, Inc., Publishers
Jefferson, North Carolina, and London

Ref
TR
855
C37

Frontispiece: Special photographic effects supervisor John P. Fulton (left) and producer-director Cecil B. DeMille confer over a trick sequence in *The Ten Commandments,* the first of several biblical epics produced and roadshown in wide gauge format. The huge VistaVision camera (numbered MVV-5) is one of the modified vertical magazine units that replaced the original "Butterfly VV" units, which had the film magazines mounted on their sides (thus looking like an enormous butterfly).

Library of Congress Cataloguing-in-Publication Data

Carr, Robert E.
  Wide screen movies.

  Filmography: p. 259.
  Includes index.
  1. Wide screen processes (Cinematography)—History.
I. Hayes, R.M., 1947–   . II. Title.
TR855.C37 1988   778.5′3   86-43093

ISBN 0-89950-242-3 (acid-free natural paper)

© 1988 Robert E. Carr and R.M. Hayes. All rights reserved.

Manufactured in the United States of America.

McFarland & Company, Inc., Publishers
  Box 611, Jefferson, North Carolina 28640

This book is dedicated to the Spirit of Showmanship as demonstrated by three filmmakers who knew just how good movies could look and sound:

Samuel Bronston • Lowell Thomas • Michael Todd

and to our families.

DISCARDED

Acknowledgments

The authors would like to extend their deep appreciation to the many individuals, companies and organizations who made invaluable contributions to this book. Without their interest and assistance this work could not have been produced as it has, and the authors would have been in the position of simply reproducing generally accepted film history instead of the facts and specifics:

Elizabeth Allen, American Cinema Editors, Inc. (ACE), American Film Institute (AFI), American Society of Cinematographers (ASC), Batjac Productions, Inc., Glen Berggren, Willem Bouwmeester, Ridgeway Callow, Enos "Yakima" Canutt, Cinerama, Inc., Cinerama Productions, Cinerama Releasing Corporation (CRC), William H. Clothier, Chris J. Condon, George Condon, Directors Guild of America (DGA), Walt Disney Archives (Walt Disney Productions), Sally Dundas, C. Robert Fine, Patrick Roper Ford, Hugo W. Friedhofer, Bill Goff, Alison Goodsall, George R. Groves, Wolf C. Hartwig, Stuart L. Hass, S. Ross Hering, Hungarian Film Institute (Magyar Filmtudományi Intézetés Filmarchivum), Hungarofilm, János Huszár, Imax Systems Corporation, International Cinerama Society (ICS), MLF Productions, Inc., Murray Lerner, Eve Miller, István Nemeskürty, A. Novikov, Tom Parris, Rapid-Film GmbH, Hazard E. Reeves, Ken Reeves, Charles "Bad Chuck" Roberson, Patrick Robertson, Victoria Silliphant, Society of Motion Picture and Television Art Directors (Local 876, IATSE), Lia Somogyi, Sovexportfilm, Jorge Stahl, Jr., StereoVision International, Inc., John Sturges, Keith H. Swadkins, M.B.K.S.T.S., Lowell Thomas, Jerry Vandeventer, King Vidor, Lothrop B. Worth, Hoyle Yarbrough, Alfred C. Ybarra, and many others.

Table of Contents

Foreword

The book you hold is the result of years of research. It was assembled to meet two basic purposes: to provide a concise, yet detailed, history of wide screen films and technologies and to be a general reference source for information on the actual films.

This book covers virtually every item of importance in wide screen technology and history, excluding only those extremely minute details that could not be unearthed or were not significant in our level of discussion. The information given for the various film systems is as accurate as possible. While every reasonable attempt was made to insure that all information was indisputable, the sad fact is that on more than one occasion reliable sources conflicted. This was usually on the tiniest detail—such as the difference in an aperture—but still it did occur. In such cases it was necessary to accept one source or another, and for that reason the reader may find (though rarely, we hope) a bit of data that conflicts with something he has read elsewhere. Naturally, anytime such a choice had to be made we hope we selected the correct one. Even so, what differences we encountered were such minor conflicts that simply mentioning the fact they existed is probably almost pointless.

Although we have covered every special film technique you are likely to encounter (or have encountered), we have not included every process utilized. There is always going to exist somewhere a novelty system for making or exhibiting films, but its use will be limited to special exhibits. Nothing given general or even rather limited commercial theatrical use has been overlooked. We have not included 3D in this book except as a mention here and there. The filmography does include some 3D films because of their use with wide screen. Stereoscopics is another book.

The reader is forewarned that the text is often out of chronological order. This might, on occasion, cause some confusion. We felt it best, however, to keep all related processes grouped together and to cover in one area the complete history of a particular format. Thus the reader will sometimes encounter mention of one process in relation to another without having been filled in on one of the processes. In such cases we hope any problems the reader has will be minor and that a quick reference to another section of the book will eliminate any confusion.

Because stereophonic sound and the wide screen have been so closely involved with each other, and because stereo is now the standard for movies, home videos, and television, a brief section is devoted to special sound processes. For the reader interested in surround sound we have included information which can be used to add a great deal of enjoyment to the home entertainment facility.

For those who remember Cinerama, Todd-AO, etc., and for those who wish they could have been there: This book has been created for you. "Movies" are just "films" now and the great 'scopes, 'visions and 'ramas are gone. We really miss them.

I. Early Wide Screen

In the Beginning

In 1907 an international agreement was reached that established 35mm as the standard commercial film gauge. Further, an aspect ratio of 1.33×1 was decided upon, with a four-perforation pulldown per frame. This was the format "developed" by W.K.L. Dickson in early 1891 for Thomas Edison's Kinetoscope viewing device, commonly called a "peepshow." (Actually, Edison stole his 35mm camera design from Frenchman Etienne Jules Marey's Chronophotographe, which was patented on October 3, 1890!) Since most films were made in the United States, it was only practical that the world at large accept the Edison standards. But by 1907 movies were no longer peepshow novelties; they were projected images on screens. A screened image of three to four proportions was adequate only for the small screen theaters that then appeared everywhere. Soon better projectors, throwing larger and brighter images onto bigger screens, made the almost square picture totally incapable of delivering the goods. Somewhat foolishly, the then-established industry held onto an already outdated format. They would continue by and large to stick to the "block ratio" until the fear of television caused a major overhaul.

Possibly Edison would have selected a wider gauge film or a narrower frame (perhaps three-perfs-per-frame pulldown) on the 35mm stock had he foreseen big and wide screen projection. But he seems to have had little foresight, being more the front for a consortium of inventors, engineers, and developers than anything else. He certainly did not create many of the items credited to him, and his involvement in the much documented Patents War clearly shows his interests were financial, not creative. (For example, Edison had his staff produce a device for synchronizing sound to film, yet discarded it when it didn't add more money to his already stuffed pockets.) His policy was very definite: Do no more than necessary to turn a buck.

Why others didn't totally sidestep the Edison standard is understandable. They, too, tended to be interested only in the money to be collected at the box office. There was no competition and, in the early years of the industry, no reason to create any. That the audience was new to the whole "picture-going experience" was enough for the vast majority of inventors — though not, thank goodness, for the real fathers of cinema.

1

Auguste and Louis Lumiere of France have often been credited with the first wide screen films. No one can deny their place as major pioneers in cinema history. Under them the first quality projectors were produced for big screen theaters. They experimented in color, 3D, extremely large screen projection and wide screen. But they did not make the first wide screen films, nor did they even develop a system that could truly be called wide screen. Any work along those lines followed the efforts of others.

In July 1896 Birt Acres of Barnet, England, shot footage of Henry Regatta on 70mm film using a ratio wider than 1.33 × 1. Since wide screen is any ratio wider than 1.33 × 1, this certainly was one of the first uses of oversize film to produce a large, wide image. But, accepted film history aside, it was not actually the first use of oversize film. In 1895 American Mutoscope and Biograph shot 62mm footage using a six-perf pulldown and a 1.36 × 1 ratio. Strictly speaking, this was a wide gauge, wide screen image. The difference in 1.33 × 1 and 1.36 × 1, however, is so slight that it would not have been possible to perceive the projected image as any wider than standard 35mm. (In fact, 16mm projectors employ a 1.37 × 1 aperture today, and they are definitely not projecting a wide screen image.) The exact ratio of Acres' film is unknown, but it seems unlikely that it would have exceeded 1.40 × 1 or so, and it probably was less than that. Acres' film was shown in London at the Palace Theatre on March 17, 1897. It was projected by a machine built in Canatosta, New York, by Herman Caster. Acres may have made other short scenes in 70mm, but if so they apparently were never exhibited.

Others were experimenting with large film about the same time. In France, Georges Demeny used 60mm film with a four-perf pulldown and a 1.22 × 1 ratio for his Chronophotographe (named after the Marey camera assembly, and possibly actually built by Marey) in 1895. Also in 1895, American Mutoscope and Biograph shot footage on film 2 7/8 inches wide with a 1.19 × 1 ratio. Britain's Prestwich made a film for Burton Holmes using 2 3/8-inch film with a 1.31 × 1 ratio and a four-perf pulldown in the late 1890s. These were experiments only and received little or no public exhibition.

In 1897, in the United States, Veriscope Company exhibited a true wide screen, wide gauge short. It was a documentary of the Corbett-Fitzsimmons prizefight filmed by Enoch J. Rector on 63mm Eastman-made film, using a five-perf pulldown and a 1.65 × 1 ratio. Regardless of prior claims, this must truly be considered the first of its type for public exhibition. Unfortunately none of this — and there were several other long-forgotten oddball films made around the same period — had any effect on the emerging film industry. The film standard was going to be 35mm, and no amount of tinkering by fringe individuals would alter that fact. (It should be noted that far more work was done on undersize film than oversize formats. Movies were then being shown on very small screens, after all.) Movie theaters grew in size and so did their screens. But the 1907 standard was to be adhered to for many years.

The Big Screen Arrives

In 1923 the Italian public was treated to the first showing of a commercial feature in wide screen, *Il sacco di Roma*. Actually only one sequence, presumably the climax, was in Panoramico Alberini, a five-perf-per-frame, 2.20 × 1 70mm process identical to that now employed worldwide. It was developed, possibly as early as 1914, by Prof. Filoteo Alberini and apparently was never used again. In 1928 Alberini would team with Englishman George Hill and attempt to sell another wide screen format in Great Britain and the United States without success. This second process would be adopted by Paramount in the early fifties under the trade name Vista-Vision. (See Chapter 4.)

The Americans were also busy in 1923 with wide gauge wide screen. Backed by Essanay Corporation, George K. Spoor and P. John Berggren developed a 63mm system they called Natural Vision (not to be confused with the Natural Vision 3-Dimension process of the fifties). Although it was promoted as stereoscopic, it in fact was not 3D but wide screen. (Claims that wide screen images were three-dimensional would really get out of hand during the first few months after CinemaScope's birth.) Essanay, no longer involved in production, did nothing with the system, and Spoor and Berggren were left to their own means. They formed Natural Vision Pictures (not to be confused with the later 3D company of that name) and produced two short films, *Rollercoaster Ride* (which would be duplicated in *This Is Cinerama*) and *Niagara Falls*. Both received limited showings in 1926. The latter film was also promoted as being in color, but this could have been no more than a tinting or toning process. While no immediate results were gained from Natural Vision, the system had been noticed.

In France two types of wide screen systems were being tried out. Hypergonar, an anamorphic process, would eventually become Cinema-Scope; and Triptych, a three-camera, three-projector system, would evolve into Magirama in 1956. (Hypergonar is covered in Chapter 3.)

Abel Gance, developer and utilizer of Triptych, also employed a format he called Polyvision. This was in no way a wide screen process, nor was the name ever used to refer to Triptych, except by recent writers. With Polyvision, several images occupied the frame in a montage. The images were almost always the same shot reduced and printed two, four, six or more times within the frame. Occasionally the Polyvision frame would include different shots, but not often. It was an interesting visual gimmick that was employed by Gance to intensify certain sequences. It worked well but was not a new gimmick; it had simply never been used to such extent or complexity before Gance's applications.

Despite what you've read, Triptych was not the mother of Cinerama. There was little similarity between the two other than the tricamera, triprojector aspect. Triptych was not used in the manner generally credited. The majority of the three scenes used by Gance generally involved different shots, the center panel being of storytelling use while the right and left panels often presented "atmospheric" scenes in mirror image to one another. That is, both outside panels might show marching troops with the soldiers facing right in the right panel and left in the left panel, achieved by flipping the negative and printing one scene with opposite orientation. All three panels were used for the same panoramic scene in only a few shots. These were quite impressive, but badly marred technically since the tricamera rig involved placement of the three cameras one above the other aimed left, center and right. The three-panel panoramic scenes did not have the same horizon and did not blend well at all. In fact they were so far off that when these films are viewed today, audiences, at first struck by the magnitude of it all, very soon start pointing out the seams and extreme misalignment. Cinerama never had such obvious misconvergence of its three panels. Triptych was never intended for a full-length feature, but was applied sparingly. The full aspect ratio was 3.66×1, compared to Cinerama's 2.72×1. (See Chapter 2 for Cinerama specifications.) Triptych was not a curved-screen process even though it was shown as such in 1956 when the name was changed to Magirama. (It was in fact shown in Paris at the Empire–Abel Gance Theatre, which was later converted into the Paris SuperCinerama Theatre.)

Gance's *Napoleon* opened in Paris in April 1927 with Triptych sequences. The film would constantly be reedited, rearranged and reshot over the years until the fifties, when a Cinerama version was considered as well as a CinemaScope edition. The latter may have actually come to pass; reports are conflicting. In 1928 Gance edited several shorts together in three-panel form, but these received extremely limited exposure and were made up entirely of footage from *Napoleon* and other films. The Triptych screen was used to show three-panel montage and not one panoramic shot, though a few of the *Napoleon* scenes may have been originally filmed with the tricamera rig. Triptych, montage, or tripanel panoramic was not a serious new film process as far as other filmmakers were concerned. It was a visual gimmick, well employed at times by Gance but nothing the world film communities cared to explore for possible general use. In so many ways Gance was ahead of his contemporaries, but as usual in such matters his ideas were just too grandiose for others. (Gance also attempted to use stereophonic sound in the thirties, but as with Triptych, few showed any interest in the technology.) Unfortunately, he was never able to rid himself of his *Napoleon* fetish, and when Cinerama became a commercial product, he was unable to embrace that process for filmmaking. Like D.W. Griffith, Edwin S. Porter, and others, Gance lived too soon in the history of motion pictures to be able to take advantage of the many technologies that would eventually be available.

In February 1929 *Napoleon,* reedited to more conventional length from its various French versions (one reportedly over five hours), arrived in the United States via MGM. Regardless of what so-called Gance authorities say, the three-panel footage, or some of it, was included in the American version. Instead of the three-projector system of presentation, MGM reduced the three frames onto one. (The home video version of the partly restored *Napoleon* has the Triptych scenes reduced in the same manner as the MGM version.) Instead of the picture expanding to three times bigger, it suddenly was reduced to one-third as large as conventional 1.33 × 1 35mm. Not only were United States audiences unimpressed, they complained en masse, and exhibitors quickly pulled the film from their theaters.

MGM may have had bigger plans for *Napoleon* than materialized. It is altogether possible they meant the Triptych scenes to be projected through Magnascope (not to be confused with MagnaScope; refer to Chapter 7 for that system). It makes sense, but nothing available to us proves that such a plan existed or that it was ever promoted to exhibitors in that way. Magnascope was the result of Paramount's desire to render a huge wide screen image from regular 35mm. A projection lens was developed in 1924 by Lorenzo del Riccio that enabled the enlargement by four times of any 35mm scene on the screen. Paramount put the unit to use on *North of '36* and *The Thundering Herd* in 1925, and *Old Ironsides* in 1926. It was utilized on several other features from that studio as well as other distributors. Initially the idea was to cover the screen in a ratio of 1.85 × 1 or whatever shape filled the stage proscenium arch. In fact the ratio varied from 1 × 1 (in a New York theater) to slightly over 2 × 1, depending entirely on the layout of the theater. Magnascope was meant only for selected scenes, though many theaters used it on many, or all, of their features to heighten the climax regardless of the subject. Westerns particularly received Magnascope presentation. It is therefore reasonable to assume that MGM at least considered the process for *Napoleon* even if theatermen didn't. The studio may have naively assumed that exhibitors would know to enlarge the screen image during the Triptych scenes. If so, then they were, and would continue to be, very foolish regarding the attitudes of most theatermen toward wide screen technology.

Magnascope was a huge success with the public, but it proved one unavoidable fact regarding 35mm: The bigger the image, the more obvious the grain, and the less sharp and bright the picture. Wide screen worked, but not well enough in Magnascope form in theaters that seated three and four thousand customers, and it was these very theaters that especially needed the bigger and wider image. Mitchell Camera Corporation offered a solution: 70mm film.

William Fox's studio quickly moved on wide gauge film. After several demonstrations of Grandeur, as they called the new technology from Mitchell and Eastman Kodak (who manufactured the film stock), they released *Fox Grandeur News* in April 1929. Basically it was just another of their newsreels, only now in 70mm widescreen. Grandeur was photographed in the same four-perf-per-frame format as regular 35mm, with the actual picture image being 22.5mm high and 48mm wide, giving a 2.13 × 1 aspect ratio. It used an oversized (literally by two) Movietone soundtrack which also rendered superior sound. Due to the width of the soundtrack and thicker framelines, the exposed image area was not quite as large as present day 70mm (see chapter 5). Grandeur started a short revolution in Hollywood. Audiences seeing the new, clear, sharp 70mm wanted more, and Fox delivered the first feature, *Fox Movietone Follies of 1929,* on May 29, 1929. It was immediately popular in the few 70mm-equipped theaters, so much so that 35mm houses equipped with Magnascope blew up the 35mm version shot simultaneously to fill their screens. Wide screen had arrived.

Wide Gauge Films: The Rise and Fall

Paramount put Lorenzo del Riccio to work on an actual film version of Magnascope. They reasoned the projection device could work doubly well if the film were also oversized. Del Riccio, sticking to his 1.85 × 1 ratio, devised Magnifilm, a 56mm system that was in all respects the same as 35mm except wider. (The camera was a modified Fox Natural Color unit. The frame was 19½mm high.) Paramount shot the short *You're in the Army Now* and possibly another film — information is conflicting — in Magnifilm and held an invitational screening in New York on July 18, 1929. The only review, indeed the only contemporary material we could find, on that presentation was extremely favorable. Paramount claimed that all theaters they owned would convert to the process and that future productions would be released in 56mm and regular 35mm, which could be cropped and enlarged via Magnascope to Magnifilm size. But nothing happened. *You're in the Army Now* was released in standard 35mm in October 1930, and quickly forgotten — as was Magnifilm.

RKO Radio contracted with Natural Vision Pictures for their 63mm process and produced the short *Campus Sweethearts.* Released on February 12, 1929, it apparently played in the only theater ever set up for the system, the State-Lake in Chicago. Because of the frame format, Natural Vision required interlocked sound. A regular 35mm projector ran the RCA Photophone soundtrack in sync with the visual presentation which was impressive over a large, wide screen. As had been done with the two previous Natural Vision shorts, the process was again promoted as stereoscopic, and this sad choice of an advertising gimmick drew the only bad criticism it received.

Fox was busy with Grandeur productions: *Happy Days* opened on February 13, 1930, along with the short *Niagara Falls,* which was culled from footage originally shot for the earlier exhibited *Fox Grandeur News. Song o' My Heart,* shot partly in Ireland, was released March 11, 1930, and *The Big Trail* opened on October 24, 1930. Fox attempted a Perspecta-type directional sound system for Grandeur, but their experiments were only marginally successful, and all prints released used standard, though oversized, Western Electric Movietone tracks. (For information on the Perspecta Stereophonic Sound System see Chapter 8.)

An actual frame from the 70mm Realife original of Billy the Kid. *Grandeur and Realife were identical in every way, just given different trade names by Fox and MGM. The wide black area on the left is for the double-size Western Electric Movietone soundtrack. Despite general belief, 70mm prints of this feature do still exist, and it was even considered for rerelease a few years ago. Today's 70mm uses five-perf-per-frame pulldown, and it would be necessary to transfer Realife-Grandeur prints to that format as well as recenter the picture image before they could be exhibited in modern theaters. The optical soundtrack would have to be replaced by a magnetic one running down both sides of the frame inside and outside the perfs.*

MGM was not going to be left out in the cold. They purchased some of the 70mm Mitchell cameras and dubbed them Realife. *Billy the Kid,* released October 19, 1930, proved, as would Fox's *The Big Trail* a few days later, just how impressive 70mm wide screen was when employed on a big, outdoors action film. Unfortunately the MGM feature was caught in an awkward position: Almost all 70mm-equipped houses were already booked for *The Big Trail.* The studio released *Billy the Kid* in regular 35mm (shot simultaneously, not reduced from the 70mm edition as claimed by other writers) for Magnascope presentation. Interestingly, some reviewers pointed out that the MGM "70mm" was not as clear and sharp as the Fox version, unaware they were actually seeing a 35mm Magnascope version and not an actual Realife print. Nevertheless, the MGM film was a huge success.

Roland West purchased one of the Mitchell cameras and shot *The Bat Whispers* in 70mm "Wide Film," as he called it. Recent claims are that this was filmed in Magnifilm or 65mm. One recent writer has stated it was probably shot with the Fearless Super Picture camera made by Ralph M. Fear, but a contemporary trade ad from Mitchell Camera clearly states *The Bat Whispers* was shot with one of their units. (The Fearless Super Picture, a.k.a. Fearless Wide Picture, camera was an all-purpose unit that shot regular 35mm, wide gauge 35mm [10 perf horizontal movement], and two-color Multicolor process. It was briefly considered as the unit to be called MGM Camera 65 in the mid fifties, but ultimately rejected in favor of a modified Grandeur-Realife system with anamorphics by Panavision. The Fearless wide screen process was never used on a film.) *The Bat Whispers* is credited as containing the first regular 35mm 1.33×1 to 70mm wide screen blowup footage, but this is only partly correct. All the miniature and special effects scenes were shot only in 35mm, but they were not optically enlarged by the lab. Instead they were projected onto a screen and rephoto-graphed in 70mm via the system called process photography.

The first, and only, Natural Vision feature, *Danger Lights,* was released by RKO Radio on December 14, 1930. Like *Campus Sweethearts* it played only the Chicago equipped theater in 63mm, with other wide screen engagements courtesy of 35mm Magnascope.

First National and Warner Bros., the last major studio not involved in wide gauge production, entered the game with Vitascope, a 65mm system. Information is conflicting, but apparently Vitascope required an inter-locked Movietone soundtrack (one source indicates it was Vitaphone sound on disc) in the same way Natural Vision did. (Natural Vision used RCA Photophone sound, but all optical audio formats were compatible.) Warners released *A Soldier's Plaything* on November 1, 1930, though infor-mation is conflicting regarding whether this was actually exhibited in Vita-scope. This was followed by *The Lash* (a.k.a. *Adios*) on January 1, 1931, and *Kismet* on January 18, 1931. The last two received very limited wide gauge presentation but got the usual Magnascope 35mm treatment and were very profitable. *A Soldier's Plaything* was released in standard 35mm in May 1931 with additional footage, to dismal box-office.

MGM finally got 70mm playdates when they released the last of the wide gauge features of the period, *The Great Meadow*, in Realife on March 15, 1931.

The attempt by Hollywood to improve the screen image was killed by the exhibitors. Already strafed by the heavy outlay for dual sound systems (for sound-on-film and sound-on-disc noncompatible formats), few were willing to put up more funds for three different wide film formats. (In all, fewer than twenty theaters had been equipped for 63mm, 65mm and 70mm projection. None apparently actually installed 56mm units except for the one demonstration screening in New York.) Most of the films had been shown in wide screen by projecting the simultaneously filmed 35mm ver-sions with Magnascope (and probably other) enlarging lenses. Why bother with new projection equipment if the same results could be obtained with 35mm? Of course there were two or three problems, like grain, brightness, and the simple fact the 35mm editions had not been framed for cropping.

Some in Hollywood tried to reason with the exhibitors. All the new wide gauge systems had been so developed that 35mm projectors could be converted to play them. Some Grandeur dual 35mm–70mm machines had been manufactured. But pleas to the theater owners were wasted. The ex-hibitors, other than a few truly interested in the improvement of the in-dustry, refused to continue with wide gauge. Those who supported the new technology were in too much of a minority to make continued use of the large formats profitable. But Magnascope would still be applied in many theaters to give regular releases wide screen presentation.

Despite popular belief, cropping was not limited to a few big theaters in a few large cities. Many small neighborhood theaters had acquired en-larging lenses and would still be using them when cropping became the official industry standard for spherical 35mm wide screen in the early fifties. In those theaters the wider image so hyped by Hollywood would be nothing new. Cropping had, in fact, become so common by 1930 that veteran cinematographer Gilbert Warrenton suggested to all in the industry that a 2×1 safe area be included in the framing of all features, thus allowing the many houses already filling their wide screens the benefit of prints that did not require constant frame adjustment by projectionists. Others also backed such an idea, most thinking the 1.85×1 ratio was better. The studios, however, ignored these suggestions and continued with 1.33×1 framing until cropping was adopted as part of the war against television. Little by little most theaters replaced their wide screens for smaller, narrower 1.33×1 ratio size. But some still kept the wider shape. (The authors know of two theaters that used undersize apertures, as the projectionists called them, to render wide screen presentation from the late twenties on. Both these cinemas were in small towns, one in Georgia and one in Alabama!)

The Mitchell 70mm Grandeur and Realife cameras and other equipment would go into storage, where they would stay until the early fifties. They would emerge, be modified and revamped, and serve as the basis for Todd-AO, MGM Camera 65, Super Panavision 70, and CinemaScope 55. Wide gauge wasn't dead; it was only sleeping, awaiting the chance to prove once more the superiority of large format over regular 35mm.

The Early Wide Screen Films

Further information on each of these films can be found in the Filmography.

PANORAMICO ALBERINI

Il sacco di Roma (1923)*

NATURAL VISON

Rollercoaster Ride (Natural Vision Pictures, 1926)**
Niagara Falls (Natural Vision Pictures, 1926)**
Campus Sweethearts (RKO Radio, 1930)**
Danger Lights (RKO Radio, 1930)**

TRIPTYCH

Cristallisation (1928)**
Danses (1928)**
Galops (1928)**

*certain sequence(s) only.
**short subject.

Marine (1928)**
Napoleon (MGM, 1928)*
14 juillet 1953 (1954)†

GRANDEUR

Fox Grandeur News (Fox, 1929)**
Fox Movietone Follies of 1929 (Fox, 1929)
Happy Days (Fox, 1930)
Niagara Falls (Fox, 1930)**
Song o' My Heart (Fox, 1930)
The Big Trail (Fox, 1930)

MAGNIFILM

You're in the Army Now (Paramount, 1929)**

REALIFE

Billy the Kid (MGM, 1930)
The Great Meadow (MGM, 1931)

70MM WIDE FILM

The Bat Whispers (UA, 1930)

VITASCOPE

A Soldier's Plaything (WB, 1930)
The Lash (aka *Adios*) (WB, 1931)
Kismet (WB, 1931)

MAGIRAMA

Magirama (1956)†

(A listing of Magnascope presentations is impossible. All wide gauge films were shown in 35mm using the system, and most major features were given the treatment in some theaters, while many cinemas applied the technique in part or whole to all their engagements for several years. A few used the enlarging lenses on all films into the fifties and beyond.)

†*included in this listing because of text coverage.*

II. The Multiple-Film and Deep Curved Screen Processes

Cinerama

The first public showing of a Cinerama film was at the Broadway Theatre in New York City, on the night of September 30, 1952. The film was appropriately entitled *This Is Cinerama*. That first audience was not prepared for what they were about to experience. Nothing like it had ever been seen or heard in a motion picture theater.

The film opened with a black-and-white prologue segment featuring veteran newscaster Lowell Thomas. As he reviewed a brief history of the movies, his image on the screen was normal in size and shape, and his voice came from the center of the screen as usual. The audience began to murmur and ask each other, "What's the big deal with this Cinerama stuff? Did we get all dressed up to come see a boring documentary on the movies?"

Suddenly, the huge curtains began to open and the audience found itself almost physically pulled into the picture, being rocketed along in the front car of Cinerama's famous roller coaster ride. Instead of the single-channel sound to which audiences were accustomed, the auditorium was filled with sound from *six* different channels! Five speakers behind the giant, curved screen, as well as several surround speakers around the auditorium, completely engulfed the audience. Along with the roller coaster sounds were recorded screams, almost as if the producers were trying to cue the audience for a response. And the audience did scream. They also held tightly to the seat armrests and swayed from side to side with the action on the screen. For the first time in the history of commercial motion pictures, an audience was taking part in a moviegoing experience which was entirely new and different — it was *real*. They were there in the picture, participating in the action on the screen, hearing all the sounds of the scene from all directions, and loving every minute of it.

The process of Cinerama was revolutionary. Experimental films had touched on similarities in the past, but until the first feature film was available for viewing by the masses, there was simply nothing else in the world like it.

Although Cinerama was not unveiled to the public until 1952, it had

11

CINERAMA...
one full year on Broadway, still smashing box office records!

Yes, Cinerama—the film medium that ushered in a new era of entertainment—celebrates its first Broadway birthday—and box office has never been better!

In just one year of public showings Cinerama has been eagerly accepted by an overwhelmed public. It is acclaimed as the most dramatic addition to motion picture entertainment in 25 years! The silent "flickers" provided action, the "Jazz Singer" introduced sound and Technicolor showed the subject in natural color. But it is Cinerama and only Cinerama, which surrounds *you*, the viewer, with movement, color and sound so realistic—with such dynamic impact—that *you* become a part of every brilliant sequence.

Since its first showing, Cinerama has become one of the world's outstanding theatrical attractions. It has *yet* to be equalled. It can *never* be excelled.

There is only *one* Cinerama! The whole country *knows* it! Box office receipts *prove* it!

NEW YORK . . . Warner Theatre
52nd Week
2 million patrons

DETROIT . . . Music Hall Theatre
28th Week

PHILADELPHIA . . . Boyd Theatre
Opening October 5th—largest
advance sale for this city

CHICAGO . . . Palace Theatre
9th Week

LOS ANGELES . . . Hollywood
Theatre
22nd Week

WASHINGTON, D. C.
Warner Theatre
Opening day—November 5th

there is only one
CINERAMA

PRINT BY TECHNICOLOR
A LOWELL THOMAS AND MERIAN C. COOPER PRESENTATION

A September 1953 trade ad. Notice the title is not given as This Is Cinerama.

been tested and refined in laboratory situations since the mid-1930s. An inventive genius named Fred Waller had been intrigued by the enhanced illusion of reality created by the use of wide-angle photography. His experiments led to an exhibit at the 1939 World's Fair in New York that featured a motion picture process known as Vitarama. A multiple-projector process utilizing a curved screen, Vitarama generated considerable excitement at that special showing, but was deemed impractical for theatrical exhibition.

The Vitarama process was kept alive by, of all things, World War II. Waller's huge, curved-screen invention found invaluable use as a gunnery trainer for the Army Air Force. Motion pictures of enemy planes were projected onto the inner surface of a dome in front of which were mounted several electronic machine guns. Student gunners were able to perfect their skills in a somewhat lifelike environment.

Waller was a scientist searching for a method of recreating reality in a motion picture setting. Early in his experiments, he had discovered that "peripheral vision," the things we see out of the corners of our eyes, helps produce our sense of depth and space. He reasoned that if he could reproduce on the screen an image that approximated what we normally see, he could create an illusion of reality.

His solution to the problem was in the design of the screen itself. Waller developed a screen that covered an arc of 146 degrees in width and 55 degrees in height. Normal human vision covers a field of 160 degrees and 60 degrees, respectively. Theoretically, Waller's screen could come very close to approximating the field of view of the human eye. (For more on this unusual screen, see page 23.)

To shoot a film that would cover this field, Waller decided to use three 35mm cameras equipped with 27mm lenses, approximately the focal length of the human eye. Each camera photographed one-third of the overall scene. The left camera shot the right third of the picture, the right camera the left third, and the center camera shot straight ahead. These three cameras were mounted as one unit, set at 48-degree angles to each other. The three pictures were shot simultaneously on three separate rolls of film. A single rotating shutter in front of the three lenses assured simultaneous exposure on each of the films.

The cameras for Cinerama were standard 35mm studio cameras with only slight modifications. Apertures were redesigned to allow a photographed frame to be six sprocket holes in height instead of the normal four. Camera speed was changed from 24 to 26 frames per second. Until Cinerama, the standard film speed for 35mm film had been established at 90 feet per minute. The new cameras for the new medium ran at 146.25 feet per minute.

In the theater, projectors for Cinerama were located left, center and right, and were housed in three separate booths. Like the cameras, projectors were standard 35mm with matching modifications to allow for the larger frame height and increased speed of the film. The three machines

Fred Waller and Vitarama camera rig.

were electronically interlocked with selsyn motors that automatically kept
the three images in perfect synchronization on the screen.

Visually, Cinerama put the audience in the picture and allowed them
to experience sights from around the world that many of them would never
be allowed to witness personally. Cinerama needed a sound system to
match that visual realism — one as sensational and revolutionary as the
screen presentation.

The answer was found by Hazard Reeves, one of the entrepreneurs behind Cinerama and a noted electronic engineer. It was obvious to Reeves
that only a multi-channel sound system could do justice to the wide picture
on the deeply curved screen. Early research and experimentation pointed
to a five-channel sound system. This would be adequate to spread out the
sound across the full picture area. Additional information would have to
be assigned to speakers placed around the auditorium in order to obtain a
sound "umbrella" for certain scenes. The standard that eventually developed was a separate sound film, in sync with the three picture panels, carrying six discrete (fully directional) soundtracks on fully coated magnetic
35mm film. These soundtracks remained the standard for Cinerama until
the utilization of the process for dramatic feature films. Both *The Wonderful World of the Brothers Grimm* and *How the West Was Won*—feature
films of 1962 and 1963, respectively, that represented the final form of three-
strip Cinerama—were presented with seven-channel sound: the standard
five behind the screen, plus two surround channels, one for each side of the

auditorium. Early printed material on Cinerama mentions only six channels of sound, while later publications emphasize that the system had always been seven channels. Apparently, some Cinerama films were six-channel and others seven-channel. It was simply a matter of patching the appropriate channels to speakers from the projection booth sound system.

The Cinerama Sound system was truly stereophonic. Many scenes were recorded on location with multiple microphones (but not *all* the sound as claimed. Much was pot-panned in rerecording, as with other stereophonic systems.) As mentioned earlier, the high speed of the film through the projection machines was a departure from the norm. This greater speed enhanced the sound record, which was reproduced "double-system" from 35mm magnetic film on an interlocked reproducer. This multi-track sound system now made it possible to follow the action of the film, not only with the eyes, but with the ears as well.

When discussing Cinerama Sound with its discrete multi-channels, it is important to note the impact the sound system alone had on an unsuspecting audience. In 1952, when Cinerama premiered, there was, realistically no such thing as stereophonic sound. (Fantasound and Vitasound had not been widely used. See information on them in Chapter 8.) Stereo recordings were not available for home use until the mid-1950s, and then only on reel-to-reel tape. Stereo phonograph records did not become available for home use until 1957. Stereo was not available in motion pictures. The first audiences to view Cinerama were, in general, completely unaware of what to expect from the soundtrack. After all, they had nothing with which to compare it — except the real world.

No one in the audience for that first Cinerama presentation will ever forget the entr'acte. Lowell Thomas' voice was heard first from the left of the auditorium, then from the right, center, surrounds, and then from every speaker in the house. Over the sounds of an orchestra tuning up, he was yelling only one word: "Quiet!" Then, in a more normal tone, Thomas delivered a historic message: "I apologize for shouting at you. It's all a part of the conspiracy. For a few moments now, we are going to give you a demonstration of our stereophonic sound. Please note the enormous power, without distortion, when the full orchestra plays!" A symphonic orchestra then showed its stuff by having individual instruments cover the entire frequency range, from sassy piccolo to aristocratic bass. This was probably the most comprehensive demonstration of stereo sound ever heard in a motion picture theater — a unique and exciting experience for the audience wherever the film played.

It should be noted that when that first theatrical feature in Cinerama was shown to a paying audience, it was still considered to be an experimental film and process by all concerned with its production and exhibition. A single theater in New York had been converted, at great expense, in order to show the new process. No one involved with it knew for sure if the public would accept or reject it. Careers were on the line. Large amounts of money needed to be recouped to satisfy investors. It was a gamble that many would not want to take. Yet, the Cinerama engineers and innovative executives were willing to "lay it all on the line," for they believed that the public would embrace the new process, as much as or more than they had the coming of sound to motion pictures 25 years earlier.

The gamble payed off. The opening of *This Is Cinerama* was a historic event in motion pictures. The film played in New York, at the same theater of its opening, for two years. With admission prices around $2.00, it grossed almost $5 million. The morning after the premiere on September 30, 1952, a review of the film appeared on the front page of the *New York Times.* Never before had the *Times* given that important and prestigious space to a motion picture — but never before had theater audiences experienced an event with as much impact as Cinerama.

The souvenir program book to *This Is Cinerama* summed it up this way:

> The whole world was opened up by Cinerama. Its three-eyed camera burst out of the flat frame that enclosed conventional film story telling. The illusion of depth and the sense of movement that Cinerama provided was as real as depth or movement itself.... Cinerama can roam the world as no kind of film making ever did, and can bring it to you.... Cinerama can take you as far and as wide as your own imagination.... Cinerama changed the course of history. It was introduced in a film without a star and without a story. It was a film in which Cinerama was the star.... Cinerama's story telling possibilities have barely been touched. They are limitless. The days of revolution are not past. They are still with us, and with Cinerama.

Even the projection process of Cinerama was a new and exciting, and sometimes disastrous, experience. Seasoned projectionists, some of whom had been operating motion picture machinery since the silent days, were suddenly confronted with an entirely new system and procedure. Their expertise was on the line. Millions of dollars could be spent on the development of the process and the release of the first feature, but the success of Cinerama lay finally on the shoulders of the individuals actually running the performance.

In the medium's early stages of development, the Cinerama heads had wisely decided that a strict set of standards must be utilized by every theater exhibiting this new process. Blueprints were carefully examined, recommendations given for further improvements, and a final decision made as to the proper presentation requirements. Theaters desiring to convert to Cinerama but lacking in any one of the requirements were rejected. New theaters, of course, had no problem since they could be designed from the ground up to accommodate the process.

From the very outset, with the premiere film *This Is Cinerama,* presentation requirements were such that five operators were necessary for each performance of Cinerama. Initially, they included three projectionists, a sound control engineer and a picture control engineer. As the original process evolved over the years to its final form with *How the West Was Won,*

TO: LIBERTY MUTUAL Employees, Families and Friends
Announcing SPECIAL PRICES for YOU on
NOVEMBER 21 at 8 PM and NOVEMBER 24 at 2 PM

FOR THE FIRST TIME CINERAMA'S GREATEST THRILLS TOGETHER IN ONE BREATHTAKING ENTERTAINMENT!

From The History-Making Roller-Coaster Ride To The Sultry South Seas...From A Hurtling Bob-Sled Ride To The Pounding Pulse-Dances Of The African Watusi...YOU Are There...Swept Into The Picture...You Live...Breathe Your Every Wildest Dream In A Fantastic Trip Around A Spectacle-Studded World!

CINERAMA INC. Presents

THE BEST OF CINERAMA

A DECADE OF THE WORLD'S GREATEST ENTERTAINMENT

TECHNICOLOR®

YOU JUMP with the giant Nambus... savages the world has forgotten...in a death-defying leap into space!

YOU LIVE a thousand dreams as the serene beauty of Japan's Mt. Fujiyama and Cherry Blossom Dances transport you to a world of ancient traditions!

Now You Are Catapulted Across Five Continents and 100 Centuries!

YOU GASP at the fight to death between a cobra and a mongoose in India's colorful native-packed streets!

YOU SHOOT the surf in a Pacific Paradise and dare the racing breakers that crash around you!

YOU ZOOM into space at the controls of a jet plane as it is catapulted from a carrier!

IMITATIONS COME AND GO BUT ONLY CINERAMA PUTS YOU IN THE PICTURE!

Martin **CINERAMA**
583 PEACHTREE STREET N.E.
ATLANTA 8, GA. · DIAL 875-9405

This anthology co-produced by MERIAN C. COOPER · THOMAS CONROY · Narration by LOWELL THOMAS · Produced by LOWELL THOMAS, MERIAN C. COOPER, ROBERT BENDICK, LOUIS De ROCHEMONT and CARL DUDLEY

TICKETS AVAILABLE FROM YOUR CLUB REPRESENATIVE

THURS. NOV. 21 at 8 PM
SUN. NOV. 24 at 2 PM

ORCHESTRA RESERVED SEAT ..$1.80 (reg.$2.20)____
BALCONY RESERVED SEAT.....$1.40 (reg.$1.75)____
CHILDREN under 12, ANY SEAT.....$1.00 ... ____

Inclosed is my remittance in the amount of $_____

Make checks payable to Martin CINERAMA Theater

ORDERS IN BY NOVEMBER 20th
or
NOON, NOVEMBER 22nd

A reserved seat order form for The Best of Cinerama. *Note the ticket prices.*

five men were still required, but their job description had changed somewhat since the first performances nearly ten years prior. The Cinerama theater still had the three projectionists, but the picture control and sound control engineer positions had been incorporated into one. Now, there were three projectionists, a "chief Cinerama engineer," and a fifth man whose sole duties were to open and close the curtain and to control the house lights for each performance. The five-man operation was also a union requirement for Cinerama theaters. Needless to say, the expense of five operators for *each* performance of Cinerama was taxing for even the largest and most profitable theaters.

Each projectionist was assigned to a particular projector. His duty was to thread the machine at the proper point on the special Cinerama leader and monitor the picture panel for that particular projector during the performance. He also maintained proper carbon trim, framing and focus.

The Cinerama engineer was stationed in the center booth, along with another operator and the sound reproducing equipment. Once all three picture machines were correctly threaded and in the "on" position, the engineer had threaded the sound film onto its machine. The film projectors and sound reproducer could then be started remotely by the Cinerama engineer. When he pushed a button labeled "Start," all three picture machines, as well as the sound machine, started at the same time and in perfect synchronization.

The Cinerama engineer was the only member of the five-man crew who was officially allowed to start and stop the show. It would have been extremely awkward for any of the other four operators to take this responsibility on themselves, since the necessary control switches were found only in the center booth, the one occupied by the chief engineer. However, each booth did contain its own control panel of sorts, and one of those controls was labeled "Emergency Stop." If an emergency occurred during the show, any operator could stop the performance, but only the chief engineer could restart the presentation.

Synchronization of the three picture panels was of extreme importance, and was accomplished by the use of selsyn motors. The main motor was assigned to the sound machine, with the projector motors acting as "slaves" to it. Sound reproduction speed remained constant, while the projectors were continually able to slightly advance or retard their speed to keep the picture panels in sync with the sound. It was mandatory that the sound remain at a constant speed since any variance in sound pitch due to speed fluctuation would be immediately noticed by the audience. Slight variations in the picture speed, however, would be unnoticed and therefore acceptable.

The problem of maintaining synchronization was most noticeable when there was a film break in one of the picture panels. All reels were edge-numbered at one-foot intervals. In the event of a film break, the performance was stopped and each projectionist pulled the film from his respective reel down to the next convenient footage number and rethreaded his projector. Of course, a scene change made the chore much easier. The operators simply placed the very first frame of the new scene in the projector aperture, and all three picture machines were again in perfect sync. The Cinerama engineer, being the sole person in charge of the sound reel, then had the task of determining by edge numbers the correct placement of the magnetic track of his film over the playback head of the reproducer for proper sound sync.

Many of the inherent problems of synchronization had already been

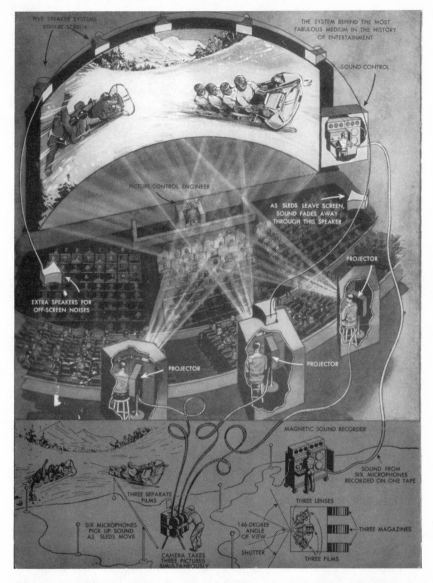

The Cinerama presentation as depicted in the souvenir program book for Cinerama Holiday.

encountered in the early days of sound films. In the late 1920s, with sound reproduction on a synchronized disc, if a film break occurred *below* the projector intermittent, the operator simply stopped the show and, using a handwheel, manually ran down enough film needed for winding around the take-up reel. If the film had not been disturbed at the aperture plate, the sound record, which was still mechanically attached to the drive gears of

no change
after Seven Wonders

SEARCH FOR PARADISE

1- Start Prologue (Walk-in music 3 mins. 28 sec.) Everybody remote/lock.

2- L. Thomas (Close-up) "Has been hounded by the memory of Alexander
The Great." - S.A.B.C. take-ups and strike arcs.

3- "Where are you going to move to next"; Stand-by for motor Start.

4- "Hey Major" (looking out window of aircraft) Push start button
and Hand & Sync dousers.

5- "What a Sight"; Open curtain. Large screen.

To End ACT 1

Robert Merrill starts to sing; Stand-by for curtain, etc.

On Fade out of picture; Close curtain.

To Start ACT 2

Everybody remote/lock.

Take-ups and Arcs.

Sound start your Walk-in music (optical sound) 2 mins. 45 secs.

After 2 mins. of walk-in music; S.A.B.C. Stand-by for motor Start.

After 2 mins. 35 secs. of walk-in music; push start button; hand
& sync dousers.

Picture hits curtain; Open large screen.

To End ACT 2

TITLES - RIVER SEQUENCES - Supervised by BUS & DON HATCH: Stand-by
for Curtain, etc.

ADVANCE ARRANGEMENTS - E. THOMAS GILLIARD, etc.; Close curtain.

Original Cinerama projectionists' cue sheet for Search for Paradise. *The Lowell Thomas prologue and the entr'acte were run on a regular 35mm projector using standard mono optical sound. Note the penciled-in message from someone at Cinerama, Inc., in the upper right hand corner. Cue sheets like this were supplied for* every *roadshow released regardless of film format.*

the projector, remained in sync with the film. The operator then restarted the show and the picture and sound were as perfectly in sync as they had been before the film break. However, a break *above* the intermittent meant that synchronization was totally lost for the remainder of that reel of film. These principles also applied to the synchronized reels of film for Cinerama. With edge-numbering of all reels in the Cinerama process, the procedure was considerably simplified.

The Cinerama engineers had taken into account that emergencies would eventually occur, and from the very beginning of theatrical presentations of the process, a regular 35mm projector was standard equipment in

SOUND CONTROL SETTINGS

SEARCH FOR PARADISE

Full House Setting_____ Half House Setting_____

ACT. 1 CUE	Speaker 7	Speaker 8	6 - 6 & 7 7-8
Beginning Act. 1	OPEN	OPEN	RIGHT
Eiffel Tower		OFF	LEFT
Breaking Camp In The Morning	OFF	OPEN	RIGHT
Horses Crossing Stream	OPEN	OFF	LEFT
End of Sword Dance	OFF	OPEN	RIGHT
Night Camp Scene	OPEN	OFF	LEFT
When Raft Leaves Shore		OPEN	RIGHT
Where Raft Returns To Shore		OFF	LEFT
ACT 2			
Start of Act. 2	OPEN	OFF	LEFT
Fade of Night Garden Scene – All Pots Up 1½ D.B.			
Fade of Coronation Sequence – All Pots Up Another 1½ D.B.			
Inside Frozen Hangar	OFF	OPEN	RIGHT
Silent Approach of Jets	OPEN		
End of Picture		OFF	LEFT
Credits and Walk Out Music			
On Normal Theatre Setting			

NOTE: Speaker Pot 1-6 to be set at proper level and remain set until the end of each Act.

Original Cinerama sound control engineers' cue sheet for Search for Paradise. *Note that the volume was set depending on the audience size and that for act two it was necessary to alter the audio D.B.S. It appears track seven was encoded with a Perspecta Stereophonic–type switching signal to render eight channels of sound. If you read these sound cues correctly you can see how the sound panned across the screen and auditorium for various sequences. This can give you some idea of the complete aural surround Cinerama Sound delivered. It has never been surpassed.*

the center booth of the theater. With *This Is Cinerama,* it was used for the prologue sequence. Also in the booth, from the very first to the very last presentation of three-panel Cinerama, was a standard-format 35mm reel of film that explained the process and showed behind-the-scenes shots of a Cinerama production. This reel was used only during those "nail-biting" times when a massive breakdown occurred. Operators and engineers alike then worked frantically to reset the Cinerama program before the 35mm reel ended. This film, it was hoped, would keep the customers in their seats during the feature interruption while giving them some explanation about the complexities of the Cinerama process.

The first Cinerama prints were mounted complete, with one reel per projector for each half of the performance. In all, one showing required a total of six picture reels and two sound reels. There were no changeovers, and every presentation required an intermission. Because of physical limitations encountered with the use of standard, but modified, 35mm projectors, reel size was adequate to hold enough film for only one-half of a normal Cinerama performance.

When Cinerama was finally used for dramatic feature presentations, increased film length necessitated changing the speed from 26 to 24 frames per second and using larger-than-normal reels. Initially, reels held approximately 7,500 feet of film — 50 minutes of picture at 26 frames per second. This in itself was a big departure from the standard 2,000-foot reels used in "normal" 35mm presentations. This reel size seemed aptly suited for the travelog films of Cinerama, but when the process evolved into dramatic feature film "roadshows," it quickly became obvious that the established reel size was inadequate. Since the Cinerama projectors did not require soundheads to reproduce the audio, there was enough space available between the projector head and the booth floor to allow the accommodation of larger reels. These new reels were capable of holding approximately 13,000 feet of film. And so, even with no changeovers possible, *The Wonderful World of the Brothers Grimm* (at 134 minutes) and *How the West Was Won* (at 162 minutes) were able to be projected in the established Cinerama process.

Though necessary for the longer feature films, these new, larger reels presented another problem for projectionists. They were so heavy that hydraulic lifts were necessary to raise them onto the upper reel shaft of the projector. At the end of a showing, the take-up reel was simply rolled across the floor of the booth to the rewind table or its shipping can. Projectionists often referred to these oversized reels as "wagon wheels."

In the event of a break in any one of the reels that resulted in the loss of only a few frames, the corresponding frames in the other reels were cut out to match the damaged footage. Another method was optional for the chief projectionist: to simply replace the damaged footage with black "spacer" film. This meant that if only one reel had suffered damage, the other three were left intact, and when the reel with the spacer film was projected, that panel merely went blank for a fraction of a second in the performance. Naturally, this could be done only with the picture reels. A blank space in the sound reel would have been totally unacceptable. This procedure was also a holdover from the early days of sound films using synchronized records.

In the beginning, all three projection booths were equipped with their own rewind tables. As the process later became more refined, all three projectors and sound machine were in the same booth, centrally located. Communication between the operators and the chief engineer was now instantaneous, allowing problems to be solved more quickly and drastically reducing down-time. The new arrangement was also convenient for the repair and splicing of all *four* films simultaneously, assuring perfect sync between the reels. The booth's rewind table could accommodate all four reels at the same time. The three picture reels and the sound reel could be rewound simultaneously, and in the event that a splice needed to be made in one of the reels, a special "sync-block" was used. It was almost identical to the device employed in studio editing facilities for matching several different picture reels with a sound record. It consisted of four sprocket and roller assemblies mounted side by side on a heavy-duty metal base that was securely bolted to the rewind table. All four sprockets were on a single shaft. Film from the four reels was threaded through this sync device, allowing repair work to be done to any one of the reels without disturbing synchronization.

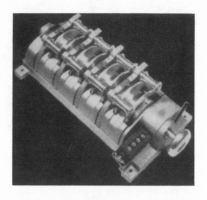

Synchronizing device used in repair work on either one or all four Cinerama film reels simultaneously.

Splices to Cinerama films were made by a "new," and necessary, means: adhesive-backed cellophane tape, especially manufactured for motion picture film. Conventional cement splices would have done the job temporarily, but for normal runs of several months, Cinerama found them unreliable. Tape splices were faster to make and moved through the projectors easier than those made with cement. Tape splices remain with us today, necessitated by automation and platter systems, where the entire feature program is often spliced together into a single run through one projector with no changeovers.

No writings on the subject of Cinerama would be complete without mention of the process's unique screen. Prior to the premiere presentation of Cinerama to a paying public, experimentation had proven that a conventional motion picture screen placed on Waller's desired arc of 146 degrees presented a special problem: Light from each side of the screen tended to be reflected to the opposite sides. To combat this problem, Waller devised a totally new type of screen. It consisted of hundreds of small, individual strips of screen material placed in a side-by-side, vertical configuration that, when inspected up close, resembled a giant venetian blind turned on its side. Thus positioned, each strip reflected light onto the backside of the strip next to it. The light was then deflected into the dark behind the screen instead of outward toward the audience. The louvered screen appeared to the audience to be an unbroken surface. (An interesting fringe benefit of this configuration was that one could actually go behind the screen during a performance and look out at the audience without their knowledge, as one would peer through the slats of a venetian blind.)

The strips, cut from the same material used in normal theater screens, were approximately 7/8 inches wide. They were shipped from the factory in rolls and installed one by one to make up the composite screen. They included a hook at each end for easy mounting on the screen frame, with the

DISCARDED
399289
LIBRARY
MURRAY STATE UNIVERSITY

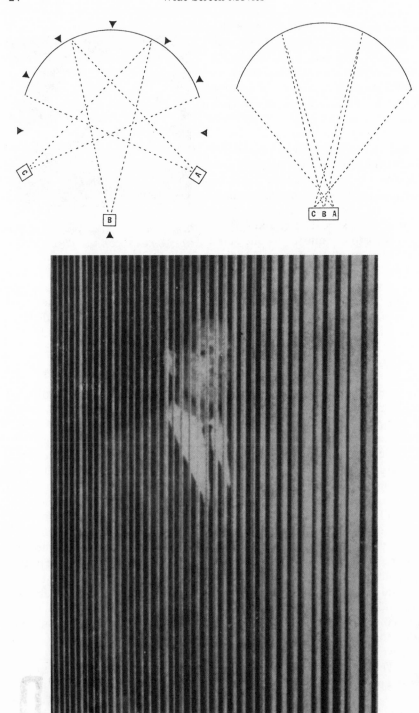

top end of the screen material attached to an elastic band between the hook and strip to maintain tautness. In the event that an individual strip of any Cinerama screen needed to be replaced, it was a simple matter of unhooking that strip from the top of the screen frame, letting it fall to the floor, and substituting another.

In the beginning, the standard Cinerama screen measured 75 feet in width and was 26 feet tall. Eleven hundred strips were needed to fill the vast expanse. This louvered screen was approximately 1700 square feet. With the move toward dramatic feature films and *The Wonderful World of the Brothers Grimm,* the *minimum* screen installed for Cinerama was a staggering 3,000 square feet! Naturally, Cinerama houses kept an adequate supply of replacement strips at all times.

As the Cinerama process increased in popularity and spread to every major city in the country, as well as key locations in Europe, South America and the Far East, the dimensions of the screen also increased. In its final days, the Cinerama screen in the largest houses measured approximately 94 feet in width and was 32½ feet tall, almost the height of a three-story building!

Cinerama Three-Panel Specifications*

*These are the standardized specifications issued by Cinerama, Inc., covering all three-camera, three-projector processes. There were slight variations from show to show which required minor repositioning of right and left panel projectors and re-patching of audio lines depending on sound channeling and number of tracks employed. The reader should understand that although these specs are dealing with hundredths of an inch, by the time the three films passed through various camera gates, optical printers and projector apertures and hit the giant screen, any slight deviation from these standards, no matter how miniscule, would result in a difference from four inches to two feet per film panel depending on screen size, projection throw, etc. And, of course, Cinerama and its offspring were always in a state of evolution which resulted in the changes in sound, frames per second and aspect ratio.

Camera and negative:

Film(s)	3 × 35 mm
Lenses	3 × 27mm
Perf-to-perf 3 × 35mm	2.895″
Between matchlines	.9478″
Overlap from perfs for each film	.051″
Aperture height for each film	1.116″
Aperture width for each film	1.014″

Opposite, top left: *Original Cinerama configuration showing the relative location of each of the three projection booths. Note the five channels of sound behind the screen, plus left, right and rear effects channel.* Top right: *Revised Super Cinerama and Cinemiracle configuration with all three projectors in the same booth. Stage and surround speaker placement remained the same as in the original Cinerama but was increased to seven-track separation.* Bottom: *The louvered Cinerama screen.*

Optical printer aperture height for each
    film   1.115″

Optical printer aperture width for each
    film   .996″

Perfs per frame   6

Frames per second:
    Cinerama and Cinemiracle   26
    Super Cinerama and Kinopanorama   24

Film speed:
    Cinerama and Cinemiracle   146.25 ft. per min.
    Super Cinerama and Kinopanorama   135 ft. per min.

Horizontal angular visual field   146°

Vertical angular visual field   55.5°

Individual camera visual field   50° overlapping

Aspect ratio:
    Cinerama, Cinemiracle and
      Kinopanorama   variable between
                                2.72×1 and
                                2.77×1

    Super Cinerama 2.59×1

Release print:
    Film(s) 3×35mm
    Projected image height for each film   1.088″
    Projected image width for each film   .985″
    Perfs per frame   6
    Frames per second:
      Cinerama and Cinemiracle   26
      Super Cinerama and Kinopanorama   24
    Film speed:
      Cinerama and Cinemiracle   146.25 ft. per min.
      Super Cinerama and Kinopanorama   135 ft. per min.
    Screen curvature:
      Cinerama, Cinemiracle and
        Kinopanorama   146°
      Super Cinerama   146° or 120°
    Sound system   35mm interlocked
                                  magnetic

    Sound format   discrete stereo-
                                  phonic

    Soundtracks:
      Cinerama   six or seven with
                                  eight possible by
                                  Perspecta type
                                encoding

      Cinemiracle and Super Cinerama   seven

Kinopanorama   nine (repatched to
                                      six or seven for
                                      U.S.)

Super Cinerama

With the involvement of MGM in 1960, the Cinerama process made some changes. When the two outfits combined forces for *The Wonderful World of the Brothers Grimm* (1962) and *How the West Was Won* (1963), they decided to increase considerably the size of the screen, increase the sound from six to seven channels, and incorporate some of the Cinemiracle (see pages 40–45) technology (Cinerama, Inc., having bought that company). The camera and projector speeds were changed from Cinerama's 26 to the standard 24 frames per second to make optical conversion to 70mm and 35mm easier. This revamped process was dubbed Super Cinerama, actually the first phase of what would be a three-phase development. The souvenir books made reference to the new name, as did all company-issued information, but neither film was ever advertised as Super Cinerama in the United States, and all ads simply bore the old Cinerama logo.

In addition to the two MGM-Cinerama coproductions released in the States, the new technology was applied to *The Golden Head* (1964; see pages 30–40) before that feature converted to Super Technirama 70. *Cleopatra* (1963) began shooting in CinemaScope, then switched over to the new Super Cinerama, then to Todd-AO. The anamorphic and tripanel scenes were discarded. *The Greatest Story Ever Told* (1965) also started production in the tripanel format, but ended up being made in Ultra Panavision 70. While it was released in 70mm Super Cinerama (see below), none of the three-strip sequences were retained, all such scenes having been reshot.

The improvements in the Cinerama system that led to the development of Super Cinerama paralleled physical improvements in the theaters, now being designed from the ground up as Cinerama houses. The stage area was completely eliminated; the screen filled the entire front of the auditorium, floor to ceiling and wall to wall, and was available in curvatures of 146 and 120 degrees. The three projection booths and picture and sound control monitors were consolidated into one room. (A triple-image projector was also designed and built, but the three-panel process was discontinued before many, if any, installations.) The idea was that these new theaters would be Super Cinerama houses, and older houses that had been converted to Cinerama could just keep that format, rather than converting a second time. (Cinerama, Inc., exercised almost total control of the design — layout, color, drapes, lights, etc. — of all Super Cinerama theaters. Nothing could be done without their approval.) To the authors' knowledge, however, the Super Cinerama name was never much exploited by theaters in the United States, though it was heavily advertised in European theaters. (The Europeans, with a rich heritage of theatrical presentations, have always been justly proud of their showcase theaters, legitimate and cinematographic. The Abel Gance Empire Theater in Paris ran a two-page ad in *Variety* showing its new screen and announcing that it was now the Super Cinerama Paris Theater.)

The second version of Super Cinerama came about with the introduction of the "new single-lens Super Cinerama projection": 70mm. The first feature in this process was *It's a Mad, Mad, Mad, Mad World,* filmed in Ultra Panavision 70 (see Chapter 5). In fact, this "new" version was simply Ultra Panavision 70 projected through an enlarging lens made for Cinerama, Inc. The anamorphic compression wasn't even corrected. Anything in the center of the screen appeared somewhat squeezed, while objects on the right and left sides looked fairly normal. This was to be the Super Cinerama process and replace completely the three-panel system. It was then decided that rather than limit the curved screen to one 70mm format, an anamorphic compression would be added to the sides of spherical 70mm and make it presentable as well. The results were the opposite of Ultra Panavision 70's look: Center-screen objects looked a bit fatter than normal and side-view objects appeared even fatter despite the added squeeze. The reason was simple: Ultra Panavision 70 was meant to cover a 2.76×1 ratio screen, but Super Panavision 70 and Todd-AO (see Chapter 5) could only cover 2.21×1 if they had no soundtrack. The 70mm Super Cinerama version took the difference in the frame normally covered by the sound strips and squeezed it into the standard 2.05×1 70mm projected frame. This still left quite a difference in the area the spherical original material had to fill, and the only way to fill it was to stretch the image out over the right and left of the screen. Apparently no one thought to add more compression, which would have fairly well corrected the problem. Still, all in all, Cinerama had always looked considerably different from other wide screen formats, so few complained. After all, the dividing lines were gone — but for that matter, so was the actual visual field. Regardless of the photographic system employed, 70mm Super Cinerama could not encompass the wraparound panoramics of the three-camera process.

The third, and last, phase of Super Cinerama was dubbed the New Super Cinerama Process. The louvered screen was eliminated, being replaced with standard screen material; the curvature was reduced to 120 degrees; the aspect ratio was brought in line with standard spherical 70mm; and all films were to be shot in spherical format with no optical correction. Other than the size of the screen, the final Cinerama process was actually Mike Todd's "Cinerama out of one hole": Todd-AO! Of course Cinerama could not allow any unauthorized films to be presented in their theaters over the entire screen, since they would not be receiving a royalty, so all theaters were required to project nonlicensed features smaller than the full New Super Cinerama process. Theaters therefore had to stock a 70mm Super Cinerama lens pair, another 70mm lens pair for non–Cinerama

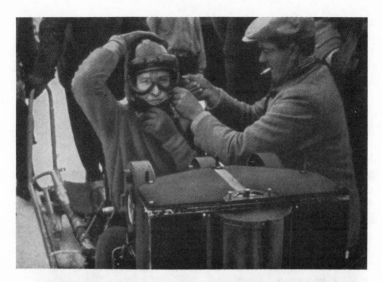

Top: *The Cinerama camera in 1954, on location in Switzerland for* Cinerama Holiday, *with operators Jack Priestly and Gayne Rescher.* Center: *This behind-the-scenes shot from* How the West Was Won *(1963) shows the modified Super Cinerama camera after MGM's involvement. Actor John Wayne and director John Ford are shown at MGM Studios.* Bottom: *The Super Cinerama logo.*

features, 35mm anamorphic pairs, and 35mm spherical pairs in order to be capable of presenting all available wide screen formats.

With 70mm single lens projection, the revolutionary process was dead. It had thrilled millions with its visual realism and had given the world a new household word: "stereophonic sound." The depth perception and perspective so recognizable with the original process was barely evident in the new "improved" version. Instead, the camera moved in more conventional, standard ways. Now, Super Cinerama had close-ups, elaborate tracking shots, complicated matte compositions and zoom shots. The new process would transfer very well to smaller screens in 35mm reductions and, eventually, would be seen on television. It became just a big picture on a deeply curved screen. Cinerama was now only a name for theater marquees.

The times put an end to roadshows in general and thus to Super Cinerama. The company's last 70mm feature, ironically titled *The Last Valley*,* was given only limited bookings in Todd-AO and none in the New Super Cinerama process. There were no more Cinerama theaters to book it in.

The Lost Cinerama Film

(We are extremely grateful to film historian István Nemeskürty, manager of the Hungarian Film Institute and former head of Budapest Studio, for providing the production information and stills that appear here, and to János Huszár and Lia Somogy at Hungarofilm in Budapest for contacting Mr. Nemeskürty for us. Without them the events regarding this almost totally unknown 70mm Super Cinerama feature would never have been uncovered.)

Today it is not unusual for "lost" episodes of television series to suddenly appear with much fanfare. Episodes of "I Love Lucy," "Perry Mason," "The Twilight Zone" and "The Honeymooners," as well as more recent shows such as "Mary Tyler Moore" and "The Barbara Mandrell Show" have been exhumed from storage vaults and syndicated for the first time. These programs were not really lost, of course; they were deliberately withheld from release for various reasons. With motion pictures the term "lost" can be more accurately applied. It has been estimated that more than 80 per cent of pre–1960 features no longer exist in their original form. (Duplicates, of course, do exist on almost all major studio product.) Even an epic such as *How the West Was Won* can no longer be seen as it was originally made: MGM has destroyed all Super Cinerama prints, keeping only a 70mm Super Cinerama dupe. Many films have suffered similar fates. One film that does exist, somewhere, is *The Golden Head* in 70mm Super Cinerama. But while it does still exist, it was never shown in the United States and in all likelihood never will be.

Alexander Paal, a Hungarian who had been involved as a producer on several minor features, had begun his career as a stageplay still photog-

A later film, The Great Waltz, was officially the last film licensed as a Cinerama presentation, but it was shot in 35mm and blown up to 70mm; it was apparently never intended for the big curved screen.

rapher. He moved to London and worked as a stillman for Alexander Korda, the transplanted Hungarian producer who was always willing to give a fellow countryman the opportunity to establish himself in the British industry. (Korda's efforts can be compared to those of Samuel Bronston, a filmmaker who never shied away from quality production values even though the finished film didn't always justify the expense.) Paal selected a British crime novel called *Nepomuk of the River* by Roger Pilkington for production. The final script bore little relationship to the book, but it offered several potentials, which the producer seized upon. (A brief synopsis: An international conference is being held in Budapest by worldwide criminal investigators. Two members of a robber gang decide it is the perfect opportunity to steal the golden bust of Saint László, Hungarian king of the Middle Ages, from the cathedral of Györ. While the police run around in circles, the children of a British inspector jump onto the crooks' trail and eventually bring the culprits to justice.)

American and Hungarian relations were not at their best, so Paal, now based in Great Britain, reasoned that a motion picture jointly financed by major studios in each country could only help in bringing the two governments together for the benefit of both. His film property offered the perfect chance to do just that plus give employment to his homeland's technicians and show off their capital city to the world. And what better film process to use than Super Cinerama, which would guarantee a worldwide market and first-class theaters?

MGM and Cinerama, Inc., were still pulling in monies from their co-productions *The Wonderful World of the Brothers Grimm,* which had been shot in part on European locations, and *How the West Was Won.* Cinerama had always been a globetrotting film medium, and Hungary certainly offered a classic city to add to their many other international location sites. Robert H. O'Brien, president of MGM, and Nicolas Reisini, president and chairman of Cinerama, Inc., agreed to back the project from the States, with Hungarofilm and Hunnia Film supporting from Budapest. Paal would produce with help from Cinerama's William R. Forman and Coleman Thomas Conroy, Jr., who as executive producer would be in overall charge for the Americans. The project was officially to be an MGM and Group No. 4 (of the Hunnia Film Studio) coproduction. Cinerama and Hungarofilm would be "presenters." British director James Hill, a former partner with Harold Hecht and Burt Lancaster on several prestigious films, was commissioned to helm, and shooting began in early fall 1963. The film was called *Millie Goes to Budapest and Who Is Millie?*

Production problems immediately arose around Hill. He was not getting along well with the Hungarians and was completely at odds with the Americans. He was a respected filmmaker, but for various reasons there were conflicts that just could not be resolved. In addition the show faced a serious weather problem: The story was set in summer and it was already October. Filming was halted and Nicholas Reisini flew to Budapest with his advisers. Paal and Conroy promoted continuation of the show. After three days of private meetings and a guarantee of acceptable weather from studio executive István Nemeskürty, the decision to resume production was made. Hill was replaced by veteran American director Richard Thorpe, who would redo Hill's scenes. Actress Hayley Mills was replaced by Lorraine Power, though it is unclear if she had actually been in any footage already shot or if her recasting was connected to Hill's situation. (Brief footage had been shot in London with Otto Preminger cameoing as a British butler. This was done as a favor to Paal, who was a still photographer on Preminger's roadshows, *Exodus* (1960) and *The Cardinal* (1963). [See entries on both films in Filmography.] Mills may have been in this sequence. The London material presumably does appear in the final film.)

Shooting took off at an accelerated pace. The three-panel process was abandoned in favor of Super Technirama 70 (see Chapter 4). (The opening sequence was optically converted to 70mm and used as is without reshooting.) There were no further problems, and the international crew and cast worked well together. Whatever political differences there were did not in any way interfere with the cooperative efforts of all. Filming ended in November just as word of United States President John F. Kennedy's assassination swept the world. Once again American and Hungarian relations became cool. Fortunately the friendships developed during production overcame political fears and postproduction was not affected adversely. Mixing and dubbing were carried out in London in January 1964, and the retitled *The Golden Head* (*Az aranyfej* in Hungarian) was ready for the 70mm Super Cinerama screen.

What went wrong next is a mystery. The world premiere was held in London in April 1964. The Hungarian opening was on December 10, 1964. The film received only modest, and limited, reviews and vanished from the giant screen. It would never appear in the United States. It was trade reviewed for *Variety,* and a forthcoming release from MGM was promised. But nothing happened. The film, as far as America was concerned, simply vanished. There would be several other 70mm Super Cinerama features, but the MGM-Cinerama association soured. Reisini would lose control of Cinerama, Inc., to William Forman and Pacific Theaters. (Before the end came there would be a long, bloody stockholders' feud to save Cinerama, Inc., from Pacific Theaters and its ultimate demise, but to no avail.) Cinerama would sell off their interests in *The Wonderful World of the Brothers Grimm* and *How the West Was Won* to MGM. It can only be assumed that *The Golden Head* was also sold to MGM, but if so, then what became of it? Forman would later strike up deals with Warner Bros. for *Battle of the Bulge* and ABC for *Custer of the West, Krakatoa East of Java, Song of Norway* and *The Last Valley.* There would be other production deals, including two MGM projects, *2001: A Space Odyssey* and *Ice Station Zebra,* as well as Paramount and United Artists projects and at least three Columbia features which were not marketed in the U.S. under the Super Cinerama banner. But from *The Golden Head* no more would ever be heard.

Soon Cinerama was totally absorbed by Pacific Theaters and the

Here and on the following pages is all anyone may ever see of The Golden Head. Top: *Richard Thorpe, who replaced James Hill as director for* The Golden Head *when conflicts arose, signals action for a scene involving the 150-member State Folk Ensemble of Hungary.* Bottom: *Cast and crew of* The Golden Head *on location in Hungary.*

Top: *Jess Conrad (left), Cecilia Esztergályos, Lorraine Power and Denis Gilmore tour the streets of Budapest.* Bottom: *Lorraine Power has language problems with Zoltán Makláry while shopping in a Budapest street market.*

Top: *Denis Gilmore enjoys Hungarian watermelon.* Bottom: *Romance blossoms between Cecilia Esztergályos and Jess Conrad.*

Top: *The scene of the crime: Lorraine Power visits the historical and beautiful Cathedral of Gyór.* Bottom: *Lionel Jeffries enjoys the rewards of robbery in this scene directed by James Hill. The scene was later reshot by Richard Thorpe, with George Sanders in Jeffries's role.*

Top: *Lorraine Power on the Danube ferryboat* Huba, *which was refurbished and renamed the* White Rabbit *for the film.* Bottom: *Lorraine Power and Cecilia Esztergályos have a "woman-to-woman" talk aboard the* White Rabbit.

Top: *Buddy Hackett greedily clutches the Herm while George Sanders devises a plan to smuggle the artifact out of Hungary on the children's ferryboat.* Bottom: *Lionel Jeffries and Buddy Hackett are confronted by László Ungvári and Denis Gilmore after the children discover they stole the Golden Head. This scene was directed by James Hill and later reshot by Richard Thorpe, with George Sanders replacing Jeffries.*

Top: *Denis Gilmore and Lorraine Power discover the Herm has been hidden on their ferryboat by the thieves.* Bottom: *Jess Conrad and Cecilia Esztergályos are delighted to hear that Lorraine Power and Denis Gilmore have put the Golden Head in the thieves' room and called the police.*

trademark attached to, of all things, hotels. The giant screen process died; not long after, so did William Forman.

The failure of *The Golden Head* is sad indeed. It was the first American-Hungarian coproduction and of great historical value from that standpoint alone. It was photographed in majestic Budapest, an ancient city that should have been seen by American audiences as only 70mm Super Cinerama could show it, and along the Danube River, perhaps Europe's most romantic waterway. It could have been a great incentive for Hungarian tourism. All the historical sites of the capital city were used as locations, including the just-constructed Elizabeth Bridge of which the Hungarians were justly proud. The film was a massive, well-executed coproduction, if not a great story. It was shot under the adverse conditions of political tension by dedicated filmmakers who proved that different cultures, languages and governments need not separate the people of the world.

Cinemiracle

The Cinemiracle process was almost identical in every respect with Cinerama. The main difference, apparently, was that it was a far superior presentation.

Like Cinerama, Cinemiracle presented a wide screen picture composed of three films synchronously projected side by side onto a deeply curved screen. (The screen was not louvered.) Only one feature, *Windjammer,* was shot in the process. *Windjammer* premiered at the Chinese Theatre in Hollywood on April 8, 1958. (Warner Bros. began production of *The Miracle* [1959] in Cinemiracle, but switched to Technirama. Part of this original three-strip footage still exists.)

Though the similarities to Cinerama were striking, Cinemiracle had two things going for it that the older process did not. All three projectors were located in a single booth at the rear of the theater, and the "join lines" where the three images came together on the screen were virtually nonexistent. An official announcement to the press hailed the Cinemiracle process as a "seamless Cinerama!"

The problem of perfectly matching the three strips of film into a panoramic whole on the giant, deeply curved screen had plagued the Cinerama engineers from the very outset of experimentation. The inventor of Cinerama, Fred Waller, had addressed the problem with an ingenious device for obscuring the join lines where the three separate images met on the screen. He had installed tiny comblike bits of steel onto each projector at the side of the film gate. These rapidly moved up and down along the edges of the film, causing the image on the screen to be slightly blurred at the edge of each picture and minimizing the lines between them. All 35mm Cinerama projectors used these devices, which were commonly referred to as "gigolos" or "jiggolos" — because they jiggled the image. (They also

Trade ad for It's a Mad, Mad, Mad, Mad World, *the first feature to use the "new single-lens Super Cinerama projection" process—i.e., Ultra Panavision 70 projected through an enlarging lens made for Cinerama, Inc.*

served to correct another vital technical problem: even light distribution across the vast screen. Where the three panels overlapped, a double light intensity was created by the arc lamps. The oscillating sawteeth decreased the light at this conjunction point by 50 percent, giving equal light on the screen from each projector and smoothly blending the dividing lines of the three separate images into one.)

Cinemiracle overcame the problem of join lines very simply: It used mirrors! Any magician would have been proud.

In 1955, National Theatres acquired exclusive rights to patents covering a new electronic camera lens system. It used a special three-lens optical arrangement mounted to three standard 35mm motion picture cameras.

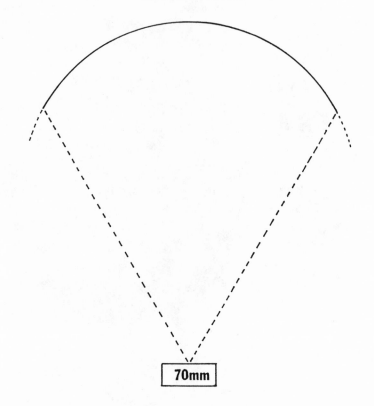

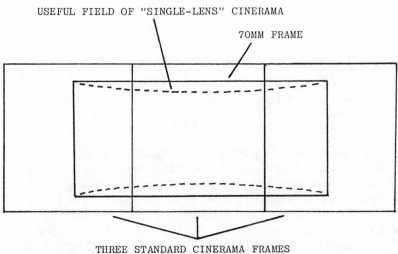

USEFUL FIELD OF "SINGLE-LENS" CINERAMA

70MM FRAME

THREE STANDARD CINERAMA FRAMES

Top: *The "New Super Cinerama" process, actually Todd-AO format 70mm, covered a somewhat narrower screen area which was only 120°.* Bottom: *Showing the useful field of "Single-Lens" Cinerama.*

Now the **BIG ONE**

We are proud to announce the first production in **CINEMIRACLE** is at **NTA**

LOUIS DE ROCHEMONT'S **WINDJAMMER**

In Gorgeous **EASTMAN COLOR**

is now ready for road show engagements in key cities throughout the country after record breaking engagements of 36 weeks at Grauman's Chinese, L. A., 24 weeks Roxy, N. Y., 33 weeks Boston, Boston, 32 weeks Century, Minneapolis, 16 weeks Boyd, Philadelphia, 13 weeks Paramount, Seattle, 15 weeks Chicago Opera House.

Flash—Strand Theatre, Milwaukee reports biggest first week hard ticket gross in the all time history of the theatre (advance sale tops every previous attraction).

In the first handful of engagements WINDJAMMER has already amassed the amazing box office gross of over $6,000,000.

N.T.A. invites the nation's top showmen to set their box office sails and take advantage of the proven enormous power of WINDJAMMER.

Set your date now for an exclusive reserved seat long run in your territory.

Now available as part of your film deal...*new* wrap-around projection and sound system installed in your theatre by our engineers.

Contact **NTA** **PICTURES, INC.**
LEONARD S. GRUENBERG, General Manager
COLISEUM TOWER • 10 COLUMBUS CIRCLE • NEW YORK 19, N. Y.

Shortly after the first Cinemiracle feature, Windjammer, *was released, it was relegated by a jealous Cinerama, Inc., to playing only Cinerama houses. Cinemiracle was dead almost before it began. Nevertheless, they had time to develop two logos (see above and right).*

CINEMIRACLE

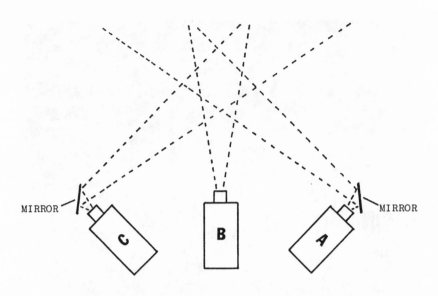

The Cinemiracle projection system.

The center camera recorded the center panel of the scene directly through the camera lens. The two side cameras, each at a precise angle, photographed the right and left sides of the scene, which were reflected by mirrors. The design and placement of the mirrors reduced the problem of parallax to a minimum.

In the theater, three specially designed projectors were interlocked with a seven-channel sound reproducer. All four machines were located in a central projection room at the rear of the theater. The projection optical system included mirrors on the two end projectors. When the image from these two machines met on the screen with the center projected panel, they became one combined elongated picture on a deeply curved screen. (Cinerama later adopted an almost identical arrangement in booths of its newer theaters.)

Four machines in one booth also meant four projectionists confined to a single room. Theaters built expressly with this arrangement in mind were able to allow for needed work space in the initial design of the structure, but theaters that had been converted to show the process of Cinerama or Cinemiracle often had to "make-do" with the physical limitations of the existing structure. Needless to say, some of these booths were very close quarters! Since the light source for the projectors in those pre–Xenon days was carbon arc lamps, these booths were also extremely warm. It was not unusual to find the operators working in undershirts, while outside it was the dead of winter.

The Cinemiracle sound system was identical with Cinerama's in that

The cramped Cinerama/Cinemiracle booth housing the three projectors, sound reproducer and rewind table for all four reels of film. The five-man crew has finished the last show of the day.

it also presented seven channels of discrete stereophonic sound. Speaker placement in the auditorium was the same, with five behind the giant screen and numerous surround units placed along the sidewalls and rear wall of the room. Cinemiracle claimed to be the first motion picture system to use the new RCA transistorized amplifiers.

Whether Cinemiracle was better than Cinerama in its overall presentation could be debated. After all, how many people today can say they remember ever seeing the process? By the time the authors had an opportunity to see *Windjammer* it was playing in a conventional Cinerama house. To the average patron in that theater, it looked like any other Cinerama presentation. It was a nice movie, was pretty to look at, and yet seemed no different from what one would have expected to see or hear in that environment.

Apparently, the original Cinemiracle presentation was very impressive and somehow stood out from the Cinerama travelogues. One fact is certain: It was impressive enough for Cinerama to want it out of existence. Shortly after *Windjammer* opened and box office receipts proved it was a hit with the public, Cinerama, Inc., and National Theatres, Inc., entered into a merger agreement. *Windjammer* played worldwide in Cinerama houses (no mirrors reflected any frame onto the screen), and the "miracle" of Cinemiracle was dead.

Kinopanorama

The Soviet version of Cinerama* was actually the blueprint for the United States Cinemiracle process in a number of ways. The two real differences in Kinopanorama and the later American system were in the amount of overlap for each frame, Kinopanorama images matting over considerably more, and the film speed, which in the Soviet process was the

The Soviets actually call their process "panoramikh" but in their own English translations always refer to it as Kinopanorama.

FIRST NATIONAL BANK CLUB

Special prices have been arranged for employees of the bank to see.......

THE **NEW**

CINERAMA

PRESENTATION!

THRILL to the exciting sea voyages . . . and the many fascinating ports of call . . . in the Caribbean . . . and around the world!

THRILL to the Portuguese New Year celebrations in Funchal, Madeira...its breath-taking scenes . . . native dances and songs!

LOUIS DE ROCHEMONT'S

"WINDJAMMER"

THRILL to the artistry of the Boston Pops Orchestra...world famous Pablo Casals' cello in San Juan . . . festivals in Dutch Curacao!

THRILL to the spine tingling dancers and singers in Trinidad's fabulous Port of Spain ...the haunting music of Puerto Rico... and More and More and More!

FEBRUARY 28 at 8 P.M.

MARTIN CINERAMA THEATRE
583 PEACHTREE ST., N.E. • ATLANTA 8, GA. • 875-9405

ORCHESTRA RESERVED SEATS----------------SPECIAL PRICE $1.80 (Reg. Price $2.20)
BALCONY RESERVED SEATS-----------------SPECIAL PRICE $1.40 (Reg. Price $1.75)
CHILDREN SEATS (Under 12)---------------$1.25

TICKETS AVAILABLE FROM BANK CLUB SECRETARY, JEANNENE RUTLEDGE, PHONE EXTENSION 637.

--------------------------Clip---------------------Clip--------------------------

TO: JEANNENE RUTLEDGE   ORDERS MUST BE IN BY FEBRUARY 26th.

I wish to order _____ ORCHESTRA Reserved Seats @ $1.80 for Date _____

I wish to order _____ BALCONY Reserved Seats @ $1.40 for Date _____

I wish to order _____ CHILDRENS (Under 12) Seats @ $1.25 for Date _____

Name _____Address _____

Enclosed is my check in the amount of $_____(Make Checks Payable MARTIN CINERAMA).

Above: *A reserved seat order form for "The New Cinerama presentation!"—formerly a Cinemiracle presentation, until that process was squelched by Cinerama, Inc. They even changed the title logo (see page 43).*

Opposite, left: *An unblimped, open, Kinopanorama three-strip camera.* Right: *Kinopanorama 70 camera. Note the incredible triangular lens. The arrangement seems more practical than the American Cinerama and Cinemiracle cameras.*

standard 24 frames per second. Projection was via mirror system by one projector with triple-reel magazines, apertures, lenses, etc. When exhibited in the United States, Kinopanorama films were shown in Cinemiracle and Super Cinerama since there was compatability between all three. Relatively minor changes to projectors allowed for the difference in film speed, and the nine-track magnetic stereophonic sound was mixable to six or seven tracks with no loss of information. (The extra sound information might have involved Perspecta-type encoding, though this is unclear. See Chapter 8 for information on Perspecta Stereophonic Sound.) Just as Cinerama adopted 70mm, the Soviets dropped the three-panel photographic technique in favor of 70mm filming. That was where Kinopanorama 70, as it was dubbed, and 70mm Super Cinerama lost their similarities. The Soviets built cameras that incorporated a special three-section lens splitter so that the visual field covered by the prime lens was equal to that of the original tricamera system. From the 70mm camera film (the Soviets do not use 65mm for photography) three separate panels were optically extracted and projected in the original Kinopanorama format. The results, excluding the dividing lines, seem to have been superior to 70mm Super Cinerama since the visual perspective was correct for the screen while the American technique was not. (Three films shot in standard 70mm were also optically converted to tripanel format. They, obviously, did not have the same visual field as true Kinopanorama, with results being even less than single lens Super Cinerama presentation.)

Kinopanorama was discontinued in the U.S.S.R. in the mid-sixties. Its life was even shorter than Cinerama's. The trade name, however, lives on and is generally applied to any specialty Soviet film technique. (The Soviets also refer to these novelty processes as cinerama, with a small *c*.) Circular Kinopanorama uses multiple cameras and projectors (usually eleven, but occasionally twenty-two with screens stacked) to render a 360-degree visual field backed with nine-channel magnetic stereophonic sound. Polyscreen, Variscope (also called Polyscopic and Variscopic) and Multifilm are 70mm presentations in which the frame is split into several different scenes at once. Projection seems always to be onto a flat screen, and magnetic stereo (presumably nine channels) is employed. These films have so far been documentaries made up almost entirely of stock footage bridged with new material and have not been used for dramatic storytelling. As elsewhere, the Soviets have generally discarded curved screens and adopted flat 70mm presentation for their prestigious features.

Dimension 150

In 1963 Dr. Richard Vetter and Carl Williams came up with a system intended to be competitive with 70mm Super Cinerama. Like that format, it would employ standard 65mm camera film with 70mm release prints. The projected image actually filled a 120-degree, curved screen in a 2×1 ratio.

The name and the advertising material were meant to deliberately mislead audiences, making them think the system was more visually encompassing than Super Cinerama.

The Dimension 150 system was completely compatible with existing spherical 70mm formats. In fact nothing was really new. There were four specially made D-150 lenses that covered fields of view at 50, 70, 120 and 150 degrees, but any lenses for 70mm were usable. The 150-degree lens was considered the main photographic element; from this lens, the highly misleading process name was taken. A special optical device fitted in front of the projection lens and gave even light, density and clarity over the entire curvature of the specially surfaced screen. When properly set up it worked as it was supposed to. (The 70mm Super Cinerama projection lens, by comparison, was little more than an enlarging device.) The sound system was six-track magnetic discrete as developed by Todd-AO (see Chapter 5). The cameras were 65mm Mitchells, the same as then used for Todd-AO and Super Panavision 70.

But the D-150 projection just did not have the visual impact of 70mm Super Cinerama. Theaters that installed the format tended to be smaller than those set up for Cinerama, and while the curvature was the same, the screen was not really floor-to-ceiling like Cinerama's. It was not louvered, either; but then, Cinerama dropped that particularity after adoption of the 70mm format. The D-150 system was packaged as "all-purpose," and unlike Cinerama, it did not ignore other formats. If a theater installed the complete system it was possible not only to change the aspect ratio for each film format (35mm spherical at 1.85×1, 35mm anamorphic at substandard 2.20×1, 70mm spherical and D-150 at 2×1), but also to seemingly alter the curvature of the screen. The screen maskings were set so that spherical 35mm was one size; 35mm anamorphic was a bit larger in height and considerably wider; 70mm was somewhat higher and wider than 35mm 'scope (anamorphic); and D-150 filled the entire available screen area. Cinerama theaters were left to their own devices for non–Cinerama engagements, which often resulted in some rather poor presentations. D-150 was designed so that all film formats would look good, though 1.85×1 35mm tended to be most unimpressive. Some theaters, of course, disregarded the specifications and showed films over more of the screen area than they were supposed to. Understandably, they felt that a 70mm print should take full advantage of the giant screen. (No doubt some felt the same about 35mm 'scope.)

Todd-AO was so impressed by Dimension 150 that they bought into the project with Vetter and Williams and formed D-150, Inc., to market, license and service productions and theaters. Todd-AO apparently reasoned that if there was going to be a true competitor to 70mm Super Cinerama then it would be in their best interests to control it. (D-150, Inc., was not a happy company, and the Vetter-Williams faction would soon be in legal opposition with the Todd-AO folks.)

D-150 did not exactly fly. It was an acceptable process, but it was never a serious competitor for Super Cinerama or any other 70mm system. Only

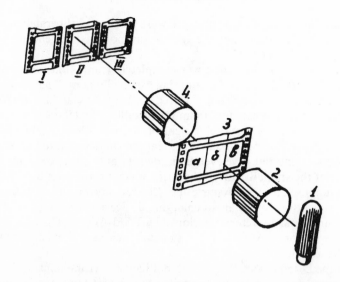

The patent drawing demonstrating the optical conversion from 70mm to three-strip Kinopanorama format. This is the same technique, sans 1.25 × 1 anamorphics, used to convert Ultra Panavision 70 footage to Super Cinerama for How the West Was Won *in the United States.*

two features would utilize the format, though it was employed for some international fair exhibition shorts. D-150 died in 1970. While 70mm Super Cinerama lasted a little longer, these two systems were the last of the big screen processes to go. (Almost all recent 70mm films have been blowups, and since literally all of the giant screen cinemas have been demolished, no attempt has been made in the production of these pictures — excepting the *Star Wars* saga and *Brainstorm* — to tailor them for big screen effects.)

Dimension 150 Specifications

Camera and negative:
Film   65mm
Exposed image height   .906"
Exposed image width   2.072"
Perfs per frame   5
Film speed   112.5 ft. per min.
Frames per second   24
Cameras   Mitchell
Lenses   D-150
Release print:
Film   70mm
Aspect ratio   2.21 × 1 sans
                                          soundtrack
Projected aspect ratio   2 × 1

Above: *The Dimension 150 screen as viewed from the theater balcony (from which it appears considerably flatter than the 120 degrees it actually was). Note how close the front seats are. The uncomfortable viewing did not help it compete against Super Cinerama, whose screen was ceiling-to-floor and seating not nearly so extreme.* Right: *The Dimension 150 logo.*

THE NEW DIMENSION IN MOTION PICTURES

Rectified aspect ratio	2.20 × 1*
Projected image height	.866″ uncropped
Projected image width	1.913″
Perfs per frame	5
Film speed	112.5 ft. per min.
Frames per second	24
Compression	1.25 × 1 on each side*
Sound system	six-track stereophonic
Sound format	magnetic sound-on-film

For some specially produced prints, which, when projected onto a 120-degree screen, appeared normal in a 2 × 1 aspect ratio.

Thrillarama

The brainchild of Albert H. Reynolds and Dowlen Russell of Texas, this ridiculous process was an unsuccessful attempt to create the Cinerama effect with two cameras and two projectors. The foolishness lies in the fact that the same results rendered by Thrillarama could have been obtained by anamorphic 35mm shot with wide angle prime lenses backing the 'scope lens and projected with a 1.33×1 aperture instead of the normal 1.18×1 'scope plate. The camera lenses would have covered the same visual field, and the screen image would have had the same aspect ratio of 2.66×1 without the noticeable center blend strip of dual film projection.

As usual with new systems of this type, the first feature was a travelog, *Thrillarama Adventure*. It opened in Houston on August 9, 1956, and closed after a week's run. It was briefly shown in other cities. An announced second film was never made, or at least never completed. The process disappeared.

On the surface Thrillarama did seem exploitable. It had a curved screen and stereophonic sound; it employed regular 35mm and could be set up in a theater in seventeen hours. The two images were photographed with cross beams, the right camera picking up the left image and the left camera picking up the right image. Projection followed this pattern. A device (patent applied for) dovetailed the two at the center to (attempt to) eliminate the slight overlap of the two frames. Another device attached to the projectors to allow proper horizontal adjustment, or so the press material claimed. Actually, adjusting the frame on each machine would have done the same thing without any additional equipment. Oversized reels, originally made for dual film 3D projection, were used, but an intermission was still required. Oddly, the publicity information stated that no alteration was needed for regular booth equipment, but if the machines crossed their projection beams, then they most definitely had to be repositioned, though in most theaters this is a very minor movement to make. Presumably a projector interlock system left over from 3D usage was employed.

Thrillarama actually did generate some industry talk, and reviews of the process were generally favorable, but hopes of it becoming another Cinerama were pipe dreams at best. Hollywood has always been quick to talk but slow to act, especially when the system really isn't worth the effort. Interestingly, Thrillarama-type photography and projection were adopted by several 8mm and 16mm amateur filmmakers for home use.

Wonderama

This was Walter Reade-Sterling's version of 70mm Super Cinerama and was applied to limited engagements of *Mediterranean Holiday** in

---

*Filmed in Superpanorama 70 and generally roadshown in 70mm Super Cinerama.

1965. The screen had a 120 degree curvature, and a special ARC-120 projection device was employed that split the 70mm film as it came out of the projector into two images, allowing separate focus (of sorts) for each half of the screen, then reconstituted them as one image on the screen. While the process worked, it did render a noticeable blur in the center of the curved screen.

Other Multiple-Film
and Deep Curved Screen Processes

Cinema 160

This system was devised by Frank Caldwell, first as Super VistaVision, then in 1955 as Cyclotrona and finally as Cinema 160 in 1958. No features were produced in the process, though it may have been utilized on one or more specialty shorts.

The camera photographed the image over three frames of standard 35mm film running through the camera horizontally. It is unclear if special optics were employed in photography or on the projector. The final image was to be projected on a large, curved screen of 160 degrees. Presumably projection was to be from a standard 35mm unit modified for horizontal film travel. The aspect ratio probably was about 2.10 × 1 (assuming no anamorphics were applied) and the sound interlocked.

Cineorama

A ten-camera, ten-projector system by Raoul Grimoin-Sanson, first used on short travelogs in 1896. We were not able to uncover specific information on any of the films, or for that matter, even how many were actually produced.

Cinerama 360

The first film to utilize this system was the fifteen-minute *Journey to the Stars* in 1962. Boeing Company commissioned Cinerama to engineer a special film for their United States Science Exhibit in the Spacearium at the Seattle World's Fair. The company came up with an extreme wide angle image covering the area of two 70mm frames and utilizing an interlocked four-track magnetic sound system. The film was then projected from the floor into a dome. The audience stood during each screening. After the fair closed, 35mm reduction prints were made and shown in novelty theaters around the country still using the Cinerama 360 logo. Despite some claims, only the Seattle screenings were in 70mm.

Cinerama 360 was only a gimmick process and really little different from the many specialty dome and hemispheric fair and trade exhibition films. It was distinct only in that it received national distribution after its carnival screenings, and then only because the Cinerama name was established with the public. The process was actually not even 360 degrees, though a viewer, looking up, had to turn his head in a wide arc to see the entire screen area.

Film Effects of Hollywood engineered a double height 70mm frame system they called Dynavision in the early seventies. This format, with an extreme wide angle lens, would be used for the thirty-three minute short *To the Moon and Beyond* in 1974. This was exhibited at San Diego's Reuben H. Fleet Space Theater and advertised in Cinerama 360 with six-track magnetic stereo sound. It would later be blown up to OMNIMAX size and be released internationally as *Cosmos*.

Few remember, or even saw, Cinerama 360. It was that minor.

Circle-Vision

This multi-camera, multi-projector system was introduced at Disneyland in 16mm in the mid 1950s. It has since evolved into a 35mm process and depending on the show is from nine to eleven screens covering from a 200- to a 360-degree viewing field. The audio playback is via magnetic stereo in various number of tracks. The screens originally did not blend together, but recently an attempt has been made to eliminate definite dividing sections by overlapping each image slightly.

Circlorama

A British circular film (multiple cameras and projectors) system with stereo sound, used on the short *Circlorama Cavalcade* in 1964. It was developed by Leonard Urry and Leon Hepner of Circlorama Theatres, Ltd., London. It apparently was used only once.

Cyclotrona

See Cinema 160.

Quadravision

A four-camera, four-projector and four-channel-sound system used by Ford Motor Company on their 12-minute commercial *Design for Suburban Living* (1959), which toured the country in a tent theater. Also the name applied to an anamorphic, side-by-side, single-strip 3D system by StereoVision International, Inc.

The Multiple-Film and Deep Curved Screen Process Films

Filming process, if different from projection process, is noted in parentheses (usually following the studio name). Further information on each of these films can be found in the Filmography.

CINERAMA

This Is Cinerama (Cinerama, 1952)
Cinerama Holiday (Cinerama, 1955)
Seven Wonders of the World (Stanley Warner, 1955)
Search for Paradise (Cinerama, 1957)
Cinerama South Seas Adventure (Cinerama, 1958)
Windjammer (National Theatres; Cinemiracle, 1958)*
Renault Dauphin (Renault commercial short; 1960)

*presented in Cinerama only in certain theaters

SUPER CINERAMA

Holiday in Spain (MT, 1961)*
Lafayette (Cinerama, 1962)**
The Wonderful World of the Brothers Grimm (MGM and Cinerama, 1962)
The Best of Cinerama (Cinerama, 1963)
How the West Was Won (MGM and Cinerama, 1963)
Cinerama's Russian Adventure (United Roadshows; Kinopanorama, 1966)

*optically converted from Todd-70
*optically converted from Super Technirama 70 and exhibited in Super Cinerama

70MM SUPER CINERAMA

It's a Mad, Mad, Mad, Mad World (UA; Ultra Panavision 70, 1963)
Circus World (Par; Super Technirama 70, 1964)*
The Golden Head (Cinerama; Super Technirama 70, 1964)*
Mediterranean Holiday (Continental; Superpanorama 70, 1964)**
Battle of the Bulge (WB; Ultra Panavision 70, 1965)
The Greatest Story Ever Told (UA; Ultra Panavision 70, 1965)
The Hallelujah Trail (UA; Ultra Panavision 70, 1965)
Shellarama (Shell Oil commercial short; 70mm; 1965)
Cinerama's Russian Adventure (United Roadshows, Kinopanorama, 1966)†
Grand Prix (MGM; Super Panavision 70, 1966)
Khartoum (UA; Ultra Panavision 70, 1966)
Custer of the West (CRC; Super Technirama 70, 1967)
Ice Station Zebra (MGM; Super Panavision 70, 1968)
2001: A Space Odyssey (MGM; Super Panavision 70 and Todd-AO, 1968)
Krakatoa East of Java (CRC; Super Panavision 70 and Todd-AO, 1969)
Song of Norway (CRC; Super Panavision 70, 1970)
The Last Valley (CRC; Todd-AO, 1971)††
The Great Waltz (MGM; Panavision 70, 1972)
This Is Cinerama (CRC, 1972)†

*one sequence optically converted from three-panel process
**shown in Wonderama in some theaters
†optically converted from three-panel process
††not shown in 70mm Super Cinerama

CINEMIRACLE

Windjammer (NTA, 1958)*
Great Is My Country (Sovexportfilm; Kinopanorama, 1959)
The Enchanted Mirror (Sovexportfilm; Kinopanorama, 1959)

*presented in Cinerama in certain theaters

KINOPANORAMA

Studios are given where known. Photographic processes other than Kinopanorama are noted.

Great Is My Country (Tsentrnauchfilm, 1957)*†
The Enchanted Mirror (Tsentraliniy dokumentaliniy film studiya, 1958)*†
Chas neozkhidannykh puteshestviy v polyote na vertolyote (Tsentraliniy dokumentaliniy film studiya, 1960)†
Chetvyortaya programma panoramikh filmov "Tsirkovoye predstavleniye" i "Na Krasnoy ploshchadyu" (Tsentraliniy dokumentaliniy film studiya, 1961)†
Opasnie povoroti (1961)
SSSR s otkritim serddem (Tsentrnauchfilm, 1961)†
The Story of Flaming Years (Kievskaya kinostudiya im. A.P. Dovzenko–Mosfilm; Todd-AO, 1961)
V Antarktiku za kitami (1961)†
The Trial of Madmen (Mosfilm; Sovscope 70, 1962)
Batmanova, Singing Slave (Mosfilm; Kinopanorama 70, 1963)
Na podvodnikh skuterakh (Kinopanorama 70, 1963)
The Optimistic Tragedy (Mosfilm; Sovscope 70, 1963)
The Volga Flows On (Kinostudiya im. M. Gorikogo, 1963)
Zimnie ztyutsi (1963)
The Sleeping Beauty (Lenfilm; Kinopanorama 70, 1964)
Delifini prikhodyat k lyudyam (Kinopanorama 70, 1966)
Na samom bolishom stadione (Kinopanorama 70, 1966)

presented in the United States in Cinemiracle
†*excerpts incorporated into* Cinerama's Russian Adventure

DIMENSION 150

Excluding international fair shorts.

The Bible: In the Beginning ... (20th–Fox, 1966)*
Patton (20th–Fox, 1970)**

credited as D-150
**credited as Dimension 150*

THRILLARAMA

Thrillarama Adventure (Thrillarama, Inc., 1956)

WONDERAMA

Mediterranean Holiday (Continental, 1965)*

filmed in Superpanorama 70 and generally roadshown in 70mm Super Cinerama

III. The Anamorphic Processes

CinemaScope

December 18, 1952: 20th Century-Fox purchases rights to the Hypergonar process. The technology of filmmaking was about to change drastically and permanently. The anamorphic system was to be renamed CinemaScope, which would soon become the most hyped word in the history of the free press.

Hollywood did not discover the anamorphic process. Unlike Edison, they acquired it legally and did what others had been unable to: make it commercial. The basic technique, a squeeze added photographically and removed during projection to produce a wider image, was applied to movies as early as 1898 by Professor Ernst Abbe and Zeiss Company in Germany. It had been used with still photography as early as 1862 by Sir David Brewster, who is credited with discovering the anamorphosis theory. The credit is of course ridiculous; certain glass, manufactured for many, many years, produced the effect, as did some metallic items going back to the Roman Empire and before. Brewster, however, was granted the first patent.

Pour construire un feu was made in 1927, utilizing the Hypergonar lens. Most, but not all, sources give credit for this lens to Professor Henri Chrétien; some claim his 'scope lens was not made until 1931. At any rate, 'scope footage was apparently limited to certain sequences, and it is possible the film was not publicly exhibited until 1929. Information from this period is extremely conflicting. *La merveilleuse vie de Jeanne d'Arc* (1929) also used Hypergonar for some scenes.

Dr. H. Sidney Newcomer tried to convince the United States film industry to use his Anamorphosa in 1929, but the community wasn't interested in special lens devices. The consensus in New York (which then controlled Hollywood) was wide gauge wide screen, not alteration to the accepted 35mm format.

Chrétien continued to promote his Anamorphoscope, as it was renamed, temporarily. Demonstrations, possibly with the showing of short films or even features, occurred in 1931 and 1935. Paramount Pictures acquired the lens for experimentation but passed on purchasing it. Further demonstrations in 1951 brought no real interest.

20th Century-Fox Announces

First Demonstrations of

CINEMASCOPE

for Producers, Exhibitors and the Press

This week, a momentous new era in motion pictures is being launched at our Hollywood studios with the first demonstrations of CinemaScope, the most eagerly anticipated development in the history of entertainment.

In addition to showings for industry executives, studio heads, producers, technicians and representatives of the guilds and the press, Mr. Spyros P. Skouras, president of our company, has scheduled a series of showings for exhibitors, personally prepared by Mr. Darryl F. Zanuck and revealing the unparalleled new vista of entertainment potentialities created by the advent of CinemaScope.

A Series of Four Demonstrations Especially for the EXHIBITORS OF THE UNITED STATES AND CANADA will be held

FRIDAY, MARCH 20th, at 2:30 P.M.

and SATURDAY, MARCH 21st,

at 10:30 A.M., 2:30 P.M. and 5 P.M.

ON STAGE 6 OF OUR STUDIO LOCATED AT WESTERN AVE. AND SUNSET, HOLLYWOOD, CALIF.

We hope you will be able to attend these demonstrations, along with those of your associates who should share this wonderful experience.

Al Lichtman, Director of Distribution, 20th Century-Fox

However, when *This Is Cinerama* opened in September 1952, film-makers opened their eyes . . . a bit slowly at first, but wide open at last. The Cinerama process had been around for years, mostly gathering dust, but when Lowell Thomas, Michael Todd, Louis B. Mayer and others jumped in and produced the first feature travelog (they didn't know what else to do with the process, so far off base was it from normal movies) and people began to line up around the block to see a wide screen film with directional sound, it was time mainstream Hollywood got on the move. Chrétien's 'scope lens (a box device that fit into a frame rig in front of the regular prime lens) was put on display again, and 20th Century–Fox bought it.

Not everyone at the studio was happy with the decision to go wide screen. Cameramen and other technicians had no interest in the system. Neither did most producers, directors and executives. But fortunately Darryl F. Zanuck and many of his top staffers realized that here was an immediate, inexpensive (compared to Cinerama) means of going to big, wide screen presentation without any of the numerous problems inherent in multiple-camera formats, wide gauge systems or 3D, which was just about to pop up (and out). And there was good reason to be interested just now: CRTs, the Box, the Tube, the dread-of-dreads, free home entertainment as never before—TeleVision!

After World War II the development of television took off. The United States was initially far behind England and the Soviet Union, but soon after the hostilities ceased, the new medium created the ultimate horror for Hollywood. By late 1952 many American homes were receiving programs every night (and usually morning and afternoon as well). It often was a community thing: Several families would gather at a friend's home to watch the new magic box. Theater attendance nosedived. Many cinemas closed. The last gasp of vaudeville was heard. Traveling medicine shows came to an end. Here was for free what had once cost. Here was the real fulfillment of the American Dream.

Hollywood, for the most part, ignored the bandwagon. Although most minor studios and independent producers saw the gold mine, sold their old movies to television, and began producing for the networks and for syndication, the major studios held onto the insane theory that it would all go away. But by 1952 it was clear the intruder was here to stay. It couldn't be driven out—but it could, maybe, be defeated.

The first step was color. Hollywood grabbed at every process available. Trucolor, Cinecolor and Technicolor all improved their facilities. Eastman Color was getting final development. But this wasn't going to work for long: RCA and others had color TV waiting in the wings (some engineers were promising color telecasts by 1954). Hollywood got scared.

Cinerama, offering sights and sounds that no television could reproduce, provided an answer—but how to get an economical version?

Opposite: *The March 1953 two-page trade ad that would change a worldwide industry.*

Twentieth Century-Fox had it! And they were gladly going to share it with all their fellow studios. The enemy would be faced head-on, no more retreating, no more ignoring. This was the time for open warfare.

CinemaScope was born. The name was catchy, and 20th Century-Fox had a beautiful logo for it. They also had a minor problem to overcome: The name was already a trademark, owned by Don Federson. A signed check eliminated that little difficulty.

The wide screen system worked, as 20th Century-Fox demonstrated over and over again to all in Hollywood, but the sound didn't: It was too small, too confined. The answer was again provided by Cinerama: Stereophonic sound recorded onto magnetic stripes, either interlocked with the picture film or placed directly onto the film. Twentieth Century-Fox chose the latter, while some studios at first elected the former audio format. Either way, television was now at a distinct disadvantage: It might eventually provide color, but it would never be able to match the height and width of the screen nor deliver fully directional sound ... never, reasoned Hollywood. (Now we do have color TV, much longer in arriving than promised; and finally stereo sound that is for the most part superior to theatrical stereo. In fact, stereo TV has caused the revival of many early stereophonic features originally exhibited on a limited basis in their multi-channel versions.)

Twentieth Century-Fox immediately put two CinemaScope features into production: *How to Marry a Millionaire* and *The Robe,* a project that had been around awhile at RKO Radio, but was finally rejected by them and was picked up by 20th Century-Fox. While ... *Millionaire* was completed first, *The Robe* was considered the bigger, more spectacular item and deemed the first CinemaScope release. (Twentieth Century-Fox and the other studios weren't sure if the process would fly with the exhibitors and shot all their earlier 'scope pictures in anamorphic and regular 35mm simultaneously. After all, there was no assurance that the foreign market would go for the system since television was not yet a box office drain outside the United States.)

CinemaScope was a resounding success. The first theaters equipped with the new screens, lenses and stereophonic sound systems saw their box office intake skyrocket. Within a few short months all major studios had anamorphic features in production except Paramount, which was still thinking in terms of wide gauge exhibition (see Chapter 4).

Since there were limited quantities of the Chrétien lenses, 20th Century-Fox contracted with Bausch & Lomb, the world's most respected optics manufacturer, to produce new lenses that would service the entire industry as well as give 20th Century-Fox control of licensing. But licensing soon proved to be beyond the studio's control: The anamorphic process itself was not patentable. MGM assigned Robert E. Gottschalk to develop an anamorphic device to render 'scope pictures in a manner unlike the Bausch & Lomb lens. (MGM wasn't sure about the actual lenses being patentable, but they knew the technology wasn't, so it was better to produce

Twentieth Century–Fox heralded The Robe *with many multiple-page ads. The ad above is the most common one and even today is remembered by many. The CinemaScope logo and curved-screen art would be standard in 'scope advertising for years.*

the same results with a different system.) The Gottschalk Lens was a prismatic device that compressed the image in the same shape as CinemaScope but was not *per se* a copy of 20th Century–Fox's lens. The MGM anamorphic unit would soon be known as Panatar (Bausch & Lomb called their lenses Baltar) and finally as Panavision. (Panavision would quickly discard the prisms in favor of actual squeeze lenses.) Others followed suit, and various anamorphic devices from Delrama (following the original Panavision policy of compression via mirror device), Vistarama, etc., appeared. Twentieth Century–Fox was naturally unhappy about their failure to capture the lens licensing market. They were, however, consoled by one fact: Most in the industry wanted standardization and regardless of the 'scope system employed agreed to use the CinemaScope trademark in advertising and screen credits. This policy didn't make the various other 'scope and 'vision manufacturers happy, but after a few years they too would start to receive proper billing. The CinemaScope process became a permanent fixture in filmmaking, even though the Bausch & Lomb lenses and the trademark would be discontinued in the late 1960s, replaced by Panavision, Technovision, Todd-AO 35, and others.

Initially the aspect ratio of CinemaScope was 2.66×1 since the only camera change was the addition of the anamorphic lens with a 2×1 optical

A Clear Statement As To The Equipment Required For CinemaScope Pictures

AND NEWS OF GREAT IMPORTANCE TO EVERY EXHIBITOR

For the perfect projection of CinemaScope pictures, exhibitors will require the following equipment:

THE CinemaScope LENS

Because of the tremendous volume of orders which have been placed with Bausch & Lomb and leading lens manufacturers of Europe for the CinemaScope anamorphic lenses, making mass production possible, the manufacturers have been able to effect large savings in the cost of the lenses and, effective immediately, this saving is being passed on to the exhibitor. **The new prices are $1900 per pair for the large lenses (for use with long focal length lenses), and $1800 per pair for the smaller lenses (for use with short focal length lenses), retroactive to all orders already received.** The original price was $2875 per pair, regardless of size. By acquiring the CinemaScope lenses, you will be able to show any picture photographed in the anamorphic process and in the same aspect ratio.

THE CinemaScope SCREENS

In order to clear up any confusion which may exist, we would like to spell out the facts about the screen required for the projection of CinemaScope pictures. CinemaScope is a quality product and it can be given full justice only through the highest quality equipment. The right screen is just as important to the proper exhibition of CinemaScope as the right lenses and the single-film magnetic stereophonic sound system.

We have found, by scientific test, that only the screens offered with the CinemaScope process, distributed by the dealer of your choice, can capture and reflect the true and full glory of the CinemaScope process.

This is true of the Miracle Mirror Screen, which is already in substantial supply and whose volume is being increased daily. The only other screen CinemaScope Products has contracted for is the Magniglow Astrolite Screen. The Radiant Manufacturing Corporation, of Chicago, is now completing plans for full-scale production of the Magniglow Astrolite Screen so that we will be able to meet the great demand for these superior screens. To date, these two screens are the only ones our engineers have found which will ensure the perfection necessary for the complete enjoyment of CinemaScope pictures.

These screens give 2-for-1 light without need for boosting amperage, an important economic factor.

They provide maximum utilization of the light reaching the screen from the projector.

They are precisely designed to reflect and distribute the light evenly over the large surface required for CinemaScope projection, thus making every seat a good seat because the picture is uniformly bright from any seat in the theatre, and the light does not fall off on either side of the screen.

They are the best by test all-purpose screens, and you can use them not only for CinemaScope but for standard 2-D, 3-D, and any other wide-screen projection systems.

THE CinemaScope MAGNETIC SOUND SYSTEM

Every 20th Century-Fox CinemaScope picture will be produced for exhibition in the revolutionary new single-film stereophonic sound system. The new CinemaScope magnetic sound head will be in full production in September and ready for continuous delivery by all the leading sound manufacturers.

The sound heads for the CinemaScope process go by various names; some manufacturers call them the Button-On sound heads, some call them "The Penthouse"...but all of them give you four tracks, one of which is an overall track for auditorium effects, on a single strip of standard 35-millimeter film. They eliminate the "double system" of using motion picture and sound separately, do away with any separate sound reproducers, eliminate extra work and enforced intermissions, prevent errors in matching film and sound, and avoid the risk of going "out of sync."

Once the new sound head has been installed, your projector can be used just as you have always used it in the past, including standard 2-D films. When you order your sound heads you will receive from the equipment dealer of your choice a complete kit for the minor changes needed in sprockets, aperture plates and other minor parts required for conversion of your present standard projector.

Our first CinemaScope picture, "The Robe" in Color by Technicolor, will open at the Roxy Theatre, New York, on September 16th. During October, we expect to launch "The Robe" in most of the principal cities of the United States and Canada, and in all the capital cities of the world before the end of this year. This will be followed by "How To Marry A Millionaire,""Beneath The 12-Mile Reef," "Prince Valiant," "Hell And High Water," and "River Of No Return." There will also be many other wonderful CinemaScope pictures coming your way. M-G-M already has two big CinemaScope pictures in production—the first of which, "Knights of the Round Table," will be released in November, soon to be followed by "Rose Marie" and many others being readied for production. From Walt Disney there will be "Lady and the Tramp," "20,000 Leagues Under the Sea," and an unlimited number of short subjects; from United Artists, Errol Flynn in "The Story of William Tell" and W. R. Frank's "Sitting Bull"; from Allied Artists, "The Black Prince." Columbia will produce a number of top quality productions in CinemaScope.

If you intend to show these great attractions, please contact *the equipment dealer of your choice* immediately for the equipment herein described, if you have not already done so.

AL LICHTMAN, 20th Century-Fox

compression. The standard 1.33 × 1 aperture was retained. This ratio was reduced to 2.55 × 1 by the addition of MagOptical Stereophonic Sound, which slightly cut into the picture area on each side. Regular optical sound and Perspecta Stereophonic Sound prints retained the 2.66 × 1 shape. Soon the 1.33 × 1 aperture was replaced with a 1.18 × 1 aperture, and the resulting image was standardized in an aspect ratio of 2.35 × 1 regardless of soundtrack format. All of this has led to much confusion over the years as to the actual aspect ratio of CinemaScope, a debate further fueled by the fact that 16mm and 8mm 'scope ratios are always given as 2.66 × 1. Actually, 16mm anamorphic is 2.74 × 1 and 8mm is 2.66 × 1 because of the difference in their camera apertures, 1.37 × 1 and 1.33 × 1 respectively. There was a difference in the ratios of some early 'scope pictures, but standardization came very quickly. Twentieth Century–Fox also tampered with the perforations, reducing them in an attempt to make the magnetic-coated prints run more stably through projectors, but the smaller holes tended to tear easily and damage the MagOptical tracks, reducing print life substantially. (Perspecta stereo optical prints did not have this problem.)

CinemaScope and the other wide screen processes did not save the industry. Despite what you've read elsewhere, CinemaScope and stereophonic sound were a blessing to only a third or so of the existing theaters in the early fifties — those that could absorb the high expense of adding the new screen technologies. Most neighborhood theaters, depleted of their audience by television, only dug their own graves more quickly by shelling out thousands of dollars for new equipment. Others cut corners in the wrong places: Theatermen most often refused to add the proper stereo audio systems and cheated the public of the benefit of correct sound reproduction. Those houses that could not accommodate the added screen width tended to crop the sides of 'scope pictures, offering a presentation far below the prescribed intentions. Theaters continued to close at a staggering rate. Indeed, only in the late 1980s would there be resurgence in new theater contruction — and even today it is not common practice for newly constructed theaters to install a screen wider than 2 × 1, making it necessary to crop .35 from the sides of anamorphic pictures.

CinemaScope's impact was also deadened by the quick adoption of cropped wide screen. The studios could not agree on the best ratio for cropping regular 35mm and variously recommended 1.66 × 1, 1.75 × 1, 1.85 × 1 and 2 × 1. Theaters often selected the ratio that filled their screens. When 1.85 × 1 was finally agreed upon by all the major studios (except Disney, which still holds to 1.75 × 1), it was too late for standardization. Today most features shot for cropping are shown between 1.85 × 1 and 2 × 1 by the

Opposite: *An August 1953 trade ad. Twentieth Century–Fox, attempting to provide the public with quality, would be waylaid by cheap exhibitors. MGM, Warner Bros. and Paramount would try to counter some of the exhibitors' tightness by offering prints in Perspecta Stereophonic Sound, an inexpensive optical system, as well as magnetic stereo. But the public would continue to be ripped off.*

CinemaScope 55: The modified Mitchell Grandeur-Realife Camera with anamor-
phics by Bausch & Lomb. Twentieth Century–Fox's Grover Laube, studio engineer,
is at left, and Sol Halprin, executive director of photography, is at right, on the
studio backlot. The day's shooting camera report sheet is taped to the rear magazine
section. This photo was presumably made during the filming of Carousel.

majority of theaters in the United States. In Europe the fight over a correct
cropped ratio is still being waged between 1.66×1 and 1.75×1. In the Iron
Curtain countries and the Middle and Far East 1.37×1 is the standard for
nonanamorphic 35mm. All too often in modern cinemas the ratio decided
upon for spherical is the ratio retained for anamorphic. Hollywood,
however, still frames for 2.35×1 'scope even though only a very small per-
entage of theaters are set up to show an image that wide. No wonder most
filmgoers today have no idea what 'scope means. The anamorphic process
would eventually fall out of favor with studios, since the principal life of
movies would be television, but recently the format has seen a very minor
revival.

'Scope pictures weren't always released in anamorphic format only.
Some were shot in 'scope and flat versions simultaneously while others were
issued in a flat edition optically extracted from the anamorphic original.
Among those offered in two versions: *The Robe, The Command, Seven
Brides for Seven Brothers, Sign of the Pagan, Brigadoon, 20,000 Leagues
Under the Sea, Bad Day at Black Rock* and *The Great Locomotive Chase.*

A clipping from Universal-International's pressbook for *The Land Unknown* (1957) warns, "If your theatre is showing 'The Land Unknown' in any form other than CinemaScope be sure to eliminate reference to CinemaScope from review, picture captions and stories on these publicity pages before releasing this material."

CinemaScope 55

When Todd-AO proved to be a money maker with *Oklahoma!* and other wide gauge systems (or variations of Todd-AO) began development at other studios, 20th Century–Fox decided it was time to create a new roadshow format of their own. CinemaScope had been successful, at first, but had not defeated television. Cinerama and Todd-AO were drawing big audiences, and the next step for 20th Century–Fox was the logical one: wide gauge, wide format.

Warner Brothers is producing in CinemaScope ... M-G-M is producing in CinemaScope ... Walt Disney is producing in CinemaScope ... Columbia is producing in CinemaScope ... Universal-International is producing in CinemaScope ...United Artists is producing in CinemaScope ..20th Century-Fox is producing in CinemaScope

A November 1953 trade ad from 20th Century-Fox. Notice that Paramount is not on the bandwagon. They had a little thing called VistaVision.

The old Mitchell Grandeur cameras were pulled from storage and revamped for the new "CinemaScope 4 × 35," as it was to be called. In actuality the system was the same as 35mm CinemaScope except it was four times the negative size, photographed on 55mm film made specially by Eastman Kodak. The perfs were the same, as were the aspect ratio and the four-track MagOptical Stereophonic Sound. Studio executives were determined the system would be adoptable by any 35mm CinemaScope theater by a few simple changes to existing projectors. While it was necessary for Bausch & Lomb to manufacture new camera lenses, the standard anamorphic projection units were usable. The idea was eventually to change the sound system from four-channel to six channel-stereophonic, but that would be sometime in the future.

CinemaScope 4 × 35 was renamed CinemaScope 55 and put to use on *Carousel* (1956). Twentieth Century–Fox wasn't sure about optically converting the 55mm to 35mm and had the film shot simultaneously in Cinema-Scope. Midway through production the 35mm unit was disbanded and the feature completed entirely in 55mm. The optical reduction had been worked out and rendered a sharp, clear 35mm 'scope edition. Soon *The

Trade ad for The King and I. *It was the second film to be shot in CinemaScope 55, but the first to be released in the 55mm format.*

King and I (1956) was shooting in CinemaScope 55, and *The Greatest Story Ever Told* was announced to follow, along with other roadshows.

Upon its completion, *Carousel* was trade-screened in 35mm and then released only in that format! Studio executives felt the 35mm reduction was so superior to regular CinemaScope that it was not necessary to make actual 55mm release prints. *The King and I,* however, would be issued in both 55mm and 35mm roadshow versions. *De Luxe Tour,* a short, was shot in

55mm, shown in one Bronx theater in 1957, and shelved until the 1960s when it would be screened, with new narration, in 35mm only. *The Greatest Story Ever Told* was shelved for the time being.

Despite the huge financial success of *Carousel* and *The King and I*, 20th Century-Fox did not follow with other features in CinemaScope 55. The process died. Nevertheless, it was an extremely impressive system and actually clearer, sharper and wider (when decompressed) than 70mm. Twentieth Century-Fox had built new cameras, and the Bausch & Lomb lenses were superior to existing anamorphic units. Like other studios, however, 20th Century-Fox decided on 70mm as the best wide gauge format. Future roadshows from the studio would utilize Todd-AO. Interestingly, *The King and I* would be reissued as a roadshow in 1961, optically converted to spherical 70mm and advertised in Grandeur 70 with six-track stereophonic sound! *The Greatest Story Ever Told* would be rescheduled for production in the early 1960s in Todd-AO, then cancelled after the failure of *Cleopatra* (also in Todd-AO) and the property sold to United Artists, who would finance its filming in 70mm Super Cinerama (Ultra Panavision 70).

Today CinemaScope 55 is a forgotten process. Existing prints of *Carousel* and *The King and I* no longer bear the attractive logo which originally introduced them: "A CinemaScope Picture in CinemaScope 55." The 55mm preprint on both films has either been destroyed or has deteriorated to the point of unsalvageability. Even the 70mm preprint on *The King and I* has turned purple. Fortunately, the pristine 35mm reduction material for both films with the original stereophonic sound has been saved.

*Super*Scope

Say *Super*Scope to most people and they think of Sony electronic equipment. The logo is still on display at many Sony dealerships. Yes, *Super*Scope, Inc., was at one time the exclusive United States distributor of Sony products, which in those days all bore the logo shown on the film ads on pages 70 and 71. But before *Super*Scope meant radios, stereos, etc., it meant a wide screen process developed by the same entrepreneurial Tushinsky brothers who later became famous as electronics importers.

When CinemaScope took hold in Hollywood, the various studios immediately set out to ascertain the correct aspect ratio for movies. With CinemaScope it was finally decided on at 2.35 × 1 (after flirting with 2.66 × 1 and 2.55 × 1). At Paramount, VistaVision began at 2 × 1, then settled on 1.85 × 1. Cropped spherical films would be framed for various ratios from 1.66 × 1 to 2 × 1. Nobody was in agreement, and they still aren't totally. Everybody had his reasons for selecting this or that shape.

At RKO Radio, Howard Hughes, never a man to share with others, decided that if the screen was to be wider, then he would have his own system. He was not about to pay 20th Century-Fox or anybody else a franchise fee for camera lenses. He put the Tushinskys to work to create a CinemaScope-

Will project any ratio Anamorphic print.

SUPERSCOPE*

The widely acclaimed Tushinsky-Superscope Variable Anamorphic lens— can now be purchased for the amazingly new low price of:

$395 PER PAIR

effective immediately

THE SAME LENS · THE SAME FEATURES · THE SAME HIGH QUALITY

All Sales on a Direct Factory to Exhibitor Basis... **IMMEDIATE DELIVERY!**

Our appreciation to NATIONAL SCREEN SERVICE for relinquishing its exclusive distribution rights. This gesture and world-wide acceptance of the Superscope lens permit this new price.

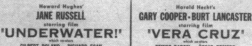

TWO GREAT FILMS IN SUPERSCOPE
Color by *Technicolor*

Howard Hughes'
JANE RUSSELL
starring film
"UNDERWATER!"
which co-stars
GILBERT ROLAND · RICHARD EGAN
and LORI NELSON
An RKO Radio Production

Harold Hecht's
GARY COOPER · BURT LANCASTER
starring film
"VERA CRUZ"
which co-stars
DENISE DARCEL · CESAR ROMERO
A Hecht-Lancaster Production
For United Artists release

Projection of these great pictures is, in our opinion, best with the Superscope lens— but for the benefit of any exhibitor who has already purchased Cinemascope equipment, Superscope prints are compatible with all anamorphic lenses.

All sales F.O.B. Los Angeles. Enclose $100 for each pair of SUPERSCOPE lenses ordered—the balance C.O.D. Specify shipping instructions, Railway Express, Air Express or Air Freight.

address... **SUPERSCOPE** INC.
780 NORTH GOWER STREET
HOLLYWOOD 28, CALIFORNIA

Trademark

compatible system that would best meet the theater needs; after all, if it wasn't accepted by the exhibitors, no process had a chance of success.

The first thing the two engineers determined was screen width: It would be impractical to install a screen with a ratio wider than 2×1 since few theaters were structured for such. (This conclusion was borne out by the observation that most theaters already equipped with CinemaScope were either cropping the image to approximately 2×1 or projecting a very small, narrow picture, defeating the big screen idea.) Their second conclusion was that anamorphic lenses were large, heavy, awkward affairs, with little depth of field, poor focus and a need for extra light.

The Tushinskys' recommendations were simple and immediately accepted by Hughes: *Super*Scope would utilize standard cameras and lenses. There was no sacrifice of focus or depth of field, nor were there any additional lighting requirements. The only concession to be made was that all action be framed to fit into a 2×1 aspect ratio with equal cropping from the top and bottom of the frame. The film was then cropped to 2×1; a 2×1 anamorphic squeeze was added, and the film was printed by Technicolor in 'scope format with .715″ height and .715″ width. A narrow black strip appeared on the right side of release print frames to fill in the difference in the .715″ *Super*Scope width and .839″ width of CinemaScope. Projection was via any 2×1 compression anamorphic device. Films not originally shot for *Super*Scope could be converted in the lab (and several were).

Additionally, *Super*Scope, Inc., manufactured variable anamorphic projection devices that were aimed at meeting any existing or future compression factor. By turning one knob on the side of the prismatic devices, the squeeze could be adjusted from neutral (no compression) to 3×1 squeeze ratio. The units could actually remain on the projectors for all films if the theater was still showing regular 35mm uncropped. To convert to 'scope meant only changing the aperture plate (which wasn't absolutely necessary) and adjusting the compression knob on the *Super*Scope device. Since VistaVision was then being offered in 'scope format with a 1.5×1 compression, it was not compatible with CinemaScope, and the Tushinsky projection device was contracted by Paramount for use in those theaters that wanted anamorphic VistaVision prints. (Hi-Lux, Panavision and others would also offer variable compression 'scope projection devices, but

Opposite, top: A trade ad for the Tushinsky-SuperScope lens. Bottom: SuperScope frames (somewhat retouched) from Underwater!, the first SuperScope feature to go into production (though not the first released). At left is the spherical camera original. The center frames show the 2×1 cropped spherical image awaiting the addition of a 2×1 anamorphic compression. At right, the 2×1 (in both anamorphic compression and aspect ratio) release print. The final .715″ by .715″ image required realignment of projectors in order that the slight black border would be even on both sides of the screen. SuperScope 235 eliminated the black release print area by using a 2.35×1 crop of the original photography, thus filling the entire release print frame area.

Skin Diver Action... Aqua-lung Thrills!
HOWARD HUGHES presents
JANE RUSSELL
IN
UNDERWATER!
COME ON BELOW to that new, exciting Underwater World...with Jane Russell as you've never seen her before! It took 3 years to make...cost $3,000,000!
THE NEW ANAMORPHIC PROCESS
SUPERSCOPE
ON THE GIANT WIDE SCREEN
color by
TECHNICOLOR
co-starring
GILBERT ROLAND · RICHARD EGAN · LORI NELSON
Directed by JOHN STURGES · Screenplay by WALTER NEWMAN · Produced by HARRY TATELMAN

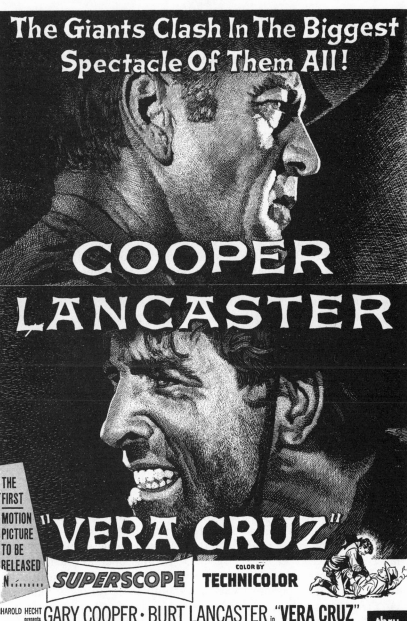

The Giants Clash In The Biggest Spectacle Of Them All!

COOPER
LANCASTER

THE FIRST MOTION PICTURE TO BE RELEASED N.......

"VERA CRUZ"

SUPERSCOPE · COLOR BY **TECHNICOLOR**

HAROLD HECHT presents **GARY COOPER** · **BURT LANCASTER** in **"VERA CRUZ"**

co-starring **DENISE DARCEL** · **CESAR ROMERO** with GEORGE MACREADY · ERNEST BORGNINE and introducing **SARITA MONTIEL**

Screenplay by ROLAND KIBBEE and JAMES R. WEBB · Story by BORDEN CHASE · Produced by JAMES HILL · Directed by ROBERT ALDRICH
A HECHT-LANCASTER PRODUCTION

thru UA

Vera Cruz *(above) was the first SuperScope release, even though* Underwater! *(op-posite) went into production first. Howard Hughes' obsessive perfectionism caused* Underwater! *to go way over budget and schedule, allowing other SuperScope features to reach the screen first.*

it soon became evident that the 2×1 squeeze ratio was going to be the standard, and Paramount stopped releasing VistaVision anamorphic prints.)

The first RKO Radio production in *Super*Scope was *Underwater!* (1955) but Hughes' attempts at perfection stretched the shooting time out so long that United Artists' *Vera Cruz* (1954) was released first. In 1956 *Super*Scope 235 was introduced. The only difference in photography was that the taking camera had a widened aperture that exposed over the soundtrack area and the crop factor allowed for a 2.35×1 ratio. Technicolor cropped to the wider ratio and printed in standard CinemaScope frame .715″ height and .839″ width. After the Tushinskys severed relations with RKO Radio, the studio continued to use *Super*Scope 235 under the moniker RKO-Scope. Superama also used the same technique.

The *Super*Scope logo is now seen only as faded displays in Sony dealers' shops, but the process survives. It is commonly employed for the conversion of stock shots and for special effects photography. The Soviets occasionally utilize it under their all-embracing "Sovscope" tag, and it is often employed on Far East–made features. Today, films shot in the *Super*Scope 235 technique are billed as Super Techniscope when processed by Technicolor and System 35 when processed by other labs.

Techniscope

In Italy, more than the United States, anamorphic cinematography was desirable in the 1960s. Unlike the American studios, Italian producers did not have unlimited funds, and the added cost of 'scope lenses often meant a reduction in some other production aspect. Technicolor in Rome came up with the solution: Techniscope. The system employed standard cameras and lenses, but the camera movement was modified to expose a two-perforation area instead of the normal four perf, and the aperture was 2.35×1. The film stock was thus extended twice over that used for 'scope photography. Spherical lenses effectively became double focal length because of the smaller frame area covered. In the lab, Technicolor added a 2×1 compression and optically blew the half frame image to full 'scope format. Despite this 50 percent enlargement, Techniscope was usually clearer and sharper than anamorphic processes with a substantial increase in depth of field. While the laboratory work was slightly more expensive than normal, the production savings were cut in half in film stock, and further cut by not having to hire anamorphic lenses.

The system was quickly seized upon in Italy, Spain and other European countries. The first feature, *The Pharaoh's Woman* (1960 in Italy, 1961 in the United States), demonstrated beyond doubt that Techniscope was a quality wide screen process. That first release carried an attractive logo stating, "In Techniscope High Fidelity Wide Screen." To our knowledge the logo was never used again. The quick acceptance of the process in Europe took Technicolor in Hollywood by surprise, but soon they set up facilities

Techniscope®

CUTS NEGATIVE COSTS BY OVER 50%

With this entirely new method of shooting 'Scope-type films the negative frame covers the height of only two perforations, thus only half the usual amount of negative is used in the camera. At the optical printing stage the two perforation frame is stretched vertically to twice the height, giving on the positive print a normal 'Scope-type four perforation frame.

Techniscope®

OFFERS ALL THESE OTHER ADVANTAGES

● No distortion of the image.

● Greater depth of field due to the short focus lenses generally used, but no limitation on the use of any type of lens.

● Use of any type of "zoom" lens.

● Wider horizontal angle of view than normal 'Scope lenses. An 18mm lens can be used (which corresponds to a 35mm 'Scope) and even shorter focal lengths.

● Full utilization of all the light that hits the projector aperture.

● The possibility of shooting longer scenes with less risk of the film running out, and halving the possibility of picking up emulsion in the aperture with consequent unsteadiness.

● Half the changes of magazines, with consequent less loss of expensive time and infinitely less strain on the part of actors and, indeed, all concerned with shooting on the set.

● Half the cost of negative developing.

● A complete saving on the hiring of anamorphic camera lenses and total elimination of their weight and encumbrance. It's really true—anamorphic lenses are no longer used in the photography stage!

● More speed in the lenses and consequent possibility of shooting at lower light levels.

● The producer who intends to release his film in black and white can—by means of using Techniscope—make a colour negative at approximately the same cost and look forward to enjoying the additional residual values from colour television, Pay-TV, re-issues in colour, etc.

Technicolor's trade announcement for Techniscope.

to process (optical print) Techniscope, and began hawking it to the studios.

Amazingly, few took much notice other than independent producers. Then Paramount utilized the process on a series of two-week, very low-budget westerns produced by A.C. Lyles. (*The Law of the Lawless* [1964], second in the series, is often erroneously credited as the first Techniscope film.) The photographic success of the Paramount-Lyles series led to the studio employing the process on several other features and influenced Universal to adopt Techniscope as the system for all their features, with the exception of a few coproductions with independent producers and super budget projects that used Panavision. (Universal's policy changed in 1970 as the studio decreased their 'scope productions and started shooting more films in spherical format for cropping.) More and more minor league producers started using the process until it eventually all but died out in the late seventies. Rarely is the system employed in the United States today. In fact, Technicolor strongly discourages its use and has on several occasions farmed out the optical conversion to other labs, notably Opticals West.

Techniscope. Left: *camera original.* Right: *optical conversion to CinemaScope format.*

In its heyday in Europe this system was so commonly used that Technicolor could not handle all the labwork and licensed other processing plants to develop Techniscope under the trade name Cromoscope. (European prints often bore the Cromoscope credit, but when Technicolor did the United States release prints, the billing would be changed to Techniscope. This has caused some confusion among those unaware that the two names applied to the same process.)

The Techniscope trademark lives on as Super Techniscope, which is actually the *Super*Scope 235 process.

Techniscope Specifications*

Camera and negative:
Film	35mm
Frames per second	24
Pulldown	2 perfs per frame
Aspect ratio	2.35 × 1
Frame image	0.868″ × 0.373″
Aperture	0.868″ × 0.355″
Centerline	0.738″ from guided edge

The Techniscope trademark was utilized only on prints manufactured by Technicolor. Production processing and prints by licensed laboratories were to carry a credit for Cromoscope. Films processed by a licensed lab but release-printed by Technicolor bore the Techniscope trademark.

These are the finalized specs for Techniscope by Technicolor and vary slightly from the particulars first applied to the system.

Ground glass markings:

2.35 × 1	0.839″ × 0.355″
1.85 × 1 (for 16mm reduction in "adapted scope" format)	0.660″ × 0.355″
1.33 × 1 (unscanned television extraction)	0.422″ × 0.317″
Cameras (individual manufacturers' specs apply to their adapted equipment	Mitchell, Arriflex, Eclair, etc.
Lenses (spherical)	18.5mm to 300mm

Release print:

Film	35mm
Optical conversion	Technicolor or licensed lab
Frames per second	24
Pulldown	4 perfs per frame
Aspect ratio	2.35 × 1
Projected image	0.839″ × 0.715″
Sound system	optical or Mag-Optical
Sound format	mono or stereophonic

Other Anamorphic Processes

Actionscope

See Toeiscope.

AgaScope

This Swedish anamorphic lens was CinemaScope–compatible and produced the standard 2.35 × 1 ratio from a 2 × 1 optical squeeze. It was owned by Aga Laboratories, who also had their own color system (Agacolor) and variable area sound system (Aga-Baltic).

Astravision

Presumably a CinemaScope–compatible system.

Camerascope

See Cinepanoramic.

Centralscope

Presumably a 2 × 1 compression anamorphic system, used on *Hentai* in 1966.

Producer, director and cameraman Charles B. Pierce rides a (homemade?) camera boom with an Arriflex Techniscope camera during production of Winterhawk *(Howco, 1976).*

Chinascope

A CinemaScope-compatible system possibly derived from Techniscope- or *Super*Scope 235-type original photography.

Cinepanoramic

A French anamorphic lens compatible with CinemaScope. The lens was built by Professor Ernst Abbe, who, in his announcement of availability of the unit, clearly stated that the anamorphic process was public domain and not patentable. This was no doubt unsettling to 20th Century–Fox, who had paid much to Henri Chrétien for exclusive rights (which they fully intended to franchise to others) to the lens they called CinemaScope. Abbe had, in fact, been experimenting with squeeze lenses for years. He managed to sell units in England, where it was called Camerascope, and to Republic Studios, who promptly redubbed it Naturama and claimed authorship by the screen billing *Naturama by Republic Pictures Corporation* (sic). Almost all features shot with the lens credited it as Franscope. This may be the same lens as Parscope.

Cinescope

Also billed as Supercinescope, though there appears to have been little or no difference in the anamorphic lenses offered. It was made in Italy and used on numerous features, often under the standard CinemaScope trademark. It may have also been called Superfilmscope, though not on any screen credits we've seen.

Cinetotalscope
See Totalscope.

ColorScope
An overall catch word used in advertising to note the film was in color and anamorphic format. It was favored by American International and a few independent companies and was occasionally advertised as Eastman ColorScope or some other slight variation. Kodak had nothing to do with the anamorphics; they simply manufactured the color film stock. Color-Scope was not a registered trademark and referred to no actual lens.

Cromoscope
The service mark applied to films employing the Techniscope system when not processed by Technicolor. Very often Cromoscope features were advertised (at least in the United States) as Techniscope when Technicolor did the release prints but another lab, licensed by Technicolor, did the production processing. While the Cromoscope billing appeared on many European ads, it never appeared in the screen credits of any feature we've seen.

Daieiscope
Anamorphic process of Daiei Motion Picture Company, Ltd. The system was sometimes billed as CinemaScope and appeared on Japanese credits as Daiei Scope.

Delrama
A variable compression mirror device invented by Albert Bouwers, noted for his x-ray work. The unit could be adjusted to produce an anamorphic image compatible with CinemaScope or any other system. Because of this it was applied to the Technirama process in Europe. In fact the only credit for the unit we recall appeared on a Technirama film.

Duo-Vision
The process utilized on **Wicked, Wicked** (MGM, 1973), which gave the audience two different scenes to view simultaneously with occasional single-view bridges. The two views were shot in 35mm spherical and optically printed in 2.35×1 'scope.

Dyaliscope
A very popular, French-made anamorphic lens giving the standard 2.35×1 aspect ratio. It was widely used in Europe, including England.

Dynavision
United Producers applied the name to *Nature Girl and the Slaver* in 1959, and it is assumed to have been an anamorphic process like CinemaScope. The trade name is now used by Film Effects of Hollywood for two 70mm processes: one using a single frame covering the same area as two normal 70mm images for blowup to IMAX format and the other

UNCONQUERABLE WARRIORS OF THE DAMNED!

WAR OF THE **ZOMBIES**

COLORSCOPE

EDGAR ALLAN POE'S

VINCENT PRICE

TOMB OF **LIGEIA**

IN — COLORSCOPE —

STUDY IN TERRIFYING EVIL!

HOUSE OF FRIGHT

COLOR and SCOPE

The mightiest adventure of them all!

American-International presents

GOLIATH AND THE DRAGON

IN COLORSCOPE

SEE GOLIATH

BATTLE the mammoth dragon in the seven caves of Moloch!

CONQUER the killer elephants!

DARE the black pit of terror!

using the two-frame area to provide right and left stereo pairs for over-and-under 3D.

Euroscope
As the name implies, a European version of CinemaScope.

Fantascope
An anamorphic system owned by actor-filmmaker Jon Hall. It was the same as CinemaScope and should not be confused with the special photographic effects technique of the same name by Howard A. Anderson Company, which used full-frame 35mm for reduction to Academy standard in order to reduce grain in optical photography.

Franscope
See Cinepanoramic.

GrandScope
Shochiku Films' CinemaScope-compatible lens. On Japanese credits it was billed as Shochiku Grand Scope.

Hammerscope
Presumably the same as MegaScope (q.v.). Some Hammer Film Productions, Ltd., pictures bore a MegaScope credit on the head and "A Hammerscope Production" on the end titles. In some cases MegaScope would appear in advertising and Hammerscope on the credits, or vice versa. (*The Abominable Snowman of the Himalayas* [20th–Fox, 1957] had "A Regalscope Picture" on the main titles and "A Hammerscope Production" on the end titles. It was produced by Exclusive Films, Ltd., Hammer's parent company, and presented by Regal Films, Inc. (See also Regalscope.)

Hi-Fi Scope
Anamorphic 2.35×1 system credited on *Karate, the Hand of Death* (AA, 1961).

ImageVision
A tape-to-film process in which hi-band video is used with an anamorphic lens having a 1.25×1 compression. The videotape is decompressed and converted to film with a 1.85×1 aspect ratio (hard matte). The results, at least on *Monty Python Live at the Hollywood Bowl* (1982), appeared no better than other tape-to-film systems.

Opposite: *Although all these ads were from American International, neither they nor anyone else held a trademark on "colorscope." An industry catch word, it signified only color and anamorphic format and referred to no specific lens or process.*

Iscovision

This anamorphic system uses 1.5×1 compression and, with a 1.33×1 camera aperture, gives a 2×1 aspect ratio. (This is the same anamorphic format applied to VistaVision.) It actually renders a superior 'scope image with substantially more depth of field, far less distortion and finer grain with a brighter projected image. The original Iscovision lenses were made for 16mm and 8mm amateur use and have been around for almost thirty years. Recently an attempt has been made to market them for 35mm theatrical use, but as of this writing there have been no takers. The 35mm version would use the standard anamorphic 1.18×1 camera aperture, giving a 1.77×1 aspect ratio, not the 1.85×1 ratio claimed in their technical material.

J-D-C Scope

Also called J-D-C Widescreen and J-D-C Anamorphic. It is a 2.35×1 system from Joe Dunton Cameras, Ltd. It is quickly becoming popular and all indications are that it will replace Panavision as the most often used anamorphic lens.

MegaScope

A British anamorphic system like CinemaScope. It was used by Hammer on several features and shorts. See Hammerscope.

Multiple Screen and Multiscreen

Two advertising names applied to rockumentaries released in anamorphic format. The films were all photographed in standard 16mm and then optically printed onto 35mm with 2×1 compression. This allowed the screen to include two or more scenes at one time. Of the several features released using this technique only *Elvis on Tour* (MGM, 1972) actually converted any single 16mm scene over the whole screen; the others always retained a small, narrow image when only one scene occupied the screen.

Naturama

Republic Pictures finally gave in to the anamorphic idea and introduced their own lens under the above name. While most of the films shot with it declared *Naturama by Republic Pictures Corporation,* it was, in fact, the Cinepanoramic unit manufactured in France (see Cinepanoramic).

Naturescope

While this is credited as a 3D system (developed by Dr. Edgar I. Fuller), the aspect ratio is given as 2.17×1. It is probable that this was an anamorphic process, since hawkers tended to call wide screen systems "3D" in the early 1950s when this one was announced. It was never employed on a film.

Nikkatsuscope

The 2×1 compression, 2.35×1 ratio process used by Nikkatsu of Japan. It was often billed as Nikkatsu Scope.

PanaScope

Manufactured by Goerz Optical Company, this lens used an anamorphic compression of 1.5×1 and an aspect ratio of 2×1. It could not be properly projected through a fixed 2×1 anamorphic compression unit, instead requiring a projection lens of the variable anamorphic type. In the 1950s and 1960s such projection units were common, but they are no longer made. The PanaScope lens had extremely limited use in feature production, but may have also been marketed as a variable anamorphic projection system.

Panoramic

See Panoramica.

Panoramica

An Italian anamorphic system occasionally referred to as Panoramic. This may be another trademark applied to the Techniscope format when not processed by Technicolor. It is compatible with CinemaScope.

Parscope

A French-made anamorphic lens, which may be another name for Cinepanoramic.

Regalscope

A CinemaScope-compatible lens used on films made by Regal Films, Inc., for 20th Century–Fox. One source says the lens was manufactured by Bausch & Lomb and was an actual CinemaScope lens. This is very likely. Regal Films became Associated Producers, Inc., and the Regalscope billing was replaced by CinemaScope, with Bausch & Lomb getting screen credit for lenses.

RKO-Scope

After the Tushinksy brothers parted with RKO the studio felt no need to continue using their *Super*Scope trademark. They just applied the same technology of *Super*Scope 235 using their own name.

Samcinescope

The system, or technique, used by Samuelson Film Service, Ltd., on the making of the sports documentary *G'Ole!* (1983). The film was photographed with standard cameras with the viewfinders marked with a 2.35×1

ratio. 'Scope prints were then extracted in the manner of *Super*Scope for theatrical release while spherical prints were struck for nontheatrical use. Unlike *Super*Scope 235 a widened aperture was not used in the cameras. The result was something comparable to Techniscope, without the benefit of savings in film stock during production, but with the advantage of not having to pan-and-scan a spherical version.

Scanoscope

A variable-compression anamorphic lens once marketed in the United States by F & B/Ceco. The name was also applied by MGM to 'scope prints with 1.5×1 squeeze and 2×1 aspect ratio derived from 2×1 compression and 2.35×1 original material.

Shawscope

The CinemaScope-compatible system used by Shaw Brothers, Ltd., of Hong Kong. Recent Shawscope pictures have been shot with Panavision lenses. Some Shawscope productions, mostly those of the chopsocky genre, have used a Techniscope or *Super*Scope 235 format.

Sonoptic

One source gives this as a French version of *Super*Scope 235.

Sovscope

A Soviet version of CinemaScope. Some credits issued by Artkino, the United States–based, Soviet-owned distributor, even bill CinemaScope. While anamorphics are most often used, the *Super*Scope 235 format is also utilized for some Sovscope prints. (The Soviets do not crop their spherical films but project them in 1.37×1 ratio. Most theaters are equipped only for this format, and all Sovscope films are released in anamorphic and panned-and-scanned spherical formats simultaneously.)

SpectraScope

2.35×1 anamorphic system used on *Flight of the Lost Balloon* (AIP, 1961).

Starsea Scope

A Chinese anamorphic system compatible with CinemaScope and probably derived from *Super*Scope 235 or Techniscope format original photography.

Stereorama

Presumably an Italian anamorphic system compatible with Cinema-Scope. One film, *Mondo balordo* (Italian, 1963; U.S.: Crown, 1967), was advertised in the process (if it is a process). It most definitely was not a stereoscopic system.

Sovscope anamorphic camera lenses.

SuperActionscope
See Toeiscope.

Super Techniscope
Identical to *Super*Scope 235 except that the system is applied to films meant for blowup to 70mm and not just to any feature. The same technique is called System 35 when processed by labs other than Technicolor.

Super Vistarama 70
See Vistarama.

Superama

Superama was another version of *Super*Scope. The idea was simple and practical: Frame for whatever ratio desired, crop to that ratio in the laboratory, add a 2×1 compression and print as a 'scope release. On the few features released with the Superama trademark the aspect ratio was 2.35×1. A variable-compression anamorphic projection lens was marketed in both 35mm and 16mm versions.

Supercinescope

See Cinescope.

Superfilmscope

See Cinescope.

Supertotalscope

See Totalscope.

System 35

The same as Super Techniscope (q.v.), but applied to films not processed by Technicolor. It is used on features meant for blowup to 70mm.

Taichang-scope

The credited 2.35×1 anamorphic system used by Tai Chang.

Technovision

Lenses of T.C. Technovision, Ltd., either anamorphic 2×1 compression or spherical. Usually "Filmed in Technovision" appears on flat prints for cropping, but it can also mean 'scope format. As with Panavision, Technovision credits can be misleading.

Todd-AO 35

Todd-AO's 35mm lenses, the name being applied to both anamorphic 2.35×1 format and spherical lenses. "Filmed in Todd-AO 35" generally refers to 'scope format, but not always. Some producers, notably Dino De Laurentiis, ignore "35" and give credit to "Todd-AO," causing more confusion when the film being shown is in 70mm, but a blowup. It is obvious what these filmmakers think of their audience.

Toeiscope

The standard 'scope format used by Toei Company, Ltd., of Japan. They have been shooting with Panavision lenses for a number of years, but Toeiscope is still being credited in advertising. The anamorphic lens has also been billed as Actionscope and SuperActionscope.

Tohoscope

Toho Company, Ltd.'s, anamorphic 2.35×1 system. On early features the process was often credited as CinemaScope. In recent years Panavision lenses have been used even thought the Tohoscope trademark (which on Japanese prints appears as Toho Scope) still appears in some advertising.

Totalscope

A CinemaScope-compatible lens made in Italy by ACT. It was often credited as Supertotalscope, but there seems to be little or no difference in the anamorphic units marketed. Indeed some films were advertised in Totalscope when the screen credits billed Supertotalscope, and vice versa. Totalscope Super/100, Totalvision and Cinetotalscope are assumed to be the same lens.

Totalscope Super/100

See Totalscope. The Super/100 probably refers to a 100mm prime lens used with the anamorphics. It doesn't refer to the film gauge. It might, though not likely, refer to the intention to project the anamorphic image onto a curved screen of 100 degrees. The credit appeared on only one feature that we are aware of.

Totalvision

See Totalscope.

Ultrascope

An Italian anamorphic lens that was marketed in the United States by F & B/Ceco. It was popular in many countries, especially West Germany, and even found use on a few American features.

Ultrascope 50

Presumably the same as Ultrascope. The added "50" probably refers to a 50mm prime lens used with the anamorphics. It most definitely does not refer to the film gauge.

Uniscope

Presumably a 2.35 × 1 anamorphic system.

Vistarama

An anamorphic lens using 2 × 1 optical compression and 2.35 × 1 aspect ratio. It was completely compatible with CinemaScope, and the first feature on which it was employed, *The Command* (WB, 1954), used the wider 2.55 × 1 ratio. In fact only two features — *Frontier Woman* (Top, 1956) and *East of Kilimanjaro* (Parade, 1962; filmed in 1957) — and a few shorts released by Republic actually credited the system. On all the other films (the exact number is unknown but it was used at Warner Bros. on probably several features) it was given the standardized CinemaScope credit. Vistarama was owned by Carl Dudley Pictures, Inc., and manufactured by Simpson Optical Company. In addition to the 35mm camera unit,

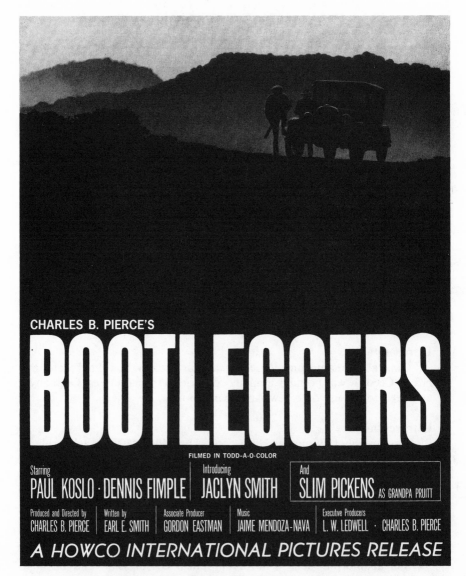

CHARLES B. PIERCE'S

BOOTLEGGERS

FILMED IN TODD-A-O-COLOR

Starring		Introducing	And
PAUL KOSLO · DENNIS FIMPLE		JACLYN SMITH	SLIM PICKENS AS GRANDPA PRUITT

Produced and Directed by	Written by	Associate Producer	Music	Executive Producers
CHARLES B. PIERCE	EARL E. SMITH	GORDON EASTMAN	JAIME MENDOZA-NAVA	L. W. LEDWELL · CHARLES B. PIERCE

A HOWCO INTERNATIONAL PICTURES RELEASE

Just one of several Todd-AO 35 features misleadingly advertised without the 35 after the process name. Also note the misspelling of the system (extra hyphen), another common error. Bootleggers *(later reissued as* The Bootlegger's Angel *to cash in on Jaclyn Smith's* Charlie's Angels *television fame) did at least give the correct screen credit. Among the Todd-AO 35 films that have not bothered to include the 35 notation in their credits:* Hurricane, Flash Gordon, Conan the Barbarian, Logan's Run *and* Dune. *Just as crediting Panavision instead of Spherical Panavision has led to confusion, Todd-AO 35 without the 35 gives the theatergoer the wrong impression regarding the photographic quality of the film. But then that's the idea!*

NEW LENS BRINGS A NEW BEAUTY, SCOPE TO SCREEN

Within the past few years new processes have been developed for the more natural and beautiful presentation of motion pictures. The big and wide screen has successfully competed with the miniature movie on the television screen. Among the most promising new developments is the new Vistarama lens which was used in filming "Frontier Woman" (Daughter of Davy Crockett) in the wild and beautiful frontier settings. Combined with Eastman Color, the lens developed and manufactured by Carl Dudley of Hollywood, brings scenes to the screen with breathtaking photographic quality never before attained. Size and ratio of the picture is the same as CinemaScope, but sharpness and brilliance have been greatly improved.

Lloyd Royal, producer of Frontier Woman" claims the sharp focus and high quality of Vistavision and the scope and dramatic effect of Cinerama have been combined into the new anamorphic process leaving little to be desired in this exciting presentation. "Frontier Woman," telling the little heard story of the Daughter of Davy Crockett and her exciting adventures on the frontier was a "natural" for showing the full possibilities of the lens.

A pressbook clipping showing the type hype used by producers and lens suppliers.

a 16mm version was also marketed, as well as projection lenses. (The projection lens is not to be confused with the curved screen projection system introduced in the 1960s under the same trademark and with which Dudley had no connection.)

Super Vistarama 70, using a 65mm taking stock and anamorphics (presumably with a 1.25×1 compression), was announced in the mid–1950s but never used and possibly never manufactured. Specific information on it was unavailable.

Vistarama was also the trademark applied to a 70mm Super Cinerama–type projection system manufactured and marketed by Andrew Smith Harkness, Ltd. The idea was to provide an all-purpose projection system in the manner of D-150, complete with screen and rigging and specially

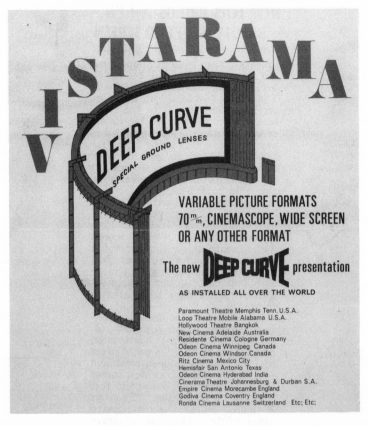

VARIABLE PICTURE FORMATS
70 ^m_m, CINEMASCOPE, WIDE SCREEN
OR ANY OTHER FORMAT

The new **DEEP CURVE** presentation

AS INSTALLED ALL OVER THE WORLD

Paramount Theatre Memphis Tenn. U.S.A.
Loop Theatre Mobile Alabama U.S.A.
Hollywood Theatre Bangkok
New Cinema Adelaide Australia
Residente Cinema Cologne Germany
Odeon Cinema Winnipeg Canada
Odeon Cinema Windsor Canada
Ritz Cinema Mexico City
Hemisfair San Antonio Texas
Odeon Cinema Hyderabad India
Cinerama Theatre Johannesburg & Durban S.A.
Empire Cinema Morecambe England
Godiva Cinema Coventry England
Ronda Cinema Lausanne Switzerland Etc; Etc;

The name Vistarama was actually applied to two different processes. One was an anamorphic lens. The ad above is for the other, a 70mm Super Cinerama–type all-purpose projection system. Despite this drawing and the use of the System in some 70mm Super Cinerama theaters, the screen had a curvature of only 70 degrees.

made Vistarama projection lenses. As with D-150, only 70mm filled the entire screen area and was to be advertised in Vistarama, though changing the 35mm 'scope lenses could make regular anamorphic cover the full screen. It is interesting to note that some 70mm Super Cinerama houses were actually Vistarama theaters.

Vistascope

A CinemaScope-compatible anamorphic system that probably was derived from *Super*Scope 235 format. Two films were made by Roger Corman under the trade name; one was anamorphic but the other was spherical, apparently never having been given the anamorphic conversion, though still advertised as if it had. Vistascope was also the name attached by Columbia Pictures in 1953 to their features cropped in 1.85 × 1 aspect ratio, but the term was quickly discarded.

WarnerScope

First announced as WarnerSuperScope in an outrageous two-page trade ad that must be read to be believed (see page 90), the name was finally shortened to WarnerScope. The lens was manufactured by Zeiss in West Germany and was an anamorphic unit compatible with CinemaScope. The name appeared on very few films; Warners, like most everyone else, opted to standardize anamorphic shows under the CinemaScope trademark.

One strange footnote: When Warners took over distribution of *The Naked and the Dead* from RKO, they had new credits shot that included "in WarnerScope," which was also billed on the ads and other publicity materials. RKO's original credits read "in RKO-Scope," which was a variation on *Super*Scope 235. Depending on which print you see on television these days, you can view the original RKO credits *and* the redone Warner titles. Both television editions are scanned, unfortunately, and were not taken from the spherical original as are most 16mm prints of *Super*Scope films.

WarnerSuperScope

See WarnerScope.

The Anamorphic Process Films

The following list is meant to be a basic guide to 35mm anamorphic feature releases in the United States. Cartoons, shorts and novelty items are not included. There are missing titles; martial arts, very minor foreign and independent films are not well documented and probably a fair number of these escaped inclusion. Additionally many foreign features made in 'scope have gone directly to United States television and did not receive theatrical playdates stateside. And of course there have been many overseas movies never released in this country that were shot anamorphic.

Films are listed according to credited or known lens system, in the order in which those systems are covered in the text. When the overall CinemaScope trademark was applied it is given here unless the actual lens is known. Almost all MGM, Columbia and UI pictures supposedly were shot with Panavision lenses, but only when such is actually known to be true is the credit given to Panavision instead of CinemaScope. Twentieth Century–Fox generally changed the credits on their pickups from foreign and independent producers to bill CinemaScope regardless of the system used. Whenever possible the actual system is credited here. Often credits on a foreign print would differ from those on the United States version, or the ad billing would be different. Sorting the actual lenses out wasn't easy at times. Films crediting ColorScope and such non-lens terms are listed an "uncredited." It should be noted that many films were shot with two or more anamorphics from different manufacturers and thus giving a single system credit is arbitrary at best. *Edge of Eternity,* for example, used Bausch & Lomb and Panavision lenses but was credited as CinemaScope. This was, and is today, very common. Converting spherical footage to 'scope is also often done, but to attempt to credit *Super*Scope 235 to all films including such enlargements would be impossible. The authors had to settle on what is before you.

Once again Look to Warner Bros. for the New Look!

To the members of the motion picture industry—worldwide—who rightfully look to Warner Bros. to make the firmest and surest advancements in modernizing our always improving techniques, this is our announcement that

WarnerSuperScope IS HERE!

This again confirms a confidence in pathfinding and leadership that began when the art and business of making motion pictures was very young. For those who are concerned with the future aspect of the motion picture screen, industry as well as the aspect ratio of the motion picture screen, we have never made an announcement of more importance.

WarnerSuperScope is not a sudden discovery presented to meet a sudden new interest in the photographic shape of things to come.

Scope as a word and as a science is the result of a Warner research development long underway. That development is here and ready; perfected to the ultimate of modern scientific know-how for screen size, for clarity, for the closer-to-nature values it gives to WarnerColor and for the tonal enhancement of WarnerPhonic Sound so that WarnerSuperScope will be welcomed as a magnificent new sensation in the motion picture theatre.

WarnerSuperScope will play its full power and beauty on the largest screens in the largest theatres, or the next to largest screens, or the screens next in size — any size within the 2.66 to 1 ratio on which its photographing and projecting lenses are based. This emphatically is not a blown-up film but a complete new photographic and projecting process produced for us by Zeiss-Opton.

The sweeping trend, as we know it, is for bigger theatre screens. We are in step with that trend.

Our own Warner All-Media Camera is now ready to photograph the following productions in WarnerSuperScope, transporting the story to WarnerColor film for projection on every wide screen installation now in use or contemplated for the future: "A Star Is Born" starring Judy Garland; "Lucky Me" starring Doris Day; "Rear Guard" starring Guy Madison; the classic spectacle of "Helen of Troy"; the world-renowned stage hit, "Mr. Roberts"; and John Steinbeck's current best-selling novel,"East of Eden" produced and directed by Elia Kazan. WarnerSuperScope is not only super in size, but super in its anticipation of our industry's needs in production and exhibition for years to come.

Jack L. Warner

Because we know the impact of an announcement of this kind and because we believe that action should accompany words — within the first few weeks of production we contemplate a worldwide WarnerSuperScope demonstration for press and exhibitors who share with us the will to make the motion picture industry thrive and prosper. We will show completed scenes precisely as they will appear on your screens.

This demonstration should run about ten minutes — nine minutes longer than anyone will need to realize what a sturdy and far-reaching contribution WarnerSuperScope makes to our business.

In line with our policy of concentrating only on the production and distributing phases of our business, and with no wish to enter into the separate field of selling theatre equipment, we will make WarnerSuperScope projection lenses available to exhibitors with each picture on a very nominal rental basis within reach of even the smallest theatre operator.

Apart from the screen the only equipment that exhibitors will need for the success of WarnerSuperScope is their own enthusiasm to recognize and exploit to the fullest Warner Bros.' latest contribution to our industry.

Roy Johnson

ALL PRODUCTIONS IN WarnerSuperScope WILL ALSO BE PHOTOGRAPHED BY THE WARNER ALL-MEDIA CAMERA IN WARNERCOLOR, 3D AND 2D TO MEET ANY DESIRED ASPECT RATIO, AND WITH WARNERPHONIC SOUND.

WARNER BROS. PICTURES INC.

Of special interest to "sound-minded" souls are the stereophonic releases noted with *. This listing is also inconclusive since information was available only from MGM and 20th Century-Fox, and then incomplete. Other films so credited are culled from memory, ads, and other sources. The use of stereo was not as limited as our * indicates, but neither was it as widespread as some have claimed. Stereophonic sound was most definitely not used on every 'scope release of the fifties! It was, however, utilized with several more films than those we are able to note here.

Further information on titles appearing in **boldface** can be found in the Filmography.

CINEMASCOPE

Beneath the 12 Mile Reef (20th-Fox, 1953)*
How to Marry a Millionaire (20th-Fox, 1953)*
King of the Khyber Rifles (20th-Fox, 1953)*
Knights of the Round Table (MGM, 1953)*
The Robe (20th-Fox, 1953)*
The Adventures of Hajji Baba (20th-Fox, 1954)*
Bad Day at Black Rock (MGM, 1954)*
The Black Shield of Falworth (UA, 1954)*
Black Widow (20th-Fox, 1954)*
Brigadoon (MGM, 1954)*
Broken Lance (20th-Fox, 1954)*
Carmen Jones (20th-Fox, 1954)*
The Command (WB, 1954)*
Demetrius and the Gladiators (20th-Fox, 1954)*
Desiree (20th-Fox, 1954)*

Opposite: *An incredible July 1953 trade ad from Warner Bros. There is much of interest in what at first appears as ultimate hype. Warners was making it clear that this was an anamorphic system, not a cropping of spherical footage; that it would cover the full frame area (2.66 × 1 being the 1.33 × 1 aperture expanded by the 2 × 1 anamorphics); that only a wide screen and the projection anamorphics were needed (the theater would use its old 1.33 × 1 aperture) on the exhibition end; and that WarnerPhonic Sound and WarnerColor would also be employed. The so-called Warner All-Media Camera was just a Mitchell equipped with the anamorphic unit. The 3D referred to is very misleading. At this early stage in the use of 'scope the panoramic process was being hyped as "3D without glasses." Reference to "any size within the 2.66 to 1 ratio" meant that 1.66 × 1 and 1.33 × 1 prints could be optically extracted from the anamorphic original. (But then, a flat version was shot simultaneously of the first couple of features just in case the 'scope idea didn't receive full acceptance by exhibitors.) The Zeiss lenses did not arrive in time for use on* Rear Guard, *which was filmed with Carl Dudley's Vistarama lens as well as spherical and released as* The Command *in CinemaScope. Warners, like all the other studios, agreed to standardize all 'scope releases under the CinemaScope trademark in order not to cause confusion among patrons. WarnerPhonic Sound (interlocked magnetic three-track, one optical track on film) was soon discarded in favor of Perspecta Stereophonic Sound (three-track optical) and limited four-track magnetic stereo on film. In the late 1950s the Warner Zeiss lens would finally get screen credit as WarnerScope. Warners' actual 3D camera would be called Warner-Vision. By the way, Warners' rental lenses were SuperScope and that might very well be the reason for the original name of their system.*

Drum Beat (WB, 1954)*
The Egyptian (20th-Fox, 1954)*
Garden of Evil (20th-Fox, 1954)*
Green Fire (MGM, 1954)*
Hell and High Water (20th-Fox, 1954)*
The High and the Mighty (WB, 1954)*
King Richard and the Crusaders (WB, 1954)*
Lucky Me (WB, 1954)*
New Faces (20th-Fox, 1954)*
Night People (20th-Fox, 1954)*
Prince Valiant (20th-Fox, 1954)*
Ring of Fear (WB, 1954)*
River of No Return (20th-Fox, 1954)*
Rose Marie (MGM, 1954)*
The Royal Tour of Queen Elizabeth and Philip (20th-Fox, 1954)
Seven Brides for Seven Brothers (MGM, 1954)*
Sign of the Pagan (UI, 1954)*
The Silver Chalice (WB, 1954)*
Sitting Bull (UA, 1954)
A Star Is Born (WB, 1954)*
The Student Prince (MGM, 1954)*
There's No Business Like Show Business (20th-Fox, 1954)*
Three Coins in the Fountain (20th-Fox, 1954)*
Track of the Cat (WB, 1954)*
20,000 Leagues Under the Sea (BVD, 1954)*
Woman's World (20th-Fox, 1954)*
At Gunpoint (AA, 1955)
Battle Cry (WB, 1955)*
Bedevilled (MGM, 1955)*
Blood Alley (WB, 1955)*
Captain Lightfoot (UI, 1955)
Chief Crazy Horse (UI, 1955)
The Cobweb (MGM, 1955)*
Count Three and Pray (Col, 1955)
The Court Martial of Billy Mitchell (WB, 1955)*
Daddy Long Legs (20th-Fox, 1955)*
The Deep Blue Sea (20th-Fox, 1955)*
Diane (MGM, 1955)*
East of Eden (WB, 1955)*
Gentlemen Marry Brunettes (UA, 1955)
The Girl in the Red Velvet Swing (20th-Fox, 1955)*
Good Morning, Miss Dove (20th-Fox, 1955)*
Guys and Dolls (MGM, 1955)*
Helen of Troy (WB, 1955)
Hell on Frisco Bay (WB, 1955)
Hit the Deck (MGM, 1955)*
House of Bamboo (20th-Fox, 1955)*
How to Be Very, Very Popular (20th-Fox, 1955)*
I Died a Thousand Times (WB, 1955)
The Indian Fighter (UA, 1955)
Interrupted Melody (MGM, 1955)*
It's a Dog's Life (MGM, 1955)*

It's Always Fair Weather (MGM, 1955)*
Jupiter's Darling (MGM, 1955)*
The Kentuckian (UA, 1955)
The King's Thief (MGM, 1955)*
Kismet (MGM, 1955)*
Lady and the Tramp (BVD, 1955)*
Land of the Pharaohs (WB, 1955)*
The Last Frontier (Col, 1955)
The Left Hand of God (20th-Fox, 1955)*
The Long Grey Line (Col, 1955)*
Long John Silver (DCA, 1955)
Love Is a Many Splendored Thing (20th-Fox, 1955)*
Love Me or Leave Me (MGM, 1955)*
The McConnell Story (WB, 1955)*
The Magnificent Matador (20th-Fox, 1955)*
A Man Called Peter (20th-Fox, 1955)*
The Man From Laramie (Col, 1955)
Many Rivers to Cross (MGM, 1955)*
Mister Roberts (WB, 1955)*
Moonfleet (MGM, 1955)*
My Sister Eileen (Col, 1955)
Pete Kelly's Blues (WB, 1955)*
Picnic (Col, 1955)
Prince of Players (20th-Fox, 1955)*
The Prodigal (MGM, 1955)*
The Purple Mask (UI, 1955)
Quentin Durward (MGM, 1955)*
The Racers (20th-Fox, 1955)*
The Rains of Ranchipur (20th-Fox, 1955)*
Rebel Without a Cause (WB, 1955)*
The Scarlet Coat (MGM, 1955)*
The Sea Chase (WB, 1955)*
The Second Greatest Sex (UI, 1955)
Seven Cities of Gold (20th-Fox, 1955)*
The Seven Year Itch (20th-Fox, 1955)*
Soldier of Fortune (20th-Fox, 1955)*
Strange Lady in Town (WB, 1955)*
The Tall Men (20th-Fox, 1955)*
The Tender Trap (MGM, 1955)*
That Lady (20th-Fox, 1955)*
Three for the Show (Col, 1955)
To Hell and Back (UI, 1955)
Untamed (20th-Fox, 1955)*
The View from Pompey's Head (20th-Fox, 1955)*
The Violent Men (Col, 1955)
Violent Saturday (20th-Fox, 1955)*
The Virgin Queen (20th-Fox, 1955)*
The Warriors (AA, 1955)
White Feather (20th-Fox, 1955)*
Wichita (AA, 1955)
Alexander the Great (UA, 1956)*
The Ambassador's Daughter (UA, 1956)

Anastasia (20th–Fox, 1956)*
Bandido! (UA, 1956)
Basket of Mexican Tales (Col, 1956)
Battle Hymn (UI, 1956)
The Beast of Hollow Mountain (UA, 1956)
The Best Things in Life Are Free (20th–Fox, 1956)*
Between Heaven and Hell (20th–Fox, 1956)*
Bhowani Junction (MGM, 1956)*
Bigger Than Life (20th–Fox, 1956)*
The Bottom of the Bottle (20th–Fox, 1956)*
The Brave One (RKO, 1956)*
The Burning Hills (WB, 1956)
Bus Stop (20th–Fox, 1956)*
Canyon River (AA, 1956)
The Cockleshell Heroes (Col, 1956)
Comanche (UA, 1956)
The Conqueror (RKO, 1956)*
D-Day the Sixth of June (20th–Fox, 1956)*
The Eddy Duchin Story (Col, 1956)*
The First Texan (AA, 1956)
Forbidden Planet (MGM, 1956)*
Four Girls in Town (UI, 1956)
Gaby (MGM, 1956)*
The Girl Can't Help It (20th–Fox, 1956)*
The Great Locomotive Chase (BVD, 1956)
Hilda Crane (20th–Fox, 1956)*
Hot Blood (Col, 1956)
Jubal (Col, 1956)
The King and Four Queens (UA, 1956)
A Kiss Before Dying (UA, 1956)
The Last Hunt (MGM, 1956)*
The Last Wagon (20th–Fox, 1956)*
The Lieutenant Wore Skirts (20th–Fox, 1956)*
Love Me Tender (20th–Fox, 1956)*
Lust for Life (MGM, 1956)*
The Man in the Gray Flannel Suit (20th–Fox, 1956)*
The Man Who Never Was (20th–Fox, 1956)*
Meet Me in Las Vegas (MGM, 1956)*
Oasis (20th–Fox, 1956)*
Odongo (Col, 1956)
On the Threshold of Space (20th–Fox, 1956)*
The Opposite Sex (MGM, 1956)*
Pillars of the Sky (UI, 1956)*
The Power and the Prize (MGM, 1956)*
The Proud Ones (20th–Fox, 1956)*
The Revolt of Mamie Stover (20th–Fox, 1956)*
Safari (Col, 1956)
Satellite in the Sky (WB, 1956)
The Sharkfighters (UA, 1956)
Storm Over the Nile (Col, 1956)
The Swan (MGM, 1956)*
Tea and Sympathy (MGM, 1956)*

The Teahouse of the August Moon (MGM, 1956)*
Teenage Rebel (20th-Fox, 1956)*
Tip on a Dead Jockey (MGM, 1956)*
Trapeze (UA, 1956)
Tribute to a Bad Man (MGM, 1956)*
23 Paces to Baker Street (20th-Fox, 1956)*
Walk the Proud Land (UI, 1956)
Westward Ho the Wagons (BVD, 1956)
World Without End (AA, 1956)
You Can't Run Away from It (Col, 1956)
Action of the Tiger (MGM, 1957)*
An Affair to Remember (20th-Fox, 1957)*
And God Created Woman (Kingsley International, 1957)
April Love (20th-Fox, 1957)*
The Barretts of Wimpole Street (MGM, 1957)*
Bernardine (20th-Fox, 1957)*
Bitter Victory (Col, 1957)
Bombers B-52 (WB, 1957)
Boy on a Dolphin (20th-Fox, 1957)*
The Bridge on the River Kwai (Col, 1957)
China Gate (20th-Fox, 1957)*
The Congress Dancer (Rep, 1957)
The Deerslayer (20th-Fox, 1957)*
Designing Woman (MGM, 1957)*
Desk Set (20th-Fox, 1957)*
Don't Go Near the Water (MGM, 1957)*
Dragoon Wells Massacre (AA, 1957)
The Enemy Below (20th-Fox, 1957)*
A Farewell to Arms (20th-Fox, 1957)*
Fire Down Below (Col, 1957)
Forty Guns (20th-Fox, 1957)*
Gun for a Coward (UI, 1957)
Gun Glory (MGM, 1957)*
A Hatful of Rain (20th-Fox, 1957)*
Heaven Knows, Mr. Allison (20th-Fox, 1957)*
The Helen Morgan Story (WB, 1957)
The Hired Gun (MGM, 1957)*
House of Numbers (20th-Fox, 1957)*
How to Murder a Rich Uncle (Col, 1957)
The Hunchback of Notre Dame (AA, 1957)
Interlude (UI, 1957)
Island in the Sun (20th-Fox, 1957)*
Istanbul (UI, 1957)
Joe Butterfly (UI, 1957)
Kelly and Me (UI, 1957)
Kiss Them for Me (20th-Fox, 1957)*
The Land Unknown (UI, 1957)
Last of the Badmen (AA, 1957)*
Les Girls (MGM, 1957)*
Let's Be Happy (AA, 1957)
The Living Idol (MGM, 1957)*
Lost Continent (Lopert, 1957)

Man Afraid (UI, 1957)
Man in the Shadow (UI, 1957)
Man of a Thousand Faces (UI, 1957)
The Midnight Story (UI, 1957)
The Miller's Beautiful Wife (DCA, 1957)
Mister Cory (UI, 1957)
My Man Godfrey (UI, 1957)
No Down Payment (20th-Fox, 1957)*
Oh, Men! Oh, Women! (20th-Fox, 1957)*
The Oklahoman (AA, 1957)
Oregon Passage (AA, 1957)
Peyton Place (20th-Fox, 1957)*
Pickup Alley (Col, 1957)
Quantez (UI, 1957)
The River's Edge (20th-Fox, 1957)*
Scandal in Sorrento (DCA, 1957)
Sea Wife (20th-Fox, 1957)*
Secrets of Life (BVD, 1957)
The Seventh Sin (MGM, 1957)*
The Ship Was Loaded (Arthur, 1957)
Silk Stockings (MGM, 1957)*
Smiley (20th-Fox, 1957)
The Spirit of St. Louis (WB, 1957)*
Stopover Tokyo (20th-Fox, 1957)*
The Sun Also Rises (20th-Fox, 1957)*
The Tall Stranger (AA, 1957)
Tammy and the Bachelor (UI, 1957)
The Tarnished Angels (UI, 1957)
Ten Thousand Bedrooms (MGM, 1957)*
This Could Be the Night (MGM, 1957)*
Three Brave Men (20th-Fox, 1957)*
The Three Faces of Eve (20th-Fox, 1957)*
The True Story of Jesse James (20th-Fox, 1957)*
Until They Sail (MGM, 1957)*
The Vintage (MGM, 1957)*
The Way of the Gold (20th-Fox, 1957)*
The Wayward Bus (20th-Fox, 1957)*
Will Success Spoil Rock Hunter? (20th-Fox, 1957)*
Zarak (Col, 1957)
Appointment with a Shadow (UI, 1958)
The Badlanders (MGM, 1958)*
The Barbarian and the Geisha (20th-Fox, 1958)*
Bonjour Tristesse (Col, 1958)
The Bravados (20th-Fox, 1958)*
Bullwhip (AA, 1958)
Cattle Empire (20th-Fox, 1958)*
A Certain Smile (20th-Fox, 1958)*
Cole Younger, Gunfighter (AA, 1958)
Count Five and Die (20th-Fox, 1958)*
Day of the Bad Man (UI, 1958)
Family Doctor (20th-Fox, 1958)
The Female Animal (UI, 1958)

The Fiend Who Walked the West (20th-Fox, 1958)
Flood Tide (UI, 1958)
The Fly (20th-Fox, 1958)*
Fort Massacre (UA, 1958)
Frankenstein 1970 (AA, 1958)
Fraulein (20th-Fox, 1958)*
From Hell to Texas (20th-Fox, 1958)*
The Gift of Love (20th-Fox, 1958)*
Gigi (MGM, 1958)*
Gunman's Walk (Col, 1958)
Gunsmoke in Tucson (AA, 1958)
Harry Black and the Tiger (20th-Fox, 1958)*
The High Cost of Living (MGM, 1958)*
High Flight (Col, 1958)
High School Confidential! (MGM, 1958)*
The Hunters (20th-Fox, 1958)*
I Accuse! (MGM, 1958)*
I, Mobster (20th-Fox, 1958)
Imitation General (MGM, 1958)*
In Love and War (20th-Fox, 1958)*
The Inn of the Sixth Happiness (20th-Fox, 1958)*
Intent to Kill (20th-Fox, 1958)*
Kathy O' (UI, 1958)
The Key (Col, 1958)
The Lady Takes a Flyer (UI, 1958)
The Last of the Fast Guns (UI, 1958)
The Last Paradise (UA, 1958)
The Law and Jake Wade (MGM, 1958)*
The Long, Hot Summer (20th-Fox, 1958)*
Mam'zelle Pigalle (Films Around the World, 1958)
Man from God's Country (AA, 1958)
Mardi Gras (20th-Fox, 1958)*
Merry Andrew (MGM, 1958)*
Money, Women and Guns (UI, 1958)
Naked Earth (20th-Fox, 1958)*
A Nice Little Bank That Should Be Robbed (20th-Fox, 1958)*
The Night Heaven Fell (Kingsley, 1958)
No Sun in Venice (Kingsley, 1958)
Once Upon a Horse (UI, 1958)
Party Girl (MGM, 1958)*
The Perfect Furlough (UI, 1958)
Quantrill's Raiders (AA, 1958)
Queen of Outer Space (AA, 1958)
Rally 'Round the Flag Boys! (20th-Fox, 1958)*
Raw Wind in Eden (UI, 1958)
The Reluctant Debutante (MGM, 1958)*
The Restless Years (UI, 1958)
Ride a Crooked Trail (UI, 1958)
The Roots of Heaven (20th-Fox, 1958)*
Rx Murder (20th-Fox, 1958)*
Saddle the Wind (MGM, 1958)*
The Saga of Hemp Brown (UI, 1958)

The Sheepman (MGM, 1958)*
The Sheriff of Fractured Jaw (20th-Fox, 1958)*
Sierra Baron (20th-Fox, 1958)*
Sing, Boy, Sing (20th-Fox, 1958)*
Some Came Running (MGM, 1958)*
Tank Force (Col, 1958)
Ten North Frederick (20th-Fox, 1958)*
This Happy Feeling (UI, 1958)
Thundering Jets (20th-Fox, 1958)
A Time to Love and a Time to Die (UI, 1958)
Torpedo Run (MGM, 1958)*
Tosca (Casolaro-Giglio, 1958)
The Tunnel of Love (MGM, 1958)*
Underwater Warrior (MGM, 1958)*
Villa! (20th-Fox, 1958)*
Voice in the Mirror (UI, 1958)
Wild Heritage (UI, 1958)
The Young Lions (20th-Fox, 1958)*
The Alligator People (20th-Fox, 1959)
The Angry Hills (MGM, 1959)
Appointment with a Shadow (UI, 1959)
Ask Any Girl (MGM, 1959)*
The Bandit of Zhobe (Col, 1959)*
The Beat Generation (MGM, 1959)*
Beloved Infidel (20th-Fox, 1959)*
The Best of Everything (20th-Fox, 1959)*
The Big Operator (MGM, 1959)
The Blue Angel (20th-Fox, 1959)*
Blue Denim (20th-Fox, 1959)*
Compulsion (20th-Fox, 1959)*
Count Your Blessings (MGM, 1959)*
The Diary of Anne Frank (20th-Fox, 1959)*
Edge of Eternity (Col, 1959)
Escort West (UA, 1959)
Five Gates to Hell (20th-Fox, 1959)
The Gazebo (MGM, 1959)*
Gidget (Col, 1959)
Green Mansions (MGM, 1959)*
The Gunfight at Dodge City (UA, 1959)
Holiday for Lovers (20th-Fox, 1959)*
Horrors of the Black Museum (AIP, 1959)
Hound Dog Man (20th-Fox, 1959)*
House of Intrigue (AA, 1959)
Idle on Parade (Col, 1959)
It Started with a Kiss (MGM, 1959)*
Journey to the Center of the Earth (20th-Fox, 1959)*
Kiku and Isamu (Dalto, 1959)
King of the Wild Stallions (AA, 1959)
The Man Who Understood Women (20th-Fox, 1959)*
The Mating Game (MGM, 1959)*
The Miracle of the Hills (20th-Fox, 1959)*

The Navy Lark (20th-Fox, 1959)
Never So Few (MGM, 1959)*
Never Steal Anything Small (UI, 1959)
Night of the Quarter Moon (MGM, 1959)*
No Name on the Bullet (UI, 1959)
The Oregon Trail (20th-Fox, 1959)*
Pillow Talk (UI, 1959)
A Private's Affair (20th-Fox, 1959)*
The Remarkable Mr. Pennypacker (20th-Fox, 1959)*
The Return of the Fly (20th-Fox, 1959)
Ride Lonesome (Col, 1959)
The Sad Horse (20th-Fox, 1959)*
Say One for Me (20th-Fox, 1959)*
The Sins of Lola Montes (Transamerica, 1959)
Smiley Gets a Gun (20th-Fox, 1959)
The Son of Robin Hood (20th-Fox, 1959)
The Sound and the Fury (20th-Fox, 1959)*
Stranger in My Arms (UI, 1959)
The Tailor's Maid (Trans-Lux, 1959)
Tamango (Valiant, 1959)
These Thousand Hills (20th-Fox, 1959)*
This Earth Is Mine (UI, 1959)
3 Men in a Boat (Valiant, 1959)
Warlock (20th-Fox, 1959)*
The Wild and the Innocent (UI, 1959)
Woman Obsessed (20th-Fox, 1959)*
Babette Goes to War (Col, 1960)
Bobbikins (20th-Fox, 1960)
Crack in the Mirror (20th-Fox, 1960)
Desire in the Dust (20th-Fox, 1960)
Dinosaurus! (UI, 1960)
A Dog of Flanders (20th-Fox, 1960)*
Esther and the King (20th-Fox, 1960)*
The Fall of the House of Usher (AIP, 1960)
Flame Over India (20th-Fox, 1960)
Flaming Star (20th-Fox, 1960)
For the Love of Mike (20th-Fox, 1960)
Freckles (20th-Fox, 1960)
From the Terrace (20th-Fox, 1960)
High Time (20th-Fox, 1960)
Jazz Boat (Col, 1960)
Killers of Kilimanjaro (Col, 1960)
Let's Make Love (20th-Fox, 1960)
The Lost World (20th-Fox, 1960)
The Marriage-Go-Round (20th-Fox, 1960)
Masters of the Congo Jungle (20th-Fox, 1960)
Michael Strogoff (Continental, 1960)
Murder, Inc. (20th-Fox, 1960)
Nature's Paradise (Fanfare, 1960)
North to Alaska (20th-Fox, 1960)*
One Foot in Hell (20th-Fox, 1960)

Our Man in Havana (Col, 1960)
The Regattas of San Francisco (Col, 1960)
The Rookie (20th-Fox, 1960)
The Secret of Purple Reef (20th-Fox, 1960)
Seven Thieves (20th-Fox, 1960)
Sink the Bismarck! (20th-Fox, 1960)
Soft Singing (Par, 1960)
Sons and Lovers (20th-Fox, 1960)
The Story of Ruth (20th-Fox, 1960)
The Story on Page One (20th-Fox, 1960)
The Third Voice (20th-Fox, 1960)
13 Flying Men (20th-Fox, 1960)
Twelve Hours to Kill (20th-Fox, 1960)
Valley of the Redwoods (20th-Fox, 1960)
Wake Me When It's Over (20th-Fox, 1960)
Walk Tall (20th-Fox, 1960)
Wild River (20th-Fox, 1960)*
The Wizard of Baghdad (20th-Fox, 1960)
Young Jesse James (20th-Fox, 1960)
All Hands on Deck (20th-Fox, 1961)
Battle at Bloody Beach (20th-Fox, 1961)
The Big Gamble (20th-Fox, 1961)
The Big Show (20th-Fox, 1961)
The Canadians (20th-Fox, 1961)
Circle of Deception (20th-Fox, 1961)
The Comancheros (20th-Fox, 1961)*
Desert Warrior (Medallion, 1961)
Ferry to Hong Kong (20th-Fox, 1961)
The Fiercest Heart (20th-Fox, 1961)
Francis of Assisi (20th-Fox, 1961)
Go Naked in the World (MGM, 1961)
The Great War (Lopert, 1961)
The Guns of Navarone (Col, 1961)*
The Hustler (20th-Fox, 1961)
The Important Man (Lopert, 1961)
The Innocents (20th-Fox, 1961)
The Little Shepherd of Kingdom Come (20th-Fox, 1961)
The Long Rope (20th-Fox, 1961)
Marines, Let's Go! (20th-Fox, 1961)
The Mark (Continental, 1961)
A Midsummer Night's Dream (Showcorporation, 1961)
The Millionairess (20th-Fox, 1961)
Misty (20th-Fox, 1961)
Morgan the Pirate (MGM, 1961)
No Love for Johnnie (Emb, 1961)
Pirates of Tortuga (20th-Fox, 1961)
The Purple Hills (20th-Fox, 1961)
Return to Peyton Place (20th-Fox, 1961)
The Right Approach (20th-Fox, 1961)
The Second Time Around (20th-Fox, 1961)
Seven Women from Hell (20th-Fox, 1961)
The Silent Call (20th-Fox, 1961)

Sniper's Ridge (20th-Fox, 1961)
Snow White and the Three Stooges (20th-Fox, 1961)
The Thief of Baghdad (MGM, 1961)
20,000 Eyes (20th-Fox, 1961)
The Two Little Bears (20th-Fox, 1961)
Voyage to the Bottom of the Sea (20th-Fox, 1961)*
The Warrior Empress (Col, 1961)
Wild in the Country (20th-Fox, 1961)*
The Wonders of Aladdin (MGM, 1961)
Air Patrol (20th-Fox, 1962)
Bachelor Flat (20th-Fox, 1962)
Billy Budd (AA, 1962)
The Broken Land (20th-Fox, 1962)
The Cabinet of Caligari (20th-Fox, 1962)
Damn the Defiant! (Col, 1962)
The Firebrand (20th-Fox, 1962)
Five Weeks in a Balloon (20th-Fox, 1962)
Flame in the Streets (Atlantic, 1962)
Hand of Death (20th-Fox, 1962)
Hemingway's Adventures of a Young Man (20th-Fox, 1962)
I Like Money (20th-Fox, 1962)
I Think a Fool (MGM, 1962)
It Happened in Athens (20th-Fox, 1962)
Life Is a Circus (Schoenfeld, 1962)
The Lion (20th-Fox, 1962)
Lisa (20th-Fox, 1962)
The Longest Day (20th-Fox, 1962)*
The Loves of Salammbo (20th-Fox, 1962)
Mr. Hobbs Takes a Vacation (20th-Fox, 1962)
Nero's Mistress (Manhattan, 1962)
Panic in Year Zero! (AIP, 1962)
Rommel's Treasure (Medallion, 1962)
Satan Never Sleeps (20th-Fox, 1962)
The Savage Guns (MGM, 1962)
The Singer Not the Song (WB, 1962)
State Fair (20th-Fox, 1962)
The Story of Joseph and His Brethren (Colorama, 1962)
Sweet Ecstasy (Audobon, 1962)
Swingin' Along (20th-Fox, 1962)
Sword of the Conqueror (UA, 1962)
Swordsman of Siena (MGM, 1962)
Tender Is the Night (20th-Fox, 1962)
The 300 Spartans (20th-Fox, 1962)
The Valiant (UA, 1962)
Woman Hunt (20th-Fox, 1962)
Wonderful to Be Young! (Par, 1962)
Any Number Can Win (MGM, 1963)
Billy Liar (Continental, 1963)
The Boys (Screen Entertainment, 1963)
The Condemned of Altona (20th-Fox, 1963)
The Day Mars Invaded Earth (20th-Fox, 1963)
The Day of the Triffids (AA, 1963)

Duel of the Titans (Par, 1963)
Harbor Lights (20th-Fox, 1963)
House of the Damned (20th-Fox, 1963)
Marilyn (20th-Fox, 1963)
Move Over, Darling (20th-Fox, 1963)
Nine Hours to Rama (20th-Fox, 1963)
Paris Ooh-La-La! (American Film Distributing, 1963)
Please, Not Now! (20th-Fox, 1963)
Police Nurse (20th-Fox, 1963)
Rich Girl (Ultra, 1963)
The Slave (Son of Spartacus) (MGM, 1963)
The Stripper (20th-Fox, 1963)
Summer Holiday (AIP, 1963)
Take Her, She's Mine (20th-Fox, 1963)
Thunder Island (20th-Fox, 1963)
The Weird Love Makers (Audobon, 1963)
The Witch's Curse (Medallion, 1963)
The Yellow Canary (20th-Fox, 1963)
Young Guns of Texas (20th-Fox, 1963)
Bay of the Angels (Pate, 1964)
La Bonne Soupe (Careless Love) (International Classics, 1964)
Fate Is the Hunter (20th-Fox, 1964)
Friend of the Family (International Classics, 1964)
Gold for the Caesars (MGM, 1964)
Goodbye Charlie (20th-Fox, 1964)
Guns at Batasi (20th-Fox, 1964)
Man in the Middle (20th-Fox, 1964)
Moderato Cantabile (Royal, 1964)
My Enemy, the Sea (Isbihara, 1964)
The Pleasure Seekers (20th-Fox, 1964)
Rio Conchos (20th-Fox, 1964)
Shock Treatment (20th-Fox, 1964)
The Son of Captain Blood (Par, 1964)
Take Off Your Clothes and Live (Brode, 1964)
Tamahine (MGM, 1964)
The Thin Red Line (AA, 1964)
The Third Secret (20th-Fox, 1964)
The Visit (20th-Fox, 1964)
Voyage to the End of the Universe (AIP, 1964)
What a Way to Go! (20th-Fox, 1964)
Why Bother to Knock (7A, 1964)
A Boy Ten Feet Tall (Par, 1965)
The Brigand of Kandahar (Col, 1965)
Curse of the Fly (20th-Fox, 1965)
Dear Brigitte (20th-Fox, 1965)
Do Not Disturb (20th-Fox, 1965)
The Great Sioux Massacre (Col, 1965)
Greed in the Sun (MGM, 1965)
Gunfighters of Casa Grande (MGM, 1965)
High Wind in Jamaica (20th-Fox, 1965)
The Hours of Love (Cinema V, 1965)
John Goldfarb, Please Come Home! (20th-Fox, 1965)

The Leather Boys (AA, 1965)
Rapture (International Classics, 1965)
The Reward (20th-Fox, 1965)
Three Weeks of Love (Westminster, 1965)
Tokyo Olympiad (AIP, 1965)
Up from the Beach (20th-Fox, 1965)
Von Ryan's Express (20th-Fox, 1965)*
Wild, Wild World (Sokoler, 1965)
The Blue Max (20th-Fox, 1966)*
Cloportes (International Classics, 1966)
Center Girl (Continental, 1966)
Fantastic Voyage (20th-Fox, 1966)*
El Greco (20th-Fox, 1966)
Lemonade Joe (AA, 1966)
The Loves of Hercules (Manley, 1966)
The Mongols (Colorama, 1966)
Our Man Flint (20th-Fox, 1966)
The Sleeping Car Murder (7A, 1966)
Son of a Gunfighter (MGM, 1966)
Stagecoach (20th-Fox, 1966)
Tight Skirts, Loose Pleasures (Times, 1966)
Vietnam in Turmoil (Harrison, 1966)
Way ... Way Out (20th-Fox, 1966)
The Battle of Algiers (AA, 1967)
Caprice (20th-Fox, 1967)
In Like Flint (20th-Fox, 1967)
The Man Who Finally Died (Goldstone, 1967)
Prostitution (Stratford, 1967)
Sexy Magico (AIP, 1967)
Hagbard and Signe (Prentoulis, 1968)
The Rider in the Night (Pilkin, 1968)
Seven Against the Sun (Emerson, 1968)
The Seventh Continent (U-M, 1968)
The Concubines (Boxoffice International, 1969)
Sign of the Virgin (Brandon, 1969)
Boy (Grove, 1970)
Alicia (Tricontinental, 1977)
Bruce Lee's Deadly Kung Fu (21st Century, 1981)
The Eagle's Shadow (Cinematic, 1982)
Hands of Lightning (Almi, 1982)
Subway (Island Alive, 1985)*

CINEMASCOPE 55

Carousel (1956)†*
The King and I (1956)††*
De Luxe Tour (short subject) (1957)*

†*released in 35mm only*
††*rereleased in 70mm*

*SUPER*SCOPE

Vera Cruz (UA, 1954)
Bengazi (RKO, 1955)
Desert Sands (RKO, 1955)
Escape to Burma (RKO, 1955)
Pearl of the South Pacific (RKO, 1955)
The Return of Jack Slade (AA, 1955)
Son of Sinbad (RKO; reissue, 1955)
Tennessee's Partner (RKO, 1955)
Texas Lady (RKO, 1955)
The Treasure of Pancho Villa (RKO, 1955)
Underwater! (RKO, 1955)
The Bold and the Brave (RKO, 1956)
Fantasia (BVD; reissue, 1956)*
Glory (RKO, 1956)
Great Day in the Morning (RKO, 1956)
Henry V (UA; reissue, 1956)
Invasion of the Body Snatchers (AA, 1956)
Slightly Scarlet (RKO, 1956)
The Beggar Student (Bakros, 1958)
Drylanders (NFBC, 1965)
Second Fiddle to a Steel Guitar (Marathon, 1965)
99 Women (Commonwealth, 1969)
The Seducers (Cinemation, 1970)

TECHNISCOPE

The Pharaoh's Woman (UI, 1961)
The Postman Goes to War (Trans-Lux, 1962)
Prisoner of the Iron Mask (AIP, 1962)
The Trojan Horse (Colorama, 1962)
The Bacchantes (Medallion, 1963)
Cleopatra's Daughter (Medallion, 1963)
Goliath and the Sins of Babylon (AIP, 1963)
The Invincible Gladiator (7A, 1963)
The Rebel Gladiators (Medallion, 1963)
Behind the Nudist Curtain (Atlantic, 1964)
East of Sudan (Col, 1964)
For Those Who Think Young (UA, 1964)
Law of the Lawless (Par, 1964)
The Quick Gun (Col, 1964)
Robinson Crusoe on Mars (Par, 1964)
Roustabout (Par, 1964)
Stage to Thunder Rock (Par, 1964)
The Triumph of the Ten Gladiators (Medallion, 1964)
Where Love Has Gone (Par, 1964)
Arizona Raiders (Col, 1965)
Billie (UA, 1965)
Black Spurs (Par, 1965)
The Bounty Killer (Emb, 1965)
Coast of Skeletons (7A, 1965)

Code 7, Victim 5! (Col, 1965)
The Curse of the Mummy's Tomb (Col, 1965)
Deadwood '76 (Fairway, 1965)
Dr. Terror's House of Horrors (Par, 1965)
The Face of Fu Manchu (7A, 1965)
Finger on the Trigger (AA, 1965)
Go Go Mania (AIP, 1965)
The Ipcress File (UA, 1965)
The Moment of Truth (Rizzoli, 1965)
The Nasty Rabbit (Fairway, 1965)
One Way Wahine (United Screen Arts, 1965)
Psycho a Go-Go! (Hemisphere, 1965)
Requiem for a Gunfighter (Emb, 1965)
Revenge of the Gladiators (Par, 1965)
Sandokan the Great (MGM, 1965)
Seaside Swingers (Emb, 1965)
Seven Slaves Against the World (Par, 1965)
The Skull (Par, 1965)
Swinger's Paradise (AIP, 1965)
A Swingin' Summer (United Screen Arts, 1965)
Town Tamer (Par, 1965)
White Voices (Rizzoli, 1965)
Young Fury (Par, 1965)
Alfie (Par, 1966)
Apache Uprising (Par, 1966)
The Appaloosa (Univ, 1966)
Beau Geste (Univ, 1966)
The Corrupt Ones (W7, 1966)
Country Boy (Howco, 1966)
Dr. Who and the Daleks (Continental, 1966)
Dracula — Prince of Darkness (20th-Fox, 1966)
Funeral in Berlin (Par, 1966)
Gambit (Univ, 1966)
The Ghost and Mr. Chicken (Univ, 1966)
The Girl from Thunder Strip (American General, 1966)
Go, Go, Go World! (ABC, 1966)
Incident at Phantom Hill (Univ, 1966)
Johnny Reno (Par, 1966)
Mozambique (7A, 1966)
Nashville Rebel (1966)
The Night of the Grizzly (Par, 1966)
A Pistol for Ringo (Emb, 1966)
A Place Called Glory (Emb, 1966)
The Psychopath (Par, 1966)
Road to Nashville (Crown, 1966)
Run for Your Life (AA, 1966)
The Secret Seven (MGM, 1966)
Sunscorched (Feature Film Corp, 1966)
Swamp Country (Patrick-Sandy, 1966)
Texas Across the River (Univ, 1966)
The Texican (Col, 1966)
That Man in Istanbul (Col, 1966)

To the Shores of Hell (Crown, 1966)
24 Hours to Kill (7A, 1966)
Waco (Par, 1966)
Wild, Wild Winter (Univ, 1966)
Africa Addio (Cinemation, 1967)
Banning (Univ, 1967)
Blood Fiend (Hemisphere, 1967)
The Busy Body (Par, 1967)
La Calda Vita (Magna, 1967)
Clambake (UA, 1967)
C'mon, Let's Live a Little (Par, 1967)
The Cobra (AIP, 1967)
Daleks' Invasion Earth 2150 A.D. (Continental, 1967)
Deadlier Than the Male (Univ, 1967)
The Deadly Bees (Par, 1967)
Fistful of Dollars (UA, 1967)
For a Few Dollars More (UA, 1967)
Fort Utah (Par, 1967)
Games (Univ, 1967)
The Good, the Bad and the Ugly (UA, 1967)
Gunfight in Abilene (Univ, 1967)
The Hills Run Red (UA, 1967)
The Hired Killer (Par, 1967)
Hostile Guns (Par, 1967)
House of a Thousand Dolls (AIP, 1967)
Island of the Doomed (AA, 1967)
It's a Bikini World (Trans American, 1967)
Kill or Be Killed (Cinemation, 1967)
King of Hearts (Lopert, 1967)
Lightning Bolt (Woolner, 1967)
Made in Italy (Royal, 1967)
A Mardin for a Prince (Royal, 1967)
A Man Called Gannon (Univ, 1967)
The Million Eyes of Su-Maru (AIP, 1967)
Mission Blood Mary (Telefilm, 1967)
The Naked Runner (W7, 1967)
Navajo Joe (UA, 1967)
One-Eyed Soldiers (United Screen Arts, 1967)
Operation Kid Brother (UA, 1967)
Peace for a Gunfighter (Crown, 1967)
The Projected Man (Univ, 1967)
Rosie (Univ, 1967)
Rough Night in Jericho (Univ, 1967)
Run Like a Thief (Feature Film Corp, 1967)
The Sea Pirate (Par, 1967)
The Tall Women (AA, 1967)
Tender Scoundrel (Emb, 1967)
Tobruk (Univ, 1967)
Track of Thunder (UA, 1967)
Up the Macgregors (Col, 1967)
The Viscount (WB, 1967)
Waterhole #3 (Par, 1967)

What Am I Bid? (Emerson, 1967)
The Young Warriors (Univ, 1967)
Any Gun Can Play (RAF, 1968)
Arizona Bushwackers (Par, 1968)
Assignment K (Col, 1968)
The Ballad of Josie (Univ, 1968)
The Big Gundown (Col, 1968)
A Bullet for the General (Avco, 1968)
The Champagne Murders (Univ, 1968)
Charly (CRC, 1968)
Counterpoint (Univ, 1968)
Did You Hear the One About the Travelling Saleslady? (Univ, 1968)
Don't Just Stand There! (Univ, 1968)
Fever Heat (Par, 1968)
The Glass Sphinx (AIP, 1968)
Grand Slam (Par, 1968)
The Hell with Heroes (Univ, 1968)
In Enemy Country (Univ, 1968)
Journey to Shiloh (Univ, 1968)
Knives of the Avenger (World Entertainment, 1968)
The Last Adventure (Univ, 1968)
The Long Day's Dying (Par, 1968)
A Lovely Way to Die (Univ, 1968)
Madigan (Univ, 1968)
The Man from Nowhere (G.G., 1968)
The Man Outside (AA, 1968)
A Matter of Innocence (Univ, 1968)
The Mini-Affair (United Screen Arts, 1968)
Mission Stardust (Times, 1968)
The Narco Men (RAF, 1968)
Nobody's Perfect (Univ, 1968)
P.J. (Univ, 1968)
Paper Lion (UA, 1968)
Payment in Blood (Winchester for Hire) (Col, 1968)
Pierrot le Fou (Pathé, 1968)
The Pink Jungle (Univ, 1968)
The Secret War of Harry Frigg (Univ, 1968)
Seven Guns for the Macgregors (Col, 1968)
The Shakiest Gun in the West (Univ, 1968)
Shock Troops (UA, 1968)
The Strange Affair (Par, 1968)
Thunderbirds Are Go (UA, 1968)
Up the Junction (Par, 1968)
The Violent Four (Par, 1968)
What's So Bad About Feeling Good? (Univ, 1968)
The Wild Eye (AIP, 1968)
Ace High (Par, 1969)
Adalen (Par, 1969)
Angel in My Pocket (Univ, 1969)
Assassination (Barry, 1969)
Dare the Devil (Cinar, 1969)
Day of Anger (NG, 1969)

Death Rides a Horse (UA, 1969)
Dirty Heroes (Golden Eagle, 1969)
The Fantastic Plastic Machine (Crown, 1969)
Five Bloody Graves (II, 1969)
The Girl Who Couldn't Say No (20th-Fox, 1969)
House of Cards (Univ, 1969)
The Last Mercenary (Excelsion, 1969)
Listen, Let's Make Love (Lopert, 1969)
The Love God? (Univ, 1969)
Loving Feeling (U-M, 1969)
The Murder Clinic (Europix-Consolidated, 1969)
Once Upon a Time in the West (Par, 1969)
Playmates (VIP, 1969)
The Ruthless Four (Goldstone, 1969)
The Sex of Angels (Lopert, 1969)
The Southern Star (Col, 1969)
They Came to Rob Las Vegas (W7, 1969)
Three Nights of Love (Magna, 1969)
The Wanderer (Pennebacker, 1969)
Wise Guys (Univ, 1969)
The Witchmaker (Excelsion, 1969)
The Bird with the Crystal Plumage (U-M, 1970)
Bora Bora (AIP, 1970)
A Bullet for Sandoval (U-M, 1970)
Captain Milkshake (Richmark, 1970)
Eugenie . . . The Story of Her Journey into Perversion (Distinction, 1970)
Kill Them All and Come Back Alone (Fanfare, 1970)
Like It Is (Brode, 1970)
Machine Gun McCain (Col, 1970)
The Mercenary (UA, 1970)
The Olympics in Mexico (Col, 1970)
A Quiet Place in the Country (Lopert, 1970)
Sabata (UA, 1970)
The Savage Wild (AIP, 1970)
Threesome (Mahler, 1970)
Two or Three Things I Know About Her (New Yorker, 1970)
Adios, Sabata (UA, 1971)
Black Jesus (Plaza, 1971)
Blue Water, White Death (NG, 1971)
The Brotherhood of Satan (Col, 1971)
The Cat o' Nine Tails (NG, 1971)
Death of Summer (Plaza, 1971)
The Dirty Heroes (Golden Eagle, 1971)
A Man Called Sledge (Col, 1971)
Medicine Ball Caravan (WB, 1971)
THX 1138 (WB, 1971)
Bewitched Love (El amor brujo) (España, 1972)
Blindman (20th-Fox, 1972)
Compañeros (GSF, 1972)
A Fistful of Dynamite (Duck, You Sucker) (UA, 1972)
Four Flies on Grey Velvet (Par, 1972)
Johnnie Hamlet (Transvue, 1972)

Return of Sabata (UA, 1972)
Slaughterhouse Five (Univ, 1972)
Weekend Murders (MGM, 1972)
American Graffiti (Univ, 1973)*
Eagle Over London (Cine Globe, 1973)
The Family (International Coproductions, 1973)
The Legend of Boggy Creek (Howco, 1973)*
Man from Deep River (Brenner, 1973)
Steel Arena (L-T, 1973)
The Arena (New World, 1974)
Count Dracula (Crystal, 1974)
Holy Mountain (ABKCO, 1974)
Partner (New Yorker, 1974)
A Reason to Live, a Reason to Die (Massacre at Fort Holman) (K-tel, 1974)
The Tongfather (Aquarius, 1974)
The Vampire's Night Orgy (International Amusements, 1974)
A Boy and His Dog (LQ Jaf, 1975)
Counselor at Crime (Green, 1975)
Fury of the Black Belt (Lana, 1975)
The Kung Fu Massacre (Aquarius, 1975)
Messiah of Evil (International Cinefilm, 1975)
Voodoo Black Exorcist (Horizon, 1975)
Winterhawk (Howco, 1975)
The Adventures of Frontier Fremont (Sunn, 1976)
Death Machines (Crown, 1976)
Execution Squad (Fanfare, 1976)
Get Mean (Cec Note, 1976)
Goodbye, Norma Jean (Stirling Gold, 1976)
Shanghai Joe (United International, 1976)
The Valley (The Valley Obscured by Clouds) (Circle, 1977)
Nightmare in Blood (PFE, 1978)
Sacrifice (Brenner, 1980)
Safari Express (Green, 1980)

AGASCOPE

The Flute and the Arrow (Janus, 1960)
A Matter of Morals (UA, 1961)
Gorilla (Herts-Lion, 1964)
The Swedish Mistress (Janus, 1964)
Short Is the Summer (Shaw, 1968)
The Boys of Paul Street (20th-Fox, 1969)
The Red and the White (Brandon, 1969)
The Round Up (Altura, 1969)
Winter Wind (Grove, 1970)

ASTRAVISION

Orgy of the Dead (F.O.G., 1965)
Bachelor's Dream (Sack, 1967)
Motel Confidential (Sack, 1967)

CENTRALSCOPE

Hentai (Olympic International, 1966)

CHINASCOPE

Blood of the Sun (Centaur, 1974)

CINEPANORAMIC

Terror-Creatures from the Grave (Pacemaker, 1967)

CINESCOPE

Marine Battleground (Manson, 1966)

CINETOTALSCOPE

The Sword and the Cross (The Slaves of Carthage) (Valiant, 1960)

CROMOSCOPE

Hercules Against the Moon Men (Governor, 1965)
Hercules vs. the Gaint Warriors (Alexander, 1965)
The She Beast (Europix-Consolidated, 1966)
Romeo and Juliet (World Entertainment, 1968)
The Young, the Evil and the Savage (AIP, 1968)
Paranoia (Commonwealth, 1969)
Superargo vs. Diabolicus (Col, 1969)
The Sweet Body of Deborah (W7, 1969)
A Bullet for Sandoval (UMC, 1971)
Superargo and the Faceless Giants (Fanfare, 1971)
The Black Belly of the Tarantula (MGM, 1972)

DAIEISCOPE

The White Heron (Daiei, 1959)
Angry Island (Bentley, 1960)
The Key (WB, 1960)
Odd Obsession (Harrison, 1961)
Fires on the Plain (Harrison, 1962)
Majin (Daiei, 1968)
Passion (Daiei, 1968)
Zatoichi (Daiei, 1968)
The Blind Beast (Daiei, 1969)
Broken Swords (Daiei, 1969)
Devil's Temple (Daiei, 1969)
Secrets of a Woman's Temple (Daiei, 1969)
Thousand Cranes (Daiei, 1969)

The Falcon Fighters (Daiei, 1970)
Gateway to Glory (Daiei, 1970)
The Magoichi Saga (Daiei, 1970)
Play It Cool (Daieiscope, 1970)
Tenchu! (Daiei, 1970)
Vixen (Daiei, 1970)
Way Out, Way In (Daiei, 1970)
Zatoichi Challenged (Daiei, 1970)
Zatoichi Meets Yojimbo (Daiei, 1970)

DAIEISCOPE/TOTALSCOPE

Gammera the Invincible (World Entertainment, 1966)

DUO-VISION

Wicked, Wicked (MGM, 1973)

DYALISCOPE

400 Blows (Janus, 1959)
The Headless Ghost (AIP, 1959)
Hercules (WB, 1959)
O.S.S. 117 Is Not Dead (Rep, 1959)
Expresso Bongo (Continental, 1960)
The Female (A Woman Like Satan) (Lopert, 1960)
Hercules Unchained (WB, 1960)
Mania (Valiant, 1961)
The Secret of Monte Cristo (MGM, 1961)
The Siege of Sidney Street (United Producers, 1961)
The White Warrior (WB, 1961)
Crime Does Not Pay (Emb, 1962)
The Day the Earth Caught Fire (UI, 1962)
The Knights of the Teutonic Order (Amperol, 1962)
Last of the Vikings (Medallion, 1962)
Last Year in Marienbad (Astor, 1962)
The Long Absence (Commercial, 1962)
Shoot the Piano Player (Astor, 1962)
Siege of Syracuse (Par, 1962)
The Story of the Count of Monte Cristo (WB, 1962)
Stowaway in the Sky (Lopert, 1962)
Where the Truth Lies (Par, 1962)
Atlas Against the Cyclop (Medallion, 1963)
Erik the Conqueror (AIP, 1963)
Fury of the Pagans (Col, 1963)
The Hellfire Club (Emb, 1963)
Mill of the Stone Women (Parade, 1963)
Naked Autumn (United Motion Picture Org, 1963)
Seven Capital Sins (Emb, 1963)
Tarzan's Three Challenges (MGM, 1963)
The Adventures of Scaramouche (Emb, 1964)
Cartouche (Emb, 1964)

A Mistress for the Summer (American Film Distributing, 1964)
Sin on the Beach (American Film Distributing, 1964)
Taxi to Tobruk (7A, 1965)
The Gendarme of St. Tropez (Magna, 1966)
The Sargossa Manuscript (Amperol, 1966)
Girl Game (Cinema Distributors, 1968)
Mississippi Mermaid (UA, 1970)
The Passenger (Altura, 1970)

DYNAVISION

Nature Girl and the Slaver (United Producers, 1959)

EUROSCOPE

The Centurion (Producers International, 1962)
Gladiator of Rome (Medallion, 1963)
The Red Sheik (Medallion, 1963)
The Avenger (Medallion, 1964)
Conquest of Mycene (Emb, 1965)
Invasion 1700 (Medallion, 1965)
Adios Gringo (Trans-Lux, 1967)

FANTASCOPE

The Ecstasies of Women (United Pictures Org, 1969)
Five the Hard Way (Crown, 1969)

FRANSCOPE

The Green Mare (Zenith, 1961)
Jules and Jim (Janus, 1962)
Lola (Films Around the World, 1962)
Sundays and Cybelle (Col, 1962)
The Army Game (Consort/Orion, 1963)
The Devil and the Ten Commandments (Union, 1963)
Love on a Pillow (Royal, 1963)
La Poupée (He, She or It!) (Lionex, 1963)
Contempt (Emb, 1964)
The Day and the Hour (MGM, 1964)
Don't Tempt the Devil (United Motion Picture Org, 1964)
Joy House (MGM, 1964)
Nutty, Naughty Chateau (Lopert, 1964)
Of Flesh and Blood (Times, 1964)
Three Penny Opera (Emb, 1964)
Two Are Guilty (MGM, 1964)
A Woman Is a Woman (Pathé, 1964)
Backfire (Royal, 1965)
Circle of Love (Continental, 1965)
The Corpse of Beverly Hills (Medallion, 1965)
Diary of a Chambermaid (International Classics, 1965)
The Dirty Girls (Audobon, 1965)

My Wife's Husband (Lopert, 1965)
Vice and Virtue (MGM, 1965)
Enough Rope (Artixo, 1966)
Fantomas (Lopert, 1966)
Man from Cocody (AA, 1966)
Marco the Magnificent (MGM, 1966)
OSS 117—Mission for a Killer (Emb, 1966)
Serenade for Two Spies (United Film, 1966)
The Sucker (Royal, 1966)
Weekend in Dunkirk (20th-Fox, 1966)
The Beautiful Swindles (Continental, 1967)
The Immoral Moment (Jerand, 1967)
More Than a Miracle (MGM, 1967)
Shadow of Evil (7A, 1967)
The 25th Hour (MGM, 1967)
Two Weeks in September (Par, 1967)
The Upper Hand (Par, 1967)
Birds in Peru (Regional, 1968)
Guns for San Sebastian (MGM, 1968)
Shalako (CRC, 1968)
Action Man (Barry, 1969)
Black Sun (Barry, 1969)
The Brain (Par, 1969)
Les Creatures (New Yorker, 1969)
Peking Blonde (Barry, 1969)
Captain Apache (Scotia, 1971)
The House That Screamed (AIP, 1971)
A Town Called Hell (Scotia, 1971)
Bad Man's River (Scotia, 1975)

GRANDSCOPE

Ballad of Narayama (Films Around the World, 1961)
Naked Youth (Shochiku, 1961)
Road to Eternity (Beverly, 1961)
Youth in Fury (Shochiku, 1961)
Harakiri (Toko, 1963)
The Body (Shochiku, 1964)
Day-Dream (Green, 1964)
The Inheritance (Shochiku, 1964)
Samurai from Nowhere (Shochiku, 1964)
Twin Sister of Kyoto (Shochiku, 1964)
Women ... Oh, Women! (Shochiku, 1964)
It's a Woman's World (Shochiku, 1965)
Love Under the Crucifix (Shochiku, 1965)
The Pleasures of the Flesh (Shochiku, 1965)
The Scarlet Camellia (Shochiku, 1965)
Twilight Path (Shochiku, 1965)
Judo Showdown (Brown, 1966)
The Affair (Shochiku, 1969)
Black Lizard (Shochiku, 1969)
Black Rose (Shochiku, 1969)

Farewell, My Beloved (Shochiku, 1969)
The House of the Sleeping Virgins (Shochiku, 1969)
Snow Country (Shochiku, 1969)
Through Days and Months (Shochiku, 1969)
Fight for Glory (Shochiku, 1970)
No Greater Love (Shochiku, 1970)
The Performers (Shochiku, 1970)
A Soldier's Prayer (Shochiku, 1970)
The Song from My Heart (Schochiku, 1970)
The Last Samurai (Schochiku, 1977)

HAMMERSCOPE

The Abominable Snowman (20th-Fox, 1957)
Hell Is a City (Col, 1960)
The Pirates of Blood River (Col, 1962)
The Crimson Blade (Col, 1964)
Nightmare (Univ, 1964)
She (MGM, 1965)
These Are the Damned (Col, 1965)
Rasputin—The Mad Monk (20th-Fox, 1966)
Prehistoric Women (20th-Fox, 1967)

HI-FI SCOPE

Karate, the Hand of Death (AA, 1961)

J-D-C SCOPE

Horror Planet (Almi, 1982)
The Bounty (Orion, 1984)*
Conan the Destroyer (Univ, 1984)
Firestarter (Univ, 1984)
Sahara (MGM/UA, 1984)*
Sword of the Valiant (Cannon, 1984)*
Cat's Eye (MGM/UA, 1985)*
The Doctor and the Devils (20th-Fox, 1985)*
King Solomon's Mines (Cannon, 1985)*
Maria (MGM/UA, 1985)
Red Sonja (MGM/UA, 1985)
Silver Bullet (Par, 1985)

MEGASCOPE

The Camp on Blood Island (Col, 1958)
Yesterday's Enemy (Col, 1959)
The Stranglers of Bombay (Col, 1960)
House of Fright (The Two Faces of Dr. Jekyll) (AIP, 1961)
Never Take Candy from a Stranger (Sutton, 1961)
Stop Me Before I Kill! (Col, 1961)
Sword of Sherwood Forest (Col, 1961)
Maniac (Col, 1963)
The Devil-Ship Pirates (Col, 1964)

MULTIPLE SCREEN

Joe Cocker/Mad Dogs & Englishmen (MGM, 1971)*
Elvis on Tour (MGM, 1972)*

MULTISCREEN

Fillmore (20th-Fox, 1972)*

NATURAMA

Accused of Murder (Rep, 1956)
Lisbon (Rep, 1956)
The Maverick Queen (Rep, 1956)
Thunder Over Arizona (Rep, 1956)
Affair in Reno (Rep, 1957)
The Crooked Circle (Rep, 1957)
Duel at Apache Wells (Rep, 1957)
Gunfire at Indian Gap (Rep, 1957)
Hell's Crossroads (Rep, 1957)
Last Stagecoach West (Rep, 1957)
The Lawless Eighties (Rep, 1957)
Panama Sal (Rep, 1957)
Spoilers of the Forest (Rep, 1957)
Taming Sutton's Gal (Rep, 1957)
The Wayward Girl (Rep, 1957)
Juvenile Jungle (Rep, 1958)
Man or Gun (Rep, 1958)
The Man Who Died Twice (Rep, 1958)
No Place to Land (Rep, 1958)
The Notorious Mr. Monks (Rep, 1958)
Young and Wild (Rep, 1958)
Plunderers of Painted Flats (Rep, 1959)

NIKKATSUSCOPE

The Temptress (Nikkatsu, 1958)
The Flesh Is Hot (European Producers International, 1963)
The Temptress and the Monk (Nikkatsu, 1963)
The Assassin (Toho, 1964)
Gate of Flesh (Nikkatsu, 1964)
The Hunter's Diary (Nikkatsu, 1964)
Unholy Desire (Toho, 1964)
Whirlpool of Woman (Toho, 1966)
Asiapol Secret Service (Toho, 1969)
East China Sea (Nikkatsu, 1969)
The House of Strange Loves (United Producers, 1969)
No Greater Love Than This (Toho, 1969)
The Friendly Killer (Nikkatsu, 1970)
The Girl I Abandoned (Nikkatsu, 1970)

PANORAMIC

Eighteen in the Sun (Goldstone, 1964)
The Horrible Dr. Hitchcock (Sigma III, 1964)
Ecco (LCR, 1965)

PANASCOPE

Fury at Smugglers' Bay (Emb, 1963)

PANAVISION

Jailhouse Rock (MGM, 1957)*
The Big Circus (AA, 1959)
Four Fast Guns (UI, 1959)
They Came to Cordura (Col, 1959)
The World the Flesh and the Devil (MGM, 1959)
The Wreck of the Mary Deare (MGM, 1959)*
The Adventures of Huckleberry Finn (MGM, 1960)
All the Fine Young Cannibals (MGM, 1960)
The Apartment (UA, 1960)
Bells Are Ringing (MGM, 1960)*
Butterfield 8 (MGM, 1960)
Comanche Station (Col, 1960)
Cimarron (MGM, 1960)*
The Gazebo (MGM, 1960)
Hell Bent for Leather (UI, 1960)
Home from the Hill (MGM, 1960)*
Key Witness (MGM, 1960)
The Magnificent Seven (UA, 1960)
Never So Few (MGM, 1960)*
Ocean's 11 (WB, 1960)
Pepe (Col, 1960)*
Please Don't Eat the Daisies (MGM, 1960)
Song Without End (Col, 1960)
Strangers When We Meet (Col, 1960)
The Subterraneans (MGM, 1960)
Swiss Family Robinson (BVD, 1960)
The Unforgiven (UA, 1960)
The Wackiest Ship in the Army (Col, 1960)
Where the Boys Are (MGM, 1960)
Ada (MGM, 1961)
Bachelor in Paradise (MGM, 1961)
Blue Hawaii (Par, 1961)*
Come September (UI, 1961)
Cry for Happy (Col, 1961)
The Deadly Companions (Pathé America, 1961)
Flower Drum Song (UI, 1961)
The Honeymoon Machine (MGM, 1961)
Love in a Goldfish Bowl (Par, 1961)
Man-Trap (Par, 1961)
On the Double (Par, 1961)

One, Two, Three (UA, 1961)
The Pit and the Pendulum (AIP, 1961)
Pocketful of Miracles (UA, 1961)
Ring of Fire (MGM, 1961)
Summer and Smoke (Par, 1961)
A Thunder of Drums (MGM, 1961)
Two Loves (MGM, 1961)
X-15 (UA, 1961)
Advise and Consent (Col, 1962)
Boys' Night Out (MGM, 1962)
Dangerous Charter (Crown International, 1962)
Escape from Zahrain (Par, 1962)
Follow That Dream (UA, 1962)
The Four Horsemen of the Apocalypse (MGM, 1962)*
Geronimo (UA, 1962)
A Girl Named Tamiko (Par, 1962)
Hero's Island (UA, 1962)
The Horizontal Lieutenant (MGM, 1962)
Jessica (UA, 1962)
Jumbo (MGM, 1962)
Light in the Piazza (MGM, 1962)
Lonely Are the Brave (UI, 1962)
Period of Adjustment (MGM, 1962)
The Pigeon That Took Rome (Par, 1962)
Premature Burial (AIP, 1962)
Ride the High Country (MGM, 1962)
Sergeants 3 (UA, 1962)
Sweet Bird of Youth (MGM, 1962)
Tales of Terror (AIP, 1962)
Tarsus Bulba (UA, 1962)
Tarzan Goes to India (MGM, 1962)
That Touch of Mink (UI, 1962)
Two for the Seesaw (UA, 1962)
Two Weeks in Another Town (MGM, 1962)
Who's Got the Action? (Par, 1962)
Beach Party (AIP, 1963)
Black Zoo (AIP, 1963)
Bye Bye Birdie (Col, 1963)
Come Blow Your Horn (Par, 1963)
Come Fly with Me (MGM, 1963)
The Comedy of Terrors (AIP, 1963)
The Courtship of Eddie's Father (MGM, 1963)
Critic's Choice (WB, 1963)
Diamond Head (Col, 1963)
Follow the Boys (MGM, 1963)
Forty Pounds of Trouble (Univ, 1963)
The Girl Hunters (Colorama, 1963)
The Great Escape (UA, 1963)
Gunfight at Comanche Creek (AA, 1963)
The Haunted Palace (AIP, 1963)
The Haunting (MGM, 1963)
The Hook (MGM, 1963)

Hud (Par, 1963)
I Could Go On Singing (UA, 1963)
In the Cold of the Day (MGM, 1963)
Irma la Douce (WB, 1963)
Island of Love (WB, 1963)
It Happened at the World's Fair (MGM, 1963)
Kings of the Sun (UA, 1963)
Love Is a Ball (UA, 1963)
McLintock! (UA, 1963)
The Prize (MGM, 1963)
PT 109 (WB, 1963)
The Raven (AIP, 1963)
The Running Man (Col, 1963)
Spencer's Mountain (WB, 1963)
Sword of Lancelot (Lancelot and Guinevere) (UI, 1963)
A Ticklish Affair (MGM, 1963)
Toys in the Attic (UA, 1963)
Twilight of Honor (MGM, 1963)
The V.I.P.s (MGM, 1963)
The Victors (Col, 1963)*
The Wheeler Dealers (MGM, 1963)
Who's Been Sleeping in My Bed? (Par, 1963)
Advance to the Rear (MGM, 1964)
Bikini Beach (AIP, 1964)
A Distant Trumpet (WB, 1964)
Ensign Pulver (WB, 1964)
Flight from Ashiya (UA, 1964)
Get Yourself a College Girl (MGM, 1964)
Honeymoon Hotel (MGM, 1964)
Kiss Me, Stupid (UA, 1964)
Kissin' Cousins (MGM, 1964)
Looking for Love (MGM, 1964)
Mail Order Bride (MGM, 1964)
The Masque of the Red Death (AIP, 1964)
Muscle Beach Party (AIP, 1964)
The Outrage (MGM, 1964)
Pajama Party (AIP, 1964)
Robin and the 7 Hoods (WB, 1964)
The Secret Invasion (UA, 1964)
A Shot in the Dark (UA, 1964)
633 Squadron (UA, 1964)
Viva Las Vegas (MGM, 1964)
The World of Henry Orient (UA, 1964)
Your Cheatin' Heart (MGM, 1964)
The Amorous Adventures of Moll Flanders (Par, 1965)
The Battle of the Villa Fiorita (WB, 1965)
Beach Blanket Bingo (AIP, 1965)
Brainstorm (WB, 1965)
Bunny Lake Is Missing (Col, 1965)
Dr. Goldfoot and the Bikini Machine (AIP, 1965)
Girl Happy (MGM, 1965)
The Glory Guys (UA, 1965)

Harlow (Par, 1965)
How to Stuff a Wild Bikini (AIP, 1965)
Inside Daisy Clover (WB, 1965)
Major Dundee (Col, 1965)
Mister Moses (UA, 1965)
My Blood Runs Cold (WB, 1965)
The Naked Prey (Par, 1965)
Never Too Late (WB, 1965)
None but the Brave (WB, 1965)
Once a Thief (MGM, 1965)
Operation Crossbow (MGM, 1965)
A Patch of Blue (MGM, 1965)
Quick, Before It Melts (MGM, 1965)
A Rage to Live (UA, 1965)
Return from the Ashes (UA, 1965)
Rotten to the Core (Cinema V, 1965)
The Rounders (MGM, 1965)
The Sandpiper (MGM, 1965)
Sands of the Kalahari (Par, 1965)
The Satan Bug (UA, 1965)
The Secret of My Success (MGM, 1965)
Sergeant Deadhead (AIP, 1965)
Signpost to Murder (MGM, 1965)
The Singing Nun (MGM, 1965)
Ski Party (AIP, 1965)
The Sons of Katie Elder (Par, 1965)
The Third Day (WB, 1965)
36 Hours (MGM, 1965)
Thunderball (UA, 1965)*
Tickle Me (AA, 1965)
Two on a Guillotine (WB, 1965)
Viva Maria! (UA, 1965)
The War Lord (Univ, 1965)
When the Boys Meet the Girls (MGM, 1965)
The Yellow Rolls-Royce (MGM, 1965)
After the Fox (UA, 1966)
Alvarez Kelly (Col, 1966)
Arabesque (Univ, 1966)
Around the World Under the Sea (MGM, 1966)*
Arrivederci, Baby! (Par, 1966)
Assault on a Queen (Par, 1966)
Blindfold (Univ, 1966)
Born Free (Col, 1966)
Cast a Giant Shadow (UA, 1966)
The Chase (Col, 1966)
Fireball 500 (AIP, 1966)
The Fortune Cookie (UA, 1966)
The Ghost in the Invisible Bikini (AIP, 1966)
The Glass Bottom Boat (MGM, 1966)
Harper (WB, 1966)
Hold On! (MGM, 1966)
Hotel Paradisio (MGM, 1966)

How to Steal a Million (20th-Fox, 1966)
Judith (Par, 1966)
Lady L (MGM, 1966)
The Liquidator (MGM, 1966)
Lost Command (Col, 1966)
Mademoiselle (Lopert, 1966)
A Man Could Get Killed (Univ, 1966)
Maya (MGM, 1966)
The Money Trap (MGM, 1966)
Nevada Smith (Par, 1966)
Penelope (MGM, 1966)
The Professionals (Col, 1966)
The Quiller Memorandum (20th-Fox, 1966)
The Rare Breed (Univ, 1966)
Return of the Seven (UA, 1966)
The Russians Are Coming, the Russians Are Coming (UA, 1966)
Seven Women (MGM, 1966)
Spinout (MGM, 1966)
Tarzan and the Valley of Gold (AIP, 1966)
Walk, Don't Run (Col, 1966)
What Did You Do in the War, Daddy? (UA, 1966)
Where the Spies Are (MGM, 1966)
The Wild Angels (AIP, 1966)
Bedazzled (20th-Fox, 1967)
Billion Dollar Brain (UA, 1967)
Cool Hand Luke (WB, 1967)
The Cool Ones (WB, 1967)
Devil's Angels (AIP, 1967)
Don't Make Waves (MGM, 1967)
Double Trouble (MGM, 1967)
The Fearless Vampire Killers; or, Pardon Me but Your Teeth Are in My Neck (MGM, 1967)
First to Fight (WB, 1967)
Fitzwilly (UA, 1967)
The Flim-Flam Man (20th-Fox, 1967)*
The Game Is Over (Royal, 1967)
The Graduate (Emb, 1967)*
A Guide for the Married Man (20th-Fox, 1967)
Hombre (20th-Fox, 1967)
Hour of the Gun (UA, 1967)
How to Succeed in Business Without Really Trying (UA, 1967)
Hurry Sundown (Par, 1967)
In Cold Blood (Col, 1967)
Jack of Diamonds (MGM, 1967)
The Last Challenge (MGM, 1967)
The Long Duel (Par, 1967)
Luv (Col, 1967)
A Midsummer Night's Dream (Showcorporation, 1967)
The Night of the Generals (Col, 1967)
Point Blank (MGM, 1967)
The President's Analyst (Par, 1967)
Reflections in a Golden Eye (W7, 1967)

The St. Valentine's Day Massacre (20th-Fox, 1967)
The Taming of the Shrew (Col, 1967)
Tarzan and the Great River (Par, 1967)
Those Fantastic Flying Fools (Blast-Off) (AIP, 1967)
Three Bites of the Apple (MGM, 1967)
Thunder Alley (AIP, 1967)
A Time for Killing (Col, 1967)
Tony Rome (20th-Fox, 1967)
The Trap (Continental, 1967)
Two for the Road (20th-Fox, 1967)
Ulysses (Continental, 1967)*
Valley of the Dolls (20th-Fox, 1967)
The Venetian Affair (MGM, 1967)
The War Wagon (Univ, 1967)
The Way West (UA, 1967)
You Only Live Twice (UA, 1967)
Anzio (Col, 1968)
Bandolero! (20th-Fox, 1968)*
Barbarella (Par, 1968)
The Biggest Bundle of Them All (MGM, 1968)
Blue (Par, 1968)
Boom! (Univ, 1968)
The Boston Strangler (20th-Fox, 1968)
The Charge of the Light Brigade (UA, 1968)*
Chubasco (W7, 1968)
Countdown (W7, 1968)
A Dandy in Aspic (Col, 1968)
Dark of the Sun (MGM, 1968)
Day of the Evil Gun (MGM, 1968)
The Detective (20th-Fox, 1968)
The Devil's Brigade (UA, 1968)
Firecreek (W7, 1968)
A Flea in Her Ear (20th-Fox, 1968)
The Green Berets (W7, 1968)
Half a Sixpence (Par, 1968)*
Hell in the Pacific (CRC, 1968)
How Sweet It Is! (NG, 1968)
How to Save a Marriage—And Ruin Your Life (Col, 1968)
The Impossible Years (MGM, 1968)
Inspector Clouseau (UA, 1968)
Joanna (20th-Fox, 1968)
Kiss the Other Sheik (MGM, 1968)
Lady in Cement (20th-Fox, 1968)
The Lion in Winter (Avco, 1968)
Live a Little, Love a Little (MGM, 1968)
The Magus (20th-Fox, 1968)
Maroc 7 (Par, 1968)
Mrs. Brown, You've Got a Lovely Daughter (MGM, 1968)
The Odd Couple (Par, 1968)
The Party (UA, 1968)
Planet of the Apes (20th-Fox, 1968)*
The Power (MGM, 1968)

The Scalphunters (UA, 1968)
Skidoo (Par, 1968)
Sol Madrid (MGM, 1968)
Speedway (MGM, 1968)
The Split (MGM, 1968)
The Stalking Moon (NG, 1968)
Stay Away, Joe (MGM, 1968)
The Sweet Ride (20th-Fox, 1968)
Tarzan and the Jungle Boy (Par, 1968)
A Time to Sing (MGM, 1968)
Villa Rides! (Par, 1968)
Where Were You When the Lights Went Out? (MGM, 1968)
With Six You Get Eggroll (NG, 1968)
The Young Runaways (MGM, 1968)
Alfred the Great (MGM, 1969)
The April Fools (NG, 1969)
The Arrangement (W7, 1969)
Assignment to Kill (W7, 1969)
The Battle of Britain (UA, 1969)
Beneath the Planet of the Apes (20th-Fox, 1969)
The Big Bounce (W7, 1969)
The Bridge at Remagen (UA, 1969)
Butch Cassidy and the Sundance Kid (20th-Fox, 1969)*
Camille 2000 (Audobon, 1969)
Castle Keep (Col, 1969)
The Chairman (20th-Fox, 1969)
Changes (CRC, 1969)
Charro! (NG, 1969)
Che! (20th-Fox, 1969)
Don't Look Now (BVD, 1969)
The Extraordinary Seaman (MGM, 1969)
A Fine Pair (NG, 1969)
The Good Guys and the Bad Guys (W7, 1969)
Goyokin (Toho, 1969)
The Great Bank Robbery (W7, 1969)
Guns of the Magnificent Seven (UA, 1969)
The Happy Ending (UA, 1969)
Hard Contract (20th-Fox, 1969)
Heaven with a Gun (MGM, 1969)
The Illustrated Man (W7, 1969)
The Italian Job (Par, 1969)
John and Mary (20th-Fox, 1969)
Justine (20th-Fox, 1969)
The Learning Tree (W7, 1969)
The Lost Man (Univ, 1969)
Made in Paris (MGM, 1969)
The Madwoman of Chaillot (W7, 1969)
The Maltese Bippy (MGM, 1969)
*M*A*S*H* (20th-Fox, 1969)*
Mayerling (MGM, 1969)
My Side of the Mountain (Par, 1969)

Oh! What a Lovely War (Par, 1969)
On Her Majesty's Secret Service (UA, 1969)
Play Dirty (UA, 1969)
Portrait of Hell (Toho, 1969)
The Reivers (NG, 1969)*
The Secret of Santa Vittoria (UA, 1969)
Sinful Davey (UA, 1969)
Staircase (20th-Fox, 1969)
Tell Them Willie Boy Is Here (Univ, 1969)
They Shoot Horses, Don't They? (CRC, 1969)
The Trouble with Girls (MGM, 1969)
The Undefeated (20th-Fox, 1969)
Beyond the Valley of the Dolls (20th-Fox, 1970)
Cannon for Cordoba (UA, 1970)
Captain Nemo and the Underwater City (MGM, 1970)
Catch-22 (Par, 1970)
The Cheyenne Social Club (NG, 1970)
Chisum (WB, 1970)
Colossus (The Forbin Project) (Univ, 1970)
The Creature Called Man (Toho, 1970)
Cromwell (Col, 1970)
Darling Lili (Par, 1970)*
Dirty Dingus Magee (MGM, 1970)
Duel at Ezo (Toho, 1970)
Elvis—That's the Way It Is (MGM, 1970)*
The Executioner (Col, 1970)
Fellini Satyricon (UA, 1970)
Female Animal (Cinemation, 1970)
Flap (WB, 1970)
The Games (20th-Fox, 1970)
The Great White Hope (20th-Fox, 1970)
The Hawaiians (UA, 1970)
I Walk the Line (Col, 1970)
Julius Caesar (AIP, 1970)
The Kremlin Letter (20th-Fox, 1970)
The Last Grenade (CRC, 1970)
Little Big Man (NG, 1970)
Little Fauss and Big Halsy (Par, 1970)
The Looking Glass War (Col, 1970)
Macho Callahan (Avco, 1970)
A Man Called Horse (NG, 1970)
The Molly Maguires (Par, 1970)
Monte Walsh (NG, 1970)
Move (20th-Fox, 1970)
Myra Breckenridge (20th-Fox, 1970)
No Blade of Grass (MGM, 1970)
On a Clear Day You Can See Forever (Par, 1970)*
The Owl and the Pussycat (Col, 1970)
The Pizza Triangle (WB, 1970)
The Private Life of Sherlock Holmes (UA, 1970)
The Scandalous Adventures of Buraikan (Toho, 1970)

Scrooge (NG, 1970)*
The Sicilian Clan (20th-Fox, 1970)
Skullduggery (Univ, 1970)
Soldier Blue (Avco, 1970)
There Was a Crooked Man (WB, 1970)
... tick ... tick ... tick ... (MGM, 1970)
Two Mules for Sister Sara (Univ, 1970)
WUSA (Par, 1970)
A Walk in the Spring Rain (Col, 1970)
The Walking Stick (MGM, 1970)
You Can't Win 'Em All (Col, 1970)
Zabriskie Point (MGM, 1970)
Zigzag (MGM, 1970)
The African Elephant (NG, 1971)
The Andromeda Strain (Univ, 1971)
Big Jake (NG, 1971)*
The Buttercup Chain (Col, 1971)
Carnal Knowledge (Avco, 1971)
Death in Venice (WB, 1971)
The Deserter (Par, 1971)
Diamonds Are Forever (UA, 1971)
Dirty Harry (WB, 1971)
The Emperor and the General (Toho, 1971)
Escape from the Planet of the Apes (20th-Fox, 1971)
Figures in a Landscape (NG, 1971)
Honky (Harris, 1971)
The Horsemen (Col, 1971)
Julius Caesar (AIP, 1971)
Kidnapped (AIP, 1971)
Klute (WB, 1971)
The Last Run (MGM, 1971)
Le Mans (NG, 1971)*
Man in the Wilderness (WB, 1971)
McCabe & Mrs. Miller (WB, 1971)
Murphy's War (Par, 1971)
The Omega Man (WB, 1971)
Rabbit Run (WB, 1971)
Road to Salina (Avco, 1971)
Scandalous John (BVD, 1971)
Skin Game (WB, 1971)
The Todd Killings (A Dangerous Friend) (NG, 1971)
Villian (MGM, 1971)
Waterloo (Par, 1971)
When Eight Bells Toll (CRC, 1971)
Yog — Monster from Space (AIP, 1971)
Zeppelin (WB, 1971)
Adam's Woman (WB, 1972)
The Burglars (Col, 1972)
The Carey Treatment (MGM, 1972)
Chandler (MGM, 1972)
Corky (MGM, 1972)
Dealing: Or the Berkeley-to-Boston Forty-Brick Lost-Bag Blues (WB, 1972)

The Devil's Widow (Tam Lin) (AIP, 1972)
The Groundstar Conspiracy (Univ, 1972)
Hannie Caulder (Par, 1972)
The Hot Rock (20th-Fox, 1972)
Images (Col, 1972)
Jeremiah Johnson (WB, 1972)
Joe Kidd (Univ, 1972)
Lady Sings the Blues (Par, 1972)
The Life and Times of Judge Roy Bean (NG, 1972)
The Little Ark (NG, 1972)
The New Centurions (Col, 1972)
Pete 'n' Tillie (Univ, 1972)
Pope Joan (Col, 1972)
Portnoy's Complaint (WB, 1972)
Portrait of Hell (Toho, 1972)
The Poseidon Adventure (20th-Fox, 1972)*
Prime Cut (NG, 1972)
The Public Eye (Univ, 1972)
Rage (WB, 1972)
The Revengers (NG, 1972)
1776 (Col, 1972)
Shaft's Big Score (MGM, 1972)
Skyjacked (MGM, 1972)
Snow Job (WB, 1972)
Sounder (20th-Fox, 1972)
Travels with My Aunt (MGM, 1972)
The Wild Pack (Sandpit General) (AIP, 1972)
The Wrath of God (MGM, 1972)
Ace Eli and Rodger of the Skies (20th-Fox, 1973)
The All-American Boy (WB, 1973)
Battle for the Planet of the Apes (20th-Fox, 1973)
Cahill, United States Marshal (WB, 1973)
Cinderella Liberty (20th-Fox, 1973)
Class of '44 (WB, 1973)
Cleopatra Jones (WB, 1973)
The Day of the Dolphin (Avco, 1973)
Detroit 9000 (General, 1973)*
Fear Is the Key (Par, 1973)
High Plains Drifter (Univ, 1973)
Hit! (Par, 1973)
Jonathan Livingston Seagull (Par, 1973)*
Kid Blue (20th-Fox, 1973)
Lady Ice (NG, 1973)
Lake of Dracula (Toho, 1973)
The Last American Hero (Hard Driver) (20th-Fox, 1973)
Lolly-Madonna XXX (MGM, 1973)
The Long Goodbye (UA, 1973)
Ludwig (MGM, 1973)
The Mackintosh Man (WB, 1973)
Magnum Force (WB, 1973)
The Man Who Loved Cat Dancing (MGM, 1973)
The Militarists (Toho, 1973)

The Nelson Affair (Univ, 1973)
Night Watch (Avco, 1973)
Oklahoma Crude (Col, 1973)
The Paper Chase (20th-Fox, 1973)
Papillon (AA, 1973)
Pat Garrett and Billy the Kid (MGM, 1973)
A Reflection of Fear (Col, 1973)
Scarecrow (WB, 1973)
The Serpent (Avco, 1973)
Shaft in Africa (MGM, 1973)
Siddhartha (Col, 1973)
The Soul of Nigger Charley (Par, 1973)
Soylent Green (MGM, 1973)
Super Fly T.N.T. (Par, 1973)
Sweet Suzy (Blacksnake) (Signal 166, 1973)
Sword of Vengeance (Toho, 1973)
A Touch of Class (Avco, 1973)
The Train Robbers (WB, 1973)
The Way We Were (Col, 1973)
Wedding in White (Avco, 1973)
Westworld (MGM, 1973)*
Zatoichi at Large (Toho, 1973)
Airport 1975 (Univ, 1974)
Bank Shot (UA, 1974)
The Black Windmill (Univ, 1974)
Blazing Saddles (WB, 1974)
The Blockhouse (Cannon, 1974)
California Split (Col, 1974)
Chinatown (Par, 1974)
Conrack (20th-Fox, 1974)
The Dove (Par, 1974)
Eleven Harrowhouse (20th-Fox, 1974)
Face the Wind (WB, 1974)
Freebie and the Bean (WB, 1974)
The Front Page (Univ, 1974)
The Girl in Blue (CRC, 1974)
Gold (AA, 1974)
Huckleberry Finn (UA, 1974)*
In the Devil's Garden (Assault) (Hemisphere, 1974)
Mame (WB, 1974)*
McQ (WB, 1974)
My Name Is Nobody (Univ, 1974)
99 44/100% Dead (The Hood) (20th-Fox, 1974)
The Odessa File (Col, 1974)
The Parallax View (Par, 1974)
The Savage Is Loose (Campbell Devon, 1974)
The Sugarland Express (Univ, 1974)
The Tamarind Seed (Avco, 1974)
Thunderbolt and Lightfoot (UA, 1974)
The Towering Inferno (20th-Fox, 1974)*
The Trial of Billy Jack (Taylor-Laughlin, 1974)
Zandy's Bride (WB, 1974)

Zardoz (20th-Fox, 1974)
Bite the Bullet (Col, 1975)
Brannigan (UA, 1975)
Breakout (Col, 1975)
Cleopatra Jones and the Casino of Gold (WB, 1975)
The Dragon Flies (20th-Fox, 1975)
The Drowning Pool (WB, 1975)
The Eiger Sanction (Univ, 1975)
The Fortune (Col, 1975)
Funny Lady (Col, 1975)*
Hard Times (Col, 1975)
Jaws (Univ, 1975)*
Johnny Firecloud (Entertainment Ventures, 1975)
The Killer Elite (UA, 1975)
Lepke (Univ, 1975)
Lucky Pierre (Seaberg, 1975)
Mahogany (Par, 1975)
The Man Who Would Be King (AA, 1975)
The Master Gunfighter (Taylor-Laughlin, 1975)
Mr. Quilp (Avco, 1975)
My Pleasure Is My Business (Brian, 1975)
Nashville (Par, 1975)*
Old Dracula (Vampira, 1975)
Once Is Not Enough (Par, 1975)
Posse (Par, 1975)
The Prisoner of Second Avenue (WB, 1975)
Rafferty and the Gold Dust Twins (WB, 1975)
The Return of the Pink Panther (UA, 1975)
Rooster Cogburn (Univ, 1975)
Rosebud (UA, 1975)
The Taste of the Savage (World Wide, 1975)
Three Days of the Condor (Par, 1975)
Tidal Wave (New World, 1975)
The Wind and the Lion (MGM, 1975)*
The Yakuza (WB, 1975)
Adios Amigo (Atlas, 1976)
Assault on Precinct 13 (Turtle, 1976)
The Bingo Long Travelling All-Stars and Motor Kings (Univ, 1976)
Buffalo Bill and the Indians or Sitting Bull's History Lesson (UA, 1976)*
Caravan to Vaccares (Bryanston, 1976)
Death Journey (Atlas, 1976)
Doc Hooker's Bunch (ESI, 1976)
The Duchess and the Dirtwater Fox (20th-Fox, 1976)
Emmanuelle — The Joys of a Woman (Par, 1976)
The Enforcer (WB, 1976)
The Front (Col, 1976)
Godzilla vs. Megalion (Cinema Shares, 1976)
The Gumball Rally (WB, 1976)
Harry and Walter Go to New York (Col, 1976)
I Will, I Will ... for Now (20th-Fox, 1976)
The Last Hard Men (20th-Fox, 1976)
The Last Tycoon (Par, 1976)

Mad Dog (Mad Dog Morgan) (Cinema Shares, 1976)
The Making of a Lady (Sunset, 1976)
The Man Who Fell to Earth (Cinema V, 1976)*
Midway (Univ, 1976)*
Mother, Jugs & Speed (20th-Fox, 1976)
Obsession (Col, 1976)
The Omen (20th-Fox, 1976)*
The Outlaw Josey Wales (WB, 1976)
The Pink Panther Strikes Again (UA, 1976)
Serail (Caribou, 1976)
The Slipper and the Rose (Univ, 1976)*
The Stranger and the Gunfighter (Col, 1976)
Swashbuckler (Univ, 1976)*
Two-Minute Warning (Univ, 1976)
The Winds of Autumn (Howco, 1976)
Airport '77 (Univ, 1977)
Black Sunday (Par, 1977)
Bobby Deerfield (Col, 1977)
A Bridge Too Far (UA, 1977)*
The Car (Univ, 1977)*
Charge of the Model-T's (Ry-Mac, 1977)
Cinderella (Group 1, 1977)
Crash (Group 1, 1977)
Damnation Alley (20th-Fox, 1977)*
The Deep (Col, 1977)*
Devil's Express (Mahler, 1977)
The Gauntlet (WB, 1977)
Godzilla on Monster Island (Cinema Shares, 1977)
Godzilla vs. the Bionic Monster (Godzilla vs. the Cosmic Monster) (Cinema
    Shares, 1977)
Grayeagle (AIP, 1977)
Herowork (NBS, 1977)
Infra-Man (Brenner, 1977)*
Islands in the Stream (Par, 1977)
The Minister and Me (Rioma, 1977)
Orca (Par, 1977)
Raggedy Ann and Andy (20th-Fox, 1977)
The Spy Who Loved Me (UA, 1977)
Strange Shadows in an Empty Room (AIP, 1977)
Three Women (20th-Fox, 1977)
The Town That Dreaded Sundown (AIP, 1977)
The True Nature of Bernadette (Campagnie France, 1977)
Viva Knievel! (WB, 1977)
The Amsterdam Kill (Col, 1978)
Big Wednesday (WB, 1978)*
The Boys in Company C (Col, 1978)
Caravans (Univ, 1978)
Casey's Shadow (Col, 1978)
Comes a Horseman (UA, 1978)
Convoy (UA, 1978)
Crossed Swords (The Prince and the Pauper) (WB, 1978)*
Damien — Omen II (20th-Fox, 1978)*

Force Ten from Navarone (AIP, 1978)*
Gray Lady Down (Univ, 1978)
Halloween (Compass, 1978)
Jaws 2 (Universal, 1978)
The Norseman (AIP, 1978)
Revenge of the Pink Panther (UA, 1978)
Shadow Mountain (Wishbone Cutter) (Par, 1978)
The Swarm (WB, 1978)
That's Country (1978)*
Up in Smoke (Par, 1978)
We Will All Meet in Paradise (First Artists, 1978)
A Wedding (20th-Fox, 1978)*
Ashanti (WB, 1979)
Avalanche Express (20th-Fox, 1979)
Beyond the Poseidon Adventure (WB, 1979)
The Dark (FVI, 1979)
Don Giovanni (New Yorker, 1979)*
Dracula (Univ, 1979)*
The Electric Horseman (Univ, 1979)
Escape from Alcatraz (Par, 1979)
The Evictors (AIP, 1979)
Manhattan (UA, 1979)
Meteor (AIP, 1979)*
More American Graffiti (Univ, 1979)*
Norma Rae (20th-Fox, 1979)*
A Perfect Couple (20th-Fox, 1979)*
The Promise (Univ, 1979)
Prophecy (Par, 1979)*
She Came to the Valley (R.G.V., 1979)
"10" (Orion, 1979)
Time After Time (WB, 1979)*
The Apple (Cannon, 1980)*
Bear Island (Taft, 1980)*
The Big Brawl (WB, 1980)
Breaking Glass (Par, 1980)*
The Chant of Jimmy Blacksmith (New Yorker, 1980)
The Day Time Ended (Compass, 1980)
Dressed to Kill (Filmways, 1980)
Eagle's Wing (IPS, 1980)
The Elephant Man (Par, 1980)*
The Final Countdown (UA, 1980)*
The Fog (Avco, 1980)
Galaxina (Crown, 1980)
Goliathon (The Mighty Peking Man) (World Northal, 1980)
Goodbye Emmanuelle (Miramax, 1980)
Health (20th-Fox, 1980)
Hide in Plain Sight (MGM, 1980)
Honeysuckle Rose (On the Road Again) (WB, 1980)*
Inside Moves (AFD, 1980)
Little Darlings (Par, 1980)
The Mountain Men (Last of the Mountain Men) (Col, 1980)
Roadie (UA, 1980)*

Shogun Assassin (New World, 1980)*
Tom Horn (WB, 1980)
Up the Academy (WB, 1980)*
Urban Cowboy (Par, 1980)
When Time Ran Out (WB, 1980)
Worlds Apart (Scanlon, 1980)
Zulu Dawn (American Cinema, 1980)*
Absence of Malice (Col, 1981)
Back Roads (WB, 1981)
Blow Out (Filmways, 1981)*
Buddy Buddy (MGM, 1981)
Caboblanca (Avco, 1981)*
Carbon Copy (Avco, 1981)
Condorman (BVD, 1981)*
Escape from New York (Avco, 1981)*
The Final Conflict (Omen III) (20th-Fox, 1981)*
First Monday in October (Par, 1981)
For Your Eyes Only (UA, 1981)*
The Funhouse (Univ, 1981)*
Gallipoli (Par, 1981)
Halloween II (Univ, 1981)*
The Haunting of Julia (Full Circle) (Discovery, 1981)
Heartbeeps (Univ, 1981)
The High Country (Crown, 1981)
History of the World Part I (20th-Fox, 1981)*
The Legend of the Lone Ranger (Univ, 1981)*
Lion of the Desert (Omar Mukhtar, Lion of the Desert) (UFD, 1981)*
Looker (Ladd, 1981)*
The Pilot (Summit, 1981)
Road Games (Avco, 1981)
S.O.B. (Par, 1981)
Sphinx (Orion, 1981)*
Strange Behavior (Dead Kids) (World Northal, 1981)
Striking Back (FVI, 1981)
Thirst (New Line, 1981)
Victory (Escape to Victory) (Par, 1981)*
The Avenging (Dayton, 1982)
Barbarosa (Univ, 1982)
Halloween III: Season of the Witch (Univ, 1982)
Safari 3000 (MGM/UA, 1982)
The Sword and the Sorcerer (Group 1, 1982)*
Tootsie (Col, 1982)
Trail of the Pink Panther (MGM/UA, 1982)
Victor/Victoria (MGM, 1982)*
Americana (Crown, 1983)*
Beyond a Reasonable Doubt (Satori, 1983)
Christine (Col, 1983)*
Curse of the Pink Panther (MGM/UA, 1983)
Double Exposure (Crown, 1983)
The Man from Snowy River (20th-Fox, 1983)*
The Outsiders (WB, 1983)*

The Pirates of Penzance (Univ, 1983)*
Scarface (Univ, 1983)*
Silkwood (20th-Fox, 1983)
Smokey and the Bandit Part 3 (Univ, 1983)
Strange Invaders (Orion, 1983)
Sudden Impact (WB, 1983)
The Survivors (Col, 1983)
Vigilante (Street Gang) (FVI, 1983)*
The Year of Living Dangerously (MGM/UA, 1983)
The Adventures of Buckaroo Banzai Across the 8th Dimension (20th-Fox, 1984)*
Carmen (Triumph, 1984)*
Careful, He Might Hear You (20th-Fox, 1984)*
Deadline (New Images, 1984)
The House by the Cemetery (Almi, 1984)
Iceman (Univ, 1984)*
Micki and Maude (Col, 1984)
Phar Lap (20th-Fox, 1984)*
Purple Hearts (WB, 1984)*
Rhinestone (20th-Fox, 1984)*
The Riddle of the Sands (Satori, 1984)
Romancing the Stone (20th-Fox, 1984)*
Runaway (Tri-Star, 1984)*
Sheena (Col, 1984)*
Treasure of the Yankee Zephyr (FVI, 1984)
Yellow Hair and the Fortress of Gold (Crown, 1984)*
D.A.R.Y.L. (Par, 1985)*
Fright Night (Col, 1985)*
Godzilla 1985 (New World, 1985)*
Murphy's Romance (Col, 1985)
My Science Project (BVD, 1985)*
The Perils of Gwendoline in the Land of the Yik Yak (Goldwyn, 1985)*
Plenty (20th-Fox, 1985)*
Prizzi's Honor (20th-Fox, 1985)*
Ran (20th-Fox, 1985)*
Razorback (WB, 1985)*
St. Elmo's Fire (Col, 1985)*
Turk 182! (20th-Fox, 1985)*
April Fool's Day (Par, 1986)
At Close Range (Orion, 1986)
Ferris Bueller's Day Off (Par, 1986)*
A Fine Mess (Col, 1986)
The Hitcher (Tri-Star, 1986)*
Running Scared (MGM/UA, 1986)*
Short Circuit (Tri-Star, 1986)*

REGALSCOPE

The Black Whip (20th-Fox, 1956)
The Desperadoes Are in Town (20th-Fox, 1956)
Stagecoach to Fury (20th-Fox, 1956)

The Women of Pitcairn Island (20th-Fox, 1956)
The Abductors (20th-Fox, 1957)
Apache Warrior (20th-Fox, 1957)
Back from the Dead (20th-Fox, 1957)
Badlands of Montana (20th-Fox, 1957)
Copper Sky (20th-Fox, 1957)
Ghost Diver (20th-Fox, 1957)
God Is My Partner (20th-Fox, 1957)
Hell on Devil's Island (20th-Fox, 1957)
Kronos (20th-Fox, 1957)
Lure of the Swamp (20th-Fox, 1957)
Plunder Road (20th-Fox, 1957)
The Quiet Gun (20th-Fox, 1957)
Ride a Violent Mile (20th-Fox, 1957)
Rockabilly Baby (20th-Fox, 1957)
She Devil (20th-Fox, 1957)
The Storm Rider (20th-Fox, 1957)
The Tattered Dress (UI, 1957)
Under Fire (20th-Fox, 1957)
The Unknown Terror (20th-Fox, 1957)
Young and Dangerous (20th-Fox, 1957)
Ambush at Cimarron Pass (20th-Fox, 1958)
Blood Arrow (20th-Fox, 1958)
Desert Hell (20th-Fox, 1958)
Escape from Red Rock (20th-Fox, 1958)
Flaming Frontier (20th-Fox, 1958)
Frontier Gun (20th-Fox, 1958)
Gang War (20th-Fox, 1958)
Showdown at Boot Hill (20th-Fox, 1958)
Space Master X-7 (20th-Fox, 1958)
Alaska Passage (20th-Fox, 1959)
Blood and Steel (20th-Fox, 1959)
Here Come the Jets (20th-Fox, 1959)
Little Savage (20th-Fox, 1959)
Lone Texan (20th-Fox, 1959)

RKO-SCOPE

While the City Sleeps (RKO, 1956)
Jet Pilot (UI, 1957)
Run of the Arrow (UI, 1957)
The Naked and the Dead (WB, 1958)
Tarzan and the Lost Safari (RKO, 1958)

SCANOSCOPE

The Double-Barreled Detective Story (Saloon, 1965)
Kimberly Jim (Emb, 1965)

SHAWSCOPE

Madame White Snake (Lee, 1963)

The Last Woman of Shang (Lee, 1964)
The Love Eterne (Lee, 1964)
The Magnificent Concubine (Lee, 1964)
The Grand Substitution (Lee, 1965)
The Mermaid (Lee, 1966)
Vermilion Door (Shaw, 1969)
Fists of Fury II (NG, 1973)
Five Fingers of Death (WB, 1973)
Seven Blows of the Dragon (New World, 1973)
Triple Irons (NG, 1973)
Lightning Swords of Death (Col, 1974)
The Sacred Knives of Vengeance (WB, 1974)
Street Gangs of Hong Kong (CRC, 1974)
Bruce Lee and I (Pacific Grove, 1975)
The Empress Dowager (Shaw, 1975)
Killer Snakes (Mahler, 1975)
Shanghai Lil and the Sun Luck Kid (Bardene, 1975)
Bamboo House of Dolls (Peppercorn-Wormser, 1976)
Exit the Dragon Enter the Tiger (Dimension, 1976)
Seven-Man Army (Shaw, 1976)
The Deadly Angels (World Northal, 1979)
Master Killer (World Northal, 1979)
Bruce Lee: His Last Days, His Last Nights (World Northal, 1980)
Dirty-Ho (World Northal, 1981)
The Flying Guillotine (World Northal, 1981)
Mortal Combat (World Northal, 1981)
Ten Tigers of Kwangtung (World Northal, 1981)
The Destroyers (World Northal, 1982)
Instructors of Death (World Northal, 1982)
Masked Avenger (World Northal, 1982)
Return of the Master Killer (World Northal, 1982)
Two Champions of Death (World Northal, 1982)
Kung Fu Warriors (World Northal, 1983)
Kung Fu Warriors Part II (World Northal, 1983)
The Spearman of Death (World Northal, 1984)

SOVSCOPE

The Cranes Are Flying (WB, 1958)
Circus Stars (Par, 1960)
Journey Beyond Three Stars (Artkino, 1960)
The Sword and the Dragon (Valiant, 1960)
Don Quixote (MGM, 1961)
The Day the Earth Froze (AIP, 1964)
The Last Game (Artkino, 1964)
The Tear's Bride (Artkino, 1966)
Portrait of Lenin (Artkino, 1967)
Anna Karenina (Corinth, 1979)
Spartacus (Corinth, 1979)
The Trans-Siberian Express (IFEX, 1979)

SPECTRASCOPE

Flight of the Lost Balloon (Woolner, 1961)

SUPERAMA

The Bonnie Parker Story (AIP, 1958)
Machine Gun Kelly (AIP, 1958)
Teenage Caveman (AIP, 1958)

SUPERCINESCOPE

The Warrior and the Slave Girl (Col, 1959)
Hannibal (WB, 1960)
Legions of the Nile (20th-Fox, 1960)
Trapped in Tangiers (20th-Fox, 1960)
... And the Wild, Wild Woman (Trans-Lux, 1961)
The Pirate of the Black Hawk (Filmgroup, 1961)
Queen of the Pirates (Col, 1961)
Marco Polo (AIP, 1962)
Queen of the Nile (S.F., 1964)
The Sword of El Cid (Production Releasing, 1964)

*SUPER*SCOPE 235

Run for the Sun (UA, 1956)
The Three Outlaws (1956)
Mark of the Hawk (UI, 1958)
The Chinese Mack (Ellman, 1976)

SUPERTOTALSCOPE

Last Days of Pompeii (UA, 1960)
The Colossus of Rhodes (MGM, 1961)
Africa Sexy (Filmarco, 1963)
Goliath Against the Giants (Medallion, 1963)
Orient by Night (Filmarco, 1963)

SYSTEM 35

Revolution (WB, 1985)*
Absolute Beginners (Orion, 1985)*

TAICHANG-SCOPE

Bearded General (Chang, 1969)

TECHNOVISION

Suspira (20th-Fox, 1977)*
Tentacles (AIP, 1977)
The Chosen (Holocaust 4000) (AIP, 1978)

The Greek Tycoon (Univ, 1978)
Silver Bears (Col, 1978)
The Innocent (Analysis, 1979)
The Passage (UA, 1979)
Bad Timing/A Sensual Obsession (World Northal, 1980)
The Godsend (Cannon, 1980)
Popeye (Par, 1980)*
City of Women (New Yorker, 1981)
Reds (Par, 1981)
Hearts and Armor (WB, 1983)*
We of the Never Never (Triumph, 1983)
The Black Cat (World Northal, 1984)
China 9, Liberty 37 (Lorimar, 1984)
Flesh and Blood (Orion, 1985)

TODD-AO 35

Macbeth (Col, 1971)
Alice's Adventures in Wonderland (American National, 1972)
Conquest of the Planet of the Apes (20th-Fox, 1972)
The Getaway (NG, 1972)
Junior Bonner (CRC, 1972)
Slaughter (AIP, 1972)
Antony and Cleopatra (Rank, 1973)
The Asphyx (Paragon, 1973)*
Jesus Christ Superstar (Univ, 1973)*
Showdown (Univ, 1973)
Slaughter's Big Ripoff (AIP, 1973)
Bootleggers (The Bootlegger's Angel) (Howes, 1974)
Against a Crooked Sky (Doty-Dayton, 1975)
Children of Rage (LSV, 1975)
The Devil's Rain (Bryanston, 1975)
The Great Waldo Pepper (Univ, 1975)
The Creature from Black Lake (Howco, 1976)
Evil in the Deep (Golden, 1976)
Gator (UA, 1976)
Sky Riders (20th-Fox, 1976)
The Witch Who Came from the Sea (Moonstone, 1976)
Cinderella 2000 (II, 1977)
Day of the Animals (FVI, 1977)
Free Spirit (Brenner, 1978)
Flash Gordon (Univ, 1980)*
Mad Max (AIP, 1980)
Ragtime (Par, 1981)
Conan the Barbarian (Univ, 1982)

TOEISCOPE

The Lord Takes a Bride (Toei, 1958)
The Story of Pure Love (Toei, 1958)
Alakazam the Great (AIP, 1961)
Magic Boy (MGM, 1961)

The Final War (Lake, 1961)
Bushido (Toei, 1964)
The Green Slime (MGM, 1969)
The World of Hans Christian Andersen (UA, 1971)
The Street Fighter (New Line, 1974)
The Return of the Streetfighter (New Line, 1975)
Sister Streetfighter (New Line, 1976)
Champion of Death (UA, 1977)
The Tattooed Hit Man (New Line, 1977)
The Executioner (Trans Continental, 1978)
The Streetfighter's Last Revenge (New Line, 1979)
Shogun's Ninja (American National, 1984)

TOHOSCOPE

The H-Man (Col, 1959)*
The Hidden Fortress (Toho, 1959)*
The Mysterians (MGM, 1959)
The Nude General (Toho, 1959)
Battle in Outer Space (Col, 1960)
The Rikisha Man (Cory, 1960)
The Three Treasurers (Toho, 1960)
The Angry Sea (Toho, 1961)
The Dangerous Kiss (Toho, 1961)
Daredevil in the Castle (Lee, 1961)
Death on the Mountain (Toho, 1961)
Eternity of Love (Toho, 1961)
I Bombed Pearl Harbor (Parade, 1961)
Life of a Country Doctor (Toho, 1961)
Man Against Man (Toho, 1961)
The Man from the East (Toho, 1961)
A Night in Hong Kong (Toho, 1961)
Secret of the Telegian (Toho, 1961)
This Greedy Old Skin (Toho, 1961)
Throne of Blood (Brandon, 1961)
Westward Desperado (Toho, 1961)
Yojimbo (Seneca, 1961)
Bandits of the Wind (Toho, 1962)
Bull of the Campus (Toho, 1962)
Challenge to Live (Toho, 1962)
Early Autumn (New Yorker, 1962)
Happiness of Us Alone (Toho, 1962)
Mothra (Col, 1962)
Sanjuro (Toho, 1962)
Star of Hong Kong (Toho, 1962)
Tatsu (Toho, 1962)
Till Tomorrow Comes (Toho, 1962)
Varan the Unbelievable (Crown International, 1962)
The Wayside Pebble (Toho, 1962)
The Wiser Age (Toho, 1962)
The Bad Sleep Well (Toho, 1963)
Born in Sin (Toho, 1963)

Chushingura (Toho, 1963)
High and Low (Continental, 1963)
Honolulu-Tokyo-Hong Kong (Toho, 1963)
King Kong vs. Godzilla (UI, 1963)
Lonely Lane (Toho, 1963)
Madame Aki (Toho, 1963)
Operation X (Toho, 1963)
Snow in the South Seas (Toho, 1963)
Wall-Eyed Nippon (Toho, 1963)
Warring Clans (Toho, 1963)
When a Woman Ascends the Stairs (Toho, 1963)
The Youth and His Amulet (Toho, 1963)
Atragon (AIP, 1964)
Ayako (Toho, 1964)
Godzilla vs. the Thing (AIP, 1964)
Gorath (Brenco, 1964)*
The Human Vapor (Brenco, 1964)*
Kwaidan (Continental, 1964)
The Legacy of the 500,000 (Toho, 1964)
The Naked General (Toho, 1964)
Operation Enemy Fort (Toho, 1964)
Saga of the Vagabonds (Toho, 1964)
Two in the Shadow (Toho, 1964)
A Woman's Life (Toho, 1964)
You Can Succeed Too (Toho, 1964)
The Blue Beast (Toho, 1965)
Brand of Evil (Toho, 1965)
Could I But Live (Toho, 1965)
Five Gents' Trick Boot (Toho, 1965)
The Gay Braggart (Toho, 1965)
Ghidrah the Three-Headed Monster (Continental, 1965)
The Lost World of Sinbad (Samurai Pirate) (AIP, 1965)
Onibaba (Toho, 1965)
Samurai Assassin (Toho, 1965)
The Sandal Keeper (Toho, 1965)
Tiger Flight (Toho, 1965)
White Rose of Hong Kong (Toho, 1965)
Beast Alley (Toho, 1966)
The Call of Flesh (Gold Star, 1966)
Campus a Go-Go (Toho, 1966)
Conquest (Toho, 1966)
Don't Call Me a Con Man (Toho, 1966)
Fort Graveyard (Toho, 1966)
Frankenstein Conquers the World (AIP, 1966)
Illusion of Blood (Lee, 1966)
It Started in the Alps (Toho, 1966)
Night in Bangkok (Toho, 1966)
Outpost of Hell (Toho, 1966)
Red Beard (Lee, 1966)*
Rise Against the Sword (Toho, 1966)
School of Love (Toho, 1966)
The Sword of Doom (Toho, 1966)

Tale of a Carpenter (Toho, 1966)
Three Dolls from Hong Kong (Toho, 1966)
We Will Remember (Official, 1966)
What's Up, Tiger Lily? (AIP, 1966)
Big Wind from Tokyo (Toho, 1967)
Bride of the Andes (Toho, 1967)
Bwana Toshi (Brandon, 1967)
Come Marry Me (Toho, 1967)
The Daphne (Toho, 1967)
5 Gents on the Spot (Toho, 1967)
Green Light of Joy (Toho, 1967)
Kojiro (Toho, 1967)
Las Vegas Free-for-All (Toho, 1967)
Let's Go, Young Guy! (Toho, 1967)
The Mad Atlantic (Toho, 1967)
Once a Rainy Day (Toho, 1967)
Rebellion (Toho, 1967)
River of Forever (Toho, 1967)
Secret Scrolls, Part II (Toho, 1967)
Siege of Fort Bismarck (Toho, 1967)
The Thin Line (Toho, 1967)
Whirlwind (Toho, 1967)
Admiral Yamamato (Toho, 1968)
The Emperor and the General (Toho, 1968)
Eyes, the Sea and a Ball (Toho, 1968)
The Gangster VIP (Toho, 1968)
Kill (Lee, 1968)
King Kong Escapes (Univ, 1968)
Kuroneko (Toho, 1968)
Destroy All Monsters (AIP, 1969)
Moment of Terror (Toho, 1969)
Our Silent Love (Toho, 1969)
Latitude Zero (NG, 1970)
Monster Zero (Godzilla vs. Monster Zero) (Macon, 1970)
The Rabble (Toho, 1970)
The War of the Gargantuans (Macon, 1970)
Godzilla vs. the Smog Monster (AIP, 1972)

TOTALSCOPE

Behind the Great Wall (Continental, 1959)*
Goliath and the Barbarians (AIP, 1959)
The Cossacks (UI, 1960)
The Giant of Marathon (MGM, 1960)
The Goddess of Love (20th–Fox, 1960)
Head of a Tyrant (UI, 1960)
Herod the Great (AA, 1960)
Journey to the Lost City (AIP, 1960)
The Nights of Lucretia Borgia (Col, 1960)
Prisoner of the Volga (Par, 1960)
David and Goliath (AA, 1961)
La dolce vita (AIP, 1961)

Guns of the Black Witch (AIP, 1961)
The Minotaur (UA, 1961)
The Revolt of the Slaves (UA, 1961)
Samson (Medallion, 1961)
Constantine and the Cross (Emb, 1962)
The Huns (Producers International, 1962)
The Lovers of Teruel (Continental, 1962)
Mighty Ursus (UA, 1962)
Nude Odyssey (Royal, 1962)
Son of Samson (Medallion, 1962)
The Tartars (MGM, 1962)
White Slave Ship (AIP, 1962)
Alone Against Rome (Medallion, 1963)
Caesar the Conqueror (Medallion, 1963)
The Fall of Rome (Medallion, 1963)
Love at Twenty (Emb, 1963)
A Monkey in Winter (MGM, 1963)
Rage of the Buccaneers (Colorama, 1963)
The Secret Mask of D'Artagnan (Medallion, 1963)
The Seven Tasks of Ali Baba (Medallion, 1963)
Son of the Red Corsair (Medallion, 1963)
The Steppe (Royal, 1963)
Suleiman the Conqueror (Medallion, 1963)
Crazy Desire (Emb, 1964)
Duel of the Champions (Medallion, 1964)
Gladiators Seven (MGM, 1964)
Goliath vs. the Vampires (AIP, 1964)
Love on the Riviera (Ultra, 1964)
Panic Button (Gorton, 1964)
Revolt of the Mercenaries (WB, 1964)
Gunmen of the Rio Grande (AA, 1965)
Horror Castle (Zodiac, 1965)
The Road to Fort Alamo (World Entertainment, 1966)
The Lion of St. Mark (Liber, 1967)
Naked Among the Wolves (Lopert, 1967)
The Seven Revenges (Avco, 1967)
The Flying Matchmaker (National Showmanship, 1970)
We Are All Naked (Citel/USA, 1970)

TOTALSCOPE SUPER/100

Hercules in the Haunted World (Woolner, 1964)

TOTALVISION

First Spaceship on Venus (Crown, 1962)
Dr. Terror's Gallery of Horrors (The Blood Suckers; Return from the Past) (American General, 1965)
A Few Bullets More (RAF, 1968)
Paris in the Month of August (Trans-Lux, 1968)
A Nun at the Crossroads (Univ, 1971)

ULTRASCOPE

The Magic Fountain (Classic World, 1961)
I Love, You Love (Royal, 1962)
Apache Gold (Col, 1965)
Treasure of Silver Lake (Col, 1965)
The Alley Cats (Audobon, 1966)
Frontier Hellcat (Col, 1966)
Last of the Renegades (Col, 1966)
Rampage of Apache Wells (Col, 1966)
Carmen, Baby (Audobon, 1967)
The Desperado Trail (Col, 1967)
The Monster of London City (PRO, 1967)
The Phantom of Soho (PRO, 1967)
Red Dragon (Woolner, 1967)
Flaming Frontier (W7, 1967)
The Taming (Times, 1968)
Therese and Isabelle (Audobon, 1968)

ULTRASCOPE 50

Savage! (J.C., 1962)

UNISCOPE

Dragon Inn (Union, 1967)
Why Russians Are Revolting (Mutual, 1970)

VISTARAMA

Frontier Woman, Daughter of Davy Crockett (Top, 1956)
East of Kilimanjaro (Parade, 1962)

VISTASCOPE

Atlas (Realant, 1961)

WARNERSCOPE

Up Periscope (WB, 1959)
Gold of the Seven Saints (WB, 1961)

UNCREDITED

Sign of the Gladiator (AIP, 1959)
Goliath and the Dragon (AIP, 1960)
Santa Claus (Murray, 1960)
The Pirate and the Slave Girl (Crest, 1961)
Samson and the Seven Miracles of the World (AIP, 1962)
Samson and the Slave Queen (AIP, 1963)
The Last Man on Earth (AIP, 1964)
Die, Monster, Die (AIP, 1965)

The Tomb of Ligeia (AIP, 1965)
The War of the Zombies (AIP, 1965)
Minnesota Clay (Harlequin, 1966)
Planet of the Vampires (AIP, 1966)
Bill Wallace of China (Logos, 1967)
The Glory Stompers (AIP, 1967)
Sadismo (Trans American, 1967)
The Shoemaker and the Elves (Trans-International, 1967)
Big Enough n' Old Enough (Trans-International, 1968)
The Royal Hunt of the Sun (NG, 1969)
Madame O (Audobon, 1970)
Santa and the Three Bears (Ellman, 1970)
Sesso (Sherpix, 1970)
Blood of the Dragon (Harnell, 1973)
Deadly China Doll (MGM, 1973)
Deep Thrust (AIP, 1973)
Duel of the Iron Fist (Mahler, 1973)
Enter the Dragon (WB, 1973)
Fists of Fury (NG, 1973)
Fists of the Double K (Cannon, 1973)
The Hammer of God (Hallmark, 1973)
The Hong Kong Cat (AIP, 1973)
Kung Fu the Invisible Fist (Mahler, 1973)
Lady Kung Fu (NG, 1973)
Screaming Tiger (AIP, 1973)
The Shanghai Killers (Hallmark, 1973)
The Thunder Kick (Cannon, 1973)
Attack of the Kung Fu Girls (Cinemation, 1974)
The Bamboo Brotherhood (Mahler, 1974)
The Black Dragon (Mahler, 1974)
Blood Fingers (Sands, 1974)
The Chinese Godfather (1974)
Chinese Hercules (Bryanston, 1974)
The Chinese Professionals (NG, 1974)
The Dragon's Vengeance (Mahler, 1974)
Fearless Fighters (Ellman, 1974)
From China with Death (Mahler, 1974)
The Godfathers of Hong Kong (Cannon, 1974)
The Hong Kong Connection (Cannon, 1974)
Karate Killer (Mahler, 1974)
Kung Fu Mama (Crown, 1974)
Kung Fu Queen (The Queen Boxer) (Aquarius, 1974)
Kung Fu, the Punch of Death (Lana, 1974)
Man of Iron (Bardene, 1974)
The Mandarin Magician (Mahler, 1974)
Return of the Dragon (Bryanston, 1974)
The Steel Edge of Revenge (Kelly-Jordan, 1974)
Sting of the Dragon Masters (Cinemation, 1974)
Thunderfist (Artisan, 1974)
The Black Dragon's Revenge (Mahler, 1975)
Challenge of the Dragon (Cannon, 1975)
The Dragon Dies Hard (AA, 1975)

Dragon Squad (In-Frame, 1975)
Kung Fu Gold (Cinema Shares, 1975)
King Fu-ry (Green, 1975)
Super Manchu (Capital, 1975)
Thou Shalt Not Kill . . . But Once (In-Frame, 1975)
The Black Dragon vs. the Yellow Tiger (Aquarius, 1976)
Bruce Lee — Super Dragon (AA, 1976)
Dragons Never Die (JMG, 1976)
Duel in the Tiger Den (Tower, 1976)
Goodbye Bruce Lee: His Last Game of Death (Game of Death) (Aquarius, 1976)
Karate: One by One (In-Frame, 1976)
The Killing Machine (Cinema Shares, 1976)
Kung Fu Master: Bruce Lee Style (Goldstone, 1976)
Return of the Panther (In-Frame, 1976)
Super Dragon (In-Frame, 1976)
Bruce Lee: The Man/The Myth (1977)
A Girl Called Tigress (Chang, 1977)
Jaws of the Dragon (Worldwide, 1977)
The Kung Fu Brothers (Goldstone, 1977)
Master of the Flying Guillotine (Borde, 1977)
One-Armed Boxer vs. the Flying Guillotine (In-Frame, 1977)
Seven to One (Independent, 1977)
Bruce vs. the Black Dragon (Ark, 1978)
The Dragon Lives (FVI, 1978)
Eagles' Claws (1978)
Fists of Bruce Lee (Cinema Shares, 1978)
The Furious Monk from Shao-Lin (Cinema Shares, 1978)
Hong Kong Strongman (Cinema Shares, 1978)
The Last Challenge of the Dragon (CineWorld, 1978)
Soul Brothers of Kung Fu (Cinema Shares, 1978)
Tiger from Hong Kong (Monarch, 1978)
Challenge of Death (Tan, 1979)
The Tattoo Connection (World Northal, 1979)
Deadly Shaolin Longfist (1980)
A Hard Way to Die (Transmedia, 1980)
The Hound of the Baskervilles (Atlantic, 1980)
King of Kung Fu (Cinematic, 1980)
Mad Mad Kung Fu (1980)
Snake Fist vs. the Dragon (21st Century, 1980)
The Ways of Kung Fu (1980)
The Woman Avenger (1980)
Dynamo (World Northal, 1981)
Edge of Fury (Mid-Broadway, 1981)
18 Fatal Strikes (World Northal, 1981)
Enter Three Dragons (Cinematic, 1981)
Jade Claw (Transmedia, 1981)
Karate Warriors (Silverstein, 1981)
Kill the Shogun (New American, 1981)
Kung Fu Executioner (Transmedia, 1981)
Kung Fu Halloween (New American, 1981)
A Man Called Tiger (World Northal, 1981)
Revenge of the Dragon (Saturn, 1981)

Revenge of the Patriots (World Northal, 1981)
Sixty-Second Assassin (East-West, 1981)
Slaughter in San Francisco (World Northal, 1981)
Snake Fist Fighter (21st Century, 1981)
Super Power (Transmedia, 1981)
Tattooed Dragon (World Northal, 1981)
When Taekwondo Strikes (World Northal, 1981)
Budo: Grand Masters of the Martial Arts (Crown International, 1982)
The Crippled Masters (New Line, 1982)
Death Mask of the Ninja (Essex, 1982)
Dragon on Fire (Trans-Continental, 1982)
Fatal Needles Fatal Fist (1982)
The Fearless Jackal (Marvin, 1982)
Fighting Dragon vs. the Deadly Tiger (Fury, 1982)
The Furious Killer (1982)
Gold Constables (1982)
Grand Master of Shaolin Fu (1982)
Justice of the Dragon (Almi, 1982)
Kung Fu Zombie (1982)
Lightning Kung Fu (East-West, 1982)
Raging Dragon (Bidford Entertainment, 1982)
The Return of the Grandmasters (Marvin, 1982)
The Seven Grandmasters (Marvin, 1982)
The Shaolin Red Master (1982)
Two Crippled Heroes (1982)
Weapons of Death (Independent Artists, 1982)
The World of the Drunken Master (Marvin, 1982)
Coil of the Snake (Almi, 1983)
Eagle vs. Silver Fox (Almi, 1983)
Fist of Golden Monkey (Almi, 1983)
A Fist Full of Talons (Transmedia, 1983)
Tiger Claws (Almi, 1983)
Assault of Final Rival (1984)
The Deadly Mantis (World Northal, 1984)
Enter the Fat Dragon (World Northal, 1984)
The Jade Warriors (World Northal, 1984)
Ninja Mission (New Line, 1984)
Shaolin: The Blood Mission (1984)
The Illusionist (Film Forum, 1985)
The Jewel of the Nile (20th–Fox, 1985)*

IV. The Wide Frame Processes

VistaVision Motion Picture High Fidelity

In 1928 British cinetechnician George Hill and Italian inventor Professor Filoteo Alberini promoted a double frame 35mm wide screen system in which the film was exposed horizontally in the camera and projected in a like manner. They called it Panoramico Alberini. It was the same name as had been applied to Alberini's 70mm wide screen process used on *Il sacco di Roma* (1923). The system was hawked to filmmakers in London and Hollywood but rejected in favor of other wide gauge formats.

With the introduction of CinemaScope, Paramount decided it was time to develop their own process. They were impressed with anamorphic films from the standpoint of the larger screen and wider ratio but were completely against the other CinemaScope factors: anamorphic lenses, high grain, poor focus and depth of field, etc. They immediately released some of their completed features in Panoramic Screen, which was no more than cropping the top and bottom of the frame from 1.47 × 1 to 1.66 × 1 (depending on the film, all which had been shot in 1.33 × 1 ratio). The results were adequate, but the grain problem was not eliminated. Researching their past efforts, Paramount dismissed Magnifilm *per se* but did believe the 1.85 × 1 aspect ratio was the proper shape for the screen. Lorenzo del Riccio, Magnifilm's developer, uncovered the Hill-Alberini system and after experimentation developed the Paramount Lazy 8 Butterfly Camera, so called because the film moved horizontally through the camera and exposed eight perforations (two frames) instead of the regular four frames of vertical movement, and the side-mounted magazines looked like butterfly wings. The system, renamed VistaVision, was refined by Loren L. Ryder, John R. Bishop and others at the studio.

Initially VistaVision was to be released in three formats: horizontal double frame, regular 35mm reduced from Lazy 8 format and anamorphic. The 'scope prints were cropped to 2 × 1, a 1.5 × 1 compression was added and the image was printed over the whole 35mm frame. Paramount was aware that the anamorphic VistaVision prints would not be compatible with CinemaScope. They settled on the *Super*Scope variable anamorphic projection device after rejecting Goertz Optical Company's similar unit (Panoscope). They would provide, at a modest fee, *Super*Scope prismatic anamorphosizers to any theater that wanted VistaVision 'scope prints but

Another trade ad for the SuperScope *lens, this time associated with* VistaVision *and the 1954* White Christmas, *the first VistaVision feature.*

did not already have variable compression units. Many theaters, not yet equipped for CinemaScope, purchased *Super*Scope devices since they offered the versatility of all existing, and presumably any yet-to-be-developed, squeeze factors. VistaVision may have been a boon for them. Theaters already with CinemaScope or other fixed anamorphic lenses either rented *Super*Scope units or purchased them as backup.

White Christmas (1954) was the first VistaVision feature and was shot before the improved cameras were ready. The results were still outstanding, but not up to the quality of the films that followed. The first engagements were presented in anamorphic format, with regular 35mm prints offered for second-run playdates in theaters without (or that didn't want) 'scope. The film also apparently played two Los Angeles theaters in horizontal format, according to Loren L. Ryder, but not according to Paramount. The Ryder claim is probably true, but officially *Strategic Air Command* (1955) was the first of many VistaVision prints released in double frame horizontal format. We suspect *White Christmas* was shown in wide gauge system only in Los Angeles as an experiment of sorts and not given national release in that format. It is also probable that it was not exhibited wide frame until after the first engagements of *Strategic Air Command.* Exactly how many Vista-Vision 'scope releases there were is now impossible to ascertain, but there were surely several. VistaVision anamorphic projector aperture plates were commercially manufactured (they bore the legend VV 2×1) and we have it on good authority that *White Christmas* was not the only film to receive the anamorphic treatment. Today no one remembers VistaVision as a 'scope process — but it was!

Paramount, having tried magnetic stereophonic sound with previous features, was not pleased with the idea of double print cost for directional sound, but they realized that monophonic sound was impractical for their horizontal presentations and wholly undesirable for regular 35mm runs. The answer came from MGM, which had just adopted the stereo optical system developed by Fine Recording in New York: Perspecta Stereophonic Sound, an inexpensive, mono-compatible optical audio system that separated its stereo channels with electronic subaudible cues.

The idea behind horizontal VistaVision was impressive. Theaters equipped with CinemaScope were to retain their screen width but increase the screen height to encompass the 1.85×1 (the image was cropped somewhat) aspect ratio of VistaVision. Thus the Paramount process, properly projected, was as wide as anamorphic and considerably higher. Paramount also hoped theaters running regular 35mm prints from VistaVision would follow the same policy. The studios that had adopted CinemaScope were obviously not happy about such a plan, but they had little to fear: Extremely few theaters went to the expense of installing yet another screen if they had purchased a CinemaScope ratio screen (most were in fact considerably narrower than the 2.55×1 prescribed 'scope width), and Vista-Vision was generally presented no larger than any other spherical film, even when in horizontal format. Theaters showing anamorphic VistaVision prints usually filled their screens with the 2×1 ratio, or very nearly so if their screens were wider. (In order to differentiate horizontal presentations from regular 35mm engagements a special logo like the one shown on page 149 was used with the addition of "Presented through," set with "Presented" on the left side of the "V" and "through" on the right side of it. Regular print playdates simply had the logo, in much smaller character, placed strategically in the advertising material. 'Scope presentations seem to have been treated no differently from regular 35mm, with no special logo or presentation announcement. Theaters were expected to utilize the Perspecta Stereophonic Sound—though very few did—and make such note in the advertising, but there were no special logos or blurbs included in publicity material, though Paramount did include such notation on ads they purchased for premiere engagements.

Paramount offered VistaVision to other producers, and a few used it in the United States. The Rank Organisation adopted the system in England, and some European filmmakers utilized it sparingly. Two cameras were sold to Daiei in Japan, who shot two features, *Buddha* (1963) and *The Great Wall* (1965), but had them converted to 70mm and dubbed the process Super 70 Technirama (see *Super Technirama 70,* page 159). Due to the expense (approximately four times that of spherical 35mm), VistaVision never gained wide use outside Paramount and Rank. It did inspire the development of Technirama, and MGM, on recommendation of chief cinetechnician John Arnold, briefly considered the Fearless Super Picture process (which used a ten-perf-per-frame horizontal movement and was first proposed in 1927) as the basis for Camera 65. Today VistaVision is commonly used in special effects photography for rear screen and traveling matte shots but is no longer employed as a production process.

VistaVision Motion Picture High Fidelity Specifications*

Camera and negative:
Film	35mm
Frame ratio	1.50×1
Aperture width	1.485"
Aperture height	0.991"
Ground glassing markings:	
1.66×1	$1.3365" \times 0.805"$
1.85×1	$1.3365" \times 0.723"$
2×1	not indicated
Pulldown (horizontal)	8 perfs
Film movement	left to right

These are the original Paramount VistaVision specifications. Current cameras in use solely for special photographic effects work have been modified by various companies to include reflex viewing, undersize magazines, etc. VistaVision is no longer a general production process.

The Industry's Most Important Event At The World's Largest Theatre

PARAMOUNT'S
East Coast Demonstration Of

VistaVision

RADIO CITY MUSIC HALL
8:30 A.M., Tuesday, April 27th

YOU ARE INVITED!

RESERVE APRIL 27,
MR. EXHIBITOR —
See VistaVision for your-
self and be convinced.
Your tickets will be sent
you shortly.

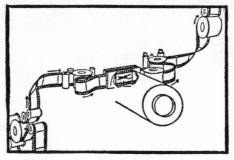

Top: *VistaVision's logo.* Bottom: *Detail from an ad showing the horizontal projection system.*

Frames per second	24
Variable frames per second	0 to 96
Film speed	180 ft. per min.
Movement and camera	Mitchell
Registration pins	dual
Pulldown claws	dual fork engaging 4 perfs simultaneously
Aperture and pressure plates	removable
Shutter	0 to 195° (can be preset, but not changeable during operation)
Focusing	through lens ground glass by racking down movement

Opposite: *An April 1954 trade ad.*

VistaVision negative frames. With the addition of anamorphic compression the system became Technirama. Later VistaVision cameras had a reduced aperture that blocked the top area of the frame that would be filled in by the Perspecta Stereophonic Soundtrack. Technirama cameras always exposed over the full frame area as shown here. If you think this looks exactly like the image exposed by your 35mm still camera, you are right. In fact, a still camera, modified to hold an oversize roll of film, was used to shoot the stop-motion animation special effects footage for Indiana Jones and the Temple of Doom *(1984).*

Focusing power	5 and 10
Mounts	single lens
Lenses	28mm, 35mm, 40mm, 50mm, 75mm, 85mm, 100mm, 150mm, 12 ½", 60mm to 240mm zoom, others adaptable
Motor drives	220v, 3 phase AC and 96v DC
Motor synchronous	AC at 220v in 50 and 60 cycles
Stop motion motor drive	110v AC
High speed motor drive	110v AC or DC
Magazines	2000 ft with built-in clutch and brake driven directly off motor
Viewfinder	over lens eliminating horizontal parallax with vertical parallax adjustment
Slater	automatic
Tachometer	electric remote operatable

Effects lineup	possible
Counters	footage and frames
Filter holder	inside
Blimp	Aluminumized
Release print(s):	
Film	35mm
Frames per second	24
Horizontal format:	
Pullcross	8 perfs per frame
Film speed	180 ft. per min.
Aspect ratio (cropped)	1.66×1, 1.85×1 and 2×1
Aspect ratio (uncropped)	1.50×1 with squared corners
Sound system	optical running horizontal across top of film
Sound format	Perspecta Stereophonic
Standard reduction format:	
Pulldown	4 perfs per frame
Film speed	90 ft. per min.
Aspect ratio (cropped)	1.66×1, 1.85×1 and 2×1
Aspect ratio (uncropped)	1.50×1 with rounded corners
Sound system	optical
Sound format	Perspecta Stereophonic
Anamorphic reduction format (original version):	
Pulldown	4 perfs per frame
Film speed	90 ft. per min.
Aspect ratio	2×1 with squared corners
Compression	1.5×1
Anamorphics (prismatic)	*Super*Scope
Sound system	optical
Sound format	Perspecta Stereophonic
Anamorphic reduction format (special effects only):*	

---

*No complete feature has been made using this technology, only special effects scenes which are to be intergrated into films shot in anamorphic format. The footage is generally blown up to spherical 70mm after the 35mm anamorphic pre-print material is assembled.

Pulldown	4 perfs per frame
Film speed	90 ft. per min.
Aspect ratio	2.35 × 1
Compression	2 × 1
Anamorphics	various types
Sound system	optical
Sound format	generally S.V.A. (stereo variable area) depending on release program

Technirama

Technicolor, ever on the lookout for increasing their revenue so sorely cut into by Eastman Color and other monopack color processes, decided to get into the big screen business with their own system.

At first 70mm seemed too restrictive; after all, how many such films would be made in a year? The system therefore had to be compatible with existing 35mm equipment but of such striking difference as to be saleable. VistaVision seemed to be the perfect starting point since standard film and only marginally modified cameras and projectors would be necessary. Of course no modification would be needed for general release prints. Vista-Vision had demonstrated the striking picture improvements rendered by double frame horizontal photography and projection. Technicolor personnel reasoned that the same technology could be employed with the addition of anamorphics to render a huge, wide screen image playable on Vista-Vision eight-perf projectors and optically convertible to standard Cinema-Scope format. From such reasoning, Technirama was developed.

It became immediately apparent that the VistaVision frame width (horizontally) of eight perfs was completely acceptable, but the height, when coupled with the anamorphic compression, rendered too wide an image. Since the VistaVision camera aperture allowed for placement of an optical soundtrack, Technicolor decided Technirama needed no such blank space and the aperture was given more height, thus exposing over the full film width (vertically) perforation to perforation. The addition of a 1.5 × 1 compression would give, when projected, a CinemaScope-shaped screen image. Thus the sharpness of VistaVision plus the width of CinemaScope assured Technicolor a process unlike any from other sources. The intention was to provide horizontal prints with magnetic sound outside the perfs, thus avoiding the cutoff of picture area an optical track would require.

While Technicolor definitely demonstrated Technirama in horizontal projection, it is extremely unlikely that many, if any, features were released in that format. Certainly all general release prints were in CinemaScope format.

The Technirama cameras were modified three-strip Technicolor units originally constructed in the 1930s. Since all fixed-compression anamorphic lenses were set at 2×1 the company had to decide on the type and supplier of the squeeze devices. Whether *Super*Scope was considered is unknown. It is to be assumed that it was, since Technicolor was using their prismatic devices for optical work and probably continued to do so for the optical conversions of Technirama to standard 35mm anamorphic format. In any event the final anamorphics were made by Panavision using their Panatar prismatic system. Additionally, mirror-type compression units from Delrama were employed, mostly in Europe. While Paramount adopted Perspecta Stereophonic Sound for VistaVision, Technicolor specified no particular sound system, except for horizontal projection where magnetic would have been mandatory.

Technirama was an expensive system. It involved not only twice the film in production but required huge, outdated, noisy cameras. Further, while the projected image was superior to CinemaScope-type wide screen, it was not so superior as to be an additional box office aid. To the audience, 'scope was 'scope. Some looked better than others, but that was about it. Technicolor was faced with an expensive system that failed to capture the market as hoped. Producers, when faced with the choice, generally went with VistaVision if they wanted a large format negative. Technicolor rethought its stand on 70mm and came to a conclusion—Super Technirama 70.

Technirama Specifications

Camera and negative:

Film	35mm
Exposed image height	.992″
Exposed image width	1.486″
Pulldown (horizontal)	8 perfs
Film speed	180 ft. per min.
Compression (horizontal)	1.5×1
Anamorphics	Panavision prismatics or Delrama mirrors

Release prints:

Film	35mm
Aspect ratio	2.34×1
Projected image height	.715″
Projected image width	.839″
Perfs per frame	4
Film speed	90 ft. per min. 24 frames per sec.
Compression	2×1
Sound system	MagOptical or optical
Sound format	stereophonic or monaural

TECHNIRAMA, the spectacular new large-screen color motion picture product developed by TECHNICOLOR® is now ready to excite theater audiences the world over.

TECHNICOLOR Corporation proudly announces that TECHNIRAMA was selected for production of the great color motion pictures listed here...soon to be released for premiere showings...

☆ **DAVY**—Ealing Production—Metro-Goldwyn-Mayer

☆ **ESCAPADE IN JAPAN**—RKO Radio Pictures, Inc.

☆ **LEGEND OF THE LOST**—A Batjac Production—United Artists

☆ **NIGHT PASSAGE**—Universal Pictures Co., Inc.

☆ **SAYONARA**—Goetz Pictures, Inc.—Warner Bros. Pictures, Inc.

☆ **SEA WALL**—De Laurentiis—Columbia

☆ **SLEEPING BEAUTY**—Walt Disney Production—Buena Vista Film Dist. Co., Inc.

☆ **SOUVENIR D'ITALIE**—Athena-Rank

☆ **THE MONTE CARLO STORY**—Titanus Films—United Artists

'TECHNICOLOR
through **TECHNIRAMA**
offers:

Large area negative photography using standard 35mm film

•

Most efficient use of negative area

•

Versatility—<u>Standard</u> or <u>road-show</u> prints all from one original negative

•

Greatly improved picture sharpness

•

Freedom from graininess

•

Increased depth of focus

•

Minimum image distortion

A Technicolor Technirama trade ad.

Opposite: *On location in Toledo, Spain, for* Custer of the West. *The cameras are Technicolor's Technirama. The one on the crane is blimped, while the one on the platform is not. Director Robert Siodmak and director of photography Cecilio Paniagua ride the boom. Others in the photo include operators Eduardo Noe and Salvador Gil, first assistant director Jose Maria Ochoa, and script girl Eva del Castillo among the grips, electricians, extras, and others.*

THE BIGGEST BLOCKBUSTER EVER MADE FOR BIG SCREENS!

SOLOMON AND SHEBA

Will Introduce the Matchless Miracles of

TODAY'S SUPER TECHNIRAMA 70

Before the New Year, selected engagements of the most colorful Biblical spectacle yet produced will launch throughout the world the biggest newsmaking large-screen projection system yet devised.

* * *

For many months the Technicolor Companies have marked "Top-Secret" **TODAY'S SUPER TECHNIRAMA 70,** the ultimate marvel in panoramic screen presentation. Now perfection has been reached.

The Technicolor Companies are revealing this "secret weapon" for bigger boxoffice results everywhere not only on **SOLOMON AND SHEBA,** but on all subsequent big screen attractions. No exhibitor can afford to be without the advantages inherent in **TODAY'S SUPER TECHNIRAMA 70.** These advantages which are many, are due chiefly to revolutionizing cameras and lenses.

A large negative — two and a half times the area of conventional film — is obtained by running 35mm negative horizontally through the new Technirama cameras. This results in a clarity and depth of focus never before possible. However, engineers know that, at a point, increased frame size diminishes visibility and image-definition. **TODAY'S SUPER TECHNIRAMA 70** rigidly controls this factor.

Lenses — developed after long research — incorporate an exclusive anamorphic device of glass prisms and mirrors which compresses the wide view sideways before it is photographed on the large negative, thus eliminating all distortions and losses common to other systems.

If attendance is to climb, every presentation improvement is vital to theatre profit. Even to so powerful an attraction as **SOLOMON AND SHEBA, TODAY'S SUPER TECHNIRAMA 70** is a potent plus. The sharpness, brilliance, size, shape of picture, color fidelity are surpassingly dramatic.

Previous processes for large, wide angled pictures will, we believe, be made obsolete by the multiple advances that **TODAY'S SUPER TECHNIRAMA 70** provides. We are confident that not only will **SOLOMON AND SHEBA** set worldwide records, but that the transcendent excellence of its presentation in **TODAY'S SUPER TECHNIRAMA 70** will be a forceful incentive to exhibitors everywhere to convert their screens to the system which will most effectively stimulate business for this and all other important film entertainment ahead.

UA Pulls Out All The Stops To Hard-Sell Your Public on "Solomon and Sheba" In TODAY'S SUPER TECHNIRAMA 70

A huge consumer budget has been allocated to promote TODAY'S SUPER TECHNIRAMA 70 in the smash worldwide campaign on SOLOMON AND SHEBA:

SPECIAL TRAILER EXPLOITATION / CONSUMER ADS / LOBBY DISPLAYS
POSTERS — (including 24-sheets) / RADIO SPOTS / TV SPOTS
CAR CARDS / SPECIAL PRESSBOOK SUPPLEMENT

ALL THESE — AND MORE FOR THE NEW "STAR" SYSTEM OF BIG SCREEN PROJECTION!

THRU UA
40th Anniversary
1919-1959

Super Technirama 70

Todd-AO was providing huge income to its backers. MGM saw 70mm as the perfect roadshow format and, while adopting a system somewhat different from the Todd-AO process, proved the further benefit of large negative, large screen presentation for selected pictures in certain cities.

Technicolor already had a large format system with Technirama. It was the same height as 70mm and, once decompressed, wider. By making Technirama into Super Technirama 70 they had a system that could compete with Todd-AO and MGM Camera 65 and could be made compatible with either. For whatever reasons they decided the spherical 70mm format was better than the slightly squeezed version. If, however, a producer wanted to release an anamorphic version there would be no problems. To convert Technirama to 70mm was simply accomplished: The horizontal 35mm was decompressed and printed directly onto 70mm. There were no additional steps. Technicolor already had plenty of cameras and lens units in stock, as opposed to the limited 65mm cameras available, and any producer then shooting or planning to shoot in Technirama had the immediate advantage of being able to go 70mm.

The producers of *Solomon and Sheba,* financially badly drained due to the death of Tyrone Power during production and the necessity of replacing him with Yul Brynner and reshooting almost a complete feature, were happy to be able to turn their Biblical epic into a 70mm roadshow, thus adding, potentially, considerably more class and dollars to their film. It worked. A first-class picture became an "event" with advanced admission prices and reserved-seat playdates. Additionally, 35mm general release prints, though still only Technirama, benefited from being advertised as "photographed in 70mm."

Technicolor wasted no time in advising the industry of the benefits of "today's Super Technirama 70." (What was yesterday's version?) *Sleeping Beauty,* being shot at Disney in Technirama, suddenly became a roadshow. Other expensive features, all originally intended for 35mm release and then using or about to use Technirama—including *The Trials of Oscar Wilde, Spartacus, Carthage in Flames* and *The Savage Innocents*—received the 70mm treatment.

Super Technirama 70 was heaven-sent for Samuel Bronston. His independently (and somewhat insufficiently) financed *King of Kings* was in production in Spain in Technirama. MGM was looking for a roadshow to follow *Ben-Hur: A Tale of the Christ* and, after screening Bronston's half-finished film, bought into it. Bronston became a supplier of several major roadshows over the next few years before eventually going into semiretirement and moving back to the United States.

An offshoot of Super Technirama 70 was Super 70 Technirama, which

Opposite: *A trade ad by Technicolor and United Artists promoting Super Technirama 70 and the first feature to utilize the process.*

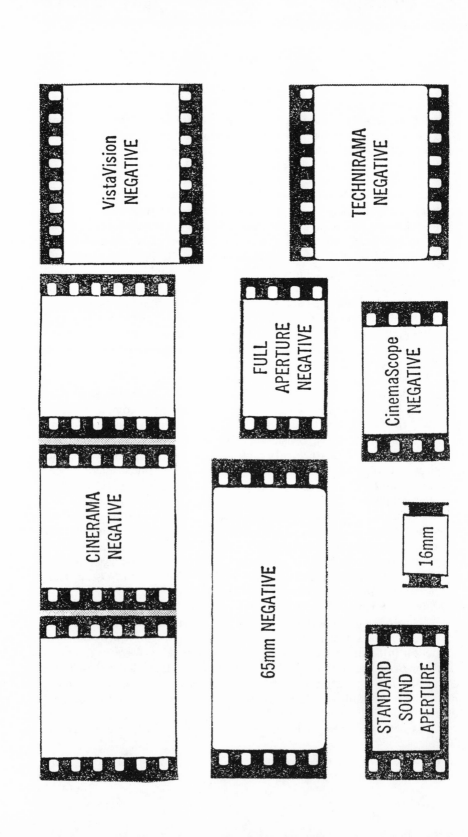

was advertised in the United States under the former trademark. This system was actually VistaVision, which Technicolor in London optically converted to 70mm by cropping the frame slightly and blowing up the image somewhat to fill the larger picture area. It was utilized on two Japanese features, *Buddha* (1963) and *The Great Wall* (1965). Both films also contained some footage shot in 35mm 'scope and blown up. It was necessary to do the optical work in London because Japan had no 70mm laboratory facilities. *Buddha,* in fact, contains the first conversions of 35mm anamorphic to 70mm spherical wide screen. (*The Bat Whispers* [1930] contains blowup footage, but this was done via process photography technique as opposed to optical conversion by the laboratory. *The Cardinal* [1963] was the first full-length feature completely blown up from 35mm to 70mm.)

Super Technirama 70 would eventually be employed on more roadshows than any other single process, though Todd-AO format would be the most common 70mm system since it was the basis for several more or less identical processes.

Super Technirama 70 Specifications

Camera and negative:
Film	35mm
Exposed image height	.992″
Exposed image width	1.486″
Pulldown (horizontal)	8 perfs
Film speed	180 ft. per min.
Compression (horizontal)	1.5×1
Anamorphics	Panavision prismatics or Delrama mirrors

Release print:
Film	70mm
Optical conversion	Technicolor exclusively
Aspect ratio	2.21×1 sans soundtrack
Projected aspect ratio	2.05×1
Projected image height	.866″
Projected image width	1.913″
Perfs per frame	5
Film speed	112.5 ft. per min.
Sound system	six track stereophonic

Opposite: *The drawings at left, showing the various negative sizes in relation to one another, are taken from a Technicolor trade ad. (Techniscope had not been invented when the ad was published.)*

Sound format   magnetic sound-
on-film

The Wide Frame Process Films

The following is a complete listing of Technirama, VistaVision and Super Technirama 70 features released in the United States. (Paramount also released nine short travelogs called *VistaVision Visits* . . . as well as other VistaVision novelty items. Those films are not listed here.) Stereophonic sound releases are noted by *, but available information was limited and the total number of stereophonic films was probably considerably greater. Further information on VistaVision and Technirama titles appearing in **boldface** can be found in the Filmography. Further information on *all* Super Technirama 70 titles can also be found in the Filmography.

VISTAVISION

Three Ring Circus (Par, 1954)*
White Christmas (Par, 1954)*
Artists and Models (Par, 1955)*
The Desperate Hours (Par, 1955)*
The Far Horizons (Par, 1955)*
The Girl Rush (Par, 1955)*
Hell's Island (South Seas Fury) (Par, 1955)*
Lucy Gallant (Par, 1955)*
The Rose Tatto (Par, 1955)*
Run for Cover (Colorado) (Par, 1955)*
The Seven Little Foys (Par, 1955)*
Strategic Air Command (Par, 1955)*
To Catch a Thief (Par, 1955)*
The Trouble with Harry (Par, 1955)*
We're No Angels (Par, 1955)*
You're Never Too Young (Par, 1955)*
Anything Goes (Par, 1956)*
Away All Boats (UI, 1956)
The Birds and the Bees (Par, 1956)*
Doctor at Sea (Par, 1956)*
High Society (MGM, 1956)*
Hollywood or Bust (Par, 1956)*
The Iron Petticoat (MGM, 1956)*
The Leather Saint (Par, 1956)*
The Man Who Knew Too Much (Par, 1956)*
The Mountain (Par, 1956)*
Pardners (Par, 1956)*
The Proud and the Profane (Par, 1956)*
The Rainmaker (Par, 1956)*
Richard III (Lopert, 1956)
The Scarlet Hour (Par, 1956)*
The Search for Bridey Murphy (Par, 1956)*
The Searchers (WB, 1956)
Simon and Laura (UI, 1956)
The Ten Commandments (Par, 1956)*
That Certain Feeling (Par, 1956)*

Three Violent People (Par, 1956)*
The Vagabond King (Par, 1956)*
War and Peace (Par, 1956)*
An Alligator Named Daisy (Rank, 1957)
Beau James (Par, 1957)*
The Black Tent (Rank, 1957)
The Buster Keaton Story (Par, 1957)*
The Delicate Delinquent (Par, 1957)*
The Devil's Hairpin (Par, 1957)*
Doctor at Large (UI, 1957)
Fear Strikes Out (Par, 1957)*
Funny Face (Par, 1957)*
Gunfight at the O.K. Corral (Par, 1957)*
Hear Me Good (Par, 1957)*
The Joker Is Wild (All the Way) (Par, 1957)*
The Lonely Man (Par, 1957)*
Loving You (Par, 1957)*
Omar Khayyam (Par, 1957)*
The Pride and the Passion (UA, 1957)
Pursuit of the Graf Spee (Rank, 1957)
The Sad Sack (Par, 1957)*
Short Cut to Hell (Par, 1957)*
The Spanish Gardener (Rank, 1957)
The Tin Star (Par, 1957)*
Triple Deception (Rank, 1957)
Value for Money (Rank, 1957)
Wild Is the Wind (Par, 1957)*
Another Time, Another Place (Par, 1958)*
The Buccaneer (Par, 1958)*
Dangerous Exile (Rank, 1958)
Desire Under the Elms (Par, 1958)*
The Geisha Boy (Par, 1958)*
Hot Spell (Par, 1958)*
King Creole (Par, 1958)*
Maracaibo (Par, 1958)*
The Matchmaker (Par, 1958)*
Night Ambush (Rank, 1958)
Rock-a-Bye Baby (Par, 1958)*
Spanish Affair (Par, 1958)*
Teacher's Pet (Par, 1958)*
Vertigo (Par, 1958)*
The Five Pennies (Par, 1959)*
The Jayhawkers (Par, 1959)*
Last Train from Gun Hill (Par, 1959)*
L'il Abner (Par, 1959)*
North by Northwest (MGM, 1959)*
A Breath of Scandal (Par, 1960)*
One-Eyed Jacks (Par, 1961)
Big Money (Lopert, 1962)
My Six Loves (Par, 1963)

TECHNIRAMA

Escapade in Japan (UI, 1957)

Legend of the Lost (UA, 1957)
The Monte Carlo Story (UA, 1957)
Night Passage (UI, 1957)
Sayonara (WB, 1957)*
Auntie Mame (WB, 1958)*
The Big Country (UA, 1958)
Paris Holiday (UA, 1958)
This Angry Age (Col, 1958)
The Seven Hills of Rome (MGM, 1958)*
The Vikings (UA, 1958)
For the First Time (MGM, 1959)*
John Paul Jones (WB, 1959)*
The Miracle (WB, 1959)*
The Naked Maja (UA, 1959)
Tempest (Par, 1959)*
Fast and Sexy (Col, 1960)*
The Grass Is Greener (UI, 1960)
Blood and Roses (Par, 1961)
World by Night (WB, 1961)
The Best of Enemies (Col, 1962)
Gypsy (WB, 1962)
The Hellions (Col, 1962)
Merrill's Marauders (WB, 1962)
My Geisha (Par, 1962)
The Leopard (20th-Fox, 1963)
The Golden Arrow (MGM, 1964)
Journey Beneath the Desert (Emb, 1967)

SUPER TECHNIRAMA 70

Solomon and Sheba (UA, 1959)
Sleeping Beauty (BVD, 1959)
Spartacus (UI, 1960)
The Trials of Oscar Wilde (Kingsley, 1960)
Carthage in Flames (Col, 1961)
El Cid (AA, 1961)
King of Kings (MGM, 1961)
The Savage Innocents (Par, 1961)
Barabbas (Col, 1962)
Black Tights (Magna, 1962)
55 Days at Peking (AA, 1962)
The Music Man (WB, 1962)
World by Night No. 2 (WB, 1962)
Buddha (Lopert, 1963)†
Hercules and the Captive Women (Woolner, 1963)
Lafayette (Maco, 1963)†††
Madame (Emb, 1963)
Circus World (Par, 1964)††

†*filmed in Super 70 Technirama*
††*presented in 70mm Super Cinerama*
†††*optically converted to Super Cinerama for selected European engagements*

The Golden Head (1964)††
The Long Ships (Col, 1964)
The Pink Panther (UA, 1964)
Zulu (Emb, 1964)
Le corsaire (1965)
The Great Wall (Magna, 1965)†
Clint the Lonely Nevedan (1968)
Custer of the West (CRC, 1968)††
The Black Cauldron (BVD, 1985)

V. The 70mm Processes

As movie screens became larger, they required more light as well as improved sharpness and steadiness. The use of 70mm film for projection satisfied all these requirements.

The 70mm projector has an aperture that is approximately four times larger than that of the standard 35mm machines. This larger aperture allows more light to reach the screen. As pointed out by the Phillips Company, manufacturers of the Todd-AO projectors, with a 44-foot picture the rate of magnification for 70mm film is 80,400 times. With standard 35mm film projected on the same screen, the magnification is 406,000 times.

Seventy mm theatrical motion picture film is twice as wide as conventional 35mm with a frame height of five perforations instead of the normal four. At the standard rate of projection of 24 frames per second, the 70mm film speed is 25 percent faster than normal, and at 30 frames per second it is 56 percent faster. This increased rate results in a much steadier image on the screen and, with increased brightness, a picture that is much more pleasant to watch. Using 70mm, a mediocre film can be enhanced considerably; a good film can become a great film. Often, the presentation makes all the difference.

Todd-AO

This process is one of the most documented in the history of motion pictures, probably because it was the "first" of the new 70mm processes developed in the early 1950s.

Hollywood experienced rapid changes following the highly successful premiere of *This Is Cinerama* in 1952. Television had been a reality for the entertainment of the masses since the late 1940s. Though in its infancy, and still somewhat in the fad stage, the medium provided free entertainment in the home and was overwhelmingly embraced by the general public. It soon became obvious that the motion picture industry had to do something dramatic to entice the public back into the theaters.

Many different exhibition processes had been developed by Hollywood over the past decades. Most were promptly put on the shelf to gather dust. Wide gauge, cropped wide screen, 3D and stereophonic sound had all proven successful in the past for various reasons had come and gone with little effect. Now the industry was scrambling to give new life to *any* process it owned, or had access to, in order to interest the public in movies again.

This Is Cinerama eventually played for two years at the same theater in New York, grossing $4.5 million with admission prices around $2.00. Hollywood definitely sat up and took notice. To many in the film community, it was inconceivable that an independently made film, using a process that no other theater could show, would do the business that it did. But the public apparently was ready for change and enthusiastically hailed the Cinerama process as an exciting experience. Patrons would often drive many miles and stand in long lines to see the film. They weren't doing the same for any other Hollywood product from the major studios, who were still stuck with the 1.33 × 1 ratio and single channel sound.

One of the original financial backers and staunch supporters of the Cinerama process was veteran showman Michael Todd. He had long before made a name for himself as a flamboyant, often unpredictable producer of "extravaganzas," and he had several successful Broadway shows to his credit. Todd's idea about the presentation of Cinerama was to treat it as an "event," not just a motion picture. A film with an intermission and advance ticket sales was certainly out of the norm for the times. Initially, *This Is Cinerama* played in only 17 theaters throughout the world. When it completed its run, it was the third-largest-grossing motion picture in history.

Todd had felt all along that even though the Cinerama process was revolutionary and exciting, there were inherent flaws that had to be overcome if the system were ever to be used to tell a dramatic story. The most obvious was the "join lines" where the three pictures met on the screen. Todd also felt very strongly that the public couldn't ride roller coasters forever. His enthusiasm and his views on how Cinerama should develop in the future often caused dissension between Todd and the Cinerama executives. A rift developed, and Todd divorced himself from Cinerama, Inc., intent upon giving the public what it wanted: a large-scale motion picture experience unprecedented in the history of the medium.

Todd already had a vision of the process that he felt would eventually be universally acceptable and economically practical. Immediately following the New York opening of *This Is Cinerama* and the rave reviews from the public and critics, he instructed his staff to find out who was the most gifted optical scientist in the country. That person turned out to be Dr. Brian O'Brien, head of the Institute of Optics at the University of Rochester. Todd's one request was that he devise a motion picture process like Cinerama, but one in which "everything comes out of one hole." The complex Cinerama process utilized three projectors in separate booths, synchronized with a six-channel sound reproducer. Todd felt that a less expensive, less complicated process could do the same job with comparable effect.

Michael Todd had stumbled onto a potential gold mine. Dr. O'Brien, coincidentally, was just being named as head of research for the American Optical Company. Meetings were arranged between Todd and American

Optical executives, and in short order agreements were finalized whereby American Optical, under the direction of O'Brien, was in the business of putting together the first really new motion picture system in thirty years!

Since its opening on Broadway in 1943, the major producers and studios in Hollywood had been trying, unsuccessfully, to land the motion picture rights to the highly successful stage musical *Oklahoma!* Master showman Todd went after them, too. He felt the play had the greatest motion picture potential of any theatrical property then available. Eventually, after several meetings and much haggling over particulars, Todd's new company had secured the rights to Rodgers and Hammerstein's *Oklahoma!*

Meanwhile, Dr. O'Brien was still at the drawing board, working out the particulars of the new wide screen system that Todd desperately hoped would, frankly, imitate Cinerama. O'Brien had decided that in order to fill such a giant screen as Todd had imagined, a larger camera negative would be necessary. By doubling the size of standard motion picture film and using specially designed lenses, he felt that a picture even sharper than Cinerama's could be expected. It was then decided that the camera negative should be 65mm in width, with the frame five sprocket holes in height instead of the normal four. This large negative image was approximately four times bigger than that of standard 35mm. In order for the accompanying soundtrack to be close to that of Cinerama presentations, a six-channel magnetic system was chosen. Where Cinerama had been interlocked, the new Todd system would include magnetic stripes along the edges of the film. The extra space necessary for the sound striping made the release prints 70mm wide. The co-efforts of Michael Todd and the American Optical Company in perfecting this new process resulted in the trade name Todd-AO.

In 1929 Fox, MGM and United Artists had briefly introduced 70mm in a somewhat different format (see Chapter 1). The old Mitchell-made cameras were still in storage in a New York warehouse. Todd learned about them and arranged to use them for Todd-AO test footage while Mitchell Camera Company was undertaking the task of constructing new cameras for the process. The Phillips Company in Holland was contracted to build the special projectors necessary to show the wide 70mm film. With minor adjustments, these projectors could easily be converted to run standard 35mm. Thus, in this one projection machine, virtually all current film formats could be run in any theater equipped for wide screen and stereophonic sound. Being a horizontal format, the VistaVision projectors were a special breed unto themselves.

The Todd-AO system became the standard for wide film exhibition. Regardless of the various 70mm techniques that were later developed by other motion picture companies, the resultant positive print could be shown in any theater using Todd-AO projectors.

Imagine, if you will, the scenario up to this point. A successful, imaginative Broadway producer is literally gambling a fortune on an idea. He has enticed a leading optical company to join forces with him, a major exhibition chain (United Artists Theatres) to put up considerable financing, and

At Last! It's Here!

Public World Premiere Thursday, October 13th

RODGERS & HAMMERSTEIN'S

OKLAHOMA!

IN THE NEW MOTION PICTURE PROCESS

When the magic that is "Oklahoma!" meets the miracle that is Todd-AO...something wonderful happens! Suddenly you're there...in the land that is grand, in the surrey, on the prairie! You live it, you're a part of it...you're *in* "Oklahoma!"

Because this is a completely new and unique presentation, without precedent in modern entertainment, all seats for "Oklahoma!" will be reserved as in the legitimate theatre.

You're in the show with

NEW sight! NEW sound! NEW screen!

SOUND BY TODD-AO
IN EASTMAN COLOR

Starring

GORDON MacRAE · GLORIA GRAHAME · GENE NELSON · CHARLOTTE GREENWOOD · EDDIE ALBERT

JAMES WHITMORE · ROD STEIGER · SHIRLEY JONES

Directed by
FRED ZINNEMANN · Produced by
ARTHUR HORNBLOW, JR. · Dances Staged by
AGNES DE MILLE · Screen Play by
SONYA LEVIEN AND WILLIAM LUDWIG

RIVOLI THEATRE
B'way at 49th St. Circle 7-1633

ORDER TICKETS NOW! ALL SEATS RESERVED
2 Shows Daily   3 Shows Sat., Sun. and Hols.

PRICES (Incl. Tax):

MATINEES:	EVENINGS:
Orch. & Loge $2.75	Orch. & Loge $3.50
Balcony $1.75, $1.50	Balcony $2.25, $1.75

DISTRIBUTED BY MAGNA THEATRE CORP.

RIVOLI THEATRE, B'way at 49th St., New York 19, N.Y. · CI 7-1633

loge ☐
Please send_____ orch. ☐ tickets at $_____
balc. ☐

for Mat. ☐ performance on_____(date)
Eve. ☐

Alternate Dates_____

NAME_____

ADDRESS_____
(Please Print Name and Address Clearly)

CITY_____Zone_____State_____

Enclose check or money order (no stamps) payable to RIVOLI THEATRE
addressed to BOX-OFFICE with self addressed and stamped envelope.
V-1

Ad for the premiere Todd-AO production, Oklahoma! *Seats were ordered in advance and reserved as in the "legitimate" theater.*

he is embarking on a project no other producer has been able to sew up
(Oklahoma!). To top it off, he plans to film the story in a process that no
theater in the world can show! He has Eastman Kodak manufacture special
film for his company, a camera manufacturer build special cameras, and
another company build new projectors just for his project. A completely
new magnetic sound format has to be developed for the process, and new
screens have to be designed. All of this is in the works before the first scene
of the first production is shot. Few showmen today would have the confidence, or gambling instinct, to even consider such a venture.

Following a formula worked out earlier by Cinerama, Todd's company leased theaters across the country, equipping them specifically to
show the Todd-AO process. Like Cinerama, *Oklahoma!* was shown with
an intermission. The total running time of the 70mm print was 148 minutes.
Advance ticket sales were available. Todd envisioned his process as one for
which audiences would plan ahead. He could see them entering the theater
in tuxedos and evening gowns, as one would attend the opera. With this at-
mosphere in mind, Todd personally decreed that no popcorn would be sold
during any performance of Todd-AO!

Although theater exhibitors had balked at some of Todd's unorthodox
ideas about the presentation of Todd-AO, the system was a smash hit with
the public. The picture was sharp and bright; the stereo sound was the ultimate in high fidelity. Best of all, any theater equipped with Todd-AO could
show 70mm, CinemaScope or standard "flat" 35mm films.

Initially, the Todd-AO process was photographed and projected at 30
frames per second. During its research period, experimentation with different film speeds had shown that the 30 frames-per-second rate was very
pleasing to look at and helped considerably to eliminate the "picket-fence"
effect while panning from one side of the scene to the other. Sound quality
was also enhanced because of the faster film speed of 140.6 frames per
minute (35mm normally ran at 90 frames per minute). However, only the
first two films in Todd-AO, *Oklahoma!* and *Around the World in 80 Days,*
were shot at 30 frames per second. With the third film in the process, *South
Pacific,* the frame rate was reduced to 24 frames per second, with no ap-
preciable difference in the projected image.

It is interesting to note that those first two Todd-AO productions were
also photographed in 35mm anamorphic. Dual camera setups were used on
both films. This was done for two reasons. First, even after *Oklahoma!* was
launched in Todd's specially equipped theaters, it was not a certainty that
the process would last beyond that one film. A 35mm print was necessary
in order to show the film in those cities that had no Todd-AO house. Sec-
ondly, and most importantly, a suitable optical printer had not yet been
constructed that could render a faultless 35mm anamorphic print from the
original 65mm negative. So, to protect the large investment at hand, if the
70mm process did not find acceptance with the public there was a crisp
35mm camera negative available for showing anamorphic prints in any
theater in the world equipped for CinemaScope. These are the 35mm prints

You're in the **DOUGH** with TODD-AO!

THE NEW MOTION PICTURE ERA!

NEW sight! NEW sound! NEW screen!

Like Rodgers & Hammerstein's "OKLAHOMA!", all great motion pictures of the future will bear the distinctive imprint— PRODUCED IN TODD-AO . . . This is the new motion picture era . . . it's TODD-AO! . . . Truly revolutionary . . . Ecstatic in its realism . . . supreme in its audience emotional involvement and participation . . . TODD-AO is supersonic in its possibilities . . . you live the action . . . you're part of it . . . TODD-AO is the entertainment miracle born of inspired boldness and determination through the happy marriage of science and the motion picture art.

UNITED ARTISTS THEATRE CIRCUIT INC.

A 1955 trade ad. Note that United Artists Theaters, not Magna Theaters, is the promoter. The UA circuit eventually bought Todd-AO Corporation and is still the owner.

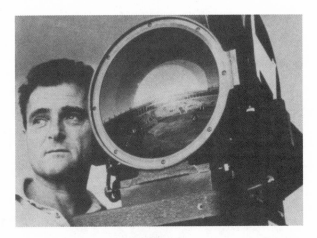

Top: *Mike Todd, Sr., and his favorite photo of himself and his Todd-AO camera. This still was made in Chinchon, Spain, on location for* Around the World in 80 Days. *The huge wide angle AO lens reflects the arena location.* Bottom: *The logo used by 20th Century–Fox on some of their roadshows in the sixties. 35mm prints had the same logo except "70mm" was removed and replaced with "CinemaScope." By contract the Todd-AO screen credit had to be removed from 35mm nonroadshow prints.*

seen today when either *Oklahoma!* or *Around the World in 80 Days* plays neighborhood houses or on television. There were no reduction prints made from the 65mm negative of *Oklahoma!*, but by the time of *80 Days* an optical printing unit was available. The second Todd-AO feature was released in 30 frames per second 35mm 'scope (see page 172) and regular CinemaScope.

Todd-AO was not merely wide screen. It was large screen and wide angle. Its lenses for 65mm photography were classified according to angle of coverage, whereas lenses for 35mm cameras are rated by focal length. Todd-AO had a selection of four lenses that covered everything from a closeup to distant scenic shots. These ranged from the huge 128-degree "bug-eye" wide angle lens down through the 64-, 48- and 37-degree lenses.

Even official trade publications from Hollywood contain conflicting information about the Todd-AO sound system. The original souvenir book for *Around the World in 80 Days* contained a section entitled "What Is Todd-AO?" Therein, the author states that its new high-fidelity system employed seven channels — six sound channels plus one control. Other printed material indicates that the premiere engagement of *Oklahoma!*

A rehearsal for Krakatoa East of Java. *This film was shot in Todd-AO and Super Panavision 70 and presented in 70mm Super Cinerama. On board the actual steamer used for much of the shooting are actors Barbara Werle, Brian Keith, Sal Mineo, J.D. Cannon, Maximilian Schell, John Leyton, and Geoffrey Holder. The Mitchell Todd-AO camera sits on an "applebox." Look at the deck and you can see the shadow of the whole camera and, presumably, operator Eduardo Noe.*

used an eight-channel sound system, possibly incorporating Perspecta encoding. (For information on this sound technique see Chapter VII). This would indicate that the first showings of Todd-AO used an interlock arrangement. However, these must be considered "special" presentations. The "official" Todd-AO sound record was reproduced by six magnetic tracks on the film itself, with five channels behind the screen for main dialogue and the sixth used for the surround speakers, located throughout the auditorium, to reproduce additional music and sound effects.

Although at first an independent venture, 20th Century–Fox quickly saw the advantages of Todd-AO's larger negative for production. It had experimented with its own 70mm Grandeur process in 1929 and a wide gauge CinemaScope photographic system (with modified Grandeur cameras) that used 55mm negative. CinemaScope 55 was used in 1956 on *Carousel* and *The King and I* and in 1957 for *De Luxe Tour*. Twentieth Century–Fox abandoned further development or use of the 55mm system after these three films and adopted the 65mm Todd-AO format for their future blockbusters. Most noteworthy of these was *The Sound of Music* (1965).

Todd-AO was the culmination of Michael Todd's dream of perfecting Cinerama. It was executed by a small army of scientists at the American Optical Company and supervised by a man who had spent a lifetime translating dreams into reality. Ironically, Todd would eventually be pushed out as producer for *Oklahoma!* and have little control over this first Todd-AO production. But Todd-AO is still alive, waiting for some other dreamer or master showman to resurrect it and thrill anew the generations of movie fans around the world.

Cinestage

This system was the official 35mm version of the original Todd-AO format. It was a direct reduction from the 65mm original running at 30 frames per second. The aspect ratio was the same since a 1.5 × 1 squeeze was used instead of the standard 2 × 1 anamorphics. The soundtrack was four-track MagOptical, rendering three screen channels and three surround channels (from one track via Perspecta Sound). Cinestage had to be projected on 35-70 machines since regular 35mm equipment could not operate at 30 frames per second. The process came about because Michael Todd wanted his Todd-AO process exhibited throughout the United Kingdom, but commonwealth laws attached such a high tax to 70mm film that it was prohibitive to ship it overseas. Since 35mm movies were also heavily taxed, the producer had the prints trimmed by one millimeter, making them 34mm and not subject to taxation. As the theaters were already set up for 30 frames per second Todd-AO they were usable for Cinestage. The process was never employed again after the frame rate for 70mm was altered to 24 frames per second and standard 35mm 'scope reductions were possible. Interestingly Cinestage was also the name of Mike Todd's first Todd-AO built theater in Chicago.

Of all Mike Todd's remarkable traits, inventiveness may have been his best. His son would eventually demonstrate the same capacity for bending the rules to meet the situation with Todd-70.

MGM Camera 65 and Ultra Panavision 70

Early in the spring of 1955, Metro-Goldwyn-Mayer studio manager Eddie J. Mannix announced to the press that the studio would switch to 65mm photography for all of its top productions. They had rejected the 35mm 10-perf-per-frame horizontal movement Fearless Super Picture process originally developed in 1927 after testing; owner Ralph G. Fear had already announced to the industry that his system would be used as the basis for MGM Camera 65. They had prior experience with 70mm wide screen, having employed it on *Billy the Kid* (1930) and *The Great Meadow* (1931).

Panavision, Inc., developed the lenses necessary for the photographing and projection of the MGM wide gauge format. Its president, Robert Gottschalk, declared that the 65mm taking process, known as Apo Panatar (later as Ultra Panatar and finally as Ultra Panavision 70), would utilize a revolutionary new optical system. Panavision had incorporated a spherical objective lens and an anamorphic element (wedged prisms) that imparted a slight horizontal squeeze to the image on the film. The anamorphic compression ratio was variable from 1.25×1 to 1.33×1. This combination anamorphosizer and objective lens in one integrated unit would also be coupled with a new optical printing technique to produce 35mm release prints from the original 65mm negative. Apparently, MGM was as concerned with higher-quality 35mm prints as they were with introducing a new wide film format.

It should be noted that at this time (spring 1955), the first production in Todd-AO, and the first release in 70mm as far as the general public was concerned (early wide gauge features had had very limited exposure), was still in production. *Oklahoma!* was not released until late in 1955. However, word had already swept through the industry that the Todd-AO process had the potential for all the impact of Cinerama at the box office. The Todd-AO format is still the industry standard for 70mm theatrical release prints.

MGM chose to call their new wide film format MGM Camera 65. A subheading in initial announcements, as well as the first image to hit the screen in their first feature in the process, was "The Window of the World."

Even though MGM had announced that *all* of its future big productions would be in Camera 65, only two features were actually made utilizing the process. *Raintree County* premiered in October 1957, followed by *Ben-Hur: A Tale of the Christ* in November 1959. Thirty-five mm anamorphic prints of *Raintree County*, which was advertised in Camera 65, had a 2.55×1 aspect ratio instead of the usual 2.35×1. This was done in order to retain the "visual purity." The same format was not followed on *Ben-Hur*.

The Camera 65 logo. On screen, the little window opened and the camera peeked out in a delightful animated sequence.

Cinerama's research had already proven that five channels of sound behind the screen was an adequate number to properly reproduce a stereophonic soundtrack in a large, curved screen environment. Todd-AO had chosen this configuration, and MGM Camera 65 followed suit. Initially, Camera 65 was available in either 65mm *or* 70mm prints. For the 65mm prints, a separate six-track magnetic film (35mm full-coated) was provided for those theaters with audio interlock equipment. For the 70mm prints, six magnetic stripes were placed on the print itself, as is the standard practice today.

Following *Ben-Hur, The Big Fisherman* utilized the Camera 65 units. The cameras were extremely heavy, oversized and difficult to maneuver. The original units had been built over Mitchell Realife cameras. Panavision decided to completely reconstruct the camera and improve upon the prismatic compression device. They had always wanted the process referred to as Ultra Panavision 70, Camera 65 being MGM's moniker, but Panavision 65, 65mm Panavision and Panavision 70mm were at various times used to identify the system. The new cameras, with "Ultra Panavision 70" blazoned over the light blue blimp, were introduced in time for principal photography on *Mutiny on the Bounty* (MGM's prerelease publicity still called the process Camera 65). The cameras were lighter, quieter and more manageable and the anamorphosis was set at a fixed 1.25×1 compression.

Panavision quickly attempted to exploit Ultra Panavision 70 as an alternate photographic system for Super Cinerama. Their idea was that 65mm be employed for all photography; then a three-panel print would be optically extracted from the 65mm footage. The logic was simple: better color continuity, lighter equipment, variable lenses and no breaking of straight lines at the panel joints. They ignored the fact that a single lens system, unless extreme distortion optics are used, cannot cover the visual field of Cinerama.

THIS IS M-G-M's FABULOUS CAMERA 65—*"Window of the World"* whose magic brings the screen M-G-M's wonderful attraction

"RAINTREE COUNTY"

IN THE GREAT TRADITION OF CIVIL WAR ROMANCE

An MGM trade ad showing the blimped 65mm Mitchell camera with matte box and Ultra Panatar anamorphics by Panavision. The blimp alone weighed 300 lbs. Note the operator's viewfinder on the side.

How the West Was Won utilized Ultra Panavision 70 for numerous sequences including all involving rear screen projection (Cinerama would have seen well past and "around" the flat background screen) and much of the action footage. The conversion to Super Cinerama from the original three-panel footage was immediately noticeable, and the depth effect was substantially less; however, the color was more even and there were less-noticeable blend lines. But with the adoption of 70mm Super Cinerama single lens projection, Ultra Panavision 70 came into its own. (70mm Super Cinerama projection lenses were spherical and Ultra Panavision 70 prints were projected with the squeeze intact and no optical conversion was used. People and objects appeared thinner than normal in the middle of the screen but approximately normal on the sides due to "screen stretch.")

MGM Camera 65 and Ultra Panavision 70 Specifications

Camera and negative:
Film	65mm
Exposed image height	.906″
Exposed image width	2.072″
Perfs per frame	5
Film speed	112.5 ft. per min.
Frames per second	24
Compression	variable from 1.25 × 1 to 1.33 × 1*
Anamorphics	Ultra Panatar

Release print:
Film	70mm
Aspect ratio	2.94 × 1 sans soundtrack
Projected aspect ratio	2.76 × 1
Perfs per frame	5
Film speed	112.5 ft. per min.
Frames per second	24
Compression	1.25 × 1
Anamorphics	Panavision
Sound system	six track stereophonic
Sound format	magnetic sound on-film

Compression was variable on MGM Camera 65 but standardized at 1.25 × 1 on Ultra Panavision 70.

Opposite: *The newly redesigned Ultra Panavision 70 camera (revamped from the much heavier Camera 65) shoots a native dance on location in Tahiti for* Mutiny on the Bounty. *Director Lewis Milestone and director of photography Robert Surtees are next to the camera, which is mounted on a boom. The full-sized reconstructed H.M.S.* Bounty *floats at anchor in the upper left corner.*

Super Panavision 70

Continuing their research on wide gauge film processes, begun in conjunction with MGM and the Camera 65 format, Panavision soon followed with their own 70mm wide film system.

Panavision developed their own set of lenses for the new cameras, arranged with a manufacturer to build them to their own exact specifications, and promptly dubbed the system New Panavision 70. It utilized spherical lenses with no anamorphic attachments. The Panavision 70 ("New" was dropped from the name very quickly), both in the taking and projection process, was identical in every technical specification with the Todd-AO process. The *only* difference in the two was in the manufacture of the cameras and lenses. Panavision had their lenses made with varying focal lengths, while the Todd-AO lenses, manufactured by the American Optical Company, ranged from 128 degrees (12.8mm) to 19 degrees (150mm), according to angle of coverage and focal length.

Panavision's spherical 65mm process produced an aspect ratio of 2.35×1 with four-channel magnetic sound for 35mm prints, and an aspect ratio of 2.05×1 with six-channel magnetic sound for 70mm prints.

Super Panavision 70 (as it was finally named) was used on the photography of *Exodus* in 1960 and *West Side Story* in 1961.

In 1964, Panavision introduced an optical printing method that allowed very sharp 70mm release prints to be made from anamorphic 35mm original negatives. This process was now referred to as Panavision 70. Super and Ultra Panavision 70 continued to use 65mm negative, while Panavision 70 now meant that the original negative was 35mm anamorphic resulting in a 70mm release print. Within two years spherical 35mm was given blowup treatment.

The first of these 35 to 70 blowups was Otto Preminger's *The Cardinal,* soon followed by *Becket, The Carpetbaggers* and *The Unsinkable Molly Brown.*

Panavision's president, Robert Gottschalk, pointed out that the print-up process was not meant to replace Super or Ultra Panavision 70. They were considered to be the ultimate in image sharpness and quality. Commenting further on his company's 70mm processes, Gottschalk added:

> They produce a "velvet" appearance, an almost three-dimensional effect which, when the projection is especially good, makes the screen seem almost to disappear completely. These processes, naturally, have far greater quality on the screen than any print-up process could ever have.

Gottschalk would live long enough to see the almost complete disappearance of 65mm original photography (except in special effects work, where today it is being used more and more) and the widespread use of 70mm blowups from various 35mm formats.

The Super Panavision 70 camera is unblimped in this exterior of West Side Story *being shot at Samuel Goldwyn Studios. Director of photography Daniel Fapp is on the camera boom with director Jerome Robbins.*

Todd-70

Todd-70, Michael Todd, Jr.'s, variation of Todd-AO, was used on *The Tale of Old Whiff* and *Scent of Mystery.* The system came about because Todd, Jr., did not want to utilize equipment from a company from which he and his father had been removed. He realized the process had to be compatible with Todd-AO but different enough to make it another system.

Mitchell cameras with the same aperture specs and frames-per-second speed as Todd-AO and Super Panavision 70 were purchased. Lenses by Panavision replaced American Optical's Todd-AO originals. The release prints had framelines at slight variance from Todd-AO — so slight that the difference was noticeable only when the image hit the screen and had to be reframed or spliced. Additionally, the Todd-AO six-track magnetic sound-on-film format was expanded by two channels. Apparently the sixth track

COLUMBIA PICTURES Presents A JOHN FRANKENHEIMER-EDWARD LEWIS Production starring

OMAR SHARIF·LEIGH TAYLOR-YOUNG·JACK PALANCE

*Father and son
battle for glory in the
wildest land on earth.*

The Horsemen

Screenplay by DALTON TRUMBO
Based on the novel by JOSEPH KESSEL
Super Panavision° · COLOR GP

Produced by EDWARD LEWIS Directed by JOHN FRANKENHEIMER

What's wrong with this ad? Not a whole lot, except that the film wasn't shot in Super Panavision 70. Columbia had intended to blow the Panavision original up to 70mm, and the ads were prepared. Even so the credit should have been Panavision 70 and not Super Panavision. As it turned out the film was substantially reedited and released only in 35mm anamorphic. The already-produced publicity was never changed, and many have wrongly assumed this to have been a 70mm release. The screen credits were quite clear on the matter: Filmed in Panavision.

was Perspecta-encoded since the film had only six-channel information space. Todd-AO became Super Panavision 70 by replacing the lenses, and Super Panavision 70 became Todd-70 by changing the framelines and altering the sound output—but all frame and projection specs were identical otherwise. Todd-70 also incorporated Smell-O-Vision, a scent-dispensing process (see Chapter VII).

Superpanorama 70

Also known as MCS-70 and Cinevision 70, this European system is identical to Todd-AO and was engineered by Jacobsen for MCS-Film (Modern Cinema Systems) of West Germany.

Sovscope 70

This is the service mark applied to *all* Soviet-produced 70mm films. The first two Soviet 70mm features were apparently shot with Mitchell Todd-AO cameras, but later films were made with U.S.S.R.-manufactured units based initially on the Ultra Panavision 70 (minus the 1.25 × 1 anamorphics) camera. The most recent Sovscope 70 cameras look exactly like Super Panavision 70 units. Unlike Free World production, where 65mm is employed for photography and 70mm for release prints, the Soviets use 70mm shooting *and* print stock. The frame dimensions and other specs are identical to Todd-AO. Six-track magnetic sound-on-film audio format is used. Many Sovscope 70 prints are blowups from Sovscope 35mm anamorphic and 1.37 × 1 spherical originals. Unfortunately the Soviets make no distinction between 70mm original process and blowup prints.

Hi Fi Stereo 70mm

A Todd-AO format system owned by Hi Fi Stereo 70 KG, Munich, West Germany. It was employed on *Mark of the Devil* (Hallmark, 1972).

Todd-AO, Super Panavision 70, Todd-70, Superpanorama 70, Sovscope 70, Hi Fi Stereo 70mm Specifications*

Camera and negative:	
Film	65mm**
Exposed image height	.906″
Exposed image width	2.072″
Perfs per frame	5
Film speed	112.5 ft. per min.***
Frames per second	24†
Cameras	Mitchell, Panavision, MCS, etc.
Lenses	American Optical,

*While all specs are standard on these spherical 70mm processes there still was such difference in camera or lenses as to not infringe upon others' patents. For example, the frame corners of Superpanorama 70 were rounded, not squared. This roundness was blocked out by the overlaid magnetic soundtrack, but it was enough to vary the process so that it could not be called an exact duplication of Todd-AO. But, of course, it really was exactly the same when it appeared on the screen, and the fact that the image had slightly rounded corners did not alter the compatibility in any way.

**Sovscope 70 employs 70mm camera stock.

***Todd-AO originally ran 140.6 ft. per min.

†Todd-AO was originally 30 frames per second.

Top: *A blimped Sovscope 70 camera looking just like an Ultra Panavision 70 unit minus the anamorphics.* Center and bottom: *Sovscope 70* (center) *blown up from Sovscope 35mm anamorphic. Note the optical soundtrack is based on the RCA Photophone format. This type of variable area system was marketed in Europe by Tobis Klangfilm. The 70mm print has not been magnetically soundtracked but would have six tracks in the same format as Todd-AO.*

	Todd-AO, Panavision, etc.
Release print:	
Film	70mm
Aspect ratio	2.21 × 1 sans soundtrack
Projected aspect ratio	2.05 × 1
Projected image height	.866″
Projected image width	1.913″
Perfs per frame	5
Film speed	112.5 ft. per min.***
Frames per second	24†
Sound system	six-track stereo-phonic††
Sound format	magnetic sound-on-film

IMAX and OMNIMAX

Tiger Child introduced the world to IMAX at Expo '70. It was such a success that theaters have since opened worldwide to show the numerous shorts made just for IMAX. (All IMAX films have been less than an hour long even though they are often referred to as "features" in press material.)

The system employs 65mm camera stock moving horizontally at 15 perfs per frame and exposing the area equal to three standard 65mm vertical frames. The speed is 24 frames per second, making reductions to 35mm and 16mm easy. Several IMAX films have been released in the smaller gauges. The release prints are on 70mm but do not use sound-on-film. Instead, the old interlock system is utilized, offering six tracks from magnetic-coated 35mm film. Recent releases have added Dolby noise reduction to the playback equipment.

OMNIMAX premiered in August 1973 with *Garden Isle.* In effect it was no more than IMAX with an extremely wide angle lens for projection onto a concave screen instead of a flat one. Indeed, since then IMAX and OMNIMAX releases have been interchangeable in projection. OMNIMAX prints play IMAX theaters and IMAX prints, with or without optical conversion for the concave, play OMNIMAX theaters. Of course there are artistic differences in shooting for flat and concave screens, and such differences must be closely monitored lest the filmed image become unviewable in one or the other projected format.

Expo '86 was the site for the unveiling of the latest IMAX format: 3D. The stereoscopic process was the dual camera configuration popular in

††*seven and eight track sound possible with use of Perspecta Sound*

Top: *The Wilcam IW5 IMAX camera is demonstrated by Bill Reeve (far right) of Imax Systems Corporation Camera Department. (Still by David Walton.)* Center: *The Wilcam W-4 IMAX camera from Wilcam Photo Research, Inc. This 15-perf, 65mm camera operates from 1 to 40 frames per second. The shutter is a single blade mirror at 45 degrees with conical back to give focal plane cutting, 175 degrees open. The ultra-bright reflex viewfinder has ×2 magnification and 12mm exit pupil. The high-efficiency motor (pancake type DC) is crystal controlled at 24 frames per second and variable between 1 to 40 frames per second. It operates in forward and reverse, and the motor drives the movement directly without belts or gears. Side-mounted magazines have footage indicator, are held by quick-release snap fittings and have their own torque motor for take-up in forward and reverse. The tonque is automatically regulated. In addition to IMAX use, the camera is an extraordinary special effects unit. The exposed film area is almost four times that of VistaVision.* Bottom: *The IMAX/OMNIMAX logo.*

Hollywood in 1953. Twin projectors provided right and left stereo images beamed through polarized filters. The audience wore polaroid viewers. IMAX 3D may be the most awesome motion picture technique developed.

Regardless of the extremely high definition and clarity of IMAX (and its two children), it will never be a general film process. The very high expense, wear on equipment (both photographic and projection) and inherent problems of interlocking picture and sound put it into a novelty class. Additionally, the oversize screens employed may work with travelogs, but not for dramatic screenplays. Reducing the image to more conventional screen size (or even Cinerama size) does not work because of the aspect ratio. IMAX is destined to remain a special process exhibited in specially made novelty cinemas.

IMAX Specifications

Camera negative:
Film	65mm
Aspect ratio	1.338 × 1
Area	5.744 sq. in.
Diagonal	3.461″
Pulldown (horizontal)	15 perfs
Pullcross (15 perfs)	2.799″
Exposed image height	2.072″
Exposed image width	2.772″
Frame height	2.558″
Pitch	.1866″

Camera:
Format	65mm
Film transport	horizontal
Perfs per frame	15
Pulldown	Claw, pin registered
Speed	24 fps standard
Shutter	155° fixed
Ground glass markings	2.072 × 2.772 camera aperture 1.913 × 2.74 projection aperture
Motor	Rheostat controlled, 18 VDC
Viewfinder	reflex
Movement	clam drive claw mechanism (double claws, double pullcross) Cam actuated

	register pins; 30-tooth feed and takeup sprockets; timing beltdrive train
Release print:	
Film	70mm
Aspect ratio	1.432 × 1
Area	5.242 sq. in. (3.3382 sq. mm)
Diagonal	3.342″ (84.89mm)
Pulldown (horizontal)	15 perfs
Pullcross (15 perfs)	3.805″ (71.25mm)
Projected image height	1.913″ (48.59mm)
Projected image width	2.74″ (69.60mm)
Frame height	2.754″ (69.95mm)
Pitch	.1870″
Sound system	interlocked 35mm
Sound format	six track magnetic

The 70mm Process Films

Further information on each film can be found in the Filmography.

TODD-AO

Oklahoma! (Magna, 1955)
The Thrill of Todd-AO (Magna, 1955)*
Around the World in 80 Days (UA, 1956)
Poema o morye (1958)**
South Pacific (Magna, 1958)***
Porgy and Bess (Col, 1959)
The Alamo (UA, 1960)
Can-Can (20th–Fox, 1960)
Povest plamennikh let (1961)**
Cleopatra (20th–Fox, 1965)
The Agony and the Ecstasy (20th–Fox, 1965)
The Sound of Music (20th–Fox, 1965)
Those Magnificent Men in Their Flying Machines or How I Flew from London to Paris in 25 Hours and 11 Minutes (20th–Fox, 1965)

*short subject
**Soviet credits bill Todd-AO but it is unclear if they actually used Mitchell Todd-AO cameras or copied them, as their Sovscope 70 is identical
***filmed with Panavision lenses, thus actually Super Panavision 70

Opposite: *Scenes from* Hail Columbia! *reproduced in different formats (actual size frames shown). From top left: 16mm with RCA Photophone soundtrack, 1.37 × 1 aspect ratio; 35mm with RCA Photophone soundtrack, 1.33 × 1 aspect ratio; 70mm sans soundtrack, 2.20 × 1 aspect ratio; 70mm IMAX; 70mm OMNIMAX.*

Doctor Dolittle (20th–Fox, 1967)
Star! (20th–Fox, 1968)
2001: A Space Odyssey (MGM, 1968)****
Airport (Univ, 1969)
Krakatoa East of Java (CRC, 1969)****
The Last Valley (CRC, 1971)

*****filmed in Todd-AO and Super Panavision 70 and presented in 70mm Super Cinerama*

MGM CAMERA 65

Raintree County (MGM, 1957)
Ben-Hur: A Tale of the Christ (MGM, 1959)

ULTRA PANAVISION 70

The Big Fisherman (BVD, 1959)§
Mutiny on the Bounty (MGM, 1962)
It's a Mad, Mad, Mad, Mad World (UA, 1963)§§
The Fall of the Roman Empire (Par, 1964)
Battle of the Bulge (WB, 1965)§§
The Greatest Story Ever Told (UA, 1965)§§
The Hallelujah Trail (UA, 1965)§§
Khartoum (UA, 1966)§§

§*actually photographed with Camera 65 units*
§§*presented in 70mm Super Cinerama*

SUPER PANAVISION 70

Exodus (UA, 1960)
West Side Story (UA, 1961)
Lawrence of Arabia (Col, 1962)
Cheyenne Autumn (WB, 1964)
My Fair Lady (WB, 1964)
Lord Jim (Col, 1965)
Grand Prix (MGM, 1966)§§
Ice Station Zebra (MGM, 1968)§§
Chitty Chitty Bang Bang (UA, 1968)
2001: A Space Odyssey (MGM, 1968)****
Mackenna's Gold (Col., 1969)
Krakatoa East of Java (CRC, 1969)****
Ryan's Daughter (MGM, 1970)
Song of Norway (CRC, 1970)§§
Tron (BVD, 1982)
Brainstorm (MGM/UA, 1983)

SUPERPANORAMA 70

Mediterranean Holiday (Continental, 1964)§§§
Scheherazade (Shawn, 1965)
The Sound of Music ((20th-Fox, 1965)††††

§§§*presented in Wonderama and 70mm Super Cinerama*
††††*second unit photography only, principal photography in Todd-AO*

Der kongress amuesiert sich (1966)
La nuit des adieux (1966)§§§§
Savage Pampas (Comet, 1967)
Shatterhand (Goldstone, 1967)
Sky Over Holland (Seneca, 1967)*
Dr. Coppelius (Childhood, 1968)
Uncle Tom's Cabin (Babb, 1969)

§§§§*possibly filmed in part or whole in Sovscope 70*
*short subject

SOVSCOPE 70

(This lists *all* known 70mm Soviet films with credited process. Seventy millimeter 3D films have been omitted. Many were blown up from 35mm anamorphic or spherical. Process credits other than Sovscope 70 (e.g. Kinopanorama 70) are given in brackets. English titles are given when they were assigned by Sovexportfilm or when the films were released in the United States. Dates in brackets [following parentheses] are for United States release.)

Poem of the Sea [Todd-AO] (1958)
The Story of Flaming Years [presented in Kinopanorama] (1961)
The Trial of Madmen [presented in Kinopanorama] (1962)
V mire tantsa (1962)
Batmanova, Singing Slave [Kinopanorama 70] (1963)
Krepostnaya aktrisa (1963)
The Law of the Antarctic (1963)
The Optimistic Tragedy [presented in Kinopanorama] (1963) [1964]
The Enchanted Desna (1964)
Kosmicheskiy splav (1964)
Meteli (1964)
Moskva pervomayskaya (1964)
Na podvodnikh skuterakh [Kinopanorama 70] (1964)
The Sleeping Beauty [Kinopanorama 70] (1964) [1966]
S O N (1964)
Bolshoi Ballet 67 (1965) [1966]
Mi, russkiy narod (1965)
Velet ("Aeroport") (1965)
Zalp "Avrori" (1965)
Delifini prikhodyat k lyudam [Kinopanorama 70] (1966)
God kak zizni (1966)
Na samom bolishom stadione [Kinopanorama 70] (1966)
Nights of Farewell [uncredited] (1966)
War and Peace, Leo Tolstoy's (1966) [1968]
Yarosti (1966)
Andromeda Nebula (1967)
Arena (1967)
Aybolit-66 (1967)
Geroy nashego vremeni (1967)
The Iron Flood (1967)
Katerina Izmailova (1967) [1969]
Royal Regatta (1967)

The Shores of Hope (1967)
The Tale of Tzar Saltan (1967)
The Three Fat Men (1967)
Viy (1967)
Vozimite nas s soboy, turisti [presented in "Roundframe"] (1967)
Wedding in Malinovke (1967)
Anna Karenina (1968)
The Brothers Karamazov (1968) [1980]
Daytime Stars (1968)
Strana moya (1968)
Swan Lake (1968)
They Live Close By (1968)
The Unforgettable (1968) [1969]
V nebe toliko devushki (1968)
Vechev nakanune Ivana Kupala (1968)
Daleko na zapade (1969)
Khozyain taygi (1969)
Krakh (1969)
Neytralinie vodi (1969)
Novie priklyucheniya neulovimikh (1969)
Razgovor s tovarishchem Leninim (1969)
Shiroka strana moya rodnaya (1969)
Baperina (1970)
Duma o Britanke (1970)
The Golden Gate (1970)
Koroli maneza (1970)
Liberation (1970)
Moya Moskva (1970)
Our March [presented in Polyscreen] (1970)
Pochtoviy roman (1970)
The Red Tent (1970) [1971]
Tchaikovsky (1970) [1972]
Chermen (1971)
Direktor (1971)
Flight (1971)
Goluboy led (1971)
International (1971)
Knyazi Igori (1971)
Koroli gor i drugie (1971)
Krushenie imperii (1971)
Leningrad (1971)
Lika-Chekhov's Love (1971)
Lyubovi Yarovaya (1971)
The Newlyweds (1971)
Prizvanie (1971)
Vozrashchenie "Svyatogo Luki" (1971)
Zvezdi ne gashut (1971)
Belaya ptitsa s chernoy otmetinoy (1972)
Committee of 19 (1972)
Dauria (1972)
A Farewell to St. Petersburg (1972)
Goyya, ili Tyazkiy puti poznaniya (1972)

I Am a Citizen of the Soviet Union [presented in Polyscreen] (1972)
Lyudi na Nile (1972)
Only You (1972)
Russian Field (1972)
The Sea in Flames (1972)
Sestra muzikanta (1972)
Taming of the Flame (1972)
Tsena bistrikh sekund (1972)
Zakhar Berkut (1972)
Commander of the Lucky "Pike" (1973)
A Courtesy Call (1973)
For Love of Man (1973)
The Headless Horseman (1973)
Hot Snow (1973)
Lautare (1973)
Lofty Title (1973)
Machekha (1973)
Mnogo shuma iz nichego (1973)
Privalov's Millions (1973)
Racers (1973)
Rustam and Sukhrab (1973)
The Siberian Woman (1973)
About Those I Remember and Love (1974)
Affairs of the Heart (1974)
Cities and Years (1974)
The Hottest Month (1974)
I na Tikhom okeane... (1974)
Iskateli zatonuvshego goroda (1974)
Lovers' Romance (1974)
Moya Poltava (1974)
Neylon 100% (1974)
No Return (1974)
Potseluy Chaniti (1974)
The Sources (1974)
Zvezda zkrana (1974)
Aeronaut (1975)
Automobile, Violin and the Dog Blob (1975)
Beliy bashlik (1975)
Blockade (1975)
Blow, Breeze! (1975)
Bolishoy attraktsion (1975)
Earthly Love (1975)
Eleven Hopefuls (1975)
Front Without Flanks (1975)
Garmoniya (1975)
Godi boribi i ispitaniy (1975)
Mothers and Daughters (1975)
Nebo so mnoy (1975)
Semiya Ivanovikh (1975)
They Fought for Their Motherland (1975)
Tovarishch Sibiri (1975)
Confidence (1976)

Dersu Uzala (1976) [1976]
From Dawn to Dusk (1976)
Gorozane (1976)
The Last Victim (1976)
Mr. McKinley's Flight (1976)
Queen of the Gypsies (1976) [1979]
The Story of How Tsar Peter Married Off His Blackamoor (1976)
Vibor tseli (1976)
Yaroslav Dombrovskiy (1976)
A Bit of Fooling (1977)
The Blue Bird (1977) [1976]
Isotope Cafe (1977)
Ivan the Terrible (1977) [1979]
The Legend of Tile (1977)
The Life and Death of Ferdinand Luce (1977)
Our Debts (1977)
Soldiers of Freedom (1977)
Soldiers on the March (1977)
Suvenir (1977)
Sweet Woman (1977)
White Bim the Black Ear (1977)
Witness for the Defense (1977)
Zdravstvuy, Sochi! (1977)
Alimanakh kinoputeshestviy (1978)
Armed and Dangerous (1978)
The Black Birch (1978)
Destiny (1978)
Duma o Kovpake (1978)
A Front Behind the Front Line (1978)
Govorit Oktyabri (1978)
Mimino (1978)
Po yuznomy beregu Krima (1978)
Pravo na lyubovi (1978)
The Red Diplomatic Couriers (1978)
The Shooting Party (1978) [1981]
A Tavern on Pyatnitskaya Street (1978)
13-y film Leonida Gaydaya (1978)
Zuravli v nebe (1978)
The Centaurs (1979)
The Siberiad (1979) [1979]
The Star of Hope (1979)
The Taste of Bread (1979)
Volshebnoe ozero (1979)
Vse reshaet mgnovenie (1979)
Yemelyan Pugachov (1979)
Znetsi (1979)
The Crew (1980)
Forget the Word Death (1980)
Krutoe pole (1980)
People in the Ocean (1980)
Poem of Wings (1980)
Poslednyaya Okhota (1980)

Take-Off (1980)
With Fidelity and Truth (1980)
Zdesi, na moey zemle (1980)
Facts of the Past Day (1981)
Fantasy on the Love Theme (1981)
The Flying Hussar Squadron (1981)
Igri zivotnikh (1981)
Kogda poyut muzchini (1981)
One Doesn't Change Horses in Midstream (1981)
Pervie starti (1981)
Rasskaz o film "Koney na pereprave ne menyayut" (1981)
Special Assignment (1981)
Teheran, 43 (1981)
To the Stars by Hard Ways (1981) [1982]
V Bolgariyu zimoy (1981)
Vishneviy omut (1981)
Zerebenok v yablokakh (1981)
Across the Gobi and the Khingans (1982)
Andrus (1982)
Baykal, krasota—to kakaya (1982)
Dusha (1982)
Express on Fire (1982)
Front v tilu vraga (1982)
An Incident in Map Grid 36-80 (1982)
Koga ozivayut ostrova (1982)
Lesnaya pesnya, Mavka (1982)
The Man in the Hat (1982)
Moya Moldova (1982)
Oslinaya shkura (1982)
Pokhishchenie veka (1982)
Predislovie v bitve (1982)
Red Bells (1982)
The Secret of St. Jur (1982)
Visokiy pereval (1982)
Vladivostok, god 1918 (1982)
Yaroslav the Wise (1982)
Anna Pavlova (1983)
The Demidovs (1983)
Fateful Sunday (1983)
A Hot Summer in Kabul (1983)
Moon Rainbow (1983)
Skorosti (1983)
Taste of Immortality (1983)
The Doctor's Apprentice (1984)
The First Cavalry Army (1984)
Legend of Love (1984)
The Legend of Princess Olga (1984)
Moya Moldova (1984)
Na ves zolota (1984)
Pristupiti k likvidatsii (1984)
Return from Orbit (1984)
The Secret of Her Youth (1984)

Shans (1984)
The Shore (1984)
The Sparkling World (1984)
Tayna "Chernikh drozdov" (1984)
Zaloznik (1984)
Ancient Russia (1985)
The Black Arrow (1985)
The Follower (1985)
Her Mr. Right (1985)
I Am Here Talking to You (1985)
The Most Charming and Attractive (1985)
One More Night of Scheherezade (1985)
Poruchiti generalu in Nesterovu (1985)
Prikhodi svobodnim (1985)
Semi stikhiy (1985)
Then Came Bumbo (1985)
Two Versions of a Collision (1985)
Zil otvazniy kapitan (1985)
The Battle of Moscow (1986)
Detached Mission (1986)
Matvey's Joy (1986)
Nachni snachala (1986)
Captain of the "Pilgrim" (1987)
Mournful Unconcern (1987)

IMAX and OMNIMAX

(Process is noted.)

Tiger Child (1970; IMAX)
North of Superior (1971; IMAX)
Labyrinth (1972; IMAX)
Catch the Sun (1973; IMAX)
Garden Isle (1973; OMNIMAX)
Standing Up Country (1973; IMAX)
Volcano (1973; IMAX)
Voyage to the Outer Planets (1973; IMAX°)
Circus World (1974; IMAX)
Cosmos (1974; OMNIMAX°)
Man Belongs to the Earth (1974; IMAX)
Snow Job (1974; IMAX)
Energy (1975; IMAX)
Viva Baja (1975; OMNIMAX)
Ontario/Summertime (1976; IMAX)
To Fly (1976; IMAX)
Ocean (1977; OMNIMAX)
Silent Sky (1977; IMAX)
Alfa 78 (1978; OMNIMAX)
Genesis (1979; OMNIMAX)
Living Planet (1979; IMAX)
Nomads of the Deep (1979; IMAX)

°*filmed in Dynavision double frame 70mm and blown up to OMNIMAX format*

Atmos (1980; OMNIMAX)
The Eruption of Mount St. Helens (1980; OMNIMAX)
The Great Barrier Reef (1980; OMNIMAX)
Space Library (1980; OMNIMAX)
An American Adventure (1981; IMAX)
My Strange Uncle (1981; IMAX)
World Coaster (1981; OMNIMAX)
Hail Columbia! (1982; IMAX and OMNIMAX)
Flyers (1982; IMAX)
Tomorrow in Space (1982; OMNIMAX)
Behold Hawaii (1983; IMAX)
Darwin and the Galapagos (1983; OMNIMAX)
El pueblo del sol (1983; OMNIMAX)
Dance of Life (1984; IMAX)
Faces of Japan (1984; IMAX)
Grand Canyon, the Hidden Secrets (1984; IMAX)
Journey of Discovery (1984; IMAX)
Magic Egg (1984; OMNIMAX)
River Journey (1984; IMAX)
Speed (1984; IMAX)
Chronos (1985; IMAX and OMNIMAX)
The Dream Is Alive (1985; IMAX and OMNIMAX)
A Freedom to Move (1985; OMNIMAX)
Water and Man (1985; OMNIMAX)
We Are Born of Stars (1985; IMAX 3D and OMNIMAX 3D°°)
Dance of the East (1986; IMAX)
On the Wing (1986; IMAX and OMNIMAX)
Picture Holland (1986; OMNIMAX)
Sacred Site (1986; OMNIMAX)
Skyward (1986; IMAX)
Transitions (1986; IMAX 3D°°°)
Indonesian Child (1987; IMAX)
Niagara: Miracles, Myths & Magic (1987; IMAX)
Parallel 50 (1987; IMAX)
Seasons (1987; OMNIMAX)

°°*filmed in anaglyphic duo-color format*
°°°*filmed with a twin camera rig and projected in dual polarized format*

VI. The 70mm Blowups

With the release of *The Cardinal* (Columbia, 1963) a new break-through was heralded by the industry: Panavision 70. Yes, the old trade name first applied to Super Panavision 70 was back. Now, however, it referred not to original photography but rather to presentation format. Panavision 70 was no more than 35mm anamorphic Panavision decompressed and optically enlarged to fill the 70mm frame. The technology was not new: Seventy millimeter had been reduced to 35mm anamorphic format for several years, so it was just a matter of reversing the procedure in the optical laboratory. In fact some blowup footage had been produced before, but until *The Cardinal* no full-length 70mm roadshow had been produced entirely from 35mm preprint footage. (Super Technirama 70 is derived from 35mm, but that was wide frame, not standard format.)

Suddenly a new market was opened up to producers. It was now possible to shoot their films on lower, even relatively modest, budgets and still be able to have a roadshow version in 70mm if the finished product were of sufficient quality or interest to warrant that type of exhibition. In the next few years a rash of blowups were announced, but in fact few were made in the United States. This has caused tremendous confusion for some researchers who, relying solely on trade announcements, have attempted listing 70mm releases. Their final compilations have tended to be way overlong and for the most part inaccurate. Such listings are further distorted by the release overseas of several United States features in 70mm blowup that received only 35mm domestic playdates. In some cases only one print was actually made in 70mm and given showcase treatment in one city, usually Los Angeles or New York. There have also been at least two cases where a blowup was produced and never exhibited in any theater.

Perhaps one of the more interesting aspects of blowing anamorphic 35mm to 70mm was the selection of format. For almost ten years 70mm release prints had been produced in two formats: anamorphic (Ultra Panavision) and spherical (Todd-AO type). The majority of roadshow theaters were equipped with spherical projection, but there were many also set up for anamorphic presentation. Both types of films were still being shot. In fact, Ultra Panavision 70 was growing in popularity, though by nature of the system still relatively restricted in use. (70mm Super Cinerama would no doubt expand its use by several years.) Anamorphic 35mm, when shown in its full width, seemed much closer in shape and ratio to Ultra Panavision than to spherical 70mm, which, depending on the width of the inside magnetic soundtrack, could not be more than 2.08×1 and was generally approximately 2.05×1. Conversion of 35mm 2.35×1 anamorphic to full Ultra Panavision 70 ratio, by slight cropping of the top and/or bottom of the frame, would have reproduced more of the originally photographed image than the side-lopping necessary to convert the preprint material to spherical 70mm format. (Since extremely few 35mm houses actually projected, or are now projecting, 'scope in a ratio much wider than 2×1 [some even less than that!] it really didn't do much, if any, artistic damage to the original films. In fact, of the many 70mm blowups from anamorphic the authors have screened we can recall only one which was noticeably marred: Some of the credits on *Quest for Fire* were partly trimmed off.) Economics were most likely the deciding factor: There were more theaters with spherical 70mm lenses, and even if the films were going to receive only a few wide gauge playdates it was to the producers' advantage to have the greater availability of cinemas. Oddly, this selection of spherical over anamorphic format seems never before to have been addressed in print. We bring it to the reader's attention mainly for that reason.

With the successful adaptation of 35mm anamorphic to 70mm, it was understandable that 35mm spherical would soon be given the same treatment. In late 1966, more than a full year before it would actually open in theaters, full page newspaper ads with reserved seat order forms began appearing for the reissue of *Gone with the Wind* in 2×1 70mm wide screen and six-track magnetic stereophonic sound. *The Wind,* or *GWTW,* as it is affectionally known in the industry, set new records when it opened in October 1967. It would continue to run as a hard-ticket attraction for over two years in some areas and even today, after much television and home video exposure, is still being booked "In New Screen Splendor" as the ads proclaimed. The newly reframed, enlarged and multitrack expanded version was a success beyond anybody's wildest dreams. This is especially impressive when one considers that in 1967 the film was almost thirty years old and had already been reissued twice since 1961. (And it had been given a spherical widescreen and Perspecta Stereophonic Sound treatment in the early fifties. It seemed to belong on the huge, wide screen. Oddly, by comparison, the 35mm wide screen version with its Perspecta Sound was far more impressive. The 70mm blowup was often irritatingly misframed, with poor color and a pseudostereophonic soundtrack that was not even directional, as was the fifties version, but simply a "polyphonic" expansion of the mono audio over the six channels. But people flocked in hordes to see it and the reason was the new size, shape and presumed-to-be stereophonic sound.) Of course, *The Wind* was no ordinary film. It never had been. It never will be.

While *The Wind* swept into movie history as the first spherical 35mm-to-70mm wide screen blowup, it was not actually the first to be exhibited. It was the first to receive the laboratory optical treatment, but several months prior to its opening, with success already determined by advance ticket sales, and the quality of that feature at least acceptable to MGM, the same studio issued *The Dirty Dozen* in selected theaters in Metroscope 70, i.e., shot in Metroscope (35mm spherical with a 1.75 × 1 hard matte) and blown up to 70mm. Like *The Wind,* that film was an astromonical success. Soon other spherical films, along with the growing number of anamorphic features, were receiving roadshow presentation in this form of wide gauge.

By the mid-seventies the Panavision 70 trademark was discontinued in the States (it is still applied in Europe) and movies were simply advertised in 70mm. (The blowups for *The Carpetbaggers* and *Close Encounters of the Third Kind* were dishonestly billed as Super Panavision 70!) Occasionally in Europe other anamorphic processes, such as Deltavision 70 and Totalscope 70mm, were advertised. The addition of the "70" denoted the difference in original 70mm material, which usually carried a "Super" (or some such catchword) before the process name, and anamorphic 35mm converted to the larger frame. By and large, however, audiences were uneducated to that fact. To them "70" meant bigger and better screen images and more encompassing sound. Of course there were still many large cinemas in those days which greatly enhanced the whole movie-going experience. This confusion is compounded even more today since most films are shot in spherical format and blown up, not over the full frame (though that is still occasionally done), but in ratios normally of 1.66 × 1, 1.75 × 1 or 1.85 × 1. *One from the Heart, Metropolis,* and most of *Napoleon* were actually 1.33 × 1. Many theater patrons, expecting a film promoted in 70mm to fill the huge screen in the few cinemas still having one, have been sorely disappointed to end up viewing a screen image that is actually smaller than 35mm 'scope in the same house. Of course if the source material was anamorphic, they do see the full-size image they expected, but 'scope features are very much in the minority these days. (See Chapter III.)

The reader no doubt wonders why so many more films were and are given 70mm release in Europe than in the United States. The reasons involve unions and government-imposed restrictions. In the United States the unions control exhibition with a strong iron claw. Refusing to give the theater owner (and as a result, the ticket buyer) an even break, the American guilds have forced cinemas to double, and in some cases quadruple, projection staffs for 70mm engagements. Faced with already overpriced operators' wage scales, the exhibitors have been forced to keep costs low by booking 35mm prints rather than paying the extra personnel for 70mm, except in those rare cases where audience attendance is always so great as to justify such expenditure, or in nonunion controlled situations. The theatermen have not been backed by Hollywood, and the customer once again has been the victim. In Europe there are no such union demands — the projectionists perform their duties regardless of the film format — but there are various government restrictions. These, in general, state that theaters cannot charge higher admission fees for regular film presentations. Thus, when a film comes along with greater-than-average potential, it is often blown up to 70mm and exhibited at a higher ticket price. This meets the laws imposed and results in many more wide gauge releases. It is not at all uncommon for films of such minor quality and interest that they are never even shown in the States on television to be treated as roadshows in foreign cities. Everything from low-budget horror films in Spain to "spaghetti westerns" in Italy to slapstick comedies in France have been blown up to 70mm. Many hundreds of films you never heard of have been better treated in Europe than major releases have been in the United States.

Since 70mm blowups are rather common today in larger cities it might be assumed by the reader who has never seen one that the quality of presentation must be substantially improved over 35mm engagements of the same film. This, unfortunately, is not always the case. While 70mm does *always* render a brighter screen image, this is often sabotaged by theater owners who reduce the projector light output to save a few dollars. Most theaters do not have huge screens and cannot provide the increased image 70mm is intended to give. But in the few houses that do, the difference is often highly impressive. Also a large number of theaters crop spherical 35mm in a wider ratio than that of many 70mm blowups, resulting in the wide gauge print actually appearing smaller. Then, too, many blowups have not been very good. Some, such as *Quest for Fire* (from anamorphic) and *Cocoon* (from spherical in 1.85 × 1 ratio), have been dark, grainy and little improved over their 35mm originals. Others, such as *Starman* (from anamorphic) and *Days of Heaven* (from spherical in 1.85 × 1 ratio) have been so pristine as to stagger the viewer with their clarity. But whatever shortcomings 70mm blowups may have in pictorial imagery, they do provide the added benefit of six-track magnetic stereophonic sound. (A very few have utilized four-track or five-track audio reproduction.) No matter how good the sound delivered from 35mm stereo optical or MagOptical Stereophonic audio, it cannot match the quality of 70mm magnetic sound with its capacity for extended bass and higher frequency response. Indeed, in most cinemas, it is the sound that sets the 70mm blowup so far apart from 35mm. (This, of course, shouldn't be the case, but until theaters install much larger screens and keep the projector beam set at the proper level, it is the sad fact.)

We do want to point out, however, that no matter how excellent the blowup — and we strongly recommend the reader always support 70mm-equipped theaters — or how good the sound, no 35mm-to-70mm enlargement can match the clarity and overall majesty of true, originally photographed 70mm wide screen. As much as *Silverado,* for example, makes regular 35mm look dull and unimpressive, then so does that film pale by comparison with, say, *Patton,* which was so sharp the threads holding George C. Scott's jacket buttons could be counted! Nor is the current system of stereophonic sound mixing and playback remotely as encompassing and directional as the original six-channel discrete format applied to Todd-AO, Super Technirama 70, etc. (A very few recent blowups have employed the original discrete format for some engagements, but this is very rare. Recent reports indicate some interest in returning to true directional separation. For more on stereophonic sound see Chapter VIII.)

The 70mm Blowup Films

The following is a list of most 70mm blowups released in the United States. Because the blowups themselves, rather than the photographic processes used in the originals, are the subject of this chapter, these films have not been grouped according to process as in previous chapters; however, the original photographic process is noted for each.

While 35mm to 70mm blowups are now common in the United States they are much more so in Europe, as explained in the previous pages. In the early seventies, Fotofilm, Spain's largest lab, had already processed or printed nearly 300 70mm films. Needless to say the vast majority were blowups. It would be very difficult to list them all. Most were shown in the United States in 35mm only, if at all.

Further information on titles appearing in **boldface** can be found in the Filmography.

Bye, Bye Birdie! (Col, 1963; Panavision)
The Cardinal (Col, 1963; Panavision)
Becket (Par, 1964; Panavision)
The Carpetbaggers (Par, 1964; Panavision)
First Men IN the Moon (Col, 1964; Panavision)
The Unsinkable Molly Brown (MGM, 1964; Panavision)
Dr. Zhivago (MGM, 1965; Panavision)
Genghis Khan (Col, 1965; Panavision)
The Great Race (WB, 1965; Panavision)
In Harm's Way (Par, 1965; Panavision)
Marriage on the Rocks (WB, 1965; Panavision)
Hawaii (UA, 1966; Panavision)
The Heroes of Telemark (Col, 1966; Panavision)
Is Paris Burning? (Par, 1966; Panavision)
The Professionals (Col, 1966; Panavision)
The Sand Pebbles ((20th-Fox, 1966; Panavision)
Camelot (W7, 1967; Panavision)
Casino Royale (Col, 1967; Panavision)
The Comedians (MGM, 1967; Panavision)
The Dirty Dozen (MGM, 1967; Metroscope)
Far from the Madding Crowd (MGM, 1967; Panavision)
Gone with the Wind (MGM; reissue, 1967; spherical 1.33×1)
Marooned (Col, 1967; Panavision)
Finian's Rainbow (W7, 1968; Panavision)
Funny Girl (Col, 1968; Panavision)
Hellfighters (Univ, 1968; Panavision)
The Jolson Story (Col; reissue, 1968; spherical 1.33×1)
Julius Caesar (MGM; reissue, 1968; spherical 1.33×1)
Oliver! (Col, 1968; Panavision)
The Shoes of the Fisherman (MGM, 1968; Panavision)
Sweet Charity (Univ, 1968; Panavision)
The Young Girls of Rochefort (W7, 1968; spherical 1.66×1)

All Quiet on the Western Front (Univ; reissue, 1969; spherical 1.33 × 1)*
Goodbye, Mr. Chips (MGM, 1969; Panavision)
Paint Your Wagon (Par, 1969; Panavision)
Those Daring Young Men in Their Jaunty Jalopies (Par, 1969; Panavision)
Where Eagles Dare (MGM, 1969; Panavision)
The Wild Bunch (W7, 1969; Panavision)
The Young Rebel (Cervantes) (AIP, 1969; Totalscope)
The Adventurers (Par, 1970; Panavision)
Anne of the Thousand Days (Univ, 1970; Panavision)
Brewster McCloud (MGM, 1970; Panavision)
Kelly's Heroes (MGM, 1970; Panavision)
The Stewardesses (Sherpix, 1970; StereoVision 3D)
Too Late the Hero (CRC, 1970; Metroscope)
Tora! Tora! Tora! ((20th-Fox, 1970; Panavision)
Two Mules for Sister Sara (Univ, 1970; Panavision)
Winning (Univ, 1970; Panavision)
Battle of Neretva (AIP, 1971; Panavision)
The Boy Friend (MGM, 1971; Panavision)
The Devils (WB, 1971; Panavision)
Fiddler on the Roof (UA, 1971; Panavision)
The Light at the Edge of the World (NG, 1971; Panavision)
Mary, Queen of Scots (Univ, 1971; Panavision)
The Music Lovers (UA, 1971; Panavision)
Nicholas and Alexandra (Col, 1971; Panavision)
The Ten Commandments (Par; reissue, 1971; VistaVision)
Waterloo (Par, 1971; Panavision)
Wild Rovers (MGM, 1971; Panavision)
The Concert for Bangladesh (20th-Fox, 1972; 16mm 1.33 × 1)
The Cowboys (WB, 1972; Panavision)
Deliverance (WB, 1972; Panavision)
The Great Waltz (MGM, 1972; Panavision)
House of Wax (StereoVision; reissue, 1972; 1.33 × 1 StereoVision 3D)
Man of La Mancha (UA, 1972; spherical 1.85 × 1)
Young Winston (Col, 1972; Panavision)
Electra Glide in Blue (UA, 1973; Panavision)
Lost Horizon (Col, 1973; Panavision)
The Neptune Factor ((20th-Fox, 1973; Panavision)
Playtime (Continental, 1973; spherical 1.66 × 1)
Tom Sawyer (UA, 1973; Panavision)
Earthquake (Univ, 1974; Panavision)
That's Entertainment (MGM, 1974; various ratios)
The Hindenburg (Univ, 1975; Panavision)
Paper Tiger (Avco, 1975; Panavision)
Rollerball (UA, 1975; Spherical Panavision)
Tommy (Col, 1975; spherical 1.85 × 1)
Grizzly (FVI, 1976; Todd-AO 35)*
King Kong (Par, 1976; Panavision)
Logan's Run (MGM, 1976; Todd-AO 35)
The Return of a Man Called Horse (UA, 1976; Panavision)
A Star Is Born (WB, 1976; Spherical Panavision)

apparently never released

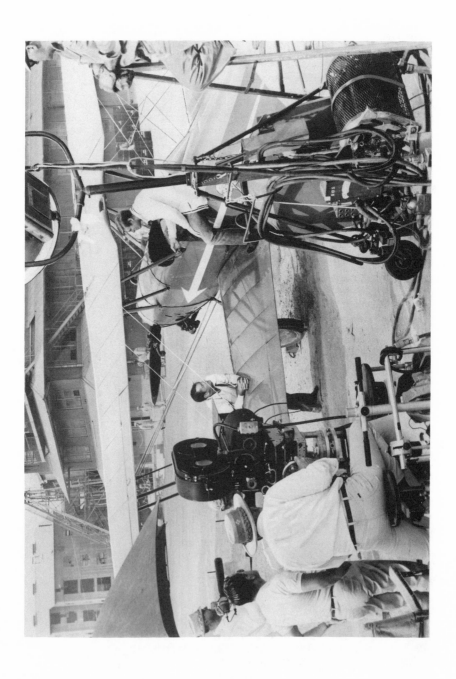

Opposite and above: *Filming* The Carpetbaggers. *Despite publicity crediting Super Panavision 70, this film was shot in Panavision and blown up to 70mm, as these production stills prove. The actors are Alan Ladd and George Peppard. Among others in the stills are director Edward Dmytryk (with pipe), operator Andrew "Duke" Callaghan (third from left in opposite photo), focus puller Dewey Wrigly, Jr., (far right in photo above), and mikeman Bud Parman (far left in opposite photo). The cameras are Mitchells.*

That's Entertainment, Part II (MGM, 1976; various ratios)
Billy Jack Goes to Washington (Taylor-Laughlin, 1977; Panavision)
A Bridge Too Far (UA, 1977; Panavision)
Close Encounters of the Third Kind (Col, 1977; Panavision)
Mohammad, Messenger of God (Tarik, 1977; Panavision)
Star Wars (20th-Fox, 1977; Panavision)
Capricorn One (WB, 1978; Panavision)
Days of Heaven (Par, 1978; Spherical Panavision)
The Deer Hunter (Univ, 1978; Panavision)
Grease (Par, 1978; Panavision)
The Manitou (Avco, 1978; Panavision)
Metamorphoses (Sanrio, 1978; Panavision)
The Punk Rock Movie (Cinematic, 1978; Todd-AO 35)
Sergeant Pepper's Lonely Hearts' Club Band (Univ, 1978; Panavision)
Superman (WB, 1978; Panavision)
Alien (20th-Fox, 1979; Panavision)
Apocalypse Now (UA, 1979; Technovision)
The Black Hole (BVD, 1979; Technovision)
The Black Stallion (UA, 1979; spherical 1.85 × 1)
The Champ (MGM, 1979; Spherical Panavision)

The filming of Lost Horizon. *Sally Kellerman (on dais, left) and Olivia Hussey (on dais, right) are being filmed with a Panavision R200 camera with Panavision anamorphics for blowup to 70mm. Director Charles Jarrott is on the extreme left. The focus puller, operator, stillman and other individuals are not known.*

The Exorcist (WB; reissue, 1979; Spherical Panavision)
Hanover Street (Col, 1979; Panavision)
Hurricane (Par, 1979; Todd-AO 35)
Moonraker (UA, 1979; Panavision)
The Muppet Movie (AFD, 1979; spherical)
1941 (Univ, 1979; Panavision)
The Rose (20th–Fox, 1979; Panavision)
Star Trek (Par, 1979; Panavision)
Winds of Change (Sanrio, 1979; Panavision)
Altered States (WB, 1980; Spherical Panavision)
The Blue Lagoon (Col, 1980; Spherical Panavision)
Can't Stop the Music (AFD, 1980; Panavision)
Close Encounters of the Third Kind (Col; special edition, 1980; Panavision)
Divine Madness (WB, 1980; Panavision)
The Empire Strikes Back (20th–Fox, 1980; Panavision)
Fame (MGM, 1980; Spherical Panavision)
Heaven's Gate (UA, 1980; Panavision)·
The Island (Univ, 1980; Panavision)
The Jazz Singer (AFD, 1980; Spherical Panavision)
Raise the Titanic! (AFD, 1980; Technovision)
Saturn 3 (AFD, 1980; spherical 1.85 × 1)
Tess (Col, 1980; Panavision)

Twinkle, Twinkle Killer Kane (UFD, 1980; Spherical Panavision)
Chariots of Fire (Ladd, 1981; spherical 1.66 × 1)
Dragonslayer (Par, 1981; Panavision)
Heaven's Gate (UA; reedited, 1981; Panavision)
Napoleon (Univ, 1981; Triptych)
Outland (Ladd, 1981; Panavision)
Raiders of the Lost Ark (Par, 1981; Panavision)
Sharkey's Machine (Orion, 1981; Spherical Panavision)
Superman II (WB, 1981; Panavision)
Wolfen (Orion, 1981; Panavision)
Zoot Suit (Univ, 1981; Spherical Panavision)
Annie (Col, 1982; Panavision)
Blade Runner (Ladd, 1982; Panavision)
Dance Craze (Nu-Image, 1982; spherical 1.85 × 1)
The Dark Crystal (Univ, 1982; Panavision)
Das Boot (The Boat; Col, 1982; Arriflex 1.66 × 1)
E.T. the Extra-Terrestrial (Univ, 1982; Spherical Panavision)
Firefox (WB, 1982; Panavision)
Gandhi (Col, 1982; Panavision)
Grease 2 (Par, 1982; Panavision)
One from the Heart (Col, 1982; Spherical Technovision)
Pink Floyd—The Wall (MGM/UA, 1982; Panavision)
Poltergeist (MGM/UA, 1982; J-D-C Scope)
Quest for Fire (20th-Fox, 1982; Panavision)
The Road Warrior (Mad Max II) (WB, 1982; Panavision)
Rocky III (MGM/UA, 1982; Spherical Panavision)
Star Trek II: The Wrath of Kahn (Par, 1982; Panavision)
Tempest (Col, 1982; Spherical Panavision)
Yes, Giorgio (MGM/UA, 1982; Spherical Panavision)
Blue Thunder (Col, 1983; Panavision)
The Keep (Par, 1983; Panavision)
Let's Spend the Night Together (Emb, 1983; Spherical Panavision)
Never Say Never Again (WB, 1983; Panavision)
Octopussy (MGM/UA, 1983; Panavision)
The Right Stuff (WB, 1983; Spherical Panavision)
Staying Alive (MGM/UA, 1983; Spherical Panavision)
Superman III (WB, 1983; Panavision)
War Games (MGM/UA, 1983; Spherical Panavision)
Amadeus (Orion, 1984; Panavision)
The Bear (Emb, 1984; Spherical Panavision)
City Heat (WB, 1984; Panavision)
The Cotton Club (Orion, 1984; Panavision)
Country (BVD, 1984; Spherical Panavision)
Dune (Univ, 1984; Todd-AO 35)
Ghostbusters (Col, 1984; Panavision)
Gremlins (WB, 1984; Spherical Panavision)
Greystoke the Legend of Tarzan Lord of the Apes (WB, 1984; Super Techniscope)
Indiana Jones and the Temple of Doom (Par, 1984; Panavision)
The Killing Fields (WB, 1984; spherical)
The Last Starfighter (Univ, 1984; Panavision)
The Neverending Story (WB, 1984; Technovision)
The Razor's Edge (Col, 1984; J-D-C Scope)

The River (Univ, 1984; Panavision)
Star Trek III: The Search of Spock (Par, 1984; Panavision)
Starman (Col, 1984; Panavision)
Streets of Fire (Univ, 1984; Spherical Panavision)
2010 (MGM/UA, 1984; Panavision)
Absolute Beginners (Orion, 1985; System 35)
American Flyers (WB, 1985; Panavision)
We Will Rock You (Swimmer, 1984; 1.33 × 1 to double from 70mm)
Baby ... Secret of the Lost Legend (BVD, 1985; Super Techniscope)
Back to the Future (Univ, 1985; Spherical Panavision)
A Chorus Line (Col, 1985; Panavision)
Cocoon (20th-Fox, 1985; Spherical Panavision)
The Emerald Forest (20th-Fox, 1985; Panavision)
Enemy Mine (20th-Fox, 1985; lenses by Arriflex [System 35?])
The Entity (20th-Fox, 1985; Panavision)
Explorers (Par, 1985; Ultracam 35)
The Goonies (WB, 1985; Panavision)
King David (Par, 1985; Panavision)
Ladyhawke (WB, 1985; Technovision)
The Last Dragon (WB, 1985; Spherical Panavision)
Lifeforce (Tri-Star, 1985; J-D-C Scope)
Mad Max Beyond Thunderdome (WB, 1985; Panavision)
Out of Africa (Univ, 1985; Spherical Technovision)
Pale Rider (WB, 1985; Panavision)
Rambo: First Blood Part II (Tri-Star, 1985; Panavision)
Return to Oz (BVD, 1985; spherical 1.85 × 1)
Rocky IV (MGM/UA, 1985; Spherical Panavision)
Santa Claus (Tri-Star, 1985; J-D-C Scope)
Silverado (Col, 1985; Super Techniscope)
Spies Like Us (WB, 1985; spherical 1.85 × 1)
Starchaser the Legend of Orin (Atlantic, 1985; over-and-under 3D)
A View to a Kill (MGM/UA, 1985; Panavision)
White Nights (Col, 1985; uncredited)
Year of the Dragon (MGM/UA, 1985; J-D-C Scope)
Young Sherlock Holmes (Par, 1985; Panavision)
The Adventures of Buckeroo Banzai Across the 8th Dimension (20th-Fox, 1986; Panavision)
Aliens (20th-Fox, 1986; Movicam 1.85 × 1)
Big Trouble in Little China (20th-Fox, 1986; Panavision)
The Clan of the Cave Bear (WB, 1986; Technovision)
Cobra (WB, 1986; Spherical Panavision)
The Fly (20th-Fox, 1986; Spherical Panavision)
Howard the Duck (Univ, 1986; Spherical Panavision)
Iron Eagle (Tri-Star, 1986; spherical 1.85 × 1)
Labyrinth (Tri-Star, 1986; J-D-C Scope)
Legal Eagles (Univ, 1986; Panavision)
Legend (Univ, 1986; Panavision)
The Money Pit (Univ, 1986; Spherical Panavision)
Poltergeist II: The Other Side (MGM, 1986; Panavision)
Star Trek IV (Par, 1986; Panavision)
Top Gun (Par, 1986; System 35)
Tough Guys (BVD, 1986; Panavision)

VII. Other Processes

This section is devoted to all those other systems, many just one-shot attempts, some only experimental, and others not processes at all but hype — gimmicks used in connection with a film or the name of equipment. We have tried to include all such items you are likely to run upon anywhere, but some tidbit may have escaped us. If so, surely something identical is already covered.

Further information on titles appearing in **boldface** in the following pages can be found in the Filmography.

AMP-O-Vision

A cropped wide screen system, presumably an enlarging lens, credited to Albert M. Pickus.

Anton Process Super-Vision 70

See Super-Vision.

Aquascope

According to one source this was a CinemaScope-type lens, or advertising name attached to such. Since this was applied only to a very low budget feature released by Roger Corman (*The Mermaids of Tiburon,* Filmgroup 1962), we suspect it was only publicity hype and not an anamorphic system at all.

AromaRama

Behind the Great Wall (Continental, 1959) showcased this scent-dispensing system, which was developed by Charles Weiss. During the film, 72 odors were expelled and withdrawn through the air conditioning ducts in sync with the film action. Unfortunately not everyone in the audience received the smells on cue, nor was it always possible to withdraw the aromas totally. Generally, however, the process was workable. *Behind the Great Wall* was the only feature that utilized the system in the United States. The Japanese feature *Baranokini baranohanssaku* (Daiei, 1960) may have been released in the Far East with the process; it was announced as an Aroma-Rama presentation, but information on whether it actually received the odor treatment was unavailable. AromaRama should not be confused with the far more complex Smell-O-Vision (q.v.).

Trade ad for AromaRama, a scent-dispensing system.

Artscope

Norman Maurer's process for making live action appear to be an animated cartoon. It was used for a brief scene in *The Three Stooges in Orbit* (Columbia, 1962). Basically it involved drawn sets, special costumes and makeup and negative printing of black-and-white film. A variation was called Cinemagic (q.v.).

Astrovision

Not a photographic process, but an aerial camera mounting system. The unit has been used with anamorphic lenses.

Automotion

A split-image traveling matte technique improved by Thomas Howard at MGM British Studios. The system wasn't new, but Howard's use of it during the late 1950s gave rise to the trade name and all sorts of majestic claims. It was certainly well rendered under his control but in fact was (and is) no more than blue screen optical photography.

Cinedome

See Hemispheric and Dome Systems.

Cinemagic

An interesting but very eye-straining effect used on *The Angry Red Planet* (American International, 1960). The Cinemagic scenes were all exterior shots of Mars and were shot in black-and-white. Special makeup, lighting, sets and costumes were utilized to keep shadows under control. The black-and-white footage was printed in negative with red replacing the gray scale. The effect was often startling and glaring and occasionally quite good. The eyestrain was, however, a tremendous drawback. The process was based on Norman Maurer's Artscope process (q.v.) in which live action was made to look like cartoon animation.

Cinetarium

See Hemispheric and Dome Systems.

Cycloramic Screen

The servicemark attached to the big screen presentations of **Portrait of Jennie** (Selznick, 1948), which employed the Magnascope enlarger to expand the hurricane sequence over as wide a screen as the theater could install. Needless to say the ratio was variable from theater to theater.

Dinovision

The name applied to the spherical (hard matted at 1.66×1) format used on a number of Spanish special effects pictures. Actually a manner of simultaneously shooting miniatures and live action with long lenses to avoid matte work, it is often very effective.

Dynamagic

An attempt by American International to attract fans of Dynamation (q.v.) to *Master of the World* (1961) with a similar trade name attached to the special effects scenes.

Dynamation

Ray Harryhausen's perfected "sandwich matte" technique, first called Electrolitic Dynamation when used in black-and-white and shortened to Dynamation when applied to color photography. It was renamed Super-dynamation when the blue screen optical photography technique was replaced by Rank's yellow screen (sodium light) process. It was called Dynamation 90 (reason unknown) for one feature, then returned to just Dynamation after the Rank traveling matte system was discarded. It is now called Dynarama, but nothing has changed in the way the system is used. At one point the trade name Giant Panamation was to be applied (Panavision anamorphics were to be used), but the name was dropped when the film on which the term was to be attached was shot spherical.

Dynamation 90

See Dynamation.

Dynarama

See Dynamation.

Ecosphere

See Hemispheric and Dome Systems.

Electrolitic Dynamation

See Dynamation.

Electronovision Theatrofilm

A hi-band video system in which regular multi-camera television production techniques are applied to feature production. The videotape, edited "in camera," was converted to film. The results were amazingly good but the image was black-and-white. It was used on *Hamlet* (Warner Bros., 1964) and *Harlow* (Magna, 1965). Color tape-to-film technology quickly replaced it. (At least one other film using a similar system was made in the 1960s, but information is unavailable regarding it, other than that Donald E. Davison was producer and director.)

Electrorama

A color video system from which Technicolor made 35mm release prints. It was used on *The Big T.N.T. Show* in 1966.

Emergo

Not a photographic process but a physical gimmick rigged in a few

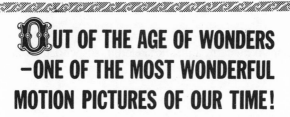

OUT OF THE AGE OF WONDERS
—ONE OF THE MOST WONDERFUL
MOTION PICTURES OF OUR TIME!

filmed in

DYNAMATION !

THE 8th WONDER OF THE WORLD!

THE
**7th VOYAGE
OF SINBAD**

SEE Sinbad in the clutch of the two-headed Roc!

SEE Princess Parisa in the palm of her lover!

SEE the chained Dragon unleashed!

SEE the murderous Skeleton stalking Sinbad!

DYNAMATION Technicolor®

starring **KERWIN MATHEWS · KATHRYN GRANT**
co-starring **RICHARD EYER** as THE GENIE with **TORIN THATCHER**
Written by KENNETH KOLB · Visual Effects Created by RAY HARRYHAUSEN
Produced by CHARLES H. SCHNEER · Directed by NATHAN JURAN
A MORNINGSIDE PRODUCTION · A COLUMBIA PICTURE

Dynamation was, and is, a "sandwich matte" technique, but it is now called Dynarama.

theaters for *House on Haunted Hill* (Allied Artists, 1958). As a continuation of a scene in the film, a plastic skeleton, suspended from wires, would float over the audience.

Fantamation
Another trade name applied to the same sandwich matting technique used for Dynamation (q.v.). It was credited on *The Crater Lake Monster* (1977).

Futurevision 360
A gimmick system unveiled in 1986 at a trade demonstration. The process used Panavision photographic lenses, presumably spherical, and Orc/Isco projection lenses.

Garutso Balanced Lenses
The clearest, sharpest lenses ever used in the film industry. Each lens was made up of two lenses, each focusing within a different visual field. The unit had to be focused for both fields, but the result was a multi-plane image of incredible depth. Indeed, Garutso-shot features were often advertised with the catchline "Filmed with Garutso Balanced Lenses for 3-Dimensional Effect." When scenes were staged to take advantage of the lens's capacity the resulting screen image was often astonishing. In the late 1950s the name was changed to Garutso Plastorama and applied to some West German features. The lenses were used in the United States from the late 1940s to the mid-1950s.

Garutso Plastorama
See Garutso Balanced Lenses.

Giantscope
See Super 1.85.

Glamorama
The trade name applied by advertising executive Douglas Leigh to the 10-perf horizontal 35mm Fearless Super Picture process (see Chapter I).

Hemispheric and Dome Systems
Septorama (seven screens), Ecosphere (70mm), Cinetarium (by Adalbert Baltes), Vista-Dome (by Jim Handy), Cinedome, and Polycran are some of the names applied to novelty films made for world fairs, international exhibitions, traveling fairs and such. These often are multi-camera films or single films projected into domes or curved screens. They are occasionally ingenious but never anything meant for use beyond their specialty showings.

Holography

One of the great myths of film technology. All holographic films exhibited at fairs, theme parks, etc., are not really holographic displays at all but just special projection techniques, usually involving silver-specked glass (the silver particles pick up the projected image, which can be viewed from any side). True holography cannot be applied to motion picutres, and all claims about the future of movies riding on the development of such is pure fantasy. Holography is no more than an optical illusion and probably will never be applicable to stereoscopic filmmaking. (True 3D film systems have already been perfected, accepted by the public, and destroyed by the theater operators.)

HypnoMagic

Nothing more than a spinning wheel effect used on *The Hypnotic Eye* (Allied Artists, 1960) to suggest to the audience that they could be mesmerized by looking at it. Not a photographic, or any other, process at all.

Hypnovision

"Warning! Unlike Anything Before! You Are Surrounded by Monsters! Not 3-D but Real FLESH-and-BLOOD Monsters!" And so it was. During certain scenes (and of course in certain theaters only), when a spiraling, mesmerizing wheel would appear on screen, theater personnel wearing masks like the makeups in the film (well, close to 'em) would run through the audience with fake axes. This was great fun for kids. The film was *The Incredibly Strange Creatures Who Stopped Living and Became Mixed-Up Zombies* (1964).

Ikegami EC-35

A video camera that gives tape the look of 35mm film. It operates like and has the same accessories as 35mm cameras.

Illusion-O

A photographic gimmick devised by William Castle and created by Butler-Glouner, Inc., for *13 Ghosts* (Columbia, 1960). The process was simple and almost effective. A mono-color ghost was printed over the black-and-white scene. The audience was given duo-color viewers. When they looked through one side the ghost became visible; through the other the ghost was invisible. (Actually the color saturation was such on the prints that the ghosts were not totally neutralized by the viewer's colored cell.) This is often referred to as being a stereoscopic process. It was, even though it wasn't meant to be. The ghosts did appear to float free of the other screen action, and when viewed through duo-color 3D glasses, the film took on all the characteristics of the stereoscopic process.

MagnaScope

A two-perf system meant for use with Super-Vision projection lenses.

The Ikegami EC-35 video camera.

The idea, so far applied on some foreign features yet to be released in the United States, is to use the Techniscope format but print as is instead of going to four-perf anamorphic. Thus there is a 50 percent savings all down the line. In addition, the MagnaScope process could be obtained by 16mm anamorphic photography which would be decompressed, slightly cropped on the sides and printed with very slight blowup (none if the 2.74 × 1 ratio was kept) onto two-perf 35mm. Super 16 could also be used with only the most minor blowup required. The system, extremely practical and inexpensive, has been ignored totally in the United States.

Metroscan
The trade name applied by MGM Laboratories to their pan-and-scan system for converting 2.35 × 1 anamorphic films to 1.37 × 1 spherical format.

Metroscope
This spherical system was no more than the hard matting of a 1.66 × 1 or 1.75 × 1 frameline by MGM Laboratories onto the release print. Oddly, in the mid-1960s, the trade name appeared on a couple of MGM's 'scope releases, including the Hammer production *She* (advertised in CinemaScope, but shot in Hammerscope), which carried an attractive curved-screen–type logo on the U.S. prints' screen credits. But despite the application of the name Metroscope to a few anamorphic releases, it never was a lens system.

Metroscope 70
Not a process any more than was Metroscope (q.v.), this was simply the blowing up of spherical 35mm to 70mm widescreen by MGM Labs.

Metrovision

Despite what you've read elsewhere, this was not the trade name applied by MGM to cropped wide screen (see Metroscope). Metrovision Tri-Dee was the studio's 3D system.

Mexiscope

The trade name applied in Mexico to films framed for cropping. Despite the fact that the name and an attractive logo often appear in screen credits, it is not an anamorphic system. Unlike prints from other countries, which more often than not hard-matte a wide frameline on films to be shown cropped, Mexiscope prints are always full image area. This avoids reframing problems when 16mm prints are struck. (Most cinemas in Central and South America are 16mm).

MiracleVision

The trademark used by one independent producer, Donald E. Davidson, for duo-color 3D, even though his publicity material stated it was something along the lines of Super Cinerama and 3D combined. The system was actually a duo-color lens from F & B/Ceco used to shoot inserts to *She Freak* so that it could be reissued as *Asylum of the Insane* (Lion-Dog Films, 1971).

Mitchell System 35

Standard 35mm Mitchell cameras employed in the manner of live video production: i.e., each operator is in touch with the director via earphones and the action is "cut in the camera" during shooting. While this was advertised on *Stop the World—I Want to Get Off* (WB, 1966), it is not a photographic process at all, but simply a production technique.

MobileVision

A large format system developed by Saul Swimmer for use in large auditoriums instead of presenting a live concert. It has been used on the feature *We Will Rock You* (1984). The process uses regular 35mm in photography and blows it up over two 70mm frames. This blowup is projected onto a gigantic screen in a 1.33 × 1 aspect ratio. The 70mm projectors have to be modified to run twice as fast due to the double frame size. The sound system is magnetic interlock with eight channels. A double frame 70mm version for photography has been announced.

Monstascope

This was simply a spherical film, meant for 1.85 × 1 cropping, given a wider look ... well, wider in the advertising, not on the screen.

Moviecam

Even though the credit "Filmed in Moviecam" has appeared in advertising and screen credits, it is not a special process but an overall camera

Monstascope existed more in the minds of the advertisers than on the screen.

system similar to other lightweight, low noise, compact units. There are no Moviecam anamorphics, but the cameras have been employed with Technovision lenses.

Mysti-Mation

An incredibly effective and very complex system for making a film appear to be a woodblock carving. It was first used on *The Fabulous World of Jules Verne* (Warner Bros., 1961) in black-and-white and then with color tints on other Czechoslovakian features made by Karel Zeman. It was a photographic process but also involved all phases of physical production mounting. (On the screen credits it is spelled as above, but on advertising it was rendered as Mystimation.)

Norwayscope

Not a photographic system but a special, all-purpose projection system that supposedly allowed 8mm, 16mm and 35mm to be handled by one machine. The anamorphic lens employed was of the variable compression, prism type.

Odorama

Despite the "Filmed in Odorama" credit, the system was not an interlocked process at all. It was a "scratch-and-sniff" card with numbered odors that were to be sniffed when the corresponding number appeared in the corner of the screen. This inexpensive and fun gimmick was used on John Water's "underground classic" *Polyester* (New Line Cinema, 1981). Not to be confused with AromaRama or Smell-O-Vision (q.v.).

Panacam

Panavision's "ultimate experience in electronic cinematography." This video unit is not for theatrical use but is meant to give a film look to videotape. It has been employed on a number of television productions.

Panaflex

Not a special lens system, but the name of Panavision's most popular lightweight camera unit. The company calls it the Rolls Royce of Cameras.

Panaglide

See Steadicam.

Panastar

One of several cameras made by Panavision.

Panoram

A French 16mm camera by Eclair that converts from 16mm to Super 16 for blowup to 35mm 1.66 × 1 spherical widescreen. Eclair refers to it as Caméra Bi-Format 16 + Super 16 "Varigate."

Panorama Cinevision

Cropped wide screen trade name used by Shiga in Japan.

Panoramic Screen

The early name applied by Paramount to their cropped films.

Paravision

Sometimes referred to as ParaVision or Para-Vision, this is generally given as the servicemark applied by Paramount Pictures to their cropped

The Odorama "scratch-and-sniff" card. (The two photos above show front and back of the two-sided card.) Audiences loved this goofy gimmick, but it was never used again after its debut in Polyester.

wide screen (see Panoramic Screen), but Paravision was actually the name of their 3D system.

Percepto
An amusing mechanical gimmick utilized in some theaters for *The Tingler* (Columbia, 1959) by which a slight electrical shock or vibration was sent to selected seats during a sequence in the movie where the Tingler escaped in a theater.

Perceptovision
A catch name applied by Bert I. Gordon to his special photographic effects, which were nothing new or unusual.

Perfect Tone
One source gives this as a Swiss cropped wide screen enlarging lens by Jean Jacques Bessire, but the name seems to be that of a sound system. It is included here for the record.

The Panaflex camera unit.

Photorama

Presumably an enlarging lens by Robert Hanover for cropping spherical films to wide screen ratio(s).

Plastorama

See Garutso Balanced Lenses.

Polycran

See Hemispheric and Dome Systems.

Polyvision

Abel Gance's trade name applied to multiple images appearing in the same frame. It was not a wide screen process in any way.

Psychorama

The so-called Precon Process was in fact no more than the superimposing of words or images over scenes for a split second (usually four frames) to suggest subconscious feelings, generally of fear or disgust. The Psychorama moniker was advertised on two low-budget horror features, *My World Dies Screaming* (a.k.a. *Terror in the Haunted House*) and *A Date with Death,* but the technique has been utilized on other films, notably *The Exorcist.* It has also been attempted in television commercials and rock videos. A similar process of barely audible sound effects has also been tried. The effectiveness of these subconscious cues is extremely debatable, but the FCC has banned their use with TV even though the ban has been ignored by rock video makers.

ScenicScope

The term used by RKO Radio for cropped wide screen in 1.66 × 1 to 1.85 × 1 ratio.

Septorama

See Hemispheric and Dome Systems.

Showscan

Douglas Trumbull's much-publicized 70mm system photographs and projects at 60 frames per second, twice the original Todd-AO speed and two and a half times standard film rate. This speed was decided upon supposedly because it is the highest rate practical without causing extensive wear on photographic and projection equipment (which still must be substantially modified) and it completely eliminates optical strobing. (For example, wagon wheels do not appear to be turning in reverse in Showscan, while they do in all other photographic processes.) The image size was originally full 70mm (2.072″ × 0.906″) and release prints were not soundtracked. Audio utilized 35mm magnetic film with six tracks feeding right, center and left screen information plus surround and subwoofer noises. Recent prints have jettisoned the interlock format for standard six-track magnetic sound-on-film with a standard 70mm ratio picture. Projection is onto a slightly curved, unmasked screen very similar to CinemaScope's early Magic Mirror screens. The first two Showscan shorts were made specially for Showbiz Piazza locations and were shot with modified Ultra Panavision 70 cameras sans the Ultra-Panatar anamorphics. Recent films, made for special venue engagements, have utilized a newly constructed camera patterned after the Panaflex 35mm units made by Panavision. Showscan has also been used in concert with activated seats that react to the screen image. As of this writing Showscan Film Corporation has gone public and a feature production is being planned.

Made in Showscan so far are the following films:

New Magic	1984
Big Ball	1984

Let's Go	1985
Deep Sea Rescue	1986*
Tour of the Universe	1986*
Night of Dreams	1986
Earthwatch	1986
Discovery	1986
Rollercoaster	1986*
Alpine Thrills	1986*
Chevrolet 75th Anniversary	1986
Niagara Wonders	1987
Kiwi Experience	1987

*presented in Dynamic Motion in which the theater seats move in relation to the action on the screen to simulate audience participation in the filmed events.

Sin*ascope

The most exciting process ever invented? Sin*ascope (sic) was nothing but hype. The 1959 comedy *Happy Anniversary* was shot spherical for cropped wide screen presentation.

Smell-O-Vision

Prof. Hans Laube, a world famous osmologist, developed a system for clearing the air of large auditoriums in the thirties. He reasoned that the technology could be applied in reverse to *add* aromas and created Scentovision, Inc., to market the device. The Swiss government utilized the process with a short novelty film, the title and subject of which has long been forgotten, at the 1939 New York World's Fair. Laube continued to make a very good living with his air-cleaning system until he was contracted by Michael Todd, Jr., to provide the technology for *Scent of Mystery*.

Smell-O-Vision, as Todd renamed the process (much to Laube's displeasure — he felt it cheapened the system, but Todd thought it was funny), involved a complex mechanical arrangement that dispensed 30 different odors into the theater and then sucked them back. Each theater seat was rigged so that all in the audience received the smells simultaneously. The length of time each odor remained was determined by the action on the screen. The Smell-O-Vision device operated in sync with the film, controlled by electronic cues encoded in the soundtrack.

In addition to its use in **Scent of Mystery,** the process was utilized with the companion animated short, **The Tale of Old Whiff,** which employed fourteen of the aromas.

It should be noted that attempts to put smells into theaters had been made in the 1920s, both for movies and stage plays. The technique was always the same: Spray the auditorium with a scent. These attempts involved no special technology and were always limited to one aroma. In the case of movies, such attempts were never the intention or recommendation of the studios; rather they represented rare creativity on the part of theater owners.

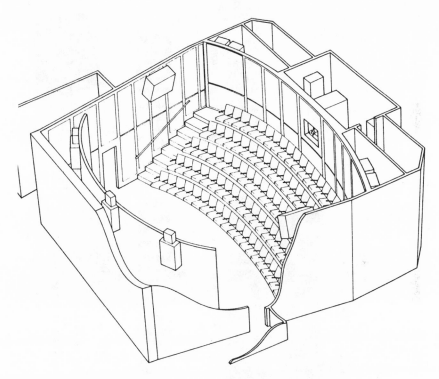

Above: *Diagram of a Showbiz Piazza Palace Showscan SuperCinema. Fewer than half a dozen were built.* Opposite, top left: *Showscan frames from* New Magic. Top right: *The same scene in 1.85 × 1 35mm spherical widescreen. Neither film has been soundtracked.* Bottom left: *The new Showscan camera, which has obviously been modelled after the Panaflex.* Bottom right: *The Showscan logo.*

The Smell-O-Vision system is not to be confused with Aromarama or Odorama (q.v.).

Spacevision

(Also known as Space-Vision Tri-Optiscope, Trioptiscope, Tru-D and SpaceVision.) Col. Robert V. Brenier's over-and-under wide screen 3D system.

SpectaMation

Trade name applied by Herman Cohen to the special photo effects seen in his films. Nothing new.

Spectrum X

A trade name applied by Independent International Pictures to a number of films in which black-and-white footage was tinted and intercut with color scenes. The effect of the tinting ranged from excellent to tacky.

FIELDS PRODUCTIONS Presents

Happy Anniversary

The Motion Picture Dedicated To The Proposition!

THRU UA

DAVID NIVEN · MITZI GAYNOR

co-starring

CARL REINER · LORING SMITH · MONIQUE VAN VOOREN · PHYLLIS POVAH and PATTY DUKE

Screenplay by JOSEPH FIELDS and JEROME CHODOROV · Based on their play "Anniversary Waltz" · Music by SOL KAPLAN and ROBERT ALLEN

Songs: "I Don't Regret A Thing" and "Happy Anniversary" Music by ROBERT ALLEN · Lyrics by AL STILLMAN · Directed by DAVID MILLER

Produced by RALPH FIELDS. A Fields Productions, Inc. Presentation

THE FIRST COMEDY FILMED IN IN·ASCOPE THE MOST EXCITING PROCESS EVER INVENTED

FIRST (1893) They Moved.

THEN (1927) They Talked

NOW (1959) They Smell

MICHAEL TODD, Jr.
presents

SCENT OF
MYSTERY

IN GLORIOUS

SMELL-O-VISION

The Process of all Processes

Scent of Mystery *and its companion animated short,* The Tale of Old Whiff, *were the only films to use the Smell-O-Vision scent-dispensing process.*

Spherical Panavision

Cropped wide screen shot with Panavision cameras and/or spherical Panavision lenses. "Filmed in Spherical Panavision" appeared on European credits in the early 1970s, but now it is more common to see "Filmed

Opposite: *It may have been the most ridiculous name ever conceived for advertising hype, but Sin*ascope was not a special process at all.*

in Panavision" or "Panaflex Cameras and Lenses by Panavision" in screen titles. Needless to say this is a most confusing situation since Panavision was so long associated with anamorphic lenses. It is rather ironic to see the Panavision credit on many television shows, especially those from Lorimar-Telepictures, which simply have the word Panavision in the technical billing.

Steadicam
Not a photographic process but a hand-held, vibration-eliminating camera rig developed by Garrett Brown. The unit was offered to Panavision, who rejected it and then produced their own version, called Panaglide.

Stereocolor
A color and wide screen process by Dr. R.E. Schensted. A color wheel was used to separate the three colors. The aspect ratio given is 2.44 × 1, but it is unknown how the wide screen shape was achieved — via cropping, wide gauge (the system was supposedly 35mm) or anamorphics. It was never applied to a film.

Super 1.85
The technique of photographing over the full frame area (including soundtrack space) and then reducing to regular 35mm. The system has been used for years in optical photography and saw brief employment in the 1950s as Giantscope.

Super Panoramascope
Supposedly a 70mm Todd-AO format process employed on **Panorama Blue,** but we seriously question the existence of the system. We suspect it was a blowup from 35mm, if indeed any 70mm prints were ever made.

Super-Vision
The full name is Anton Process Super-Vision 70. This is a projection lens developed by Evan J. Anton which allows Super 8 to be thrown onto a 16mm-size screen (rather pointless since Super 8 lenses are superior to 16mm and fill a larger area on the screen anyway), 16mm to cover the same area as 35mm spherical (1.85 × 1 ratio) and spherical 35mm (cropped) to cover the full 2.35 × 1 'scope or larger (so-called 70mm) screen. It supposedly allows up to a 180-degree curvature without distortion. It is not a camera lens, though it could be used as one. Its companion process is MagnaScope. Super-Vision is not the same as Supervision (q.v.).

Supervision
This was credited on *Ironmaster* (American National Enterprises, 1983), an Italian and French coproduction. It apparently was no more than a hard matte 1.66 × 1 format and is not to be confused with Super-Vision (q.v.).

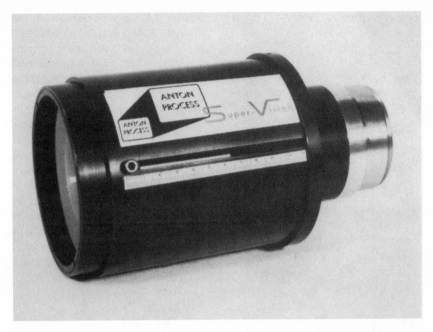

The Anton Process Super-Vision 70 (or simply "Super-Vision") projection lens.

Super VistaVision
See Cinema 160.

Superdynamation
See Dynamation.

Supra Motion
This appears to be nothing but an advertising come-on.

Thomascolor
A 1942 color process by Richard Thomas, supposedly shot in 65mm. No features used the system.

3D
There are numerous stereoscopic processes in use worldwide. Of particular interest to the reader are the names Stereovision 70, Stereo 70 and 70mm Triarama, all trade names applied to the Jacobsen system controlled by Munchener Filmtheaterbesellschaft. A 70mm camera is utilized with 2 × 1 anamorphics to render a side-by-side squeezed 3D 'scope print in 2 × 1 aspect ratio. The sound format is four-track magnetic with the audio stripes appearing only on the outside of the frame. The full frame is used for picture except for a "dark bar" center vertical frame. Three features have been shot with the system and two, **Love in 3-D** and **Frankenstein's Bloody**

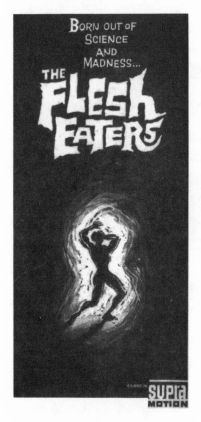

Supra Motion ad.

Terror, have been exhibited in the United States optically converted to 35mm over-and-under format. The latter film was also released stateside in 2.35×1 anamorphic 35mm. Two United States companies offer the system for use, but so far it has been ignored in America. The Soviets have a similar system, also called Stereofilm, which is basically the same except a 1.33×1 image is rendered without anamorphics and the image size of the stereo pairs is slightly smaller. The Soviet format has been used in the United States by StereoVision International under the trademark StereoVision 70.

Tri-Ergon

The name of a German company and apparently the name applied to both their optical sound system and a 42mm wide screen format used on a demo film, title unknown though also called *Tri-Ergon* by one source, shown in 1924 in New York.

Trioptiscope

See Spacevision.

Tru-D

See Spacevision.

Ultracam 35

This is not a special process but a camera system owned by Leonetti Cine Rentals. There are no Ultracam 35 anamorphics, but the cameras have been used on several features with J-D-C Scope.

UltraVision

Developed by Wil-Kin, Inc., this was a 70mm Super Cinerama–type projection system. It involved a floor-to-ceiling, wall-to-wall, deeply curved screen with a unique means of throwing the picture evenly over the full screen area: The film was projected and focused onto a large mirror in the booth and the mirror reflected the picture onto the screen. This actually

The Ultracam 35 camera.

worked amazingly well (a variation was employed with Cinemiracle and is fairly standard practice in the Soviet Union), but almost, if not all, of the UltraVision theaters have been multiplexed and the system is no longer utilized. A mirror bouncing system is employed, considerably less effectively, in many theaters today, but these units and their flat 2×1 (and usually lesser width) screens bear no resemblance to UltraVision. Development engineers E.H. Geissler and Glen M. Berggren received a 1972 Scientific or Technical Award, Class III, from the Academy of Motion Picture Arts and Sciences for UltraVision. (The Oscar citation was displayed in Atlanta at the first UltraVision theater until the mid-1970s, when that theater was duplexed. Officially UltraVision ceased to exist at that time.)

UltraVision is also the name of an equipment supplier in Hollywood. The occasional screen credit *Cameras and Lenses by UltraVision* refers to them. (The name was temporarily applied to the Dimension 3 stereoscopic wide screen process but was dropped after the projection system trademark was discovered to be registered.)

Uraniscope

A European wide screen system, presumably CinemaScope-compatible, though the process may be no more than cropped spherical.

Variscope

MGM's spherical system in which films were shot allowing for projection in any ratio to 1.75×1. The Soviets also have a technique under the same name (see Kinopanorama).

An impressive May 1953 trade ad from Universal-International. Wide-Vision was
actually 1.85×1 cropping and had been used on a number of features prior to
Thunder Bay. *However this was the first film of the fifties actually photographed*
allowing for cropping and was meant to be shown on a curved screen up to 2×1
ratio.

VastVision
Republic's trade name, applied to cropped wide screen between
1.66×1 and 1.85×1.

Wondra-Scope was not an anamorphic process, but a hype term for special effects.

Vista-Dome
See Hemispheric and Dome Systems.

Vitarama
See Chapter II.

VitaScope
Not to be confused with the Warner Bros. 65mm process (see Chapter I), this was no more than cropped spherical.

Widescope
A 1921 process developed by George W. Bingham in which double-width film was exposed with a twin-lens camera, the film split and then projected by two machines. A demo film was produced, but the system was pointless and never used commercially. (See Thrillarama.) The Widescope name also appeared in the 1960s on at least one Italian feature shot in 2.35×1 anamorphic format.

Wide-Vision
A servicemark used first by Universal-International, then by MGM, 20th Century–Fox and others, to indicate cropped wide screen.

Wondra-Scope

This was not an anamorphic process or any other kind of system. Basically it was hype for the special effects scenes. Oddly, the prints were released in two formats: 1.33×1 for cropping and 1.85×1 hard matte. It was also printed by Technicolor, a rarity for MGM releases, which almost always employed Metrocolor regardless of the screen or advertising billing.

VIII. Special Sound Processes

Stereophonic and directional sound movies are not new. Experimentation had been conducted in the 1920s (and very probably much earlier) by all the major audio firms. You might be tempted to ask, "Why did it take so long to develop?" But you must keep in mind that the film industry was and is controlled by men whose main objective is to make money as cheaply as possible. Of course the less you offer the less expense there is. But while this stupidity controls the minds of the producing executives, it is pure genius next to the thinking of the theatermen (exhibitors) and unions.

Theatermen have never been motivated to improve their houses and presentations except in dire straits, and then it was usually too late. They have never showed inclination toward invention. They fought sound, they fought color, they did all in their power to ignore 3D and wide screen, and they plain sabotaged stereophonic sound. They found a fast ally in IATSE, who officially took the stand that stereo sound was unwanted by the public, useless, troublesome, and to be avoided at all costs. Their magazine, *International Projectionist,* approached stereo with a vileness and hatred that Chancellor Hitler would have envied. Stereo-equipped theaters would receive stereo prints and the booth operators would deliberately run them monaurally. (This happens today with stereo optical sound, which involves no additional effort on the projectionist's part except flipping a switch!)

In the 1950s, interlocked magnetic stereo and MagOptical stereo fell immediate victims to the terrorism of organized labor. So did Perspecta. (See Magnetic Sound and Perspecta in this chapter.) Since the theater owners had no love for any improvement, they were overjoyed by their united front against stereo. They had managed to destroy 3D (admittedly with help from the producers), but had lost the wide screen war. Defeating stereo was at least some consolation. They had to put in wider screens, but as sure as the sun shines they were not going to put out more money to have decent sound systems. As always the paying customer was robbed.

Only in very recent years has this exhibitor attitude changed ever so slightly. Still the vast majority of theatermen are as dead-set against stereo sound as ever. They install it only in their "showcase" houses, and then only because of industry pressure. The power of some producers — notably George Lucas — has been the only reason theatrical stereo sound survives today. Video cassette recorders, with their hi-fi stereo capacity, have put

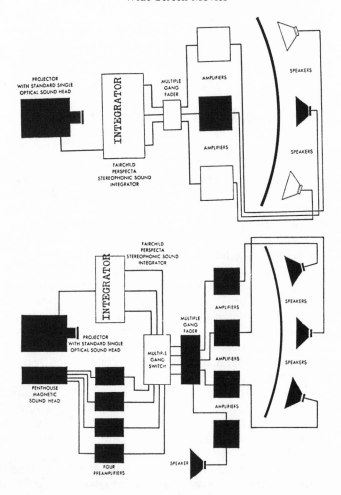

Drawings showing the introduction of stereophonic sound to an existing theater mono audio system: The top drawing shows in dark the original sound reproduction layout and equipment. The light items are those needed to convert the theater to Perspecta Stereophonic Sound. The bottom sketch shows the layout of a theater with MagOptical Stereophonic Sound (including surround), shown in dark, with the needed items for Perspecta Stereophonic Sound shown in light. The Penthouse Magnetic Sound Head was actually an add-on part of the projector, not a separate item, but is shown here detached because it was auxiliary to existing mono equipment.

such a dent into theater attendance that video rentals now exceed theater tickets sold. Beta Hi-Fi and VHS Hi-Fi Stereo are actually better than theater sound; dbx MTS (multiple television sound, q.v.) stereo has also demonstrated that TV can sound better than theaters. Exhibitors can't understand why anyone would rather watch a clear, bright video picture with excellent stereo sound than go to their small-screen cinemas and watch a very dark, cropped movie in poor mono sound. But then they didn't understand why people wanted to hear sound in theaters in the late 1920s ... or preferred color over black-and-white ... or liked those wide screens ....

Further information on film titles appearing in **boldface** in the following pages can be found in the Filmography.

Belock 8-Channel Sound

Also known as Todd-Belock, this eight-channel system was magnetic six-track sound-on-film. It was engineered by Todd-AO using Westrex equipment and provided five screen channels (right, right center, center, left center and left) and three surround channels (right wall, left wall and rear wall). Apparently the surround information was encoded with Perspecta directional cues. (See Cinestage Sound.) One feature and a short utilized the system, both released in 1960 by the Michael Todd company:

Scent of Mystery (feature)   Mixers: Joseph I. Kane and Fred
                                                         Hynes

The Tale of Old Whiff   Mixer: Fred Hynes
(short)

CinemaScope Sound

See Magnetic and MagOptical Stereophonic Sound.

Cinemiracle Sound

A seven-track magnetic stereo interlocked format employed on the feature *Windjammer*. The system employed solid state RCA recording and playback equipment and was compatible with Cinerama Sound.

Cinerama Sound

The Cinerama sound system utilized interlocked magnetic tracks on a separate 35mm film recorded and reproduced with Westrex equipment. Depending on the feature, six or seven tracks were employed. In the case of *Seven Wonders of the World,* eight channels of sound were derived from seven tracks by incorporation of a Perspecta-type tone shifter which converted the seventh track into two different channels. With the introduction of 70mm Super Cinerama, Westrex six-track magnetic sound-on-film was utilized.

Cinestage Sound

This MagOptical system (see Magnetic and MagOptical Stereophonic Sound) was used on some 35mm prints of **Around the World in 80 Days.** Three tracks fed right, center and left screen speakers, and the fourth track fed surround information right wall, left wall or rear, or all three simultaneously by use of Perspecta (q.v.) encoding.

Cyclophonic Sound

A special audio expanding system utilized for some engagements of

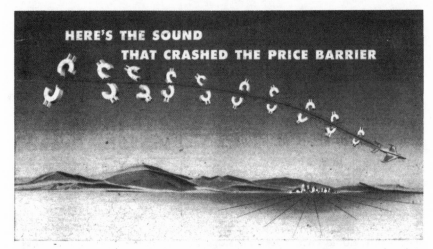

HERE'S THE SOUND
THAT CRASHED THE PRICE BARRIER

RCA now presents the lowest priced
QUALITY STEREOPHONIC SOUND

For the first time ever . . . here is a quality stereophonic sound system—built to let the small- and medium-sized theatre enjoy the increased grosses of the new types of films . . . on a rock-bottom budget.

Through a brand-new, dual-cone speaker design—through important manufacturing economies—RCA can offer many exclusive RCA design features—many items now in use in the largest houses—to the theatre that must operate on a small budget.

Developed specifically for RCA's new "Smaller-Theatre" line, is the all-new, reflex-baffle speaker . . . a true, wide-range, big-power speaker for houses up to 1200 seats. In this speaker you'll find RCA has again put its vast facilities and technical background to work . . . to bring you quality at a low, low price.

For the finest in stereophonic sound, equip your house with RCA's superb Stereo-scope Sound, including:

- **RCA BUTTON-ON SOUNDHEAD**
  utilizing the soft-loop system for flutter-free sound

- **RCA AUDIO-SYNC AMPLIFIERS**
  for complete operator convenience, most faithful reproduction

- **RCA EXPONENTIAL-FLARE SPEAKERS**
  for complete coverage in any type of house

 THEATRE EQUIPMENT
RADIO CORPORATION of AMERICA
ENGINEERING PRODUCTS　　　　　**CAMDEN, N.J.**
In Canada: RCA VICTOR Company Limited, Montreal

Here and on facing page, two ads touting stereophonic sound systems.

Portrait of Jennie (Selznick, 1948; mixers, Don McKay, Fred Hynes). The process involved surround sound. During the hurricane segment the screen enlarged to fill the stage area (or at least was supposed to, but screens varied in size and shape from house to house) and the sound filled the auditorium. The system apparently was a version of Vitasound (q.v.). It was not an interlock process but was stereophonic in that dialog did not shift into the surround speakers. It was developed under the supervision of James L. Stewart.

Digital Sound

Perhaps the most heralded recent sound achievement has been digital. Home video, compact discs, and now movies are boasting this new process. Digital, however, is an extremely overused term and possibly an overrated technology. Radios, tape and video decks and all sorts of other consumer items claim they are digital. In fact, most have only the LED readout in anything approaching digital format. As for "digital sound," it also falls short of what the public assumes it is, and far short of what the manufacturers market it as. While many videocassettes bear the "digitally mastered" catchline, the actual soundtrack(s) are standard Beta Hi-Fi and VHS Hi-Fi format derived from a digitally rerecorded (and occasionally remixed) original source. Audio reproduction on the home level is not digital at all, nor is the actual soundtrack. The results most often are not even as good as normal Hi-Fi video masters. The digital mastering does eliminate all noise, but it also clips consonances, flattens the spatial effect of most music, deadens extreme bass and generally renders a soundtrack that lacks the dramatic scope of normal Hi-Fi. Digital sound may be perfect sound, but the human voice, music instruments and nature fail to produce perfection. Digital mastering rather than improving upon what is there, more often than not just "cleans up" the audio, and by so doing destroys the very effectiveness it is supposed to enhance. Still, digital sound is here to stay, and once more a "perfect technology" is being accepted by the public regardless of its imperfections. As with most technologies, the future is bright for digital. With its wide acceptance and eventual use throughout all phases of sound recording and reproduction, it will become an advantage instead of the (general) liability it now is.

In digital sound within the theatrical film, there are even more problems to overcome than on the home video level. (Numerous VCRs can actually record and reproduce digital sound, but not with a video picture. They work only as audio recorders-reproducers. Probably in the next few years the ability to have both digital sound *and* picture image will evolve.) While the cost of home video equipment may be increased only 50 percent or so, the cost of converting a cinema to handle true digital sound reproduction will run into the many thousands of dollars and require complete replacement of all existing speakers and wiring. Additionally, to produce dramatic soundtracks that aren't plagued with "clipping," it will be necessary to do all original recording in digital. The cost of such will skyrocket feature sound and postproduction budgets. Release prints, too, will cost more, and theater ticket prices will immediately show the difference. Sadly, the results probably are not going to be worth the difference to most cinema patrons. Nevertheless, it can be expected that by the end of this century, digital sound will be a theater standard in most, if not all, larger cities, probably completely replacing stereo optical. As of this writing, three features, the reworked *Fantasia* (BVD, 1984), *Robocop* and *Throw Momma from the Train* (both Orion, 1987), have already had extremely limited (fewer than twenty total) theatrical engagements in digital sound, and a short made in collaboration by Glen Glenn Sound, Eastman Kodak and others has been shown in some areas. The major studios are not overlooking digital sound, with Disney, MGM and others now producing digital masters on part or all their films for future use. Disney is currently utilizing digital sound on all Disneyland and Disney World/EPCOT film presentations. Dolby Laboratories has, with *Robocop* and *Throw Momma from the Train*, introduced their digital system, dubbed Spectral Recording Dolby Stereo. Other sound labs and dubbing theaters will be following suit. Sony already has the necessary audio equipment available for film application as does Dolby. There is no doubt that more and more features will be released in digital format, and manufacturers of stereo optical theater sound reproducers will get on the bandwagon and provide digital sound units. Television sound, already using high fidelity MTS (q.v.), will probably follow, or may even lead in this area.

Fantasound

Without doubt Fantasound caused more interest than any sound format until the introduction of magnetic sound (q.v.) in the early 1950s, and rightly so. It was developed by RCA and Walt Disney Studios to meet Disney's demand for a fully directional system for **Fantasia** (RKO Radio) in 1940 (mixers: William E. Garity, C.O. Slyfield and John N.A. Hawkins). Basically it was four tracks of RCA Photophone format printed onto a 35mm film run in sync with the picture film, which carried a regular mono RCA Photophone track in the event of problems. The playback system was right, center and left screen speakers with surround speakers on right and left walls. Despite what you have read there was directional dialog as well as music. The system could easily have been employed with any dramatic film, and such was the eventual intention. The process was successful and very well received but discontinued with the outbreak of World War II. For whatever reasons it was not revised after the war, though the same audio distribution system would be utilized with magnetic stereo in the 1950s.

Western Electric also developed a similar system for use with a live-action concert film trade-screened in 1940, but the title of the film and all detailed information has long since been lost. It is assumed the film was of feature length but the only information uncovered was not specific.

Feelarama

See Sensurround.

Kinopanorama Sound

This Soviet audio system was compatible with the United States' Cinerama sound format, but utilized nine channels of discrete information. Apparently seven tracks were employed, with Perspecta-type encoding for two additional tracks. When exhibited in the United States, Kinopanorama films were presented with seven tracks only.

Magnetic and MagOptical Stereophonic Sound

CinemaScope films were not the first to employ magnetic soundtracks as often credited. **This Is Cinerama** used interlocked magnetic sound with six discrete tracks, and a similar system, employing fewer tracks (usually three, sometimes four), was adopted by Warner Bros. for WarnerPhonic

Sound and by Paramount, Universal-International, and others for their first stereophonic releases. *Bwana Devil,* the first United States–produced full color 3D feature, utilized interlocked mono magnetic sound. All dual-film 3D pictures have used interlock magnetic for their stereo sound.

Obviously, interlock sound came with numerous built-in problems. Not only was the dual-print inventory extremely expensive, it was subject to all the problems inherent to separate but dependent items: loss, damage, mis-synchronization (especially the latter). Twentieth Century–Fox realized that changes had to be made quickly or magnetic stereo was doomed. They introduced MagOptical Stereophonic Sound with their first 'scope release, **The Robe.** (Despite popular belief, 20th Century–Fox's early CinemaScope films were not meant to be run interlocked. Some limited prints were made for theaters set up for interlock sound, but the vast majority of stereo prints were MagOptical.) This format allowed magnetic sound-on-film tracks plus the advantage of a backup optical track for mono use or fallback if the stereo reproducing system went out. Other studios quickly discarded interlock and adopted the MagOptical format for their magnetic releases. (Perspecta Sound, q.v., would be used for stereo optical prints.) Even today MagOptical Stereophonic Sound is often called CinemaScope Sound by soundmen and theater operators.

Todd-AO produced magnetic sound-on-film for 70mm with **Oklahoma!** The system used six tracks of discrete sound played back through five screen speakers (right, right center, center, left center and left) and multiple surround speakers (all carrying one sound source). Seven- and eight-track versions rendering separate right wall and left wall or separate right wall, left wall and rear wall surround information apparently incorporated Perspecta encoding, since the film area allowed only six-track space. 70mm prints still employ the same soundtrack format but not necessarily the same channeling. Almost all recent 70mm prints have used the so-called "baby boom" audio layout in which screen channels one (left), three (center) and five (right) are used for dialog, music and effects, channels two (left center) and four (right center) are for subwoofer sounds to increase effectiveness of explosions, crashes, etc., and track six supplies surround information, which may or may not be separate right wall and left wall sound (being so directed by the out-of-phase encoding commonly associated with Dolby Surround). A few prints have used the same channeling except with tracks two and four also supplying surround information by sending rumbles from explosions, etc., into the wall speakers. The least-employed system is the Todd-AO format discussed above. In fact, when a film is now mixed with true directional dialog and effects for playback over all five 70mm screen speakers or three 35mm screen speakers, it is said to have Todd-AO Sound. (Dolby Stereo films rarely use directional dialog, which is why they sound bad when compared with older stereophonic pictures.)

MagOptical solved almost all the problems of interlocked sound: no loss, no mis-sync. However, damage, due mostly to perf misalignment and poorly maintained reproducing heads, plagued MagOptical pitilessly. Then there was just the weather; humidity was a real toll-taker on the magnetic tracks. Additionally, the cost of magnetic striping and recording doubled the expense of each print. A mint MagOptical print, properly presented, was an audio treat, but the system was doomed to virtual extinction because of uncontrollable problems and superior stereo optical.

Stereo optical (technically S.V.A., or stereo variable area, q.v.) is now the standard for 35mm even though an occasional release will be MagOptical. (Recent MagOptical releases include: *The Blues Brothers, White "Pop" Jesus, Nine to Five* and *Dawn of the Dead* in 1980; *Tarzan the Ape Man* and *Train Ride to Hollywood* in 1981; *The Best Little Whore House in Texas* in 1982; and *Yentl* [also released in stereo optical] and *Scarface* in 1983.) During the 1970s, such advertised trade names as Screaming Stereo, Multi Channel Sound, Dimensional Sound, Space Sound 4, and Future Sound, were all MagOptical.

Magnetic sound was outdated in less than two years, but failed to disappear. Cinerama continued to use the interlock method with all their three-panel films until the mid-1960s. 70mm still employs magnetic sound-on-film format. It is a mystery why 70mm has not replaced the extremely expensive, high-maintenance magnetic track with stereo optical.

MagOptical Stereophonic Sound

See Magnetic and MagOptical Stereophonic Sound.

MegaSound

During 1980 Warner Bros. installed special subwoofers in certain theaters playing some of their 70mm releases. The new sound system added a much wider bass range on explosions and crashes, and was really no more than a rumble effect. After the four films on which MegaSound was credited (listed below), the servicemark was seen no more. All were recorded in six-track Dolby Stereo magnetic, with tracks one, three and five being used for music, effects and dialog; track six was surround information, and tracks two and four contained the subwoofer information. Most 70mm films now use the same sound layout without the trademark.

Outland	Mixers: Robin Gregory, John Keene Wilkinson, Robert W. Glass, Jr. and Robert M. Thirlwell
Superman II	Mixers: Roy Charman, John Richards and Gerry Humphries
Wolfen	Mixers: Dennis Maitland, Sr., Daniel Wallin, Michael Minkler, Ken S. Polk and James A. Corbett
Altered States	Mixers: Willie Burton, Lester Fresholtz, Arthur Piantadosi and Michael Minkler

MTS (Multiple Television Sound)

To say that MTS, developed by Zenith and dbx, Inc., has revolution-

THE GROSSES CONTINUE
WHERE The **Robe**
LEFT OFF!

VARIETY

'DEMETRIUS' GREAT!
Los Angeles

'DEMETRIUS' TALL!
Indianapolis

'DEMETRIUS' BANGUP!
St. Louis

'DEMETRIUS' SOCKO!
Denver

'DEMETRIUS' HEFTY!
Boston

'DEMETRIUS' WOW!
Cincinnati

'DEMETRIUS' TALL!
New York

'DEMETRIUS' TERRIF!
Pittsburgh

'DEMETRIUS' HUGE!
Providence

'DEMETRIUS' ROBUST!
Seattle

'DEMETRIUS' MIGHTY!
Omaha

'DEMETRIUS' WOW!
Cleveland

'DEMETRIUS' WHAM!
Detroit

'DEMETRIUS' SMASH!
Buffalo

20th Century-Fox presents
DEMETRIUS and
The GLADIATORS
Color by TECHNICOLOR
CINEMASCOPE

starring
VICTOR **MATURE** · SUSAN **HAYWARD**
AS DEMETRIUS   AS MESSALINA

Produced by
FRANK ROSS

Michael Rennie · Debra Paget · Anne Bancroft · Jay Robinson · with Barry Jones · William Marshall

Directed by DELMER DAVES Written by PHILIP DUNNE

Play it in your choice of
CINEMASCOPE
equipment!
4-TRACK HIGH-FIDELITY MAGNETIC
STEREOPHONIC SOUND
1-TRACK HIGH-FIDELITY MAGNETIC SOUND
1-TRACK OPTICAL SOUND

By mid-1954 the majority of theatermen had their steal-from-the-public way, and 20th Century–Fox was forced to offer inferior mono optical sound versions of their hi-fi stereophonic pictures (note lower right-hand corner of these two ads). A few not-too-cheap operators had installed magnetic reproducing units but refused to complete the system with stereo channeling. Twentieth Century–Fox offered hi-fi mono magnetic prints for those exhibitors.

Original sin...drawing them like a magnet...to this place...to each other!

GARY · SUSAN · RICHARD
COOPER · HAYWARD · WIDMARK

TRESPASS INTO THE

GARDEN OF EVIL

Hooker struck a match...and the light fell on Leah, to reveal her as she really was...so deceptively innocent, so inwardly bold...and then the flame slowly flickered to mirror Fiske, the gambler, who was now playing for the highest stakes of all...the woman!

This is Hooker...
who led!

This is Leah...
who tempted!

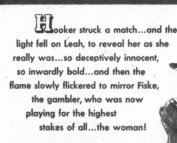

One of the powerful pressbook ads on this great attraction!

This is Fiske...
who cheated!

20th Century-Fox's Production in

CinemaScope

takes you beyond the treacherous torrents of Los Concheros...
beyond the land of the Black Sand...with these three!

Color by TECHNICOLOR

with Hugh MARLOWE · Cameron MITCHELL · Rita Moreno
Victor Manuel Mendoza

Produced by   Directed by   Screen Play by
Charles BRACKETT · Henry HATHAWAY · Frank FENTON

From a story by FRED FREIBERGER and WILLIAM TUNBERG

Play it in GENUINE
**4-TRACK MAGNETIC
HIGH-FIDELITY DIRECTIONAL
STEREOPHONIC SOUND**

Also available in
1-TRACK HIGH-FIDELITY
MAGNETIC SOUND

1-TRACK OPTICAL SOUND

AVAILABLE FOR JULY 4th! See Your 20th Century-Fox Branch Manager Now!

ized television audio is an understatement! This high fidelity stereophonic system has been accepted by NBC, ABC, Fox and PBS as the standard. As of this writing, CBS, always the least forward-thinking of the networks, has virtually ignored it, but only the most backward network affiliates and independent stations have not converted over. In effect MTS is two channels of audio, one which is dbx noise reduction–encoded, which is fully compatible with mono TV audio. As with S.V.A. Sound (q.v.), the system is capable of rendering right, center (if you have a decoder with center channel locking based on the "common information" placement used with SVA) and left front and right and left surround sound (by phase shifting — see S.V.A.). The results are astonishing, especially on movies and programs with surround information — and there are many. Additionally, MTS can be used, via its SAP (Second Audio Program) ability, to provide shows in two different languages simultaneously. This has led to many TV sets (some with surround decoders built in) and VCRs being manufactured with MTS, along with numerous inexpensive decoders which can be purchased and simply added to your mono TV and video equipment. Hundreds of features made in various stereophonic formats are now available to television stations in full directional sound. Many features originally produced in mono have also been converted to stereo for TV syndication. When heard in all its capacity, MTS is as different from mono TV audio as color is from black-and-white. It is that dramatic an improvement. It also puts many theatrical systems in the Dark Ages.

Perspecta Stereophonic Sound

Without doubt Perspecta Stereophonic Sound was the single most important sound development of the 1950s. The fact that theatermen ignored it shows the total contempt they had for their audience.

Perspecta was a stereo system that was usable with any sound format, optical or magnetic. Developed by Robert Fine of Fine Sound, Inc., it was a three-channel directional system that utilized subaudible tones (30 cycle for left, 35 cycle for center and 40 cycle for right) to separate into its proper screen speaker locations. As originally employed, a surround track was not incorporated into the channeling but could have easily been added. The only drawback to the process, and one which would have been overcome had the exhibitors backed it, was its inability to render all three channels separately, simultaneously. Perspecta was only able to send sound in one direction at a time. Music, crowd noises, etc., were directed to all three speakers, or they could be sent to right and left speakers if the theater audio playback system was so arranged as to exclude a center screen speaker (in which case the 35 cycle center information would be split and sent both right and left during regular directional channeling). While this might seem a big fault, it should be noted that all contemporary reports indicate that few in the audience were able to ascertain the difference in Perspecta three-channel stereo optical and MagOptical four-track stereophonic sound. Apparently the fidelity of the music was such that it had a "spread-out-sound" even though it actually was monaural. Of course Perspecta dialog and general sound effects were completely directional. (This is the opposite of today's stereo optical, which tends to have mono dialog, very limited directional sound effects, and stereo music. Obviously the Perspecta format was more realistic and probably more impressive.)

While Perspecta was intended for use with standard optical soundtracks it was employable with magnetic sound and was used on the Cinestage prints of **Around the World in 80 Days** to give three separate surround channels (right wall, left wall and rear wall or right and left simultaneously) from the one magnetic surround track. A variation was also utilized on one Cinerama feature and presumably with the Soviet Kinopanorama process and Belock 8-Channel Sound.

MGM saw Perspecta for what it was: an extremely cheap, highly effective, directional process. It was possible to mix (pan the sound and encode the three tones) a Perspecta soundtrack in less than half a day. MagOptical usually took a minimum of four days after all premixing had been laid down. There were no additional print costs, and all Perspecta prints were playable on all optical sound systems. (Current stereo optical depreciates considerably when played through a mono theater system.) Once encoded with the Perspecta stereo cues the sound would always retain its capacity for directional playback. Other than the lack of true stereophonic music, the process was perfect for the industry.

Paramount agreed. They almost immediately announced that all VistaVision releases would incorporate only Perspecta Stereophonic Sound. They had had their fill of the problems inherent with interlock magnetic and even MagOptical stereo (see Magnetic Sound). Warner Bros. and Columbia also decided Perspecta was an excellent idea. Like MGM, they would also release many of their A pictures in MagOptical as well as Perspecta in order to service those theaters that had not bothered to add stereo optical to their directional playback systems. (The addition of a tone decoder was all that was necessary to convert a MagOptical or interlock stereo playback system to Perspecta. The Perspecta system purchased by itself was substantially cheaper than a MagOptical system; however, the stereo optical could not as easily be converted to handle magnetic sound playback.)

Why the industry did not go all out with Perspecta can only be chalked up to insanity. Its inexpensiveness alone made it the sensible choice over magnetic sound. With the introduction of solid state components it would have been relatively simple to add surround information as well as to make it possible for full, three-channel simultaneous separation. Alas, Perspecta Stereophonic Sound was murdered by lack of interest at the exhibitors' level. MGM, who employed it on more features than any other company (including the first Perspecta film to be released, 1953's **Knights of the Round Table**) and even used it on their cartoons and shorts, would discontinue the process in 1960. The other studios had already dropped it. A few foreign releases were encoded for directional playback into the mid-1960s. Japan, the last holdout, dropped the process by 1965. (The Iron Curtain

GREATEST NEWS YET IN THEATRE SOUND!

Multi-directional sound on a standard optical track

This is it! The simple, permanent sound system that solves all the exhibitor's stereophonic sound problems — and it's fully compatible with conventional sound systems. Projection procedures remain the same, too.

Exhibitors with stereophonic sound can switch to Perspecta Stereophonic Sound by installing only an integrator unit, design-engineered by Fairchild. Theatres equipped for conventional sound need only that single miracle unit plus additional power amplifiers, loudspeakers and a multiple gang fader.

REMEMBER! *MGM, Paramount and Warner Bros. are now filming all productions with this new technique.*

See your theatre supply dealer for full information or write:

FAIRCHILD RECORDING EQUIPMENT

MOTION PICTURE SOUND DIVISION ● WHITESTONE 57, NEW YORK

Above and facing page: *Two 1954 trade ads promoting the Perspecta Stereophonic Sound system to theater owners. The system cost $990.*

countries used a stereo optical system by Tobis Klangfilm that was four separate variable area tracks on the film. They have recently been converting to Dolby Stereo.) Interestingly, Dolby Laboratories has recently manufactured a Perspecta decoding element for their stereo optical reproducers so that theaters exhibiting features made in the 1950s can now present them with the proper directional sound.

Polydimensional Sound

This system is a mystery but appears to be no more than the use of various frequencies to create the aural illusion of spatial sound. Jaime Mendoza Nava, a composer-conductor and postproduction supervisor, was

HERE'S SOUND ADVICE!

If the confusion that surrounds the various sound systems being offered today has delayed your decision on just what you should install in your theatre, consider these facts:

Three of the majors — M·G·M, Paramount and Warner Brothers — have already announced that *all* future productions will have Perspecta Stereophonic Sound. Other studios are following their example.

Why has Perspecta Stereophonic Sound been chosen as standard — a standard certain to remain for years to come? For three very good reasons:

1. The movie industry wants to make money. To do this they know they must keep your box-office busy. Perspecta Stereophonic Sound will do just that by giving the movie-going public the dramatic realism they want.

2. Perspecta Stereophonic Sound is a system every movie exhibitor can afford to install.

3. Perspecta Stereophonic Sound Track operates identically with the optical sound track you've been using for years except for the inclusion of three low-level, low-frequency tones "heard" only by the Integrator, which automatically controls volume and direction for true stereophonic effect.

The Perspecta Stereophonic Sound Integrator, design-engineered by Fairchild, makes this system available to you at a price you can afford. Only one Fairchild Integrator serves all projectors in the booth — controls Perspecta Stereophonic Sound through any 3-channel sound system of standard make. And projector modifications are not required.

Call, wire or write *now* for full information on your specific theatre sound problem.

FAIRCHILD RECORDING EQUIPMENT

MOTION PICTURE SOUND DIVISION • WHITESTONE 57, NEW YORK

credited as developer and creator on the one feature that used the technique, *The Legend of Boggy Creek* (Howco, 1973; mixers, Lyle Burbridge, Harry Warren Tetrick, and Bill McCoy). Rerecording was done at MGM using Westrex equipment. It is possible Polydimensional Sound was Perspecta Stereophonic or a variation thereof.

Todd-Belock Sound

See Belock 8-Channel Sound.

Quadrophonic Sound

This was a variation on four-track MagOptical stereo, except instead of right, center, left and surround channels, the audio was fed into a right screen speaker, left screen speaker, right wall speaker and left wall speaker. The effect was interesting, but not especially different from normal four-track stereo except in the use of the wall speakers. Very few films used the

M-G-M's POLICY ON CINEMASCOPE PICTURES AND STEREOPHONIC SOUND....

A Statement by Charles M. Reagan, General Manager of Sales

In response to the demands of many motion picture exhibitors, M-G-M announces that it will release its CinemaScope pictures to all theatres capable of presenting them on a wide screen and with anamorphic projection.

Up to this time M-G-M CinemaScope productions have been available solely to those theatres which had installed stereophonic equipment suitable for magnetic sound tracks.

The new policy is designed to service theatres which present the single channel track as well as those equipped for magnetic sound and the new Perspecta sound.

Many theatres have voiced the opinion that motion picture distributing companies should furnish their CinemaScope productions to the many thousands of theatres which are not yet prepared to expand their sound facilities.

M-G-M has released only two CinemaScope productions. They are "KNIGHTS OF THE ROUND TABLE" and "ROSE MARIE." These productions will be made available to all theatres equipped with a screen wide enough to encompass the projection via the anamorphic lens.

Other M-G-M pictures announced for CinemaScope are "THE STUDENT PRINCE," "SEVEN BRIDES," "BRIGADOON," "ATHENA," "GREEN FIRE" and "JUPITER'S DARLING."

In connection with this announcement it is important for exhibitors to realize that all M-G-M pictures, in whatever dimension, will be released with Perspecta sound tracks permitting exhibitors to employ either stereophonic sound or single channel sound.

Exhibitors would be short-sighted if they did not take full advantage of this opportunity for improved presentation.

The exhibition without stereophonic sound of CinemaScope or other M-G-M pictures would eliminate an effect essential to their full enjoyment.

We cannot urge exhibitors strongly enough to install stereophonic devices.

To ignore the advantages of new sound techniques is a disservice to the public and an obstruction to the great future development of motion pictures. We are on the threshold of tremendous achievement and an improvement in presentation techniques. The failure of exhibitors to cooperate fully in the new advances would be to retard and discourage the great future which has already been revealed and is only in its early stages of development.

It would be sad indeed if exhibitors were induced into a lethargy and not inspired to take advantage of the wonderful opportunities presented by the inventions and achievements of great technicians working in the Studios.

Furthermore, we believe that the theatres which are equipped with stereophonic sound devices will have a great box-office advantage over those theatres not so equipped, and that the movie-going public, which has already put its stamp of approval on CinemaScope with stereophonic sound will further demonstrate its acceptance by preferring to attend those theatres properly equipped for the new type of presentation.

An exhibitor who does not wish to see motion pictures presented under the best possible circumstances is not keeping faith with his public and we sincerely hope and strongly recommend that those theatres playing M-G-M pictures will install stereophonic sound devices if they have not already done so.

A May 1954 trade ad shows the tension that by then had developed between studios and exhibitors over the installation of stereophonic sound.

technique (see list below), even though many theaters are actually channeling stereo optical sound in the same matter. The lack of a center channel is not particularly noticeable.

Made in Quadrophonic:

The Asphyx (Paragon; 1973)*	4 Track Quadrophonic Sound
	Mixer: unavailable
Beyond the Door (FVI; 1974)	Quadrophonic Possessosound
	Mixer: uncredited
Dynasty (JAD; 1977)	Real-A-Rama Quadrophonic Sound
	Mixer: uncredited

Quintophonic Sound

Developed by John Mosley's Quinta Enterprises, Inc., this complex system employed three magnetic tracks and two optical tracks fed through a Dolby noise reduction unit. The sound led to three screen speakers (right, center and left) and speakers on each wall. Only one film, **Tommy** (Col. 1975; mixers, Ron Nevison, Ian Bruce and Bill Rowe),** used this soundtrack format of MagOptical since it soon became possible to create five channels from stereo optical. In fact most stereo optical films after 1978 have been quintophonic.

Sensurround

Developed by MCA and RCA under the guidance of former Universal City Studios sound department head Waldon O. Watson, the Sensurround Special Effects System, as it was billed on later releases, employed subaudible sound to create vibrations that made the audience feel the effects of earthquakes, explosions, crashes and the like. For 35mm engagements, prints were offered in three different formats: MagOptical with three-channel stereo on three magnetic tracks and the Sensurround information on one optical track; MagOptical with one magnetic track containing mono channeled music, dialogue and effects and one optical track containing the Sensurround information; and single track optical containing all audio information. For 70mm prints, six magnetic tracks were employed in the same manner as MegaSound (q.v.). Sensurround changed with each feature even though the soundtrack pattern was followed as noted. For example, *Earthquake* had only rumbles in the Sensurround information; *Midway* included rumbles and sound effects; *Rollercoaster* incorporated music into the Sensurround rumble along with sound effects; and *Zoot Suit,* which introduced Sensurround Plus, utilized the full system plus Lightsurround, a synced light cueing system for in-auditorium effects. Feelarama, a variation of Sensurround, was utilized for the mid-1970s European reissue of *Krakatoa East of Java,* retitled *Volcano.* Another variation, called Vibrasound, was originally to have been employed on *The Boat*

TV title Horror of Death
Tommy *was released in several different sound formats. See the note after the credits in the Filmography.*

(Das Boot), but that film was released in the United States in Dolby Stereo only; it is unclear if the rumble effects system was actually utilized elsewhere.

Made in Sensurround:

Earthquake* (Univ., 1974)	Mixers: Melvin M. Metcalfe, Sr., Ronald Pierce and Robert Leonard
Midway* (Univ., 1976)	Mixers: Robert Martin and Leonard Peterson
King Kong (Par., 1976)	Mixers: Jack Solomon, Daniel Wallin, Aaron Rochin, Harry Warren Tetrick and William Mc-Caughey**
Rollercoaster* (Univ., 1977)	Mixers: James Alexander and Edwin J. Somers
Battlestar Galactica* (Univ., 1978)	Mixers: James Alexander, Robert L. Hoyt, John Stephens, Lowell Harris, Eddie Brackett and Earl Madery

*Richard Stumpf was sound supervisor and Waldon O. Watson sound consultant on the Universal releases.
**Released in Sensurround only outside the United States.

In Sensurround Plus*:

Zoot Suit (Univ., 1981)	Mixers: unavailable

*Incorporated Lightsurround in auditorium effects.

In Feelarama:

Krakatoa East of Java* (re titled **Volcano**, CRC, 1975?)	Mixers: Wallace H. Milner and Gordon K. McCallum

*Europe only.

In Vibrasound:

The Boat (Das Boot, Col., (1982)*	Mixers: Milan Bor, Trevor Pyke, Tommy Klemt, Werner Bohm, Karsten Ullrich, Heinz Schurer, Stani Litere and Albrecht von Bethmann

*Not released in the United States in Vibrasound; use in Europe is uncertain.

Sound 360

This was a variation by 20th Century–Fox on MagOptical stereo. It differed somewhat from MagOptical, but not nearly to the degree 20th Century–Fox hawked. In fact it was playable through any old magnetic four-track stereo reproducer with almost the same results.

Twentieth Century–Fox executives decided to relocate the sound and thus surround the audience. All that was done was to take the sound that normally on four-track stereo would have fed the right and left screen speakers and send it to the right and left sides. (One speaker was used for each channel, not several, thus the side track information came from only one speaker on the right and one of the left placed midway on the auditorium walls.) The surround track, which would have fed side speakers, was sent to one speaker in the center of the auditorium rear wall. Thus four-channel, four-speaker surround. (The distance between the front speaker and the side speakers and the rear speaker and the side speakers was to be the same.) This worked okay but was rather flat sounding when sound came only from the front. Music was channeled from all speakers, but predominately from the sides. (Some theaters still use a setup like this for stereo optical sound, and you can try it out in your home if you have stereo video equipment.) The system also used an altered MagOptical track layout in that only three channels were magnetic and one was optical.

Only one film was made using this system:

Damnation Alley (1977)　　　　Mixers: Bruce Bisenz and Theodore Soderberg

Sound 360 was a financial and artistic success, and 20th Century–Fox announced that *The Driver* (1978) and *Damien — Omen II* (1978) would utilize the system. The former film was apparently released only in mono, and the latter appeared in standard four-track MagOptical format though it most likely was mixed for Sound 360 playback. Since stereo optical was considerably cheaper, 20th Century–Fox abandoned their process.

Super SpectraSound

By the midseventies Dolby Laboratories was beginning to make a strong push toward industry use of its noise reduction system and S.V.A. (stereo variable area) audio derived from separate RCA Photophone tracks. The vast majority of filmmakers did what was normal with the introduction and promotion of an improved technology: They simply ignored it! A few independent producers actually utilized Dolby Stereo on their features, but with an extremely limited number of theaters equipped for proper stereophonic playback, and those not inclined toward exhibiting anything but major releases, few, if any, were heard except in mono. **Tommy** (Columbia, 1975) had been the only major production to apply the stereo optical sound format, and it was for that film alone that United States theaters had installed the decoding unit necessary to separate the multi-tracks. Indeed some of the **Tommy** theaters hadn't actually purchased stereo optical sound processors at all, but simply the noise reduction decoder, since the film was really MagOptical in format and not totally stereo optical. **Tommy,** however, had its effect, and several top-name independent filmmakers started backing Dolby Stereo. Dubbing houses, little by little, began incorporating the capacity to produce the soundtrack. Ken Russell, then totally behind Dolby (and since going back to mono sound for some of his films!) and responsible for **Tommy,** followed that film a few months later with *Lisztomania* (Warner Bros., 1975), advertised "in New Dolby Stereo Sound." The industry suddenly took notice. Not overwhelming notice, of course, but interest was spreading, and some big-budget films were being announced for the process (though it would take 1977's *Star Wars* and *Close Encounters of the Third Kind* before even the slightest interest would be shown by very many theater owners).

As usual, when something appeared to be getting even the smallest foothold into any technology, competition developed. Thus was born Super SpectraSound. Like Dolby Stereo, this was a stereo optical format requiring a special decoding unit for proper playback, but compatible with existing mono theater sound systems. Unlike Dolby there was no noise reduction applied. The format worked by having four individual audio tracks the size of 16mm optical soundtracks separately color coded. The stereo optical decoder "read" the color of the track and channeled it to screen right, screen center, screen left and surround speakers. (One source says the audio distribution was screen right, screen left, right surround and left surround, but this is unlikely, even though press material did refer to the sound as quadraphonic.) The backers of the system seem to have spent more time debasing Dolby's noise reduction unit, which they declared unnecessary, than actually promoting their own technology. If the very little published information is even remotely correct, color-coded stereo optical seemed to have had quite a few supporters and very, very briefly appeared to be on the verge of taking the industry by storm.

Super SpectraSound did not emerge from a cloudburst with thunderclaps sounding. It barely made even a spring sprinkle, and there was definitely no thunder heard. In fact there appear to have been only two features ever made in the system, and neither played more than a very few (probably fewer than a dozen) theaters in stereo. The first out was *Moses* (Avco Embassy, 1976), reedited from the six-hour television miniseries *Moses the Lawgiver* with additional footage thrown in. While theaters everywhere promoted the film "in spectacular Super SpectraSound," only audiences in Los Angeles and New York heard the intended multichannel audio. (The home video version has the full stereophonic sound.) Few patrons complained. (One of the authors did complain directly to Avco Embassy and was informed by one of their executives that Super SpectraSound wasn't anything at all but an advertising gimmick! The executive further stated he had seen the film—how nice that he would go to such trouble!—and he clearly remembered it was not stereophonic! At that point in the conversation he turned to others in the office and asked: "It isn't in stereo, is it?" He received blank stares and then continued to assure the complainer that it definitely did not have any kind of special soundtrack.)

No more was heard of Super SpectraSound as such, and the rather attractive logo was not seen on other advertising. Then a few years later a strange thing occurred: Robert Altman, one of the most productive Dolby supporters, made *Popeye* (1980) as a coproduction between Paramount and Disney in a "new" stereo optical color-coded sound system. (Altman, after several Dolby Stereo features, would abandon stereophonic sound altogether and make his films with outdated mono audio.) This so-called new system could only have been Super SpectraSound, but no trade name, to our knowledge, was ever applied to it. *Popeye* was simply advertised "in stereo." It is possible the system had undergone some changes, but available information indicates it was identical to the format utilized on *Moses*. (The home video and television syndicated prints of *Popeye* are in full stereo and sound as good as other films in Dolby or any other recent stereo system.) It is also possible, but unlikely, that the color-coded format was applied to other stereo optical releases, but to our knowledge Super SpectraSound completely vanished after *Popeye*.

| *Moses* (Avco Emb, 1976) | Mixers: Luciano Welisch and Paul Carr |
| *Popeye* (Par, 1980) | Mixers: Robert Gravenor, Michael Minkler, Daniel Wallin and Steve Brimmer |

SurrounduSound

This system is assumed to be magnetic four-track in MagOptical format, but no specifics were available. One source claims the two films that used the system were in 16mm. That is a very strong possibility since both were hardcore porno. They were as follows (both produced and released by Joe Gage Films):

| *Handsome* (1975) | Mixer: unavailable |
| *Kansas City Trucking Co.* (1976) | Mixer: Glen Nathan |

S.V.A. (Stereo Variable Area) Sound

In recent years people have been much misled by the Dolby Stereo trademark on films. They mistakenly assume some magic is involved that is controlled by Dolby Laboratories, Inc., and that all current stereophonic films must employ this legendary system. Let such nonsense be set aside forever.

The system utilized by Dolby is technically called S.V.A. (stereo variable area). It was not invented by Dolby, nor is it controlled by them. Any film can be made using the format, and Dolby equipment is not necessarily involved, though of course it must be in order to use their trademark. In the early 1970s several films were made on which Dolby noise reduction was applied in the rerecording stage. These films could be played in any theater with any reproducing audio system. They did sound better with a Dolby processor, but not greatly so.

Eastman Kodak wanted an inexpensive means of release-printing 16mm films with dual soundtracks, one track being in English and the other in a different language. It was then necessary to have a magnetic track on the prints with the foreign track, but this was very expensive. They approached RCA with the idea of using the Photophone format (variable area dual track, both tracks being the same) with one side in English and the other foreign. RCA produced the necessary optical sound camera and by using a split exciter lamp was able to give Kodak the type soundtrack they wanted.

It was discovered that the split Photophone track was so small that it generated a great deal of hiss and unwanted noise. In an effort to clean this up, RCA introduced a Dolby noise reduction unit to the projection outfit.

While the two tracks were different language versions, it seemed to RCA and Kodak that it would be practical to apply the technology to stereo.

Dolby Labs was not involved in any of this experimental work, which was all done on 16mm. They entered the picture when it was decided to market the system for 35mm use. RCA made the bad error of not proceeding with the system, and Dolby took off with the idea. Still it wasn't until the release of *Star Wars* (1977) that the industry at large paid much attention. *Star Wars,* however, came four years after the first Dolby Stereo release. There were several, but only *Tommy* had gotten many playdates in theaters equipped with Dolby System, as it was then known. While several of the early stereo optical sound releases played Dolby equipped theaters, it was often in mono. Dolby was marketing both mono and stereo versions of their reproducing units, and a number of theaters purchased the mono playbacks for financial considerations or simple ignorance.

The success of *Star Wars* changed things. Producers and wiser theatermen decided stereo optical sound was the way to go. Unfortunately, the first few years were hard on all, with many stereo recorded films going out only in mono versions or in very limited stereo print runs. A large number of these films are now on video in their true stereo version, and many people have been surprised to learn just how many features have been produced using the S.V.A system (as of this writing, close to 1,500). But the S.V.A. system is not limited to those films bearing the Dolby Stereo trademark. Films in Todd-AO Stereo, Ultra-Stereo, and Eagle-Stereo all employ the same technology. Likewise theaters calling their system StarScope Stereo, Kintek All Stereo, THX Sound, Wide Screen Stereo, Ultra-Stereo, HSP 4000 Sound and Total Stereo all use S.V.A. equipment from the several manufacturers now supplying such. The patron should make sure he attends a stereo film being exhibited in a stereo equipped theater; otherwise he is supporting an operation that wants to provide little for the ticket purchased. (S.V.A. theater processors can be purchased for less than a $1,000. A first-run theater makes that in one weekend from its concession stand.)

S.V.A. works in this manner: The actual soundtrack is the old Photophone track, except each track is different. One track feeds the right sound, the other feeds the left sound. Center channel sound (not all theaters use a center speaker) is on both tracks, is read by the audio processor as common information, and is sent to the center speaker. Right and left surround sound is on the right and left tracks, out of phase. This is picked up by the processor, decoded (as Dolby likes to say), and channeled into the surround speakers. Not all theaters with S.V.A. have surround speakers, and, depending on the processor they have, are either sending surround information to the respective right and left screen speakers or more than likely not retrieving it at all. A few theaters also have a right and left (or just a center screen) subwoofer speaker(s) that pulls extra bass for explosions and such from the soundtrack. However, many films do not have this extra bass material in their soundtrack.

A problem that should be mentioned is cheating. Many theaters, especially long narrow ones, install S.V.A. processors but have only one screen speaker and then one rear (totally unacceptable) surround speaker or limited right and left surround speakers. The theatergoer is not hearing true stereo in these theaters, but is getting surround. Another cheat, and one that actually works very, very well even if the sound is being misdirected, is when one screen speaker is used, right and left channels are sent to right and left surrounds, and surround information is either not used or is sent to rear speakers. Actually this rigging of speakers gives extremely impressive sound.

All films are not soundtracked equally, and many do not employ surround sound or may use identical right and left surround. And all S.V.A. processors aren't equal either, though the differences are usually in the setup of the system and not in the quality of the equipment.

If you own a stereo VCR, TV or video disc (CED or LaserVision player) you can get all the surround information in your home at little or no cost depending on what you have at hand. Processing surround sound (and the Dolby Surround logo means nothing regardless what you've read or heard; you do not need a Dolby-approved system to get all the sound) is easy and well worth the effort to rig. Here's how to do it: From the R + on your amplifier run a speaker wire to your R + surround speaker. From the L + on your amplifier run a speaker wire to your L + surround speaker. The wires running to the surround speakers should be opposite to those in the amp. That is, if one wire is clear and one is dark, then use the opposite for the surrounds. If the amp + is clear then use the dark for the surround + . The R − and L − wires are not to be used. Leave them covered, or better yet, cut them away. Finally, from the R − surround speaker run the − wire to the L − surround speaker. Turn up the volume of your TV to get center dialog stabilization.

And that is it. You now have the same wiring system used in theaters. No magic. No secret devices. Just a means of pulling the out-of-phase surround sound out. This system gives you the surround information exactly as it is meant to be heard, which is half as loud as the front speakers. But if you are like most people you might not be satisfied and you'll want to control the surround volume. In that case run the surround + wires into another amp and then repeat off the second amp the procedures as above. You can also run the aux out into the aux in on the second amp and then rig the surrounds. Either way works. But do not mix tube and solid state amps. Use only solid state amps. And be sure to start with the volume low, then turn it up until you get what you want. You can also add subwoofers in the front, but then the sound can really get overpowering for a TV picture. This system works on all home video stereo systems: VCR, TV and disc. But the source material has to be stereo or hi-fi. It will not work on a mono source, though it will work on a simulated stereo source. Some hi-fi mono video tapes and discs have surround tracks, but these are simply repeats of the front speaker material. Some stereo tapes and discs which had surround information theatrically do not have it on the home version.

Several stereo TV series including "Miami Vice," "Amazing Stories," "Crime Story," and "L.A. Law" have true surround sound, but not always on every episode. All dbx TV stereo sound has surround, but this is usually repeat front information. You will just have to check each program out. (See MTS.)

Vibrasound

See Sensurround.

Vitasound

Even Louis B. Mayer envied Warner Bros. for the quality of their sound. It is therefore not surprising that Warners was the first studio to produce stereophonic features for general release.

In 1940 the studio decided monophonic sound did not produce the added audio kick wanted for certain scenes. Under Nathan Levinson and George R. Groves, the sound department approached a method to expand the sound. Using the RCA Photophone format, they decided to make the two tracks separate channels. (Photophone uses two identical variable density tracks printed on the film side by side, half size.) By incorporating an audio triggering system they were able to switch on additional amplifiers (necessary because once the tracks were used as separate channels the volume of each was reduced considerably) that powered speakers on the right, center and left of the screen. Dialog was centered, while sound effects and music were sent to right and left speakers. The music and effects were not stereophonic as the same information came from both sides, but they were separate from the dialog.

Unfortunately Vitasound was not used for the whole show but only during selected sequences, and as might be expected, was installed in very few theaters. It had a very short childhood, slept through a long adolescence, and then was awakened to a shaky but soon-to-prosper adulthood: From Vitasound came today's S.V.A. systems.

The Vitasound films are listed below.* All were from Warner Bros. — First National. Nathan E. Levinson was sound supervisor.

Santa Fe Trail (Dec. 1940)	Mixers: Robert B. Lee and George R. Groves
Four Mothers (Jan. 1941)	Mixer: George R. Groves
Affectionately Yours (May (1941)	Mixers: Clare A. Riggs and George R. Groves

A recently discovered studio memo implies "all films" shown at Warner Bros.' two Los Angeles showcase theaters were mixed in part or in whole in Vitasound. While the memo opens up all kinds of possibilities, it should be taken into account that at the time it was written—early 1941—probably only the first couple of Vitasound features had been made and had indeed played there. Information from George R. Groves is very clear that only the films listed above used the sound system. Still it is not beyond logic to accept that there may have been others.

Shining Victory (June 1941)	Mixers: Dolph Thomas and George R. Groves
Dive Bomber (Aug. 1941)	Mixers: Francis J. Scheid and George R. Groves
Sergeant York (Sep. 1941)	Mixers: Oliver S. Garretson and George R. Groves

WarnerPhonic Sound

With the opening of *This Is Cinerama,* the industry took notice of magnetic stereophonic sound. Warner Bros., always a leader in sound engineering, quickly decided stereo should not be limited just to novelty films but should be applied to all A features. They developed their Warner-Phonic Sound to be showcased with their first 3D feature, *House of Wax,* in early 1953. It utilized the basic idea of Cinerama Sound: directional dialog, music and effects on magnetic striped film run in interlock with the picture film. Warners settled on four tracks instead of the six used with Cinerama. Their reasoning was understandable since the screen standard for 35mm was still 1.33×1 aspect ratio. For their two 3D films Warner-Phonic used the magnetic tracks as right, center and left screen speaker supplier. Right and left tracks contained only the music. The middle track contained the dialog and effects, encoded with a Perspecta-type tone shifter that appropriately sent the audio information right, center or left as required by the on-screen action. The dual film prints (3D at that time required two picture films run in sync) each contained an RCA Photophone optical track. One of the picture prints carried the rear (and fourth) WarnerPhonic channel, while the other carried a composite mono track of all the screen (right, center and left) information but not the rear track. Thus a theater could run the films in full WarnerPhonic Sound, an abbreviated version of WarnerPhonic using just the front mono optical track and rear optical track, or regular mono sound if the magnetic reproducer was down or if the theater had not installed WarnerPhonic at all. (It should be noted that the fourth WarnerPhonic track was not a surround channel but was meant strictly for rear sound location. When *House of Wax* was reissued in 70mm in 1971 with four-channel magnetic stereo, theaters incorrectly placed the rear information into all surround speakers, ruining the intended audio effect.)

For the only flat feature released in WarnerPhonic Sound the audio format was slightly different. The magnetic tracks were the same and the picture film carried a composite RCA Photophone track, but there was no rear channel.

WarnerPhonic was soon outmoded by MagOptical (see Magnetic and MagOptical Stereophonic Sound) and Perspecta Stereophonic (q.v.) systems. Both systems were adopted by Warners since neither required a separate sound film.

The WarnerPhonic films are listed below. All were released by Warner Bros. William A. Mueller was sound supervisor.

House of Wax (Natural Vi-   Mixers: Charles Lang and George R.
    sion 3-Dimension, April   Groves
    1953)

The Charge at Feather River Mixers: Charles Lang and George R.
    (Natural Vision 3-   Groves
    Dimension, July 1953)

Island in the Sky (Sept. 1953)   Mixers: Earl Crain, Sr., Ed Borschell
                                       and George R. Groves

Filmography: Wide Gauge, Large Format, and Other Technologically Significant Films — Credits and Casts

The following material includes the most detailed and accurate credit and cast lists we could assemble. Very often these lists are considerably longer than those appearing on the films. At other times, most particularly on foreign productions, they are not as long or complete.

The data appearing here were assembled from many sources, including actual screen billing, production notes, unit lists, studio files, publicity materials, souvenir program books, pressbooks, letters from individuals involved, interviews, and trade publications. We have made no effort to discredit any individual's work on the films; however, research often uncovered the fact that the final, "official" billing was not necessarily accurate and most definitely not conclusive. When such conflicted with totally reliable sources we have retained all given credits; thus the reader will very often find names listed here that did not get the same screen billing. The problem of ascertaining and assigning duly deserved credits to the films was approached from the standpoint that as long as the source was reliable the credit would be included here. We were not influenced by the rules often dictated by unions and studio policies that mandated certain credits to certain individuals only. Still, for no reason other than to expand our files, we would like to hear from anyone who can add further data for the films covered herein, and most definitely from anyone who can make any addition to the list of films, for in all likelihood there are unintentional omissions.

Our credit listings resemble as closely as possible the screen titles and other sources from which they have been taken; we have attempted to retain the original billing and terminology in order that the reader might get some of the "flavor" of the original sources, especially for foreign-made films. In some cases, however, the credits for the foreign films were so different from the terminology applied in English-speaking countries as to make them incomprehensible to the average reader. In those cases more familiar English terms have been substituted.

This filmography covers every film of note mentioned in the text. All wide gauge and special format films are included. Additionally, we have included solely for historical reference some films not directly involved with the subject of this book but whose place in the overall history of cinema makes them noteworthy. Thus the reader will find the credits and casts for the first full-color feature and the first all-talking feature, among other items.

We have attempted the first-ever, first-anywhere documentation of Soviet 70mm films. Most of these productions have previously been unknown outside the U.S.S.R. Many are blowups from 35mm and by all rights might seem undeserving of inclusion; however, the very fact they have never before been so much as listed makes their

259

appearance in this book all the more important and necessary. For the first time it is now possible to have an overview of a cinematic world only vaguely glimpsed before.

In most cases the Russian material has been transliterated, rather than translated or anglicized, from the original Cyrillic material provided us. (The exception is well-known non-Russian names—e.g. Elizabeth Taylor, Johann Sebastian Bach, Georges Bizet—which are given here in their customary roman-alphabet spellings.) Because Russian nouns are inflected, direct transliteration occasionally results in a name being given in its inflected form, which may strike the English-speaking reader as unusual: "Tolstogo," for example, is a transliteration of "Tolstoy" in the genitive case.

The Russian films, like the other foreign films, are listed under their international title in English when given. The existence of such a title does not mean that an English-language version was produced or even that the film was ever exhibited outside the Soviet Union. It means only that Sovexportfilm assigned an English title—a common practice worldwide—and that in some, but not all, cases the films were made available for screening outside the U.S.S.R. Only an extremely limited number have been shown in the United States. The English titles given are not always direct translations of the Soviet titles, and no attempt has been made to give English titles (or translations) to those films not assigned such titles by the Soviets.

The running times are for the Soviet versions and not for such international editions as were released. Usually the international running times were less than the original length.

It should be noted that we have deliberately omitted all Soviet 70mm 3D films. They are excluded here because wide screen technology is not applied to their production.

Sovexportfilm is credited on all Soviet films as international distributor. Any interested company seeking distribution of these films in any market must contact that agency, which can provide all the films in any format and aspect ratio desired, including video.

The reader might well wonder why, if all the Soviet 70mm blowups are included, no effort was made to fully document all the English-language VistaVision, Technirama and 70mm blowups, as well as wide gauge enlargements from other countries. We have not done so because information on the English-language films, even if limited, is readily available from numerous and easily obtainable sources. Also, those films regularly appear on television, and many are available in various video formats. As for films made elsewhere and blown up, it was a matter of research time and book space. There were literally hundreds of 70mm blowups made in Europe. While someone perhaps should attempt a complete assembly of credits and casts, or at the very least a listing of them, to do so was simply beyond reason for this book. The Soviet films are covered because information on them cannot be obtained by general research. With time, the European films could be relatively easily documented.

Specific release dates (month, day and year) are for United States release; only the year of release is given for films not released in the States. Running times (except for Soviet films) are also for the United States versions, but notes are included giving additional information—not only on length variations, but on alternate titles and anything else considered of importance or special interest.

We would like to point out that several of the roadshow features covered in this book are now available on home video in restored editions with fully directional stereophonic sound. One can now see and hear some of these films in versions that, given the limits of various video systems, are as near to their original hard-ticket versions as possible. Notable restorations include *Cheyenne Autumn, Hello, Dolly!* and *How the West Was Won,* as well as others, and they are far more impressive in their video editions than they ever were in the reedited 35mm general release mono prints most people have seen. Of course, they do suffer somewhat from the considerable reduction in screen size and width, but the reader is advised they are more than worth the effort of seeking them out for purchase or rental.

This filmography is our salute to those named and the so many unnamed whose contributions to world cinema cannot be overlooked.

About Those I Remember and Love (1974). Filmed in Sovscope 70. *Screen author* Budimer Metalinikov. *Based on the story "Devichiya" by* P. Zavodchikova and S. Samoylova. *Directors* Anatoli Bekhotko and Natalia Troshshenko. *Operator* Aleksandr Chetsulin. *Artist* Valeri Yurkeviy. *Composer* Sergei Slonimskiy. *Sound operators* E. Nesterov and G. Lukina. ¶A Lenfilm production. International distribution Sovexportfilm. Sovcolor. Six-track magnetic stereophonic sound. 80 minutes. Filmed at Lenfilm Studios, Leningrad, R.S.F.S.R. ¶CAST: *Lt. Vasiliev* Valeri Zolotukhin. *With* Ekaterina Vasilieva, Viktoriya Fedorova, Evgeniya Sabelinikov, V. Zukhimovich, N. Karpushina, L. Staritsina, A. Inozemtsev and D. Omaev. ¶A Soviet production released in Russia in 1974 as *O tekh, kogo pomnyu i lyudlyu.*

Across the Gobi and the Khingans (1982). Filmed in Sovscope 70. *Screen authors* Vadim Trunin and Vassily Ordinskiy *in collaboration with* Lodongiyn Tudev. *Directors* Vassily Ordinskiy and Badrakhin Sumkhu. *Operators* Nickolai Vasilikov and Zambaly Asalbay. *Artists* Yu. Kladtsenko and O. Myagmor. *Composers* Yu. Butsko and B. Damdinsurzn. *Sound operators* S. Litvinov and Ts. Dolzinsurzn. ¶A Mosfilm-Mongolkino-DEFA production. International distribution Sovexportfilm. Sovcolor. Six-track magnetic sterophonic sound. 208 minutes plus intermission. Filmed at Mosfilm Studios, Moscow, R.S.F.S.R. and on location in Mongolia, Central Asia. ¶CAST: Aleksandr Ovchinnikov, Lyudmila Petrova, Vladimir Ivashev, Bolot Beyshenaliev, A. Kobaladze, Ch. Nzrguy, Ts. Timurbator, L. Zolotukhin, V. Larionov, V. Ezepov, A. Bekmurazov, E. Lazarev and A. Martinov. ¶A Soviet, Mongolian and East German coproduction released in Russia in 1982 as *Cherez Gobi i khingan* in two parts running 102 minutes and 106 minutes.

Adios *see* **The Lash.**

Aeronaut (1975). Filmed in Sovscope 70. *Screen author* Vladimir Kunin. *Directors* Natalia Troshchenko and Anatoly Vekhotko. *Operator* Aleksandr Chechulin. *Artist* Valery Yurkevich. *Composer* I. Tsvetkov. *Sound operator* R. Belenikiy.

¶A Lenfilm production. International distribution Sovexportfilm. Sovcolor. Six-track magnetic stereophonic sound. 117 minutes. Filmed at Lenfilm Studios, Leningrad, R.S.F.S.R. ¶CAST: *Ivan Zaikin* Leonard Varfolomeev. *Baroness Clautilde de Laroche* Ekaterina Vasilieva. *Alexander Kuprin* Armen Dzigarkhanyan. *Henri Farman* Anatoly Solonitsin. *Rigaut* Leonkhard Merzin. *Gaber-Vlinsky* Valery Olshansky. *Matsievich* Vladimir Zamanskiy. *French flyer* Georgi Drozd. *Efimov* Nikolay Fedortsov. *With* V. Nikulin, A. Ravinovich, V. Iliichev, O. Basilashvili, A. Merzin and S. Dreyden. ¶A Soviet production released in Russia in 1975 as *Vozdukhoplavateli.*

Affairs of the Heart (1974). Filmed in Sovscope 70. *Screen authors* Vladimir Kunin and Semyon Laskin. *Director* Izkhdar Ibragimov. *Operator* Margarita Pilikhina. *Artist* Gennady Myasnikov. *Composer* Arif Melikov. *Sound operator* S. Litvinov. ¶A Mosfilm production. International distribution Sovexportfilm. Sovcolor. Six-track magnetic stereophonic sound. 115 minutes. Filmed at Mosfilm Studios, Moscow, R.S.F.S.R. ¶CAST: *Alexei* Georgi Taratorkin. *Lida* Antonina Shuranova. *Boris Ivanovich* Anatoli Papanov. *Natasha* Ekaterina Markova. *With* P. Vinnik, I. Kondratieva, G. Kulikov, D. Masanov, D. Netrebin, L. Dranovskaya, N. Zvachkina, P. Merkuriev and E. Tyapkina. ¶A Soviet production released in Russia in 1974 as *Dela serdechnie.*

(Irving Stone's) The Agony and the Ecstasy (October 7, 1965). Filmed in Todd-AO. *Executive producer* Darryl F. Zanuck. *Associate executive producer* Elmo Williams. *Producer and director* Carol Reed. *Screen story and screenplay* Philip Dunne. *Based on the novel by* Irving Stone. *Music composer and conductor* Alex North. *Director of photography* Leon Shamroy. *Art direction* Jack Martin Smith. *Production designer* John De Cuir. *Choral music composer and conductor* Franco Potenza. *Film editor* Samuel E. Beetley. *Set decorations* Dario Simoni. *Special photographic effects* L.B. Abbott, Emil Kosa, Jr. and Art Cruickshank. *Assistant director* Gus Agosti. *Sound* Carlton W. Faulkner and Douglas O. Williams *Costume designer* Vittorio Nino

Novarese. *Wardrobe makers* Casa d'Arte-Firenze of R. Peruzzi. *Makeup* Amato Garbini. *Hair stylist* Grazia de Rossi. *Prop master* Sam Gordon. *Orchestration* Alexander Courage. *Second unit director* Robert D. Webb. *Second unit photography* Piero Portalupi. *Italian production manager* Giorgio Zambon. *Todd-AO developers* American Optical Company and Magna Theatre Corp. *Production executive* Doc Merman. *Prolog music* Jerry Goldsmith. *Sound studio* Fono Roma. *Sound supervision* James Corcoran. *Music recording* Douglas O. Williams *Technical advisers* Prof. Igino Cupelloni and Vincent Labello *Camera operator* Irving Rosenberg. *Assistant cameraman* Lee "Red" Crawford. *Still photographers* Art Kane and Emil Schutkess. *Unit publicist* Howard Liebling. *Supervising music editor* George Adams. *Sound editor* Peter Thornton. ¶A Carol Reed production. An International Classics, Inc. picture. Released by 20th Century–Fox. Color by De Luxe. Westrex six-track magnetic stereophonic sound. 140 minutes plus intermission. Filmed in the Studio of Dino De Laurentiis Cinematografica S.p.A. and Studio Cinecitta, Rome and on location in Rome, Carrara, Florence, Todi, Bracciano and Monterano, Italy. ¶CAST: *Michelangelo Buonarroti* Charlton Heston. *Pope Julius II* Rex Harrison. *Contessina de' Medici* Diane Cilento. *Bramante* Harry Andrews. *The Duke of Urbino* Alberto Lupo. *Giovanni de' Medici* Adolfo Celi. *Paris de Grassis* Venantino Venantini. *Sangallo* John Stacy. *The stone quarry foreman* Fausto Tozzi. *A woman from Michelangelo's past* Maxine Audley. *Raphael* Tomas Milian. *Cardinal* Richard Pearson. ¶The prolog and intermission were removed from 35mm general release and 16mm nontheatrical prints. The prolog has been restored to some television prints and the video cassette edition.

Agression *see* **The Battle of Moscow.**

Agressiya *see* **The Battle of Moscow.**

Airport (May 5, 1970). Filmed in Todd-AO. *Producer* Ross Hunter. *Directors* George Seaton and Henry Hathaway. *Screenplay* George Seaton. *Based on the novel by* Arthur Hailey. *Director of photography* Ernest Laszlo. *Music* Alfred Newman. *Film editor* Stuart Gilmore. *Associate producer* Jacques Mapes. *Unit production manager* Raymond Gosnell, Jr. *Assistant directors* Donald Roberts and Peter Bogart. *Art directors* Alexander Golitzen and E. Preston Ames. *Set decorations* Jack D. Moore and Mickey S. Michaels. *Men's costumes* Ross Hunter. *Women's costumes* Edith Head and Richard Hopper. *Makeup* Bud Westmore. *Hair stylist* Larry Germain. *Sound* Waldon O. Watson, David H. Moriarty and Ronald Pierce. *Special photographic effects* Film Effects of Hollywood, Don W. Weed, James B. Gordon, Linwood G. Dunn and Cecil Love. *Script supervisor* Betty Abbott. *Technical advisers* John N. Denend and Capt. Lee Danielson. *Cosmetics* Universal Pictures Professional Cosmetics. ¶A Ross Hunter Productions, Inc. picture. Released by Universal Pictures. Technicolor. Westrex six-track magnetic stereophonic sound. 137 minutes. Filmed at Universal City Studios and on location at Minneapolis-St. Paul International Airport, Minnesota. ¶CAST: *Mel Bakersfeld* Burt Lancaster. *Capt. Vernon Demerest* Dean Martin. *Tanya Livingston* Jean Seberg. *Gwen Meighen* Jacqueline Bisset. *Joe Patroni* George Kennedy. *Ada Quonsett* Helen Hayes. *D.O. Guerrero* Van Heflin. *Inez Guerrero* Maureen Stapleton. *Lt. Anson Harris* Barry Nelson. *Cindy Bakersfeld* Dana Wynter. *Harry Standish* Lloyd Nolan. *Sarah Bakersfeld Demerest* Barbara Hale. *Cy Jordan* Gary Collins. *Peter Coakley* John Findlater. *Harriet DuBarry Mossman* Jessie Royce Landis. *Commissioner Ackerman* Larry Gates. *Marcus Rathbone* Peter Turgeon. *Mr. Davidson* Whit Bissell. *Mrs. Schultz* Virginia Grey. *Judy* Eileen Wesson. *Dr. Compagno* Paul Picerni. *Capt. Benson* Robert Patten. *Bert Weatherby* Clark Howat. *Reynolds* Lew Brown. *Roberta Bakersfeld* Ilana Dowding. *Libby Bakersfeld* Lisa Gerritson. *Father Steven Lonigan* Jim Nolan. *Joan* Patty Poulsen. *Ruth* Ena Hartman. *Maria* Malila Saint Duval. *Sally* Sharon Harvey. *Lt. Ordway* Albert Reed. *Marie Patroni* Jodean Russo. *Bunnie* Nancy Ann Nelson. *Mr. Schultz* Dick Winslow. *Schuyler Schultz* Lou Wagner. *Sister Katherine Grace* Janis Hansen. *Sister Felice* Mary Jackson. *Rollings* Shelly Novack. *Parks* Chuck Daniel. *Diller* Charles Brewer. *Cindy's father* Walter Woolf King. *Praying* *father* Damian London. *Airport security man* Richard Van Vleet. ¶Henry Hathaway took over direction during George Seaton's illness. Sequels, all featuring George Kennedy as Joe Patroni, were *Airport 1975, Airport '77* and *The Concorde—Airport '79.*

The Alamo (October 24, 1960). Filmed in Todd-AO. *Producer and director* John Wayne. *Associate producer and original screenplay* James Edward Grant. *Story* Patrick Roper Ford. *Second unit directors* Cliff Lyons, John Ford and Ray Kellogg. *Director of photography* William H. Clothier. *Music composer and conductor* Dimitri Tiomkin. *Film editor* Stuart Gilmore. *Technical supervision* Jack Pennick and Frank C. Beetson, Sr. *Art director and construction manager* Alfred Ybarra. *Interior construction foreman* Fred La Tour. *Set decorations* Victor A. Gangelin. *Property master* Joseph La-Bella. *Special effects* Lee Zavitz. *Stunt coordinator* Cliff Lyons. *Assistant directors* Robert E. Relyea and Robert Saunders. *Costumers* Frank C. Beetson, Sr. and Ann Peck. *Production manager* Nate H. Edwards. *Unit manager* Thomas J. Andre. *Makeup supervision* Webster Overlander. *Hair stylist* Fae M. Smith. *Sound recording supervisors* Fred Hynes and Gordon E. Sawyer. *Sound* Jack Solomon. *Music recorders* Murray Spivack and Vinton Vernon. *Sound recording* Todd-AO and Samuel Goldwyn Studios. *Sound editor* Don Hall, Jr. *Music editor* Robert Tracy. *Assistant to producer* Michael A. Wayne. *Main title* Pacific Title & Art Studio. *Livestock coordinator* Billy Jones. *Transportation coordinator* George Coleman. *Public relations* Russell Birdwell. *Production executive* Jim Henaghen. *Production assistant* Thomas J. Kane. *Camera operators* Lou Jennings and Art Lane. *Assistant cameramen* Robert Rhea and Joe Raue. *Chief electrician* Ralph Owen. *Technical advisers* J. Frank Dobie and Lon Tinkle. *Animal protection* American Humane Association. *Longhorns suppliers* Milby Butler, J.D. Phillips, Cap Yates and Bill Daniel. *Associated with the production* Clinton W. Murchison, Sr., Clinton W. Murchison, Jr., John Dabney Murchison, O.J. McCullough and I.J. McCullough. *"Ballad of the Alamo," "Tennessee Babe," "The Green Leaves of Summer"* and

"Here's to the Ladies" music Dimitri Tiomkin, *lyrics* Paul Francis Webster. *"Eyes of Texas" courtesy of* Student Association, University of Texas. *Negative* Eastman Color. ¶A Batjac Productions, Inc. picture for The Alamo Company. Released by United Artists. Technicolor. Westrex six-track magnetic stereophonic sound. 161 minutes plus overture and intermission. Filmed at Samuel Goldwyn Studios and on location at Alamo Village, Brackettville, Texas. ¶CAST: *Col. David Crockett* John Wayne. *Col. James Bowie* Richard Widmark. *Col. William Barret Travis* Laurence Harvey. *John W. "Smitty" Smith* Frankie Avalon. *Capt. James Butler Bonham* Patrick Wayne. *Maria "Flaca" de Lopez Bexar* Linda Cristal. *Susannah (Sue) Dickinson* Joan O'Brien. *Beekeeper* Chill Wills. *Alcalde Juan Seguin* Joseph Calleia. *Capt. Almeron Dickinson* Ken Curtis. *Lt. Reyes* Carlos Arruza. *Jethro* Jester Hairston. *Blind Nell Robertson* Veda Ann Borg. *James "Jocko" Robertson* John Dierkes. *Thimberig* Denver Pyle. *Angelina "Lisa" Dickinson* Aissa Wayne. *Parson* Hank Worden. *Dr. William D. Sutherland* William (Bill) Henry. *Col. James C. Neill* William (Bill) Daniel. *Emil Sande* Wesley Lau. *"Do it mean what I think it do" Tennessean* Charles (Chuck) Roberson. *Acting Lt. Finn* Guinn "Big Boy" Williams. *Mrs. Stephen Dennison* Olive Carey. *Gen. Antonio Lopez de Santa Anna* Ruben Padilla. *Gen. Sam Houston* Richard Boone. *Sgt. William J. Lightfoot* Jack Pennick. *Silverio Seguin* Julian Trevino. *Pete Denison* Cy Malis. *Bearded defender* Fred Graham. *Bull* Tom Hennesy. *Defenders* William F. McGaha, Chester Harvey Smith, Slim Hightower, Jack Williams, Dean Smith, Bob Morgan and Cliff Lyons. *Tennessean Boyd "Red"* Morgan. *Tennessean cannoneer* Charles (Chuck) Hayward. *Women* Le Jean Guyo Ethridge and Carol Berlin. *Teenager* Carol Baxter. ¶Premiered at 192 minutes plus overture and intermission. All other versions were 161 minutes during initial release. The overture and intermission were removed from the 35mm general release version. Reissued in 1967 running 140 minutes. Wayne had tried for years to produce the film while at Republic. He had at that time intended to shoot it in Peru. Republic kept delaying the project, and Wayne left the studio and set up opera-

On the set of The Alamo, *producer, director and star John Wayne (left) leans over the Todd-AO camera to adjust Carlos Arruza's chinstrap. Cinematographer William H. Clothier can be glimpsed behind Wayne's arms. The individual under the lamp may be gaffer Ralph Owen.*

tions at Warner Bros., where it again was delayed. Republic then produced their own version, *Lost Command* (1955), partly on Texas locations. Wayne moved to United Artists and finally shot his film. Footage was later incorporated into *How the West Was Won*. As so much footage was eventually cut from the various versions of this film, a cataloging of excised material is in order. All the material below appeared in the 70mm premiere print, but the 70mm and 35mm roadshow versions were edited considerably. Italics denote material that was retained in part or whole in the roadshow and general release version, was later removed, but now appears in the excellent home video version, which also has the original, fully directional stereophonic soundtrack. (The video version does not have the overture, intermission or exit music.) The footage was: *Bowie, with a hangover, discovers Travis has been placed in command of the garrison at San Antonio; Travis and Dickinson discuss how much the garrison should know about their true situation;* Crockett, Bowie, Parson and Beekeeper are confronted by Emil Sande and his henchmen in the town church where Sande has secreted arms and munitions from the rebels, a fight ensues and Crockett kills Sande; Crockett advises Flaca of the fight with Sande; Flaca speaks to Mrs. Guy during movement of the settlers; *Bowie defends Smitty's abilities as a soldier;* Crockett and Bowie discuss explosives; Crockett explains a ridgepole to Flaca; *Travis and Bowie conflict over defense of the garrison after the first assault against the fort;* a patrol led by Dickinson is ambushed; a few reinforcements arrive; a birthday party is held for Lisa Dickinson (a still from which appears in the souvenir program book); Crockett prays over the dying Parson; *religious attitudes are debated by some of the defenders the night before the last assault; and Bowie speaks during the final assault concerning the north wall.* Additional, often nonsensical, cuts were made for network television presentation. While John Ford worked uncredited on the production, it has been written by others that his involvement was far greater than that of second unit director. In fact Ford, who never claimed credit at all, directed only the following footage: Mexican artillery crossing the river; a panoramic sweep of the Mexican army approaching the fort; the Mexican dance on the river bank; the Mexican cavalryman shot from his horse by Travis; Dickinson's patrol swimming across the river (part of the deleted ambush sequence); and Smitty's delivery of the last message from the Alamo to Houston, who then berates his officers for their men's attitude. Cliff Lyons functioned not only as second unit director but "Wayne's right hand during the entire production," to quote the souvenir program book. Ray Kellogg, uncredited, also aided in the action footage. However, no footage was shot without Wayne's supervision, and despite the use of second units (a common practice on most films) he *was* the producer and director in charge. Let the detractors be silenced once and for all!

Alfa 78 (1978). Filmed in OMNIMAX. *Producer* Les Novros. *Director* Robert Amram. *Photographer* J. Barry Herron. ¶A Graphic Films Corporation production. Released by Centro Cultural Alfa. Filmed in Mexico. Eastman Color. Six-track magnetic stereophonic sound. 26 minutes. ¶Originally made as a visual annual report of the corporate activities of Grupo Industrial Alfa in Mexico for Centro Cultural Alfa, Monterrey, Mexico.

Alimanakh kinoputeshestviy (1978). Filmed in Sovscope 70. International distribution Sovexportfilm. Sovcolor. Six-track magnetic stereophonic sound. ¶A Soviet production released in Russia in 1978.

Alpine Thrills (June 1986). Filmed in Showscan. Presented in Dynamic Motion. ¶Produced and released by Showscan Film Corporation in collaboration with Intamin Corporation, Inc., Establishment. Eastman Color. Six-track magnetic Dolby Stereo. Approximately 3 minutes. ¶An American and Liechtensteinian coproduction, made for showing in a Dynamic Motion Theater (in which the seats move in sync with the action on the screen to give the audience the feeling of participating in the filmed action).

An American Adventure (1981). Filmed in IMAX. *Producer* David Dwiggins. *Director and photographer* Timothy Galfas. ¶A William McCaffery, Inc.–Dove Films production. Released by Marriott's Great

America. Eastman Color. Six-track magnetic stereophonic sound. 25 minutes. ¶Filmed throughout the United States. Originally made for Marriott Corp., it duplicates Cinerama's rollercoaster ride on a loop Demon Roller Coaster.

Ancient Russia (1985). Filmed in Sovscope 70. *Screen authors* Gennady Vasiliev and Mikhail Vorfolomeyev. *Based on the novel "Ruz iznachalnaya" by* Valentin Ivanov. *Director* Gennady Vasiliev. *Operator* Avetis Garibyan. *Artist* Alfred Talantsev. *Costumier* Lyudmila Chekulaeva. *Composer* Alexey Rybnikov. *Sound operator* Leonid Veitkov. ¶A Tsentra studiya detskikh i yunosheskikh filmov im. M. Gorikogo production. International distribution Sovexportfilm. Sovcolor. Six-track magnetic stereophonic sound. 146 minutes. Filmed at Tsentraliniy studiya detskikh i yunosheskikh filmov im. M. Gorikogo, Moscow, and on location in Sudak, Crimea, Askania Nova and Uyborg, R.S.F.S.R. ¶CAST: *Ratibor* Vladimir Antonick. *Voyevoda Vseslav* Boris Nevzorov. *Aleya* Lyudmila Chursina. *Mlava* Elena Kondulainen. *Emperor Yustinian* Innokenty Smoktunovskiy. *Empress Theodora* Margarita Terekhova. *Khazar girl* Alla Plotkina. *Ipatias* Evgeni Steblov. *With* Elguya Burduli. ¶A Soviet production released in Russia in 1985 as *Ruz iznachalnaya*. Also known as *The Beginning of Russia*.

Andrey Bolkonskiy *see* **Leo Tolstoy's War and Peace.**

Andromeda Nebula (1967). Filmed in Sovscope 70. *Screen authors* Vladimir Dmitrievskiy and Evgeni Sherstobitov. *Based on the novel "Tumannosti Andromedi" by* Ivan Efremova. *Director* Evgeni Sherstobitov. *Operator* Nikolay Zuravlev. *Artist* Alexey Bobrovnikov. *Composer* Yakov Lapinskiy. *Sound operator* Naum Trakhtenberg. ¶A Kievskaya kinostudya im A.P. Dovzenko production. International distribution Sovexportfilm. Sovcolor. Six-track magnetic stereophonic sound. 96 minutes. Filmed at Kievskaya kinostudiya. im. A.P. Dovzenko, Kiev, Ukrainian S.S.R. ¶CAST: *Veda Kong* Vuya Artmane. *Dar Veter* Segey Stolyarov. *Erg Noor* Nikolay Kryufkov. *Niza Krit* Tatyana Voloshina. *Mven Mas* Lado Tshvariashvili. ¶A Soviet production released in Russia in 1967 as *Tumannosti*

Andromedi. Fans of *Star Wars* films should find one of the character names interesting.

Andrus (1982). Filmed in Sovscope 70. *Screen author* Vloletta Palichinskayte. *Director* Algirdas Araminas. *Operator* Ionas Martsinkyavichyus. *Artist* Algirdas Nichyus. *Composer* Bronius Kutavichyus. *Sound operator* Yu. Tuyta. ¶A Litovskaya kinostudiya production. International distribution Sovexportfilm. Sovcolor. Six-track magnetic stereophonic sound. 63 minutes. Filmed at Litovskaya kinostudiya, Vilnius, Lithuanian S.S.R. ¶CAST: *Rauplenas* Donates Banionis. *With* Edvin Menchikov, Inga Brunzayte, Indra Andrashchyunayte and Irena-Maria Lednavichyute. ¶A Soviet production released in Russia in 1982 as *Andryus*.

Andryus *see* **Andrus.**

Angeli kosmosa *see* **To the Stars by Hard Ways**

Anna Karenina (1971). Filmed in Sovscope 70. *Screen authors* Vassili Katanyan and Aleksandr Zarkhi. *Based on the novel by* Count Leo Nikolayevich Tolstogo. *Director and producer* Aleksandr Zarkhi. *Operator* Leonid Kalashnikov. *Artists* A. Bopisov and Yu. Kladienko. *Composer* Rodion Shchedrin. *Sound operators* V. Leshchev and B. Zuev. *Editor* N. Petrykina. ¶A Mosfilm production. Released by Sovexportfilm. Sovcolor. Six-track magnetic stereophonic sound. 135 minutes. Filmed at Mosfilm Studios, Moscow, R.S.F.S.R. ¶CAST: *Anna Karenina* Tatyana Samoilova. *Kitty* Anastasia Vertinskaya. *Dolly* Iya Savvina. *Princess* Maya Plisetskaya. *Karenin* Nikolai Gritsenko. *Vronsky* Vassili Lanovoy. *Konstantine* B. Goldaev. *Lydia* L. Sukharevskaya. *Serioja* Vassia Sakhnovskiy. *With* Yu. Yakovlev, V. Vertinskaga, S. Pilyavskaya and E. Tyapkina. ¶A Soviet production released in Russia in 1968 in two parts running 95 minutes and 86 minutes. Specific U.S. release date unknown.

Anna Pavlova (1983). Filmed in Sovscope 70. *Screen author and director* Emil Latyanu. *Operators* Evgeni Guslinskiy and Vladimir Nakhabstev. *Artist* Boris Blank. *Composer* Evgeny Doga. *Sound operator* A. Pogosyan. *Music executed in the film* P.I. Chaykovskiy, Aleksandr Porfirevich

Borodina, Alyabieva, Johann Sebastian Bach, Bokkerini, Adana, Guno and Deliba. ¶A Mosfilm-Poseidon Productions, Ltd.-DEFA-ICAIC-Films Cosmos production in collaboration with Sovinfilm. International distribution Sovexportfilm. Sovcolor. Six-track magnetic stereophonic sound. 192 minutes plus intermission. Filmed at Mosfilm Studios, Moscow, R.S.F.S.R. ¶CAST: *Anna Pavlova* Galina Belyaeva. *With* L. Buldakova, Sergei Shakurov, Vsevolod Larionov, James Fox, Jacques Debarry, G. Dimitriu, P. Gusev, D. Myurrey, Svetlana Toma, N. Fateeva, V. Reshetnikova, Tiit Khyarm and Martin Scorcese. ¶A Soviet, British, East German, Cuban and French coproduction released in Russia in 1983 in two parts running 98 minutes and 94 minutes.

Arena (1967). Filmed in Sovscope 70. *Screen authors* Vladimir Kapitanovskiy and Samson Samsonov. *Director and producer* Samson Samsonov. *Operators* Nikolay Bolishako and Mikhail Suslov. *Artists* Boris Blank and Vladimir Kamskiy. *Composer* Eduard Artemiev. *Sound operator* Grigori Korenblyum. ¶A Mosfilm production. International distribution Sovexportfilm. Sovcolor. Six-track magnetic stereophonic sound. 121 minutes. Filmed at Mosfilm Studios, Moscow, R.S.F.S.R. ¶CAST: *Masha* Margarita Volodina. *Lovitor* Gleb Strizenov. *Red clown* Adolf Dimsha. *White clown* Valentin Skulme. *Commandant* Yanis Melderis. *With* P. Kvaskov, V. Preymanis and K. Zabulionis. ¶A Soviet production released in Russia in 1967. Reedited to 97 minutes.

Armed and Dangerous (1978). Filmed in Sovscope 70. *Screen authors* Vladimir Vladimirov and Pavel Finn. *Based on characters created by* Francis Brett "Bret" Harte. *Director* Vladimir Vaynshtok. *Operator* Konstantin Rizov. *Artist* Konstantin Zagorskiy. *Composer* Gennady Firtich. *Sound operator* N. Ozornov. ¶A Tsentraliniy studiya detskikh i yunosheskikh filmov im. M. Gorikogo production. International distribution Sovexportfilm. Sovcolor. Six-track magnetic stereophonic sound. 125 minutes. Filmed at Tsentraliniy studiya detskikh i yunosheskikh filmov im. M. Gorikogo, Moscow, R.S.F.S.R. and on location in Azer-

baiyuian and Baku, U.S.S.R., Ploskowice Castle, Czechoslovakia and Constanta, Rumania. ¶CAST: *Gabriel Conroy* Donantes Banionis. *Jack Hamlin* Mirca Veroyu. *Julie Prudom* Lyudmilla Senchina. *Dolores Dumphey* Maria Ployya. *Banker Dumphey* Leonid Bronevoy. *Lucky Charlie* Lev Durov. *Indian Joe* Talgat Nigmatulia. *Starbottle* Algis Masyulis. *Butler* Yan Shalines. *Trott* Sergei Martinson. *Henry York* Vsevolod Podulov. *With* V. Abdulov, Ferents Bentse, G. Lyampe and Oleg Zakov. ¶A Soviet production released in Russia in 1978 as *Vooruzen i ocheni opacen.* Released in England in 1978 by International Film Exchange (IFEX) as *Armed and Very Dangerous: The Time and Heroes of Francis Bret Harte,* running 123 minutes. This is a western!

Armed and Very Dangerous: The Time and Heroes of Francis Bret Harte *see* **Armed and Dangerous**

(Michael Todd's) Around the World in 80 Days (October 1956). Filmed in Todd-AO. *Producer* Michael Todd. *Director* Michael Anderson. *Screenplay* James Poe, John Farrow and S.J. Perelman. *Based on the novel by* Jules Verne. *Music* Victor Young. *Orchestrations* Leo Shuken and Sidney Cutner. *First assistant directors* Ronnie Rondell, Ivan Volkman and Dennis Bertera. *Director of photography* Lionel Lindon. *Directors of photography second unit* William N. Williams, David Stanley Horsley and Ellis W. Carter. *Associate producer and production designer* William Cameron Menzies. *Art direction* James Sullivan and Ken Adam (London). *Set decorator* Ross Dowd. *Sound* Joseph I. Kane and Fred Hynes. *Editors* Gene Ruggiero and Howard Epstein. *Choreographer and dance director* Paul Godkin. *Production manager* Percy Guth. *Special effects* Lee Zavitz. *Research* Ann Pearls. *Makeup* Gustaf Norin. *Hairdressing* Edith Keon. *Still cameraman* Robert Donald Christie. *Casting* William White. *Unit manager* Frank (Fox) Kowalski. *Wardrobe manager* Robert Martien. *Sound editor* Theodore Bellinger. *Music editor* Charles Clement. *Titles designer* Saul Bass. *Costumes designer* Miles White. *Assistant to the producer* Michael Todd, Jr. *Executive secretaries* Richard Handley and Midori Tsuji. *Foreign*

Locations: Second unit director and assistant to the producer Kevin O'Donovan McClory. *Cameramen* Harry Mimura and Graham (Skeets) Kelly. *Technical consultant* Edward Williams. *Properties* Thomas Erley. *Technical advisers* Koichi Kawana and Dr. R. Charles Beard. *Makeup* Yamada and John O'Gorman. *United States: Associate producer* Ned (Herbert) Mann. *Lyrics* Harold Adamson. *Second unit directors* Michael Todd and James Sullivan. *Executive assistant* Samuel Lambert. *Todd-AO technical consultant* Schuyler A. Sanford. *Negative* Eastman Kodak. *Todd-AO developers* American Optical Company and Magna Theatre Corp. *Sound system* Todd-AO. *Publicity* Bill Doll, Lou Smith, Ernest Anderson, Chuck Cochard, Jack Egan, Seymour Krawitz, Al Sharper and Tom Wood. *Secretarial* Edythe Baird, Mayme Bell, Gladys Benito, Louise Costa, Jack Frost, Margaret Kelly, Liberty Koloniar, Doris Kruse, Renee Laven, Margaret Marsh, Patricia O'Neil, Blanche Pinkussohn, Jordan Ramin, Carol Robertson, Virginia Rowe, Flora Dee Sampson, Adelaide Schneider, Marguerite Smith, Lillian Stewart, Helen Tomlinson, Matilda Wiebel and Patricia Woodward. *Accounting* Samuel Wien, Gerry Broderick, Sophia Brown, Louis Bernstein, Mazzios Damon, Charles Heiss, Harriet Iskowitz, Ethel King, Albert Kraus, Harold Lindemann, Edna Maguire, William Quinn and John Wooster. *Art direction and sets* Allan Abbott, Eugene Angel, Lois Green Cohen, Lucius O. Croxton, Leroy Deane, George Fowler, Fred Harpman, Leslie Marzoff, Ladd Hoffman, Alexander Mayer, Masaji B. Murai, Steven Pridgeon, Alfred Sheppard, Frank Smith, Marilyn Sotto and Tyrus Wong. *Casting* Frank Leyva and Ann Teague. *First assistant director, Lawton, Oklahoma* Lew Borzage. *Second assistant directors* Jack Boland, Joseph C. Boyle, Elmer Decker, Paul Feiner, George Lopez, Frank Losee, Buddy Messenger, Michael G. Messenger, Wilbur Mosier, William O'Donnell, Lewis Jeffrey Selznick, Ivan G. Thomas and Arthur R. Thompson. *Teachers of children appearing in picture* Lucie Besag, Mary Dewitt, Marcia Levin, Leon G. Lyons, Georgia Marsh, Ruth Overman, Felippa G. Rock and Ruth Victor. *Editorial* Paul Weatherwax and Donald Tomlinson. *Projectionist* Fred Beard. *Electrical* Don C. Stott,

Leland Armstrong, William Draper, Albert Gilbert, John D. Glover, Jack Griffith, Norman Lindley, Frank Milliken, John O'Malley, Glenn Pennington, Jess Salais and John Vaiana. *Electrical, Durango, Colorado* Merle Boardman, Harold G. Coulson, Francis E. Grumpp and Thomas B. Lloyd. *Floral and arboreal decoration* Harold G. Becker, Bruce Bell, Nicholas Carey, William Crider, Richard Huhn, Arthur Lang, Myron C. Peterson, Abe Siegel, William Steck and Robert Villegas. *Floral and arboreal contractor* Lou Honig. *Hair styling* Peggy Adams, Jane Aldrich, Cherie Banks, Sally Berkeley, Yvette Bernier, Lillian Burkhart, Eleanor Cole, Madine Banks, Elizabeth Detter, Katharina Detter, Lily Dirigo, Doris Durkus, Emmy Eckhardt, Ray Forman, Wava Green, Carla M. Hadley, Doris Haines, Dotha Hippe, Hazel Keithley, Ann E. Kirk, Hazel Kraft, Fritzy La Bar, Lillian Lashin, Annabell Levy *(ch),* Maudlee MacDougall, Peggy McDonald, Wenda McKee, Mildred Margulies, Louise Miehle, Eve Newing, Lily Rader, Francesca Raffa, Gladys Rasmussen, Gertrude Reade, Merle Reeves, Leonora Sabine, Ruth Sandifer, Katherine Shea, Lillian Shore, Fae M. Smith, Josephine Sweeney, Hazel R. Thompson, Peg Thomson and Marion Vaugh. *Pilots* Paul Mantz, Merle Edgerton and Stanley Reaver. *Drivers* Robert Jamieson, George F. Andrews, Leroy A. Beach, Don Bell, William S. Bethea, John Cooley, Frank Coon, Russell Coon, Ike Danning, William Ford, Albert Frederickson, Wilbur Freese, Emil Garner, Orville Hebert, Irving Hedeen, Cecil Higgins, William Hoxie, R.W. Hutchinson, Horace Irwin, John F. Jackson, John Jay Jones, Edwin Kemp, Wilkie Kleinpell, Norman Knighton, John A. O'Hara, Peter Pitassi, Nick Potskoff, Allen G. Reed, Ernest A. Reed, Edward Ritchie, Paul Romero, Hal H. Smith, George Spahn, Jr., William Trow and James R. White. *Drivers, Durango, Colorado* Ernest F. Austin, R.A. Beirley, Beryl D. Benham, Edward Douglas Brown, John D. Brown, Charles Robert Carter, William H. Craig, Pat L. Cugnini, Melvin V. Flack, Bennie Legill, Carl H. Longstrom, William Loftus, Henry C. Ludwig, Charles Harry Meador, Chester W. Meador, Samuel H. Miller, James A. Norton, Shirley B. Palmer, William A. Pryor, Robert Bruce Robertson, Edgar A.

Rowe, Fred M. Rudy, Bennet B. St. John and Harold A. Schaaf. *Makeup* Bunny Armstrong, Carl Axzelle, George T. Bau, Charles F. Blackman, Willard Buell, Edwin J. Butterworth, Jr., Larry Butterworth, Jack Byron, E. Thomas Case, Jr., Jack Casey, Jean Casey, John Chambers, Steven Clensos, Robert Cowan, Robert Dawn, Armand Delmar, Violette De Noyer, Russel Drake, Willon Fields, Charles Gemora, George G. Gray, H. Dan Greenway, Lee Greenway, Burris Grimwood, Joseph Hadley, Richard Hamilton, Robert Hickman, Louis Hippe, Gordon Hubbard, John A.D. Johnson, Newton J. Jones, A.C. Karnagel, Claire Kaufman, Grant Keats, Benjamin Lane, Ted Larsen, Frank La Rue, Charles Lauder, Harold Lierly, Robert Littlefield, Raymond Lopez, Stanley McKay, Otis Malcolm, Paul Malcolm, Harry Maret, Robert Mark, Terry Miles, Thomas P. Miller, Jr., Imogene Mollner, Bill Morley, Garret W. Morris, Dick Narr, William Oakley, Jack Obringer, Stanley Orr, E. Webster Overlander, Ernie Park, Sidney Perell, Louis Phillipi, Fred Phillips, H.W. Phillips, Webster C. Phillips, Sam Polo, Mark Reedall, Lynn Reynolds, Ray Romero, Harry Ross, Carl A. Russell, Philip Scheer, Walter Schenck, Don Schoenfeld, Charles Schram, Erroll K. Silvera, Gloria Skarstedt, Jack M. Smith, Allan Snyder, Leland Stanfield, Paul Stanhope, Jr., John A. Stone, Daniel Striepke, John F. Sweeney, Claude M. Thompson, William P. Turner, Thomas Tuttle, Nicholas Vehr, Fred T. Walker, John Wallace, Fred Williams, Joe Williams, Alice Wills, Edith Wilson, William D. Wood, E. Jean Young and Edward Zimmer. *Assistant music editor* Herbert C. Steinore. *Orchestra manager* Henry Hill. *Musicians* Doris C. Albert, Samuel Albert, Albert C. Anderson, James Arkatov, Victor Arno, Robert Bain, Robert Barene, Arnold Belnick, Morris Bercov, Haakon Bergh, Cy Bernard, Ennio Bolognini, Morris Brenner, John T. Boudreau, Huntington Burdick, Audrey Call, May Cambern, Manuel Compinsky, Marshall Cram, Leonard Dahlsten, Bonnie Jean Douglas, Alexander DuVoir, Walter Edelstein, Henry Emerson, George Faye, Dominick Fera, Robert Fleming, Dominic Frontiere, Arthur D. Gault, Richard Giese, Benny Gill, Ossip Giskin, Fred Glickman, Philip Goldberg, Alex Golden, Victor Gottlieb, Max Gralnick, Saul Grant, Charlotte Harris, Dave Harris, Stanley Harris, Jimmie Haskell, Raymond Hoback, Abraham Hochstein, Lawrence Hochstein, Milton Holland, Davida G. Jackson, Carl Jeschke, David Jeselson, Maxine Johnson, Glen Johnston, Milton Kestenbaum, Sol Kindler, Raphael Kramer, Amnon Levy, Abe Luboff, Alfred Lustgarten, Paul McLarand, Arthur Maebe, Lily Mahler, Lou Marcasie, Jack Marsh, G.R. Menhennick, Peter Mercurio, David Miller, William Miller, Elizabeth Moor, Ted Nash, Robert Nelson, William Newman, Eugene Ober, Pullman Pederson, Jack Pepper, Joseph Pepper, Alex Pierce, Nicholas Pisani, Carl Prager, Cecil Read, Joseph Reilich, Sam Rice, Joseph Rizzo, Edward Rosa, Jack Rose, Luther Roundtree, Doris Savery, Harold Schneier, Toscha Seidel, Waldmar Seliger, Bernard Senescu, Eudice Shapiro, Barbara Shik, Erno Shik, Tibor Shik, Clarence Smith, Elmer Smithers, Peter Sniadoff, Maxim Sobolewsky, Harry Solloway, Stanley Spiegelman, Maurice K. Stein, Albert Steinberg, David Sterkin, Manuel Stevens, Harry Stitman, Robert Sushel, Thomas J. Tedesco, Milton Thomas, Raymond Turner, Lloyd E. Ulyate, Jeanette Violin, George Wendt, Eunice Wennermark and Seymour Zeldin. *Singers* Jacqueline Allen, Gurney N. Bell, Dick Byron, Lee Gotch, Homer Hall, Delos Jewkes, Dudley Kuzel, Ray L. Linn, Jr., Dorothy McCarty, Charles Prescott, Jr., Charles Schroeder and Allan Watson. *Photography* Landon Arnett, Alfred Baalas, Donald H. Birnkrant, Haskell Boggs, Emilio Calori, Edward Chaffin, Alfred Cline, Walter Craig, James Daly, Arthur Jock Feindel, James Grout, Harold Harmon, S.J. Hoffberg, Roy Ivey, Richard H. Kline, Arthur Lindsley Lane, George Le Picard, Sr., Cliff MacDonald, Fred Mautino, Harry Parsons, Otto Pierce, William Rankin, Maynard B. Rugg, Lester Shorr, George Smart, William Snyder, Charles Straumer, Charles Termini, John D. Weiler and Jock Wendall. *Set construction and operation coordinator* Don Bruno. *Painters* W.R. Moore, Alex Sinel and Alfred Stroup. *Grips* John Akers, Alvin R. Cannon, Louis Kusley, Martin Kusley, Bruce Long, George Rader, Karl Reed, Saul Selznick and Marvin Wilson. *Laborers* Owen Davies, Frank Grandetta, Richard A.

Rabis, Victor Ramos and Dick Stoll. *Properties* Anthony Lombardo, Jack Gorton, John Graffeo, Jack Hallett, Ralph Harris, Willard Hartman, George MacQuarrie, Earl McKee and Paul Melnick. *Technical advisers* Eddie Box, Ernest Greenwalt, George Kishketon, Edgar Monetathchi, Francis Shields, Reginald Lal Singh and Tyrus Wong. *Set decoration* John Lester Hallett, James A. Lee, George McCrearie, Edward Parker, Allan Price, Barnard Schoefelt and Harold Worthington. *Sound* G.R. Danner, William Griffith, Guy Ingersoll, Clarence P. Kelley, John Rixley, Marvin Stoltz and Kenneth Wesson. *Special effects* W. Roy Bolton, Robert N. Bonning, John Christensen, Jack Faggard, Joseph Goss, C.B. Handley, Daniel W. Hays and Louis Hopper. *Special photographic effects* Jack R. Rabin, Louis DeWitt and Irving A. Block. *Special effects boat crew* R.N. Acquistapace, Norman Breedlove, Roscoe S. Cline, Gustav Eriksson, George Harris, Daniel W. Lee, Wiley Medearis, Fred Mitchke, Kenneth Nelson, Merle C. Newby, Leon H. Paquet, Kenneth Sneed, R.C. Stangler, Jesse J. Stone, Robert A. Tait and Jerry Welker. *Still cameramen* Jack Albin, Ernest Bachrach, William Cary, Milton Gold, Newton Hopcraft, Clifton L. Kling, Madison Lacy, Talmadge Morrison, Leonard Powers and William E. Thomas. *Wardrobe* Hazel Allensworth, Charles Arrico, Eugene Ashman, Norma Brown, Frank Butz, Frank Cardinale, Veda Carroll, Mildred Duncan, Elmer Ellsworth, Ann Fielder, Leona Forman, William Jobe, Jr., Norman Martien, G.L. Merrill, Jr., Lillian Orr, Marie Osborn, Theodore Parvin, Bernice Pontrelli, Carl Steppling, Thelma Strahm, Sophia Stutz and James W. Wallace. *Seamstresses* Justine Cavaliere and Anita Duran. *Tailor* William Guzik. *Wrangling* Sam Ashton, David Baker, Richard Brehm, James Campbell, Minyard Caudill, Harley Chambers, Ray Chandler, Edward W. Clark, Delmer Combs, Sam Cook, Howard Cramer, Robert F. Dick, Edward Duarte, Jean W. Eaton, Leslie Elder, Walter D. Elliott, George Emerson, Homer Farra, Jeff Flores, Milton Galbraith, Eugene Goebel, L.C. Goss, Clinton C. Hall, Marceline J. Herrara, Tony Gilbert Herrera, William Hines, Wayne Hobson, William L. Hostetter, Wayne Howe, Harry Hupp, Kenneth L. Jenkins, Ben Johnson, A.W. Kennard, Alvin Kimsey, Frank Klump, William Koehler, Adam Krackenberger, Frank D. Lane, Kenneth Lee, Richard A. Lee, Kester Lipscomb, Joe Lomax, John McDonald, William McNally, Charles McQuary, Burt Mattox, George Myers, Walter Noble, Fox O'Callahan, Albert Parker, Frank Potts, Russell Ray, Fess Reynolds, Alvin T. Reed, Henry Herbert Reed, A.F. Reinhardt, D.B. Richardson, Sr., D.B. Richardson, Jr., Lee Roberson, Claude L. Robinson, Alfred Roelker, Wallace C. Ross, Frank R. Sanders, Carl Scarsdale, Oscar Schaaf, Jack Shannon, Elmo Slade, Jack E. Smith, Drew Stanfield, Henry Tyndall, Norman Walke, Richard Webb, Mike Wiciniski, Leonard Douglas Winbourn and Robert Yankie. *Boat crew on the S.S. Henrietta* Robert E. Lee, *captain;* Everett D. Klaumann, *first mate;* Edward Silva, *ship's engineer. Police attache, California* Herb Felsen. *Radio operator* Willard Starr. *Society for the Prevention of Cruelty to Animals representative* Jimmy Jack. *Script supervision* Betty Levin. *Script clerk* John Franco. *Maid in Durango* Lena Henderson. *Watchman in Durango* Joe C. Valdez. *Production illustrator* Joseph F. Hurley. *Costumes* Western Costume, Metro-Goldwyn-Mayer, Paramount, 20th Century–Fox, Warner Bros., Universal City Studios and others. *Titles* Shamus Culhane Productions. *Animation executive producer* James "Shamus" Culhane. *Animation producer and director* Bill Hurtz. *London: Accounting* Irene Jay and Myra Mitford. *Construction manager* Peter Dukelow. *Property buyer* Marjory Whittington. *Scenic artist* Gilbert Wood. *Casting* Maude Spector. *Costume design* Anna Duse. *Assistant art director* Olga Lehmann. *Second assistant director* Charles Hammond. *Third assistant director* Gino A. Marotta. *Hair styling* Bette Lee. *Makeup* Tom Smith. *Photography* Neil Binney, Bill Bonner, R. Bryce, Kenneth Clark, Kevin Kavanagh, Stanley Sayer and E.H. Williams. *Production managers* Cecil F. Ford and Cecil Foster Kemp. *Research* A. Appleton. *Sound* T.R. Cotter, F. Hales and G. Saunders. *Still cameramen* Kenneth Danvers and James Swarbrick. *Wardrobe* Betty Adamson, Monty Berman, Harry Jourdan and Janet Lesley. *Script clerk* Kay Rawlings. *Costumes* Berman's Ltd. *Spain: Publicity* Juan Luis

Calleja. *Accounting* Jose Boqueron and Felix Fadrique. *Art direction and sets* Julio Molina and Juan Alberto Soler. *Second assisant directors* Alfonso Acebal and Isidore Martinez-Ferry. *Hair styling* Puyol-Suarez. *Driver* Jose Carmona. *Makeup* Alonso. *Photography* Manuel Berenguer and Luis Macasoli. *Production* Alfonso Acebal, Luis Berraquero, Alfredo Ruescas and Juanito Solorzano. *Properties* Luna and Angel Sevillano. *Wardrobe* Jose Baquera and Humberto Cornejo. *Police attache* Paulino Domingo. *Paris: Accounting* Aubart and Lavigne. *Costume design* Jacques Cottin and Mme. Rey. *Second assistant director* Charles Hammond. *Hair styling* Alex Archambault. *Makeup* Monigue Archambault, Mme. Barsky, Bordenave, Georges Bouban, Nicole Bouban, de Fast, Yvonne Gasperina, Gauthier, Mlle. Gilet, Gleboff, Klein, Simone Knapp, Denise Lemoigne, Claude Milhau, Neant, Neant, Mme. Ouvrard, Pallazolo, Quentin, Svoboda and Mme. Trieste. *Photography* Bontemps, Clunie, Andre Domage, Letouzey and Mlle. Massey. *Production* Jacques Bar, Michel Boisserand, Gilbert Bokanowski, de Masure, Lucien Denis, Louis Germain, Lahet, Rey, Rosen, Fred Sursin and Viriot. *Properties* Doublet and Dumousseau. *Technical adviser* Mme. Lourie. *Set decoration* Hinkis, Gabriel Paris, Thibault and Helene Thibault. *Special effects* Mme. Dunan. *Wardrobe* Mme. Alaphilippe, Mme. Banguarel, Colette Baudot, Fred Capel, Chivalie, Mme. Chivalie, Gasnier, Manza, Mme. Manza, Radenane, Suzanne Revillard, Mme. Sckeder and Vittonatto. *First aid* Larry Bump, Sidney Kruger and John Leber. *Script clerk* Mme. Lecouffe. *Japan: Production manager* Robert Nakai. *Camera operators* A. Matsumoto and Yanagawa. *First assistant director* Farley James. *Stills* C. Watanabe. *Second assistant director* Jack Karamoto. *Wardrobe* Shimizu. *Carpenters and special effects* Kazuo Ito and Sakae Kawakami. *Electricians* Hashiyama and Odawara Shoten. *Hong Kong: Technical staff* Li Chou and Henry Woo. *Second assistant director* Cheung. *Siam: Technical staff* Tobi Sac. *Pakistan: Technical staff* Jobakan Jerry and Karim. *Documentary: Director* Sidney Smith. *Cutter* Asa Clark. *Second assistant director* John Chulay. *Cameraman* Wallace Chewning. ¶A Michael Todd Company, Inc., production. Released by United Artists. Technicolor. Westrex six-track magnetic stereophonic sound. Filmed at MGM Studios, Paramount Studios, RKO Studios, 20th Century –Fox Studios, Warner Bros. Studios, Universal City Studios and Republic Studios, Hollywood and Shepperton Studios, London and on location in Hollywood, Chatsworth and San Francisco, California, Lawton, Oklahoma, Durango, Colorado, White Sands, New Mexico, London, England, Paris and Southern France, Chinchon, Spain, Mexico, India, Hong Kong, Pakistan, Siam, Yokohama, Japan, Egypt, on the Mediterranean Sea and on the Pacific and Atlantic oceans. ¶CAST: *Phileas Fogg* David Niven. *Passepartout* Cantinflas. *Princess Aouda* Shirley MacLaine. *Insp. Fix* Robert Newton. *M. Gasse* Charles Boyer. *Fort Kearney station master* Joe E. Brown. *Paku* Robert Cabal. *Tourist in Paris railroad station* Martine Carol. *Col. Proctor Stamp* John Carradine. *Hong Kong steamship office clerk* Charles Coburn. *Great Indian Peninsular Railway official* Ronald Colman. *R.M.S. Mongolia steward* Melville Cooper. *Roland Hesketh-Baggott* Noel Coward. *Whist player in Reform Club* Finlay Currie. *Bombay police inspector* Reginald Denny. *S.S. Henrietta first mate* Andy Devine. *Barbary Coast saloon owner* Marlene Dietrich. *Spanish bullfigher* Luis Miguel Dominguin. *Paris coachman* Fernandel. *Foster* John Gielgud. *London tart* Hermione Gingold. *Cave of the Seven Winds dancers* Jose Greco & Troupe. *Sir Francis Cromarty* Cedric Hardwicke. *Fallentin* Trevor Howard. *Tart's companion* Glynnis Johns. *American railroad conductor* Buster Keaton. *Paris flirt* Evelyn Keyes. *Revivalist group leader* Beatrice Lillie. *S.S. Carnatic steward* Peter Lorre. *S.S. Henrietta chief engineer* Edmund Lowe. *Billiard player in Reform Club* A.E. Matthews. *Drunk in Hong Kong dive* Mike Mazurki. *American cavalry commander* Col. Tim McCoy. *S.S. Henrietta helmsman* Victor McLaglen. *London cabbie* John Mills. *British consul in Suez* Alan Mowbray. *Ralph* Robert Morley. *S.S. Henrietta captain* Jack Oakie. *Barbary Coast saloon bouncer* George Raft. *Achmed Abdullah* Gilbert Roland. *Barbary Coast saloon piano player* Frank Sinatra. *Drunk in Barbary Coast saloon* Red Skelton. *Reform Club members* Ronald

Squire and Basil Sydney. *Hinshaw* Harcourt Williams. *American railroad engineer* Casey MacGregor. *American railroad fireman* Richard Wessel. *Spectator* Ava Gardner. *Londoners* Ronald Adams, Walter Fitzgerald and Frank Royde. *Prolog commentator* Edward R. Murrow. *With* Richard Aherne, Philip Ahn, Roy Aversa, Frank Baker, Alex Ball, John Benson, Leon Bouvard, Donald Brown, Ollie Brown, Theona Bryant, J.W. Burr, Al Cavens, Shih Hung Choy, Neil Collins, Cecil Combs, Louis Cortina, Ashley Cowan, Roy Darmour, Maria Delgado, Anna de Linsky, Amapola Denison, Leslie Denison, Clint Dorrington, Ed Edmonson, Carli D. Elinor, Duke Fishman, Frances Fong, Raoul Freeman, Tom Fujiwara, Joseph Garcia, Harry Gilette, Joseph Glick, Arthur Gould-Porter, Bernard Bozier, Ralph Grosh, Charles (Chuck) Hamilton, Mahgoub Hanaf [Galli Galli], Doc Harnett, Chester Hayes, Tex Holden, David B. Hughes, Joanne Jones, Paul King, Walter Kingsford, Ben Knight, Katy Koury, Freddie Letuli, Weaver Levy, Richard Loo, Manuel Lopez, Joan Lora, Keye Luke, Robert McNulty, D. Ellsworth Manning, Dewey Manning, Harry Mayo, Lorion Miller, Maria Monay, Jack Mulhall, Robert Okazaki, Manuel Paris, James Porter, Satini Puailoa, Amando Rodriguez, George Russell, Jim Salisbury, Sohi Shannan, Bhogwan Singh, Alvin Slaight, Fred O. Somers, Owen Kyoon Song, Ward Thompson, Philip Van Zandt, Frank Vessels, Jr., Al Walton, Robert Whitney, Kathryn Wilson, Thomas Quon Woo, R. Brodie, Patrick Cargill, Campbell Cotts, Felix Fetton, Cameron Hall, Maria Hanson, Roddy Hughes, Frederick Leister, N. Macowen, Frank Royd, Bill Shine, Janet Sterke, Michael Trubshawe and Richard Wattis. *Stunts:* Reginald C. Armor, Jr., Paul Baxley, Jerry Brown, Bob Burrows, Richard Crockett, Don Cunningham, Mario Dacal, Robert Folkerson, Bob Gordon, Saul Gorss, Joseph Goss, Tex Holden, Charles Horvath, Ace Clyde Hudkins, Alexander Jackson, Bert LeBaron, Boyd "Red" Morgan, Charles Mosley, Edwin Parker, Gilbert Perkins, Walter Pietila, Allen D. Pinson, George Ross, Jr., Frosty Royse, Danny Sands, Aubrey Saunders, Raymond Saunders, Russell Saunders, Clint Sharp, George Spoots, Wayne "Buddy" Van Horn, Dale Van Sickel, Frank Vincent, Bill White, Louis Williams and Bud Wolfe. *Dancers:* Marie Ardell, Douglas Burnham, Manuela De Herey, Lola De Ronda, Gloria Dewerd, Dolores Ellsworth, John Ferguson, Paul Haakon, Gitanillo Heredia, Gretchen Houser, Leona Irwin, Antonio Jimenez, Joan Kelly, Virginia Lee, John C. Lewis, Charles Lunard, William Lundy, Demita Prado, Anita Ramos, Paul Rees, Joe Rudan, Arthur Sedinger, Pepita Sevilla, Robert Street and Muriel Weldon. *Standins:* Wanda Brown, Antonion Gutierrez, Esteban Gutierrez, Leslie Raymaster, Ed Scarpa, Virginia Whitmore and John Zuniga. *Hollywood extras:* Abdullah Abbas, Leo Abby, Charles Abraham, Dinah Ace, Rosemary Ace, Boyd Ackerman, Panchita Acosta, Francis Adams, Jesse Adams, David Addar, George Agawa, Ernest Aquilar, Benny Ahuna, Fred Akahoshi, Carolos Albert, Gladys Alden, Fred Aldrich, Emil Alegata, Kurpan Ali, Leroy Allen, Sally Alonzo, Lupe Alvarado, Dick Ames, August Angelo, William Angelo, Ed Arbogast, Gene Ardell, Danny Aredas, Ray Armstrong, Ray Arnett, Larry Arnold, Russell Ash, Eula Asher, Gertrude Astor, Edward Astran, George Atsumo, Besmark Auelua, Aggie Auld, Irene Austin, Kaz Awai, Sande Aziko, Walter Bacon, Rama Bai, Al Bain, Leah Baird, Alex Ball, Benjie Bancroft, Ralph Bara, Dick Barber, Bertha Barbier, Beverly Barker, Olga Barone, Salvador Barroga, Robert Barry, Merrill F. Bates, Mary Ellen Batten, Baucine, Angelina Bauer, Brandon Beach, Elena Beattie, Eugene Beday, Ivan Bell, Helena Benda, Eleanor Bender, Norma D. Bernhart, Alfred Berumen, Audrey Betz, Ongyue Big, Bobby Birchfiel, Cathy Ann Bissutti, Richard Bissutti, George Blagoi, Tina Blagoi, Eumenio Blanco, Oscar Blank, Rosemary Blong, George Bloom, Phil Bloom, William Bloom, Toni Bond, Paul Bordman, Olga Borget, Dan Borzage, Leon Bouvard, Hazel Boyne, Virginia Bradley, Mario Bramucci, Kahala Bray, John Breneman, Ernest Brengk, Kenneth Brischof, Donald Brown, Mildred Brown, Wanda Brown, George Bruggeman, Phyllis Brunner, Helen Bruno, Joan Buckley, Al Buen, Jane Burgess, Ted Burgess, Betty Burns, Bob Burrows, Paul Busch, Guy Buscola, Boyd Cabeen, Eugene Cahn, Allen Calm, Ann Cameron, Joyce Cameron, John

Carboni, Fred Carpenter, Mick Carr, Kit Carson, Dick Carter, Louis Cartina, Gordon Carveith, Danny Casabian, Marlene L. Caspari, Perta Castneda, Steve Cavalieri, Bert Cafali, Frank Ceniceros, Dorothy Chan, Douglas Chan, Eugene Chan, Jowe Chan, Lum Chan, Mary Chan, Ronald Chan, Spencer Chan, Suey Chan, Wong Hing Chan, Pauline Chang, Irene Chapman, Jack Chefe, Huaplala Cherie, Dick Cherney, Fon Chillson, May Chinn, Nina Chirva, Noble Kid Chissell, Lee Chon, Margarite Chow, Beulah Christian, Elaine Leemoi Chu, Howard M. Chueng, Kui Sau Cui, Wong Chun, Bing Yee Chung, Jane Chung, Sue Fawn Chung, Martin Cichy, Michael Cirillo, Richard Dale Clark, Mary Loue Clifford, Walter Clinton, Bud Cokes, Neil Collins, Louise Colombet, Anthony M. Conde, Kathy Connors, Connie Conrad, Miguel Contreras, Chabling Cooper, Joan Corbett, Wilson Cornell, Dolores Corral, Barbara Correa, William J. Couch, Theresa Courtland, Lynne Craft, Paul Cristo, Catalina Cruz, Stuart W. Culp, Dorothy Curtis, Max Cutler, Gloria Dadisman, Ruth Dalbrook, Roy Damron, Anita Louise Dano, Edmund Dantez, Lawrence Daquila, Theresa Darling, Roy Darmour, Eddie Das, Richard Tate, Serafin Davidoff, Jack Davidson, Jack Davies, Jack Davis, Robert Dayo, Gloria Dea, Diana Deane, Joseph Deangelo, John Deauville, Louise Decarlo, Helen Dee, Deena, George Deer, Douglas Degioia, Maria Deglar, Denice DeLacey, John Delgado, Maria Delgado, Anna Delinsky, La Verne Dell, Jack Delrio, Rosita Delva, Rod De Medici, Angelo De Meo, Emory Dennis, Gil Dennis, Harry Denny, Kathleen Desmond, Lala Detolly, Gabriel De Valle, Gloria Deward, Angela Dewitt, Maya Kaur Dhillon, Marilyn Dialon, Sterling Dillard, James Dime, Franklin Dix, Edward Gary Dodds, Dolores Domasin, Robert Dominguez, William Dominguez, Barbara Donaldson, William Donelley, Clint Dorrington, Diane Dorsey, Julie Dorsey, Joe Dougherty, Al Dowling, Dan Dowling, Jack Downs, Fanny Drabin, Morris Drabin, Barbara Drake, Helen Drake, John Drake, Dewey Drapean, Joseph Draper, Darren Dublin, Alfonso Du Bois, Harry Duff, Arthur Dulac, Robert Dulaine, Gordon Dumont, Charles Dunbar, Renald Dupont, Lawrence Duran, William Duray, Mintan Durfee, Andre K. Duval, Hedi Duval, Bob Dyer, Joan Dyer, Mitchell Dylong, Elaine Earl, Ina Edell, Everett L. Eddy, Michka Egan, Anita Egna, Carli D. Elinor, Jerry Elliott, Jack Ellis, Richard Elmore, John Eloff, Calvin Emery, Ronald Eng, Helen Enriquez, Frank Erickson, Maude Erickson, Madge Erwin, Miguel Esquembre, Marcello Estorres, Bob Evans, Harry Evans, Joe Evans, Henry Faber, Dr. F.W. Fahrney, James Fakato, Antonio Farfan, Franklin Farnum, Amir Farr, Margaret Farrell, Joe Fay, Adolph Faylauer, Art Felix, Tony Fillion, Walter Findon, Samuel Finn, John Fioff, Carlo Fiore, Duke Fishman, Bess Flowers, Ray Flinn, Charles Fogel, Gene Hunter Foley, Bob Folkerson, Clarence Fong, Dick Fong, Richard G. Fong, Sam Fong, Yut Man Fong, Raymond Fontes, Otto Forrest, Helen Foster, John Fox, Harold Francis, Jess Franco, Oscar Freeburg, Raoul Freeman, Milton Freibrun, Wilma Friedman, John Fritz, Shela Fritz, Ben Frommer, Virginia Fuentes, Janice Fuginani, Koshihiro Fukdo, Jay Fuller, Sumi Funo, Curt Furberg, John Furukawa, M. Furukawa, Yoneka Furukawa, Carol Ann Gainey, Michael Gainey, Juliana Galic, A. Gallagher, Al Gallagher, Elias Gamboa, Charles Garcia, Capt. Fernan Garcia, Israel Garcia, Joseph Garcio, Diana Garrison, Robert Garvin, Mark Gates, Edward Gee, June Gee, Toc Yee Gee, Wong Kim Gee, Wayne Geer, Anita Gegna, Carine A. Generaux, John George, Jay Gerard, Rudolph Germane, Curly Gibson, Elaine Gilbert, Joe Gilbert, Leon Gill, Harry Gillette, H.D. Gin, Njon Tuey Gin, May Ginn, Noreen Ginn, Stephen Ginn, Jr., Kay Ginoza, Wong Git, Howard C. Glasson, Mary Ellen Gleason, Betty J. Glennie, Joseph Glick, June Glory, Albert Godderis, Joe Gold, Roy Goldman, Angela Gomez, Mar Suey Gong, Quon Gong, Soledad Gonzales, Armando Gonzalez, Alex Gonzalez, Carmen Gonzalez, Charles Gonzalez, Fernando Gonzalez, James Gonzalez, Allen Goode, Alora Gooding, Verne Goodrich, Lee Teu Gook, Eve Gordon, Richard Gordon, Ruth Gordon, Mickey Gotanda, Oxy Goto, Violet Goulet, Ann Graeff, Betty Graeff, Rita Graeff, William Graeff, Jr., Joan Graffeo, Hershel Graham, Grace Grant, Valerie Gratton, Dolly Gray, Don Gray, Elenora Norina Greco, Suzanne Greco, David Greene, David Greenwood,

Karla Gribbel, B. Pat Groom, Ralph Grosh, Sei Groves, Sei Jeri Groves, Victor Groves, Edward Grubb, Kit Guard, Tenmana Guerin, Edward A. Guerra, Jesus Guerra, Marilyn Gustafson, Paul Gustine, Georgina Gutierrez, Edward Ha, Herman Hack, Robert Haines, Betty Hall, Stuart Hall, Chuck Hamilton, Chick Hannan, Maria Haro, Silver Harr, Maj. Sam Harris, Louis G. Hart, James Hasagawa, George Hashimoto, Gus Hashimoto, Harry Hashimoto, Al Haskell, Lauren Hastings, William Hayden, Chester Hayes, Frank Heaney, Charles Heard, Shirley Heart, Bonnie Henjum, Charles Hennecke, Clarence Hennecke, Robert Hennes, Tars Hensen, George Hickman, Charles Hicks, George Higa, Sue Hikawa, Jenny Hing, Yoshio Hiraga, Kimiko Hiroshige, Hiroshi Hisamune, Fun Ho, Harlan Hoagland, Lee Yuen Hock, Yoshyo Hohamura, Tex Holden, Stuart Holmes, Syd Holtby, Yee Jock Hom, Kenny Homabe, Midori Homano, Lee Kim Hong, Janice Hood, Hans R. Hopf, James Horan, John Hoskin, Shep Houghton, Ken Hovey, Gladys Howe, Lee Yuen Hoy, Madelon Hubbard, Clyde Hudkins, Warren Huff, Tom Humphrey, Frank Hunt, S. Iguchi, Yoneo Iguchi, Joe Iino, Taruko Ikari, Kazuo Ikida, Kay Imamura, Omaru Imazaki, John Impolito, David Inez, Vi Ingraham, Leona Irvin, Merrill C. Isbell, Yoshio Ishibashi, Tom Ishikura, Ray Ishimatsu, Kinuko Ito, Roy Iwaki, Jacqueline Jackler, Diane Jackson, Marjorie Jackson, Allen Jaffe, Charles James, Idell James, Robert James, Mary Jan, Sushila Janadas, Gerald Jann, William A. Janssen, Dolly Jarvis, Michael Jeffers, Joan Jerrae, Robert Jewett, Dee Ho Joe, Edgar W. Johnson, Leroy Johnson, Dick Johnstone, Todd Joko, A. Winfield Jones, Freda Jones, Joanne Jones, Myra Jones, Sallie Jones, Madge Journeay, Raymond Joyer, S.S. Jung, Fred Kajikawa, Al Kakumi, Gee Toy Kam, Yukimi Kamaka, Joe Kameshita, Stanley Kamijama, Mary Kanae, Ken Kane, Madelynne Kane, Morris Kaneshire, Mamie Karaki, Harvey C. Karels, Bopeep Karlin, Harumi Kashaka, Ken Kato, George Katsuhiro, George Kawashima, Tak Kawashima, Sugar Willi Keeler, Valentine Kekipi, Jodi Kelley, Joan Kelly, Fannie Kennerly, Jack Heavy Kenney, Eleanor Kent, Johnny Kern, Joseph Gee Key, Allan Kila, John Kim,

Anita King, Brian King, Grace King, Paul King, Judith A. Kinnon, Ken Kinoshita, Shinyo Kita, Max Kleven, Marlene Kloss, Frank Kneeland, William J. Kollberg, King Kong, Bob Konno, James Kono, Harry Koshi, Roy Kouchi, Kay Koury, Akira Koyama, Tom Koyama, Gladys Kress, Paul Kruger, Jack Krupnick, Jo Ngau Kum, Ann Kunde, Wally Kushinaejo, Wallace Kusumajo, George Kuwashige, Sumiyo Kuwashige, Jeung Lai Kwong, Lita Laceman, Paul Lacy, Clyde Ladd, Jeanne Lafayette, Richard Lamarr, Laura Lamb, Connie Lamont, Cherokee Landrum, Frank Lane, Warren Lane, James Lang, Webster Lagrange, Frances Lara, Manuel Laraneta, Jean Larson, Lydia Latzke, June Lavere, Gustave Lax, Park Lazelle, B.M. Lee, Bik Yuk Lee, Esther Ying Lee, Fee Loon Lee, Foo Lee, Gee Sho Lee, Harold Lee, Helen Lee, Jack Lee, Margaret Lee, Nelson Lee, Ng Jung Lee, Norman Lee, Richard Goon Lee, Teng Kem Lee, Tommy Lee, Virginia Lee, Charles Legneur, Lewellyn Lem, Christopher Leng, Marian Leng, Marrilee Leng, Jeanne Lennox, Frank Leonard, Peggy Leonard, Rita Leonard, Johnny Leone, Rose Leong, Harry Leroy, Lillian Leroy, Freddie Letulli, Carl Leviness, Mabel Lew, Shirley Lew, William H. Lewin, John Lewis, Eleanor Lexaber, James Leyton, Baron Lichter, Amelia Liggett, David Lim, Gin Lim, Sing Lim, Geraldine Lindsay, Quong Ling, Yee Suey Ling, King Lockwood, Dale Logue, James Long, Kwong You Loo, Lee Duck Look, Tu Duck Look, Caroline Lopez, Marco Lopez, Richard Lopez, Joan Lora, Marie Loredo, Robert L. Lorraine, Billie Louie, Donald Louie, James Louie, Marygold Louie, Wilbert Louie, Louise Loureau, Harry Lowe, Jr., Wai Lue, Cop Lum, David Lum, Pauline Lum, Lupe Lvarado, Bessie Ma, Bruce MacCallister, Duncan MacDonell, Ann Macomber, Michael M. Macy, Celeste Madamba, Ralph Madlener, T. Maeshiro, Roy Maeua, Guadelope Malasig, Cy Malis, Shoji Malyama, Max Manues, Tela Mansfield, Joseph Marievsky, Ramon Marintz, Joseph Mariunsky, John Marlin, Rena Marlin, Sandee Marriott, Gloria Marshall, Joseph Marsico, Carlos Martinez, Rickey Martin, Thomas F. Martin, Mary D. Mascari, Rudy Masson, Nita Mathews, Peter Mathews, Corky Matsumoto, John Matsutani, Mack Mauda,

Dorothy May, Harry Mayo, George Mayon, Ila McAvoy, Angelita McCall, David O. McCall, Glen McCarthy, Frank L. McClure, Glen McComas, Robert McCrady, Robert F. McElroy, Donald McGuire, Bob McGurk, Lanie McIntyre, Sylvia McKaye, Dorcas McKim, Rowena McNamara, William Meada, Rudolph Medina, Russell Meeker, Marie Melesch, Ann Merman, Tommy Merrill, Sam A. Mides, Harold Miller, Frank Mills, Robert Milton, Tom Mishimoto, Lennie Mitchell, Tameo Mitsunaga, Mary Miyaji, Henry Miyamoto, Helen Miyarahara, Luther Mizukami, Irene Mizushima, Sam Mizushima, James Mohlmann, Jr., King Mojave, Joe Molina, William Monahan, Marion Monsour, Beverly Mook, Lee Kai Moon, Earl Moore, Zelinda Mora, Ralph Moratz, Ernest Morelli, Michael Morelli, Linda Moreno, Cline Morgan, Patricia Morgan, Evelyn Moriarty, Thomas Morita, Shiegeyo Moriyama, Patricia Morris, Charles Morton, Shirley Motonada, Kai Motowaki, Man Ho Moy, Thomas Mullen, Inez Murakami, Jan Murakawi, Sol Murgi, Joe Murphy, Tessie Murray, Thomas Murray, Michael Musso, George Myers, Stevie Myers, Satya Nanda Nag, Frank Nagai, Kisaduro Nagai, Hiro Nakado, Kico Nakaod, Kisabara Nakado, Tsunesuki Nakado, Joe Nakai, Charles Nakamaura, Mary Nakamura, Fred Nakano, Kay Nakashima, Ken Nakasoni, Frank E. Naley, George Nardelli, Aurora Navarro, Myra Nelson, Augie Neves, Stewart Newmark, H.B. Newton, Irving Fig Newton, Ngai Foo Ng, Woo Shee Ng, Charles Nickum, William H. Nind, Keiko Ninura, Shizuko Nishida, Bob Nishihar, Roy Noda, Lynn Noe, Joseph Nordon, Anton Northpole, Barry Norton, Faye Nuell, Daniel Nunez, Kathy O'Brien, William H. O'Brien, June O'Carroll, Jeong Wah Ock, Peggy Mae O'Connell, Kent Odell, Patricia O'Donnell, George Ogawa, Judy Ogawa, Yasu Ogawa, Monty O'Grady, Sati Ohashi, Joe Ohye, Robert Okazaki, Tak Okazaki, Ruth Oklander, George Okusu, Agnes O'Laughlin, Bob Olen, Adrian Olson, Andra Olson, Lillian O'Malley, Yui Big Ong, Helen Ono, Edna Onofrio, Charles K. Opunui, Josephine Ortega, Chiyoho Ota, Iris Ota, Mike Ota, Robert Otoi, Herb Pacheco, Emma Palmese, Norman Papson, Robert J. Paradise, George Paris, Jonni Paris, Derek Park, Patricia Patrick, Joan Patti, Renee Paul, Victor Paul, Loretta Pedroza, Robert A. Pedroza, Charles Pendleton, Fred Perce, Chip Perrin, Jack Perrin, Elsa Petersen, Harold Peterson, Paula Petris, Virginia Pherrin, Sylvia Pineira, Melvin Pixley, Joseph Ploski, Byron Poindexter, Anita Pollack, Robert Polo, Lucille Porcett, James Porta, Charlotte Portney, Alice Portugal, Jose Portugal, Ray L. Pourchot, Warren Powers, Edward M. Pozzo, Damita Prado, Donald Pulford, Rita Punay, Terry Pyne, Henry Quan, Thomas Y. Quan, Tung Him Quan, Wong Chuck Quen, Rod Quesada, Art Quigley, John Quijada, Alvin Quon, Duey Quon, Wallace Moon Quon, Concettina Ragone, William Raisch, Shine Ram, Tony Randall, Dianne Randolph, Fred Rapport, Beverly Ravel, Dianne Ravel, M. Ravenscroft, Sammy Ray, Leslie Raymaster, Anthony Raymond, Ford Raymond, Kathryn Reed, Robert Reeves, Roland Rego, Leina Ala Reid, Max Reid, Waclaw Rekwart, Peggy Remington, Fred Revelala, Fess Reynolds, Ricky Riccardi, John Rice, David Richardson, Leo C. Richmond, Suzanne Ridgeway, Don Rizzuti, Dwight F. Roberts, Robert Robinson, Edwin Rochelle, Aaron Rochin, Celia Rochin, Paul Rochin, Walter Rode, Armando Rodriquez, Lloyd Rogers, Julia Rojas, Betty Rome, Florita Romero, Kathleen Rooney, Buddy Roosevelt, Bert Rose, Milt Rose, George Ross, Jr., Joe Ross, Marion Ross, Andrew Roud, John Rousanville, Antonio Roux, John Roy, Joseph Rubino, Sylvester Rumboa, Barbara Rundell, Pola Russ, George Russell, Jamie Russell, Johnnie Russo, Dick Ryan, Loulette Sablon, Tulip Gee Sack, Yoshitaro Sadato, Joe Sadd, Jose Saenz, Robert St. Angelo, John Saito, Clifford Sakai, Henry Sakato, James Salsbury, Lew Sam, Tanya Samova, Raymond Sanchez, Danny Sands, George Santell, Jack Santoro, Cosmo Sardo, Noriko Saruwatari, Edna Sato, Dean Savant, Gen. Sam Savitsky, Jeffrey Sayre, Edward Scarpa, Rube Schaffer, Fred Scheiwiller, Maria Scheue, Nancy Schiro, Joseph Leopold Schneider, John Scholtman, Kathleen Schoon, Millie Schottland, Phillip Schumacher, Harry Schwartz, James Scobie, James Robert Scott, Peter Seal, Eddie Searless, Robert E. Sease, Scott Seaton, Duke Seba, Bernard Sell, James Selwyn, Jack Semple, George Sesaki, Ya Mee Tuk Seto, Sammy

Shack, Earl Shafer, Dee Sharon, Clint Sharp, Lee Tom She, Yee Shee, Bobbie Sheehan, Edith P. Sheets, A. Sheffield, Jordan Shelley, Ariel Sherry, Amy Shibata, Min Shigezani, Jack Shin, Kumakichi Shirano, Renato Siauss, Arthur Siegel, Irene K. Silva, Chen Sing, Basanta Singh, Bhogwan Singh, Reginald Lal Singh, Bonnie Sinka, Leslie Sketchley, Roy Skluth, Charles Slay, June Smaney, Mabel Smaney, Ted Smile, Albert Smith, J. Lewis Smith, Julian Smith, Michael Smith, Valerie Smith, Winona Smith, Beverly Snyder, Don Snyder,Leonard Van Snow, Channon Sohi, Ray Solari, Charles Soldani, Stephen Soldi, Tanya Somova, Laciba Sonami, May Song, Owen Kyoon Song, Kaluk Sonkur, Eileen Soo Hoo, Helen Soo Hoo, Howard Soo Hoo, Ilene Soo Hoo, Lester Soo Hoo, Walter Soo Hoo, Wo She Soo Hoo, Littlie Sotomayor, Annette Sottile, Colleen Spealman, Edwana Spence, Jimmy Spencer, Ray Spiker, Fred Spitz, John Stack, Scherry Staiger, Larry Stamps, Ed Stanbridge, John Stanley, Murray Steckler, Anna Stein, Phil Steinberg, Miles Stephenson, Rita Stetson, Norman Stevans, Bert Stevens, Joy Stewart, Keahi Stone, Jack Stoney, Bruce Stowell, Martin Strader, Jane Strangis, Robert Strong, Kam Wong Sui, Lianne Sui, Lily Sui, Bill Suiter, Mits Sumoze, Joseph R. Sun, Jew Sung, Richard Sung, Mitzi Sutherland, Mahmed Tahir, Wong Tai, Arnold Takaki, Fumi Tamura, Tak Tanino, Everett Tannahill, Ruth Tarshis, Tyra Tashireo, Tatsu Tashiro, Blanche Taylor, Maxine Taylor, Tim Taylor, Michael Tellegen, Lilliam Teneyck, Terry Terril, Barbara Terry, Theresa Testa, Delmar Thomas, Loretta Thomas, Richard Thorne, Ken Thorpe, Julio Tijero, Kimi Togawa, Allen Tom, Chon Lem Tom, C.Y. Tom, Herb Tom, Ronald Tom, Masu Tomita, Miyako Tomita, Alfred H. Tonkel, Byron Topetchy, Jack Tornek, Arthur Tovey, Lee Kay Toy, Bebe Trad, Danny Truppi, Kuka Tuitama, Mary Turbay, Blaine Turner, Barbara Uchiyamada, Laura Udall, Junior Ugarte, Evelyn Underwood, Christine Ung, Fay Ung, Judy Ung, Tony Urchel, Manuel Valdez, June Valentine, Albano Valerio, Lisle Valetti, Charles Van, Shirley Van Dyke, James Van Horn, Gloria B. Varela, Luz Vasquez, Ronald Veto, Sailor B. Vincent, Bill Yahuhara, Mickey Yamaguchi, Harriet Yamaka, Sally Yarnell, Bill Yashuhara, Phil Yashuhara, Bob Yani, Conha Ybarra, Manuel Ybarra, Roque Ybarra, Helen Yee, Shion Sim Yee, Shuy Ching Yee, Archie Yim, Anna Yip, Yee Oak Yip, William Yokata, Peggy Yomanchi, Yas Yongawa, Roy Yoshimara, Harold Yoshimura, Lily Yoshizaki, Min Yoshizaki, Gracie Young, Mary Lou Young, May Young, Ernesto Zambrano, Margaret Zane, Allen Zeidman, Esther Zeithen and John Zuniga. ¶Advertised as *Michael Todd's Around the World in 80 Days*. Production began using the Grandeur camera while Mitchell Camera Corporation was building new Todd-AO units. Filmed simultaneously in CinemaScope. According to Shamus Culhane the animated credits were shot in 35mm 'scope. The footage from the rocket was filmed in 35mm and blown up. Also released in Cinestage. Purchased by Warner Bros. in 1983 and reedited to 141 minutes and rereleased in CinemaScope and Dolby Stereo. Fortunately the 70mm version was left intact and the full-length edition is available on video cassette. A documentary of the production, running approximately 2 hours, was made but where it is today, or even its original use, is unknown.

Ati-bati shli soldati *see* **Soldiers on the March**

Atmos (1980). Filmed in OMNIMAX. *Producers* John Spotton and Michael Sullivan. *Director* Colin Low. *Codirectors and photographers* Douglas Keifer and Ernie McNabb. ¶Released by Quest Management and National Film Board of Canada. Eastman Color. Six-track magnetic stereophonic sound. 27 minutes. Also known as *Storm*. ¶A Canadian, American and Mexican coproduction originally made for National Film Board of Canada, Reuben H. Fleet Space Theater, Science Museum of Minnesota, Detroit Science Center and Centro Cultural Alfa.

Aupres de ma blonde *see* **Magirama**

Automobile, Violin and the Dog Blob (1975). Filmed in Sovscope 70. *Screen author* Alla Akhundova. *Director* Rolan Bikov. *Operator* Mikhail Ardabievskiy. *Artist* Aleksandr Kuznetsov. *Composer* Maxim Dunaevskiy. *Sound operator* Yun.

Rabinovich. *Song texts* S. Marshchaka, A. Agundovoy, Rolan Bikov and R. Sefa. ¶A Mosfilm production. International distribution Sovexportfilm. Sovcolor. Six-track magnetic stereophonic sound. 127 minutes. Filmed at Mosfilm Studios, Moscow, R.S.F.S.R. ¶CAST: *Kuza* Sasha Chernyavskiy. *Ania* Natasha Tenischeva. *Oleg* Andrey Gusev. *Davidik* Tzolak Vartazarin. *Band leader* Rolan Bikov. *Adults* Oleg Anofriev, Georgi Vitsin, Zinovy Gerdt, Galina Poliskikh, Nikolay Griniko, Mikhail Kozakov, Alexey O. Smirnov, Spartak Mishulin and Z. Fedorova. ¶A Soviet production released in Russia in 1975 as *Avtomobili, skripka i sobaka Klyaksa.*

Avtomobili, skripka i sobaka Klyaksa *see* **Automobile, Violin and the Dog Blob**

Aybolit-66 (1967). Filmed in Sovscope 70. *Screen authors* Vadim Korostilev and Rolan Bikov. *Based on the story by* K. Chukovskogo. *Director and producer* Rolan Bikov. *Operators* Gennadi Tsekaviy and Viktor Yakushev. *Artist* Aleksandr Kuznetsov. *Composer* Boris Chaykovskiy. *Sound operator* Yun Rabinovich. ¶A Mosfilm production. International distribution Sovexportfilm. Sovcolor. Six-track magnetic stereophonic sound. 125 minutes. Filmed at Mosfilm Studios, Moscow, R.S.F.S.R. ¶CAST: *Dr. Aybolit* Oleg Efremov. *Chicki* Lidia Knyazeva. *Avva* Evgeni Vasiliev. *Barmaley* Rolan Bikov. *Merry servant* Alexei Smirnov. *Melancholy servant* F. Mkrtchyan. ¶A Soviet production released in Russia in 1967. Reedited to 99 minutes.

Az aranyfej *see* **The Golden Head**

Baperina (1970). Filmed in Sovscope 70. *Based on the ballet "Paymonda." Director and operator* V. Derdenev. *Artist* L. Shengeliya. *Sound operator* Ya. Khoron. Tanpuet M. Plistetskaya *fragments from the ballet "Paymonda" by* Glazunova. *"Prelude and fugue"* Johann Sebastian Bach. *"Umirayushshiy lebedi"* Sen-Sansa. *"Carmen suite"* Georges Bizet. ¶A Mosfilm production. International distribution Sovexportfilm. Sovcolor. Six track magnetic stereophonic sound. 87 minutes. Filmed at Mosfilm Studios, Moscow, R.S.F.S.R. ¶A Soviet production released in Russia in 1970.

Barabbas (October 10, 1962). Filmed in Super Technirama 70. *Producer* Dino De Laurentiis. *Director* Richard Fleischer. *Screenplay* Christopher Fry, Ivo Perilli, Diego Fabbri and Nigel Balchin. *Based on the book by* Pär Lagerkvist. *Publisher* Albert Bonnier Forlag, A.B., Stockholm. *Director of photography* Aldo Tonti. *Art direction* Mario Chiari. *Costumes* Maria De Matteis. *Set dressing* Maurizio Chiari. *Assistant to producer* Ralph Serpe. *Associate producer* Luigi Luraschin. *Editors* Raymond Poulton and Alberto Gallitti. *Musical score* Mario Nascimbene. *Conductor* Franco Ferrara. *Musical copyright* "Dino" Roma. *Casting* Paola Rolli. *Production manager* Bruno Todini. *Assistant director* Alberto Cardone. *Assistant operator* Luciano Tonti. *Still photographers* Nino Di Giovanni, Auguste Di Giovanni, Tazo Secchiaroli and Tony Luraschi. *Publicity director* G. Lon Jones. *Consultant for eclipse* Capt. Ottavio Vittori, Osservatorio de Mt. Cimone. *Production assistant* Caryl Gunn. *Riding master* Count Frederich Ledebur. *Sound studio* RCA Italiana S.p.A. ¶A Dino De Laurentiis Cinematografica, S.p.A. production. Released by Columbia Pictures. Filmed at Studio Dinocitta, Rome and on location in Verona and Roccastrada, Italy and Mt. Etna, Sicily. Technicolor. Westrex six-track magnetic stereophonic sound. 144 minutes including intermission. ¶CAST: *Jesus Barabbas* Anthony Quinn. *Rachel* Silvana Mangano. *Pontius Pilate* Arthur Kennedy. *Sara* Katy Jurado. *Simon-Peter* Harry Andrews. *Sahak* Vittorio Gassman. *Sicilian Governor Rufio* Norman Wooland. *Julia* Valentina Cortese. *Gladiator Captain Torvald* Jack Palance. *Lucius* Ernest Borgnine. *Joseph of Arimathaea* Arnoldo Foa. *Lazarus* Michael Gwynn. *Disciples* Laurence Payne, Ed McReedy and Bill Kuehl. *Vasasio* Douglas V. Fowley. *Scorpius* Guido Celano. *Important man* Enrico Glori. *First Roman officer* Carlo Giustini. *Third Roman officer* Gianni Di Benedetto. *Commander of gladiators* Robert Hall. *Reveller in tavern* Rina Braido. *Jacopo* Tullio Tomadini. *Second gladiator* Joe Robinson. *Second Roman officer* Count Frederich Ledebur. *Second slave overseer* Spartaco Nale. *Mendicants* Maria Zanoli, John Stacey, Aubrey Fairfax, Joseph Pilcher and David Maunsell. *Second man in potters' street*

Gustavo de Nardo. *Farm superintendent* Vladimiro Piccafuochi. *First man in group* Colm Caffrey. *Second man in group* John Farksen. *Jesus Christ* Roy Mangano. *Women in tavern* Marilyn Tosatti, Caroline de Fonseca, Anna Maria Ferara and Marilyn Lombardo. *Drinker in tavern* Eugene Gervasi. *Mary the Mother* Emma Baron. *Mary Magdalene* Paola Pitagora. *Princess Salome* Vera Drudi. *Mary of Cleofe* Rina Franchetti. *Mary's sister* Miranda Campa. *Nicodemus* Piero Pastore. *John* Antonio Segurini. *Thomas* Jacopo Tecchio. *First man in potters' street* Richard Watson. *Third man in potters' street* Fernando Hillbeck. *People in potters' street* Marghé Sala, Maria Marchi, Livia Cordaro and Carlo Alberto Lolli. *First outlaw* Jay Weston. *Second outlaw* John Palance. *Third outlaw* Ralph Dammers. *Fourth outlaw* David Crowley. *First priest* Paul Muller. *Second priest* Robert Gardett. *Blacksmith* Vladimiro Tucovith. *Awaken slave* Van Aikens. *First slave overseer* Remington Olmsted. *Ploughman* Dan Sturkie. *Mounted Roman officer* Massimo Righi. *Attendant* James Clark. *Third gladiator* Bill Brown. *Gladiator trainer* Alfio Caltabiano. *Fourth gladiator* Dale Cummings. *Fifth gladiator* George Ehling. *Emperor of Rome* Ivan Triesault. *Woman in the catacombs* Ela Gerber. *Man during the burning of Rome* A. Valentinsich. *Woman during the burning of Rome* Veronica Welles. *Rich man during the burning of Rome* Jody Excell. *Roman officer during the burning of Rome* Burt Nelson. *First prisoner* Larry Hall. *Second prisoner* Jim Dolen. *Fourth Roman officer* Roland Rartrop. *Prisoners* Honore Singer, John Horne, George Birt, Joan Maslow, David Montresor and Inna Alexandieff. *With* Nando Angelini, Marcello Di Martire, Rick Howes, Curt Lowens, Walter Maslow and Circo di Togni. ¶An Italian production released in Italy in December 1961 as *Barabba*. Advertised in Technirama 70. The screen credits state "Westrex Electric Recording" (sic!).

The Bat Whispers (November 13, 1930). Filmed in 70mm Wide Film. *Executive producer* Joseph M. Schenck. *Producer, director, adaptation and dialog* Roland West. *Based on "The Bat: A Play of Mystery in Three Acts" by* Mary Roberts Rinehart and Avery Hopwood, *as produced on the stage by* Wagenhals & Kemper, *from the novel "The Circular Staircase" by* Mary Roberts Rinehart. *Supervisor of Wide Film photography and 35mm photographer* Ray June. *Wide Film photographer* Robert H. Planck. *Settings designer and executor* Paul Roe Crawley. *Wide Film editor* Hal C. Kern. *35mm film editor* James Smith. *In charge of sound* J.T. Reed. *Sound technician* Oscar E. Lagerstrom. *Sound and music consultant* Dr. Hugo Riesenfeld. *Assistant director* Roger H. Heman. *Production assistant* Helen Hallett. *Technical effects* Ned (Herbert) Mann. *Dialog director* Charles H. Smith. *Makeup artist* S.E. Jennings. *Paintings* Thomas Lawless. *Scenic artist* Harvey Meyers. *Electrical effects* William McClellan. *Special technician* Charles Cline. *Wide Film second cameraman* Stanley Cortez. *35mm second cameraman* Stuart Thompson. *35mm assistant cameraman* Bert Shipman. *Special photography* Edward Colman and Harry Zech. *Wide Film camera* Mitchell Camera Corporation. ¶A Joseph M. Schenck presentation. A Roland West production. An Art Cinema Corporation–Feature Productions picture. Released by United Artists. Western Electric Movietone recording. 85 minutes. Filmed at United Artists Studios. ¶CAST: *False Det. Anderson and The Bat* Chester Morris. *Dale Van Gorder* Una Merkel. *Police lieutenant* Chance Ward. *Gideon Bell* Richard Tucker. *Butler* Wilson Benge. *Police captain* De Witt Jennings. *Police sergeant* Sidney D'Albrook. *Man in black mask* S.E. Jennings. *Cornelia Van Gorder* Grayce Hampton. *Lizzie Allen* Maude Eburne. *Old caretaker* Spencer Charters. *Brook Bailey* William Bakewell. *Dr. Venrees* Gustav von Seyffeitia. *Richard Fleming* Hugh Huntley. *Det. Jones* Charles Dow Clark. *Real Det. Anderson* Ben Bard. ¶Working titles were *Love in Chicago* and *Whispers*. Other versions were *The Bat* (United Artists, 1926; also produced, written and directed by Roland West) and *The Bat* (Allied Artists, 1959). Miniature and trick photography sequences were shot only in 35mm and converted to 70mm via process photography and not by optical printing. Unlike most films shot simultaneously in two formats, *The Bat Whispers* was staged differently for the two ratios. The 35mm version was fluid with many angles and cuts, while the 70mm edition was shot stiff with no closeups or camera moves, giving the impression, almost, of a filmed stageplay. Most sources claim this was shot in Magnifilm; one source says it was filmed with Ralph G. Fear's Fearless Super Picture camera. They are all wrong. It was photographed with the same cameras used for Grandeur and Realife made by Mitchell Camera Corporation.

Batmanova, Singing Slave (1963). Filmed in Kinopanorama 70. *Screen authors* L. Zakharov, E. Guerken and S. Vogelson. *Director* Roman Tikhomirov. *Operator* E. Chapiri. *Composer* Nikolai Streinikov. *Editor* M. Penn. ¶A Mosfilm production. International distribution Sovexportfilm. Sovcolor. Nine-track magnetic Kinopanorama Sound. 92 minutes. Filmed at Mosfilm Studios, Moscow, R.S.F.S.R. ¶CAST: *Batmanova* Tamara Semina. *Andrei* Dmitri Smirnov. *Nikita* Evgeni Leonov. *Prince* Sergue Filippov. ¶A Soviet production released in Russia in 1963. The first Kinopanorama 70 feature.

La battaglia di Fort Apache *see* **Shatterhand**

Battle for Berlin *see* **Liberation**

The Battle of Moscow (1986). Filmed in Sovscope 70. *Screen author and director* Yuri Ozerov. *Operators* Igor Chernikh and V. Gusev. *Artists* Aleksandr Myagkov and Tatiana Lapshina. *Composer* Aleksandr Pakhmutova. *Sound operators* V. Shmelikin and V. Toropov. *Announcers* V. Tikhonov and A. Karapetyan. *Song text* N. Dobronravova. ¶A Mosfilm production in collaboration with Barrandov, DEFA and Fafim. International distribution Sovexportfilm. Sovcolor. Six-track magnetic stereophonic sound. Part one: 220 minutes plus intermission. Part two: 217 minutes plus intermission. Filmed at Mosfilm Studios, Moscow, R.S.F.S.R. and on location in Czechoslovakia and Vietnam. ¶CAST: Yakov Tripoliskiy, Mikhail Uliyanov, Aleksandr Goloborodiko, B. Freyndlikh, Nikolai Zasukhin, A. Nikitin, Vladimir Troshin. S. Mikoyan, V. Ezepov, Yuozas Budraytis, M. Mikiver, G. Sayfulin, L. Prigunov, Akhim Petrov, Konstantin Stepankov, R. Yankovskiy, Yuri Yakovlev, A. Martinov, V. Kuznetsov, Vitaly Rassatalnoy, Yizri Kholt, Vitaly Yur-

chenko, Romyaldas Anunas, Emmanil Vitorgan and Irina Shmeleva. ¶A Soviet, Czechoslovakian, East German and Vietnamese coproduction released in Russia in 1986 as *Bitva za Moskvu* in two parts: *Agressiya (Aggression)* in two parts running 103 minutes and 117 minutes; and *Tayfun (Typhoon)* in two parts running 109 minutes and 118 minutes.

Battle of the Bulge (December 16, 1965). Filmed in Ultra Panavision 70. Presented in 70mm Super Cinerama. *Executive producers* Jack L. Warner, William R. Forman and Sidney Harmon. *Producers* Milton Sperling and Philip Yordan. *Director* Ken Annakin *Writers* Philip Yordan, Milton Sperling and John Melson. *Director of photography* Jack Hildyard. *Art direction and special effects sequences* Eugene Lourie. *Supervising editor* Derek Parsons. *Sound editors* Kurt Herrnfeld and Alban Streeter. *Sound recordists* David Hildyard and Gordon K. McCallum. *Chief of special effects* Alex C. Weldon. *Costume design* Laure De Zarate. *Dialog coach* Janet Brandt. *Production supervisor* Bernard Glasser. *Unit managers* Leon Chooluck, Miguel Perez and Juan Estelrich. *Music composer and conductor* Benjamin Frankel. *Players* The New Philharmonia Orchestra. *Production managers* Tibor Reves and Gregorio Sacristan. *Postproduction executive* Lester A. Sansom. *Production coordinator* Lou Brandt. *Script supervisors* Joy Mercer and Marie Wachman. *Second unit photography* John Cabrera. *Aerial photography* Jack Willoughby. *Assistant directors* Jose Lopez Rodero, Martin Sacristan and Luis Garcia. *Second unit directors* Eugene Lourie and William Conrad. *Technical advisers* Maj. Edward King and Lt. John Sims. *Military advisers* Maj. Gen. (a.D.) Meinrad von Lauchert, Lt. Col. Luis Martin de Pozuelo and Lt. Col. Sherman Joffe. *Warner Bros. production representative* William Conrad. *Wardrobe* Charles Simminger. *Makeup artists* Trevor Crole-Rees and Jose Maria Sanchez. *Special effectsmen* Richard Parker, Kit West and Basilio Cortijo. *Miniature construction* Henri Assola. *Camera operator* Dudley Lovell. *Camera assistant* Ronald Anscombe. *"Panzerlied" lyrics* Kurt Wiehle. *Special effects photography* Manuel Berenguer. *Construction supervisor* Francisco Prosper. *Production*

The November 1964 trade announcement for Battle of the Bulge. *(The title would lose "The.") The single lens used would be Ultra Panavision 70. Notice that the announcement is being made by Cinerama. Their name would appear only on the roadshow version and the restored television edition. Forman did not take a screen credit even though a page of the souvenir program would be devoted to him (with a photo) and the Cinerama process. Cinerama, Inc., Warner Bros. Pictures, Inc., and several others would eventually lose a lawsuit over rights to the story material. In the end Warner Bros. would own the film outright.*

illustrator Manolo Mampasso. ¶A Cinerama, Inc., production. A Sidney Harmon in association with United States Pictures, Inc., production. Released by Warner Bros. Pictures. Technicolor. Westrex six-track magnetic stereophonic sound. 162 minutes plus intermission. Filmed at Estudios Sevilla and Estudios Roma, Madrid and on location in Segovia and Sierra Guadarrama, Spain. ¶CAST: *Lt. Col. Kiley* Henry Fonda. *Col. Hessler* Robert Shaw. *Gen. Grey* Robert Ryan. *Col. Pritchard* Dana Andrews. *Sgt. Duquesne* George Montgomery. *Lt. Schumacher* Ty Hardin. *Louise* Pier Angeli. *Elena* Barbara Werle. *Maj. Wolenski* Charles Bronson. *Gen. Kohler* Werner Peters. *Cpl. Conrad* Hans Christian Blech. *Lt. Weaver* James MacArthur. *Sgt. Guffy* Telly Savalas. *Von Diepel* Karl

Otto Alberty. *Maj. Burke* Charles Stalnaker. *Mother Superior* Janet Brandt. *Narrator* William Conrad. *With* Steve Rowland, Robert Woods, David Thomson, Roul Perez, Sebastian Cavalieri, Jack Gaskins, Max Slaten, Carl Rapp, Axel Anderson, Bud Strait, Ben Zatan, Richard Zeidman, Donald Pickering, Peter Herendeen, Paul Eshelman, John Schereschewsky, Victor Brandt, William Boone, Ward Maule, Freddie Toehl, Richard Baxter, John Clark, Paul Polansky, Leland Wyler, Quinn Donoghue, Reginald Gillam, Richard Lava, Derek Robertson, Robert Royal, John Fries, Peter Grzcegorczyk, Ross Stoddard, Harry von der Linden and Martin Roland. ¶"This picture is dedicated to the one million men who fought in this great battle. To encompass the whole of the heroic contributions of all the participants, places, names and characters have been generalized and action has been synthesized in order to convey the spirit and essence of the battle." ¶Working title: *The Battle of the Bulge.* 35mm general release version was 140 minutes without an intermission. The television edition is complete and even has the Cinerama logo on the head.

Baykal, krasota—to kakaya (1982). Filmed in Sovscope 70. International distribution Sovexportfilm. Sovcolor. Six-track magnetic stereophonic sound. A Soviet production released in Russia in 1982.

Becky Sharp (June 14, 1935). Filmed in Technicolor. *Executive producer* Merian C. Cooper. *Producer* Kenneth Macgowan. *Director* Rouben Mamoulian. *Designer* Robert Edmond Jones. *Screenplay* Francis Edward Faragoh. *Based on the play "Becky Sharp" by* Langdon Mitchell. *From the novel "Vanity Fair" by* William Makepeace Thackeray. *Photographer* Ray Rennahan. *Associate art director* Wiard B. Ihnen. *Assistant director* W. Argyle Nelson. *Musical director* Roy Webb. *Dance director* Russell Lewis. *Makeup artist* Robert J. Schiffer. *Chief electrician* Bert Wayne. *Properties* George Hazenbush. *Recorder* Earl A. Wolcott. *Editor* Archie S. Marshek. ¶A Pioneer Pictures, Inc. production. Released by RKO Radio Pictures. RCA Victor High Fidelity Sound System. 83 minutes. Filmed at RKO Radio Studios. ¶CAST: *Becky Sharp* Miriam Hopkins. *Amelia Sedley* Frances Dee. *Marquis de Steyne* Cedric Hardwicke. *Lady Bareacres* Billie Burke. *Julia Crawley* Alison Skipworth. *Joseph Sedley* Nigel Bruce. *Capt. Randon Crawley* Alan Mowbray. *George Osborne* G.P. Huntley, Jr. *Pitt Crawley* William Stack. *Sir Pitt Crawley* George Hassell. *Duke of Wellington* William Haversham. *Gen. Tufto* George Richman. *Duchess of Richmond* Doris Lloyd. *Capt. William Dobbins* Colin Tapley. *Lloyd Tarquin* Leonard Mudie. *Lady Blanche* Bunny Beatty. *Bowles* Charles Coleman. *Briggs* May Beatty. *Miss Flowery* Finis Barton. *Prince Regent* Olaf Hytten. *Fifine* Pauline Garon. *Page* James "Hambone" Robinson. *Miss Pinkerton* Elspeth Dudgeon. *Charwoman* Tempe Pigott. *Lady Jane Crawley* Ottola Nesmith. *Young girl* Margaret Dee. *Ballroom dancer* Pat Ryan

Nixon. *Officers* Pat Somerset and Creighton Hale. ¶The first complete feature in full three-color Technicolor. Director Lowell Sherman died three weeks into production and was replaced by Rouben Mamoulian, who reshot all scenes already filmed. Rereleased in Cinecolor and in black-and-white. A recent attempt to restore the three-color version netted only fair results at best.

Beg *see* **Flight.**

The Beginning of Russia *see* **Ancient Russia.**

Begone Dull Care *see* **Magirama.**

Begstvo mistera Mak-Kinli *see* **Mr. McKinley's Flight.**

Behind the Great Wall (December 8, 1959). Presented in AromaRama. *Executive producer for U.S. version* Walter Reade. *Producer* Leonardo Bonzi. *Director* Carlo Lizzani. *Story* Ennio de Concini. *Photography* Pierludovico Pavoni. *Second unit photography* Alesandro d'Eva. *Artistic supervision* Giancarlo Vigorelli. *Music* Angelo Francesco Lavagnino. *Film editor* Mario Serandrei. *Writers and adapters for AromaRama* Sidney Kaufman and Thomas Orchard. *AromaRama process conceiver and developer* Charles Weiss. *AromaRama editing* Lou Rothstein. *Fragrances compounders* Rhodia, Inc. *Automation mechanisms* Industrial Timer Corporation. *Triggering devices* Camera Equipment Company. *Odor control* Statronic. *Prints* De Luxe. ¶A Walter Reade presentation. An Astra Cinematografica-Leonardo Bonzi production. Released by Continental Distributing, Inc. Totalscope. Eastman Color. Four-track Mag-Optical stereophonic sound. 98 minutes. Filmed in China with a prolog shot in New York City. ¶CAST: *Himself* Chet Huntley. ¶An Italian production released in Italy in 1959 as *La muraglia cinese.* A prolog with Chet Huntley and AromaRama were added for U.S. release. This was the only AromaRama release even though Walter Reade announced production of *The Scent of New Mown Hay.*

Behold Hawaii (April 1983). Filmed in IMAX. *Producer, director and photographer* Greg MacGillivray. *Music* Basil

Poledouris. *Sound effects* Alan Howarth and Mark Mangini and Richard Anderson of Thundertracks. *Mixing* Michael Minkler at Lion's Gate Sound. *Minicrane designers* Don Weegar and Calgar of San Luis Obispo. *Underwater camera casing* Mart Toggweiler. *Gyro camera mounts* Nelson Tyler. ¶A MacGillivray Freeman Films production. Released by MacGillivray Freeman Films Distribution Company. Eastman Color. Six-track magnetic Dolby Stereo. 40 minutes. ¶CAST: *Keola* Blaine Kia. ¶Originally made for McDonald's Development Corporation.

Belaya ptitsa s chernoy otmetinoy (1972). Filmed in Sovscope 70. *Screen authors* Yu. Ilienko and I. Mikolaychuk. *Director* Yu. Ilienko. *Operator* V. Kalyuta. *Artist* A. Mamontov. *Sound operator* L. Vachi. ¶A Kievskaya kinostudiya im. A.P. Dovzenko production. International distribution Sovexportfilm. Sovcolor. Six-track magnetic stereophonic sound. 125 minutes. Filmed at Kievskaya kinostudiya im. A.P. Dovzenko, Kiev, Ukrainian S.S.R. ¶CAST: L. Kadochnikova, I. Mikolaychuk, B. Stupka, Yu. Mikolaychuk, N. Naum, D. Firsova, A. Plotnikov, V. Simchich, L. Bakshtaev, O. Polstvin, M. Ilienko and V. Shakalo. ¶A Soviet production released in Russia in 1972.

Beliy bashlik (1975). Filmed in Sovscope 70. *Screen author* B. Shinkuba. *Based on the poem "Pesnya o skale" by* B. Shinkubi. *Director* V. Saveliev. *Operator* V. Ilienko. *Artist* A. Bobrovnikov. *Composer* V. Guba. *Sound operators* L. Vachi and A. Kuzimin. ¶A Kievskaya kinostudiya im. A.P. Dovzenko production. International distribution Sovexportfilm. Sovcolor. Six-track magnetic stereophonic sound. 123 minutes. Filmed at Kievskaya kinostudiya im. A.P. Dovzenko, Kiev, Ukrainian S.S.R. ¶CAST: T. Kokoskir, A. Kochetkov, N. Kamkia, L. Kaslandzia, Z. Kove, I. Gunba, A. Tania and Sh. Pachalka. ¶A Soviet production released in Russia in 1975.

Beliy Bim Chernoe Ukho *see* **White Bim the Black Ear**

Ben-Hur: A Tale of the Christ (November 1959). Filmed in Camera 65. *Producers* Sam Zimbalist and William Wyler. *Director* William Wyler. *Screenplay* Karl Tunberg, Christopher Fry, Maxwell Anderson, S.N. Behrman and Gore Vidal. *Based on the novel by* Lew Wallace. *Music* Miklos Rozsa. *Director of photography* Robert L. Surtees. *Additional photography* Harold E. Wellman and Pietro Portalupi. *Art directors* William A. Horning and Edward Carfagno. *Set decorations* Hugh Hunt. *Special photographic effects* A. Arnold Gillespie, Lee LeBlanc, Matthew Yuricich and Robert R. Hoag. *Color consultant, settings* Charles K. Hagedon. *Film editors* Ralph E. Winters and John D. Dunning. *Second unit directors* Andrew Marton, Yakima Canutt, Mario Soldati and Richard Thorpe. *Assistant directors* Gus Agosti, Alberto Cardone, Sergio Leone, Ferdinando Baldi and Donald C. Klune. *Makeup* Charles Parker and Charles Schram. *Unit production manager* Edward Woehler. *Recording supervisor* Franklin E. Milton. *Sound recordists* Alexander Sash Fisher and William Steinkamp. *Costume designer* Elizabeth Haffenden. *Color consultant, costumes* Joan Bridge. *Hair styles* Gabriella Borzelli. *Production executive* Joseph J. Cohn. *Production supervisor* Henry Henigson. *Wardrobe* Jack Martell. *Chariot builders* Danesi Brothers, Rome. *Chariot master* Alfredo Danesi. *Horse trainer* Glenn Randall. *Special effects* A.D. Flowers, Robert A. MacDonald and Glen Robinson. *Music editor* William Saracino. *Sound editor* Milo Lory. *Editorial coordinator* Frederic Steinkamp. *Assistant production supervisor* Maurizio Lodi-Fe. *Unit publicist* Morgan Hudgins. *Camera operator* John Schmitz. *Assistant cameramen* Edward Phillips and Edward Wahrman. *Still photographers* Eric Carpenter and Nino Di Giovanni. *Assistant art director* Ken Adam. *Photographic lenses* Panavision. ¶A William Wyler presentation. A Loew's Inc. production. Released by Metro-Goldwyn-Mayer. Technicolor. Westrex six-track magnetic stereophonic sound. 212 minutes plus intermission. Filmed at Studio Cinecitta, Rome and MGM Studios and on location in Arcinazzo, Anzio and other sites in Italy. ¶CAST: *Judah Ben-Hur* Charlton Heston. *Quintus Arrius* Jack Hawkins. *Messala* Stephen Boyd. *Esther* Haya Harareet. *Sheik Ilderim* Hugh Griffith. *Miriam* Martha Scott. *Simonides* Sam Jaffe. *Tirzan* Cathy O'Donnell. *Balthasar* Finlay Currie. *Pontius Pilate* Frank Thring. *Drusus* Terence Longden. *Sextus*

A SPECIAL OPPORTUNITY TO ENJOY THE EXPERIENCE OF YOUR THEATRE-GOING LIFETIME!

A SPECIAL THEATRE PARTY

BEN-HUR—Prince of Judea.
Who challenged the evil
might of pagan Rome!

QUINTUS ARRIUS—Admiral
of the Roman Fleet. A deadly
enemy, but a steadfast friend!

ESTHER—The Beautiful.
Whose love was stronger than
the bonds of slavery!

MESSALA—The Roman Warrior.
Who traded loyalty for power
and trust for treachery!

ILDERIM—The Lusty Sheik.
He believed one God and fifty
wives enough for any man!

MIRIAM—The Loving.
All the cruelties of Rome
could not destroy her faith!

A reserved seat order form sans theater imprint information.

Andre Morell. *Flavi* Marina Berti. *Tiberius* George Relph. *Malluch* Adi Berber. *Amrah* Stella Vitelleschi. *Mary Jose* Greci. *Joseph* Laurence Payne. *Spintho* John Horsley. *Metellus* Richard Coleman. *Marius* Duncan Lamont. *Tiberius' aide* Ralph Truman. *Gaspar* Richard Hale. *Melchior* Reginald Lal Singh. *Quaestor* David Davies. *Jailer* Dervis Ward. *The Christ* Claude Heater. *Gratus* Mino Doro. *Chief of rowers* Robert Brown. *Rower no. 42* John Glenn. *Rower no. 43* Maxwell Shaw. *Rower no. 28* Emile Carrer. *Leper* Tutte Lemkow. *Hortator* Howard Lang. *Rescue ship captain* Ferdy Mayne. *Doctor* John Le Mesurier. *Blind man* Stevenson Lang. *Barca* Aldo Mozele. *Race starter* Thomas O'Leary. *Centurion* Noel Sheldon. *Officer* Hector Ross. *Soldier* Bill Kuehl. *Man in Nazareth* Aldo Silvani. *Villager* Diego Pozzetto. *Marcello* Dino Fazio. *Raimondo* Michael Cosmo. *Cavalry officer* Aldo Pini. *Decurian* Remington Olmstead. *First galley officer* Victor De La Foose. *Second galley officer* Enzo Fiermonte. *Mario* Hugh Billingsley. *Roman at bath* Tiberio Mitri. *Pilate's servant* Pietro Tordi. *Corinthian charioteer* Jerry Brown. *Byzantine charioteer* Otello Capanna. *Syrian charioteer* Luigi Marra. *Lubian charioteer* Cliff Lyons. *Athenian charioteer* Edward J. Auregui. *Egyptian charioteer* Joseph Yrigoyan. *Armenian charioteer* Alfredo Danesi. *Old man* Raimondo Van Riel. *Seaman* Mike Dugan. *Sportsman* Joe Canutt. *Aristocratic guests at Roman party* Prince Emanuele Ruspoli, Prince Raimondo, Count Santiago Oneto, Prince Hohenlohe, Princess Wassilchikoff, Count Mariglians del Monte, Baroness Lillian de Balzo and Duchess Nona Medici. *Stuntmen* Cliff Lyons, Joseph Yrigoyan, Tap Canutt, Joe Canutt, Mickey Gilbert, Edward J. Auregui, Jerry Brown, Alfredo Danesi, Otello Capanna and Luigi Marra. ¶A remake of the 1925 Metro-Goldwyn feature. Reedited to 165 minutes without an intermission. Restored to original length for rerelease and television syndication. All current 70mm prints have been converted from anamorphic to spherical format with approximately .57 reduction in width and are in Metrocolor. Some 35mm prints may have been released with Perspecta Stereophonic Sound. Sam Zimbalist died during production and William Wyler took over as uncredited producer.

Bereg *see* **The Shore.**

Bereg nadezdi *see* **The Shores of Hope.**

The Best of Cinerama (November 21, 1963). Filmed in Cinerama. *Anthology executive producer* Max E. Youngstein. *Anthology coproducers* Merian C. Cooper and Coleman Thomas Conroy, Jr. *Producers* Lowell Thomas, Merian C. Cooper, Robert Bendick, Louis de Rochemont and Carl Dudley. *Narration* Lowell Thomas. *Supervising film editor* Lovel S. Ellis. *Film editors* Norman Karlin and William E. Wild. ¶Produced and released by Cinerama, Inc. Technicolor. Seven-track magnetic Cinerama Sound. 142 minutes plus overture, intermission and exit music. ¶Excerpts from *This Is Cinerama, Louis de Rochemont's Cinerama Holiday, Seven Wonders of the World, Search for Paradise* and *Cinerama South Seas Adventure.*

La Bibbia *see* **The Bible: In the Beginning . . .**

The Bible: In the Beginning . . . (September 28, 1966). Filmed in Dimension 150. *Producer* Dino De Laurentiis. *Director* John Huston. *Screenplay* Christopher Fry, *assisted by* Jonathan Griffin, Ivo Perilli and Vittorio Bonicelli. *Based on the first 22 chapters of the Book of Genesis in the Old Testament. Musical score* Toshiro Mayuzumi. *Conductor of Orchestra Cinefonica Italiana and Chorus Carapellucci* Franco Ferrara. *Director of photography* Giuseppe Rotunno. *Art director* Mario Chiari. *Costumes* Maria de Matteis. *Associate art director* Stephen Grimes. *Production manager* Bruno Todini. *Associate producer* Luigi Luraschi. *Assistant to producer* Ralph Serpe. *Film editor* Ralph Kemplen. *Assistant directors* Vana Caruso and Ottavio Oppo. *Associate to John Huston* Gladys Hill. *Makeup supervision* Alberto de Rossi. *Sound recording supervisor* Fred Hynes. *Sound recorders* Murray Spivack and Basil Fenton Smith. *Music recorder* Murray Spivack. *Sound editor* Leslie Hodgson. *Music editor* Gilbert D. Marchant. *Assistant art director* Pasquale Romano. *Casting director* Guidarino Guidi. *Set construction* Aldo Puccini and Mario Scisi. *Set dressing* Enzo Eusepi and Bruno Avesani. *Script girl* Yvonne Axworthy. *Assistant to film editor*

Eunice Mountjoy. *Zoological consultant* Angelo Lombardi. *Hairdresser* Elda Magnanti. *Production assistants* Roman Dandi and Giorgio Morra. *Special optical effects* Technicolor, Ltd., Linwood G. Dunn, Cecil Love and Film Effects of Hollywood. *Second unit direction for "The Creation"* Ernst Haas. *Choreography* Katherine Dunham. *Special effects* August J. Lohman and Carlo Rambaldi. *Set dressing accessories* Tani-Cappellini. *Wigs* Rocchetti. *Costumes* Tigano e Lo Faro. *Ava Gardner's costumes* Sorelle Fontana, Rome. *Sun effects-special projector* Zeus-Ianiro. *Cooperating artists* Corrado Cagli [Colliea] and Mirko. *Music recording* RCA Italiana, S.p.A. *Musical edition* Edizioni Musicali DINO. *Second unit photography for "The Creation"* Lupino Latourno. *Story consultant* Emilio Villa. *Camera operator* Giuseppe Maccari. *Makeup* Giuliano Laurenti. *Production inspectors* Marco Tamburella, Antonio Girasante and Fernando Cinquini. *Sound engineer* Mario Celentano. *Sound recording* Todd-AO. *Consultants* Rev. W.M. Merchant and Mon. Salvatore Garofalo. *Sculptor* Giacomo Manzu. *Still photographers* Paul Ronald and Louis Goldman. *Unit publicists* Robert Thiele and Peter DeAngelis. *Dimension 150 process consultants* Richard Vetter and Carl Williams. *Negative* Eastman Color. ¶A Dino De Laurentiis Cinematografica, S.p.A. production. Released by 20th Century-Fox in association with Seven Arts Pictures. Color by Technicolor. Prints by De Luxe. RCA and Westrex six-track magnetic stereophonic sound. 174 minutes plus intermission. Filmed in the studio of Dino De Laurentiis Cinematografica, Rome and on location in Sicily, Sardinia and Egypt. ¶CAST: *Adam* Michael Parks. *Eve* Ulla Bergryd. *Cain* Richard Harris. *Noah and narrator* John Huston. *Nimrod* Stephen Boyd. *Abraham* George C. Scott. *Sarah* Ava Gardner. *Three Angels* Peter O'Toole. *Hagar* Zoe Sallis. *Lot* Gabriele Ferzetti. *Lot's wife* Eleonra Rossi Drago. *Abel* Franco Nero. *Noah's wife* Pupella Maggio. *Isaac* Alberto Lucantoni. *Ishmael* Luciano Conversi. *Abraham's steward* Robert Rietty. *Lot's daughters* Adriana Ambesi and Maria Grazia Spina. *Nimrod's queen* Claudie Lange. *Shem* Angelo Boscariol. *Ham* Peter Heinze. *Shem's wife* Anna Maria Orso. *Japheth* Eric Leutzinger. *Japheth's*

wife Rossana di Rocco. *Ham's wife* Gabriella Pallotta. *Serpent* Flavio Bennati. *With* Roger Beaumont, Gianluigi Crescenzi, Michael Steinpichter and Giovanna Galletti. ¶An Italian production released in Italy in 1966 as *La Bibbia*. Advertised as *The Bible . . . In the Beginning.* There were two advertising campaigns, one stating "Filmed and Presented in D-150" and the other crediting "Produced in 70mm." This was to have been the first in a series of possibly six films covering the Old Testament. There were no others.

Big Ball (1984). Filmed in Showscan. Produced and released by Showscan Film Corporation. Eastman Color. Six-track magnetic Dolby Stereo. This short was made specially for showing in Showbiz Piazza SuperCinemas.

The Big Fisherman (August 1959). Filmed in Ultra Panavision 70. *Producer* Rowland V. Lee. *Associate producer* Eric G. Stacey. *Director* Frank Borzage. *Screenplay* Howard Estabrook and Rowland V. Lee. *Based on the novel by* Lloyd C. Douglas. *Photographer* Lee Garmes. *Production design* John De Cuir. *Music composer* Albert Hay Malotte. *Music supervision* Joseph Gershenson. *Orchestrations* David Tamkin. *Set decoration* Julia Heron. *Costumes* Renie. *Makeup* Bud Westmore and Frank Westmore. *Hair stylist* Larry Germain. *Casting* James Ryan. *Script supervisor* Anita Speer. *Costume supervision* Wesley Jeffries. *Technical adviser* George M. Lamsa. *Unit manager* Edward Dodds. *Assistant director* Richard Moder. *Sound* Leslie I. Carey and Frank H. Wilkinson. *Editorial supervision* Paul Weatherwax. *Associate editors* William Andrews *(sound)* and Arnold Schwarzwald *(music).* *Camera operator* Eddie Garvin. *Negative* Eastman Color. ¶A Centurion Films Inc. presentation. A Rowland V. Lee production. Released by Buena Vista Distribution Co. Inc. Technicolor. Westrex six-track magnetic stereophonic sound. 180 minutes plus intermission. Filmed at Universal City Studios and on location in the San Fernando Valley, Palm Springs and Lake Chatsworth, California. ¶CAST: *Simon-Peter* Howard Keel. *Princess Fara* Susan Kohner. *Prince Voldi* John Saxon. *Herodias* Martha Hyer. *King Herod-Antipas* Herbert Lom, *King Deran* Ray Stricklyn.

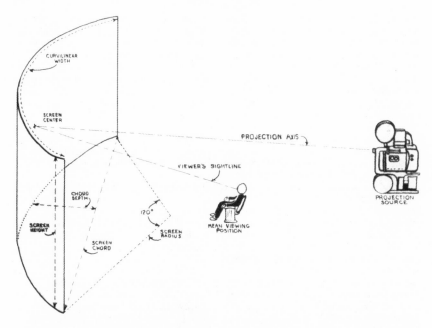

Top: *Original D-150, Inc., drawing showing theater projection layout and perspective. Despite the name and the advertisements for films such as* The Bible: In the Beginning . . . , *which read, "Presented in D-150," the screen was only 120 degrees.* Bottom: *The rather amazing D-150 projection lens, manufactured by Kollmorgen Corporation. The lens delivered a bright, undistorted, perfectly focused image over the full screen area, and incorporated a so-called "Curvulon" optical correction system.*

Arnon Marian Seldes. *David Ben-Zadok* Alexander Scourby. *Hannah* Beulah Bondi. *John the Baptist* Jay Barney. *Rennah* Charlotte Fletcher. *Zendi* Mark Dana. *Andrew* Rhodes Reason. *Menicus* Henry Brandon. *John* Brian Hutton. *James* Thomas Troupe. *Ione* Marianne Stewart. *Lysias* Jonathan Stewart. *Ilderan* Leonard Mudie. *Beggar* James Griffith. *Phillip* Peter Adams. *Deborah* Jo Gilbert. *Innkeeper* Michael Mark. *Assassin* Joseph Di Reda. *Aretas* Stuart Randall. *Tiberius* Herbert Rudley. *Lucius* Phillip Pine. *Scribe spokesman* Francis J. McDonald. *Pharisee spokesman* Perry Ivins. *Aged pharisee* Ralph Moody. *Sadducee spokesman* Tony Jochim. *Roman centurion* Don Turner. ¶"With deep appreciation to the other members of the cast, all of the highly trained extras, and the skilled technicians." ¶The screen credits read "Photographic Process by Panavision" while advertising billed "70mm Panavision" and "Panavision 70mm." Some of the publicity material referred to "Panavision 65." Recut to 166 minutes, 150 minutes and 144 minutes. One of the very few non–Walt Disney Productions features released by that firm's distribution arm.

The Big Trail (October 24, 1930). Filmed in Grandeur. *Executive producer* William Fox. *Producer* Winfield Sheehan. *Director* Raoul Walsh. *Screenplay and dialog* Jack Peabody, Marie Boyle and Florence Postal. *Scenario* Fred Sersen. *Story* Hal G. Evarts. *Grandeur photographer* Arthur Edeson. *35mm photographer* Lucien Andriot. *Film editor* Jack Dennis. *Sound supervisor* Edmund H. Hansen. *Chief sound technicians* George Leverett and William Donald Flick. *Sound recordists* Bill Brent and Paul Heihly. *Production manager* Archibald Buchanan. *Business managers* George Busch and Benjamin Wurtzel. *Production assistants* John Padjeon and Joe Flores. *Assistant directors* Archibald Buchanan, Edmund Goulding, Ewing Scott, Sidney Bowen, Clay Crapnell, George Walsh, Virgil Hart and Earl Rettig. *Art director* Harold Miles. *Photographic effects* Fred Sersen and Ray Kellogg. *Chief technicians* William Donald Flick and Louis Witte. *Grandeur camera crew* David Ragin, Sol Halprin, Curt Fetters, Max Cohn, Harry Smith, L. Kunkel and Harry Dawe. *35mm camera crew* Don Anderson, Roger Shearman, Bobby Mack, Henry Pollack and Bill McDonald. *"Song of the Big Trail"* by Joseph McCarthy and James F. Hanley. *Incidental music* Hugo Friedhofer, Reginald H. Bassett, Jack Virgil and Arthur Kay. *Musical direction* Arthur Kay. *Master of wardrobe* Earl Moser. *Makeup* Jack Dawn and Louise Sloane. *Props* Don Greenwood and Tom Plews. *Chief carpenter* Les Shaw. *Chief electrician* L.E. Barber. *Stills* Frank Powolny. ¶A William Fox presentation. A Raoul Walsh production. Released by Fox Film Corp. Western Electric Movietone recording. 158 minutes. ¶CAST: *Breck Coleman* John Wayne. *Ruth Cameron* Marguerite Churchill. *Gussie* El Brendel. *Zeke* Tully Marshall. *Red Flack* Frederick Tyrone Power, Sr. *Dave Cameron* David Rollins. *Bill Thorpe* Ian Keith. *Pa Bascom* Frederick Burton. *Windy Bill* Russ Powell. *Lopez* Charles Stevens. *Honey Girl* Helen Parrish. *Gussie's mother-in-law* Louise Carver. *Wellmore* William V. Mong. *Abigail* Dodo Newton. *Bill Gillis* Jack Peabody. *Sid Bascom* Ward Bond. *Mrs. Riggs* Marcia Harris. *Mary Riggs* Marjorie Leet. *Sairey* Emslie Emerson. *Ohio man* Frank Rainboth. *Ohio man's son* Andy Shufford. *Missouri sisters* Gertrude and Lucille Van Lent. *Boat captain* De Witt Jennings. *Marshall* Alphonze Ethier. *Youth* Robert Parrish. *Indian* Chief John Big Tree. *Pioneer* John Padjeon. ¶Simultaneously filmed in regular 35mm. Released in 35mm on November 1, 1930 running 125 minutes. Also filmed in a German version, *Die grosse fahrt,* and a French version directed by P. Couderc, *La piste des géants,* presumably in 35mm only. In 1985 the 70mm version was converted to 35mm 'scope format.

Billy the Kid (October 19, 1930). Filmed in Realife. *Producer and director* King Vidor. *Screenplay* Wanda Tuchock and Laurence Stallings. *Additional dialog* Charles McArthur. *Based on the book "The Saga of Billy the Kid"* by Walter Noble Barnes. *Photographer* Gordon Avil. *Film editor* Hugh Wynn. *Recording director* Douglas Shearer. *Sound engineers* Paul Neal and Jack Jordan. *Art director* Cedric Gibbons. *Costumes* David Cox. *Technical adviser* William S. Hart. ¶A King Vidor production. Controlled by Loew's Inc. Released by Metro-Goldwyn-Mayer. Western Electric Movietone recording. 90 minutes. Filmed at MGM

Studios and on location in Arizona. ¶CAST: *Billy the Kid* Johnny Mack Brown. *Sheriff Pat Garrett* Wallace Beery. *Claire Kay* Johnson. *Swenson* Karl Dane. *Tunston* Wyndham Standing. *McSween* Russell Simpson. *Mrs. McSween* Blanche Frederici. *Old Stuff* Roscoe Ates. *Ballinger* Warner P. Richmond. *Donovan* James Marcus. *Butterworth* John Beck. *Nicky Whoosiz* Marguerita Padula. *Mrs. Hatfield* Aggie Herring. *Santiago* Christopher Martin. *With* Nelson McDowell, Jack Carlyle, Hank Bell, Soledad Jiminez, Don Coleman and Lucille Powers. ¶Some sources claim this was shot in 35mm and blown up to Realife format; others claim it was never shown in the wide gauge format. Still others claim the 35mm version was shot for cropping in 2×1 ratio. The fact is a Realife and standard 35mm version were shot simultaneously, and the 35mm edition was given cropped presentation in some theaters. Also filmed in German and Spanish versions, apparently in 35mm only. Remade by MGM as *Billy the Kid* (1941) and *Pat Garrett and Billy the Kid* (1973). Many other films have concerned the same lead characters.

A Bit of Fooling (1977). Filmed in Sovscope 70. *Screen author* Semyon Lunzin. *Director* Vladimir Menishov. *Operator* Mikhail Bits. *Artist* Boris Blank. *Composer* Aleksandr Flyarkovskiy. *Sound operators* V. Alekseeva and V. Popov. *Song text* A. Didurova. ¶A Mosfilm production. International distribution Sovexportfilm. Sovcolor. Six-track magnetic stereophonic sound. 96 minutes. Filmed at Mosfilm Studios, Moscow, R.S.F.S.R. ¶CAST: *Old teacher* Evgenia Khanaeva. *Taya* Natalia Fateeva. *Oleg Komarovsky* Andrei Gusev. *Igor Grushko* Dima Kharatiyan. *With* Zinovy Gerdt, Harry Bardin, Pavel Vinnik, Musa Krepkogorskaya, Lubov Misheva, Oleg Tabakov, N. Vavilova, A. Zilitsov and D. Germanova. ¶A Soviet production released in Russia in 1977 as *Rozigrish.*

Bitva za Moskvu *see* **The Battle of Moscow.**

The Black Arrow (1985). Filmed in Sovscope 70. *Screen author and director* Sergei Tarasov. *Based on the novel "The Black Arrow" by* Robert Louis Stevenson. *Operator* Mikhail Ardabievskiy. *Artist* Aleksandr Kuznetsev. *Composer* Igor

Kantyukov. *Sound operator* E. Popova. ¶A Mosfilm production. International distribution Sovexportfilm. Sovcolor. Six-track magnetic stereophonic sound. 113 minutes. Filmed at Mosfilm Studios, Moscow, R.S.F.S.R. ¶CAST: *Dick Shelton* Igor Shavlak. *Joan Sadely* Galina Belyaeva. *Richard Gloucester* Aleksandr Filippenko. *David Brackley* Leonid Kulagin. *Sir Oliver* Yuri Smirnov. *Bennett Hatch* Algimantas Masyulis. *Lord Grace* Boris Khmelnitsky. *With* B. Khimichev and Sergei Tarasov. ¶A Soviet production released in Russia in 1985 as *Chernaya strela.*

The Black Birch (1978). Filmed in Sovscope 70. *Screen authors* Boris Arhipovets, Mikhail Berezko and Samson Polyakov. *Director* Vitaly Chetverikov. *Operator* Dmitry Zaytsev. *Artist* Leonid Ershov. *Composer* Alexei Muravlev. *Sound operator* B. Shangin. ¶A Belorusfilm production. International distribution Sovexportfilm. Sovcolor. Six-track magnetic sterephonic sound. 181 minutes plus intermission. Filmed at Belorusfilm Studios, R.S.F.S.R. ¶CAST: *Andrei Khmara* Evgeny Kareliskin. *Tanya* Irina Alfyerova. *Doctor* Demma Firsova. *With* Natalia Braznikova, Irina Reznikova, Vladimir Kuleshov, O. Khabalov, L. Danchishin, V. Duchkovskiy, Z. Gabrinayte and A. Vasilevskiy. ¶A Soviet production released in Russia in 1978 as *Chernaya bereza.*

The Black Cauldron (July 1985). Filmed in Super Technirama 70. *Executive producer* Ron Miller. *Producer* Joe Hale. *Directors* Ted Berman, Richard Rich and Art Stevens. *Story* David Jonas, Vance Gerry, Ted Berman, Richard Rich, Joe Hale, Al Wilson, Roy Morita, Peter Young and Art Stevens. *Additional dialog* Rosemary Anne Sisson and Roy Edward Disney. *Adaptation* Mel Shaw. *Based on the novels "The Book of Three" and "The Black Cauldron" by* Lloyd Alexander. *Music* Elmer Bernstein. *Character design* Andreas Deja, Mike Ploog, Phil Nibbelink, Al Wilson and David Jonas. *"Fflewddur's Song" music and lyrics by* Richard Bowden and Richard Rich. *Animators* Andreas Deja, Hendel Butoy, Dale Baer, Ron Husband, Jack Jackson, Barry Temple, Phil Nibbelink, Steve Gordon, Doug Krohn, Shawn Keller, Mike Gabriel, Phillip Young, Tom Ferriter,

Jesse Cosio, Ruben Procopio, Viki Anderson, David Block, Charlie Downs, Sandra Borgmeyer, Ruben Aquino, Cyndee Whitney, George Scribner, Mark Henn, Terry Harrison, Dick Huemer and David Pacheco. *Key coordinating animator* Walt Stanchfield. *Layout* Don Griffith, Guy Vasilovich, Glenn Vilppu, Dan Hansen and William Fraker, 3rd. *Layout styling* Mike Hodgson. *Color styling* James Coleman. *Backgrounds* Donald Towns, Brian Sebern, John Emerson, Tiaw Kratter, Lisa Keene and Andrew Phillipson. *Effects animators* Don Paul, Mark Dindal, Jeff Howard, Patricia Peraza, Scott Santoro, Glenn Chaika, Barry Cook, Ted Kierscey, Kelvin Yasuda, Bruce Woodside, Kimberley Knowlton and Allen Gonzales. *Xeroxgraphy* Dave Spencer. *Lithography* Bernie Gagliano. *Special photographic effects* Philip Meador, Ron Osenbaugh and Bill Kilduff. *Film editors* James Melton, Jim Koford and Armetta Jackson. *Orchestration* Peter Bernstein. *Production manager* Don Hahn. *Assistant directors* Mark Hester, Terry Noss and Randy Paton. *Sound effects design* Mike McDonough. *Sound supervisor* Bob Hathaway. *Lenses* Panavision. ¶A Walt Disney Pictures presentation. Produced by Walt Disney Productions in association with Silver Screen Partners II. Released by Buena Vista Distribution Co. Technicolor. Six-track magnetic Dolby Stereo. 80 minutes. Filmed at Walt Disney Studios. MPAA rating: PG. ¶CAST: (Voice Characterizations): *Taran the assistant enchanter* Grant Bardsley. *Princess Eilonwy* Susan Sheridan. *Dallben the Enchanter* Freddie Jones. *King Fflewddur Fflam* Nigel Hawthorne. *King Eidilleg* Arthur Malet. *Gurgi and Doli* John Byner. *Horned King* John Hurt. *Fairfolk* Lindsay Rich, Brandon Call and Gregory Levinson. *Orddu* Eda Reiss Merin. *Orwen* Adele Malis-Morey. *Orgoch* Billie Hayes. *Creepers* Phil Fondcaro, Peter Renaday, James Almanzar and Wayne Allwine. *Henchmen* Steve Hale, Phil Nibbelink and Jack Laing. *Prolog narrator* John Huston. ¶Disney's second 70mm animated feature. One source credits this as being shot in "Super Panavision Widescreen," but the Technirama format was used with Panavision lenses. Jonathan Winters' voice for King Eidilleg was rerecorded by Arthur Malet. Originally this was to have included a 3D sequence involving holography (sic).

Black Tights (February 1962). Filmed in Super Technirama 70. *Producer* Joseph Kauffman. *Director* Terence Young. *"The Diamond Cruncher" story* Roland Petit and Alfred Adam. *"Cyrano de Bergerac" (based on the play by Edmond Rostand), "A Merry Mourning" and "Carmen" (based on the opera by Georges Bizet, Henri Meilhac and Ludovic Halevy) stories* Roland Petit. *Director of photography* Henri Alekan. *Film editor* Francoise Javet. *Associate producer* Simon Schiffrin. *Music director and "Cyrano de Bergerac" music* Marius Constant. *"The Diamond Cruncher" music* Jean-Michel Damase. *"A Merry Mourning" music* Maurice Thiriet. *"The Diamond Cruncher" lyrics* Raymond Queneau, *English version* Herbert Kretzmer. *Orchestra* Concerts Lamoreaux. *Choreography* Roland Petit. *Maitre de ballet* Francoise Adret and Raoul Celada. *Art directors* Georges Wakhevitch and Henri Morin. *"The Diamond Cruncher" decor and costumes* Georges Wakhevitch. *"Cyrano de Bergerac" decor* Bazarte. *"Cyrano de Bergerac" costumes* Yves Saint-Laurent. *"A Merry Mourning" and "Carmen" decor and costumes* Antoni Clave. *Sound engineer* Jacques Lebreton. *Assistant director* Bernard Farrel. ¶A Joseph Kauffman presentation. A Grandes Projections Cinematographiques–Talma Films–Doperfilme production. Released by Magna Pictures. Technicolor. Westrex six-track magnetic stereophonic sound. 120 minutes. Filmed in Paris. ¶CAST: *Introduction by* Maurice Chevalier. *Dancers* Ballets de Roland Petit. **The Diamond Cruncher:** *Diamond cruncher* Zizi Jeanmaire. *Pierrot* Dirk Sanders. *Proprietor* Bertie Eckhart. **Cyrano de Bergerac:** *Roxanne* Moira Shearer. *Cyrano de Bergerac* Roland Petit. *Christian* Georges Reich. **A Merry Mourning:** *Widow* Cyd Charisse. *Young man* Roland Petit. *Husband* Hans Van Manen. *Waiter* Gerard Lemaitre. *Soubrettes* Danielle Jossi and Regine Boury. *Narrator* Maurice Chevalier. **Carmen:** *Carmen* Zizi Jeanmaire. *Don Jose* Roland Petit. *Toreador* Henning Kronstam. *Female bandit* Josette Clavier. *Smuggler* Fredbjørn Bjørnsson. *Male bandit* Hans Van Manen. ¶A French production released in France in 1962 as *Les collants noirs* running 140 minutes.

IN SUPER TECHNIRAMA 70

Starring

CYD CHARISSE • MOIRA SHEARER • ZIZI JEANMAIRE
ROLAND PETIT and MAURICE CHEVALIER

Ad for the 1962 French production Black Tights (Les collants noirs).

Working and preview title was *Un, deux, trois, quatre!*

Blistayushchiy mir *see* **The Sparkling World.**

Blockade (1975). Filmed in Sovscope 70. *Screen authors* Aleksandr Chakovsky and Arnold Vitoli. *Based on the novel "Blokada" by* Aleksandr Chakovskogo. *Director* Mikhail Ershov. *Operator* Anatoly Nazarov. *Artist* Mikhail Ivanov. *Composer* Veniamin Basner. *Sound operator* I. Volkova. *Song text* M. Matusovskogo. ¶A Lenfilm production. International distribution Sovexportfilm. Sovcolor. Six-track magnetic stereophonic sound. Filmed at Lenfilm Studios, Leningrad, R.S.F.S.R. ¶CAST: *Gen. Zhukov* Mikhail Uliyanov. *Maj. Zvyagintsev* Yuri Solomin. *Valitsky* Vladislav Strzelichik. *Zhdanov* Sergei Kharchenka. *With* Irina Akulova, Nikolai E. Lebedev, Aleksandr Razin, Yuozas Budraits, L. Zolotukhin, B. Gorbatov, D. Sagal, V. Minin, V. Abramov, A. Verbitskiy, Yu. Malitsev, A Bershchachskiy, O. Korchikov, L. Lemke, A. Afanasiev and V. Zelidin. ¶A Soviet production released in Russia in 1975 as *Blokada* in four parts: *Luzskiy rubez (The Luzhsky Defense Line)* running 139 minutes, *Pulkovskiy meridian (The Pulkovo*

Meridan) running 96 minutes, *Leningrad-skiy metronom (The Leningrad Metronome),* running time unknown, and *Operatsiya Iskra (Operation Spark),* running time unknown. The last two parts were not in general release until 1978.

Blokada *see* **Blockade.**

Blow, Breeze! (1975). Filmed in Sovscope 70. *Screen authors* Imant Ziedonis and Gunar Piesis. *Based on the play "Vey, veterok!" by* Yanis Raynisa. *Director* Gunar Piesis. *Operator* Martin Kleyn. *Artist* D. Rozlapa. *Composer* Imant Kalnini. *Sound operator* V. Lyuchev. ¶A Rizskaya kinostudiya production. International distribution Sovexportfilm. Sovcolor. Six-track magnetic stereophonic sound. 120 minutes. Filmed at Rizskaya kinostudiya, Riga, Latvian S.S.R. and on location on the Daugava River. ¶CAST: *Baiba* Emeralda Ermale. *Zane* Astrida Kairisha. *Mother* Elza Radzinya. *Uldis* Girt Yakovlev. *Gatyn* Petr Gaudinish. *With* Z. Krastinya, A. Liedskalninya and L. Freymane. ¶A Soviet production released in Russia in 1975 as *Vey, veterok!*

The Blue Bird (May 1976). Filmed in Sovscope and Panavision. *Executive producer* Edward Lewis. *Producer* Paul Maslansky. *Coproducers* Paul Radin and Lee Savin. *General director of production* Aleksandr Archanskiy. *Director* George Cukor. *Screenplay* Hugh Whitemore and Alfred Hayes. *Screen author (Soviet version)* Alexei Kapler. *Based on the play by* Maurice Maeterlinck. *Director of photography* Frederick A. Young. *Chief operator* Ionas Gritsyus. *Music supervisors, arrangers and conductors* Irwin Kostal and Lionel Newman. *Songs and ballet music* Andrei Petrova. *Lyrics* Tony Harrison. *Film editors* Ernest Walter, Tatiana Shapiro and Stanford C. Allen. *Production designer* Brian Wildsmith. *Artist* Valery Yurkevich. *Decorators* Evgeny Starikovitch, Eduard Isaev and Tamara Polyansaka. *Choreographers* I. Beliskiy and L. Yakobson. *Sound recordists* John Bramall and Gordon Everett. *Sound operators* Georgi Elibert and G. Ebert. *Costume designer* Edith Head. *Costumier* Mariana Azizian. *Rerecording* Theodore Soderberg. *Assistant directors* Mike Gowans, Evgeny Tatarskiy, Liliana Markova and Stirlin Harris. *Panavision*

cameras and lenses Samuelson Film Service, Ltd. *Services* Bluebird Productions, Ltd. ¶A 20th Century–Fox Film Corporation–Wenles Films, Ltd.–Lenfilm production in association with Robert H. Greenberg and Harry N. Blum. Produced in cooperation with Tower International. Released by 20th Century–Fox. Sovcolor. Prints De Luxe. Westrex recording system. 100 minutes. Filmed at Lenfilm Studios, Leningrad, R.S.F.S.R. MPAA rating: G. ¶CAST: *Mother, Maternal Love, Witch and Light* Elizabeth Taylor. *Night* Jane Fonda. *Luxury* Ava Gardner. *Cat* Cecily Tyson. *Father Time* Robert Morley. *Oak* Harry Andrews. *Tyltyl* Todd Lookinland. *Myltyl* Patsy Kensit. *Grandfather* Will Geer. *Grandmother* Mona Washbourne. *Dog* George Cole. *Bread* Richard Pearson. *Blue Bird* Nadia Pavlova. *Sugar* George Vitsin. *Milk* Margareta Terekhova. *Fat Laughter* Oleg Popov. *Father* Leonid Nevedomskiy. *Water* Valentina Ganilae Ganibalova. *Fire* Evgeny Scherbakov. *Sick girl* Pheona McLellen. *With* Leningrad Kirov Ballet. ¶An American, British and Soviet coproduction released in Russia in 1977 as *Sinyaya ptitsa* in 70mm and six-track magnetic stereophonic sound running 100 minutes. Released in the U.S. in 35mm only. Postproduction work was done principally in Hollywood. A remake of the 1918 silent feature and 20th Century–Fox's 1940 Technicolor classic.

Bolishoy attraktsion (1975). Filmed in Sovscope 70. *Screen authors* A. Basargin and V. Georgiev. *Director* V. Georgiev. *Operator* Z. Savelieva. *Artist* G. Shabanova. *Composer* G. Podzliskiy. *Sound operator* V. Kurganskiy. *Song text* L. Derbeneva. ¶A Mosfilm production. International distribution Sovexportfilm. Sovcolor. Six-track magnetic stereophonic sound. 81 minutes. Filmed at Mosfilm Studios, Moscow, R.S.F.S.R. ¶CAST: N. Varley, G. Tsilinskiy, M. Menglet, G. Vitsin, S. Martinson, E. Morgunov, S. Kramarov, T. Pelittser, V. Grammatikov, A. Akopyan, B. Amarantov and M. Georgiev. ¶A Soviet production released in Russia in 1975.

Bolshoi Ballet 67 (September 29, 1966). Filmed in Sovscope 70. *Directors and producers* Leonid Lavrovskiy and Aleksandr Shelenkov. *Screen authors* Lev Arnshtam,

Leonid Lavrovskiy and Aleksandr Shelenkov. *English narration* Sidney Carroll. *English version supervision* Celebrity Concert Corporation. *Chief operators* Aleksandr Shelenkov and Iolanda Chen-F-Lan. *Operator* S. Armand. *Artist* A. Parkhomenko. *Editor* L. Feyginova. *Ballet directors* T. Kuyava-Dzkhevetska, T. Ustinova and S. Golovkina. *Choreographer* Leonid Lavrovskiy. *Sound operators* B. Voliskiy and Grigoriy Korenblyum. *Assistant director* L. Brozkhovskiy. *Manager of production* I. Khlopyeva. *Costumes* A. Danduryan. *Costume for ballet "Rhapsody on a theme by Paganini"* V. Ryndina. *Makeup* M. Maslova and T. Krylova. *Special effects* G. Ayzenberg, N. Spiridonova and Ya. Korablyov. *"Valses nobles et sentimentales" and "Bolero" composer* Maurice Joseph Ravel. *"Giselle" composer* Adolphe Charles Adam. *"Laurensiya" composer* Aleksandr Abramovich Kreyn. *"Don Kikhot" composer* Ludwig Minkus. *"Le cygne" composer* Camille Saint-Saens. *"Skaz o kamennom tsvetke" composer* Sergei Sergeevich. *"Rhapsody on a theme by Paganini" composer* Sergei Rachmaninoff. *Music selections* P.I. Chaykovskogo. *Special music composer and arranger* Nikolay Yakovlev. *Performers* Bolshoi Theatre Orchestra and Bolshoi Symphony Orchestra of Radio and Television, *conductor* Gennadiy Rozhdestivenskiy, *concertmaster* I. Zaytseva, and Bolshoi Theatre Violin Ensemble, *conductor* Y. Reyentovich. *Prints* Technicolor. ¶DANCERS: *"Valses nobles et sentimentales"* Natalya Bessmertnova and Mikhail Lavrovskiy. *"Giselle"* Nina Sorokina. *"Laurensiya"* Nina Timofeeva. *"Don Kikhot"* Nayya Samkhvalova. *"Rhapsody on a theme by Paganini"* Yaroslav Sekh and Ekaterina Maksimova. *"Bolero"* Elena Kholina, Aleksandr Lavreniuk and S. Radchenko. *"Le cygne"* A. Osipenko. *"Skaz o kamennom tsvetke"* Raisa Struchkova, Yu. Grigoryev, Vladimir Levashyov, Natalya Kasatkina and A. Simachyov. *Narrator* Ariane. *With* Bolshoi Theatre Ballet and students of Moscow Choreographic School. ¶A Celebrity Concert Corporation presentation. A Mosfilm production. Released by Paramount Pictures by arrangement with Sovexportfilm. Sovcolor. Six-track magnetic stereophonic sound. 82 minutes including intermission. Filmed at Mosfilm Studios, Moscow, R.S.F.S.R. ¶A Soviet production released in Russia in 1965 as *Sekret uspekha* running 98 minutes. The running time for the U.S. version includes a 7-minute intermission.

Brainstorm (September 30, 1983). Filmed in Super Panavision 70. *Executive producer* Joel L. Freeman. *Producer and director* Douglas Trumbull. *Screenplay* Bruce Joel Rubin, Robert Stitzel, Philip Frank Messina and Robert Getchell. *Story* Bruce Joel Rubin. *Associate producer and director of photography* Richard Yuricich. *Music composer* James Horner. *Film editors* Edward Warshilka, Sr. and Freeman Davies. *Casting* Lynn Stalmaster and Associates and Toni Howard. *Costume designer* Donfeld. *Production designer* John Vallone. *Executive in charge of production* Jack Grossberg. *Unit production managers* Jack Grossberg and John G. Wilson. *First assistant directors* David McGiffert, Brian Frankish, Robert Jeffords and Eugene Mazzola. *Second assistant director* Patrick Cosgrove. *Art director* David L. Snyder. *Set decorators* Tom Pedigo and Linda DeScenna. *Set designer* Marjorie Stone. *Script supervisor* Ana Maria Quintana. *Second unit director of photography* Robert Haagensen. *Camera operators* Daniel Lerner and Al Bettcher. *First assistant cameramen* Craig Haagensen and Steve Smith. *Second assistant cameraman* Bruce McCallum. *Still photographers* Josh Bener, Len Hedel and Christine Loss. *Video engineer* Gregory L. McMurray. *Video technician* Rhonda Gunner. *Chief lighting technician* Theodore Porterholt. *Assistant chief lighting technicians* Jim Ross, Thomes Hoes and James T. Blerienburg. *Key grip* Tim Ryan. *Grip best boy* Carl Gibson, Jr. *Second grip* Leonardo Chavez. *Dolly grip* Dennis W. Greene. *First assistant film editor* Scott Wallace. *Assistant film editors* Edward Warschilka, Jr. and Barbara Dunning. *Music editor* William Saracino. *Sound editors* Bill Sawyer, Teri E. Dorman, Don Hall, Jr., Joe Ippolito, John Larsen and Victoria Rose Sampson. *Assistant sound editor* Eric Whitfield. *ADR editor* Jay Engel. *Source music consultant* Bill Croft. *Supervising rerecording mixer* Don MacDougall. *Rerecording mixers* Richard Tyler and John Mack. *Orchestration* Greg McRitchie. *Music supervisor* Harry V. Lojewski. *Sound mixer* Art Rochester.

Boomman Richard Thornton. *Cableman* Peter Martinez. *Property master* Jackie Adelman. *Assistant property* Phil Calhoun. *Propmaker* Dick Connister. *Special effects* Robert Spurlock, Eric Allard and Martin Bresin. *Women's costumer* Aida Swinson. *Men's costumer* Dick Butz. *Costumers* DeeDee Burch and John George. *Ms. Wood's hair stylist* Kaye Pownall. *Ms. Wood's makeup artist* Edwin Butterworth. *Makeup artists* Edward C. Ternes and Robert Jiras. *Special makeup artist* William Munns. *Hair stylist* Bette L. Mason. *Location manager* Paul Pav. *Production office coordinator* Barbara Spitz. *Unit publicists* Don Levy and Vic Heltsohn. *Assistant art directors* Stephen Dane and Tom Melton. *Set construction* Wynand Productions. *Construction coordinators* Claude Powell and Steven Lincoln. *Standby painter* Phil Campanella. *Craft services* Michael Knutsen. *Leadman* Joe DeRosa. *Stunt coordinator* Bill Couch. *Transportation coordinator* Randy Peters. *Transportation captains* Don Perce and Frank Melcarea. *Music recording supervisor* Shawn Murphy. *Special synthesizer effects* Frank Serafine, Ian Underwood and Jack Manning. *Computer controlled robots* ASEA. *The Duke University Choir conductor* J. Benjamin Smith. *California Boy Choir conductor* Douglas Nicland. *Experimental sequence consultants* Stanislav and Christina Grof. *Scientific consultants* Durk Pearson and Sandy Shaw. *Assistance* Gov. James B. Hunt, Jr., North Carolina Film Commission, Research Triangle Foundation, Burroughs Wellcome Company, Wright Brothers National Memorial, Duke University, Pinehurst Hotel and Country Club and Sandy Lane Farm. *"The Tonight Show" courtesy* Carson Productions, Inc. *Flight simulator courtesy* Northrop Corporation Aircraft Division. *Rerecording* Gomillion Sound, Inc. *Special purpose lenses courtesy* Omnivision. *Color timer* William Pine. *Super Panavision 70 and Panaflex cameras and lenses* Panavision. *Special visual effects creators* Entertainment Effects Group. *Visual effects directors* Douglas Trumbull and Richard Yuricich. *Director of photography* Dave Stewart. *Optical effects supervisor* Robert Hall. *Compsy effects supervisor* Don Baker. *Visual effects supervisor* Alison Yerxa. *Action props and miniatures supervisor* Mark Stetson. *Matte artist* Matthew Yuricich. *Postproduction coordinator* Robert Hippard. *Assistant editor of visual effects* Jack Hinkle. *Optical lineup* Michael Backauskas. *Compsy designer and technical supervisor* Richard Hollander. *Animation and graphics* John C. Wash. *Additional photography* James R. Dickson. *Consulting engineer* Evans Wetmore. *Programmer* John Piner. *Visual consultant and still photographer* Virgil Mirano. *Cinetechnician* George Polkingorne. *Illustrators* Tom Cranham and Dick Lasley. *Effects artistic consultants* Robert Hickson, Paul Olsen, Peggy Weil and Adolph Schaller. *Assistant matte artist* Dana Yuricich. *Mechanical technicians* Stephen C. Fog and Mark J. West. *Effects grip* Pat van Auken. *Electronic technicians* Gary Lynnlove, Robin Leyden, Paul Van Camp and William Goddard. *Film technician* Beth Parker. *Still lab technician* Ernest Garza. *Assistant to Mr. Trumbull* Allen Yamashita. *Assistant to Mr. Yuricich* Joyce Goldberg. *Postproduction office coordinator* Terry Ladin. *Postproduction aides* Jess Katz, George Pryor, Robert Wilson and Dan Scharf. *Optical camera operator* Chuck Cowles. *Lead camera technician* Alan Harding. *Camera technicians* David Hardburger, Tama Takahashi and Joshua Morton. *Camera operators* William Asman, Joe Valentine, Ralph Gerling, Michael Gershman and Ronald Vidor. *Negative cutter* Jeanne Smith. *Artistic consultants* Michael Gibson, Jerry Morawski and Ann Vidor. *Action props and miniatures* Paul Curley, Leslie Ekker, Kent Gebo, Ronald Gress, Robert Johnston, Mike McMillen, Thomas Pahk, Robin Reilly, Christopher Ross, Dennis Schultz, David Schwartz and Richard Thompson. *Visual effects assistant* Carolyn Bates. *Rotoscope artist* Bob Seeley. *Angel costume designers* Anne Theodore and Alison Yerxa. ¶A Metro-Goldwyn-Mayer presentation. A JF production. A Douglas Trumbull film. Released by MGM/UA Entertainment Co. Metrocolor. Six-track magnetic Dolby Stereo. 106 minutes. Filmed at EEG Studios and on location in North Carolina. MPAA rating: PG. ¶CAST: *Michael Brace* Christopher Walken. *Karen Brace* Natalie Wood. *Lillian Reynolds* Louise Fletcher. *Alex Terson* Cliff Robertson. *Gordy Forbes* Jordan Christopher. *Landon Marks* Donald Hotton. *Robert Jenkins*

Alan Fudge. *Hal Abramson* Joe Dorsey. *James Zimbach* Bill Morey. *Chris Brace* Jason Lively. *Security technician* Darrell Larsen. *Wendy Abramson* Georgianne Walken. *Chef* Lou Walker. *Andrea* Stacey Kuhne-Adams. *Animal lab technician* John Hugh. *Barry* David Wood. *Dr. Ted Harris* Keith Colbert. *Dr. Janet Bock* Jerry Bennett. *Realtor* Mary-Frann Lyman. *Col. Howe* Jim Boyd. *Col. Easterbrook* Charlie Briggs. *Security guard* Jack Harmon. *Simulator technician* Nina Axelrod. *Race car man* Kelly W. Brown. *First bikini girl* Desiree Ayres. *Second bikini girl* Debbie Porter. *First man at party* Allen G. Butler. *Second man at party* Robert Bloodworth. *Terson's secretary* Ann Lincoln. *Minister at bell tower* Rev. Robert Terry Young. *Emergency room doctor* Bill Willens. *Tape lab technician* Jim Burk. *Tape library technician* Jimmy Casino. *Screaming man* Robert Hippard. *Dr. Pederson* John Gladstein. *Dr. Graf* Herbert Hirschman. *Bellhop* John Vidor. *First agent* Bill Couch. *Second agent* Robert Gooden. *Third agent* Wallace Merck. *Fourth agent* Glen Lee. *First stunt guard* Ernie Robinson. *Bob Burns* Roger Black. *Second stunt guard* Tommy Huff. *Tape library woman* May Raymond Boss. *Tape library man* Clay Boss. *Doug* Peter Harrell. *Angels* Susan Kampe. *Chimpanzee* Doc. ¶Leading lady Natalie Wood died in a boating accident before filming was completed, but through careful editing and some reshooting the film was finished and released. Working titles were *The George Dunlap Tape* and *The Light Fantastic*. The project was rejected by Paramount. Trumbull wanted to shoot in Showscan but MGM agreed only to 70mm filming. The dream sequences were in Super Panavision 70 with the principal scenes in Spherical Panavision 1.85×1. The difference in the two ratios is barely noticeable in most theaters. While it was shot partly in 70mm this footage was most likely reduced to 35mm anamorphic, the spherical footage converted to 1.85×1 anamorphic and the whole show blown up to 70mm. This was advertised in Super Panavision, and some involved with the production claim the 35mm footage was blown up and cut with the 70mm material. This seems unlikely, but MGM would not confirm which way the 70mm version was produced. We believe the reduction-and-then-blowup

pattern. If so then this really does not belong in this filmography section and is included here for the record only.

Bratiya *see* **The Sources.**

Bratiya Karamazovi *see* **The Brothers Karamazov.**

The Breakthrough *see* **Liberation.**

Brothers *see* **The Sources.**

The Brothers Karamazov (June 1980). Filmed in Sovscope 70. *Screen author and director* Ivan Piriev. *Based on the novel "Bratiya Karamazovi" by* Fyodor M. Dostoevskogo. *Collaborators* Mikhail Uliyanov and Kirili Lavro. *Operator* Sergev Vronskiy. *Artist* S. Volkov. *Composer* Isaak Shvarts. *Sound operator* E. Kashkevich. ¶A Mosfilm production. Released by Columbia Pictures by arrangement with Soxexportfilm. Sovcolor. 125 minutes. Filmed at Mosfilm Studios, Moscow, R.S.F.S.R. ¶CAST: *Dmitry Karamazov* Mikhail Uliyanov. *Grushenka* Lionella Pirieva. *Ivan Karamazov* Kirili Lavrov. *Alyosha* Andrei Myatkov. *Fyodor Pavolvich* Marc Prudkin. *Svetlana* Katerina Ivanovna. *Smerdiakov* Valentin Nikulin. *With* S. Korkoshko, P. Pavlenko, N. Svetlovidov, A. Abrikosov, N. Podgorniy, O. Chuvaeva, A. Khvilya, T. Nosova, R. Rizov, G. Kirillov, L. Korneva, N. Bubnov, G. Yukhtin, V. Matov, I. Vlasov, G. Kolpakov, E. Urusova, S. Chekan, A. Danilova and I. Lapikov. ¶A Soviet production released in Russia in 1968 as *Bratiya Karamazovi* in 70mm and six-track magnetic stereophonic sound in three parts running 102 minutes, 92 minutes and 95 minutes. Uliyanov and Lavro completed part three. Released in the U.S. in 35mm only. The U.S. version may be culled from only the first two parts. Some of the above cast probably do not appear in the U.S. version. Previously filmed in the U.S. by Avon Productions and MGM in 1958.

The Bubble (December 21, 1966). Filmed in Space-Vision Tri-Optiscope 4-D. *Producer, writer, director and photographic designer* Arch Oboler. *Director of photography* Charles F. Wheeler. *Director for Space-Vision technology* Col. Robert V.

Bernier. *Music* Paul Sawtell and Bert Shefter. *Film editor and music supervisor* Igo Kanter. *Producer's assistant* Jerry Kay. *Associate producer, production manager and art director* Marvin Chomsky. *Sound* Alfred Overton and Carl Daniels. *Rerecording* Don Minkler, Bill Mumford and Buddy Myers at Producer's Sound Service Inc. *Lighting* Don Stott and Harry Hopkins. *Head grip* Arthur Brooker. *Second grip* Henry Briere. *Camera crew* Donald Peterman, Fred Pearce, Serge Haignere and Robert D. Sharp. *Sound effects* Edit-Rite Inc. *Script supervisor* Dorothy Hughes *Assistant director* Richard Dixon. *Makeup* Harry Thomas. *Special effects* George Schlicher and Samuel Dockery. *Color backgrounds* George Guard and Joe Chavez of Mobile Colorfx of Hollywood. *Space-Vision licensing* The Tru-D Company. *Processing, titles, opticals and prints* Consolidated Film Industries. ¶A Midwestern Magic-Vuers, Inc. production. An Arch Oboler film. Released by Arch Oboler Productions. Dimensional Color [Eastman Color]. Westrex recording system. 112 minutes. Filmed at CBS Studio Center and on location in Southern California. ¶CAST: *Mark* Michael Cole. *Catherine* Deborah Walley. *Tony* Johnny Desmond. *Ticket cashier* Virginia Gregg. *Watch repairman* Olan Soule. *Newspaper vendor* Chester Jones. *Taxi driver* Victor Perrin. *Doctor* Kassie McMahon. *Talent* Barbara Eiler. ¶The first U.S. film in over-and-under wide screen 3D. Space-Vision was later called Spacevision. While the first lenses made bore the Tri-Optiscope trade name, improved lenses carried only the Spacevision trademark. Rereleased in 1972 by Sherpix, Inc., running 94 minutes. Rereleased in March 1977 by Monarch Releasing Corporation as an Allan Shackleton presentation titled *Fantastic Invasion of Planet Earth* and advertised in StereoVision 3D, since StereoVision International, Inc. was supplying all projection lenses and viewers.

Buddha (July 2, 1963). Filmed in Super 70 Technirama. *Producer* Masaichi Nagata. *Associate producer* Akinari Suzuki. *Director* Kenji Misumi. *Screenplay* Fuji Yahiro Yahiro. *Photography* Hiroshi Imai. *Lighting* Kenichi Okamoto. *Music* Akira Ifukube. *Music conductor* Jin Ueda. *Performers* Tokyo Symphony Orchestra. *Film editor* Kanji Suganuma. *Sound recording supervisor* Masao Osumi. *Costume designer* Hachiro Nakajima. *Art director* Kisaku Ito. *Art* Akira Naito. *Set decorator* Teruo Kajitani. *Production manager* Masatsugu Hashimoto. *Assistant directors* Akira Inoue and Yoshiyuki Kuroda. *Animation* Tomio Sagisu. *Drawings* Yoshio Watanabe. *Color Consultant* Yoshiaki Kiura. *Decoration consultant* Toshiharu Takatsu. *Costume consultant* Yoshio Ueno. *Choreography* Kiitsu Sakakibara. *Special photographic effects* Tooru Matoba and Chishi Makiura. *Special effects* Tatsuyuki Yokota and So-Ichi Aisaka. *Technical advisers* Gakuro Nakamura and Takio Nakamura. ¶A Masaichi Nagata Presentation. A Daiei Motion Picture Co., Ltd. production. Released by Lopert Pictures [United Artists]. Technicolor. Six track magnetic stereophonic sound. 139 minutes. Filmed at Daiei Studios, Kyoto and on location in Japan. ¶CAST: *Prince Siddhartha* Kojiro Hongo. *Princess Yashodhara* Charito Solis. *Devadatta* Shintaro Katsu. *Nandabala* Machiko Kyo. *Kunala* Raizo Ichikawa. *Usha* Fujiko Yamamoto. *Ajatashatru* Hiroshi Kawaguchi. *Ananda* Katsuhiko Kobayashi. *Auttami* Tamao Nakamura. *Matangi* Junko Kano. *Amana* Mieko Kondo. *Sari* Tokiko Mita. *Naccha* Hiromi Ichida. *Kilika* Michiko Ai. *Sonna* Matasaburo Niwa. *Upali* Keizo Kawasaki. *Child's mother* Reiko Fujiwara. *Shariputra* Gen Mitamura. *Bhutika* Ryuzo Shimada. *Arama* Joji Tsurumi. *Kalodayi* Shiro Otsuji. *Kaundinya* Yoshiro Kitahara. *Mahakashyapa* Jun Negami. *Ashoka* Ganjiro Nakamura. *Graha* Toshio Chiba. *Bandhu* Ryuichi Ishii. *Maudgaliputra* Yoichi Funaki. *Rayana* Sanemon Arashi. *Jivaka* Osamu Maryuama. *Kisaka* Gen Shimizu. *Kalidevi* Isuzu Yamada. *Takshakara* Yumeji Tsukioka. *Sumi* Tanie Kitabayashi. *Maya* Chikako Hosokawa. *Vaidehi* Haruko Sugimura. *Shuddhodana* Koreya Senda. *Suratha* Eijiro Tono. *Channa* Bontaro Miyake. *Ajita* Osamu Takizawa. *Bimbisara* Jukai Ichikawa. *Suprabuddha* Koichi Katsuragi. *Bashpa* Ryonosuke Azuma. *Mahanaman* Shintaro Nanjyo. *Chunda* Kinya Ichikawa. *Bhadrika* Seishiro Hara. *Ashvajit* Saburo Date. *Sabhaya* Kongo Reiko. *Amita* Kimiko Tachibana. ¶A Japanese production released in Japan in 1963 as *Shaka* running

156 minutes. Filmed with two modified VistaVision cameras. Some scenes shot in Daieiscope and blown up to 70mm. Advertised in Super Technirama 70 in the U.S.

Buran see **Duma o Kovpake.**

Cafe isolop see **Isotope Cafe.**

Campus Sweethearts (February 12, 1930). Filmed in Natural Vision. *Supervisor* Richard Currier. *Director* J. Leo Meehan. *Book, music and lyrics* Lester Lee and Charlie Lesison. *Musical director* Alfred Newman. *Editor* Rusel C. Shields. ¶A Radio Pictures presentation. A RKO Productions, Inc. picture. Released by RKO Radio Pictures. RCA Photophone recording. 27 minutes (approximately). Filmed at RKO Pathe Studios. ¶This received extremely limited wide gauge exhibition, probably no more than one playdate. Filmed simultaneously in standard 35mm.

Cole Porter's Can-Can (March 1960). Filmed in Todd-AO. *Producer* Jack Cummings. *Director* Walter Lang. *Screenplay* Dorothy Kingsley and Charles Lederer. *Based on the play by* Abe Burrows; *with music and lyrics by* Cole Porter. *Associate producer* Saul Chaplin. *Director of photography* William H. Daniels. *Dance stager* Hermes Pan. *Art direction* Lyle R. Wheeler and Jack Martin Smith. *Set decorations* Walter M. Scott and Paul S. Fox. *Sound recording supervisor* Fred Hynes. *Sound* William Donald Flick. *Rerecording* Todd-AO Sound Department. *Music and lyrics* Cole Porter. *Music arranger and conductor* Nelson Riddle. *Vocal supervision* Robert Tucker. *Film editor* Robert Simpson. *Costume designer* Irene Sharaff. *Makeup* Ben Nye. *Hair styles* Myrl Stoltz. *Hair styling consultant* Tony Duquette. *Assistant director* Joseph E. Rickards. *Color consultant* Leonard Doss. *Costume modelmaker* Wah Chang. *Todd-AO developers* American Optical Co. and Magna Theatre Corp. ¶A Suffolk-Cummings production. Released by 20th Century-Fox. Technicolor. Westrex six-track magnetic stereophonic sound. 131 minutes plus intermission. Filmed at 20th Century-Fox Studios. ¶CAST: *Francois Durnais* Frank Sinatra. *Simone Pistache* Shirley MacLaine. *Paul Barriere* Maurice Chevalier. *Philippe*

Forrestier Louis Jourdan. *Claudine* Juliet Prowse. *Andre* Marcel Dalio. *Arturo Leon* Belasco. *First bailiff* Nestor Paiva. *Jacquesi* John A. Neris. *Judge Merceaux* Jean Del Val. *League president* Ann Codee. *Chevrolet* Eugene Borden. *Recorder* Jonathan Kidd. *Adam* Marc Wilder. *Dupont* Peter Coe. *Detective* Marcel de la Broesse. *Dowagers* Rene Godfrey and Lili Valenty. *Knife thrower* Charles Carman. *Gigi* Carole Bryan. *Camille* Barbara Carter. *Renee* Jane Earl. *Julie* Ruth Earl. *Germine* Laura Fraser. *Gabrielle* Vera Lee. *Fifi* Lisa Mitchell. *Maxine* Wanda Shannon. *Gisele* Darlene Tittle. *Lili* Wilda Taylor. *Apache dancer* Ambrogio Malerba. *Butler* Alphonse Martell. *Secretary* Genevieve Aumont. *Judge* Edward Le Veque. *Second bailiff* Maurice Marsac. ¶35mm prints by De Luxe. Advertised as *Cole Porter's Can-Can.*

Captain of the "Pilgrim" (1987). Filmed in Sovscope 70. *Screen author* Aleksandr Guselnikov. *Based on the novel "A Fifteen Year Old Captain" by* Jules Verne. *Director* Andrei Prachenko. *Operators* Vasily Trushkovsky and Alexei Zolotaryov. *Artists* Ksana Medved and Sergei Khotimsky. ¶A Kievskaya kinostudiya im. A.P. Dovzenko production. International distribution Sovexportfilm. Sovcolor. Six-track magnetic stereophonic sound. 91 minutes. Filmed at Kievskaya kinostudiya im. A.P. Dovzenko, Kiev, Ukrainian S.S.R. ¶CAST: *Capt. Hull* Lev Durov. *Dick Sand* Viacheslav Khodchenko. *Negoro* Nodar Mgaloblishvili. *Harris* Leonid Yarmolnik. *Benedict* Albert Filozov. *Hercules* Vittorio Echmedia. ¶A Soviet production released in Russia in 1987 as *Kapitan "Piligrima."* This is a remake of the 1946 Soviet feature and one of the many Russian adaptations from Jules Verne's works.

The Cardinal (December 1963). Filmed in Panavision 70. *Producer and director* Otto Preminger. *Screenplay* Robert Dozier. *Based on the novel by* Henry Morton Robinson. *Music* Jerome Moross. *Production designer* Lyle R. Wheeler. *Director of photography* Leon Shamroy. *Editor* Louis R. Loeffler. *Second unit camera* Piero Portalupi. *Camera operators* Jack Atcheler, Saul Midwall and Paul Uhl. *Chief gaffer* Fred Hall. *Best boy* Ken-

Reserved seat form for Can-Can *(1960).*

neth Lang. *Construction grip* Fred Bock-stahler. *Key grips* Leo McCreary and Morris Rosen. *Makeup* Dick Smith, Robert Jiras and Maurice Seiderman. *Hairdressing* Frederick Jones. *Wardrobe* Joseph King, Florence Transfield and George Newman. *Property masters* Tom Frewer and Art Cole. *Sound* Harold Lewis, Red Law, Walter Goss, Morris Feingold and John Cox. *Music editor* Leon Birnbaum. *Sound effects editor* Peter Thornton. *Script supervisor* Kathleen Fagan. *Set decorators* Gene Callahan and Guilio Sperabene. *Art director, Vienna* Otto Niedermoser. *Art director, Rome* Antonio Sarzi-Braga. *Executive assistant to the producer* Nat Rudich. *Associate producer* Martin C. Schute. *Dialog coach* Max Slater. *Casting* Bill Barnes. *Casting, Rome* Paola Rolli. *Production managers* Harrison Starr, Eva Monley and Henry Weinberger. *Production manager, Vienna* Paul Waldherr for Danubia Films. *Production manager, Rome* Guy Luongo for International Film Services. *Costume coordinator* Hope Bryce. *Costume designer* Donald Brooks. *Jewelry* Paltscho of Vienna. *Choreography* Buddy Schwab. *Technical adviser* Donald Hayne. *Assistant directors* Gerry O'Hara, Bob Vietro, Bryan Coates, Hermann Leitner, Robert Fiz and Eric von Stroheim, Jr. *Title designer* Saul Bass. *Assistant cameraman* Lee "Red" Crawford. *Unit publicists* Bernard Quint and Beverly Quint. *Still photographers* Paul Apoteker, Claude Azoulay, Stephen Colhoun, Louis Goldman, Alexander Paal, Steve Shapiro, Sam Shaw and Josh Weiner. *Location liaison, Vienna* Ernst Haussermann. *Location liaison, Rome* Mario Burgognini. *Song "They Haven't Got the Girls in the U.S.A.":* *music* Jerome Moross; *lyrics* Al Stillman; *singer* Robert Morse. *Liturgical chants for ordination, consecration and religious service* the Monks of the Abbey at Casamari under the direction of Dom Nivardo Bultarazzi, priest and Dom Raffaele Scaccia, prior. *"Alleluia" from the motet "Exultate Jubilate"* Wolfgang Amadeus Mozart; *singers* The Wiener Jugendchor; *soloist* Wilma Lipp. *Stereophonic rerecording* Shepperton Studios. ¶An Otto Preminger production. A Gamma Productions Inc. picture. Released by Columbia Pictures. Technicolor. Westrex six-track magnetic stereophonic sound. 175 minutes plus intermission. Filmed in

Hollywood and on location in Boston, Quincy and Stamford, Massachusetts, Rome and Casamari, Italy and Vienna and Duernstein, Austria. ¶CAST: *Stephen Fermoyle* Thomas (Tom) Tryon. *Annemarie* Romy Schneider. *Mona Fermoyle and Regina Fermoyle* Carol Lynley. *Florrie Fermoyle* Maggie McNamara. *Benny Rampell* John Saxon. *Cardinal Glennon* John Huston. *Bobby & His Adora-Belles* Robert Morse. *Monsignor "Dollar Bill" Monaghan* Cecil Kellaway. *Celia Fermoyle* Dorothy Gish. *Father Ned Halley* Burgess Meredith. *Frank Fermoyle* Bill Hayes. *Din Fermoyle* Cameron Prud'Homme. *Cornelius J. Deegan* Loring Smith. *Ramon Gongaro* Jose Duval. *Father Callahan* Peter MacLean. *Father Lyons* James Hickman. *Mrs. Rampell* Berenice Gahm. *Boston master of ceremonies* Billy Reed. *Hercule Menton* Pat Henning. *Lalage Menton* Jill Haworth. *Dr. Heller* Russ Brown. *Cardinal Quarenghi* Raf Vallone. *Cardinal Giacobbi* Tullio Carminati. *Father Gillis* Ossie Davis. *Ordination master of ceremonies* Don Francesco Mancini of Veroli. *Italian monsignor* Dino Di Luca. *Father Eberling* Donald Hayne. *Monsignor Whittle* Chill Wills. *Sheriff Dubrow* Arthur Hunnicutt. *Woman picket* Doro Merande. *Cecil Turner* Patrick O'Neal. *Lafe* Murray Hamilton. *Kurt von Hartman* Peter Weck. *Drinking man at ball* Rudolph Forster. *Cardinal Innitzer* Josef Meinrad. *Mme. Walter* Dagmar Schmedes. *Seyss-Inquart* Eric Frey. *Von Hartman's butler* Josef Krastel. *Father Neidermoser* Mathias Fuchs. *Sister Wilhelmina* Vilma Degischer. *S.S. major* Wolfgang Preiss. *Army lieutenant* Jurgen Wilke. *Bit man* Glenn Strange.¶The first film in Panavision 70.

(Rodgers & Hammerstein's) Carousel (February 17, 1956). Filmed in Cinema-Scope 55. *Producer* Henry Ephron. *Director* Henry King. *Screenplay* Phoebe and Henry Ephron. *Based on the play with book and lyrics by* Oscar Hammerstein II; *and music by* Richard Rodgers; *as produced by* The Theatre Guild; *from "Liliom" by* Ferenc Molnar; *adapted by* Benjamin F. Glazer. *Music* Richard Rodgers. *Lyrics* Oscar Hammerstein II. *Music supervisor and conductor* Alfred Newman. *Associate music supervisor* Ken Darby. *Director of photography* Charles

G. Clarke. *Choreography* Rod Alexander. *Louise's ballet* Agnes De Mille. *Costume designer* Mary Wills. *Art direction* Lyle R. Wheeler and Jack Martin Smith. *Set decorations* Walter M. Scott and Chester Bayhi. *Wardrobe direction* Charles Le-Maire. *Makeup* Ben Nye and Herman Buchman. *Hair styles* Helen Turpin. *Sound* Bernard Freericks, Harry M. Leonard and Carlton W. Faulkner. *Orchestration* Edward B. Powell, Herbert W. Spencer, Earle Hagen, Nelson Riddle, Bernard Mayers and Gus Levene. *Color consultant* Leonard Doss. *Assistant director* Stanley Hough. *Special photographic effects* Ray Kellogg, L.B. Abbott and Emil Kosa, Jr. *Film editor* William Reynolds. *CinemaScope lenses* Bausch & Lomb. ¶Produced and released by 20th Century-Fox. Color by De Luxe. Western Electric Movietone recording. Four-track MagOptical stereophonic sound. 128 minutes. Filmed at 20th Century-Fox Studios. ¶CAST: *Billy* Gordon MacRae. *Julie* Shirley Jones. *Jigger* Cameron Mitchell. *Carrie* Barbara Ruick. *Cousin Nettie* Claramae Turner. *Enoch Snow, Sr.* Robert Rounseville. *Starkeeper* Gene Lockhart. *Mrs. Mullen* Audrey Christie. *Louise* Susan Lucket. *Heavenly friend* William Le Massena. *Mr. Bascombe* John Dehner. *Louise's dancing partner* Jacques D'Amboise. *Capt. Watson* Frank Tweddell. *Policeman* Richard Deacon. *Enoch Snow, Jr.* Dee Pollock. *With* Sylvia Stanton, Mary Orozco, Tor Johnson, Harry "Duke" Johnson, Marion Dempsey, Ed Mundy and Angelo Rossitto. ¶The first film in CinemaScope 55 but released in 35mm only. Gordon MacRae replaced Frank Sinatra, who had already recorded all his songs. A remake of *Liliom* (S.A.F.-Fox Europa, 1935).

Cartagine in fiamme *see* **Carthage in Flames.**

Carthage en flammes *see* **Carthage in Flames.**

Carthage in Flames (January 25, 1961). Filmed in Super Technirama 70. *Producers* Guido Luzzato and Carmine Gallone. *Director* Carmine Gallone. *Screenplay* Ennio de Concini, Duccio Tessari and Carmine Gallone. *English version* William De Lane Lea. *Based on the novel "Cartagine in fiamme" by* Emilio Salgari.

Associate producers Marino Vecca and Carmine Gallone, Jr. *Director of photography* Piero Portalupi. *Music composer* Mario Nascimbene. *Conductor* Franco Ferrara. *Film editor* Nicolo Lazzari. *Art directors* Guido Fiorini and Amedeo Mellone. *Costumes* Veniero Colasanti. *Special effects* Ottavio Mannini. *Sound* Renato Cadueri. *Assistant directors* Franco Cirino and Andrea Volpe. ¶A Lux Film-Gallone Produzione-C.C.F. Lux production. Released by Columbia Pictures. Technicolor. 111 minutes. Filmed at Studio Lux Film, Rome. ¶CAST: *Fulvia* Anne Heywood. *Hiram* Jose Suarez. *Ophir* Ilaria Occhini. *Phegor* Daniel Gelin. *Sidone* Pierre Brasseur. *Astarito* Paolo Stoppa. *Tsour* Mario Girotti. *Hermon* Aldo Silvani. *Nurse* Edith Peters. *With* Erno Crisa, Ivo Gamani, Cesare Fantoni, Gianrico Tedeschi and Fernand Leboux. ¶An Italian and French coproduction released in Europe in 70mm and six-track magnetic stereophonic sound. Released in the U.S. in 35mm 'scope only. The U.S. version was reedited to 93 minutes. Released in Italy in January 1960 as *Cartagine in fiamme* running 120 minutes and released in France in March 1960 as *Carthage en flammes* running 115 minutes. Mario Girotti is now known as Terence Hill and lives in the U.S.

La case de l'Oncle Tom *see* **Uncle Tom's Cabin.**

Catch the Sun (1973). Filmed in IMAX. *Producer and director* David Mackay. *Photographer* Robert Ryan. *Released by* Imax Systems Corporation. Eastman Color. Six-track magnetic stereophonic sound. 22 minutes. Filmed in Ontario, Canada. A Canadian production originally made for Ontario Place. This has a duplication of Cinerama's famous rollercoaster ride.

Les cavaliers rogues *see* **Shatterhand.**

The Centaurs (1979). Filmed in Sovscope 70. *Screen author and director* Vitautas Zalakyavichyus. *Operator* Pavel Lyubeshen. *Artists* Levan Shengeliya, A. Neogradi and O. Okach. *Sound and musical composition* R. Kazaryan. ¶A Mosfilm-United Dialog-Mafilm-Barrandov-Dinpro production. International distribution Sovexportfilm. Sovcolor. Six-track magnetic stereophonic sound. 175 minutes plus intermission. Filmed at Mosfilm Studios, Moscow, R.S.F.S.R. and on location in Colombia, South America. ¶CAST: *President* Donates Banionis. *Orlando* Regimatas Adomaytis. *Anna-Marie* Elena Ivochkina. *With* Margit Lukach, Evgeny Lebedev, Dyula Benky, Gennady Bortnikov, Valentin Gaft, Bruno Oya, Mikhail Volontir, Ion Ungurianu, Tibor Gantzogi, Iren Shote, Itka Zelenogorska, Kakhi Kavsadze, Yuozas Budraitis and Anna Mokhina. ¶A Soviet, Hungarian, Czechoslovakian and Colombian coproduction released in Russia in 1979 as *Kentavri* in two parts running 84 minutes and 91 minutes.

Cento dollari d'odio *see* **Uncle Tom's Cabin.**

Chas neozkhidannykh puteshestviy v polyote na vertolyote (1960). Filmed in Kinopanorama. A Tsentraliniy dokumentaliniy film studiya production. International distribution Sovexportfilm. Sovcolor. Nine-track magnetic Kinopanorama Sound. 100 minutes. A Soviet production released in Russia in 1960. Excerpts later incorporated into *Cinerama's Russian Adventure.*

Chateaux de nuages *see* **Magirama.**

Chaykovskiy *see* **Tchaikovsky.**

The Chelsea Girls (September 15, 1966). Filmed in 16mm Dual Screen. *Producer, director and photographer* Andy Warhol. *Writers* Andy Warhol and Ronald Tavel. *Music* The Velvet Underground. *Production assistant* Paul Morrissey. *Strobe lighting* Billy Linch. ¶A Film-Makers' Cooperative presentation. An Andy Warhol Films production. Released by Film-Makers' Distribution Center. Eastman Color. Optical sound. 205 minutes. Filmed in New York City and Cambridge, Massachusetts. ¶CAST: *Reel 1: Girlfriend* Nico. *Boyfriend* Eric Emerson. *Son* Ari. *The Pope Ondine Story: Pope Ondine* Ondine [Bob Olivio]. *With* Angelina "Pepper" Davis, Ingrid Superstar [Ingrid Von Scheven], Albert Rene Ricard, Mary Might [Mary Woronov], International Velvet [Susan Bottomly] and Ronna. *The Duchess: Duchess* Brigid Polk. *The John: Ed* Ed Hood. *Patrick* Patrick Flemming. *Transvestite* Mario Montez. *With* Angelina "Pepper" Davis, International Velvet [Susan Bottomly], Mary Might [Mary Woronov], Gerard Malanga, Albert Rene Ricard and Ingrid Superstar [Ingrid Von Scheven]. *Hanoi Hanna (Queen of China): Hanoi Hanna* Mary Might [Mary Woronov]. *With* International Velvet [Susan Bottomly], Ingrid Superstar [Ingrid Von Scheven] and Angelina "Pepper" Davis. *The Gerard Malanga Story: Mother* Marie Menken. *Gerard Malanga* Gerard Malanga. *Girlfriend* Mary Might [Mary Woronov]. *The Trip and "Their Town (Toby Short)": Toby Short* Eric Emerson. *Afternoon Edie* Edie Sedgwick. *With* Ondine [Bob Olivio], Arthur Loeb, Donald Lyons and Dorothy Dean. *The Closet: Children* Nico and Randy Borscheidt. ¶Program segments were advertised as "Room 723 – Pope Ondine," "Room 422 – The Gerard Malanga Story," "Room 946 – George's Room," "Room 202 – Afternoon," "Room 116 – Hanoi Hanna," "Room 632 – The John," "Room 416 – The Trip" and "Room 822 – The Closet." Cast for "George's Room" is not known. "Reel 1" began the show on the right side of the screen. All other segments were screened on both sides. The film was in black-and-white except for "The Gerard Malanga Story" and "Their Town (Toby Short)." There may have been an intermission as the running time is also listed as 195 minutes and 210 minutes.

Cherez Gobi i Khingan *see* **Across the Gobi and the Khingans.**

Cherez ternii k zvezdam *see* **To the Stars by Hard Ways.**

Chermen (1971). Filmed in Sovscope 70. *Screen authors* Grigory Pliev and Aleksandr Misharin. *Director* Nikolai Sanishvili. *Operator* Dudar Margiev. *Artist* R. Mirzashvili. *Composer* I. Gabaraev. *Sound operators* O. Gegechkori and A. Petrusenko. ¶A Gruziya-film production. International distribution Sovexportfilm. Sovcolor. Six track magnetic stereophonic sound. 96 minutes. Filmed at

Gruziya-film studios, Tbilisi, Georgian S.S.R. ¶CAST: *Chermen* Klatov Bimbulat Vamaev. *His sweetheart* Teresa Kantemirova. *With* Zurab Kapdanidze, Veriko Andzaparidze, Vladimir Tkhapsaev, Sofiko Chiaurelli, K. Slanov, M. Abaev, K. Davshvili, U. Khurumov, F. Kalazov, A. Davaev, D. Gabaraev and U. Slanov. ¶A Soviet production released in Russia in 1971.

Chernaya bereza *see* **The Black Birch.**

Chernaya strela *see* **The Black Arrow.**

Chetvyortaya programma panoramikh filmov "Tsirkovoye predstavleniye" i "Na Krasnoy ploshchadyu" (1961). Filmed in Kinopanorama. A Tsentralniy dokumentaliniy film studiya production. International distribution Sovexportfilm. Sovcolor. Nine-track magnetic Kinopanorama Sound. 100 minutes. A Soviet production released in Russia in 1961. Excerpts were incorporated into *Cinerama's Russian Adventure.*

Chevrolet 75th Anniversary (1986). Filmed in Showscan. Produced by Showscan Film Corporation for Chevrolet Motor Division of General Motors Corporation. Eastman Color. Six-track magnetic Dolby Stereo. 60 minutes. Originally made for the Chevrolet 75th Anniversary Dealer Show in Orlando, Florida. Also produced was a theatrical commercial which, with footage from the longer film, was optically converted to standard 35mm and exhibited at several auto shows by General Motors. The 35mm version of the commercial was exhibited nationally in numerous theaters.

(John Ford's) Cheyenne Autumn (October 5, 1964). Filmed in Super Panavision 70. *Producer* Bernard Smith. *Director* John Ford. *Screenplay* James R. Webb and Patrick Ford. *Adaptation* Patrick Ford and Dudley Nichols. *Based on the book by* Mari Sandoz. *Director of photography* William H. Clothier. *Music composer and conductor* Alex North. *Film editor* Otho Lovering. *Associate producer* Patrick Ford. *Associate directors* Patrick Ford and Ray Kellogg. *Art director* Richard Day. *Set decorator* Darrell Silvera. *Costume designer* Ann Peck. *Costume coordinator* Frank Beetson, Sr. *Sound* Francis J. Stahl, Jack Solomon and George R. Groves. *Assistant directors* Wingate Smith and Russell Saunders. *Indian technical adviser* David H. Miller. *Stunt coordinator* Charles Hayward. *Camera operators* George Gordon Nogle and Eddie Garvin. *Assistant cameraman* Robert Rhea. *Gaffer* Ralph Owen. *Key grip* Kenny Taylor. *Head wrangler* Billy Jones. *Casting* Hoyt Bowers. *Unit manager* Russell Saunders. *Location production assistants* Frank Bradley and Lee Bradley. *Special effects* Ralph Webb. *Special photographic effects* Ray Kellogg. *Still photographer* John R. Hamilton. *Script supervisor* Meta Stern. *Makeup supervisor* Gordon Bau. *Makeup artist* Norman Pringle. *Supervising hair stylist* Jean Burt Rielly. *Hair stylists* Sherry Wilson and Fae M. Smith. ¶A John Ford-Bernard Smith production. A Ford–Smith Productions, Inc. picture. Released by Warner Bros. Pictures. Technicolor. RCA six-track magnetic stereophonic sound. 158 minutes plus overture and intermission. Filmed at Warner Bros. Studios and on location in Monument Valley and Moab, Utah and Gunnison, Colorado. ¶CAST: *Capt. Thomas Archer* Richard Widmark. *Deborah Wright* Carroll Baker. *Marshal Wyatt Stapp Earp* James Stewart. *Interior Sec. Carl Schurz* Edward G. Robinson. *Capt. Oskar Wessels* Karl Malden. *Red Shirt* Sal Mineo. *Spanish Woman* Dolores Del Rio. *Subchief Little Wolf* Ricardo Montalban. *Subchief Dull Knife* Gilbert Roland. *Dr. John H. Holliday* Arthur Kennedy. *2nd Lt. Scott* Patrick Wayne. *Guinevere Plantagenet* Elizabeth Allen. *Maj. Jeff Blair* John Carradine. *Chief Tall Tree* Victor Jory. *Sr. Sgt. Stanislas Wichowsky* Mike Mazurki. *Maj. Braden* George O'Brien. *Dr. O'Carberry* Sean McClory. *Mayor John "Dog" Kelly* Judson Pratt. *Pawnee Woman* Carmen D'Antonio. *Joe Homer* Ken Curtis. *Rev. Jeremy Wright* Walter Baldwin. *Skinny* George "Shug" Fisher. *Little Bird* Nancy Hsueh. *Jesse* Charles (Chuck) Roberson. *Trooper "Smitty" Smith* Harry Carey, Jr. *Trooper Plumtree* Ben Johnson. *Troopers* Danny Borzage, David Humphreys Miller, Patrick Roper Ford, James O'Hara, Charles (Chuck) Hayward, Dean Smith, John McKee, Dan Carr and Ted Mapes. *Lead Cheyenne brave* John Stanley. *Cheyenne braves* Frank Bradley and Lee Bradley. *Lt. Peter-*

Door panels (20″ × 60″) for John Ford's Cheyenne Autumn.

son Walter Reed. *Infantry colonel at Victory Cave* Willis Bouchey. *Schurz' aide* Carleton Young. *Sen. Henry* Denver Pyle. *Svenson* John Qualen. *Running Deer* Nanomba Moonbeam Morton. *Texas trailhand* Henry Wills. *Senator* Harry Holcombe. *Medicineman* Many Mules Son. *Fort Robinson sergeant-of-the-guard* James Flavin. *Miss Plantagenet's "entertainers"* Mary Statler, Donna Hall, Stephanie Epper and Jeannie Epper. *Indian Territory post telegrapher* Bing Russell. *Dodge City residents* Maj. Sam Harris and Philo McCullough. *Cheyenne woman* Louise Montana. *Infantry captain at Dodge City* William (Bill) Henry. *Newspaper publisher* Charles Seel. *Newsboy* Kevin O'Neal. *Saloon patron* Dan M. White. ¶Working title was *The Long Flight.* Contains one scene from *She Wore a Yellow Ribbon* (RKO Radio Pictures, 1949). Previewed at 179 mintues plus intermission, but audience reaction was considered poor and the studio reedited to 158 minutes plus a 1½ minute overture and intermission for roadshowing and 148 minutes without an overture and intermission for general release. The video cassette version has been restored to the original 158 minutes plus overture but minus the intermission. The stereo television version contains the restored "Battle of Dodge City" sequence but has been reedited throughout otherwise and runs just over 2 hours.

Chitty Chitty Bang Bang (December 18, 1968). Filmed in Super Panavision 70. *Producer* Albert R. Broccoli. *Director* Ken Hughes. *Associate producer* Stanley Sopel. *Screenplay* Roald Dahl and Ken Hughes. *Additional dialog* Richard Maibaum. *Based on the novel by* Ian Fleming. *Musical numbers stagers* Marc Breaux and Dee Dee Wood. *Music supervisor and conductor* Irwin Kostal. *Music and lyrics* Richard M. Sherman and Robert B. Sherman. *Director of photography* Christopher Challis. *Production designer* Ken Adam. *Production associate and supervising editor* Peter Hunt. *Color costume design* Elizabeth Haffenden and Joan Bridge. *Potts' inventions creator* Rowland Emett. *Editor* John Shirley. *Special effects* John Stears. *Matte effects* Cliff Culley. *Production supervisor* David Middlemas. *Art director* Harry Pottle. *Sound recordists* John Mitchell and Fred Hynes *Rerecording* Todd-AO. *Music editor* Robin Clark. *Dubbing editors* Harry Miller and Les Wiggins. *Assistant art directors* Robert Laing, Peter Lamont and Michael White. *Wardrobe supervisor* Jackie Cummins. *Second unit directors* Richard Taylor and Peter Hunt. *Second unit cameraman* Skeets Kelly. *Aerial cameraman* John Jordan. *Camera operator* John Harris. *Continuity* Angela Martelli. *Assistant director* Gus Agosti. *Location manager* Frank Ernst. *Associate art director* Jack Stephens. *Unit publicists* Jeffrey Newman and Roy McGregor. ¶An Albert R. Broccoli presentation. A Warfield, Ltd. production. A Dynamic Features, Inc. picture. Released by United Artists. Technicolor. Westrex six-track magnetic stereophonic sound. 145 minutes plus intermission. Filmed at Pinewood Studios, London and on location in England, Southern France and Bavaria, West Germany. CAST: *Caractacus Potts* Dick Van Dyke. *Truly Scrumptious* Sally Ann Howes. *Grandpa Potts* Lionel Jeffries. *Baron Bomburst* Gert Frobe. *Baroness Bomburst* Anna Quayle. *Toymaker* Benny Hill. *Lord Scrumptious* James Robertson-Justice. *Child catcher* Robert Helpmann. *Jemima* Heather Ripley. *Jeremy* Adrian Hall. *Blonde* Barbara Windsor. *Admiral* Davy Kaye. *First spy* Alexander Dore. *Second spy* Bernard Spear. *Chancellor* Stanley Unwin. *Captain of the guard* Peter Arne. *Coggins* Desmond Llewelyn. *Junkman* Victor Maddern. *Big man* Arthur Mullard. *Chefs* Ross Parker and John Backcomb. *Ministers* Gerald Campion, Felix Felton and Monti de Lyle. *Duchess* Totti Truman Taylor. *Lieutenant* Larry Taylor. *Orchestra leader* Max Bacon. *Inventors* Max Wall, John Heawood, Michael Darbyshire, Kenneth Maller, Gerald Taylor and Eddie Davis. *Secretary of Sweet Factory* Richard Wattis. ¶A British and American coproduction.

Chronos (Summer 1985). Filmed in OMNIMAX. Presented in OMNIMAX and IMAX. *Producers* Jeff Kirsch and Mark Magidson. *Director and photographer* Ron Fricke. *Development* Elizabeth Emerson. *Concept* Genevieve and Constantine Nicholas. *Music* Michael Stearns. *Electronics designer and animator* Wayne McGee. *Camera machinist* Dave Garcia of Dave-Co Precision. *Production manager* Alton Walpole. *Production assistant* Tove

Johnson. *Optical effects* Canticle Films, Ltd. ¶A Canticle Films, Ltd. production. Released by Canticle Films, Ltd. and San Diego Hall of Science. Eastman Color. Six-track magnetic stereophonic sound. 40 minutes.

Cica Tomina koliba *see* **Uncle Tom's Cabin.**

El Cid (December 17, 1961). Filmed in Super Technirama 70. *Executive producers* Robert Haggiag and Philip Yordan. *Producer* Samuel Bronston. *Director* Anthony Mann. *Associate producers* Jaime Prades and Michael Waszynski. *Writers* Fredric M. Frank and Philip Yordan. *Italian version* Diego Fabbri. *Music* Miklos Rozsa. *Director of photography* Robert Krasker. *Set decoration, production and costume design* Veniero Colasanti and John Moore. *Film editor* Robert Lawrence. *Director of photography second unit* Manuel Berenguer. *Special effects* Alex C. Weldon and Jack Erickson. *Second unit director* Yakima Canutt. *Production managers* Leon Chooluck and Guy Luongo. *First assistant director* Luciano Sacripanti. *Assistant directors* Jose Maria Ochoa, Jose Lopez Rodero and Ferdinando Baldi. *Property master* Stanley Detlie. *Camera operator* John Harris. *Head grip* Carl Gibson. *Supervising electrician* Norton Kurland. *Sound recordist* Jack Solomon. *Rerecorder* Gordon K. McCallum. *Sound editor* Verna Fields. *Music editor* Edna Bulluck. *Wardrobe director* Gloria Mussetta. *Hair styles* Grazia de Rossi. *Makeup creator* Mario van Riel. *Paintings and drawings* Maciek Piotrowski. *Script supervisor* Pat Miller. *Horse master* Comandant Jesus Luque. *Assistant operator* Andres. *Assistant to the editor* Magdalena Paradell. *Fencing master* Enzo Musumeci-Greco. *Costume makers* Peruzzi e Cerreitilli and Casa Cornejo. *Armorers* Hermanos Garrido. *Technical advisor* Dr. Gonzalo Menendez Pidal. *"The Falcon and the Dove" music* Miklos Rozsa, *lyrics* Paul Francis Webster. ¶A Samuel Bronston presentation in association with Philip Yordan. A Samuel Bronston Productions, Inc. picture in association with Dear Film Produzioni. Released by Allied Artists Pictures. Technicolor. Westrex six-track magnetic stereophonic sound. 184 minutes plus overture, intermission and exit music.

Filmed at Estudios Chamartin, Estudios Sevilla and Estudios CEA, Madrid and Studio Titanus Appia, Rome and on location in Madrid, Sierra Guadarrama, Villadolid, Peñiscola and La Manha, Spain. ¶CAST: *Rodrigo Diaz de Bivar* Charlton Heston. *Chimene de Bivar* Sophia Loren. *Count Ordonez* Raf Vallone. *Queen Urraca* Genevieve Page. *King Alfonso* John Fraser. *Prince Sancho* Gary Raymond. *Count Arias* Hurd Hatfield. *Fanez* Massimo Serato. *Ben Yussuf* Herbert Lom. *Emir Al Kadir* Frank Thring. *Emir Moutamin* Douglas Wilmer. *Don Diego de Bivar* Michael Hordern. *Count Gormaz* Andrew Cruickshank. *Don Pedro* Tullio Carminati. *King Ferdinand* Ralph Truman. *Don Martin de Aragon* Christopher Rhodes. *King Ramiro* Gerard Tichy. *Bermudez* Carlo Giustini. *Dolfos* Fausto Tozzi. *Mother Superior* Barbara Everest. *Soldiers* Enzo Musumeci-Greco, Tap Canutt, Joe Canutt, Jack C. Williams, Jerry Brown and Buff Brady. *With* Paul Muller, Katina Noble and Franco Fantasia. ¶Advertised as *Samuel Bronston's El Cid.* An American and Italian coproduction. This may have had British backing from The Rank Organisation and possibly Spanish backing from various sources. Sequel was *The Sword of El Cid* (1962).

(Samuel Bronston's) El Cid *see* **El Cid.**

Cinerama *see* **This Is Cinerama.**

(Louis de Rochemont's) Cinerama Holiday (February 9, 1955). Filmed in Cinerama. *Producer* Louis de Rochemont. *Directors* Robert Bendick and Philippe de Lacy. *Associate producers* Otis Carney, Borden Mace and Thomas Orchard. *Adaptation* Otis Carney and Louis de Rochemont, III. *Narration* John Stuart Martin. *Derived in part from "America Through a French Looking Glass" by* Renee and Pierre Gosset. *Published in August 1953 by* Realites. *Original music score* Morton Gold. *Additional music* Nathan Van Cleave. *Musical director* Jack Shaindlin. *Assistant musical director* Robert McBride. *Directors of photography* Joseph Brun and Harry Squire. *Operative cameramen* Jack Priestley, Gayne Rescher and Raymond Lemoigne. *Camera technician* Coleman Thomas Conroy, Jr. *Director of photography and operator for aerial sequence over the Alps* Gayne Rescher. *Chief grip* Michael

SAMUEL BRONSTON
presents
CHARLTON HESTON and SOPHIA LOREN
in

SCHEDULE OF PRICES AND PERFORMANCES

ORCHESTRA

NIGHTS at 8 P.M.
SUN., MON., TUES., WED., THURS.........................$2.00
FRI., SAT. & HOLIDAY EVES.............................$2.50

MATINEES DAILY at 2 P.M.
MONDAY.............................$1.25
TUES., WED., THURS., FRI. & SAT...........$1.50
SUNDAY & HOLIDAYS.................$2.00

All above Prices include Tax

USE THIS COUPON FOR YOUR CONVENIENCE !

FOR THE MOST DESIRED TICKETS IN THE WORLD

Special Consideration and Accommodations Given to Theatre Parties and Groups —
Phone: 7-3785
or
79-0691

CENTER THEATRE, CENTRAL AT 9th STREET, ST. PETERSBURG, FLA.
P. O. BOX 11416

Please send...orch. ☐
tickets at $......................for Mat. ☐.....................Eve. ☐
performance on...(date)
Alternate dates...
NAME...
ADDRESS...
CITY...............................ZONE.........STATE.........

Enclose check or money order (no stamps) payable to CENTER THEATRE, addressed to BOX OFFICE with self-addressed stamped return envelope.

EXCLUSIVE ENGAGEMENT STARTS THURS. EVENING, FEB. 22nd
CENTER THEATRE
CENTRAL AT NINTH STREET, ST. PETERSBURG, FLORIDA • 7-3785

Litho U. S. A.

A reserved seat order form for El Cid *(1961). Note ticket prices.*

Mahoney. *Generator operator* Harvey Genkins. *Technical assistants* Maurice Delille, Marcel Gilot, Martin Philbin and Marcel Policard. *Sound engineers* Richard J. Pietschmann, Jr. and Rolf Epstein. *Assistant sound engineers* Fred Bosch and Ray Sharples. *Technical supervision for Cinerama, Inc.* Wentworth D. Fling. *Cameras* Erik M. Rondum and Richard C. Babish. *Sound* Avery Lockner, Richard Vorisek and Stuart Rodger. *Cinerama Sound* Cinerama Laboratories. *Art direction* Joy Batchelor, John Halas and Herbert G. Andrews. *Film editors* Jack Murray, Leo Zochling and Frederick Y. Smith. *Editorial administration* Peter Ratkevich. *Sound effects editor* Lovel S. Ellis. *Music editor* Angelo Ross. *General business manager* John J. Wingerter. *Production controller* Martin Mahoney. *Production manager* Hans Sommer. *Production staff* Charles Byron, Philip Donoghue, Robert Fabian, William Hocker, Waring Jones, Francis Keenan, Francois Mesliere, Jean Pages, James A. Petrie, Georges Regnier, Michael A. Roemer, Stanley Schneider and John Walsh. *Special effects for finale* International Fireworks Company and furnaces of Bethlehem Steel Company. *"Fandango" by* Johnny Bradford and Frank Perkins, *performed at* Wilbur Clark's Desert Inn. *"Santy Anno" singers* Larry Mohr and Odetta Felious at Tin Angel. *"Luminous Pearl and Magnolia" played by* traditional Chinese orchestra. *"Men of Dartmouth" singers* Dartmouth College Glee Club. *"Come to the Fair" by* Easthope Martin and Helen Taylor, *singers* University of New Hampshire Glee Club. *"Down by the Riverside" singers* Henry A. LeRoy, Jr. and Congregation of Second Free Mission Baptist Church. *"When the Saints Go Marching In" performers* Jolly Bunch Social and Pleasure Club and Tuxedo Marching Band in Lafayette Cemetery. *"Tiger Rag" by* Original Dixieland Jazz Band, *players and singers* Oscar "Papa" Celestin and Original Tuxedo Dixieland Jazz Band in Absinthe House. *"Ballet of the Skis" composer* Morton Gould, *orchestrator* Nathan Van Cleave. *"Sentiberg Jodel" singers* Bertely Studer and Ernst Berchtold. *"Hop sah sah Waltz" performers* Bertely Studer and Ernst Berchtold. *"Entr'acte: Hop sah sah Waltz" orchestrator* Morton Gould. *"Solemn High Mass" by* Francois Couperin, *singers* Boys' Choir of the Cathedral of Notre Dame. *"Sur le pont d'avignon" arranger* Frank Engelen, *played at* Students' Ball. *"Les indes galantes" by* Jean-Philippe Rameau. *"Les fleurs" adaptors* Henri Busser and Rene Fauchois. *"Les marroniers de Paris" by* Claude Bolling, *played at* Maison Jacques Fath. *Principal "Lido" music* Garni Kramer. *"Holiday in Rio" by* Terig Tucci. *"Sambre et meuse" players* Band de la Garde Republicaine. *"Hail to Our Land" by* James Peterson and Jack Shaindlin, *singers* United States Naval Academy. *"Exit Music: Ballet of the Skis and Cinerama Holiday Theme" by* Morton Gould. ¶CAST: Betty and John Marsh of Kansas City and Beatrice and Fred Troller of Zurich. ¶A Cinerama Films, Inc. presentation. A Louis de Rochemont production. A Stanley Warner Cinerama Corporation picture. Released by Cinerama, Inc. Technicolor. Six-track magnetic Cinerama Sound. Filmed in Las Vegas, San Francisco, New Hampshire, New Orleans, Switzerland and Paris. ¶Scenes later incorporated into *The Best of Cinerama.*

Cinerama South Seas Adventure (July 16, 1958). Filmed in Cinerama. *Producer* Carl Dudley. *Coproducer* Richard Goldstone. *Directors* Francis D. Lyon, Walter Thompson, Basil Wrangell, Richard Goldstone and Carl Dudley. *Writers* Charles Kaufman, Joseph Ansen and Harold Medford. *Music composer and conductor* Alex North. *Cinerama Symphony Orchestra recorded at* Oyster Bay Cinerama Studio. *Vocals* Norman Luboff and Choir. *Director of photography* John F. Warren. *Additional photography* Paul Hill. *Supervising editors* Frederick Y. Smith and Walter Stern. *Music editor* Richard C. Harris. *Sound editor* Warner E. Leighton. *Sound* Fred Bosch, Ray Sharples, Jay Ashworth, Avery Lockner, Richard Vorisek and Hal Magargle. *Art direction* Dan Cathcart, Ray Morris and Eric Thompson. *Maps and titles* Pacific Title & Art Studio. *Production managers* Lee William Lukather and Ron Whelan. *Assistant director* James Engle. *Public relations* Jacob Y. Brodsky. *Production staff* Edward R. Evans. *Cameraman* Peter Gibbons. *Assistant cameraman* Joe Raue. *Cinerama technician* Walter Gibbons-Fly. *Musical instruments of the South Seas used by* Cinerama Symphony Orchestra *by courtesy of* American Museum of Natural History. *Cooperation of* Her Majesty, Queen Salote of Tonga, His Excellency, Governor of French Oceania, M. Jean Francois Toby, His Excellency, Sir Ronald Garvey, KCMG, MBE, Governor of Fiji, Ansett Airways, Matson Navigation Company, Qantas Airlines and United Airlines. *Negative* Eastman Color. ¶A Cinerama Films, Inc. presentation. A Carl Dudley production for Stanley Warner Cinerama Corporation. Released by Cinerama, Inc. Technicolor. Six-track magnetic Cinerama Sound. 120 minutes plus overture, intermission and exit music. Filmed in Hawaii, Tahiti, Tonga, Fiji, New Hebrides, Australia and New Zealand. ¶CAST: *Storyteller* Orson Welles. *Kay Johnson* Diane Beardmore. *Marlene Hunter* Marlene Lizzio. *Ted Hunter* Tommy Zahn. *Jean-Louis Martin* Igor Allan. *Capt. Amos Dorn* Ed Olsen. *Eng. Oley and Davy Jones* Walter Gibbons-Fly. *Pete the Cook and King Neptune* Fred Bosch. *Turia* Ramine. *Hulu dancer at Don the Beachcomber's* Leilani. *Jim Perry* Jay Ashworth. *Nurse* Maxine Stone. *Nurse's husband* Don Middleton. *Stefan Koschek* Hans Farkash. *Anna Koschek* Janice Dinnen. *David Koschek* Eric Reiman. *Bobby Koschek* Sean Scully. *Betty Koschek* Margaret Roberts. *Themselves* Commodore Harold Gillespie (captain of the *Lurline*), Don the Beachcomber, Marcel (the mate), Singing Chorus of Queen's College, Tonga Free Wesleyan Methodist Church Choir, Mrs. Gibb (schoolteacher of the air), Frank Basden (chief operator, Communications Base, Broken Hill), Dr. Huxtable (Royal Flying Doctor Service) and Vic (pilot, Royal Flying Doctor Service). *Himself and Neptune's daughter* Eddie Titiki. *Supplemental narrations* Shepherd Mencken, Walter Coy and Ted de Corsia.

Cinerama's Russian Adventure (March 29, 1966). Filmed in Kinopanorama. Presented in Super Cinerama and 70mm Super Cinerama. *Producers* Harold J. Dennis and J. Jay Frankel. *Original prolog and narration* Homer McCoy. *Directors* Leonid Kristi, Roman Karmen, Boris Dolin, Oleg Lebedev, Solomon Kogan, Vasiliy Katanyan and V. Komissarzkhevskiy. *Operators* Nikolay Generalov, Sergey Medynskiy, Anatoliy Koloshin, E. Ezov, Ilya Gutman, A. Missyura, Vladimir Vorontsov, V. Ryklin and Georgiy Kholnyy. *Original music composers* Aleksander Lokshin, Ilya Shveytser and Yuriy Efimov. *Film editor* Harold J. Dennis. *Supervising music editor* William E. Wild. *Production supervisor and prolog photography* Coleman Thomas Conroy, Jr. *Commercial consultant* E. Douglas Netter. *Negative* Agfacolor and Eastman Color. *Super Cinerama three strip prints* Technicolor. *Super Cinerama 70mm prints* Metrocolor. ¶A Harold J. Dennis-J. Jay Frankel presentation. A J. Jay Frankel production. A Tsentraliniy dokumentaliniy film studiya–Tsentrnauchfilm–Accord International–Hal Dennis Productions–Cinerama, Inc. picture. Released by United Roadshow Presentations, Inc. by arrangement with Sovexportfilm under the auspices of the Cultural Exchange Program. Sovcolor and Eastman Color. Westrex recording system. Seven-track magnetic Cinerama Sound (Super Cinerama version) and six-track magnetic stereophonic sound (70mm Super Cinerama version). 146 minutes with overture and intermission. Filmed in Moscow, Siberia, the resorts on the Black Sea, in the Sea of Okhotski, on the Tisza River, on the Volga River, in the Moyun-Kum of Central Asia, at the North Pole, in the Antarctic Circle and in Hollywood. ¶CAST: *Host and narrator* Bing Crosby. *With* Bolshoi Theatre Ballet, Bolshoi Theatre Orchestra, Moscow State Circus (featuring Clown Oleg Popov), Moiseyev Ensemble and Piantnitsky State Chorus and Dance Ensemble. ¶An American production comprised primarily of Soviet footage culled from the Kinopanorama features *Great Is My Country* (1957), *The Enchanted Mirror* (1958), *Chas neozkhidannykh puteshestviy v polyote na vertolyote* (1960), *Chetvyortaya programma panoramikh filmov "Tsirkovoye predstavleniye" i "Na Krasnoy ploshchadyu"* (1961), *SSSR s okritim serdeem* (1961), *V Antarktiku za kitami* (1961) and *Udivitelinaya okhota* (1962). (See each title individually.) The footage was exchanged for one Cinerama feature, presumably *The Best of Cinerama* (q.v.).

(Frank Capra's) Circus *see* **(Henry Hathaway's) Circus World.**

Circus World (1974). Filmed in IMAX. *Producer and director* Roman Kroitor. *Photographer* John Spotton. ¶Filmed

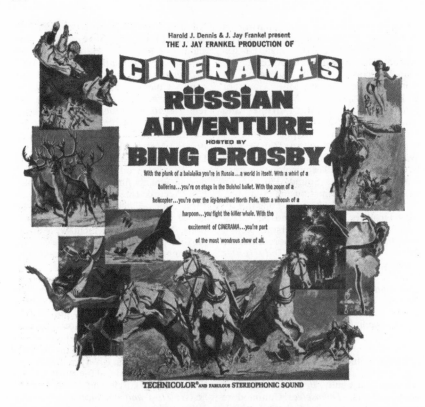

Harold J. Dennis & J. Jay Frankel present
THE J. JAY FRANKEL PRODUCTION OF

CINERAMA'S RUSSIAN ADVENTURE
HOSTED BY
BING CROSBY

With the plunk of a balalaika you're in Russia...a world in itself. With a whirl of a
ballerina...you're on stage in the Bolshoi ballet. With the zoom of a
helicopter...you're over the icy-breathed North Pole. With a whoosh of a
harpoon...you fight the killer whale. With the
excitement of CINERAMA...you're part
of the most wondrous show of all.

TECHNICOLOR® AND FABULOUS STEREOPHONIC SOUND

Ad for Cinerama's Russian Adventure.

by Imax Systems Corporation and Circus World, Inc. Produced and released by Circus World, Inc. Eastman Color. Six-track magnetic stereophonic sound. 25 minutes. Filmed at Ringling Bros. and Barnum & Bailey Circus. ¶CAST: The Flying Gaonas, Gunther Gebel-Williams, *et al.,* of Ringling Bros. and Barnum & Bailey Circus. ¶A Canadian production.

(Samuel Bronston's) Circus World *see* **(Henry Hathaway's) Circus World.**

(Henry Hathaway's) Circus World (June 25, 1964). Filmed in Super Technirama 70. Presented in 70mm Super Cinerama. *Producer* Samuel Bronston. *Director* Henry Hathaway. *Executive associate producer* Michael Waszynski. *Music composer and conductor* Dimitri Tiomkin. *Screenplay* Ben Hecht, Julian Halevy and James Edward Grant. *Story* Philip Yordan and Nicholas Ray. *Production designer* John De Cuir, Sr. *Costume designer* Renie. *Film editor* Dorothy Spencer. *Director of photography* Jack Hildyard. *Second unit director of photography* Claude Renoir. *Second unit director* Richard Talmadge. *Assistant director, first unit* Jose Lopez Rodero. *Assistant director, second unit* Terry Yorke. *Coordinator of circus operations* Frank Capra, Jr. *Sound mixer* David Hildyard. *Sound rerecorder* Gordon K. McCallum. *Dialog coach* George Tyne. *Execution production manager* C.O. Erickson. *Special effects* Alex C. Weldon, Richard Parker and Pablo Perez. *Special photographic effects consultant* Linwood G. Dunn. *Makeup* Mario van Riel. *Hairdressing* Grazia de Rossi. *Continuity* Elaine Schreyeck. *Second unit continuity* Kay Rawlings. *Supervising technician* Carl Gibson. *Supervising electrician* Bruno Pasqualini. *Master of properties* Stanley Detlie. *Casting* Maude Spector. *Head of wardrobe* Ana Maria Fea. *Titles*

Dong Kingman. *Horse trainer* Joseph Leshkov. *Coordinators of circus performances* Umberto Bedini, Bob Dover and Perezoff. *Technical advisers* Franz Althoff and Alfred Marquerie. *Special technical adviser* Bob Dover. *Assistant cameraman* Andres Berenguer. *Song "Circus World" music* Dimitri Tiomkin, *lyrics* Ned Washington. ¶A Samuel Bronston presentation. A Bronston-Midway production. Released by Paramount Pictures. Technicolor. Westrex six-track magnetic stereophonic sound. 135 minutes plus overture and intermission. Filmed at Samuel Bronston Studios, Madrid and on location in Madrid, Barcelona, Toledo, Vicalvaro, Chinchon and Aranjuez, Spain and Paris, France. ¶CAST: *Matt Masters* John Wayne. *Toni Alfredo* Claudia Cardinale. *Lili Alfredo* Rita Hayward. *Cap Carson* Lloyd Nolan. *Aldo Alfredo* Richard Conte. *Steve McCabe* John Smith. *Emile Schuman* Henri Dantes. *Frau Schuman* Wanda Rotha. *Giovana Alfredo* Katharyna. *Flo Hunt* Kay Walsh. *Anna Hunt* Margaret MacGrath. *Molly Hunt* Kathrine Ellison. *Billy Rogers* Miles Malleson. *Hilda* Katharine Kath. *Hamburg waterfront cafe bartender* Moustache. *Ringmasters* Robert Cunningham and Francois Galepides. *Bartender* Franz Althoff. *Madrid bartender* George Tyne. *Clown Max* Max Van Embden. *Clown* Pio Nock. *Circus personnel* The Franz Althoff Circus, Jose Maria Caffarel, Harry Althoff, Marianne Althoff and Franziska Althoff. ¶Advertised as *Samuel Bronston's Circus World*. Originally developed as a project for Nicholas Ray, then turned over to Frank Capra, at which point the title became *Frank Capra's Circus*. The cast was to have had David Niven in the Cap Carson role. Both Capra and Niven left after the screenplay was rewritten by James Edward Grant, and Henry Hathaway took over direction. Released in England as *The Magnificent Showman*.

Cities and Years (1974). Filmed in Sovscope 70. *Screen author* Vladimir Valutskiy and Aleksandr Zarkhi. *Based on the book "Goroda i godi" by* Konstantin Fedina. *Director* Aleksandr Zarkhi. *Operator* Aleksandr Knyazinskiy. *Artist* David Vinnitskiy. *Composer* Alfred Shnitke. *Sound operator* G. Korenblyum. ¶A Mosfilm production in association with DEFA. International distribution

Sovexportfilm. Sovcolor. Six-track magnetic stereophonic sound. 170 minutes plus intermission. Filmed at Mosfilm Studios, Moscow, R.S.F.S.R. ¶CAST: *Andrei Startsov* Igor Starigin. *Marie* Barbara Briliska. *Kurt Vahn* Vinfried Glatseder. *Rita* Irma Pechernikova. *Markgrsf Muhlen-Schonan* Friedrich Yunge. *With* Kh. Gering, Nikolai Griniko, L. Kulagin, S. Martinson, G. Burkov, V. Balon and V. Nosik. ¶A Soviet and East German coproduction released in Russia in August 1974 as *Goroda i godi* in two parts running 91 minutes and 79 minutes.

(Joseph L. Mankiewicz') Cleopatra (June 12, 1963). Filmed in Todd-AO. *Executive producer* Darryl F. Zanuck. *Producer* Walter Wanger. *Directors* Joseph L. Mankiewicz and Rouben Mamoulian. *Screenplay* Nigel Balchin, Ludi Claire, Dale Wasserman, Lawrence Durrell, Joseph L. Mankiewicz, Ranald MacDougall and Sidney Buchman. *Script consultants* Nunnally Johnson and Marc Brandel. *Based upon histories by* Plutarch, Suetonius and Appian, *other ancient sources and the book "The Life and Times of Cleopatra" by* C.M. Franzero. *Music composer and conductor* Alex North. *Choreography* Hermes Pan. *Elizabeth Taylor's costumes and additional costumes designer* Irene Sharaff. *Directors of photography* Leon Shamroy and Jack Hildyard. *Art direction* Jack Martin Smith, Hilyard Brown, Herman Blumenthal, Elven Webb, Maurice Pelling, Boris Juraga and Enzo Bulgarelli. *Production designer* John De Cuir. *Set decorations* Walter M. Scott, Paul S. Fox and Paul Ray Moyer. *Men's costumes designer* Vittorio Nino Novarese. *Women's costumes designer* Renie. *Film editor* Dorothy Spencer. *Special photographic effects* L.B. Abbott and Emil Kosa, Jr. *Sound recording supervisors* Fred Hynes and James Corcoran. *Sound recorders* Bernard Freericks and Murray Spivack. *Assistant directors* Fred R. Simpson and Richard Lang. *Production managers* Forrest E. Johnston and C.O. Erickson. *Casting consultant* Stuart Lyons. *Makeup* Alberto de Rossi. *Miss Taylor's hair stylists* Vivienne Zavitz and Sydney Guilaroff. *Second unit directors* Ray Kellogg and Andrew Marton. *Second unit photography* Claude Renoir and Pietro Portalupi. *Second unit production manager*

Saul Wurtzel. *Associate music conductor* Lionel Newman. *Color consultant* Leonard Doss. *Todd-AO developers* American Optical Company and Magna Theatre Corporation. *Assistant to the director* Christopher Mankiewicz. *Italian production manager* Franco Magli. *Casting* Owen McLean. *Supervising music editor* George Adams. *Production executive* Doc Merman. *Production supervisor* Sid Rogell. *Property masters* Samuel Gordon, Joseph LaBella and Bill Middlesat. *Production illustrators* Ed Graves and Leon Harris. *Set draughtsman* John Barry. *Costume makers* Western Costume Company. *Costume coordinator* Irina Wassilichikov. *Costume modelmaker* Wah Ming Chang. *Wardrobe supervision* Courtney Haslem and Eddie Wynigear. *Production assistant* Rosemary Mathews. *Dialog coach* Pamela Danova. *Miss Taylor's secretary* Dick Hanley. *Assistant to Miss Taylor* John Lee. *Construction supervisors* Jack Tait and Herbert Cheek. *Gaffer* Fred Hall. *Key grip* Leo McCreary. *Camera operator* Irving Rosenberg. *Assistant cameraman* Lee "Red" Crawford. *Still photographer* Bert Stern. *Script supervisors* Elaine Schreyeck and Stanley K. Scheuer. *Unit publicists* Jack Brodsky and Guilio Ascarelli. *Production accountant* Larry Rice. *Wigmakers* Stanley Hall of London. *Sound recording* Todd-AO Sound Department and 20th Century–Fox Studio Sound Department. *Music recorders* Murray Spivack and Douglas O. Williams. *Special mechanical effects* August J. Lohman and Gerald Endler. ¶An MCL Films-Walwa Films production. A 20th Century–Fox Productions, Ltd. picture. Released by 20th Century–Fox. Color by De Luxe. Westrex six-track stereophonic sound. 243 minutes plus overture, intermission and exit music. Filmed at Pinewood Studios, London and Studio Cinecitta and Studio Sperimentale, Rome and on location in England, Almeria, Spain, Alexandra, Edkou and the northern desert, Egypt and Torre, Astura, Anzio, Ischia and Lanuvro, Italy. ¶CAST: *Queen Cleopatra* Elizabeth Taylor. *General Marc Antony* Richard Burton. *Emperor Julius Caesar* Rex Harrison. *Egyptian High Priestess* Pamela Brown. *Flavius* George Cole. *Sosigenes* Hume Cronyn. *Apollodorus* Casare Danova. *Brutus* Kenneth Haigh. *Agrippa* Andrew Keir. *Octavian* Roddy McDowall. *Germanicus* Robert Stephens. *Eiras* Francesca Annis. *Pothinos* Gregoire Aslan. *Ramos* Martin Benson. *Theodotos* Herbert Berghof. *Phoebus* John Cairney. *Rufio* Martin Landau. *Lotos* Jacqui Chan. *Charmian* Isabelle Cooley. *Achillas* John Doucette. *Canidius* Andrew Faulds. *Cimber* Michael Gwynn. *Cicero* Michael Hordern. *Cassius* John Hoyt. *Euphranor* Marne Maitland. *Casca* Carroll O'Connor. *Ptolemy* Richard O'Sullivan. *Calphurnia* Gwen Watford. *Decimus* Douglas Wilmer. *Queen of Tarsus* Marina Berti. *Egyptian High Priest* John Karlsen. *Caesarion at age four years* Loris Loddi. *Octavia* Jean Marsh. *Marcellus* Gin Mart. *Mithridates* Furio Meniconi. *Caesarion at age twelve years* Kenneth Nash. *Caesarion at age seven years* Del Russell. *Valus* John Valva. *Roman soldier* Gary Collins. *Dancers* Leo Coleman and Claude Marchant. *Archesilaus* Laurence Naismith. *Titus* Finlay Currie. *First Roman officer* John Alderson. *Second Roman officer* Peter Forster. *With* Maria Badmajev, Michele Bally, Marie Devereaux, John Gayford, Maureen Lane, Kathy Martin, Gesa Meikin and Simon Mizrahi. *Narrator* Ben Wright. ¶A British and American coproduction. Elizabeth Taylor replaced Joan Collins in the lead. Production began in England at Pinewood Studios with Peter Finch as Caesar and Stephen Boyd as Antony, Rouben Mamoulian directing and Jack Hildyard photographing in Todd-AO. When Collins was to have starred the show was to have been shot in CinemaScope. The screenplay was then being credited to Nigel Balchin, Ludi Claire, Dale Wasserman and Lawrence Durrell with Nunnally Johnson and March Brandel unit listed as script consultants. Johnson claimed he rewrote the scenario and this is probably true. Mamoulian was replaced by Joe Mankiewicz, who rewrote the screenplay. Production was soon in trouble, Rex Harrison replaced Finch, and Richard Burton replaced Boyd. Leon Shamroy was brought in as director of photography. Ranald MacDougall and Sidney Buchman were added as dramatists. The production was moved to Studio Cinecitta in Rome. Some of Mamoulian's footage, as well as scenes shot by Hildyard, appear in the final film. Finch and Boyd may appear in some long shots, but this is unconfirmed. At one point footage was shot in Super

Cinerama, but none appeared in the final print. The roadshow was continuously re-edited with 222 minute, 215 minute and 166 minute (plus overture and intermission) versions being screened. The original 243 minute edition has been restored for television and video release. This was the most expensive feature made at that time and succeeded in almost destroying 20th Century-Fox. It toppled the Zanuck empire and virtually stopped the careers of Mamoulian and Walter Wanger, who was removed as producer in the last phases of production.

Clint the Lonely Nevedan (1968). Filmed in Super Technirama 70. *Executive producer* Francisco Balcazar. *Producer and director* Alfonso Balcazar. *Screenplay* Jose Antonio de la Loma and Alfonso Balcazar. *Story* Jose Antonio de la Loma, Alfonso Balcazar and Helmut Harum. *Director of photography* Victor Monreal. *Music* Nora Orlandi. *Editor* Otelo Colangeli. *Set designer* Juan Alberto Soler. *Costumes* Berenica Sparano. *Stunt director* Remo de Angelis. ¶A Producciones Cinematograficas Balcazar–Lux Film-International Germania Film production. Technicolor. 92 minutes. Filmed at Estudios Balcazar, Barcelona, Spain. ¶CAST: *Clint Harrison* Jorge Martin. *Chico Tom* Francisco Jose Huetos. *Julie* Marianne Koch. *Ross* Fernando Sancho. *Simpson* Xan Das Bolas. *Bill O'Brien* Gerhard Riedmann. *Dave Shannon* Paolo Gozlino. *McKinley* Beni Devs. *Walter Shannon* Walter Barnes. *Agriculturist* Renato Baldini. *Peabody* Gustavo Re. *Men* Remo de Angelis and Osvaldo Genazzani. ¶A Spanish, Italian and West German co-production released in Spain in 70mm and six-track magnetic stereophonic sound in 1968 by Filmex as *Clint, el solitario*. Sequel was *El retorno de Clint el solitario* (1972). U.S. distribution undetermined, but an English language version was made.

Les collants noirs *see* **Black Tights.**

Come Easy *see* **A Soldier's Plaything.**

Commander of the Lucky "Pike" (1973) Filmed in Sovscope 70. *Screen authors* Aleksandr Moldavskiy, Vladimir Valutskiy and Boris Volchek. *Director* Boris Volchek. *Operators* Boris Volchek and Valentin Makarov. *Artist* Vladimir

Aronin. *Composer* Aleksandr Zatsepin. *Sound operator* V. Shmelikin. *Song text* L. Derbeneva. ¶A Mosfilm production. International distribution Sovexportfilm. Sovcolor. Six-track magnetic stereophonic sound. 101 minutes. Filmed at Mosfilm Studios, Moscow, R.S.F.S.R. ¶CAST: *Capt. Alexei Strogov* Pyotr Vediyaminov. *Commissar Victor Sharknis* Donates Banionis. *Golik* Vladimir Ivanov. *Svetlana Vedenina* Elena Dobronravova. *With* M. Volkov, V. Kashpur, Sveltana Suhovey, S. Borodokin, Evgeni Evstigneev, N. Astakhov, P. Mazetin, Sh. Mshvenieradze, A. Belov, M. Kublinskiy, K. Raykin, I. Kultsk and Elena Solovei. ¶A Soviet production released in Russia in 1973 as *Komandir schastlivoy "Shuki."*

Committee of 19 (1972). Filmed in Sovscope 70. *Screen authors* Sergei Mikhalkov and Aleksandr Shlepyanov *with the participation of* Savva Kulish. *Director* Savva Kulish. *Operators* Vladimir Fastenko and Konstantin Brovin. *Artist* L. Pertsev. *Composer* Oleg Karavaychuk. *Sound operator* V. Krachkovskiy. ¶A Mosfilm production. International distribution Sovexportfilm. Sovcolor. Six-track magnetic stereophonic sound. 162 minutes plus intermission. Filmed at Mosfilm Studios, Moscow, R.S.F.S.R. ¶CAST: Nikolai Zasukhin, Yuri Yarvet, Naum Shopov, Voldemar Panso, Yuris Strenga, Aleksandr Vokach, Madelaine Marteon, Sveltana Smekhnova, B. Ture, R. Liensoli, S. Landgraf, G. Teyh, L. Nedovich, A. Dolo, A. Videnieks, M. Donskoy, V. Medvedev and D. Singkh. ¶A Soviet production released in Russia in 1972 as *Komitet 19-ti* in two parts running 88 minutes and 74 minutes.

Con la morte alla spalle (1967). Filmed in Stereovision 70. *Executive producers* Italo Zingarelli and Francisco Balcazar. *Producer and director* Alfonso Balcazar. *Story and screenplay* Jose Antonio de la Loma, Alfonso Balcazar and Gianni Simonelli. *Director of photography* Victor Monreal. *Music composer and conductor* Klaus [Claude] Bolling. *Editor* Gilbert Natot. *Set designer* Enzo Bulgarelli. *Costumes* Berenica Sparano. ¶A West Film, S.r.L.–Le Comptoir Francais du Film-Producciones Cinematografica Balcazar production. Eastman Color. Four-track magnetic stereophonic sound. 86 minutes.

Filmed at Estudios Balcazar, Barcelona, Spain and on location throughout Europe. ¶CAST: *Gary* George [Jorge] Martin. *Monica* Vivi Bach. *Silvana* Rosalba Neri. *Bill* Michael Monfort. *Electia* Daniele Vargas. *Ivan* Ignazio Leone. *Frau Von Hallew* Maria Badmayen. *Col. Randolph Robert* Party. *Prof. Roland* Georges Chamarat. *With* Klaus Jurgen Wussov and Juan Llusa. ¶Filmed in the Jacobsen 70mm 3D system, not the U.S. StereoVision 70 format. An Italian, French and Spanish coproduction which was apparently never released in the U.S. Released in Italy in 1967 by Delta Film. The title translates as *With Death on Your Back*.

The Concert for Bangladesh (March 1972). Filmed in 16mm. Presented in 70mm Wide Screen. *Producers* George Harrison and Allen V. Klein. *Writer and director* Saul Swimmer. *Photography* Saul Negrin, Richard Brooks, Fred Hoffman and Tohru Nakamura. *Film editor* Howard Lester. *Music recording producers* Phil Spector and George Harrison. *Production manager* Steve Bono. *Titles* Perri and Lewis. *70mm wide screen blowup* Film Effects of Hollywood. *Optical technicians* Linwood G. Dunn, Don Weed and Cecil Love. *Sound* Todd-AO. *"Bangla Dhun" writer and performer* Ravi Shankar. *"Bangladesh," "Here Comes the Sun," "While My Guitar Gently Weeps," "Beware of Darkness," "Wah-Wah," "My Sweet Lord," "Something" and "Awaiting on You All" writer and singer* George Harrison. *"That's the Way God Planned It" writer and singer* Billy Preston. *"It Don't Come Easy" writer and singer* Ringo Starr. *"Jumpin' Jack Flash" writers* Mick Jagger and Keith Richard, *singer* Leon Russell. *"Youngblood" writers* Jerry Lieber, Mike Stoller and Doc Pomus, *singer* Leon Russell. *"A Hard Rain's Gonna Fall," "It Takes a Lot to Laugh/It Takes a Lot to Cry," "Blowin' in the Wind" and "Just Like a Woman" writer and singer* Bob Dylan. ¶An Apple film. Released by 20th Century–Fox. Technicolor. Westrex six-track magnetic stereophonic sound. 100 minutes. Filmed at Madison Square Garden, N.Y.C. MPAA rating: G. CAST: *Principal performers* Eric Clapton, Bob Dylan, George Harrison, Billy Preston, Leon Russell, Ravi Shankar, Ringo Starr and Klaus Voor-

man. *Other performers* Alla Rakah, Ali Akbar Khan, Kamala Chakravarty, Badfinger, Allen Beutler, Jesse Davis, Tom Evans, Chuck Findley, Mike Gibbons, Jo Green, Jeanie Greene, Marlin Greene, Dolores Hall, Pete Ham, Jim Horn, Jackie Kelso, Jim Keltner, Claudia Linnear, Lon McCreary, Ollie Mitchell, Joey Molland, Don Nix, Don Preston and Carl Radle. *Himself* Allen V. Klein. ¶The only feature shot in 16mm and blown up to 70mm wide screen. This was originally intended for television but upon its completion those involved decided to go with a theatrical release. It was shot with six cameras at two performances on August 1, 1971, before an estimated audience of 40,000. Approximately 40 hours of footage was exposed, mostly at the evening performance. There was a prologue, consisting of a news conference held by George Harrison and Allen Klein, in 1.33 × 1 ratio, with the concert material in 2 × 1. The 35mm running time is given as 96 minutes so the press footage may have appeared only on 70mm prints. All 35mm prints were 1.33 × 1.

Confidence (1976). Filmed in Sovscope 70. *Screen authors* Mikhail Shatrov and Vladimir Loginov. *Directors* Viktor Tregubovich and Zelevin Layne. *Operator* Dmitry Meshiev. *Artist* Grachia Mekinyan. *Composer* Georgy Sviridov. *Sound operators* I. Chernyakhovskaya and Z. Lumes. ¶A Mosfilm-Fennada-film production. International distribution Sovexportfilm. Sovcolor. Six-track magnetic stereophonic sound. 96 minutes. Filmed at Mosfilm Studios, Moscow, R.S.F.S.R. and on location in Finland. ¶CAST: *Lenin* Kiriil Lavrov. *Andreyeva* Irina Miroshnichenko. *Maxim Gorki* Afansay Kochetkov. *Vladimir Bonch-Bruyevich* Igor Dmitriev. *Yakov Sverdlov* Vladimir Tatosov. *With* Margarita Terekhova, Antonia Shuranova, Leonid Nevedomskiy, Oleg Yankovskiy, Yuri Kamorny, Vilkho Spivola, Yurye Paudo, Metli Ranin, Esa Saario, Yussi Yurkkya, L. Merzin, A. Solonitsin, A. Zybozenko, Yu. Tyakhtelya and Z. Salmi. ¶A Soviet and Finnish coproduction released in Russia in 1976 as *Doverie*.

Congress of Love (1966). Filmed in Superpanorama 70. *Producers* Aldo von Pinelli and Peter Schaeffers. *Director* Geza von

The Concert for Bangladesh: *The 16mm original and the 70mm blowup shown in actual-size relation.*

Radvanyi. *Script* Fred Denger, Aldo von Pinelli and Geza von Radvanyi. *Camera* Heinz Hoelscher. *Music* Peter Thomas, Johann Strauss and Robert Stolz. *Settings* Otto Pischinger and Herta Harsiter. *Costumes* H. Reihs-Gromes and F. Sthamer. ¶A Melodie Film-Wiener Stadthaile production. Eastman Color. Six-track magnetic stereophonic sound. 96 minutes. ¶CAST: *Princess Metternich* Lilli Palmer. *Tsar Alexander* Curt [Curd] Jurgens. *Prince Talleyrand* Paul Meurisse. *Viennese guide* Walter Slezak. *Prince Metternich* Hannes Messemer. *Rosa* Anita Hoefer. *Baron Stefan* Bret Halsey. *Napoleon's double* Wolfgang Kieling. *Sophie* Bibi Jelinek. *Stefan's father* Gustav Knuth. ¶A West German and Austrian coproduction released in West Germany in May 1966 by Nora as *Der Kongress amuesiert sich.* We have listed the film here under its international title, but there does not appear to have been an English language version and most definitely not an American release in 70mm.

Le corsaire (December 8, 1965). Filmed in Super Technirama 70. *Executive producer* John Brabourne. *Producer and director* Anthony Havelock-Allan. *Music* Riccardo Drigo and Léon Minkus. *Director of photography* Geoffrey Unsworth. *Choreography* Rudolf Nureyev. *Based on original choreography by* Marius Petipa. *Film editors* Richard Marsden and James Clark. *Sound* Edgar Vetter. ¶A British Home Entertainment production. Technicolor. Filmed at the Royal Opera House, Covent Garden, London. ¶CAST: Pas de deux Rudolf Nureyev and Margot Fonteyn. *Corps de ballet* Royal Ballet. ¶This British short was shot in 1963 along with *La valse, Les Sylphides* and *Aurora's*

Wedding and edited into the 85-minute feature *An Evening with the Royal Ballet,* which was released in England in 1963 and in the U.S. in 1965 by Sigma III Corporation. Only *Le corsaire* was filmed in 70mm, but the entire show may have been blown up and given wide gauge exhibition in London. In the U.S. it was shown only in 35mm.

Cosmos *see* **To the Moon and Beyond.**

A Courtesy Call (1973). Filmed in Sovscope 70. *Screen authors* Anatoli Grebnev and Yuli Raizman. *Director* Yuli Raizman. *Operator* Naum Ardashnikov. *Composer* Nikolai Sidelinikov. *Artists* Nicolai Dvigubskiy and Felix Yasfkevich. *Sound operator* R. Kazaryan. ¶A Mosfilm production. International distribution Sovexportfilm. Sovcolor. Six-track magnetic stereophonic sound. 186 minutes plus intermission. Filmed at Mosfilm Studios, Moscow, R.S.F.S.R. and on location in Greece. CAST: *Lucy, Pompeian lady, slave girl and Hetaera* Lyubov Alibitskaya. *Lt. Capt. Andrei Glebov and foreigner* Boris Gusakov. *Kositsky* Vladimir Nosik. *Pansa* Aleksandr Vokach. *Kondakov* Nikolai Rachinskiy. *Lara* Valentina Shendrikova. *With* Alla Demidova, Vladislav Strzelchik, L. Tarabarinov, G. Pusep, A. Zybozenko, B. Khimichev, L. Selyanskaya, O. Shklovskiy and R. Filippov. ¶A Soviet production released in Russia in 1973 as *Vizit vezlivosti* in two parts running 109 minutes and 77 minutes.

The Crew (1980). Filmed in Sovscope 70. *Screen authors* Yuli Dunskiy, Valery Frid and Aleksandr Mitta *in collaboration with* Boris Urinovskiy. *Director* Aleksandr

Mitta. *Operator* Valery Shuvalov. *Artist* Anatoly Kuznetsov. *Composer* Alfred Shnitke. *Sound operators* E. Popova and V. Karasev. ¶A Mosfilm production. International distribution Sovexportfilm. Sovcolor. Six-track magnetic stereophonic sound. 144 minutes plus intermission. Filmed at Mosfilm Studios, Moscow, R.S.F.S.R. ¶CAST: *Flight Cmdr. Timchenko* Georgi Zzenov. *Valentin Nenarokov* Anatoly Vasiliev. *Skvortsov* Leonid Filatov. *Nenarokov's wife* Irina Akulova. *Timchenko's wife* Ekaterina Vasilieva. *Tamara* Aleksandr Yakovleva. *With* Yuri Gorobets, A. Pavlov, Galina Gladkova and R. Monin. ¶A Soviet production released in Russia in 1980 as *Zkipaz* in two parts running 84 minutes and 60 minutes.

Cristallisation (1928). Filmed in Triptych. *Director and editor* Abel Gance. *Original director* S.L. Mol. ¶A Societé Generale des Films production. Original production Multifilm-Haarlem. ¶A French production released in France on April 20, 1928. A montage of scenes from the 1925 French film *Krislallen* (q.v.) reedited by Gance for Triptych presentation.

Custer of the West (January 24, 1968). Filmed in Super Technirama 70. Presented in 70mm Super Cinerama. *Executive producer* Irving Lerner. *Producer* Philip Yordan. *Director* Robert Siodmak. *Writers* Bernard Gordon, Julian Halevy and Philip Yordan. *Director of photography* Cecilio Paniagua. *Production executive* Lester A. Sansom. *Art direction* Jean Pierre D'Eaubonne, Eugene Lourie and Julio Molina. *Film editor* Maurice Rootes. *Sound editors* Kurt Herrnfeld and Alban Streeter. *Production supervisor* Gregorio Sacristan. *Production manager* Jose Manuel Herrero. *Unit manager* Alejandro Perla. *Assistant director* Jose Maria Ochoa. *Casting* Lillian Kelly. *Costume designer* Laure De Zarate. *Wardrobe* Charles Simminger. *Script supervisor* Eva del Castillo. *Dialog continuity* John Kirby. *Makeup artist* Julian Ruiz. *Set dressing* Antonio Mateos. *Civil War sequence* Irving Lerner. *Music composer and conductor* Bernardo Segall. *Players* The Royal Philharmonic Orchestra. *Special effects sequences director* Eugene Lourie. *Second unit director* Noel Howard. *Second unit cameraman* John Cabrera. *Assistant editors* Jim Hopkins

and Soledad Lopez. *Camera operators* Eduardo Noe and Salvador Gil. *Sound recordists* Jim Willis and Gordon K. McCallum. *Technical effects* Joe Purcell. *Special effects* Leon Ortega. *Production consultant* Stan Torchia. *Technical adviser* Faith Clift. *Still photographer* Antonio Luengo. *Property master* Julian Mateos. ¶A Cinerama, Inc. presentation. A Louis Dolivet-Philip Yordan production. A Security Pictures, Inc. film. From the American Broadcasting Companies, Inc. Released by Cinerama Releasing Corp. Technicolor. Westrex six-track magnetic stereophonic sound. 140 minutes plus overture and intermission. Filmed at Estudios Sevilla, Madrid and on location in Madrid, Toledo and Almeria, Spain. ¶CAST: *Gen. George Armstrong Custer* Robert Shaw. *Elizabeth Custer* Mary Ure. *Lt. Frederick W. Benteen* Jeffrey Hunter. *Maj. Marcus A. Reno* Ty Hardin. *Lt. Howells* Charles Stalnaker. *Sgt. Buckley* Robert Hall. *Gen. Philip H. Sheridan* Lawrence Tierney. *Chief Dull Knife* Kiernon Moore. *Rich goldminer on train* Marc Lawrence. *Sgt. Patty Mulligan* Robert Ryan. *With* Jack Gaskin, John Clark, Bill Christmas, Joe Zboran, Jack Cooper, Carl Rapp, Bud Strait, Dennis Kilbane, Jack Taylor, Fred Kohler, Jr., Luis Rivera, Clemence Bettany, Barta Barri, John Dillon, John Underhill and Robert Reynolds. ¶An American, British, French and Spanish coproduction. Working title was *Custer*. British backing came from Cinerama International Releasing Organization Establishment, French backing from Louis Dolivet and Spanish backing from Stan Torchia. Released in 35mm in a complete edition and a 120 minute reedited version. Some of the shorter 35mm prints were retitled *A Good Day for Fighting* (after the comment Dull Knife made to Custer prior to the Little Big Horn massacre). While this is the most accurate depiction of Custer's life on screen, it also has some very odd errors: Custer had been a general, but was a colonel during the time most of the action of the film occurred; Benteen was a captain, not a lieutenant, during the same story period (and had, in fact, been a colonel during the Civil War); Sheridan was a lieutenant general, not a full general; and the Indian leader represented was not Dull Knife but Crazy Horse.

Top: *A general release ad for* Custer of the West. *This is for the complete version, not the shortened edition. The "70" has been dropped from the Super Technirama credit (lower right corner), and a large boxed catchline ("the action picture of the year . . .") occupies the area originally devoted to the Cinerama logo.* Bottom: *The crew of* Custer of the West *on location in Toledo, Spain. Director Robert Siodmak stands behind the unblimped Technirama camera. Stillman Antonio Luengo props against the camera while operator Eduardo Noe sits on a box. The clapper-loader is on the extreme right with the slate. The man sitting with the dark glasses is presumably the focus puller. Others in the still are grips and extras.*

Daleko na zapade (1969). Filmed in Sovscope 70. *Screen author* G. Mdivani. *Director* A. Faynpimmer. *Operator* L. Kraynenkov. *Artist* P. Kiselev. *Composers* V. Muradeli and V. Dekhtyarev. *Sound operator* G. Korenblyum. ¶A Mosfilm production. International distribution Sovexportfilm. Sovcolor. Six-track magnetic stereophonic sound. 111 minutes. Filmed at Mosfilm Studios, Moscow, R.S.F.S.R. ¶CAST: N. Kryuchkov, V. Safonov, N. Merzlikin, G. Yukhtin, A. Soloviev, P. Butkevich, G. Pirtshalava, V. Dvorzetskiy, V. Protasenko, R. Muratov, G. Andreeva, A. Vertogradov, G. Plasksin and Z. Matstsevskiy. ¶A Soviet production released in Russia in 1969.

Dance of Life (1984). Filmed in IMAX. *Producer, director and photographer* Greg MacGillivray. ¶A MacGillivray Freeman Films production. Released by MacGillivray Freeman Films Distribution Company. Eastman Color. Six-track magnetic Dolby Stereo. 31 minutes. Filmed in the Indonesian Archipelago. Originally made for Taman Min, Indonesia.

Dance of the East (1986). Filmed in IMAX. *Producer and director* Sokin Bae. ¶A Shindongah Group production. Released by Imax Systems Corporation. Eastman Color. Six-track magnetic stereophonic sound. 40 minutes. Filmed in Korea. A South Korean production originally made for Shindongah Group's DLI IMAX Theatre.

Danger Lights (December 14, 1930). Filmed in Natural Vision. *Executive producer* William Le Baron. *Associate producer* Myles Connolly. *Director* George B. Seitz. *Story and dialogue* James Ashmore Creelman. *Photographers* Karl Struss and John Boyle. *Film editor* Archie S. Marshek. *Dialogue director* Hugh Herbert. *Settings* Carroll Clark. *Set decorations* Thomas Little. *Costumes* Walter Plunkett. *Makeup* Mel Berns. *Sound supervisor* Carl Dreher. *Sound recorder* Clem Portman. *Sound effects* Murray Spivack. *Musical director* Max Steiner. *Photographic effects* Lloyd Knechtel and Vernon L. Walker. *Effects photographer* Linwood G. Dunn. *Optical technician* Cecil Love. *Miniatures* Donald Jahraus. *Special effects* Harry Redmond, Jr. *Operative cameramen* Robert de Grasse, Burnett

Guffey and Clifford Stine. ¶A Radio Pictures presentation. A RKO Productions, Inc. picture. Released by RKO Radio Pictures. RCA Photophone recording. 87 minutes. Filmed at Pathe Studios and on location in Southern California. ¶CAST: *Dan Thorn* Louis Wolheim. *Larry Doyle* Robert Armstrong. *Mary Ryan* Jean Arthur. *Ed Ryan* Frank Sheridan. *Engineer* Robert Edeson. *Professor* Hugh Herbert. *Joe Geraghty* James Farley. *General manager* Allan Roscoe. *Chief dispatcher* William P. Burt. ¶Filmed simultaneously in standard 35mm.

Dangerous Charter (September 19, 1962). *Producers* Robert Gottschalk and John R. Moore. *Director and original story* Robert Gottschalk. *Screenplay* Raul Strait. *Director of photography* Meredith M. Nicholson. *Music* Ted Dale. *Film editor* George White. *Sound* Franklin E. Milton and Jean Valentino. *Assistant directors* Joe Boyle and Robert C. Scrivner. *Assistant editor* Carl Mahakian. *Songs "The Sea Is My Woman" and "Lonely Guitar" by* Rod Sherwood. ¶A Panavision, Inc. production. A Dangerous Charter Productions picture. Released by Crown International Pictures. Panavision. Technicolor. Westrex recording system. Panasound. 76 minutes. Filmed on location on Santa Catalina Island, in San Pedro and off the coast of Southern California. ¶CAST: *Marty McMahon* Chris Warfield. *June Smith* Sally Fraser. *Dick Kane* Richard Foote. *Sidney Manet* Peter Forster. *Kick Smith* Chick Chandler. *Joe Gallardo* Wright King. *With* Carl Milletaire, Steve Conte, John Zaremba, John Pickard and Alex Montoya. ¶This film is being included only because of its maker, Robert Gottschalk, since his name might be of some interest to the reader. The film was shot in 1958. Panasound may have been four-track or Perspecta stereophonic. Postproduction was done at MGM Studios. Presumably this was the only theatrical feature actually produced by Panavision.

Danses (1928). Filmed in Triptych. *Producer and director* Abel Gance. *Photography* Jules Kruger. *Editors* Abel Gance and Marguerite Beauge. ¶A Societé Generale des Films production. 11 minutes. A French production released in France on February 10, 1928, this was the

Bal de victimes sequence reedited from *Napoleon.*

Darwin on the Galapagos (1983). Filmed in OMNIMAX. *Directors* Graphic Films Corporation. ¶Produced and released by Science Museum of Minnesota. Eastman Color. Six-track magnetic stereophonic sound. 47 minutes.

Dauria (1972). Filmed in Sovscope 70. *Screen authors* Yuri Klepikov and Viktor Tregubovich. *Based on the novel "Dauriya" by* K. Sedykh. *Director* Viktor Tregubovich. *Operator* Evgeni Mezentsev. *Artist* Gay Mekinyan. *Composer* Georgi Portnov. *Sound operator* I. Chernyakhovskaya. ¶A Lenfilm production. International distribution Sovexportfilm. Sovcolor. Six-track magnetic stereophonic sound. 169 minutes plus intermission. Filmed at Lenfilm Studio, Leningrad and on location in Transbaikal and Narva, Siberia, R.S.F.S.R. ¶CAST: *Roman Ulybin* Vitali Solomin. *Dauriya* Svetlana Golovina. *Alexei Kargin* Efim Kopelyan. *Anarchists* Pyotr Gitis and Mikhail Kokshenov. *Semyon Nagorny* Yuri Solomin. *With* A. Terusov, P. Shelokhonov, V. Kuznetsova, Vassili Shukshin, Z. Matlyantsev, F. Odinokov, L. Malinovskaya, Yu. Dubrovin, V. Losev and I. Efimov. ¶A Soviet production released in Russia in 1972 as *Dauriya* in two parts running 89 minutes and 80 minutes.

Dauriya *see* **Dauria.**

David-Bek *see* **The Star of Hope.**

Daytime Stars (1968). Filmed in Sovscope 70. *Screen author and director* Igor Talankin. *Based on the play "Dnevnie zvezdi" by* Olga Bergzolits. *Operator* Margarita Pilikhina. *Artists* N. Usachev and A. Makarov. *Composer* A. Shnitke. *Sound operator* Ya. Kharon. ¶A Mosfilm production. International distribution Sovexportfilm. Sovcolor. Six-track magnetic stereophonic sound. 119 minutes. Filmed at Mosfilm Studios, Moscow, R.S.F.S.R. ¶CAST: *Olga* Alla Demidova. *Nikolay* Konstantin Baranov. *Father* Andrey Popov. ¶A Soviet production released in Russia in 1968 as *Dnevnie zvezdi.*

Deep Sea Rescue (1986). Filmed in Show-

scan. Presented in Dynamic Motion. Produced and released by Showscan Film Corporation. Eastman Color. Six-track magnetic Dolby Stereo. Originally made for the British Columbia Pavilion at EXPO 86 in Vancouver. Shown with the Deep Rover Shuttle simulator to give the audience the impression of participation in a deep sea rescue mission.

Dela serdechnie *see* **Affairs of the Heart.**

Delifini prikhodyat k lyudyam (1966). Filmed in Kinopanorama 70. International distribution Sovexportfilm. Sovcolor. Nine-track magnetic Kinopanorama Sound. A Soviet production released in Russia in 1966.

De Luxe Tour (1957). Filmed in CinemaScope 55. *Executive producer* Darryl F. Zanuck. *Producer* Robert L. Jacks. *Story* Frederick Wakeman. *Director of photography* Charles G. Clarke. *Aerial supervisor* Paul Mantz. *Co-pilot* Jim Thompson. *Flight engineer* Cort Johnson. *CinemaScope lenses* Bausch & Lomb. ¶Produced and released by 20th Century-Fox. Color by De Luxe. Westrex four-track MagOptical stereophonic sound. 1 reel (?). Apparently shown in only one Bronx theater in 55mm and then withdrawn from release. It was rereleased in England, presumably in 35mm only, in 1966 with a new narrative script.

Demidovi *see* **The Demidovs.**

The Demidovs (1983). Filmed in Sovscope 70. *Screen authors* Vladimir Arimov and Eduard Volodarskiy. *Director* Yaropolk Lokshin. *Operator* Anatoly Lesnikov. *Artist* Yuri Istratov. *Composer* Yuri Levitin. *Sound operator* M. Tomilova. *Song text* V. Bokova. ¶A Sverdlovskaya kinostudiya production. International distribution Sovexportfilm. Sovcolor. Six-track magnetic stereophonic sound. 156 minutes plus intermission. Filmed at Sverdlovskaya kinostudiya, Sverdlovsk and on location in Petrodvoretz and Leningrad, R.S.F.S.R. ¶CAST: *Nikita Demidov* Evgeni Evstigneev. *Akinfy* Vadim Spiridonov. *Evdokia* Lubov Polekhina. *With* Aleksandr Lazarev, Leonid Kuravlev, Mikhail Kozakov, Tatiana Tashkova, Lyudmila Chursina, Lidia Fedoseeva-Shukshina, Valery Zolotukhin, N.

Skorobogatov, Yu. Nazarov, M. Zimin, V. Korzun, V. Balashov, N. Merzlikin, L. Borisov, M. Bocharov, Oleg Vidov and Vsevolod Larionov. ¶A Soviet production released in Russia in 1983 as *Demidovi* in two parts running 79 minutes and 77 minutes.

Les dents du diable *see* **The Savage Innocents.**

Dersu Uzala (October 5, 1976). Filmed in Sovscope 70. *Producers* Nikolai Sizov and Yoichi Matsue. *Screen authors* Akira Kurosawa and Yuri Nagibin. *Based on the book "Dersu, okhotnik" by* Vladimir K. Arsenieva. *Director* Akira Kurosawa. *Associate directors* Teruyo Nogami and Vladimir Vasiliev. *Operators* Asakadru Nakai, Yuri Gantman and Fyodor Dobronravov. *Artist* Yuri Raksha. *Composer* Isaak Shvarts. *Production manager* Karlen Korshikov. *Sound operator* O. Burkova. *Interpreter* Lev Korshikov. ¶A Roger Corman presentation. A Mosfilm-Atelie-41 production. Released by New World Pictures by arrangement with Sovexportfilm. Sovcolor. Six-track magnetic stereophonic sound. 141 minutes plus intermission. Filmed at Mosfilm Studios, Moscow and on location in Siberia, R.S.F.S.R. ¶CAST: *Dersu Uzala* Maxim Munzuk. *Capt. Vladimir K. Arsenieva* Yuri Solomin. *Mrs. Arsenieva* Svetlana Danilichenko. *Vova Arsenieva* Dima Kortishev. *Yan Rao* Schemeikl Chokmorov. *Turtwigin* Vladimir Kremena. *With* A. Pyatkov, M. Bichkov and B. Khorulev. ¶A Soviet and Japanese coproduction released in Russia in 1976 as *Dersu Uzala* running 181 minutes plus intermission (part one: 90 minutes, part two: 91 minutes) and released in Japan on August 2, 1975, by Herald Eiga as *Dersu Usara.* First shown in the U.S. in 1975 by Sovexportfilm in order to qualify for an Academy Award as Best Foreign Language Film, which it won. New World Pictures took over national distribution in Fall 1976. Toho Company, Ltd., Japan, is usually erroneously listed as coproducer.

Derusu Usara *see* **Dersu Uzala.**

Destiny (1978). Filmed in Sovscope 70. *Screen authors* Pyotr Proskurina and Evgeny Matveev. *Based on the novel "Sudiba" by* Pyotr Prosjurina. *Director* Evgeny Matveev. *Operators* Gennady Tsekaviy and Viktor Yakushen. *Artist* Semyon Volyushok. *Composer* Evgeny Ptichkin. *Sound operator* I. Mayorov. *Verses* R. Rozdestvenskogo and V. Bokova. ¶A Mosfilm production. International distribution Sovexportfilm. Sovcolor. Six-track magnetic stereophonic sound. 213 minutes plus intermission. Filmed at Mosfilm Studios, Moscow and on location at Trubino and Smolensk, R.S.F.S.R. ¶CAST: *Zakhar Deriugin and Bulavin* Evgeny Matveev. *Evfrosinya Zinaida* Kirienko. *Manya* Olga Ostroumova. *With* Yuri Yakovlev, Valeria Zaklunnaya, Algimantas Masyulis, Vladimir Samoylov, V. Spiridonov, G. Yuatov, N. Oleynik and R. Filippov. ¶A Soviet production released in Russia in 1978 as *Sudiba* in two parts running 124 minutes and 89 minutes. See *Earthly Love.*

Detached Mission (1986). Filmed in Sovscope 70. *Screen author* Evgeny Mesyatsev. *Director* Mikhail Tumanishvili. *Operator* Boris Bondarenko. *Artists* Tatiana Lapshina and Aleksandr Myagkov. *Composer* Viktor Babushkin. *Sound operator* A. Khasin. *Song text* Mikhail Nozkin. ¶A Mosfilm production. International distribution Sovexportfilm. Sovcolor. Six-track magnetic stereophonic sound. 96 minutes. Filmed at Mosfilm Studios, Moscow, R.S.F.S.R. ¶CAST: *Shatokin* Mikhail Nozkin. *Kruglov* Aleksandr Fatyushina. *Hessalt* Arnis Litststis. *With* Sergei Nasibov, Nartai Begalin, V. Zikora, O. Golubitskiy, V. Vinogradov, S. Volkosh, B. Ogorodnikov, K. Vats, Veronika Izotova and Yanis Melderis. ¶A Soviet production released in Russia in 1986 as *Odinochnoe plavanie.*

Direktor (1971). Filmed in Sovscope 70. *Screen author* Yu. Nagibin. *Director* A. Saltikov. *Operators* G. Tsekaviy and V. Yakushev. *Artist* S. Volkov. *Composer* A. Zshpay. *Sound operator* V. Kirshenbaum. ¶A Mosfilm production. International distribution Sovexportfilm. Sovcolor. Six-track magnetic stereophonic sound. 189 minutes plus intermission. Filmed at Mosfilm Studios, Moscow, R.S.F.S.R. ¶CAST: N. Gubenko, S. Zgun, V. Sedov, B. Kudryavtsev, A. Eliseev, B. Shilovskiy, B. Zakariadze, R. Daglish, V. Berezutskaya, V. Popova, L. Ivanova and A. Krtschenkov. ¶A Soviet production released in Russia in 1971 in two parts running 93 minutes and 96 minutes.

The Dirty Dozen (June 28, 1967). Filmed in Metroscope 70. *Producer* Kenneth Hyman. *Director* Robert Aldrich. *Screenplay* Nunnally Johnson and Lukas Heller. *Based on the novel by* E.M. Nathanson. *Director of photography* Edward "Ted" Scaife. *Music* Frank DeVol. *Associate producer* Raymond Anzarut. *Camera operators* Alan McCabe and Tony Spratling. *"The Bramble Bush" music* Frank DeVol, *lyrics* Mack David, *singer* Trini Lopez. *"Einbam" music* Frank DeVol, *lyrics and singer* Sibylle Seigfried. *Art director* William E. "Bill" Hutchinson. *Special effects supervisor* Cliff Richardson. *Assistant director* Bert Batt. *Unit production manager* Julian Mackintosh. *Film editor* Michael Luciano. *Continuity* Angela Allen. *Makeup* Ernest Gasser and Walter "Wally" Schneiderman. *Sound recording* Franklin E. Milton, Claude Hitchcock and Harry Warren Tetrick. *Sound editor* John Poyner. *Main title design* Walter Blake. *Technical advisers* Historical Research Unit (Eugene and Andrew Mollo). *Special effects assistant* John Richardson. *Assistant film editor* Frank J. Urioste. ¶A Kenneth Hyman production. A MKH Productions, Ltd.–MGM British Studios, Ltd.–Metro-Goldwyn-Mayer, Inc. picture. Released by Metro-Goldwyn-Mayer. Metrocolor. Westrex six-track magnetic stereophonic sound. 149 minutes plus intermission. Filmed at MGM British Studios and on location in England and completed at MGM Studios. MPAA rating: SMA. ¶CAST: *Maj. Reisman* Lee Marvin. *Gen. Worden* Ernest Borgnine. *Joseph Wladislaw* Charles Bronson. *Robert Jefferson* Jim Brown. *Victor Franko* John Cassavetes. *Sgt. Bowren* Richard Jaeckel. *Maj. Max Armbruster* George Kennedy. *Pedro Jiminez* Trini Lopez. *Capt. Stuart Kinder* Ralph Meeker. *Col. Everett Dasher-Breed* Robert Ryan. *Archer Maggott* Telly Savalas. *Vernon Pinkley* Donald Sutherland. *Samson Posey* Clint Walker. *Gen. Denton* Robert Webber. *Milo Vladek* Tom Busby. *Glenn Gilpen* Ben Carruthers. *Roscoe Lever* Stuart Cooper. *Cpl. Morgan* Robert Phillips. *Seth Sawyer* Colin Maitland. *Tassos Bravos* Al Mancini. *Pvt. Arthur James Gardner* George Ronbicek. *Worden's aide* Thick Wilson.

German whore Dora Reisser. ¶A British and American coproduction. The first feature shot in spherical 35mm widescreen (1.75 × 1 hard matte) and blown up to 70mm widescreen. Lee Marvin replaced John Wayne who dropped out before any footage was shot. Al Mancini's character is named after Aldrich's son-in-law. Sequels were *The Dirty Dozen: Next Mission* (NBC-TV, 1985) with Marvin, Borgnine and Jaeckel reprising their roles and *The Dirty Dozen: The Deadly Mission* (NBC-TV, 1987) with Borgnine repeating and Telly Savalas replacing Marvin. The reader is warned to be very careful in purchasing the home video version of *The Dirty Dozen*. This was originally released for home sales in a 137-minute version mastered from the reedited television edition, and many video shops still have this shorter tape in stock. The recently reissued video cassettes are the complete roadshow version, sans the intermission, with the full, directional stereophonic sound.

Discovery (1986). Filmed in Showscan. Produced for the British Columbia government. Special photographic effects Entertainment Effects Group. Released by Showscan Film Corporation. Eastman Color. Six-track magnetic Dolby Stereo. 16 minutes. Originally made for the British Columbia Pavilion at EXPO 86 in Vancouver.

Dnevnie zvezdi *see* **Daytime Stars.**

Dochki-materi *see* **Mothers and Daughters.**

Dr. Coppelius (December 25, 1968) Filmed in Superpanorama 70. *Executive producer* Victor Torruella. *Producers* Frank J. Hale and Ted Kneeland. *Director* Ted Kneeland. *Story, screenplay and choreography* Jo Anna Kneeland and Ted Kneeland. *Spanish version* Victor Torruella. *Based on the ballet "Coppelia" by* Clement Philibert Leo Delibes and Charles Louis Etienner Nuitter. *Director of photography* Cecillo Paniagua. *Conductor of Gran Teatro del Liceo Orquesta de Barcelona* Adrian Sardo. *Film editors* Jo Anna Kneeland, Ted Kneeland and Juan Serra. *Additional film editing* Raymond Guy Wilson. *Associate producer* James Udell. *Set designer* Gil Parrondo. *Design supervisor* Florence Lustig.

Decorator Robert Carpio. *Costumes* Robert Carpio and Marian Ribas. *Production manager* Ramon Plana. *Assistant choreographer* Richard Dodd. *Sound* Jose Mane. *Animation* Estudios Filman. *Backgrounds* Jose Maria Gimeno. *Artistic consultant* Alicia Markova. *Negative* Eastman Color. ¶A Frank J. Hale presentation. A Jo Anna and Ted Kneeland production. A Copelia S.A.-Coppelia Company picture. Released by Childhood Productions. Color by Fotofilm Madrid. Westrex six-track magnetic stereophonic sound. 97 minutes. Filmed in Spain. ¶CAST: *Dr. Coppelius* Walter Slezak. *Swanhilda and Coppelia* Claudia Corday. *Franz* Caj Selling. *Brigitta* Eileen Elliott. *Spanish doll* Carmen Rojos. *Roman doll* Veronica Kusmin. *Hungarian dance champion* Milorad Miskovitch. *Mayor* Luis Prendes. *Swanhilda's friends* Marcia Bellak, Kathy Jo Brown, Clara Cravey, Kathleen Garrison, Christine Holter and Sharon Kapner. *Voice of the bull* Terry-Thomas. *With* Helens Villarroya, Gran Teatro del Liceo Ballat, International Cine Ballet, Aurelio Bogado and Xenia Petrowsky. ¶Advertised as *Dr.?? Coppelius!!* A Spanish and American coproduction released in Spain in December 1966 as *El fantastico mundo del Dr. Coppelius.* Rereleased in the U.S. in 1976 by Bronston Releasing Company as *The Mysterious House of Dr. C.,* running 88 minutes and advertised in MCS-70. Cincom was credited as production company.

Doctor Dolittle (December 19, 1967). Filmed in Todd-AO. *Producer* Arthur P. Jacobs. *Associate producer* Mort Abrahams. *Director* Richard Fleischer. *Screenplay, music and lyrics* Leslie Bricusse. *Based on the "Doctor Dolittle" stories by* Hugh Lofting. *Costume designer* Ray Aghayan. *Music scorers and conductors* Lionel Newman and Alexander Courage. *Dances and musical numbers stager* Herbert Ross. *Director of photography* Robert Surtees. *Art direction* Jack Martin Smith and Ed Graves. *Production designer* Mario Chiari. *Set decorations* Walter M. Scott and Stuart A. Reiss. *Special photographic effects* L.B. Abbott, Art Cruickshank, Emil Kosa, Jr. and Howard Lydecker. *Music editor* Robert Mayer. *Vocal supervision* Ian Fraser. *Film editors* Samuel E. Beetley and Marjorie Fowler. *Unit production managers* William

Eckhardt and Jack Stubbs. *Assistant director* Richard Lang. *Sound supervision* James Corcoran and Murray Spivack. *Sound* Douglas O. Williams, John Myers and Bernard Freericks. *Makeup* Ben Nye, Marvin Westmore and Thomas Burman. *Hair styles* Margaret Donovan. *Todd-AO developers* American Optical Co. and Magna Theatre Corp. *Animals and birds suppliers and trainers* Jungleland, Thousand Oaks, Ca. *Titles* Pacific Title & Art Studio. *Title designer* Don Record. *Unit publicist* Harold Stern. *Camera operator* George Nogle. *Assistant cameraman* Emilio Calori. *Script supervisor* June Santantonio. *Wardrobe supervision* Wesley Sherrard. *Property master* Allen Levine. *Gaffer* Earl Gilbert. *Key grip* Lou Pazelli. *Animal and bird supervisor* Roy Kabat. *Marine coordinator* Fred Zendar. *Art department modeller* Constantin Morros. ¶An Arthur P. Jacobs production. An APJAC Productions, Inc. picture. Released by 20th Century-Fox. Color by De Luxe. Westrex six-track magnetic stereophonic sound. 152 minutes plus overture, intermission and exit music. Filmed at 20th Century-Fox Studios and on location in Castle Combe, England and Santa Lucia, British West Indies. ¶CAST: *Dr. John Dolittle* Rex Harrison. *Emma Fairfax* Samantha Eggar. *Matthew Mugg* Anthony Newley. *Albert Blossom* Richard Attenborough. *Gen. Bellowes* Peter Bull. *Mrs. Blossom* Muriel Landers. *Tommy Stubbins* William Dix. *Willie Shakespeare* Geoffrey Holder. *Sarah Dolittle* Portia Nelson. *Lady Petherington* Norma Varden.

The Doctor's Apprentice (1984). Filmed in Sovscope 70. *Screen author* Ipai Kuznetsov. *Director* Boris Ritsarev. *Operator* A. Kirillov. *Artist* Nikolai Terekhov. *Composer* Mikhail Tariverdiev. *Sound operator* S. Gurin. *Song text* V. Korostileva. *Still photo* Arkady Goltsin and Sergei Ivanov. ¶A kinostudiya im. M. Gorikogo production. International distribution Sovexportfilm. Sovcolor. Six-track magnetic stereophonic sound. 88 minutes. Filmed at kinostudiya im. M. Gorikogo, Gorki, R.S.F.S.R. ¶CAST: Oleg Kazancheev, Oleg Golubitskiy, Natalia Vavilova, Ariadna Shengelaya, Mikhail Gluzskiy, Mikhail Manukov, V. Iliichev, Yu. Chekulaev and Svetlana Orlova. ¶A Soviet production released in Russia in 1984 as *Uchenik lekarya.*

Dolgi nashi *see* **Our Debts.**

La donna dei Faraoini *see* **The Pharaohs' Woman.**

Doverie *see* **Confidence.**

The Dream Is Alive (June 1985). Filmed in IMAX and OMNIMAX. *Producer and director* Graeme Ferguson. *Photography* fourteen NASA astronauts. *Camera trainer* John Shaw. *Sound effects* Benjamin P. Burtt, Jr. *Post production* Lucasfilm, Ltd. *Distribution manager* Rod Shannon. ¶A Threshold Corporation, a division of Imax Systems Corporation, production. Released by Imax Systems Corporation. Eastman Color. Six-track magnetic Dolby Stereo. 37 minutes. ¶CAST: Astronauts Judith Resnick, Kathy Sullivan, et al. Narrator Walter Cronkite. ¶A Canadian production originally made for the Smithsonian Institution's National Air and Space Museum and Lockheed Corporation. Filmed in space by fourteen crew members of three shuttle flights.

Dugi brodovi *see* **The Long Ships.**

Duma o Britanke (1970). Filmed in Sovscope 70. *Screen author* Yu. Parkhomenko. *Based on the play "Duma o Britanke" by* Yu. Yanovskogo. *Director* N. Vinfgranovskiy. *Operator* V. Davidov. *Artist* A. Dobroleza. *Composer* P. Mayboroda. *Sound operator* G. Parakhanikov. ¶A Kievskaya kinostudiya im. A.P. Dovzenko production. International distribution Sovexportfilm. Sovcolor. Six-track magnetic stereophonic sound. 83 minutes. Filmed at Kievskaya kinostudiya im. A.P. Dovzenko, Kiev, Ukrainian S.S.R. ¶CAST: V. Miroshnichenko, N. Olyalin, N. Polishuk, K. Stepankov, N. Vinfgranovskiy, K. Ershov, V. Fushchich, V. Yanpavlis, V. Iliyashenko and V. Polishuk. ¶A Soviet production released in Russia in 1970.

Duma o Kovpake (1978). Filmed in Sovscope 70. *Screen authors* I. Bolgarin and V. Smirnov. *Director* T. Levchuk. *Operator* Z. Pluchik. *Artist* V. Agranov. *Composer* I. Shamo. *Sound operator* Yu. Rikov. *Song text* D. Lutsenko. ¶A Kievskaya kinostudiya im. A.P. Dovzenko

production. International distribution Sovexportfilm. Sovcolor. Six-track magnetic stereophonic sound. Filmed at Kievskaya kinostudiya im. A.P. Dovzenko, Kiev, Ukrainian S.S.R. ¶CAST: K. Stepankov, V. Belokhvostik, Nikolai Griniko, N. Sarantsev, M. Golubovich, N. Shutiko, Z. Kapianidze, V. Antonov, M. Koshenov, N. Merzlikin, V. Plotnikov, S. Sergeychikova, Yu. Demich and N. Gvozdikova. ¶A Soviet production released in Russia in 1978 in three parts: *Nabat* running 79 minutes, *Buran* running 73 minutes and *Karpati, karpati* running time unknown.

Dusha (1982). Filmed in Sovscope 70. *Screen authors* A. Borodyanskiy and A. Stefanovich. *Director* A. Stefanovich. *Operator* V. Klimov. *Artist* A. Speshneva. *Composer* A. Zatsepin. *Music* A. Zatsepina, A. Kutikova and A. Makarevicha. *Songs* R. Rozdestvenskogo, I. Kokhanovskogo and A. Makarevicha. *Sound operators* V. Babushkin and V. Ladigin. ¶A Mosfilm production. International distribution Sovexportfilm. Sovcolor. Six-track magnetic stereophonic sound. 117 minutes. Filmed at Mosfilm Studios, Moscow, R.S.F.S.R. ¶CAST: S. Rotaru, R. Bikov, M. Boyarskiy, V. Spesivtsev, I. Kalnini, L. Obolenskiy and O. Melik-Pashaev. ¶A Soviet production released in Russia in 1982.

Dve versii odnogo stolknoveniya *see* **Two Versions of a Collision.**

Earthly Love (1975). Filmed in Sovscope 70. *Screen authors* Pyotr Proskurina, Valentin Chernikh and Evgeni Matveev. *Based on the story "Sudiba" by* Pyotr Proskurina. *Director* Evgeni Matveev. *Operators* Gennady Tsekaviy and Viktor Yakushev. *Artist* Semion Valyushok. *Composer* Evgeny Ptichkin. *Sound operator* I. Mayorov. *Song text* R. Rozdestvenskogo. ¶A Mosfilm production. International distribution Sovexportfilm. Sovcolor. Six-track magnetic stereophonic sound. 113 minutes. Filmed at Mosfilm Studios, R.S.F.S.R. ¶CAST: *Zakhar Deriugin* Evgeni Matveev. *Evfrosinya* Zinaida Kirienko. *Maria* Olga Ostroumova. *With* V. Samoylov, V. Khohryakov, Yuri Yakovlev, Valeria Zaklunnaya, M. Krepkogorskaya and V. Nosik. ¶A Soviet production released in

Russia in 1975 as *Lyubovi zemnaya.* See also *Destiny.*

Earthquake (November 1974). Presented in Sensurround. *Executive producers* Jennings Lang, Robert Wise and Bernard Donnenfeld. *Producer and director* Mark Robson. *Writers* George Fox and Mario Puzo. *Director of photography* Philip Lathrop. *Special visual effects* Albert J. Whitlock. *Special photography* Clifford Stine. *Special effects* Frank Brendel, Jack McMasters and Lou Ami. *Production designer* Alexander Golitzen. *Art director* E. Preston Ames. *Set decorations* Frank McKelvy. *Costume designer* Burton Miller. *Costume supervisor* Sheila Mason. *Sound supervisor* Richard Stumpf. *Sound* Melvin M. Metcalfe Sr., Ronald Pierce and Robert Leonard. *Sound consultant* Waldon O. Watson. *Miniatures* Glen Robinson. *Matte photography* Roswell A. Hoffman. *Film editor* Dorothy Spencer. *Assistant film editor* Ed Broussard. *Sound editor* Jerry Christian. *Postproduction supervisor* Phil Scott. *Unit production manager* Wallace Worsley. *First Assistant director* Fred R. Simpson. *Second assistant director* Murray Schwartz. *Production coordinator* Esther Powell. *Music* John Williams. *Concertmaster* Israel Baker. *French horn soloist* Vince De Rosa. *Piano soloists* Ralph Greirson and Claire Fisher. *Drums soloist* Shelley Manne. *Percussion soloist* Jerry Williams. *Assistant art directors* Fred Tuch and Leslie Thomas. *Property master* Eddie Keys. *Unit publicist* Booker McClay. *Stunt coordinator* John Daheim. *Makeup* Nick Marcellino. *Cosmetics* Cinematigue. *Titles and optical effects* Universal Title. *Sensurround develpers* MCA, Inc. and RCA. ¶A Jennings Lang presentation. A Mark Robson production. A Red Lion Productions, Inc. picture. From The Filmmakers Group, Inc. Released by Universal Pictures. Panavision 70. Technicolor. Westrex and RCA Photophone recording. Three-track MagOptical stereophonic sound. 122 minutes. Filmed at Universal City Studios and on location in Southern California. ¶CAST: *Stewart Graff* Charlton Heston. *Remy Royce Graff* Ava Gardner. *Sgt. Lew Slade* George Kennedy. *Sam Royce* Lorne Greene. *Denise Marshall* Genevieve Bujold. *Miles Quade* Richard Roundtree. *Jody* Marjoe Gortner. *Dr. Willis Stockle*

Barry Sullivan. *Dr. Vance* Lloyd Nolan. *Rosa Amici* Victoria Principal. *Drunk in bar* Walter Matuschanskayasky [Matthau]. *Barbara* Monica Lewis. *Sal Amici* Gabriel Dell. *Ofr. Emilio Chavez* Pedro Armendariz, Jr. *Bill Cameron* Lloyd Gough. *Mayor Lewis* John Randolph. *Walter Russell* Kip Niven. *Assistant dam caretaker* Scott Hylands. *Corry Marshall* Tiger Williams. *Dr. Harvey Johnson* Donald Moffat. *Buck* Jesse Vint. *Ralph* Alan Vint. *Hank* Lionel Johnston. *Carl Leeds* John Elerick. *Chief inspector* John S. Ragin. *Army colonel* George Murdock. *Sid* Donald Mantooth. *Sandy* Michael Richardon. *First pool player* Alex A. Brown. *Dr. Frank Ames* Bob Cunningham. *Burly pool player* H.B. Haggerty. *Brawny foreman* John Dennis. *Dam caretaker* Gene Dynarski. *Farmer Griggs* Bob Gravage. *Technician* Dave Morick. *Laura* Inez Pedroza. *Las Vegas agent* Tim Herbert. *Police captain* Lonnie Chapman. *Seismologist* Ernest Harada. *Second pool player* Charles Picerni. *Third pool player* Dean Smith. *Laborer* Don Wilbanks. *First worker* Hal Bokar. *Loudspeaker voice* Stuart Nisbet. *Army private* Ric Carrott. *Studio guard* Sandy Ward. *Second worker* Clint Young. *Housewife* Frances Osborne. *Checkout cashier* Kitty Vallacher. *Ambulance driver* William Whitaker. *First policeman* Dave Cass. *Second policeman* George Sawaya. *Nurse* Shannon Christie. *First man* Bruce M. Fisher. *Second man* Jerry Hardin. *Third man* Karl Lukas. *First woman* Diana Herbert. *Second woman* Vivian Brown. *Boy with radio* Josh Albee. *Third policeman* Bernie Stettner. *Fourth policeman* Bert Kramer. *Third radio voice* Keith A. Walker. *Fourth radio voice* Ron Fortner. *Fourth man* Forrest Wood. *Stranger* Bill Burton. *Boy on Honda* Reb Brown. *Bartender* Fred Scheiwiller. *Helicopter pilot* James W. Gavin. *Secretary* Patty Elder. *Cook* Ken Endoso. *Diver* Richard Warlock. *Graduate student* Jim Nickerson. *Sports car driver* Robert Ferro. *Fifth policeman* Grant Owens. *Ofr. Scott* Ian Bruce. *Office worker* Gene Collier. *Stunts* Rick Arnold, Lorraine Baptist, Craig Baxley, Marilyn Beer, Mary R. Ross, Buff Brady, Robert Bralver, Fred Brookfield, Tony Brubaker, Jerry Brutsche, Polly Burson, Hank Calia, Joe Canutt, Mickey Caruso, William Catching, Royden Clark, Erick Cord, Paula Crist,

Richard Crockett, Evelyne Cuffee, Howard Curtis, John Daheim, Jadie David, Carol DeMent, Dottie Catching, Paula Dell, Dick Dial, Nick Dimitri, Bennie Dobbins, Gary Downey, Larry Duran, Bud Ekins, Patty Elder, Ken Endoso, Andy Epper, Gary Epper, Jeannie Epper, Stephanie Epper, Pam Estrem, Robert Ferro, Lila Finn, Donna Lee Garrett, Ralph Garrett, Mickey Gilbert, Orwin Harvey, Robert D. Herron, Eddie Hice, Fred Hice, Larry Holt, Thomas J. Huff, Victor Hunsberger, Jr., Loren Janes, Edward Jauregui, Julie Ann Johnson, Louise Johnson, Kevin Johnston, Peaches Jones, Kim Kahana, Henry Kingi, William T. Lane, Gene LeBell, Julius Le Flore, Terry Leonard, Allison Logsden, Maurice Marks, Paula Martin, Denver Mattson, Troy Melton, Robert Minor, Jon Arnold Miller, Marilyn Moe, Harry Monty, Stevie Myers, Paul Nuckles, Harvey Parry, Reg Parton, Regina Parton, Barbara Perlman, Melvin Robert Porter, Byron Quisenberry, Glenn H. Randall, Jr., Ernest Robinson, Ronald Clark Ross, Audrey H. Saunders, Russell Saunders, Felix Silla, Eddie Smith, Evelyn Smith, Tom Steele, Cyndi Swan, Bob Terhune, Jack Verbois, Rock Walker, Bud Walls, Marvin Walters, Richard Washington, Jesse Wayne, Jack J. Wilson and Brayton W. Yerkes. ¶The first film in Sensurround. Released in the U.S. in 35mm only. Working title: *Earthquake 1980*. Reedited and expanded for television with new footage (shot spherical and in no way matching the scanned 'scope original) and televised in some areas with an AFM stereo simulcast. Among the actors in the new footage was Debralee Scott as a newlywed. Several of the original cast appeared in the new material. There were no amended production credits but the main titles stated that Mark Robson produced and directed the theatrical version only.

Earthquake 1980 *see* **Earthquake.**

Earthwatch (1986). Filmed in Showscan. Produced and released by Showscan Film Corporation. Eastman Color. Six-track magnetic Dolby Stereo. 7 minutes. Originally made for the Canadian Pavilion at EXPO 86 in Vancouver.

1819 God *see* **Leo Tolstoy's War and Peace.**

Eleven Hopefuls (1975). Filmed in Sovscope 70. *Screen authors* Valentin Ezhov and Viktor Sadovsky. *Director* Viktor Sadovsky. *Operator* Vladimir Kovsel. *Artist* Boris Burmistrov. *Composer* Vladlen Christiakov. ¶A Lenfilm production. International distribution Sovexportfilm. Sovcolor. Six-track magnetic stereophonic sound. 9 reels. Filmed at Lenfilm Studios, Leningrad, R.S.F.S.R. ¶CAST: *Sports commentator* Naum Demarskiy. *Viktor Parkhomenko* Nikolai Sentimenko. *Aleksandr Sokolovskiy* Igor Dobriakov. *With* Anatoly Papanov, Lubov Virolainen, Yury Demich and Aleksandr Goloborodo. ¶A Soviet production released in Russia in 1975 as *Odinnadtsat nadezkhd.*

Emeliyan Pugachev *see* **Yemelyan Pugachov.**

The Enchanted Desna (1964). Filmed in Sovscope 70. *Executive producer* L. Kanareykina. *Director and producer* Yulia Solntseva. *Story and screen author* Aleksandr P. Dovzenko. *Chief operator* Alexei Temerin. *Chief artist* Aleksandr Borisov. *Composer* Gavriil Popov. *Sound operator* A. Bulgakov. *Crew director* L. Basov. ¶A Mosfilm-Kievskaya kinostudiya im. A.P. Dovzenko production. International distribution Sovexportfilm. Released by Mosfilm. Sovcolor. Six-track magnetic stereophonic sound. 81 minutes. Filmed at Mosfilm Studios, Moscow and kinostudiya im. A.P. Dovzenko, Kiev, Ukrainian S.S.R. ¶CAST: *Alexander Mykolayovich* Evgeni Samoylov. *Sashko* Vova Goncharov. *Father* Evkhen Bondarenko. *Mother* Zinaida Kirienko. *Semen* Vasyl Orlovsky. *Samiylo* Khrykhoriy Serdyuk. *Platon* Boris Andreev. *With* I. Pereverzev, I. Marks and D. Orlovskiy. ¶A Soviet production released in Russia in December 1964 as *Zacharovannaya Desna.*

The Enchanted Mirror (July 1959). Filmed in Kinopanorama. Presented in Cinemiracle. *Screen authors and directors* Leonid Kristi and V. Komissarzkhevskiy. *Operators* Vladimir Vorontsov, Ilya Gutman, Anatoliy Koloshin and Sergey Medynskiy. *Sound operator* I. Gunger. *Cartoon director* I. Aksenchuk. *Cartoon operators* A. Astafiev and N. Klimova. *Cartoon artists* L. Milchin, I. Shvarzman,

A. Vinokurov and T. Sazonova. ¶A Ministry of Culture of the U.S.S.R. presentation. A Tsentraliniy dokumentaliniy film studiya production. Released by Sovexportfilm. Sovcolor. Nine-track magnetic Kinopanorama Sound. 90 minutes. Filmed in Siberia, Bratskiy and Obsk Sea, R.S.F.S.R., China and Brussels, Belgium. ¶CAST: *"Swan Lake" excerpts* Galina Ulanova. *Recital* Oleinichenko. *Dance ensemble* Piatnitzky Choir. *Opera performers* Peking Classical Choir Company. ¶A Soviet production released in Russia in 1958 as *Volshevnoye zerkalo* running 140 minutes. Also known as *Magic Mirror*. Presumably the nine-channel sound was patched into Cinemiracle's seven-channel playback format. This contains the first animation in the Cinerama process. Excerpts were later incorporated into *Cinerama's Russian Adventure* (q.v.).

Energy (1975). Filmed in IMAX. *Producer and director* Len Casey. *Photographers* Don Wilder, David Douglas and Robert Ryan. ¶Released by Imax Systems Corporation. Eastman Color. Six-track magnetic stereophonic sound. 24 minutes. This Canadian production was originally made for Ontario Place.

Ercole alla conquista di Atlantide *see* **Hercules and the Captive Women.**

The Eruption of Mount St. Helens (1980). Filmed in OMNIMAX. *Writer, producer and director* George Casey. *Photographer* James Neihouse. ¶Produced and released by Graphic Films Corporation. Eastman Color. Six-track magnetic stereophonic sound. 21 minutes.

Escape from Fort Bravo (January 22, 1954). Filmed in Spherical Panavision. *Executive producer* Dore Schary. *Producer* Nicholas Nayfack. *Director* John Sturges. *Screenplay* Frank Fenton. *Story* Philip Rock and Michael Pate. *Director of photography* Robert L. Surtees. *Color consultant* Alvord Eiseman. *Art directors* Cedric Gibbons and Malcolm Brown. *Film editor* George Boemler. *Set decorators* Edwin B. Willis and Ralph S. Hurst. *Special effects* A. Arnold Gillespie and Warren Newcombe. *Women's costume designer* Helen Rose. *Hair styles* Sydney Guilaroff. *Makeup creator* William Tut-

tle. *Music* Jeff Alexander. *Recording supervisor* Douglas Shearer. *Assistant director* Arvid L. Griffen. *Songs "Yellow Stripes"* Stan Jones *and "Soothe My Lonely Heart"* Jeff Alexander. ¶A Loew's, Inc. production. Released by Metro-Goldwyn-Mayer. Ansco Color. Western Electric Movietone recording. 98 minutes. Filmed on location in Chatsworth, California and Arizona. ¶CAST: *Capt. Roper* William Holden. *Carla Forrester* Eleanor Parker. *Capt. John Marsh* John Forsythe. *Campbell* William Demarest. *Cabot Young* William Campbell. *Alice Owens* Polly Bergen. *Lt. Beecher* Richard Anderson. *Col. Owens* Carl Benton Reid. *Watson* Howard McNear. *Chavez* Alex Montoya. *Dr. Miller* Forrest Lewis. *Jones* Fred Graham. *Symore* William Newell. *Kiowa* Frank Matts. *Eilota* Charles Stevens. *Sims* Michael Dugan. *Girl in bar* Valerie Vernon. *Bartender* Phil Rich. *Sgt. Compton* Glenn Strange. *Chaplain* Harry Cheshire. *Girl* Eloise Hardt. *Confederate lieutenant* Richard P. Beedle. ¶The first feature made with Panavision spherical lenses. Filmed in MGM's Variscope, framed for 1.75×1 cropping. This was not in Perspecta Stereophonic Sound.

An Evening with the Royal Ballet. *see* **Le corsaire.**

Exodus (March 27, 1960). Filmed in Super Panavision 70. *Producer and director* Otto Preminger. *Screenplay* Dalton Trumbo and Leon Uris. *Based on the novel by* Leon Uris. *Music* Ernest Gold. *Art director* Richard Day. *Associate art director* William E. Hutchinson. *Director of photography* Sam Leavitt. *Film editor* Louis R. Loeffler. *Camera operator* Ernest Day. *Electrical supervisor* James Almand. *Key grip* Morris Rosen. *Makeup* George Lane. *Hairdressing* A.G. Scott. *Wardrobe* Joseph King, May Walding and Margo Slater. *Property master* Robert Goodstein. *Sound* Paddy Cunningham, John Cox, Red Law and Fred Hynes. *Music editor* Leon Birnbaum. *Sound effects editor* Winston Ryder. *Special effects* Cliff Richardon. *Script supervisor* Angela Martelli. *Set dressing* Dario Simoni. *Costume coordinator* Hope Bryce. *Miss Saint's clothes designer* Rudi Gernreich. *General manager* Martin C. Schute. *Production manager* Eva Monley.

OTTO PREMINGER PRESENTS

EXODUS

PAUL NEWMAN EVA MARIE SAINT
RALPH RICHARDSON LEE J. COBB
PETER LAWFORD SAL MINEO -
JOHN DEREK GREGORY RATOFF
HUGH GRIFFITH DAVID OPATOSHU
ALEXANDRA STEWART MARIUS GORING
FELIX AYLMER MICHAEL WAGER
JILL HAWORTH NEW PANAVISION 70 TECHNICOLOR®

a United Artists release

An extremely simple prerelease ad for Exodus *(1960). New Panavision 70 would be renamed Super Panavision 70 before this film went into release. To our knowledge this logo never appeared on any other publicity material even though all prerelease press information used the trade name. Panavision 70, as it was screen-billed, would shortly become the servicemark for features shot in 35mm anamorphic Panavision and blown up to spherical 70mm wide screen. Advertising billing was to credit* Super Panavision *if the engagement was not in 70mm.*

Assistant production managers Mati Raz, Ivan Lengyel and Lionel Lober. *Special effects assistant* John Richardon. *Production secretary* Noreen Hipwell. *Assistants to the producer* Max Slater and Thomas C. Ryan. *Speech consultant* Simon R. Mitchneck. *Technical advisers* Ilan Hartuv, Anan Safadi, Col. Gershon Rivlin and Maj. Gen. Francis Rome. *First assistant director* Gerry O'Hara. *Assistant directors* Otto Plaschkes, Yoel Silberg, Larry Frisch and Christopher Trumbo. *Assistant art director* Arnon Adar. *Construction manager* Peter Dukelow. *Title designer* Saul Bass. *Unit publicist* Thomas C. Ryan. *Still photographers* Gjon Mili, Stephen Colhoun, Leo Fuchs, Burt Glinn, Louis Goldman and Alexander Paal. *Location liaison* Meyer Weisgal. *Production assistant* Nat Rudich. *Rerecording* Shepperton Studios and Todd-AO. ¶An Otto Preminger presentation. A Carlyle Alpina, S.A. production. Released by United Artists. Technicolor. Westrex six-track magnetic stereophonic sound. 213 minutes plus intermission. Filmed on location in Nazareth, Kafr Kana, Jerusalem, Atlit, Caesarea, Acre and Haifa, Israel and Nicosia and Famagusta, Cyprus. ¶CAST: *Ari Ben Canaan* Paul Newman. *Kitty Fremont* Eva Marie Saint. *Gen. Sutherland* Ralph Richardson. *Maj. Caldwell* Peter Lawford. *Barak Ben Canaan* Lee J. Cobb. *Dov Landau* Sal Mineo. *Taha* John Derek. *Mandria* Hugh Griffith. *Lakavitch* Gregory Ratoff. *Dr. Lieberman* Felix Aylmer. *Akiva* David Opatoshu. *Karen* Jill Haworth. *Von Storch* Marius Goring. *Jordana* Alexandra Stewart. *David* Michael Wager. *Mordekai* Martin Benson. *Reuben* Paul Stevens. *Sarah* Betty Walker. *Dr. Odenheim* Martin Miller. *Sergeant* Victor Maddern. *Yaov* George Maharis. *Hank* John Crawford. *Proprietor* Samuel Segal. *Uzi* Dahn Ben Amotz. *Colonel* Ralph Truman. *Dr. Clement* Peter Madden. *Avidan* Joseph Furst. *Driver* Paul Stassino. *Lt. O'Hara* Marc Burns. *Mrs. Hirshberg* Esther Reichstadt. *Mrs. Frankel* Zeporah Peled. *Novak* Philo Hauser. *Burly man* Paul Smith. ¶Screen credits billed Panavision 70; prerelease advertising credited New Panavision 70; and final advertising claimed Super Panavision 70.

The Exploding Plastic Inevitable *see* **The Velvet Underground and Nico.**

Express on Fire (1982). Filmed in Sovscope 70. *Screen author* Vsevolod Ivanov. *Director* Andrei Malyukov. *Operator* Yuri Gantman. *Artist* T. Lakshina. *Composer* M. Minkov. *Sound operator* M. Bronshteyn. *Song text* O. Lukiyanovoy. ¶A Mosfilm production. International distribution Sovexportfilm. Sovcolor. Six-track magnetic stereophonic sound. 83 minutes. Filmed at Mosfilm Studios, Moscow and on location in North Caucasus, R.S.F.S.R. ¶CAST: *Clown* Lev Durov. *Animal trainer* Algimantas Masyulis. *Officer cadet* Aleksandr Rishchenkov. *With* Elena Mayorova, Aleksandr Fatyushin, P. Gaudinish, Marina Shimanskaya, Irina Pechernikova, R. Rizakov and G. Malinov. ¶A Soviet production released in Russia in 1982 as *34-y skoriy.*

Faces of Japan (1984). Filmed in IMAX. *Producers* Ray Salo and Averill Kronick. *Writer and director* Perry Schwartz. ¶A Filmmakers, Inc. production. Released by FilmMax Releasing Corporation. International distribution Imax Systems Corporation. Eastman Color. Six-track magnetic Dolby Stereo. 30 minutes.

Facts of the Past Day (1981). Filmed in Sovscope 70. *Screen authors* Yuri Skop and Vladimir Basov. *Based on the novel "Tekhnika bezopasnosti" by* Yuri Skopa. *Director* Vladimir Basov. *Operator* Ilya Minikovetskiy. *Artists* Aleksandr Parkhomenko and A. Makarov. *Composer* Veniamin Basner. *Sound operator* E. Fedorov. *Song text* M. Matusovskogo. ¶A Mosfilm production. International distribution Sovexportfilm. Sovcolor. Six-track magnetic stereophonic sound. 157 minutes plus intermission. Filmed at Mosfilm Studios, Moscow, R.S.F.S.R. ¶CAST: *Ivan Mikheyev* Mikhail Uliyanov. *Ksenya Mikheyev* Lyudmila Chursina. *Grigory Gavrilov* Aleksandr Abdulov. *Nelly* Karisa Udovichenko. *Zina* Ekaterina Vasilieva. *Alexey Kryakuin* Andrey Martinov. *With* Vladislav Strzelichik, Valentina Telichkina, L. Borisov, Vladimir Basov, N. Zasukhin, V. Filippov and V. Soshaliskaya. ¶A Soviet production released in Russia in 1981 as *Fakti minuvshego dnya* in two parts running 86 minutes and 71 minutes.

Fakti minuvshego dnya *see* **Facts of the Past Day.**

The Fall of the Roman Empire (March 26, 1964). Filmed in Ultra Panavision 70. *Producer* Samuel Bronston. *Director* Anthony Mann. *Executive associate producer* Michael Waszynski. *Screenplay* Ben Barzman, Basilio Franchina and Philip Yordan. *Music composer and conductor* Dimitri Tiomkin. *Production and costume designers and set decorators* Veniero Colasanti and John Moore. *Consultant* Dr. Will Durant. *Film editor* Robert Lawrence. *Director of photography* Robert Krasker. *Associate producer* Jaime Prades. *Director of second unit operations* Andrew Marton. *Second unit director* Yakima Canutt. *Executive production manager* C.O. Erickson. *Production manager* Leon Chooluck. *Assistant director, first unit* Jose Lopez Rodero. *Assistant director, second unit* Jose Maria Ochoa. *Casting* Maude Spector. *Camera operator* John Harris. *Second unit cameraman* Cecilio Paniagua. *Title backgrounds and murals* Maciek Piotrowski. *Sound mixer* David Hildyard. *Sound rerecorder* Gordon K. McCallum. *Sound effects editor* Milton Burrow. *Music editor* Leon Birnbaum. *Assistant film editor* Magdalena Paradell. *Special effects* Alex C. Weldon. *Master of properties* Stanley Detlie. *Supervising technician* Carl Gibson. *Supervising electrician* Bruno Pasqualini. *Head of wardrobe* Gloria Mussetta. *Costume makers* Ceratelli & Peruzzi, Italy. *Makeup* Mario van Riel. *Hairdressing* Grazia de Rossi. *Continuity* Elaine Schreyeck. *Dialog coach* George Tyne. *Master of horse* Commandant Jesus Luque. *Riding coach* Count Friedrich Ledebur. *Second assistant director* Ferdinando Baldi. *Assistant operator* Andres Berenguer. *Music publisher* Leo Feist. Inc. ¶A Samuel Bronston presentation. A Bronston-Roma production. Released by Paramount Pictures. Technicolor. Westrex six-track magnetic stereophonic sound. 180 minutes plus overture and intermission. Filmed at Samuel Bronston Studios, Madrid and Studio Cinecitta, Rome and on location in Manzanares, El Real, Sierra Guadarrama, Segovia, Las Matas, Ischia and Lake Santillana, Spain. ¶CAST: *Lucilla* Sophia Loren. *Livius* Stephen Boyd. *Marcus Aurelius* Alec Guinness. *Timonides* James Mason. *Commodus* Christopher Plummer. *Verulus* Anthony Quayle. *Ballomar* John Ireland. *Sohamus* Omar Sharif. *Cleander* Mel Ferrer. *Julianus* Eric Porter *Caecina* Finlay Currie. *Polybius* Andrew Keir. *Niger* Douglas Wilmer. *Victorinus* George Murcell. *Virgilianus* Norman Wooland. *Cornelius* Michael C. Gwynn. *Marcellus* Virgilio Texera. *Claudius* Peter Damon. *Lentulus* Rafael Luis Calvo. *Helva* Lena von Martens. *Soldiers* Tap Canutt and Jack Williams. *Officer* Count Friedrich Ledebur. *Tauna* Gabriella Licudi. *Marcis* Guy Rolfe. ¶35mm general release prints were reedited to 149 minutes without an overture, intermission or exit music. 16mm nontheatrical and television prints are also 149 minutes.

Fantasia (November 13, 1940). Presented in Fantasound. *Producer* Walt Disney. *Production supervisor* Ben Sharpstein. *Story direction* Joe Grant and Dick Huemer. *Musical director* Edward H. Plumb. *Musical film editor* Stephen Csillag. *Live action cameraman* Winton C. Hoch. *Technicolor color director* Natalie Kalmus. *Recording* William E. Garity, C.O. Slyfield and John N.A. Hawkins. *Special processes* Ub Iwerks. *Process cameraman* Art Cruickshank. *Optical cameraman* Eustace Lycett. *Optical coordinator* Robert Broughton. *Assistant director* Jack Brunner. *Music editor* George Adams. *Fantasound developers* RCA Manufacturing Company in collaboration with Walt Disney Studios. *Narrator* Deems Taylor. *Conductor* Leopold Stokowski. *Musicians* The Philadelphia Orchestra. *"Ave Maria" soloist* Julietta Novis. *Mickey Mouse's voice characterization* Walt Disney. *"Dance of the Hours" live action models* Members of the Ballet Russe featuring Roman Jasinsky, Tatiana Riabouchinska and Irina Baranova. *"Night on Bald Mountain" live action model for Tchernabog* Bela Lugosi. ***Toccata and Fugue in D Minor:*** *Composer* Johann Sebastian Bach. *Director* Samuel Armstrong. *Story development* Lee Blair, Elmer Plummer and Phil Dike. *Art director* Robert Cormack. *Animators* Cy Young, Art Palmer, Daniel MacManus, George Rowley, Edwin Aardal, Joshua Meador and Cornett Wood. *Background paintings* Joe Stanley, John Hench and Nino Carbe. ***The Nutcracker Suite:*** *Composer* Peter Ilich Tchaikovsky. *Director* Samuel Armstrong. *Story development* Sylvia Moberly-Holland, Norman Wright, Albert Heath, Bianca Majolie and Graham Held. *Character designers* John Walbridge, Elmer Plummer and Ethel Kulsar. *Art directors* Robert Cormack, Al Zinnen, Curtiss D. Perkins, Arthur Byram and Bruce Bushman. *Animators* Arthur Babbitt, Les Clark, Don Lusk, Cy Young and Robert Stokes. *Background paintings* John Hench, Ethel Kulsar and Nino Carbe. *The Sorcerer's Apprentice: Composer* Paul Dukas. *Director* James Algar. *Story development* Perce Pearce and Carl Fallberg. *Art directors* Tom Codrick, Charles Philippi and Zack Schwartz. *Animation supervision* Fred Moore and Vladimir Tytla. *Animators* Les Clark, Riley Thompson, Marvin Woodward, Preston Blair, Edward Love, Ugo D'Orsi, George Rowley and Cornett Wood. *Background paintings* Claude Coats, Stan Spohn, Albert Dempster and Eric Hansen. *The Rite of Spring: Composer* Igor Stravinsky. *Directors* Bill Roberts and Paul Satterfield. *Story development and research* William Martin, Leo Thiele, Robert Sterner and John Fraser McLeish. *Art directors* McLaren Stewart, Dick Kelsey and John Hubley. *Animation supervision* Wolfgang Reitherman and Joshua Meador. *Animators* Philip Duncan, John McManus, Paul Busch, Art Palmer, Don Tobin, Edwin Aardal and Paul B. Kossoff. *Background paintings* Ed Starr, Brice Mack and Edward Levitt. *Special camera effects* Gail Papineau and Leonard Pickley. *Pastoral Symphony Composer* Ludwig van Beethoven. *Directors* Hamilton Luske, Jim Handley and Ford I. Beebe. *Story development* Otto Englander, Webb Smith, Erdman Penner, Joseph Sabo, Bill Peet and George Stallings. *Character designers* James Bodrero, John P. Miller and Lorna S. Soderstrom. *Art directors* Hugh Hennesy, Kenneth Anderson, J. Gordon Legg, Herbert Ryman, Yale Gracey and Lance Nolley. *Animation supervision* Fred Moore, Ward Kimball, Eric Larson, Arthur Babbitt, Oliver M. Johnston, Jr. and Don Towsley. *Animators* Berny Wolf, Jack Campbell, John Bradbury, James Moore, Milt Neil, Bill Justice, John Elliotte, Walt Kelly, Don Lusk, Lynn Karp, Murray McLennan, Robert W. Youngquist and Harry Hamsel. *Background paintings* Claude Coats, Ray Huffine, W. Richard Anthony, Arthur Riley, Gerald Nevius and Roy Forkum. *Dance of the Hours: Composer* Amilcare Ponchielli. *Directors*

Thornton Hee and Norman Ferguson. *Character designers* Martin Provensen, James Bodrero, Duke Russell and Earl Hurd. *Art directors* Kendall O'Connor, Harold Doughty and Ernest Nordli. *Animation supervision* Norman Ferguson. *Animators* John Lounsbery, Howard Swift, Preston Blair, Hugh Fraser, Harvey Toombs, Norman Tate, Hicks Lokey, Art Elliott, Grant Simmons, Ray Patterson and Franklin Grundeen. *Background paintings* Albert Dempster and Charles Conner. *Night on Bald Mountain and Ave Maria: Composers (respectively)* Modest Moussorgsky and Franz Schubert. *Director* Wilfred Jackson. *Story development* Campbell Grant, Arthur Heinemann and Phil Dike. *Art directors* Kay Nielsen, Terrell Stapp, Charles Payzant and Thor Putnam. *Animation supervision* Vladimir Tytla. *Animators* John McManus, William N. Shull, Robert W. Carlson, Jr., Lester Novros and Don Patterson. *Background paintings* Merle Cox, Ray Lockrem, Robert Storms and W. Richard Anthony. *Special animation effects* Joshua Meador, Miles E. Pike, John F. Reed and Daniel MacManus. *Special camera effects* Gail Papineau and Leonard Pickley. *Special lyrics for "Ave Maria"* Rachel Field. *"Ave Maria" chorus director* Charles Henderson. ¶A Walt Disney production. Released by RKO Radio Pictures. Multiplane Technicolor. RCA Photophone recording. 135 minutes including intermission. Filmed at Walt Disney Studios and the Philadelphia Academy of Music. ¶The first U.S. film in stereophonic sound. Reedited to 120 minutes, then 88 minutes. Rereleased in 1956 and 1963 in *Super*Scope and four-track Mag-Optical stereophonic sound. Rereleased in 1969 in 1.33×1 and mono sound. Reedited, rescored by Irwin Kostal, and reissued in 1984 in 1.75×1 with digitally mastered Dolby Stereo. Leopold Stokowski was dubbed for the new version. *The Rite of Spring* was released as a short with narration added to turn it into a geological documentary (of sorts).

Fantastic Invasion of Planet Earth *see* **The Bubble.**

El fantastico mundo del Dr. Coppelius *see* **Dr. Coppelius.**

Fantasy on the Love Theme (1981). Filmed in Sovscope 70. *Screen author* Aleksandr

Mariyamov *in collaboration with* Aida Manasarova. *Director* Aida Manasarova. *Operator* Genry Abramyan. *Artist* Natalia Meshkova. *Music* Stas Namina and Aleksandr Slnzukova. *Sound operator* O. Burkova. *Songs in verse* A. Pushkina, M. Tsvetaevoy, S. Kirsanova and V. Niplinga. ¶A Mosfilm production. International distribution Sovexportfilm. Sovcolor. Six-track magnetic stereophonic sound. 107 minutes. Filmed at Mosfilm Studios, Moscow and on location in Dortmund, and Leningrad, R.S.F.S.R. and Armenia, Armenian S.S.R. ¶CAST: *Alexander* Yuri Ovchinnikov. *Nastya* Irina Skobeleva. *Stepan* Amayak Akopyan. *With* Andrei Vitman and Anastasia Voznesenskaya. ¶A Soviet production released in Russia in 1981 as *Fantaziya na temu lyubvi.*

Fantaziya na temu lyubvi *see* **Fantasy on the Love Theme.**

A Farewell to St. Petersburg (1972). Filmed in Sovscope 70. *Screen author* Natoli Grebnev. *Director* Yan Frid. *Operator* Oleg Kukhovarenko. *Artist* M. Krotkin. *Composer* Vladlen Chistyakov. *Sound operator* V. Yakovlev. ¶A Lenfilm production. International distribution Sovexportfilm. Sovcolor. Six-track magnetic stereophonic sound. 97 minutes. Filmed at Lenfilm Studios, Leningrad, R.S.F.S.R. ¶CAST: Gyrt Yakovlev, Tatyana Bedova, Tatyana Pilestsaya, Vassili Merkuriev, Pavel Kadochnikov, I. Dmitriev and S. Karnovich-Balya. ¶A Soviet production released in Russia in 1972 as *Proshchanie s Peterburgom.*

Fateful Sunday (1983). Filmed in Sovscope 70. *Screen authors* Boris Medovey, Rudolf Fruktov and Anatoly Levitov. *Director* Rudolf Fruktov. *Operator* Konstantin Suponitskiy. *Artist* Boris Tsarev. *Composer* Mikhail Ziv. *Sound operator* A. Grech. *Chief trick operator* Aleksandr Barkov. ¶A Mosfilm production. International distribution Sovexportfilm. Sovcolor. Six-track magnetic stereophonic sound. 108 minutes. Filmed at Mosfilm Studios, Moscow, R.S.F.S.R. ¶CAST: Emmanuel Vitorgan, Klara Luchko, Aleksandr Belyavskiy, Sergei Martinov, Georgi Korolichuk, Ruben Simonov, Olga Kataeva, Tatiana Tashkova, Tatiana Bozok, V. Safonov, D. Netrebin, S. Balasanov and A. Yanvarev. *Stuntman* Aleksandr Mikulin. ¶A Soviet production re-

leased in Russia in 1983 as *Trevoznoe voskresenie.*

Une fete foraine *see* **Magirama.**

55 Days at Peking (May 28, 1963). Filmed in Super Technirama 70. *Producer* Samuel Bronston. *Directors* Nicholas Ray and Guy Green. *Executive associate producer* Michael Waszynski. *Screenplay* Philip Yordan, Bernard Gordon, Ben Brazman and Betty Utey Ray. *Music composer and conductor* Dimitri Tiomkin. *Director of photography* Jack Hildyard. *Set decoration, production and costume design* Veniero Colasanti and John Moore. *Director second unit operations* Andrew Marton. *Film editor* Robert Lawrence. *Associate producer* Alan Brown. *Second unit director* Noel Howard. *Executive production manager* C.O. Erickson. *Assistant director first unit* Jose Lopez Rodero. *Assistant director second unit* Jose Maria Ochoa. *Casting* Maude Spector. *Additional dialog* Robert Hamer. *Sound mixer* David Hildyard. *Sound rerecorder* Gordon K. McCallum. *Sound effects editor* Milton Burrow. *Music editor* Richard C. Harris. *Master of properties* Stanley Detlie. *Special effects* Alex C. Weldon and Jack Erickson. *Second unit cameraman* Manuel Berenguer. *Assistant to the editor* Magdalena Paradell. *Supervising technician* Carl Gibson. *Supervising electrician* Bruno Pasqualini. *Head of wardrobe* Gloria Mussetta. *Makeup* Mario van Riel. *Hairdressing* Grazia de Rossi. *Miss Gardner's hair styles* Alexandre of Paris. *Continuity* Lucie Lichtig. *Technical adviser* Col. James R. Johnson, B.S.O., O.B.E., M.C. *Title paintings* Dong Kingman. *Special photographic effects consultant* Linwood G. Dunn. *Assistant operator* Andres Berenguer. *"So Little Time" music* Dimitri Tiomkin, *lyrics* Paul Francis Webster. ¶A Samuel Bronston production. Released by Allied Artists Pictures. Technicolor. Westrex six-track magnetic stereophonic sound. 154 minutes plus overture, intermission and exit music. Filmed at Samuel Bronston Studios, Madrid, and on location in Las Matos, Spain. ¶CAST: *Maj. Matt Lewis* Charlton Heston. *Baroness Natalie Ivanoff* Ava Gardner. *Sir Arthur Robertson* David Niven. *Empress Tzu Hsi* Flora Robson. *Sgt. Harry* John Ireland. *Father de Bearn* Harry Andrews. *Gen. Jung-lu* Leo Genn. *Prince Tuan* Robert

Helpmann. *Baron Sergei Ivanoff* Kurt Kaszner. *Julliard* Philippe LeRoy. *Dr. Steinfeldt* Paul Lukas. *Lady Sarah Robertson* Elizabeth Sellars. *Garibaldi* Massimo Serato. *Maj. Bobrinski* Jacques Sernas. *Lt. Andy Marshall* Jerome Thor. *Smythe* Geoffrey Bayldon. *Capt. Hanselman* Joseph Furst. *Capt. Hoffman* Walter Gotell. *Col. Shiba* Ichizo Itami. *Clergyman* Mervyn Jones. *Spanish minister* Alfredo Mayo. *Hugo Bergmann* Martin Miller. *Mme. Baumaire* Conchita Montes. *Italian minister* Jose Nieto. *Baron von Meck* Eric Polhmann. *M. Baumaire* Aram Stephan. *Capt. Hanley* Robert Urquhart. *Teresa* Lynn Sue Moon. *Gerald* Alfred Lynch. *Dutch minister* Felix Defauce. *Austrian minister* Andre Esterhazy. *Japanese minister* Carlos Casaravilla. *Belgian minister* Fernando Sancho. *Chiang* Michael Chow. *American marine* Mitchell Kowal. *Sgt. Britten* Ex-RSM Brittain. *Amb. Maxwell* Nicholas Ray. *Orientals* Kenji Takako, Dong Kingman, Soong Ling and Andy Ho. *Americans* Stephen Young and John A. Tinn. *Englishman* John Moulder-Brown. ¶The Rank Organisation and Valoria may have been involved in the financing. Guy Green, director, and Ben Brazman, writer, were brought in to speed up shooting.

The First Cavalry Army (1984). Filmed in Sovscope 70. *Screen authors* Valentin Ezov and Vladimir Lyubomudrov. *Director* Vladimir Lyubomudrov. *Operator* Vladimir Fridkin. *Artists* Anatoly Kuznetsev and Georgi Koshelev. *Composer* Eduard Artemiev. *Sound operator* O. Zilibershteyn. ¶A Mosfilm production. International distribution Sovexportfilm. Sovcolor. Six-track magnetic stereophonic sound. 171 minutes plus intermission. Filmed at Mosfilm Studios, Moscow, R.S.F.S.R. ¶CAST: *Cmdr. Yegorov* Vesvolod Larinov. *Kliment Voroshilov* Evgeny Zarikov. *With* Vadim Spiridonov, A. Vanin, G. Martinyuk, A. Ermakov, A. Potapov, V. Prikhodiko, Natalia Arinbasarova, M. Kokshenov, Elena Proklova, A. Tabakov, S. Prokhanov and Elena Drapeko. ¶A Soviet production released in Russia in 1984 as *Pervaya konnaya* in two parts, 85 and 86 minutes.

The Flaming Bulge *see* **Liberation.**

Flight (1971). Filmed in Sovscope 70. *Screen authors and directors* Aleksandr Alov and Vladimir Naumov. *Based on the play "Beg" and the novel "The White Guard" by* Mikhail A. Bulgakov. *Operator* Levan Paatashvili. *Artist* Aleksandr Parkhomenko. *Composer* Nikolai Karetnikov. *Sound operator* R. Kazaryan. ¶A Mosfilm production. International distribution Sovexportfilm. Sovcolor. Six-track magnetic stereophonic sound. 246 minutes plus intermission. Filmed at Mosfilm Studios, Moscow, R.S.F.S.R. ¶CAST: *Serafima Korzukhina* Savelieva. *Gen. Khludov* Vladislav Dvorzetskiy. *Sergei Golubkov* Alexei Batalov. *Gen. Charnota* Mikhail Uliyanov. *Viceminister Korzukhin* Evgeni Evstigneev. *White Guard commander-in-chief* Bruno Freydlikh. *With* T. Tkach, R. Khomyatov, V. Zamanskiy, N. Olyalin, V. Osenev, A. Yanvarev, V. Basov, T. Loginova, O. Efremov, A. Naumov and P. Shpringfelid. ¶A Soviet production released in Russia in 1971 as *Beg* in two parts running 118 minutes and 128 minutes.

Flyers (1982). Filmed in IMAX. *Producers and directors* Dennis Earl Moore and Greg MacGillivray. *Photographer* Greg MacGillivray. *Assistant cameraman* Rod Blackie. *Production manager* Richard Gelfand. ¶A MacGillivray Freeman Films–Dennis Earl Moore Productions coproduction. Sponsored by Conoco, Inc., a DuPont company. Released by Lawrence Associates, New York City. Eastman Color. Six-track magnetic stereophonic sound. 32 minutes. Filmed in the U.S. and France. Originally made for the National Air and Space Museum in Washington, D.C. A sequel to *To Fly* (1976).

Flying Clipper—Traumreise unter weissen Segeln *see* **Mediterranean Holiday.**

The Flying Hussar Squadron (1981). Filmed in Sovscope 70. *Screen author* Sergei Ermolinskiy. *Directors* Stephen Stepanov and Nikita Khubov. *Operator* Mikhail Yakovich. *Artist* N. Emeliyanov. *Composer* Aleksandr Zurbin. *Sound operator* N. Ozornov. *Text and songs in verse* Denis Davidova. ¶A kinostudiya im. M. Gorikogo production. International distribution Sovexportfilm. Sovcolor. Six-track magnetic stereophonic sound. 209 minutes plus intermission.

Filmed at kinostudiya im. M. Gorikogo, Gorki, R.S.F.S.R. ¶CAST: *Genisov* Andrei Rostotskiy. *With* Marina Shimanskaya, Lidia Kuznetsova, Evgeny Lebedev, Yuri Richkov, Nickolai Eremenko-Mladshiy, A. Semin, A. Karin and A. Zimin. ¶A Soviet production released in Russia in 1981 as *Zskadron gusar letuchikh* in two parts running 110 minutes and 99 minutes.

The Follower (1985). Filmed in Sovscope 70. *Screen authors* Yuli Nikolin and Rodion Nakhapetov. *Director* Rodion Nakhapetov. *Operator* Pavel Lebeshev. *Artists* Aleksandr Boym and Aleksandr Makarov. *Composer* Sergei Banevich. *Sound operator* V. Bobrovskiy. ¶A Mosfilm production. International distribution Sovexportfilm. Sovcolor. Six-track magnetic stereophonic sound. 92 minutes. Filmed at Mosfilm Studios, Moscow, R.S.F.S.R. ¶CAST: *Valentin Rusov* Ivar Kalnini. *Teacher* Nikolai Griniko. *With* Pyotr Glebov, Elena Smirnova, Andrei Smirnov, Vera Glagoleva, D. Germanov, V. Strzelichik and P. Markova. ¶A Soviet production released in Russia in 1985 as *Idushchiy sledom.*

For Love of Man (1973). Filmed in Sovscope 70. *Screen author and director* Sergei Gerasimov. *Operator* Vladimir Rapoport. *Artists* P. Pashkevich and P. Galadzev. *Composer* Ilya Kataev. *Sound operator* D. Flyangolits. ¶A kinostudiya im. M. Gorikogo production. International distribution Sovexportfilm. Sovcolor. Six-track magnetic stereophonic sound. 166 minutes plus intermission. Filmed at kinostudiya im. M. Gorikogo, Gorki, R.S.F.S.R. ¶CAST: *Maria* Lyubov Virolaynev. *Dmitri* Anatoli Solonitsin. *Aleksandra Vassilyevna* Tamara Makarova. *Tanya* Zkhanna Bolotova. *Prof. Paladyev* Yuri Volkov. *With* I. Neganov, M. Zimin, Yu. Kuzimenkov, N. Eremenko, L. Sokolov, N. Egorov and A. Panchenko. ¶A Soviet production released in Russia in 1973 as *Lyubiti cheloveka* in two parts running 81 minutes and 85 minutes.

For the Sake of Life on Earth *see* **Lofty Title.**

Forget the Word Death (1980). Filmed in Sovscope 70. *Screen author* Eduard

Volodarskiy. *Director* Samvel Gasparov. *Operator* Viktor Krutin. *Artist* Mikhail Kats. *Composer* Aleksandr Zobov. *Sound operators* V. Morozeviy and Z. Segal. ¶An Odesskaya kinostudiya production. International distribution Sovexportfilm. Sovcolor. Six-track magnetic stereophonic sound. 103 minutes. Filmed at Odesskaya kinostudiya, Odessa, Ukrainian S.S.R. ¶CAST: *Polishchuk* Evgeny Leonov-Gladyshev. *Ostrovoy* Bogdan Stupka. *Girl in black* Olga Gasparova. *Kalyanov* Pyotr Merkuriev. *With* Konstantin Stepankov, Elgudya Burduli, Oleg Korchikov and Aleksandr Gorbatov. ¶A Soviet production released in Russia in 1980 as *Zabudite slovo smerti.*

14 juillet 1953 (1954). Filmed in Triptych. *Director* Abel Gance. *Assistant director* Jacques Chastel. ¶A Georges Rosetti-Gaumont-Debrie production. 22 minutes. A French production released in France on July 16, 1954. This documentary was reedited from *Napoleon.* It may also have contained new material. One source claims it was shown in Cinerama. It may have been converted to 'scope and given a general release.

Fox Follies *see* **Fox Movietone Follies of 1929.**

Fox Grandeur News (August 25, 1929). Filmed in Grandeur. *Executive producer* William Fox. *Producer* Winfield Sheehan. ¶A William Fox presentation. Produced and released by Fox Film Corp. Western Electric Movietone recording. 1 reel. Promoted with the catchline "Extra Wide Film on Extra Wide Screen."

Fox Movietone Follies of 1929 (May 29, 1929). Filmed in Grandeur. *Executive producer* William Fox. *Producer* Winfield Sheehan. *Director* David Butler. *Revue director* Marcel Silver. *Story* David Butler. *Dialog* William K. Wells. *Music conductor* Arthur Kay. *Music and lyrics* Con Conrad, Sidney Mitchell and Archie Gottler. *Photographer* Charles Van Enger. *Ensembles* Archie Gottler and Fanchon & Marco. *Film editor* Ralph Dietrich. *Chief sound engineer* Edmund H. Hansen. *Recording engineer* Joseph E. Aiken. *Costumes* Sophie Wachner and Alice O'Neill. *Color sequence* Technicolor. ¶A William Fox presentation. Produced and released by Fox Film Corp.

Western Electric Movietone recording. 80 minutes. Filmed at Fox Studios. ¶CAST: *George Shelby* John Breeden. *Lila Beaumont* Lola Lane. *Jay Darrell* De Witt Jennings. *Ann Foster* Sharon Lynn. *Al Leaton* Arthur Stone. *Swifty* Stepin Fetchit. *Martin* Warren Hymer. *Stage manager* Archie Gottler. *Orchestra leader* Arthur Kay. *Le Maire* Mario Dominici. *Song and dance numbers* Sue Carol, Lola Lane, Sharon Lynn, Dixie Lee, Melva Cornell, Paula Langlen, Carolynne Snowden, David Percy, David Rollins, Bobby Burns, Frank Richardson, Henry M. Mollandin, Frank La Mont, Stepin Fetchit and Jeanette Dancey. *Adagio dancers* Vina Gale, Arthur Springer, Helen Hunt, Charles Huff, Harriet Griffith and John Griffith. ¶Filmed simultaneously in regular 35mm. Technicolor was employed on the 35mm version only. Working title was *Fox Follies*.

Frankenstein's Bloody Terror (January 1972). Filmed in Stereo 70. *Producer and director* Henry L. Egan [Enrique L. Equiluz]. *Screenplay* Jocinto Molina [Jocinto Molina Alvarez]. *Director of photography* Emil [Emilio] Foriscot. *Music* Angelo Arten [Angel Artsaga]. *Editor* Francis [Francisco] Janmandreu. *Art director* Joseph [Jose Luis R.] Ferrer. *Negative* Eastman Color. *English language version: Director* F. Neumann. *Optical conversion* Film Effects of Hollywood. *Art design* Gary Morrow. *Titles and animation* Bob Le Bar. *Advertising design* Turner & Molin. *Pressbook and special photography* Ren Patterson. ¶A Mexpar, S.A. production. Released by Independent-International Pictures. Color by Fotofilm Madrid. *Prints by* Technicolor. 83 minutes. Filmed in Madrid, Spain. MPAA rating: PG. ¶CAST: *Count Waldemar Daninski* Paul Naschy [Jocinto Molina Alvarez]. *Countess Janice* Diana Zura [Dianik Zurakowska]. *Rudolph* Michael Manza [Manuel Manzaneque]. *Count Dracula/Dr. Mikelhov* Julian Ugarte. *Wandessa de Nadashy* Rosemarie Winters [Rossana Yanni]. *With* Anita Avery [Aurora de Alba], Joseph Morton [Jose Nieto], Carl Casara [Carlos Casaravilla], Gilbert Granger [Gualberto Galban] and Victoriano Lopez. ¶A Spanish production filmed in 1967 and released in Spain in 1969 as *La marca del hombre lobo (The Mark of the Wolfman)* in anamorphic

70mm 3D and four-track magnetic stereophonic sound running 133 minutes. Converted to 35mm over-and-under wide screen 3D and 35mm anamorphic wide screen for U.S. release. First in a long-running series starring Paul Naschy as the werewolf Count Waldemar Daninski, though this was the only entry in 70mm. The American title is meaningless. A stupid prologue was attached with a narrator informing the audience that the Frankenstein family was cursed with lycanthropism and forced to change their name to Wolfstein.

A Freedom to Move (1985). Filmed in OMNIMAX. *Executive producer* Roman Kreiter. *Producer and director* Michel Brault. ¶An Imax Systems Corporation-Nanouk Films, Inc. production. Released by Imax Systems Corporation. Eastman Color. Six-track magnetic stereophonic sound. 23 minutes. A Canadian production originally made for Expo 86 Corporation, Vancouver.

From Dawn to Dusk (1976). Filmed in Sovscope 70. *Screen authors* Lev Chumichev and Gavriil Egiazarov. *Director* Gavriil Egiazarov. *Operators* Pyotr Samunovskiy and Valery Shuvalov. *Artist* Abram Freydin. *Composer* Valentin Levashov. *Sound operator* V. Alekseeva. *Song text* B. Okudzavi and M. Platskovskogo. *Verses* I. Krasnova. ¶A Mosfilm production. International distribution Sovexportfilm. Sovcolor. Six-track magnetic sterephonic sound. 125 minutes. Filmed at Mosfilm Studios, Moscow, R.S.F.S.R. ¶CAST: *Fyodor Rozkhnov* Nikolai Pastukhov. *Pelagea Rozkhnov* Lubov Sokolova. *Valentina Rozkhnov* Evgenia Sabelinikova. *Nadezhda Rozkhnov* Zkhanna Prokhorenko. *Old farmer* Nikolai Sergeev. *General* Igor Ledogorov. *With* V. Berezutskaya, B. Tokarev, E. Shutov, A. Yanvarev, V. Malishev and B. Ivanov. ¶A Soviet production released in Russia in 1976 as *Ot zari do zari*.

A Front Behind the Front Line (1978). Filmed in Sovscope 70. *Screen author* Semion Dneprov. *Based on the novel "Mi vernemeya" by* Semion K. Tsviguna. *Director* Igor Gostev. *Operator* Aleksandr Kharitonov. *Artists* Vasily Golikov and Aleksandr Samulekin. *Composer* Veniamin Basner. *Sound operator* L. Bulgakov. *Song text* Mikhail Matusovskogo.

NEW— **SICKENING HORROR**
to make your
STOMACH TURN and FLESH CRAWL!

SEE— THE "WOLF MONSTER" attack-
LUSTING, SLASHING, RIPPING
in a Gory, Flesh-Hungry, Blood-Mad Massacre!

FREE—Burial
to anyone who dies
of FRIGHT during the
performance of this film

FRANKENSTEIN'S BLOODY TERROR

Filmed In
SUPER 70mm
CHILL-O-RAMA

ALL AGES ADMITTED-PARENTAL CAUTION SUGGESTED

IN EASTMAN COLOR Released by
INDEPENDENT-INTERNATIONAL
Pictures Corp.

PG ALL AGES ADMITTED
Parental Guidance Suggested

SEE- Victims horribly mutilated by the "Walking Dead"!

Now here is showmanship at its tacky best. This ad, with its blatant mistitle—but what a great title for the right movie!—and totally misleading art promises much that was not delivered. But while the movie didn't really have what is promoted here, it was a stylish and rather classy production, even in its mutilated U.S. version. Note the curved screen background and "process" logo. The stereoscopic version was advertised with 3D in place of Chill-O-Rama. This was never shown in the U.S. in 70mm.

¶A Mosfilm production. International distribution Sovexportfilm. Sovcolor. Six-track magnetic stereophonic sound. 218 minutes plus intermission. Filmed at Mosfilm Studios, Moscow, R.S.F.S.R. ¶CAST: *Maj. Mlynsky* Viacheslav Tikhonov. *Granddad Matvey* Oleg Zkhakov. *Yerofeich* Ivan Lapikov. *Semirenko* Evgeny Matveev. *Reisner-Afanasiev* Igor Ledogorov. *Zina* Galina Poliskikh. *Field doctor* Valeria Zaklunnaya. *Prof. Belyayev* Yuri Tolubeyev. *Father Pavel* Ivan Pereverzev. *Okrim* Evgeny Shutov. *Aliev* Tofik Mirzoyev. *With* Girt Yakovlev, Harry Pietsch, O. Zakov, V. Samoylov, V. Strzelichik, N. Polishuk, A. Lukiyanov and Hanio Hasse. ¶A Soviet production released in Russia in 1978 as *Front za liniey fronta* in two parts. See *Front v tilu vroga* and *Front Without Flanks.*

Front bez flangov *see* **Front Without Flanks.**

Front v tilu vraga (1982). Filmed in Sovscope 70. *Screen author* Semion Dneprov. *Based on the novel "Mi vernemsya" by* Semion K. Tsviguna. *Director* Igor Gostev. *Operator* Aleksandr Kharitonov. *Artists* S. Volkov, A. Voleman and Kh. Reske. *Composer* Veniamin Basner. *Sound operator* L. Bulgakov. *Song text* Mikhail Matusovskogo. ¶A Mosfilm-Barrandov-DEFA production. International distribution Sovexportfilm. Sovcolor. Six-track magnetic stereophonic sound. 169 minutes plus intermission. Filmed at Mosfilm Studios, Moscow, R.S.F.S.R. ¶CAST: Viacheslav Tikhonov, Valeria Zaklunnaya, Evgeni Matveev, Ivan Lapikov, A. Mikhaylov, V. Maynelite, Tofik Mirzaev, V. Shuligin, L. Polyakov, A. Kobaladze, V. Strelichik and R. Elinek. ¶A Soviet, Czechoslovakian and East German coproduction released in Russia in 1982 in two parts, running 96 and 73 minutes. See *A Front Behind the Front Line* and *Front Without Flanks.*

Front Without Flanks (1975). Filmed in Sovscope 70. *Screen author* Semion Dneprov. *Based on the novel "Mi vernemsya!" by* Semion Tcviguna. *Director* Igor Gostev. *Operator* Aleksandr Kharitonov. *Artist* Vasily Golikov. *Composer* Veniamiy Basner. *Sound operator* L. Bulgakov. *Song text* Mikhail Matusovskiy. *History consultant* Georgi Iverin. ¶A Mosfilm production. International distri-

bution Sovexportfilm. Sovcolor. Six-track magnetic stereophonic sound. 169 minutes plus intermission. Filmed at Mosfilm Studios, Moscow, R.S.F.S.R. ¶CAST: *Maj. Mlynsky* Viacheslav Tikhonov. *Grandfather Matvei* Oleg Zakov. *Vakulenchuk* Aleksandr Denisov. *Aliev* Tofik Mirzoev. *Klavdia* Lyudmila Poliakova. *Capt. Seriogin* Semion Morozov. *Zina* Galina Poliskikh. *With* I. Pereverzev, E. Shutov, V. Ivashchov, V. Kuznetsova, E. Leonov, S. Sukhovey and V. Safonov. ¶A Soviet production released in Russia in 1975 as *Front bez flangov* in two parts running 84 minutes and 85 minutes. See *A Front Behind the Front Line* and *Front v tilu vraga.*

Front za liniey fronta *see* **A Front Behind the Front Line.**

Galops (1928). Filmed in Triptych. *Producer and director* Abel Gance. *Photography* Jules Kruger. *Editors* Abel Gance and Marguerite Beauge. ¶A Societé Generale des Films production. 11 minutes. A French production released in France on February 10, 1928. Napoleon's escape from Corscia sequence reedited from *Napoleon.*

Garden Isle (August 1973). Filmed in OMNIMAX—A New Experience in Cinema. *Executive producer for Space Theater* Preston M. Fleet. *Writer, producer and director* Roger Tilton. *Score composer and conductor* Zoltan Rozsnyai. *Photographer* Barry O. Gordon. *Editor* Jerry T. Watkins. *Narrator* Victor Perrin. *Filming pilot* Jack Harter of Hawaii Helicopters International. *Production supervisor* Philip R. Rosenberg. *Sound system* Todd-AO. *Titles* Film Effects of Hollywood. *Production assistance* Hawaiian Airlines, Hawaii Visitors Bureau, Kauai's Paradise Pacifica and Princeville of Hanalei. *OMNIMAX development* Multiscreen Corp., Ltd. *Development engineer* William Shaw. *Projection system* Spitz Laboratories. ¶A Roger Tilton Films, Inc. production. Eastman Color. Six-track magnetic stereophonic sound. 44 minutes. The first film in OMNIMAX. Initially made for the Reuben H. Fleet Space Theater, San Diego, California.

Garmoniya (1975). Filmed in Sovscope 70. International distribution Sovexportfilm. Sovcolor Six-track magnetic stereophonic sound. A Soviet production released in Russia in 1975.

Genesis (1979). Filmed in OMNIMAX. *Producer and director* George Casey. *Photographer* Averill Townsend. ¶A Graphic Films Corp. production. Released by Science Museum of Minnesota. Eastman Color. Six-track magnetic stereophonic sound. 32 minutes. Originally made for the Science Museum of Minnesota.

The George Dunlap Tape *see* **Brainstorm.**

Geroy ee romana *see* **Her Mr. Right.**

Geroy nashego vremeni (1967). Filmed in Sovscope 70. *Screen author and director* S. Rostotskiy. *Based on "Bela," the first part of the novel "Geroy nashego vremeni," by* M. Yu. Lermontova. *Operator* V. Shumskiy. *Artist* P. Pashkevich. *Composer* K. Molchanov. *Sound operator* A. Matveenko. ¶A Kinostudiya im. M. Gorikogo production. International distribution Sovexportfilm. Sovcolor. Six-track magnetic stereophonic sound. 142 minutes. Filmed at kinostudiya im. M. Gorikogo, Gorki, R.S.F.S.R. ¶CAST: V. Ivashev, S. Berova, A. Chernov, S. Mamilov, R. Borashvili, B. Mulaev, R. Kuchmazokov and V. Rudniy. ¶A Soviet production released in Russia in 1967.

The Girl in the Red Bikini *see* **September Storm.**

God kak zizni (1966). Filmed in Sovscope 70. *Screen authors* G. Serebryakova and G. Roshali. *Based on the novel "Pohishchenie ognya" by* G. Serebryakovoy. *Director and producer* G. Roshali. *Chief operators* L. Kosmatov and A. Simonov. *Chief artist* I. Shpineli. *Composer* L. Shostakovich. *Sound operator* V. Lagutina. ¶A Mosfilm production. International distribution Sovexportfilm. Sovcolor. Six-track magnetic stereophonic sound. 155 minutes plus intermission. Filmed at Mosfilm Studios, Moscow, R.S.F.S.R. ¶CAST: I. Kvasha, A. Mironov, R. Nifontova, A. Alekseev, V. Livanov, A. Soloviev, V. Balashov, S. Kharitonova, L. Zolotukhin and A. Karapetyan. ¶A Soviet production released in Russia in 1966 in two parts running 83 minutes and 72 minutes.

Godi boribi i ispitaniy (1975). Filmed in Sovscope 70. International distribution Sovexportfilm. Sovcolor. Six-track magnetic stereophonic sound. A Soviet production released in Russia in 1975.

The Golden Gate (1970). Filmed in Sovscope 70. *Screen authors* Yulia Solntseva and V. Karen. *Based on writings by* Aleksandr P. Dovzenko. *Director and producer* Yulia Solntseva. *Operator* G. Rerberg. *Artist* Aleksandr Boym. *Composer* V. Ovchinnikov. *Sound operators* G. Korenblum and M. Leksachenko. *Editor* L. Nekhoroshev. *Voice-over* Sergei Bondarchuk. ¶A Kievskaya kinostudiya im. A.P. Dovzenko-Mosfilm production. International distribution Sovexportfilm. Sovcolor. Six-track magnetic stereophonic sound. Filmed at Kievskaya kinostudiya im. A.P. Dovzenko, Kiev, Ukrainian S.S.R. A Soviet production filmed in 1968 and released in Russia in 1970 as *Zolotye vorota.*

The Golden Head (1965). Filmed in Super Technirama 70 and Super Cinerama. Presented in 70mm Super Cinerama. *Executive producer* Coleman Thomas Conroy, Jr. *Producers* Alexander Paal and William R. Forman. *Director* Richard Thorpe. *Screenplay* Stanley Goulder and Iván Boldizsár. *Based on the novel "Nepomuk of the River" by* Roger Pilkington. *Music* Peter [Szabolcs] Fényes. *"The Golden Head" and "Things I'd Like to Say" music and lyrics* Mitch Murray; *singer* Jess Conrad. *Photography* István Hildebrand. *Art director* Béla Zeichán. *Editors* Frank Clarke, Zoltán Kerényi and Imre Fehér. *Sound* Fred Bosch and Jenó Winkler. *Unit managers* Elizabeth Woodthorpe, Jenos Gotz and Tibor Hránitzky. *Assistant director* Gyula Kormos. *Camera operator* István Nyakas. *Associate producer and production manager* András Németh. *Hungarian State Folk Ensemble artistic director* Miklos Rabay. *Hungarian State Folk Ensemble music* Miklos Kocsár. *Dubbing* Éva Márkus. *Assistant to the director* Zsolt Szabó. *Costume* Erzsébet Ujhelyi. *Chief electrician* Béla Bojkovszky. *Hungarian unit* Gyorgy Prokofiev, Ivánieza, Zsuzsa Schartnér and Nándor Fazekas. *"Swan Lake" ballet music* Sergei. *President and chairman of the board, Cinerama, Inc.* Nicolas Reisini. *President, Metro-Goldwyn-Mayer, Inc.* Robert H. O'Brien. *General manager, Hungarofilm* István Dósai. *Head,*

Budapest Studio István Nemeskürty. ¶A Cinerama, Inc., and Hungarofilm presentation. A IV Art–Group of Hunnia Film Studio and Metro-Goldwyn-Mayer, Inc., production. Technicolor. RCA six-track magnetic stereophonic sound. 115 minutes plus intermission. Filmed at Budapest Studio and on location in Budapest, Szentendre and Esztergoom and on the Danube River, Hungary and completed at Shepperton Studios, London. ¶CAST: *Basil Palmer* George Sanders. *Lionel Peck* Buddy Hackett. *Michael Stevenson* Jess Conrad. *Milly Stevenson* Lorraine Power. *British Legation Official Braithwaite* Robert Coote. *Harold Stevenson* Denis Gilmore. *Anna* Cecilia Esztergályos. *Detective Inspector Stevenson* Douglas Wilmer. *Priest* Sándor Pécsi. *Old man* Zoltán Makláry. *Hatted man* Ervin Kibédi. *Police officer* László Ungvári. *Braithwaite's silent interpreter* Piri [Piroska] Joó. *"Swan Lake" solo dancers* Zsuzsa Kun and Viktor Fülöp. *"Swan Lake" dancers* Hungarian State Opera Ballet. *Folk dancers* Hungarian State Folk Ensemble. *With* László Csákányi, Endre Csonka, László Csurka, Ilona Dajbukát, Iván Darvas, János Dömsödi, József Fonyó, Dezsó Garas, Zoltán Gera, László Joó, Géza Márki, Lajos Pándy, Gellért Raksányi, Irén Sitkey, János Zách, Zoltán Látinovico and Louis Básthy. ¶An American and Hungarian coproduction which was never released in the U.S. Released in Hungary on December 10, 1965 as *Az aranyfej,* running 102 minutes. Released in England in April 1965. Working titles were *Millie Goes to Budapest* and *Millie Goes to Budapest and Who Is Millie?* Production began in Super Cinerama but switched to Super Technirama 70. Some of the three-panel footage was converted to 70mm and appears in the film. Advertised in Technirama 70. Lorraine Power replaced Hayley Mills as Milly, George Sanders replaced Lionel Jeffries as Palmer and Richard Thorpe replaced James Hill as director. Otto Preminger appeared as an English butler in three-camera footage shot in London. Since this was an unbilled cameo and neither author has seen a print of the feature, it is unknown whether his scene was part of the retained Super Cinerama footage, or if the material was reshot in Budapest (Preminger believed it to be) or not included in the final edit.

Goluboy led (1971). Filmed in Sovscope 70. *Screen authors* Yu. Nagibin and D. Solodari. *Director* B. Sokolov. *Operator* A. Chechulin. *Artists* A. Kompaneets and A. Blek. *Composer* Ya. Vaysburd. *Sound operator* B. Livshits. ¶A Mosfilm production. International distribution Sovexportfilm. Sovcolor. Six-track magnetic stereophonic sound. 88 minutes. Filmed at Mosfilm Studios, Moscow, R.S.F.S.R. ¶CAST: A. Gorelik, N. Sedikh, M. Khellastz and A. Babienko. ¶A Soviet production released in Russia in 1971.

Gone with the Wind (December 15, 1939). Fire sequence filmed in Dual Screen. *Producer* David O. Selznick. *Directors* Victor Fleming, George Cukor, Sidney Franklin and Sam Wood. *Screenplay* Sidney Howard, Oliver H.P. Garrett, David O. Selznick, Howard Hawks, John L. Balderston, F. Scott Fitzgerald, Michael Foster, Charles MacArthur, John Lee Mahin, Edwin Justus Mayer, Donald Ogden Stewart, Jo Swerling, Sr., John van Druten, Ben Hecht, Winston Miller and Bradley Foote. *Adaptation* Sidney Howard. *Based on the novel by* Margaret Mitchell. *Production designer* William Cameron Menzies. *Art direction* Lyle Reynolds Wheeler. *Photographers* Ernest Haller, Lee Garmes, Joseph Ruttenberg, Paul Ivano and Harold Rosson. *Technicolor associate photographers* Ray Rennahan, Wilfrid M. Cline, W. Howard Greene and Winton C. Hoch. *Musical score* Max Steiner. *Assistant musical director* Louis Forbes. *Special photographic effects* John R. Cosgrove and Clarence W.D. Slifer. *Fire effects* Lee Zavitz. *Costumes designer* Walter Plunkett. *Scarlett's hats* John Frederics. *Interiors* Joseph B. Platt. *Interior decoration* Edward G. Boyle and Hobe Erwin. *Supervising film editor* Hal C. Kern, Sr. *Associate film editor* James E. Newcom. *Scenario assistant* Barbara Keon. *Recorders* Frank Maher and Lucho Navarro. *Makeup* Monty Westmore. *Makeup associates* Ben Nye, Percy Westmore, Paul Stanhope, Stanley Campbell and Eddie Allen. *Hair styling* Hazel Rogers. *Hair styling associates* Martha Acker and Sydney Guilaroff. *Dance directors* Frank Floyd and Eddie Prinz. *Historian* Wilbur G. Kurtz. *Technical advisers and dialog coaches* Susan Myrick and Will Price. *Research* Lillian K. Deighton. *Production* *manager* Raymond A. Klune. *Associate production manager* Edward W. Butcher. *Technicolor color supervision* Natalie Kalmus. *Associate Technicolor color supervisors* Henri Jaffa, Richard Mueller and Giff Chamberlain. *Assistant directors* Eric G. Stacey, Edward Woehler, Harvey Foster and Ralph J. Stosser. *Second assistant directors* Ridgeway Callow, William McGarry and G. Cecil Barker. *Production continuity* Lydia Schiller, Connie Earle, George Bernard McNutly, Jerry Wright and Naomi "Dillie" Thompson. *Mechanical engineers* R. Donald Musgrave, Oskar Jarosch and Hal Corl. *Construction superintendent* Harold Fenton. *Chief grip* Fred Williams. *In charge of wardrobe* Edward P. Lambert. *Wardrobe associates* Marian Dabney and Elmer Ellsworth. *Casting managers* Charles Richards and Fred Schuessler. *Location manager* Mason Litson. *Scenic department superintendent* Henry J. Stahl. *Electrical superintendent* Wally Oettel. *Chief electrician* James Potevin. *Properties manager* Harold Coles. *On the set properties* Arden Cripe. *Greens* Roy A. McLaughlin. *Drapes* James Forney. *Special properties maker* Ross B. Jackman. *Tara landscaper* Florence Yoch. *Still photographers* Fred Parrish and Clarence Bull. *Camera operators* Arthur E. Arling, Vincent J. Farrar and Roy Clark. *Assistant film editors* Richard L. van Enger, Ernest Leadley, Hal C. Kern, Jr. and Stuart Freye. *Subtitles* Ben Hecht. *Montage scenario* Val Lewton, Winston Miller and Wilbur G. Kurtz. *Additional music* Franz Waxman, Adolph Deutsch, Hugo Friedhofer, Heinz Roemheld and David Axt. *Intermission music arranger* Albert Hay Malotte. *Sound supervisor* Thomas T. Moulton. *Sound rerecording* Samuel Goldwyn Studios. *Rerecorders* Fred Albin, Arthur W. Johns and Gordon E. Sawyer. *Boom operator* Antonio Samamiego. *Associate historian* Annie Laurie Fuller Kurtz. *Studio teacher* Priscilla Brader. *Medical adviser* Dr. Reuben D. Chier. *Research associate* Ruth Leone. *Assistant production manager and unit manager* Eric G. Stacey. *Technicolor color technician* Paul Hill. *Technicolor color timers* Bob Riley, Dave Johnson and Gerald McKenzie. *Wardrobe assistants* Helen Henley, Mary Madden, Catherine Causey, Julie Kinetter and Basia Bassett. *Clark Gable's tailoring* Oviatt. *Clark Gable's supervising tailor*

Eddie Schmidt. *Casting associates* John Darrow and Maxwell Arnow. *Casting tests directors* George Cukor and Anthony Mann. *Camera assistants* Harry Wolf, Al Cline, Bob Carney and Howard Nelson. *Stunt coordinator* Yakima Canutt. *Set draftsman* Martin Devy, Roger C. McDonald, Chris and Kelly. *Art illustrators* Joseph McMillan Johnson, Dorothea Redman, Howard Richman, Frank Bowers and Jack Martin Smith. *Second unit directors* Chester Franklin, William Cameron Menzies, B. Reeves Eason, John R. Cosgrove, James A. Fitzpatrick and Hal C. Kern, Sr. *Second unit photographer* Glenn R. Kershner. *Publicity supervisors* Howard Dietz and Howard Strickling. *Production publicists* Russell Birdwell and Victor M. Shapiro. *Associate production publicists* John Flinn, Neville Reay and George Glass. *Production accountant* Ernest L. Scanlon. *Handwritten inserts* Jack Connors. *Scarlett's portrait* Helen Carlton. *Montage opening for act two* Peter Ballbush. *Wranglers* Tracy Lane and Art Hudkins. *Horse trainer* Dick Smith. *Production executive* Henry Ginsberg. *Executive assistant to the producer* Marcella Rabwin *Producer's secretary* Betty Baldwin. *George Cukor's secretary* Dorothy Dawson. *Production secretary* Harriet Flagg. *Legal affairs* Daniel T. O'Shea. *Production doctor* Dr. Gilbert Stone. *Chorale* The Hall Johnson Choir. *Orchestral arrangements* Hugo Friedhofer, Bernard [Bernhard] Kaun, Adolph Deutsch, Reginald H. Bassett and Maurice de Packh. *Titles* Pacific Title & Art Studio. *Story editors* Val Lewton and Katharine Brown. *Matte scene artists* John R. Cosgrove, Fitch Fulton, Albert Maxwell Simpson, Byron L. Crabbe and Jack Shaw. *Process projection equipment* George Teague. *Process projectionist* Bob Cresco. *Special photograpic effects camera assistants* William Newmann, Russell Hoover and Bert Willis. *Special photographic effects Technicolor color technicians* Rube Boyce, John Hamilton, Dave Jordan and Nelson Cordes. ¶A Selznick International Pictures, Inc. presentation in association with Metro-Goldwyn-Mayer Corporation. A David O. Selznick production. A Selznick International picture. Released by Loew's, Inc. Technicolor. Western Electric Mirrophonic recording. 225 minutes plus intermission. Filmed at Selznick International

Studios and MGM Studios and on location in Busch Gardens, Pasadena, Reuss Ranch, Chico, Lasky Mesa, Agoura, Calabasas and on the Stockton River, California and in Oregon. ¶CAST: *Capt. Rhett Butler* Clark Gable. *Scarlett O'Hara* Vivien Leigh. *Melanie Hamilton* Oliva De Havilland. *Ashley Wilkes* Leslie Howard. *Gerald O'Hara* Thomas Mitchell. *Belle Watling* Ona Munson. *Aunt Pittypat Hamilton* Laura Hope Crews. *Suellen O'Hara* Evelyn Keyes. *Careen O'Hara* Ann Rutherford. *Jonas Wilkerson* Victor Jory. *Ellen O'Hara* Barbara O'Neil. *India Wilkes* Alicia Rhett. *Mammy* Hattie Mc-Daniel. *Prissy* Butterfly McQueen. *Brent Tarleton* Frederic Crane. *Stuart Tarleton* George Reeves. *Big Sam* Everett Brown. *Elijah* Zack Williams. *Pork* Oscar Polk. *Tara house servants* D. Bufford, N. Pharr, Ruth Byers and F. Driver. *Hezekiah* Clinton C. Rosemond. *Pickaninnie* Ivy Gaines. *Jeems* Ben Carter. *John Wilkes* Howard Hickman. *Charles Hamilton* Rand Brooks. *Frank Kennedy* Carrol Nye. *Cathleen Calvert* Marcella Martin. *Gossiping lady at Twelve Oaks barbecue* Marjorie Reynolds. *Young gentleman guest at barbecue* Selmer Jackson. *Gentlemen guests at barbecue* James Bush, Bryant Washburn, Jr., Carlyle Blackwell, Jr., Edward De Butts, Ralph Brooks and Phillip Trent. *Little girl guest at barbecue* Diane Fisher. *Tony Fontaine* Tom Seidel. *Cade Calvert* David Newell. *Rafe Calvert* Eric Alden. *Twelve Oaks house servants* Sarah Whitley, Marina Cortina, Inez Hatchett and Azarene Rogers. *Lady wedding guest* Frances McCardell. *Dr. Meade* Harry Davenport, Sr. *Mrs. Meade* Leona Roberts. *Mrs. Merriweather* Jane Darwell. *Rene Picard* Albert Morin. *Maybelle Merriweather* Mary Anderson. *Fanny Elsing* Terry Shero. *Old Levi* William Mc-Clain. *One-armed soldier collecting for the cause* Harry Davenport, Jr. *Soldier at the bazaar* Revel Freeman. *Lieutenant general at the bazaar* Wayne Castle. *Officer at the bazaar* Col. Tim Longeran. *Uncle Peter* Eddie "Rochester" Anderson. *Phil Meade* Jackie Moran. *Elderly band leader outside "Examiner" office* Luke Cosgrove. *Elderly band leader's wife* Louise Carter. *Mother reading casualty list* Laura B. Treadwell. *General's wife outside "Examiner" office* Edythe Elliott. *Boy outside "Examiner" office* Tommy Kelly. *Reminiscent hospital patient* Cliff Edwards. *Sergeant at the hospital* Edward Chandler. *Hospital patient in pain* George Hackathorne. *Convalescing hospital patient* Roscoe Ates. *Hospital amputation case* Eric Linden. *Dr. Wilson* Claude King. *Dying soldier in hospital* John Arledge. *Cardplaying hospital patient* Guy Wilkerson. *Hospital nurses* Joan Drake and Jean Heker. *Colored woman at hospital* Hattie Noel. *Hospital patient calling for his mammy* Clay Mercer. *Hospital patients* James Mason and Charles "Jockey" Haefeli. *Elderly men at train depot* Josef Swickard and Emmett King. *Elderly officer at train depot* Allen Cavin. *Elderly officer's wife* Mary Carr. *Women at train depot* Nell Carlo and Raida Rae. *Rig driver during the evacuation* Hank Bell. *Townswoman during the evacuation* Marian Montgomery. *Townsman during the evacuation* Fred Behrle. *Commanding officer during the evacuation* Tom Tyler. *Colored man during the evacuation* Jesse Clark. *Medical aide at the railroad station* Frank Faylen. *Nurse at the railroad station* E. Livingston. *Mounted officer during the siege* William Bakewell. *Red Horse Saloon bartender* Lee Phelps. *Belle's girls* Shirley Chambers and Yola D'Avril. *Belle's maids* Ivy Parsons and Libby Taylor. *Baby Beauregard Wilkes* Patrick Curtis. *Looters* Emerson Treacy, Trevor Bardette and Lestor Dorr. *Young soldier who collapses during the retreat* Frank Coghlan, Jr. *Officer during the retreat* Sam Garrett. *Yankee deserter at Tara* Paul Hurst. *Colored carpetbagger* Ernest Whitman. *One-legged returning veteran* John Wallace. *Bearded returning veteran* Philip Trent. *Veterans eating at Tara* William Stelling and Al Kunde. *Hungry soldier at Tara* Louis Jean Heydt. *Beau at age 11 months* Ricky Holt. *Emmy Slattery* Isabel Jewell. *Minister* William Stark. *Beau at age 1½ years* Gary Carlson. *Yankee major at the stable-jail* Robert Elliott. *Poker-playing captains at the stable-jail* George Meeker and Wallis Clark. *Corporal at the stable-jail* Irving Bacon. *Carpetbagger orator* Adrian Morris. *Townswomen during reconstruction* Mrs. Bowker and Aline Goodwin. *Johnny Gallegher* J.M. Kerrigan. *Kennedy store clerk* Fred Warren. *Kennedy store customer* Frances Goodall. *Yankee businessman* Olin Howland. *White renegade hobo at shanty town* Yakima

Canutt. *Colored renegade hobo at shanty town* Edgar "Blue" Washington. *Capt. Tom* Ward Bond. *Tom's sergeant* Harry Strang. *Tom's troopers* Charles Hamilton, H. Nellman, Kernan Cripps and W. Kirby. *Yankee on street during reconstruction* Si Jenks. *New Orleans can-can dancers* Evelyn Harding, Jolane Reynolds and Suzanne Ridgeway. *Bonnie Blue Butler at age 6 months* Julia Ann Tuck. *Bonnie at age 2½ years* Phyllis Callow. *Bonnie at age 4 years* Cammie (Eleanore) King. *Bonnie's London nurse* Lillian Kemble-Cooper. *Rhett's stable boy* D. Goff. *Young Beau* Mickey Kuhn. *Photo doubles and standins* Fay Helm, Pearl Adams, Yakima Canutt, Earl Dobbins, Cary Harrison, Aline Goodwin, Joan Rogers, Mozelle Miller, Richard Smith, Arthur Roland Tovey, Edward L. Davenport, Anne Robinson Miller, Gwen Kenyon, Tony Beard, Jr., Lew Smith, Dorothy Fargo and Si Slocum. *Ashley's horse* Rebel. *Rhett's horse* Black Chief. *Bonnie's pony* Bobby. ¶The dual-screen fire sequence was never used. Rereleased in 1954 in Wide-Vision (reframed for 1.75×1 cropping) and Perspecta Stereophonic Sound. Rereleased in 1961 in Wide-Vision and Metrocolor. Reedited to 140 minutes and briefly issued in 1963 in Wide-Vision and Metrocolor. Blown up to 70mm 2×1 wide screen with six-track magnetic Polyphonic Sound (advertised as stereophonic sound) and roadshown in 1967. Since 1968 35mm Metrocolor prints have been available reframed for 1.85×1 projection with four-track MagOptical Polyphonic Sound. These prints, and the 70mm blowup, had new main titles. Robert Glecker died during production and his scenes were reshot with Victor Jory. Mary Young as Mrs. Elsing and Bruce Lane as Hugh Elsing were edited from scenes shot by George Cukor, and new material without them was filmed by Victor Fleming. Cut prior to release were Margaret Seddon as Grandma Tarleton, George Reed as the Tarleton family coachman and John Wray as the provost marshal. Legal action has prevented MGM and others from producing a sequel.

Gonshchiki *see* **Racers.**

Goroda i godi *see* **Cities and Years.**

Gorozane (1976). Filmed in Sovscope 70.

Screen author V. Kunin. *Director* V. Rogovoy. *Operator* I. Zarafiyan. *Artist* P. Pashchkevich. *Composer* V. Khozak. *Sound operator* S. Gurin. *Song text* V. Lebedev-Kumach, E. Agranovich and S. Gurin. ¶A Tsentraliniy studiya detskikh i yunoshevskikh filimov im. M. Gorikogo production. International distribution Sovexportfilm. Sovcolor. Six-track magnetic stereophonic sound. 108 minutes. Filmed at Tsentraliniy studiya detskikh i yunoshevskikh filimov im. M. Gorikogo, Moscow, R.S.F.S.R. ¶CAST: N. Kryuchkov, M. Kukushina, M. Basikov, A. Mironov, B. Chirkov and G. Yumatov. ¶A Soviet production released in Russia in 1976.

Goryaiy sheg *see* **Hot Snow.**

Govorit Oktyabri (1978). Filmed in Sovscope 70. International distribution Sovexportfilm. Sovcolor. Six-track magnetic stereophonic sound. A Soviet production released in Russia in 1978.

Goyya, ili Tyazkiy puti poznaniya (1972). Filmed in Sovscope 70. *Screen author* A. Vagenshteyn. *Director* K. Volif. *Operators* K. Rizov and V. Bergman. *Artists* A. Khirshmayer and V. Yurkevich. *Composers* K. Karaev and F. Karaev. *Sound operators* Z. Vanunts, G. Belenikiy and E. Yudin. ¶A Lenfilm-DEFA-Bosna-film production. International distribution Sovexportfilm. Sovcolor. Six-track magnetic stereophonic sound. 206 minutes plus intermission. Filmed at Lenfilm Studios, Leningrad, R.S.F.S.R. ¶CAST: Donates Banionis, O. Katarina, F. Dyuren, T. Lolova, R. Khoppe, M. Voyt, Z. Bush, M. Kozakov, A. Shalavskiy, Lyudmila Chursina, V. Andzaparidze, A. Shengelaya and N. Khodes. ¶A Soviet, East German and Yugoslavian coproduction released in Russia in 1972 in two parts.

Grand Canyon, The Hidden Secrets (June 16, 1984). Filmed in IMAX. *Executive producer* Richard James. *Producers* O. Douglas Memmott and Kieth Merrill. *Director* Kieth Merrill. *Photography* Reed Smoot. *Music* Bill Conti. *Production manager* Richard Gelfand. *Consultant* David Douglas. *Executive in charge of production* Venetia Stevenson. *Sound design* Randy Thom. *Post production*

Lucasfilm, Ltd. ¶A Cinema Group Venture-Investmore, Ltd. presentation. A World Cinemax production. Released by Grand Canyon Theater Venture. Eastman Color. Six-track magnetic Dolby Stereo. 36 minutes.

Grand Prix (December 21, 1966). Filmed in Super Panavision 70. Presented in 70mm Super Cinerama. *Executive producers* Kirk Douglas, James Garner and John Frankenheimer. *Producer* Edward Lewis. *Director* John Frankenheimer. *Story and screenplay* John Frankenheimer and Robert Alan Arthur. *Additional dialog* William Hanley. *Music composer and conductor* Maurice Jarre. *Director of photography* Lionel Lindon. *Production designer* Richard Sylbert. *Supervising film editor* Fredric Steinkamp. *Film editors* Henry Berman, Stewart Linder and Frank Santillo. *Assistant directors* Enrico Isacco, Roger Simons, Stephen Isovesco and Sam Itzkowitch. *Sound editor* Gordon Daniels. *Special effects* Milt Rice and Robert Bonning. *Property master* Frank Agnone. *Makeup* Giuliano Laurenti and Alfio Meniconi. *Costume selection and supervision and hair styles and makeup creation* Sydney Guilaroff. *Unit production manager* William Kaplan. *Production manager, Monaco and France* Sacha Kamenka. *Production manager, Italy* Sam Gorodisky. *Production manager, England* Peter Crowhurst. *Sound recording* Franklin Milton, Roy Charman and Harry Warren Tetrick. *Racing advisers* Phil Hill, Joakim Bonnier and Richie Ginther. *Racing camera mounts* Frick Enterprises. *Technical consultant* Carroll Shelby. *Second unit cameramen* John M. Stephens, Jean-Georges Fontenelle and Yann Le Masson. *Visual consultant and montages and titles* Saul Bass. *Unit publicist* Gordon Arnell. *Music editor* William Saracino. *Camera operator* Gian Franco Maioletti. *Second unit assistant cameraman* Otto Nemenz. *Camera maintenance* Frank Sealatti. *Key grip* Gordon Meagher. *Camera helicopter pilot* Gilbert Chomat. *Aerial camera mounts* Tyler Camera Systems. *Boom operator* George Rice. *Driving instructors* Carroll Shelby, Bob Bondurant, Jim Tuminus and Jim Russell. *Chief auto mechanic* Jim Russell. *Special equipment* Alan Gordon Enterprises, Motorola, Irving Jacobson Engineering Co. and Bell Toptex. *Racing sequences filmed with the cooperation of* Assocation Sportive de l'Automobile Club d'Auvergne "Circuit de Montagne d'Auvergne"; Association Sportive de l'Automobile Club de l'Quest "24 Heures du Mans"; Automobile Club di Palermo (Sicily) "Targa Florio"; Brands Hatch Circuit Ltd.; British Racing Drivers' Club (Silverstone); Royal Automobile Club "British Grand Prix"; Comite d'Organisation du Grand Prix de Monaco "XXIVme Grand Prix de Monaco 1966"; Koninklijke Nederlandsche Automobiel Club in co-operation with Nederlandse Autorensport Vereniging (Circuit Van Zandvoort) "The Dutch Grand Prix 1966"; Royal Automobile Club de Belgique (Circuit de Francorchamps) "Grand Prix de Belgique 1966"; and Watkins Glen Grand Prix Corp. "United States Grand Prix." ¶A Douglas & Lewis production. A Joel Productions, Inc.-John Frankenheimer Productions-Cherokee Productions picture. A John Frankenheimer film. Released by Metro-Goldwyn-Mayer. Metrocolor. Westrex six-track magnetic stereophonic sound. 179 minutes plus overture and intermission. Filmed on location in the U.S., England, Italy, Monaco, France, Sicily, Holland and Belgium. ¶CAST: *Pete Aron* James Garner. *Louise Frederickson* Eva Marie Saint. *Jean-Pierre Sarti* Yves Montand. *Izo Yamura* Toshiro Mifune. *Scott Stoddard* Brian Bedford. *Pat Stoddard* Jessica Walter. *Nino Barlini* Antonio Sabato. *Lisa* Francoise Hardy. *Agostini Manetta* Adolfo Celi. *Hugo Simon* Claude Dauphin. *Guido* Enzo Fiermonte. *Monique Delvaux Sarti* Genevieve Page. *Jeff Jordan* Jack Watson. *Wallace Bennett* Donald O'Brien. *Father of killed boys* Jean Michaud. *Monte Carlo surgeon* Albert Remy. *Mrs. Stoddard* Rachel Kempson. *Mr. Stoddard* Ralph Michael. *Sportscasters* Alan Fordney, Anthony Marsh and Tommy Franklin. *Tim Randolph* Phil Hill. *Bob Turner* Graham Hill. *Journalist* Bernard Cahier. *Douglas McClendon* Bruce McLaren. *John Hogarth* Richie Ginther. *Mrs. Randolph* Evan Evans [Frankenheimer]. *Victor* Bernard Chier. *Dave* John Bryson. *Claude* Arthur Howard. *American boy* Alain Gerard. *Monza doctor* Tiziano Feroldi. *Rafael* Gilberto Mazzi. *BBC interviewer* Raymond Baxter. *Ferrari official* Eugenio Dragoni. *Japanese interpreter* Maasaki Asukai. *Press photographer* Peter

Ustinov. *Racers* Joakim Bonnier, Bob Bondurant, Ludovico Scariotti, Jack Brabham, Dan Gurney, Lorenzo Bandini, Mike Spence, Dennis Hulme, Joseph Siffert, Chris Amon, Michael Parkes, Jochen Rindt, Juan Manuel Fangio, Guiseppe "Nino" Farina, Louis "The Debonair" Chiron, Jean Pierre Beltoise, Ken Costello, Skip Scott, Jo Schlesser, Jim Russell, Peter Rovson, Paul Frere, Tony Lanfranchi, Guy Ligier, Andre Pillette and Teddy Pillette. *Stunt drivers* Carey Loftin, Tom Bamford and Max Balchowski. *Voice characterization for Toshiro Mifune* Paul Frees. ¶After the world premiere Mifune's dialog was looped by Paul Frees.

The Great Barrier Reef (1980). Filmed in OMNIMAX. *Writer, producer and director* George Casey. *Photographers* Mal Wolfe, J. Barry Herron, Stephen Craig and Soames Summerhays. ¶A Graphic Films Corp. production. Released by Science Museum of Minnesota. Eastman Color. Six-track magnetic stereophonic sound. 47 minutes. Filmed in Australia's Great Barrier Reef. ¶CAST: Ron Taylor, Valerie Taylor and Soames Summerhays. ¶Made for the Science Museum of Minnesota.

Great Is My Country (July 1959). Filmed in Kinopanorama. Presented in Cinemiracle. *Director and producer* Roman Karmen. *Codirector* Z. Feldman. *Commentary authors* E. Dolmatovskiy and Roman Karmen. *Operators* Sergey Medynskiy, V. Ryklin and Georgiy Kholniy. *Composers* K. Molchanov and V. Khushevitskiy. *Sound operator* K. Ben-Nazarov. *Editor* M. Minaeva. ¶A Ministry of Culture of the U.S.S.R. presentation. A Tsentrnauchfilm production. Released by Sovexportfilm. Sovcolor. Nine-track magnetic Kinopanorama Sound. 90 minutes. Filmed in the R.S.F.S.R. on location in Moscow, Leningrad, Ukraine, Baken, Kuibyshev, Siberia, Mount Elbrus, Black Sea, Neva River and aboard the ship Volga. ¶NARRATORS: S. Khenkina and Ya. Adamov. ¶A Soviet production released in Russia in 1957 as *Shyrokr strana moya rodnaya....* Also known as *How Wide Is My Country.* Presumably the nine-channel sound was patched into Cinemiracle's seven-channel playback system. Excerpts incorporated into *Cinerama's Russian Adventure* (q.v.).

The Great Meadow (March 15, 1931). Filmed in Realife. *Director* Charles Barbin. *Screenplay* Charles Barbin and Edith Ellis. *Based on the novel by* Elizabeth Maddox Roberts. *Photographers* William Daniels and Clyde de Vinna. *Film editors* George Hively and Anne Bauchens. *Recording director* Douglas Shearer. *Sound engineer* Ralph Shugart. *Art director* Cedric Gibbons. ¶Produced and released by MGM. Controlled by Loew's, Inc. Western Electric Movietone recording. 75 minutes. Filmed at MGM Studios and on location in California. ¶CAST: *Berk Jarvis* Johnny Mack Brown. *Diony Hall* Eleanor Boardman. *Elvira Jarvis* Lucille LaVerne. *Betty Hall* Anita Louise. *Evan Muir* Gavin Gordon. *Reuben Hall* Guinn "Big Boy" Williams. *Thomas Hall* Russell Simpson. *Mistress Hall* Sarah Padden. *Sally Toliver* Helen Jerome Eddy. ¶Filmed simultaneously in regular 35mm.

The Great Wall (September 1965). Filmed in Super 70 Technirama. *Producer* Masaichi Nagata. *Director* Shigeo Tanaka. *Screenplay* Fuji Yahiro. *Photography* Michio Takahashi. *Film editor* Tatsuji Nakashizu. *Music* Akira Ifukube. *Director of dubbed version* Brett Morrison. ¶A Masaichi Nagata-Marshall Naify presentation. A Daiei Motion Picture Co., Ltd. production. Released by Magna Pictures. Technicolor. Six-track magnetic stereophonic sound. 106 minutes. Filmed on location in Taiwan. ¶CAST: *Emperor Shih Huang Ti* Shintaro Katsu. *Princess Chu* Fujiko Yamamoto. *Crown Prince Tan* Ken Utsui. *Hsi Liang* Hiroshi Kawaguchi. *Chiango-nu* Ayako Wakao. *Li Hei* Kojiro Hongo. *Ching Ko* Raizo Ichikawa. *Hsu Fu* Ganjiro Nakamura. *Li Tang* Eijiro Tono. *Dowager empress* Isuzu Yamada. *Mencius* Ken Mitsuda. *With* Junko Kano, Kazuo Hasegawa and Machiko Kyo. ¶A Japanese production advertised in the U.S. in Super Technirama 70. Filmed with two modified Vista-Vision cameras. Some scenes may have been shot in Daieiscope and blown up. Released in Japan in 1962 as *Shin No Shikotei* running 160 minutes.

The Great Waltz (November 1972). Filmed in Panavision 70. Presented in 70mm Super Cinerama. *Writer, producer*

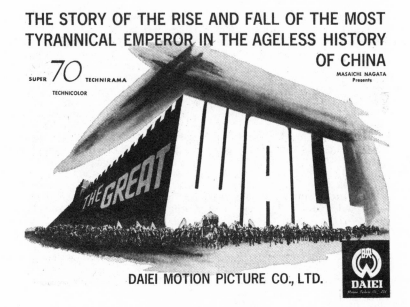

THE STORY OF THE RISE AND FALL OF THE MOST
TYRANNICAL EMPEROR IN THE AGELESS HISTORY
OF CHINA

SUPER 70 TECHNIRAMA

TECHNICOLOR

MASAICHI NAGATA
Presents

DAIEI MOTION PICTURE CO., LTD.

DAIEI

Ad for The Great Wall.

and director Andrew L. Stone. *Associate producer* Peter V. Herald. *Music* Johann Strauss, Jr., Johann Strauss, Sr., Josef Strauss and Jacques Offenbach. *Lyrics and music adaptations* Robert Craig Wright and George Forrest. *Music supervisor and conductor* Roland Shaw. *Choreographer* Onna White. *Director of photography* Davis Boulton. *Assistant director* John O'Connor. *Art director* William Albert Havenmeyer. *Editor* Ernest Walter. *Costume designers* David Walker, Emmi Minnich and Josef Wanke. *Casting director* Irene Howard. *Associate choreographer* Martin Allen. *Violin soloist* Carlos Villa. *Music coordinator* Arthur Tatler. *Dance music arranger* Ray Holder. *Sound recordist* John Aldred. *Camera operator* Kelvin Pike. *Makeup* Ernest Gasser. *Hairdresser* Alfred G. Scott. *Continuity* Trudy Von Trotha. *Re-recording* Metro-Goldwyn-Mayer, Inc. ¶An Andrew L. Stone, Inc., production. Released by Metro-Goldwyn-Mayer. Metrocolor. Westrex six-track magnetic stereophonic sound. 135 minutes plus intermission. Filmed on location in Vienna and Salzburg, Austria. ¶CAST: *Johann Strauss, Jr.* Horst Bucholz. *Jetty Treffz* Mary Costa. *Baron Tedesco* Rossano

Brazzi. *Johann Strauss, Sr.* Nigel Patrick. *Anna Strauss* Yvonne Mitchell. *Josef Strauss* James Faulkner. *Lili Weyl* Vicki Woolf. *Emilie Trampusch* Susan Robinson. *Karl Frederick Hirsch* George Howe. *Donmayer* Lauri Lupino Lane. *Karl Haslinger* Michael Tellering. *Karl Treffz* William Parker. *Theresa Strauss* Ingrid Wayland. *Olga* Lorna Nathan. *Louise* Hermione Farthingale. *Caroline Strauss* Elizabeth Muthsam. *Josef Weyl* Franz Aigner. *Havemeyer* Helmut Janatsch. *Johann Herbeck* Marty Allen. *Jacques Offenbach* Dominique Weber. *Max Steiner* Guido Wieland. *Princess Pauline Metternich* Paola Loew. *Emperor Franz Josef* Prince Johannes Schonburg-Hartenstein. *Choir* The Mike Sammes Singers. *Narration singer* Kenneth McKellar. ¶A remake, this time as a musical, of MGM's 1938 biography of Johann Stauss, Jr. While this was officially the last film licensed as a Cinerama presentation, it was shot in 35mm and blown up to 70mm, and was not actually produced with the huge curved screen in mind. (*The Last Valley* was technically the last 70mm Super Cinerama–intended production.) This film was released in the U.S. in 70mm but not exhibited in Super Cinerama. It was presented in London under the Cinerama logo, the last film known to have been so exhibited or presented.

The Greatest Story Ever Told (February 15, 1965). Filmed in Ultra Panavision 70. Presented in 70mm Super Cinerama. *Producer and director* George Stevens. *Executive producer* Frank I. Davis. *Associate producers* George Stevens, Jr. and Antonio Vellani. *Music composer and conductor* Alfred Newman. *Screenplay* James Lee Barrett and George Stevens; *in creative association with* Carl Sandburg. *Based on The Old Testament, The New Testament, other ancient writings, the book "The Greatest Story Ever Told" by* Fulton Oursler; *and the radio series "The Greatest Story Ever Told" by* Fulton Oursler and Henry Denker. *Sets creator* David Hall. *Art directors* Richard Day and William J. Creber. *Costume designer* Vittorio Nino Novarese. *Assistant costume designer* Marjorie O. Best. *Directors of photography* William C. Mellor and Loyal C. Griggs. *Special color consultant* Eliot Elisofon. *Choral supervision* Ken Darby. *Set decoration* Paul Ray Moyer, Fred M. MacLean and Norman Rockett. *Makeup creator* Del Armstrong. *Assistant makeup creator* Keester Sweeney. *Hair styles* Carmen Dirigo. *Property master* Samuel Gordon. *Construction supervisor* Jack Tait. *Second unit directors* Richard Talmadge and William Hale. *Assistant directors* Ridgeway Callow and John Veitch. *Supervising film editor* Harold F. Kress. *Film editors* W. Argyle Nelson, Jr. and Frank O'Neill. *Special visual effects* Joseph McMillan Johnson, Clarence W.D. Slifer, Robert R. Hoag, A. Arnold Gillespie and Matthew Yuricich. *Recording supervisors* Franklin E. Milton and William Steinkamp. *Sound* Charles Wallace. *Production projectionist* Charles MacLeod. *Research supervisor* Tony van Renterghem. *Script supervisor* John Dutton. *Dialog director* Bob Busch. *Casting* Lynn Stalmaster. *Production managers* Nathan E. Barragar and Eric G. Stacey. *Production staff* Thomas J. Andre, Raymònd Gosnell, Jr., Lee William Lukather and Saul Wurtzel. *Wardrobe* Jack Martell. *Stunt coordinator* Henry Wills. *Additional direction* David Lean and Jean Negulesco. *Orchestration* Leo Shuken and Jack Hayes. *Special music* Ovadia Tuvia. *Special music adaptation* Frederick Steiner and Hugo Friedhofer. *Music producer* Alan Douglas. *"Messiah"* George Frederick Handel. *Aerial sequences* Paul Mantz and Frank Tallman. *Second assistant director* Wendell Franklin. *Assistant film editor* Hal Ashby. *Special contact lenses* Dr. Morton K. Greenspoon. *Titles* Maury Nemoy. *Cinerama technical adviser* Peter Gibbons. *Camera operator* Irving Rosenberg. *Assistant cameraman* Charles Termini. *Rerecording* Metro-Goldwyn-Mayer Studios. ¶A George Stevens Productions, Inc. picture. Released by United Artists. Technicolor. Westrex six-track magnetic stereophonic sound. 197 minutes plus overture and intermission (totalling 221 minutes). Filmed at Metro-Goldwyn-Mayer Studios and Desilu Studios and on location in Glen Canyon, Utah, and Wahweap, Arizona. ¶CAST: *Jesus Christ* Max Von Sydow. *James the Younger* Michael Anderson, Jr. *Veronica* Carroll Baker. *Martha of Bethany* Ina Balin. *Angel guarding Christ's tomb* Pat Boone. *Sorak* Victor Buono. *Barabbas* Richard Conte. *Mary Magdalene* Joanna Dunham. *Herod Antipas* Jose Ferrer. *Bar Amand* Van Heflin. *John the Baptist* Charlton Heston. *Caiaphas* Martin Landau. *Claudia* Angela Lansbury. *Mary of Bethany* Janet Margolin. *Judas Iscariot* David McCallum. *Matthew* Roddy McDowall. *Mary the Mother* Dorothy McGuire. *Uriah* Sal Mineo. *Shemiah* Nehemiah Persoff. *The Dark Hermit* Donald Pleasence. *Simon of Cyrene* Sidney Poitier. *Herod the Great* Claude Rains. *Simon-Peter* Gary Raymond. *Pontius Pilate* Telly Savalas. *Nicodemus* Joseph Schildkraut. *Questor* Paul Stewart. *Centurion at crucifixion* John Wayne. *Woman who is healed* Shelley Winters. *Old Aram* Ed Wynn. *Salome's silhouette dancers* Members of the Inbal Dance Theatre of Israel. *Joseph the Carpenter* Robert Loggia. *Simon the Zealot* Robert Blake. *Andrew* Burt Brinckerhoff. *John* John Considine. *Thaddaeus* Jamie Farr. *Philip* David Hedison. *Nathanael* Peter Mann. *Thomas* Tom Reese. *James the Elder* David Sheiner. *Lazarus* Michael Tolan. *Pilate's aide* Johnny Seven. *Gen. Varus* Harold J. Stone. *Emissary* Robert Busch. *Alexander* John Crawford. *Scribe* Russell Johnson. *Speaker of Capernaum* John Lupton. *Joseph of Arimathaea* Abraham Sofaer. *Theophilus* Chet Stratton. *Annas* Ron Whelan. *Aben* John

The
GEORGE STEVENS
Production

THE
GREATEST
STORY
EVER
TOLD

Presented in
CINERAMA

Released by
UNITED ARTISTS

MAX VON SYDOW • MICHAEL ANDERSON, JR. • CARROLL BAKER • INA BALIN • PAT BOONE • VICTOR BUONO • RICHARD CONTE • JOANNA DUNHAM • JOSE FERRER • VAN HEFLIN
CHARLTON HESTON • MARTIN LANDAU • ANGELA LANSBURY • JANET MARGOLIN • DAVID McCALLUM • RODDY McDOWALL • DOROTHY McGUIRE • SAL MINEO • NEHEMIAH PERSOFF
DONALD PLEASENCE • SIDNEY POITIER • CLAUDE RAINS • GARY RAYMOND • TELLY SAVALAS • JOSEPH SCHILDKRAUT • PAUL STEWART • JOHN WAYNE • SHELLEY WINTERS • ED WYNN
with MEMBERS OF THE INBAL DANCE THEATRE OF ISRAEL • Screenplay by JAMES LEE BARRETT and GEORGE STEVENS • Produced and directed by GEORGE STEVENS
In creative association with CARL SANDBURG • Music ALFRED NEWMAN • Filmed in ULTRA PANAVISION® • TECHNICOLOR®

An unaltered ad for The Greatest Story Ever Told. *George Stevens had the Cinerama logo removed from all advertising material and replaced it with the process name in the same style type as the other credits. ("Cinerama" appeared on all publicity material the same size as "United Artists.") Stevens carried his soberness further by not having the usual press hype issued and by having the souvenir program book completely devoid of production information and bios. He did allow the publication of a cast list and general production credits, though in somewhat shorter length than the actual screen credits.*

Abbott. *Lancer captain* Rodolfo Acosta. *Herod's commander* Michael Ansara. *Chuza* Philip Coolidge. *Philip* Dal Jenkins. *Archelaus* Joe Perry. *Herodias* Marian Seldes. *Tormentor* Frank De Kova. *Dumah* Joseph Sirola. *Melchior* Cyril Delevanti. *Balthazar* Mark Lenard. *Caspar* Frank Silvera. *Jacob* Gilbert Perkins. *Dismas* Richard Bakalyan. *Focas* Marc Cavell. *Weeping woman* Renata Vanni. *Simon-Peter's second accuser* John Pickard. *Woman behind railings* Celia Lousky. *Rabble rouser* Mickey Simpson. *Men* Frank Richards, Harry Wilson and Jim Boles. *Woman* Dorothy Neumann.

Lancer Henry Wills. ¶THE PROGRAM: *Overture; main title, Jesus of Nazareth; A Prophecy; A Voice in the Wilderness; Come Unto Me; The Great Journey; A Time of Wonders; intermission; entr'acte; There Shall Come a Time to Enter; A New Commandment; The Hour Has Come; Into Thy Hands; The Triumph of The Spirit.* ¶Premiered at 238 minutes. Stevens' first version was 260 minutes but United Artists demanded it be reedited. After the premiere they demanded further cuts. 35mm general release prints were 197 minutes plus overture and intermission. A mutilated 35mm version running 127 minutes was also released, made by physically cutting the 197-minute prints. Rereleased running 141 minutes in 35mm and 16mm, which unfortunately is the only version currently available for theatrical exhibition. Restored to 197 minutes for video cassette sales. Originally announced for production in May 1955 by 20th Century-Fox to be filmed in CinemaScope 55. Postponed until 1962 when production was set to begin in Todd-AO. After the failure of *Cleopatra* the project was sold to United Artists. Shooting began in Super Cinerama, then switched to Ultra Panavision 70. None of the three-panel footage was used. David Lean and Jean Negulesco took over direction during George Stevens' illness. Alfred Newman left before completing the music, and final scoring was handled by Frederick Steiner and Hugo Friedhofer.

The Green Carnation *see* **The Trials of Oscar Wilde.**

Greystoke *see* **Greystoke the Legend of Tarzan Lord of the Apes.**

Greystoke the Legend of Tarzan Lord of the Apes (March 1984). Filmed in Super Techniscope. *Producers* Hugh Hudson and Stanley S. Canter. *Director* Hugh Hudson. *Screenplay* P.H. Vazak [Robert Towne] and Michael Austin. *Based on the novel "Tarzan of the Apes" by* Edgar Rice Burroughs. *Photographer* John Alcott. *Original music composer and conductor* John Scott. *Additional music* Sir Edward Elgar, Boccherini and D'Albert; *musical director* John Warrack; *conductor* Norman DelMar; *performers* The Royal Philharmonic Orchestra. *Costume designer* John Mollo. *Special visual effects* Albert J. Whitlock. *Special makeup effects and primate costume design and creation* Rick Baker. *Production designer* Stuart Craig. *Film editor* Anne V. Coates. *Associate producer* Garth Thomas. *Supervising art director* Simon Holland. *Art director* Norman Dorme. *Set decorator* Ann Mollo. *Andie MacDowell's costume designer* Shirley Russell. *Sound recordist* Ivan Sharrock. *First assistant directors* Ray Corbett and Simon Channing-Williams. *Second unit director of photography* Egil Woxholt. *Primate choreography* Peter Elliott. *Primate consultant* Roger Fouts, Ph.D. *Casting* Patsy Pollock. *Chief rere-cording mixer* Gordon K. McCallum. *Animal consultant* Jimmy Chipperfield. *Chief production accountant* Ron Swinburne. *Construction manager* Terry Apsey. *Cameroon construction manager* Jack Carter. *Assistant art director* Clifford Robinson. *Prop master* Charles Torbett. *Standby propmen* Michael Pugh, Steven Short and Gordon Billings. *Production buyer* Ian Giladjian. *Art department assistants* Arthur Max and Martin Hitchcock. *Camera operator* Douglas O'Neons. *Focus pullers* Michael Connor and Ronald Anscombe. *Clapper-loaders* Paul Kenward and Jeremy Jones. *Second unit camera operator* Ken Withers. *Camera maintenance* Norman Godden. *Camera grip* Ray Hall. *Second unit camera grip* John Flemming. *Video operator* Don Brown. *Boom operators* Ken Weston and Don Banks. *Sound assistant* Richard Daniel. *Production manager* Simon Bosanquet. *Cameroon unit production manager* Frank Ernst. *Cameroon production coordinator* Marie-Therese Boiche. *Script supervisor* Maggie Unsworth. *Cameroon location manager* Peter Kohn. *Scotland location manager* Bernard Hanson. *England location manager* William Lang. *Second assistant directors* Michael Zimbrich, Kiernon Phipps and Paul Tivers. *Second unit assistant director* Lee Cleary. *Production secretary* Mary Richards. *Producers' assistant* Laura Grumitt. *Unit nurse* John Brookes. *Assistant location manager* Christopher Knowles. *Chief makeup artist* Paul Engelen. *Makeup artist* Peter Frampton. *Chief hairdresser* Barry Richardson. *Hairdresser* Joan Hills. *Wardrobe supervisor* Nicolas Ede. *Costume maker* David Garrett. *Wardrobe assistants* Michael Jeffrey, Kenny Crouch and Catherine Halloran. *Special assistants to Rick Baker* Doug Beswick, Greg Cannon, Gunnar Ferdinandsen, Tom Hestor, Steve Johnson, Shawn McEnore and Elaine Baker. *Primate wardrobe supervisor* Diana Moseley. *Chief primate effects technician* Rodger Shaw. *First assistant film editor* Patrick Moore. *Dubbing editors* Les Wiggins and Roy Baker. *Dialog editor* Archie Ludski. *Effects editors* Jack Knight and Terry Busby. *Rerecording mixers* Graham V. Hartstone and Nicolas Le Messurier. *Second assistant film editors* Bill Parnell, Pat Gilbert, Alan Corder, Jean Sheffield, Robert Hambling and Tim Arrowsmith.

Special effects supervisor Peter Hutchinson. *Chief electrician* Lou Bogue. *Production accountants* Hazel Crombie, Steve Long and Brian Harris. *Unit publicist* Susan D'Arcy. *Still photographer* Murray Close. *Body development coach* Dreas Reyneke. *Voice coach* Joan Washington. *Stunt arranger* Roy Scammell. *Horses and carriages* George Mossman. *Mobile recording engineer* Bob Auger. *Music recording producers* Brian Culverhouse and Christopher Palmer. *Title design* John Gorham. *Title photography* Optical Film Effects. *Rerecording* Pinewood Studios. *Arri 35BL cameras* Arriflex. *Lenses* Zeiss. *Film* Eastman Kodak. ¶Thanks for valuable cooperation to Paul Channon, M.P.; Marthe Dame; John Guy; Earl Hopper, Ph.D.; Solomon Tandeng Muna and family; and Brian Sparrow and Antony Steel. ¶A Hugh Hudson film. Produced and released by Warner Bros. Technicolor. Six-track magnetic Dolby Stereo. 129 minutes. Filmed at Thorn–EMI Elstree Studios, Borehamwood, England and on location in Scotland at Floors Castle (by permission of the Duke of Roxbroghe), Hatfield House (by permission of Lord Salisbury), Blenheim Palace (by permission of the Duke of Marlborough) and the Natural History Museum (by permission of the trustees), and in the Republic of Cameroon, Africa. ¶CAST: *The Sixth Earl of Greystoke* Ralph Richardson. *Capitaine Phillippe D'Arnot* Ian Holm. *Lord Esker* James Fox. *John Clayton, Jr., Tarzan Lord of the Apes* Christopher Lambert. *Miss Jane Porter* Andie MacDowell. *Lady Alice Clayton* Cheryl Campbell. *Jeffson Brown* Ian Charleson. *Maj. Jack Downing* Nigel Davenport. *Sir Hugh Belcher* Nicholas Farrell. *Lord John Clayton* Paul Geoffrey. *Capt. Billings* Richard Griffiths. *Willy* Hilton McRae. *Prince Max "Buller" Von Hesse* David Suchet. *Sir Evelyn Blount* John Wells. *Deon* Ravinder. *Tarzan at age 12* Eric Langlois. *Tarzan at age 5* Daniel Potts. *Tarzan at age 1* Peter Kyriakou. *Tarzan as a baby* Tali McGregor. *Rev. Simms* Paul Brooke. *White* Tristam Jellenbok. *Observer* Roddy Maude-Roxby. *Silverbeard* Elliott W. Cane. *Kala* Ailsa Berk. *White Eyes* John Alexander. *Droppy Eyes* Christopher Beck. *Figo* Mak Wilson. *Primates* Rona Brown, Georgia Clarke, Tessa Crockett, Frances D'Arcy, David Forman, Toh Koksum, Eugene Little, Tina Maskell, Dougie Mann, Roxy Mitchell, Martin Pallot, Deep Roy, Kiran Shah, Martin Scully, Philip Tan and George Yiasoumi. *Riding stunts* Terry Forrestal. ¶Andie MacDowell was looped by another actress because of her Southern accent. Copyright was registered to Edgar Rice Burroughs, Inc., and Warner Bros. Inc. The former was coclaimant due to their licensing agreement with Warners. David Puttnam resigned as producer during preproduction. Robert Towne had his credit pseudonymized because of rewriting. Working title was *Greystoke*. The first film in Super Techniscope.

The Gypsy Camp Goes Skyward *see* **Queen of the Gypsies.**

Hail Columbia! (1982). Filmed in IMAX and OMNIMAX. *Producers* Graeme Ferguson and Roman Kroitor. *Director and principal cinematographer* Graeme Ferguson. ¶Produced and released by Imax Systems Corporation. Eastman Color. Six-track magnetic stereophonic sound. 36 minutes. ¶CAST: Flight Commander John Young, Space Shuttle Pilot Robert Crippen and scientists, engineers and support personnel of NASA. ¶This Canadian documentary covered the first space shuttle flight.

(John Sturges') The Hallelujah Trail (June 23, 1965). Filmed in Ultra Panavision 70. Presented in 70mm Super Cinerama. *Executive producer* Walter Mirisch. *Producer and director* John Sturges. *Screenplay* John Gay. *Based on the novel by* Bill Gulick. *Music* Elmer Bernstein. *Associate producer* Robert E. Relyea. *Director of photography* Robert Surtees. *Art director* Cary Odell. *Production supervisor* Allen K. Wood. *Film editor* Ferris Webster. *Costumes* Edith Head. *Production manager* Nate H. Edwards. *Unit manager* Patrick J. Palmer. *Assistant director* Jack N. Reddish. *Sound* Robert Martin. *Properties* Joseph La Bella. *Special effects* A. Paul Pollard. *Makeup* Robert J. Schiffer, Webster Phillips and Gary Liddiard. *Hairdressing* Fae M. Smith, Maudlee MacDougal and Nadine Danks. *Wardrobe* Wesley Jeffries and Angela Alexander. *Script supervisor* John Franco. *Assistant editor* Marshall M. Borden. *Music editor* Richard Carruth. *Sound effects editors* Wayne B. Fury and Gilbert

D. Marchant. *Rerecording* Clem Portman at Samuel Goldwyn Studios. *Set decorator* Hoyle Barrett. *Casting* Lynn Stalmaster. *"The Hallelujah Trail," "Stand Up, We'll March to Denver," "Denver Free Militia" and "We Will Save" lyrics* Ernie Sheldon. *Orchestration* Leo Shuken, Jack Hayes and Frederic Steiner. *Titles* Robert McGinnis. *Maps* DePatie-Freleng Enterprises Inc. *Production executives* Harold Mirisch and Marvin Mirisch. *Camera operator* William Mendenhall. *Assistant cameramen* Bruce Surtees, David M. Walsh and Tim Vanik. *Second unit director of photography* Charles F. Wheeler. *Second unit camera operator* John M. Stephens. *Set designer* Angelo Graham. *Recordist* Bert Hallberg. *Boom operator* W.C. Smith. *Sound supervisor* Gordon E. Sawyer. *Second assistant directors* Paul Cameron, Tim Zinnemann, Fred Lemoine and Thomas J. Schmidt. *Still photographer* Jack Harris. *Dialog coach* Thom Conroy. *Construction supervisor* William Maldonado. *Gaffer* Earl Gilbert. *Choral director* Jack Halloran. *Music recording* John Norman. *Music producer* Bobby Helfer. *Music publisher* United Artists Music Co. Inc. ¶A Mirisch Corp. presentation. A Mirisch-Kappa production. Released by United Artists. Technicolor. Westrex six-track magnetic stereophonic sound. 165 minutes plus overture and intermission. Filmed at Paramount Studios and on location in Gallup, New Mexico. ¶CAST: *Col. Thadeus Gearhart* Burt Lancaster. *Cora Templeton Massingale* Lee Remick. *Capt. Paul Slater* Jim Hutton. *Louise Gearhart* Pamela Tiffin. *Oracle Jones* Donald Pleasence. *Frank Wallingham* Brian Keith. *Chief Walks-Stooped-Over* Martin Landau. *Sgt. Buell* John Anderson. *Kevin O'Flaherty* Tom Stern. *Chief Five Barrels* Robert J. Wilke. *First brother-in-law* Jerry Gatlin. *Second brother-in-law* Larry Duran. *Elks-Runner* Jim Burk. *Clayton Howell* Dub Taylor. *Rafe Pike* John McKee. *Henrietta* Helen Kleeb. *Interpreter* Noam Pitlik. *Phillips* Carl Pitti. *Brady* Bill Williams. *Carter* Marshall Reed. *Simmons* Caroll Adams. *Bandmaster* Ted Markland. *Bilkins* Buff Brady. *Horner* Bing Russell. *Simpson* Billy Benedict. *Mary Ann* Karla Most. *Loretta* Elaine Martone. *Mrs. Hasselrad* Hope Summers. *"A" Company sergeant* Carroll Henry. *Hobbs* Whit Bissell. *Denver bartender* Val Avery. *Narrator*

John Dehner. ¶Some 35mm general release prints were advertised under the title *The Whiskey Trail*. Stuntman Billy Williams was killed doing the wagon-over-the-cliff gag.

Happy Days (February 13, 1930). Filmed in Grandeur. *Executive producer* William Fox. *Producer* Winfield Sheehan. *Director* Benjamin Stoloff. *Stager* Walter Catlett. *Story* Sidney Lanfield. *Dialog* Edwin Burke. *Grandeur photographer* J.O. Taylor. *35mm photographers* Lucien Androit and John Schmitz. *Film editor* Clyde Carruth. *Art director* Jack Schulze. *Music* George Olsen and His Orchestra. *Musical direction* Howard Jackson. *Musical arrangements* Hugo Friedhofer. *Dance stager* Earl Lindsay. *Assistant directors* Ad Schaumer, Michael Farley and Lew Breslow. *Costumes* Sophie Wachner. *Chief sound engineer* Edmund H. Hansen. *Recording engineer* Samuel Waite. *"Mona," "Snake Hips" and "Crazy Feet" music and lyrics* Con Conrad, Sidney Mitchell and Archie Gottler. *"Minstrel Memories" and "I'm on a Diet of Love" music and lyrics* L. Wolfe Gilbert and Abel Baer. *"We'll Build a Little World of Our Own" and "A Toast to the Girl I Love" music and lyrics* James F. Hanley and James Brockman. *"Whispering" and "Happy Days" music and lyrics* Joseph McCarthy and James F. Hanley. *"Vic and Eddie" music and lyrics* Harry Stoddard and Marcy Klauber. ¶A William Fox presentation. Produced and released by Fox Film Corp. Western Electric Movietone recording. 86 minutes. Filmed at Fox Studios. ¶CAST: *Col. Billy Batcher* Charles E. Evans. *Margie* Marjorie White. *Dick* Richard Keene. *Jig* Stuart Erwin. *Nancy Lee* Martha Lee Sparks. *Sheriff Benton* Clifford Dempsey. *Interlocutors* George MacFarlane and James J. Corbett. *"I'm on a Diet of Love"* Marjorie White and Richard Keene. *"Minstrel Memories"* George MacFarlane. *"We'll Build a Little World of Our Own"* Janet Gaynor and Charles Farrell. *"Vic and Eddie"* Victor McLaglen and Edmund Lowe. *"Crazy Feet"* Dixie Lee. *"Snake Hips"* Sharon Lynn and Ann Pennington. *"A Toast to the Girl I Love"* J. Harold Murray. *"Mona"* Frank Richardson. *"Happy Days"* Whispering Jack Smith. *Other guest stars* Will Rogers, Warner Baxter, Frank Albertson, El Brendel, Walter

CINERAMA
BURT LANCASTER   LEE REMICK
JIM HUTTON   PAMELA TIFFIN
THE MIRISCH CORPORATION presents
JOHN STURGES' THE
HALLELUJAH
TRAIL
ALSO STARRING
DONALD PLEASENCE   BRIAN KEITH MARTIN LANDAU
Produced and Directed by JOHN STURGES Screenplay by JOHN GAY Based on the novel by BILL GULICK
Filmed in **ULTRA PANAVISION** A MIRISCH-KAPPA PICTURE Color by **TECHNICOLOR**
Released thru UNITED ARTISTS

Ad for John Sturges' The Hallelujah Trail *in which Cinerama is literally billed as one of the stars.*

Catlett, William Collier, Sr., Paul Page, Tom Patricola, David Rollins, George Olsen and His Orchestra, George Jessel, Nick Stuart, Rex Bell, Lew Brice, J. Farrell MacDonald, The Slate Brothers and Flo Bert. *Gentlemen of the choral ensemble* Jack Frost, John Westerfelt, Douglas Steade, Peter Custulovich, John Lockhart, Randall Reynolds, Carter Sexton, Leo Hanley, George Scheller, Kenneth Nordyke, Marius Langan, Ralph Demaree, Glen Alden, Frank McKee, Bob McKee, Joe Holland, Ed Rockwell, Clarence Brown, Jr., Roy Rockwood, Enrico Cuccinelli, Harry Lauder, Ted Waters, Thomas Vartian, J. Harold Reeves, Phil Kolar, Frank Heller, William Hargraves and Ted Smith. *Young ladies of the choral and dancing ensembles* Helen Mann, Mary Lansing, Beverly Royed, Joan Navarro, Catherine Navarro, Joan Christensen, Dorothy McNames, Vee Maule, Hazel Sperling, Bo Peep Karlin, Georgia Pembleton, Marbeth Wright, Miriam Hellman, Margaret La Marr, Consuelo De Los Angeles, Lee Auburn, Betty Halsey, Joyce Lorme, Myra Mason, Eileen Bannon, Theresa Allen, Pear La Valle, Barbara Le Valle, Gertrude Friedly, Dorothy Krister, Doris Baker, Melissa Ten Eyck, Kay Gordon, Betty Gordon, Jean De Parva, Joan Gaylord, Charlotte Hamill, Alice Goodsell, Gwen Keate, Virginia Joyce, Le Verne Leonard, Betty Grable, Marjorie Levoe, Pat Hanne and Estella Essex. ¶Filmed simultaneously in regular 35mm. Working title was *New Orleans Frolic.* Released with the short *Niagara Falls.*

The Headless Horseman (1973). Filmed in Sovscope 70. *Screen authors* Vladimir Vladimirov and Pavel Finn. *Based on the novel "Vsadnik bez golovi" by* Mayne Reid. *Director* Vladimir Vladimirov.

Operator Konstantin Rizov. *Composer* Nikita Bogoslovskiy. *Artists* G. Mekinyan and Ya. Rivosh. *Sound operator* T. Silaev. ¶A Lenfilm production. International distribution Sovexportfilm. Sovcolor. Six-track magnetic stereophonic sound. 125 minutes. Filmed at Lenfilm Studios, Leningrad, R.S.F.S.R. ¶CAST: *Louise Poindexter* Lyudmila Savelieva. *Maurice Gerald* Oleg Vidov. *Zeb Stump* Ivan Petrov. *Calhoun* Aarne Yukskyula. *Henry Poindexter* Aleksandr Milokostiy. *Old Poindexter* Alejandro Lugo. *Isidora Covarubio* Eslina Nunez. *Miguel Diaz* Enrique Santi-Estaban. *Pluto* Alfonso Gadinez. *Major* Rolando Diaz. *With* R.D. Reyes, P. Lesli and Yu. Mariya. ¶A Soviet production released in Russia in 1973 as *Vsadnik bez golovi*. This is a western!

Hello, Dolly! (December 16, 1969). Filmed in Todd-AO. *Producer* Ernest Lehman. *Director* Gene Kelly. *Screen writer* Ernest Lehman. *Based on the play with book by* Michael Stewart; *and music and lyrics by* Jerry Herman; *from the play "The Matchmaker" by* Thornton Wilder; *as produced on the New York stage by* David Merrick; *and directed and choreographed by* Gower Champion. *Associate producer* Roger Edens. *Dances and musical numbers stager* Michael Kidd. *Music and lyrics* Jerry Herman. *Music scorers and conductors* Lennie Hayton and Lionel Newman. *Director of photography* Harry Stradling. *Production designer* John De Cuir. *Art direction* Jack Martin Smith and Herman Blumenthal. *Costume designer* Irene Sharaff. *Set decorations* Walter M. Scott, George James Hopkins and Raphael Bretton. *Film editor* William Reynolds. *Unit production managers* Francisco Day and Richard Kobritz. *Assistant director* Paul Helmick. *Sound supervision* James Corcoran. *Sound* Murray Spivack, Vinton Vernon, Jack Solomon and Douglas O. Williams. *Assistant choreographer* Shelah Hackett. *Orchestrations* Philip J. Lang, Lennie Hayton, Joseph Lipton, Don Costa, Alexander Courage, Warren Barker, Frank Comstock and Herbert W. Spencer. *Dance arrangements* Marvin Laird. *Choral arrangements* Jack Latimer. *Music editors* Robert Mayer and Kenneth Wannberg. *Scenic artist* Lawrence C. Reehling. *Special photographic effects* L.B. Abbott

and Art Cruickshank. *Makeup supervision* Daniel Striepeke. *Makeup artists* Ed Butterworth, Richard Hamilton and Thomas Burman. *Hair styling* Edith Lindon. *Wardrobe supervision* Courtney Haslam. *Wardrobe* Ed Wynigear and Barbara Westerland. *Antique jewelry* Laurence W. Ford & Company. *Public relations* Patricia Newcomb. *Script supervisor* Mollie Kent. *Dialog coach* George Eckert. *Todd-AO developers* American Optical Co. and Magna Theatre Corp. *Second assistant director* Randell Henderson. *Trainee assistant director* Jerry Ziesmer. *Casting* Hugh Fordin. *Camera operator* Richard Johnson. *Assistant cameraman* Elmer Faubion. *Aerial photography* Nelson Tyler. *Still photographers* Gordon Parks, Ernst Haas, David Bailey, Claude Azoulay, Al St. Hilaire and Mal Bullock. *Key grip* Richard Boland. *Camera crane* Economy Crane Service Inc. *Train supplier* Lindley F. Bothwell. ¶An Ernest Lehman production. A Chenault Productions, Inc. picture. Released by 20th Century-Fox. Color by De Luxe. Westrex six-track magnetic stereophonic sound. 148 minutes with intermission and exit music. Filmed at 20th Century-Fox Studios and on location in Garrison, New York. ¶*Dolly Levi* Barbra Streisand. *Horace Vandergelder* Walter Matthau. *Cornelius Hackl* Michael Crawford. *Louis Louis* Armstrong. *Irene Molloy* Marianne McAndrew. *Minnie Fay* E.J. Peaker. *Barnaby Tucker* Danny Lockin. *Ermengarde Vandergelder* Joyce Ames. *Ambrose Kemper* Tommy Tune. *Gussie Granger* Judy Knaiz. *Rudolph Reisenweber* David Hurst. *Fritz* Fritz Feld. *Joe Richard Collier*. *Policeman in park* J. Pat O'Malley. *Mr. Jones* Sherman "Scatman" Crothers. *Mr. Cassidy* Eddie Quillan. *Rhine maiden* Lisa Todd. *Onlooking workman* Morgan Farley. *Drunk* Jimmy Cross. *Woman with groceries* Jessie Garnier. *Onlooker* Russ Kimbrough. *Keystone Kop* Hubie Kerns. *Ofr. Gogarty* Patrick O'Moore. *Pushcartmen* Michael Mark and Charles Wagenheim. *Policeman* Ralph Roberts. *Sullivan* James Chanler. *Newsvendor* Billy Benedict. *Harmonica Gardens patron* Bern Hoffman. *Vandergelder's singing laborers* James MacEachin, Sam Edwards, Ralph Montgomery, Clay Tanner, Charles Lampkin, Guy Wilkerson, Tyler McVey, Jerry James, Ken Hooker and David Ahdar. ¶35mm general release prints and 16mm nontheatrical prints ran 118 minutes with the prolog and intermission removed as well as overall reediting. Restored for television syndication and video cassette sales to original length. A remake of *The Matchmaker* (Paramount, 1958).

Her Mr. Right (1985). Filmed in Sovscope 70. *Screen authors* Yacheslav Verbin and Yuri Gorkovenko. *Based on the story "Lopushok" by* A. Kaplera. *Director* Yuri Gorkovenko. *Operator* Genri Abramyan. *Artists* Valentin Virvich. *Composer* Viktor Lebedev. *Sound operator* A. Grech. *Song text* V. Verbina. ¶A Mosfilm production. International distribution Sovexportfilm. Sovcolor. Six-track magnetic stereophonic sound. 99 minutes. Filmed at Mosfilm Studios, Moscow, R.S.F.S.R. ¶CAST: Galina Belyaeva, Vladimir Shevelbkov, N. Agapova, Anatoly Romashin, Viktor Pavlov, Mikhail Kozakov, Aleksandr Shirvinot, Rolan Bikov, V. Shakalo, Mikhail Boyarskiy, Oleg Anofriev, Z. Gerdt, I. Rizkov, I. Liepa, S. Morozov, S. Migitsko, B. Puladze and Semyon Farada. ¶A Soviet production released in Russia in 1985 as *Geroy ee romana*.

Hercule à la conquete de Atlantide *see* **Hercules and the Captive Women.**

Hercules and the Captive Women (April 15, 1963). Filmed in Super Technirama 70. *Producer* Achille Piazzi. *Director* Vittorio Cottafavi. *Screenplay* Alessandro Continenza, Vittorio Cottafavi and Duccio Tessari. *Story* Archibald Zounds, Jr. *Director of photography* Carlo Carlini. *Second unit director* Giorgio Cristallini. *Set designer* Franco Lolli. *Musical score* Gino Marinuzzi and Armando Trovajoli. *Additional music for U.S. version* Gordon Zahler. *Editor* Maurizio Lucidi. *Editor of U.S. version* Hugo Grimaldi. *Choreography* Peter van der Sloot. *Sound* Umberto Picistrelli. *Costumes* Vittorio Rossi. *Production manager* Danilo Marciani. ¶A SPA Cinematografica–Comptoir Francois du Film production. Released by Woolner Bros. Pictures. Technicolor. Westrex recording system. 93 minutes. Filmed in Italy. ¶CAST: *Hercules* Reg Park. *Antinea* Fay Spain. *Androcles* Ettore Manni. *Illus* Luciano Marin. *With* Mario Petri, Mimmo Palmara, Ivo Garrani, Mario Valdemarin, Allesandro Sperli,

Laura Altan, Enrico Mario Salerno, Salvatore Furnario, Maurizio Caffarelli, Gian Maria Volonte, Luciana Angiolillo, Nicola Sperli and Mino Doro. ¶Released in Europe in 70mm and six-track magnetic stereophonic sound. Released in the U.S. in 35mm only with mono sound and advertised in Technirama. Announced for U.S. release as *Hercules Conquers Atlantis*. An Italian and French coproduction released in Italy in August 1961 as *Ercole alla conquista di Atlantide* running 101 minutes and in France in February 1962 as *Hercule à la conquete de Atlantide* running 98 minutes.

Hercules Conquers Atlantis *see* **Hercules and the Captive Women.**

The Highwayman Rides *see* **Billy the Kid.**

Holiday in Spain (December 1961). Filmed in Todd-70. Presented in Super Cinerama. ¶A Holiday in Spain company presentation. A Michael Todd, Jr. production. Released by MT Assets· Corporation. Technicolor. Super Cinerama optical conversion by Film Effects of Hollywood. Westrex recording system. Seven-track magnetic Cinerema Sound. 102 minutes plus intermission. ¶This film was simply *Scent of Mystery* (q.v.) in a new package: reedited, retitled, optically converted to three-panel format and reissued sans Smell-O-Vision. Released in Europe in 70mm Super Cinerama. (When the film was presented on U.S. television, scratch-and-sniff cards were available for viewers who wanted to recapture some of the Smell-O-Vision effect.)

Hot Snow (1973). Filmed in Sovscope 70. *Screen authors* Yuri Bondarev, Evgeni Grigoriev and Gavriil Egiazarov. *Based on the novel "Goryaiy sheg" by* Yuri Bondareva. *Director* Gavriil Egiazarov. *Operator* Yu. Fyodor Dobronravov. *Artist* V. Golikov. *Composer* Alfred Shnitke. *Sound operator* V. Kurganskiy. ¶A Mosfilm production. International distribution Sovexportfilm. Sovcolor. Six-track magnetic stereophonic sound. 130 minutes. Filmed at Mosfilm Studios, Moscow, R.S.F.S.R. ¶CAST: *Gen. Bessonov* Georgi Zzenov. *Vesnin* Anatoli Kuznetsov. *Lt. Kuzneteov* Boris Tokarev. *Tanya*

Tamara Sidelinikova. *Lt. Drozdovski* Nikolai Eremenko. *Sgt. Ukhanov* Yuri Nazarov. *With* V. Spiridonov, A. Babadzanyan, A. Panikin, V. Grachev, K. Tirtov, M. Strelkov, A. Kavalerov, B. Beyshenaliev and I. Ledogorov. ¶A Soviet production released in Russia in 1973 as *Goryaiy sheg.*

A Hot Summer in Kabul (1983). Filmed in Sovscope 70. *Screen authors* Vadim Trunin and Asudulla Habib. *Director* Ali Khamraev. *Operator* Yu. Klimenko. *Artist* Sh. Abdusalamov. *Composer* Z. Artemiev. *Sound operators* L. Terehovskaya, M. Bronshteyn and A. Sifati. ¶A Mosfilm-Afganfilm production. International distribution Sovexportfilm. Sovcolor. Six-track magnetic stereophonic sound. 86 minutes. Filmed at Afghanfilm Studios, Kabul and on location in Afghanistan. ¶CAST: O. Zakov, N. Olyalin, D. Moniava, G. Tashbaeva, M. Alimova, L. Khamraeva, L. Babakhanov, K. Faroh, B. Ikhtiarov, B. Matchanov, F. Muminova, M. Nasim, M. Maksumov and D. Muhammed. ¶A Soviet and Afghani coproduction released in Russia in 1983 as *Zarkoe leto v Kabule.*

The Hottest Month (1974). Filmed in Sovscope 70. *Screen authors* Gennady Bokarev and Yuly Karasik. *Director* Yuly Karasik. *Operators* Arkady Kolitsatiy, Ilya Minikovstskiy and Valery Shuvalov. *Artist* Boris Blank. *Composer* Eduard Khagagortyan. *Sound operator* I. Mayorov. ¶A Mosfilm production. International distribution Sovexportfilm. Sovcolor. Six-track magnetic stereophonic sound. 172 minutes plus intermission. Filmed at Mosfilm Studios, Moscow, R.S.F.S.R. ¶CAST: *Viktor Lagutin* Leonid Diyachkov. *Steel founders* Igor Okhlupin and Boris Yurchenko. *Sartakov* Ivan Lapikov. *Lena* Maria Koreneva. *With* Igor Vladimirov, Elena Drapenko and L. Kulagin. ¶A Soviet production released in Russia in 1974 as *Samiy zarkiy mesyats* in two parts running 89 minutes and 83 minutes.

How the West Was Won (February 21, 1963). Filmed in Super Cinerama. *Producer* Bernard Smith. *"The Civil War" director* John Ford. *"The Railroad" director* George Marshall. *"The Rivers," "The Plains," "The Outlaws" and additional scenes director* Henry Hathaway. *Historical transitions director* Richard Thorpe. *Writers* James R. Webb, John Gay and Henry Hathaway. *Suggested by the series appearing in "Life" magazine. Directors of photography* Joseph LaShelle *("The Civil War" and "The Railroad"),* William H. Daniels *("The Plains"),* Charles Bryant Lang, Jr. *("The Rivers")* and Milton Krasner *("The Outlaws"). Overall production supervising director of photography* Milton Krasner. *Art direction* George W. Davis, William Ferrari and Addison Hehr. *Set decoration* Henry Grace, Don Greenwood, Jr. and Jack Mills. *Color consultant* Charles K. Hagedon. *Film editors* Harold F. Kress and Margaret Booth. *Second unit photography* Harold E. Wellman, Dale Deverman, Robert L. Surtees and Peter Gibbons. *Assistant directors* George Marshall, Jr., William McGarry, Robert Saunders, William Shanks and Wingate Smith. *Production supervisor for Cinerama, Inc.* Coleman Thomas Conroy, Jr. *Special effects* Glenn E. Robinson. *Special visual effects* A. Arnold Gillespie and Robert R. Hoag. *Costume designer* Walter Plunkett. *Hair styles* Sydney Guilaroff and Mary K. Keats. *Makeup creator* William Tuttle. *Music* Alfred Newman conducting the MGM Studio Symphony Orchestra. *Music associate* Ken Darby. *Music coordinator* Robert Emmett Dolan. *Recording supervisor* Franklin E. Milton. *Sound recording* Fred Bosch, Ray Sharples, Harold V. Moss and William Steinkamp. *Sound consultant* Douglas Shearer. *Second unit directors* Yakima Canutt and Richard Talmadge. *Cinerama visual consultant* Peter Gibbons. *Cinerama technical consultant* Walter Gibbons-Fly. *Process photography* Harold E. Wellman. *Music editor* Richard C. Harris. *Sound editor* Milo Lory. *Historical technical adviser* David Humphreys Miller. *"The Civil War" technical adviser* Jack Pennick. *Livestock supervisors* Richard Webb and Vernon Mouce. *Location manager* Howard "Dutch" Horton. *"How the West Was Won" music* Alfred Newman, *lyrics* Ken Darby. *"Home in the Meadow" music adaptation* Robert Emmett Dolan, *lyric adaptation* Sammy Cahn, *conductor* Robert Armbruster. *"Raise a Ruckus" music adaptation* Robert Emmett Dolan, *lyric adaptation* Johnny Mercer. *"Wait*

The epic journey of four generations of Americans who carved out a country with their bare hands

METRO-GOLDWYN-MAYER and CINERAMA present HOW THE WEST WAS WON, starring:
CARROLL BAKER · LEE J. COBB · HENRY FONDA · CAROLYN JONES · KARL MALDEN
GREGORY PECK · GEORGE PEPPARD · ROBERT PRESTON · DEBBIE REYNOLDS
JAMES STEWART · ELI WALLACH · JOHN WAYNE · RICHARD WIDMARK · SPENCER TRACY
CO-STARRING
BRIGID BAZLEN · WALTER BRENNAN · DAVID BRIAN · ANDY DEVINE · RAYMOND MASSEY · AGNES MOOREHEAD · HENRY (HARRY) MORGAN · THELMA RITTER · MICKEY SHAUGHNESSY
RUSS TAMBLYN WRITTEN BY JAMES R. WEBB DIRECTED BY HENRY HATHAWAY, JOHN FORD, GEORGE MARSHALL PRODUCED BY BERNARD SMITH MUSIC ALFRED NEWMAN METROCOLOR MGM

G
ALL AGES ADMITTED
General Audiences

An ad for the 35mm anamorphic release of How the West Was Won.

for the Hoedown" and "What Was Your Name in the States" *lyric adaptation* Johnny Mercer. *Solo singer* Debbie Reynolds. *Folk singing* Dave Gard and The Whiskeyhill Singers and The Ken Darby Chorus. *Accordian solos* Carl Fortina. *Ultra Panavision 70 cameras and lenses* Panavision, Inc. ¶A Metro-Goldwyn-Mayer, Inc., and Cinerama, Inc., production. Released by Metro-Goldwyn-Mayer. Technicolor. Westrex recording system. Seven-track magnetic Cinerama Sound. 162 minutes including overture and intermission. Filmed at MGM Studios and on location in Custer State Park, Black Hills and Rapid City, South Dakota; Uncompaghre National Forest, Rocky Mountains, Montrose, Durango and Silverton, Colorado; on the Ohio and Cumberland rivers and in Paducah, Kentucky; Oatman, Perkinsville, Superior and Canyon de Chelly, Arizona; Monument Valley, Utah; Eugene and Grand Pass, Oregon; San Francisco, Lone Pine, Bishop, Simi and Scotia, California; Tonto National Forest and Inyo National Forest. "To the officials of the State of South Dakota, the United States Forest Service and Bureau Reclamation we express deep appreciation." ¶CAST: *Eve Prescott Rawlings* Carroll

Baker. *Gold City Marshal Lew Ramsey* Lee J. Cobb. *Jethro Stewart* Henry Fonda. *Julie Stewart Rawlings* Carolyn Jones. *Zebulon Prescott* Karl Malden. *Cleve Van Valen* Gregory Peck. *Zebulon Rawlings* George Peppard. *Wagonmaster Roger Morgan* Robert Preston. *Lilith Prescott Van Valen* Debbie Reynolds. *Linus Rawlings* James Stewart. *Charlie Gant* Eli Wallach. *Gen. William Tucumseh Sherman* John Wayne. *Railroad Superintendent Mike King* Richard Widmark. *Narrator* Spencer Tracy. *Dora Hawkins* Brigid Bazlen. *Col. Jeb Hawkins* Walter Brennan. *Lilith's attorney* David Brian. *Cpl. Peterson* Andy Devine. *Abraham Lincoln* Raymond Massey. *Rebecca Prescott* Agnes Moorehead. *Gen. Ulysses Simpson Grant* Henry (Harry) Morgan. *Agatha (Aggie) Clegg* Thelma Ritter. *Gold City Deputy Marshal Stover* Mickey Shaughnessy. *Confederate deserter from Texas* Russ Tamblyn. *Sam Prescott* Kim Charney. *Zeke Prescott* Bryan Russell. *Parson Harvey* Tubor Owen. *Angus Harvey* Barry Harvey. *Brutus Harvey* Jamie Ross. *Colin Harvey* Mack Allen. *Marty Hawkins* Lee Van Cleef. *Col. Hawkins' river pirates* Gilbert Perkins, Sol Gorss, Roy Jensen, Victor Romito and Harvey Parry. *St. Louis showgirl* Hope

Lange. *Allen Jones* James Griffith. *Dick Hargreaves* Christopher Dark. *Attorney Hylan Seabury* Clinton Sundberg. *Grimes* John Larch. *Grimes' investor friend* Clifford Osmond. *Bearded poker player in wagon* Walter Burke. *Red Hart* Boyd "Red" Morgan. *Blacksmith Bob Weston* Ken Dibbs. *Mr. Huggins* Jay C. Flippen. *El Dorado barker* Charles Briggs. *Sacramento Queen gamblers* Gene Roth, Lou Krugman and Tom Greenway. *Sacramento Queen captain* Joseph Sawyer. *Jeremiah Rawlings* Claude Johnson. *Union officers* Carleton Young, Bob Morgan and Charles (Chuck) Roberson. *Cpl. Murphy* Jack Pennick. *Union surgeon* Willis Bouchey. *Union doctor* Walter Reed. *Orderly Ben* Ken Curtis. *Second orderly* Red Perkins. *Union officer in field hospital* Bing Russell. *First staff officer* William (Bill) Henry. *Second staff officer* William A. Wellman, Jr. *Railroad clerk* Jerry Holmes. *Girl on trapeze in railroad saloon* Polly Burson. *Man who helps girl down from trapeze* Danny Sands. *Indian chiefs* Ben Black Elk, Jr., William Shake Spears, Chief Oglalla Hansaka, Chief Weasel and Red Cloud. *James Marshall* Craig Duncan. *Jim's wife* Beulah Archuletta. *Auctioneer* Edward J. McKinley. *Assistant auctioneer* Paul Bryar. *Eve Rawlings II* Kym Karath. *Linus Rawlings II* Dennis Cole. *Prescott Rawlings* Stanley Livingston. *Yaqui* Rudolfo Acosta. *Jenks* Jack Lambert. *Tom* Harry Dean Stanton. *Gold City officials* John Damler and Robert Nash. *Train conductor* Karl Swenson. *Outlaw shot from log car* Charles (Chuck) Roberson. *Outlaw* Bob Morgan. *Settlers, railroad workers, outlaws and others* John Anderson, Charles (Chuck) Hayward, Robert P. Lieb, Lew Smith, Jack C. Williams, Leroy Johnson, David H. Miller, Loren Janes, Boyd "Red" Morgan, Troy Melton, Gilbert Perkins, Henry Wills, Gregg Martell, Don Rhodes, Charles (Chuck) Roberson, Harvey Parry and Joseph Yrigoyen. *Indian population* Tribe members of Brulee Sioux, Oclalles Sioux, Minnecanjous Sioux, Arapahoe and Cheyenne Nations. ¶All action scenes in "The Civil War" were from *Raintree County*. Footage of Mexican troops marching was from *The Alamo*. Ultra Panavision 70 was used in process shots and background scenes. This 70mm footage was converted to three-panel Super Cinerama by the MGM Laboratories Optical department under the supervision of Robert R. Hoag. After the introduction of single strip Super Cinerama the whole show was converted to 70mm Metrocolor, with the seven-track sound remixed to six tracks. In order not to date the program the footage of modern San Francisco was removed. A 35mm anamorphic version with four-track stereo was also released. The overture, entr'acte and exit music were removed from this version, but the intermission title was left for those houses wishing to have a break. Three 16mm versions were produced: anamorphic (2.74 × 1 ratio), Metroscope (spherical 1.75 × 1) and Metroscan (1.37 × 1). Stuntman Bob Morgan lost a leg during production of "The Outlaws." This film was later the basis of the MGM teleseries for NBC in 1978.

How Wide Is My Country *see* **Great Is My Country.**

I Am a Citizen of the Soviet Union (1972). Filmed in Sovscope 70. Presented in Polyscreen. *Screen authors* Yakov Varshavsky and Aleksandr Shein. *Directors* Pyotr Mostovoi and Aleksandr Shein. *Operators* Abram Vinokurov, Avetis Zenyan and Boris Travkin. ¶A Mosfilm production. International distribution Sovexportfilm. Sovcolor. Six-track magnetic stereophonic sound. A Soviet documentary production released in Russia in 1972 as *Ya-grazdanin Sovetskogo Soyuza.*

I Am Here Talking to You (1985). Filmed in Sovscope 70. *Screen author* Ilya Reznik. *Director* Naum Ardashnikov. *Operator* Nikolay Olonovskiy. *Artist* Yuri Kladienko. *Composers* Alla Pugacheva and I. Nikolaev. *Sound operators* V. Babushkin and V. Klyuchnikov. *Text and songs* B. Ahmadulinoy. ¶A Mosfilm production. International distribution Sovexportfilm. Sovcolor. Six-track magnetic stereophonic sound. 89 minutes. Filmed on location in Moscow, Yerevan and Leningrad, R.S.F.S.R., and in Finland. ¶CAST: Alla Pugacheva, Evgeny Boldin, Lyudmila Dorodnova, Ivan Lobanov, Boris Moiseev, Zinaida Pugacheva, Llya Reznik, Darya Semenova, V. Trofimchuk, Kh. Talimar, L. Khitana, V. Tsoy and L. Chesnulyavichute. ¶A Soviet production released in Russia in 1985 as *Prishla i govoryu.*

I eshche odna nochi Sheherezadi ... *see* **One More Night of Scheherazade.**

I na Tikhom okeane ... (1974). Filmed in Sovscope 70. *Screen authors* A. Gorokhov, T. Ivanova and Yu. Chulyukin. *Based on the story by* Vs. Ivanova. *Director* Yu. Chulyukin. *Operators* G. Shatrov and R. Ruvinov. *Artists* N. Markin and B. Tsarev. *Composer* O. Felitsman. *Sound operator* N. Kropotov. *Song text* R. Rozdestvenskiy. ¶A Mosfilm production. International distribution Sovexportfilm. Sovcolor. Six-track magnetic stereophonic sound. 122 minutes. Filmed at Mosfilm Studios, Moscow, R.S.F.S.R. ¶CAST: A. Kuznetsov, V. Avtsyushko, L. Sokolova, L. Polyakov, N. Podgorniy, E. Shutov, K. Golovko, V. Titova, S. Kurilov, V. Basov and S. Golovanov. ¶A Soviet production released in Russia in 1974.

I Saw the Birth of a New World *see* **Red Bells.**

I, Shapovalov T.P. *see* **Lofty Title.**

I vot prishel Bumbo ... *see* **Then Came Bumbo.**

Ice Station Zebra (October 23, 1968). Filmed in Super Panavision 70. Presented in 70mm Super Cinerama. *Producer* Martin Ransohoff. *Associate producer* James C. Pratt. *Director* John Sturges. *Screenplay* Douglas Heyes. *Screen story* Harry Julian Fink. *Based on the novel by* Alistair MacLean. *Director of photography* Daniel L. Fapp. *Music composer and conductor* Michel Legrand. *Art directors* George W. Davis and Addison Hehr. *Set decoration* Henry Grace and Jack Mills. *Recording supervisor* Franklin Milton. *Assistant director* Thomas J. Schmidt. *Technical adviser* Capt. John M. Connolly, U.S.N. Retd. *Unit production manager* Ralph W. Nelson. *Special visual effects* Joseph McMillan Johnson, Carroll L. Shepphird, Clarence W.D. Slifer and Matthew Yuricich. *Optical effects* Robert R. Hoag. *Additional Arctic photography* John M. Stephens and Nelson Tyler. *Special effects* Henry E. Millar, Sr., Ralph Swartz and Earl McCoy. *Makeup* William Tuttle. *Dialog coach* Norman Stuart. *Film editor* Ferris Webster. *Sound editor* Milo Lory. *Music editor* Frank J. Urioste.

Assistant art director John Clark. *Assistant Arctic cameraman* John Kiser. *Unit publicists* John Tobias and Ted Bonnet. ¶A Martin Ransohoff production. A Filmways, Inc. picture. Released by Metro-Goldwyn-Mayer. Metrocolor. Westrex six-track magnetic stereophonic sound. 148 minutes plus overture and intermission. Filmed at MGM Studios and on location in the Arctic. ¶CAST: *Cmdr. James Ferraday* Rock Hudson. *Borsi Vaslov* Ernest Borgnine. *David Jones* Patrick McGoohan. *Capt. Leslie Anders* Jim Brown. *Lt. Russell Walker* Tony Bill. *Adm. Garvey* Lloyd Nolan. *Col. Ostrovsky* Alf Kjellin. *Lt. Cmdr. Bob Raeburn* Gerald S. O'Loughlin. *Lt. Jonathan Hansen* Ted Hartley. *Lt. George Mills* Murray Rose. *Paul Zabrinczski* Ron Masak. *Lt. Edgar Hackett* Sherwood Price. *Lt. Mitgang* Lee Stanley. *Dr. Jack Benning* Joseph Bernard. *First survivor* John Orchard. *McBain* William O'Connell. *Lt. Courtney Cartwright* Michael T. Mikler. *Russian aide* Jonathan Lippe. *Wassmeyer* Ted Kristian. *Earl MacAuliffe* Jim Dixon. *Bruce Kentner* Boyd Berlind. *Cedrick Patterson* David Wendel. *Lyle Nichols* Ronnie Rondell, Jr. *Gafferty* Craig Shreeve. *Kohler* Michael Grossman. *Parker* Wade Graham. *Fannovich* Michael Rougas. *Peter Costigan* Jed Allan. *Webson* Lloyd Haynes. *Edward Rawlins* Buddy Garion. *Lt. Carl Mingus* T.J. Escott. *Hill* Buddy Hart. *Lorrison* Gary Downey. *Kelvaney* Robert Carlson. *Timothy Hirsch* Don Newsome. *Third survivor* Jim Goodwin. *Philip Munsey* Bill Hillman. *Gambetta* Dennis Alpert. ¶Production began in Ultra Panavision 70, then converted to Super Panavision 70. One source says some Panavision footage was blown up to 70mm. Stock footage later incorporated into *Fer de Lance* (a.k.a. *Death Dive*) (Leslie Stevens Productions, 1974) and *Firefox* (Warner Bros., 1982).

Idushchiy sledom *see* **The Follower.**

Igri zivotnikh (1981). Filmed in Sovscope 70. International distribution Sovexportfilm. Sovcolor. Six-track magnetic stereophonic sound. A Soviet production released in Russia in 1981.

An Incident in Map Grid 36-80 (1982). Filmed in Sovscope 70. *Screen author*

SPA CINEMATOGRAFICA—LUX COMPAGNIE CINEMATOGRAPHIQUE DE FRANCE—EICHBERG FILM G.M.B.H. *announce:*

A Film by FOLCO QUILICI
"I MILLE FUOCHI"
Produced by ACHILLE PIAZZI

SUPERTECHNIRAMA 70mm   TECHNICOLOR

Foreign sales:

OMNIA DEUTSCHE FILM EXPORT G.M.B.H.
Herzog-Rudolf Strasse, 1
Muenchen, 22, Deutschland

Was this Italian, French and West German coproduction ever made? We don't think so. This 1962 trade ad was the only information discovered on it.

Evgeni Mesyatsev. *Director* Mikhail Tumanishvili. *Operator* Boris Bondarenko. *Artists* Gennady Novozilov and Georgy Koshelev. *Composer* Viktor Babushkin. *Sound operators* V. Shmelikin and A. Khasin. *Still photo* Gennady Lyzhin. ¶A Mosfilm production. International distribution Sovexportfilm. Sovcolor. Six-track magnetic stereophonic sound. 93 minutes. Filmed at Mosfilm Studios, Moscow, R.S.F.S.R. ¶CAST: Boris Shcherbakov, Mikhail Volontir, Anatoly Kuznetsov, Vladimir Sedov, O. Volmer, P. Butkevich, V. Tomkus and I. Kalnini. ¶A Soviet production released in Russia in 1982 as *Sluchay v kvadrate 36-80.*

Indonesian Child (1987). Filmed in IMAX. *Producer and director* Greg MacMillivray. *Photographers* Greg MacGillivray and Timothy Housel. ¶A MacGillivray Freeman Films production. Sponsored by Yayasan Harapan Kita Cultural Foundation. Released by MacGillivray Freeman Films Distribution Company. Eastman Color. Six-track magnetic Dolby Stereo. 30 minutes. Filmed in Indonesia.

International (1971). Filmed in Sovscope

70. *Screen authors* Viktor Gorokhov and Aleksandr Bovin. *Directors* Aleksandr Svetlov and Aleksandr Shein. *Operators* Samuel Rubushkin, Abram Vinokurov, Boris Aretsky and Yuri Sobolkov. ¶International distribution Sovexportfilm. Sovcolor. Six-track magnetic stereophonic sound. 29 minutes. A Soviet production released in Russia in 1971 as *Internatsional.*

Internatsional *see* **International.**

The Iron Flood (1967). Filmed in Sovscope 70. *Screen authors* Arkadi Perventsev and Efim Dzigan. *Based on the novel "Zelezniy potok" by* Aleksandr O. Serafimovicha. *Director and producer* Efim Dzigan. *Operator* Alexei Temerin. *Artist* Pyotr Kiselev. *Composer* Vano Muradel. *Sound operators* V. Sharun and N. Kalinichenko. ¶A Mosfilm production. International distribution Sovexportfilm. Sovcolor. Six-track magnetic stereophonic sound. 134 minutes. Filmed at Mosfilm Studios, Moscow, R.S.F.S.R. ¶CAST: *Kozhukh* Nikolay Alekseev. *Artyomov* Lev Frichinskiy. *Bezugly* Nikolay Denisenko. *Prikhodko* Vladimir Ivashov. *Smirnyuk* Yakov Gladkikh. *Klavdia* Nina Alisova. *Denikin* Leonid Gallis. *With* A. Degtyari, N. Dutsak, I. Murzaeva and G. Zaslavets. ¶A Soviet production released in Russia in 1967 as *Zelezniy potok.*

Iskateli zatonuvshego goroda (1974). Filmed in Sovscope 70. *Screen author* M. Saralidze. *Director* D. Abashidze. *Operator* N. Sukhishvili. *Artist* Sh. Gogolashvili. *Composer* R. Lagidze. *Sound operator* V. Machaidze. ¶A Gruziya-film production. International distribution Sovexportfilm. Sovcolor. Six-track magnetic stereophonic sound. 73 minutes. Filmed at Gruziya-film Studios, Tbilisi, Georgian S.S.R. ¶CAST: K. Tavartkiladze, L. Andronikashvili, D. Kuparadze, P. Kalandadze, M. Vashadze, V. Nindze, L. Budchrashvili, I. Kahiani, D. Tserodze, O. Koberidze and O. Mezvinetuhutsesi. ¶A Soviet production released in Russia in 1974.

Isotope Cafe (1977). Filmed in Sovscope 70. *Screen authors* Vasily Soloviev and Mikhail Kalatozov. *Based on the opera "Pravo vibova" by* M. Kolesnikova. *Director* Georgi Kalatozishvili. *Operator*

Sergei Vronskiy. *Artist* Felix Yasyukevich. *Composer* Gia Kancheli. *Sound operator* M. Bronshteyn. ¶A Mosfilm production. International distribution Sovexportfilm. Sovcolor. Six-track magnetic stereophonic sound. 106 minutes. Filmed at Mosfilm Studios, Moscow, R.S.F.S.R. ¶CAST: *Volodya Prokhorov* Aleksandr Safronov. *Lena Skuratora* Lyudmilla Maksakova. *Tanya* Nadezhda Butirtseva. *With* Igor Vasiliev, Yuri Nazarov, V. Nosik, O. Gudkova, V. Gulyaev, G. Korolikov, V. Kozelkov, G. Krashennikov and G. Sovchis. ¶A Soviet production released in Russia in 1977 as *Kafe "Izotop."*

Istoki *see* **The Sources.**

It's a Mad, Mad, Mad, Mad World (November 7, 1963). Filmed in Ultra Panavision 70. Presented in 70mm Super Cinerama. *Producer and director* Stanley Kramer. *Story and screenplay* William and Tania Rose. *Director of photography* Ernest Laszlo. *Music* Ernest Gold *conducting the* Los Angeles Philharmonic Orchestra. *Aerial supervision* Paul Mantz and Frank Tallman. *Production design* Rudolph Sternad. *Art director* Gordon Gurnee. *Costume design* Bill Thomas. *Costume supervision* Joseph King. *Assistant to the director* Ivan Volkman. *Assistant directors* Charles Scott, Jr., Bert Chervin and George Batcheller. *Production manager* Clem Beauchamp. *Location manager* William Mull. *Stunt supervisor* Carey Loftin. *Special photographic effects* Linwood G. Dunn, James B. Gordon, Film Effects of Hollywood, Cecil Love, Howard Fisher, Howard Lydecker, Willis H. O'Brien, James Danforth, Marcel Delgado, Don Weed and Bill Reinhold. *Special effects* Danny Lee. *Process photography* Farciot Edouart. *Title designer* Saul Bass. *Casting* Stalmaster-Lister Co. *Film editors* Frederic Knudtson, Robert C. Jones and Gene Fowler, Jr. *Music editor* Art Dunham. *Sound* Samuel Goldwyn Studios. *Sound supervision* Gordon E. Sawyer. *Sound engineer* James Keene. *Rerecording* Clem Portman, Vinton Vernon and Roy Granville. *Sound editor* Walter G. Elliott. *Assistant to the producer* Anne Kramer. *Property master* Art Cole. *Set decorator* Joseph Kish. *Construction coordinator* Arnold "Bud" Pine. *Aerial photography* Albert Wetzel.

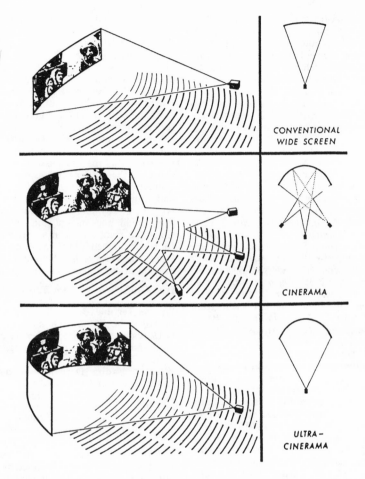

A 1962 Cinerama, Inc., press handout for the United Kingdom, in which 70mm Super Cinerama is called "Ultra-Cinerama." Only It's a Mad, Mad, Mad, Mad World *was advertised in the U.K. under the Ultra-Cinerama banner, which was apparently never applied anywhere else. After* Mad World *all U.K. presentations were simply heralded as Cinerama, regardless of format.*

Additional photography Irmin Roberts and Hal A. McAlpin. *Camera operator* Charles F. Wheeler. *Camera assistant* Richard Johnson. *Chief gaffer* Joseph Edesa. *Company grip* Morris Rosen. *Assistant company grip* Martin Kaschuk. *Script supervisor* Marshall Scholm. *Makeup* George Lane, Lynn Reynolds and Dick Smith. *Hair stylist* Connie Nichols. *Music recording* William Britton. *Orchestration* Albert Woodbury. *Music production assistant* Bobby Helfer.

Titles Playhouse Pictures. *Title producer* Bill Melendez. *Title animation photography* Allen Childs. *Title editor* Hugh Kelley. *Studio security* Vance Boyd. *Songs* "It's a Mad, Mad, Mad, Mad World," "31 Flavors" and "You Satisfy My Soul": *music* Ernest Gold; *lyrics* Mack David; *dance music singers* The Shirelles; *players* The Four Mads. ¶A Stanley Kramer presentation. A Cinerama, Inc., production. A Casey Productions, Inc., picture. Released by United Artists. Technicolor.

Westrex six-track magnetic stereophonic sound. 210 minutes including overture (8 minutes) and intermission (16 minutes). Filmed at Revue Studios (Universal City Studios) and on location in Colorado and in Santa Rosita Beach State Park, San Diego, Agoura, Kernville, Long Beach, Malibu, Palm Desert, Palm Springs (Palos Verdes Estates), San Pedro, Santa Ana, Santa Barbara, Santa Monica, 29 Palms and Yucca Valley, California. ¶*Capt T.G. Culpepper* Spencer Tracy. *J. Russell Finch* Milton Berle. *Melville Crump* Sid Caesar. *Bengy Benjamin* Buddy Hackett. *Mrs. Marcus* Ethel Merman. *Ding Bell* Mickey Rooney. *Sylvester Marcus* Dick Shawn. *Otto Meyer* Phil Silvers. *Lt. Col. J. Algernon Hawthorne* Tery-Thomas. *Lennie Pike* Jonathan Winters. *Monica Crump* Edie Adams. *Emmeline Finch* Dorothy Provine. *First taxi driver* Eddie "Rochester" Anderson. *Second taxi driver* Peter Falk. *Third taxi driver* Leo Gorcey. *Tyler Fitzgerald* Jim Backus. *Biplane pilot* Ben Blue. *Police sergeant* Alan Carney. *Mrs. Halliburton* Barrie Chase. *Police Chief Alouisous O'Hara* William Demarest. *Col. Wilberforce* Paul Ford. *Mr. Dinckler* Edward Everett Horton. *Jimmy the Crook* Buster Keaton. *Nervous driver* Don Knotts. *Airport tower controller* Carl Reiner. *Airport firemen* The Three Stooges (Moe Howard, Larry Fine and Curly Joe De Rita). *Union official* Joe E. Brown. *Sheriff Mason* Andy Devine. *City fire chief* Sterling Holloway. *Irwin* Marvin Kaplan. *Airport manager* Charles Lane. *Lt. Matthews* Charles McGraw. *Gertie* Zasu Pitts. *Schwartz* Madlyn Rhue. *Ray* Arnold Stang. *Airport tower radio operator* Jesse White. *City mayor* Lloyd Corrigan. *Voice of Ginger Culpepper* Selma Diamond. *Deputy sheriff* Stan Freberg. *Voice of Billie Sue Culpepper* Louise Glenn. *George* Ben Lessy. *Biplane pilot's wife* Bobo Lewis. *Miner* Mike Mazurki. *Negro truck driver* Nick Stewart. *Chinese laundryman* Sammee Tong. *First detective at Grogan's accident* Norman Fell. *Second detective at Grogan's accident* Nicholas Georgiade. *Smiler Grogan* Jimmy Durante. *Detective* Stanley Clements. *Police officer* Allan Jenkins. *Police radio operator* Harry Lauter. *Dinckler's store salesman* Doodles Weaver. *Traffic officer* Tom Kennedy. *Airport tower radioman* Eddie Ryder. *Helicopter observer* Don C.

Harvey. *Patrolmen* Roy Engel and Paul Birch. *Helpful motorist* Jack Benney. *Prankster who runs over Culpepper's hat* Jerry Lewis. *Airport officer* Howard da Silva. *Bits* Chick Chandler, Barbara Pepper, Cliff Norton and Roy Roberts. *Stuntmen* Dale Van Sickel, Harvey Parry, Max Balchowski and Carey Loftin. ¶Released in 70mm reedited to 162 minutes plus overture and intermission. Released in 35mm running 154 minutes without an overture and with the music and informational reports during the intermission removed. Cut from the shorter versions were Chick Chandler, Barbara Pepper, Cliff Norton and Roy Roberts. Cinerama became involved midway through production and their credit appears only on the Super Cinerama prints. English advertisements for the film billed it in "Ultra-Cinerama." Home video version is 154 minutes but has original discrete stereo sound.

Ivan Grozni *see* **Ivan the Terrible.**

Ivan the Terrible (December 1979). Filmed in Sovscope 70. *Screen authors* Yuri Grigorvich and Vadim Derbenev. *Based on the ballet "Ivan Grozni" by* Sergei Prokofiev. *Film director* L. Chrimanko. *Stage director* Vadim Derbenev. *Producer* Adolf Fradis. *Choreographer* Yuri Grigorvich. *Chief operators* Vadim Derbenev and Viktor Pishchalnikov. *Artists* Valentin Vyrvich and Yuri Kokyaiam. *Music* Sergei Prokofiev. *Music composition and editing* Mikhail Chulaki. *Conductor of Bolshoi Theatre Orchestra* Algis Youritis. ¶A Mosfilm production. Released by Corinth Films by arrangement with Sovexportfilm. Sovcolor. 97 minutes. Filmed at Mosfilm Studios, Moscow, R.S.F.S.R. ¶CAST: *Ivan the Terrible* Yuri Vladimirov. *Anastasya* Natalia Bessmertnova. *Prince Kurbsky* Boris Akimov. *With* Members of Bolshoi Ballet and Orchestra. ¶A Soviet production released in Russia in 1977 in 70mm and six-track magnetic stereophonic sound as *Ivan Grozni* running 91 minutes. Released in the U.S. in 35mm only and advertised in CinemaScope.

J'accuse *see* **Magirama.**

John Reed *see* **Red Bells.**

Journey of Discovery (1984). Filmed in IMAX. *Executive producer* Barry Bittle. *Producer* Candace Conacher. *Director*

John Sebert. ¶A Boardwalk Motion Pictures, Ltd. production. Released by Imax Systems Corporation. Eastman Color. Six-track magnetic stereophonic sound. 21 minutes. Filmed in Ontario, Canada. A Canadian production originally made for Ontario Place.

Journey to the Stars (June 1962). Filmed in Cinerama 360. *Producer and director* John Wilson. *Chief cameraman* Eugene Borghi. *Program manager and project coordinator* William D. Liittschwager. *Special photographic effects* Linwood G. Dunn and Don Weed. *Camera* Cinerama Camera Corporation. *Lens design* Curtis Optical. *Optics* Fairchild. *Photographic and projection equipment* Benson-Lehner Corporation. *Processing* Technicolor. *Printing equipment, optical effects and release printing* Film Effects of Hollywood. *Filmed by* Fine Arts Productions, Inc. ¶A Cinerama, Inc., production for Boeing Company. Released by Cinerama, Inc. Eastman Color. Ampex four-track magnetic stereophonic sound. 15 minutes. Originally shown at Boeing's United States Science Exhibit in the Spacearium at the Seattle World's Fair. Later shown in various cities, usually in 35mm.

Kafe "Izotop" *see* **Isotope Cafe.**

Karpati, karpati *see* **Duma o Kovpake.**

Kapitan "Piligrima" *see* **Captain of the "Pilgrim."**

Katerina Izmailova (April 25, 1969). Filmed in Sovscope 70. *Screen author and composer* Dimitri Dmitriyevich Shostakovich. *Based on the opera "Katerina Izmaylova" by* Dimitri Dmitriyevich Shostakovich and A. Preys. *From the story "Ledi Makbet Mtsenskogo uezda" by* Nikolay Semyonovich Leskova. *Director* Mikhail Shapiro. *Operators* Rostislav Davidov and Vladimir Ponomarev. *Conductor* Konstantin Simeonov. *Players* Shevchenko Opera and Ballet Theatre Orchestra. *Artist* Evgeniy Eney. *Sound operator* Ilya Volk. *Manager of production* G. Khokhlov. *Assistant director* A. Tubenshlyak. ¶A Lenfilm production. International distribution Sovexportfilm. Released by Artkino Pictures. Sovcolor. 118 minutes. Filmed at Lenfilm Studios, Leningrad, R.S.F.S.R. ¶DRAMATIC CAST: *Katerina Lvovna Izmaylova* Galina Vishnevskaya. *Boris Timofeyevich* Aleksandr Sokolov. *Zinoviy Borisovich* Nikolay Boyarskiy. *Sergey* Artyom Inozemtsev. *Sonyetka* Tatyana Gavrilova. *Village drunk* S. Strezkhnev. *With* V. Titova and R. Tkachuk. ¶SINGING CAST: *Boris Timofeyevich* Aleksandr Vedernikov. *Zinoviy Borisovich* Vyacheslav Radziyevskiy. *Sergey* Vasili Tretyakov. *Sonyetka* Valentina Ryeka. *With* Shevchenko Opera and Ballet Theatre Chorus. ¶A Soviet production released in Russia in April 1967 as *Katerina Izmaylova* in 70mm and six-track magnetic stereophonic sound running 149 minutes. Released in the U.S. in 35mm 'scope with mono sound only.

Katerina Izmaylova *see* **Katerina Izmailova.**

Kentavri *see* **The Centaurs.**

Khartoum (June 15, 1966). Filmed in Ultra Panavision 70. Presented in 70mm Super Cinerama. *Producer* Julian Blaustein. *Director* Basil Dearden. *Writer* Robert Ardery. *Music composer and conductor* Frank Cordell. *Director of photography* Edward Scaife. *Second unit director* Yakima Canutt. *Second unit photography* Harry Waxman. *Special effects* Richard Parker and Nick Allder. *Art director* John Howell. *Editor* Fergus McDonell. *Production supervisor* Charles Orme. *Unit managers* Basil Appleby and Frank Ernst. *Research* Mary Bruce. *Assistant directors* John Peverell and Bluey Hill. *Camera operators* Jack Atcheler, H.A.R. (Robert) Thomson, Ray Parslow, Kelvin Pike and Jeff (Geoffrey) Seaholme. *Sound recordists* Bert Ross, Laurie Clarkson, Gordon K. McCallum and John S. Dennis. *Sound editor* Dino Di Campo. *Introductory scenes director* Eliot Elisofen. *Associate art directors* Scott MacGregor and Ted Tester. *Set dressers* Pamela Cornell and John Dodimeade. *Continuity* Eileen Head and Kay Rawlings. *Makeup* William Lodge and Tom Smith. *Wardrobe supervisor* John McCorry. *Hairdressing* Hilda Fox. *Special photographic effects* Cliff Culley. *Special location consultant* Maj. Gen. S.E. Sabbour. *Negative* Eastman Kodak. ¶A Julian Blaustein Productions, Ltd. presentation. Released by United Artists. Technicolor. Westrex six-track magnetic stereophonic sound. 134

minutes plus intermission. Filmed in England and on location in Sudan. ¶CAST: *Gen. Charles "Chinese" Gordon* Charlton Heston. *Mahdi* Laurence Olivier. *Col. J.D.H. Stewart* Richard Johnson. *Mr. Gladstone* Ralph Richardson. *Sir Evelyn Baring* Alexander Knox. *Khaleed* Johnny Sekka. *Lord Granville* Michael Hordern. *Zobeir Pasha* Zia Mohyeddin. *Sheikh Osman* Marne Maitland. *Gen. Wolseley* Nigel Green. *Lord Hartington* Hugh Williams. *Sir Charles Dilke* Ralph Michael. *Khalifa Abdullah* Douglas Wilmer. *Col. Hicks* Edward Underdown. *Maj. Kitchener* Peter Arne. *Awaan* Alan Tilvern. *Bordeini Bey* Alex Mango. *Frank Power* Jerome Willis. *Herbin* Michael Anthony. *Dancer* Leila. *Lord Northbrook* Ronald Leigh-Hunt. *Giriagio Bey* George Pastell. *Stunt double for Charlton Heston* Tap Canutt. *Narrator* Leo Genn. ¶A British production released in England in March 1966 with a BBFC "U" certificate. Within a few weeks of this film's U.S. opening stock footage of the battle sequences appeared in *The Time Tunnel* television series episode *Raiders from Outer Space.*

Khleb i lyudi *see* **The Taste of Bread.**

Khleb i zemlya *see* **The Taste of Bread.**

Khleb nash nasushchniy *see* **The Taste of Bread.**

Khleb otechestva *see* **The Taste of Bread.**

Khozyain taygi (1969). Filmed in Sovscope 70. *Screen author* B. Mozaev. *Director* V. Nazarov. *Operator* V. Nikolaev. *Artist* S. Uskhakov and I. Shreter. *Composer* L. Afanasiev. *Sound operator* E. Fedorov. *Songs* V. Visotskogo. ¶A Mosfilm production. International distribution Sovexportfilm. Sovcolor. Six-track magnetic stereophonic sound. 83 minutes. Filmed at Mosfilm Studios, Moscow, R.S.F.S.R. ¶CAST: V. Zolotukhin, V. Visotskiy, L. Pirieva, M. Kokshenov, D. Masanov, L. Kmit and Z. Bredun. ¶A Soviet production released in Russia in 1969.

The King and I (June 29, 1956). Filmed in CinemaScope 55. *Executive producer* Darryl F. Zanuck. *Producer* Charles Brackett. *Director* Walter Lang. *Screenplay* Ernest Lehman. *Based on the play with book and lyrics by* Oscar Hammer-

stein II; *and music by* Richard Rodgers; *from the book "Anna and the King of Siam" by* Margaret Landon. *Music* Richard Rodgers. *Lyrics* Oscar Hammerstein II. *Music supervisor and conductor* Alfred Newman. *Associate music supervisor* Ken Darby. *Director of photography* Leon Shamroy. *Film editor* Robert Simpson. *Choreography* Jerome Robbins. *Art direction* Lyle R. Wheeler and John De Cuir. *Set decorations* Walter M. Scott and Paul S. Fox. *Costume designer* Irene Sharaff. *Wardrobe direction* Charles LeMaire. *Makeup* Ben Nye, Sr. and Robert Dawn. *Hair styles* Helen Turpin. *Sound* E. Clayton Ward, A. Murray Jarvis, Warren B. Delaplain and Carlton W. Faulkner. *Orchestrations* Edward B. Powell, Gus Levene, Bernard Mayers and Robert Russell Bennett. *Ballet arrangement* Trude Rittman. *Oriental music consultant* Michike. *Assistant director* Eli Dunn. *Special photographic effects* Ray Kellogg, L.B. Abbott and Emil Kosa, Jr. *Assistant cameraman* Lee "Red" Crawford. *Production illustrator* Dale Hennesy. *Color consultant* Leonard Doss. *Music editor* Earl Dearth. *CinemaScope lenses* Bausch & Lomb. ¶A Darryl F. Zanuck presentation. Produced and released by 20th Century–Fox. Color by De Luxe. Western Electric Movietone recording. Four-track MagOptical stereophonic sound. 133 minutes plus intermission. Filmed at 20th Century–Fox Studios. ¶CAST: *Anna Leonowens* Deborah Kerr. *King Mongkut* Yul Brynner. *Tuptim* Rita Moreno. *Kralahome* Martin Benson. *Lady Thiang* Terry Saunders. *Louis Leonowens* Rex Thompson. *Lun Tha* Carlos Rivas. *Prince Chulalongkorn* Patrick Adiarte. *British ambassador* Alan Mowbray. *Ramsey* Geoffrey Toone. *Eliza in ballet* Yuriko. *Simon Legree in ballet* Marion Jim. *Keeper of the dogs* Robert Banas. *Uncle Thomas in ballet* Dusty Worrall. *Specialty dancer* Gemze de Lappe. *Twins* Thomas and Dennis Bonilla. *Angel in ballet* Michiki Iseri. *Ship's captain* Charles Irwin. *Interpreter* Leonard Strong. *Whipping guards* Fuji and Weaver Levy. *High priest* William Yip. *Messenger* Eddie Luke. *Princess Ying Yoowalak* Jocelyn Lew. *Siamese girl* Irene James. *Amazons* Jadin and Jean Wong. *Palace guest* Joseph Smith. *Deborah Kerr's vocals* Marni Nixon. ¶Previously filmed as a nonmusical, *Anna and*

Ad for the 70mm conversion of The King and I, *which was filmed in CinemaScope 55 using modified Grandeur cameras.*

the King of Siam (20th Century–Fox, 1946). Converted to 70mm and rereleased March 23, 1961 and advertised in Grandeur 70.

King of Kings (October 11, 1961). Filmed in Super Technirama 70. *Producer* Samuel Bronston. *Associate producers* Alan Brown and Jaime Prades. *Director* Nicholas Ray. *Screenplay* Philip Yordan. *Narration* Ray Bradbury. *Music* Miklos Rozsa. *Directors of photography* Franz F. Planer, Milton Krasner and Manuel Berenguer. *Sets and costumes designer* Georges Wakhevitch. *Set decorations* Enrique Alarcon. *Special photographic*

effects Lee LeBlanc. *General production manager* Stanley Goldsmith. *Master of properties* Stanley Detlie. *Supervising technician* Carl Gibson. *Supervising electrician* Norton Kurland. *Special effects* Alex C. Weldon. *Film editors* Harold F. Kress and Renee Lichtig. *Murals* Maciek Piotrowski. *Second unit directors* Noel Howard and Sumner Williams. *Assistant directors* Carlo Lastricati, Jose Maria Ochoa and Jose Lopez Rodero. *Makeup creators* Mario van Riel and Charles Parker. *Recording supervisor* Franklin E. Milton. *Sound recordist* Basil Fenton Smith. *Rerecording* William Steinkamp at Metro-Goldwyn-Mayer Studios. *Super-*

visor of costuming Eric Seelig. *Hair styles* Anna Cristofani. *Choreography for Salome's dance* Betty Utey Ray. *Assistant operator* Andres Berenguer. ¶A Samuel Bronston Productions, Inc. picture. Technicolor. Westrex six-track magnetic stereophonic sound. 168 minutes plus overture, intermission and exit music. Filmed at Estudios Sevilla and Estudios Chamartin, Madrid, and on location in Chinchon, Manzanares, Aldea del Fresno, Navacerrada, Lake Alberche, Venta de Frascuela and Almeria, Spain. ¶CAST: *Jesus Christ* Jeffrey Hunter. *Mary the Mother* Siobhan McKenna. *Pontius Pilate* Hurd Hatfield. *Lucius the Centurian* Ron Randell. *Claudia* Viveca Lindfors. *Herodias* Rita Gam. *Mary Magdalene* Carmen Sevilla. *Salome* Brigid Bazlen. *Barabbas* Harry Guardino. *Judas Iscariot* Rip Torn. *Herod Antipas* Frank Thring. *Caiphas* Guy Rolfe. *Nicodemus* Maurice Marsac. *Herod the Great* Gregoire Aslan. *Simon-Peter* Royal Dano. *John the Baptist* Robert Ryan. *Balthazar* Edric Connor. *Camel driver* George Coulouris. *Gen. Pompey* Conrado San Martin. *Joseph the Carpenter* Gerard Tichy. *John the Younger* Jose Antonio. *The good thief* Luis Prendes. *Burly man* David Davies. *Caspar* Jose Nieto. *Matthew* Ruben Rojo. *Insane man* Fernando Sancho. *Thomas* Michael Wager. *Joseph of Arimathea* Felix de Pomes. *Melchior* Adriano Rimoldi. *The bad thief* Barry Keegan. *Simon of Cyrene* Rafael Luis Calvo. *Andrew* Tino Barrero. *Blind man* Francisco Moran. *Narrator* Orson Welles. ¶Current prints run 151 minutes with the overture, intermission and exit music removed and some of the music reedited.

Kismet (January 18, 1931). Filmed in Vitascope. *Producer* Robert North. *Director* John Francis Dillon. *Screenplay and dialog* Howard Estabrook. *Based on the play "Kismet: An 'Arabian Night' in Three Acts" by* Edward Knoblock. *Photographer* John B. Seitz. *Film editor* Al Hall. *Recording supervisor* Nathan Levinson. *Recording engineer* Joseph I. Kane. ¶A First National picture. Released by Warner Bros. Pictures. Western Electric Movietone recording. 87 minutes. Filmed at First National Studios. ¶CAST: *Hajj* Otis Skinner. *Marsinah* Loretta Young. *Wazir Mansur* Sidney Blackmer. *Zeleekha* Mary Duncan. *Caliph Abdallah* David

Manners. *Amru* Ford Sterling. *Jailer* Montagu Love. *Wazir* Charles Clary. *Kafur* Noble Johnson. *Narjis* Blanche Frederici. *Miskah* Carol Wines. *Muezzin* Richard Carlyle. *Iman mahmud* John St. Polis. *Guide Hazir* Theodore von Eltz. *Kazim* John Sheehan. *Azef* Otto Hoffman. *Jawan* Edmund Breese. *Chamberlain* Sidney Jarvis. *Zayd* Lorris Baker. *Captain of the guard* Olin Francis. *Herald* William Walling. ¶A 1 minute prolog showed the difference between Vitascope and 35mm using silent scenes from the film. Filmed simultaneously in regular 35mm. A German-language version was also filmed, but it is not known if Vitascope was employed. The director of that version was William Dieterle. Ulrich Steindorff and Karl Etlinger wrote the dialog. The cast was toplined by Gustav Froehlich, Dita Parlo, Vladimir Sokoloff, Anton Pointer and Karl Etlinger.

Kiwi Experience (1987). Filmed in Showscan. Produced and released by Showscan Film Corporation. Eastman Color. Six-track magnetic Dolby Stereo. 18 minutes. Originally made for Showscan theaters in Rotorua and Queenstown, New Zealand.

Knights of the Round Table (December 23, 1953). Presented in Perspecta Stereophonic Sound. *Executive producer* Dore Schary. *Producer* Pandro S. Berman. *Director* Richard Thorpe. *Screenplay* Talbot Jennings, Jan Lustig and Noel Langley. *Based on the novel "Le mort d'Arthur" by* Sir Thomas Malory. *Directors of photography* Frederick A. Young and Stephen Dade. *Music* Miklos Rozsa. *Assistant director* Jack Martin. *Second unit director* Yakima Canutt. *Art directors* Alfred Junge and Hans Peters. *Costume designer* Roger Furse. *Photographic effects* Thomas Howard. *Film editor* Frank Clarke. *Makeup* Charles Parker. *Recording supervisor* Anthony W. Watkins. *Rerecording supervisors* Douglas Shearer and Dr. Wesley C. Miller. *Assistant editor* Ernest Walter. *Processing* Denham Laboratories, Ltd. *Prints* Technicolor. ¶A Loew's, Inc. production. Released by Metro-Goldwyn-Mayer. CinemaScope. Eastman Color. Western Electric Movietone recording. 115 minutes. Filmed at MGM British Studios, Ltd., Borehamwood, and on location in

A reserved seat order form for King of Kings. *Note admission prices.*

Tintagel, England. ¶CAST: *Sir Lancelot du Lac* Robert Taylor. *Queen Guinevere* Ava Gardner. *King Arthur* Mel Ferrer. *Morgan le Fay* Anne Crawford. *Sir Mordred* Stanley Baker. *Merlin the Magician* Felix Aylmer. *Lady Elaine* Maureen Swanson. *Sir Percival* Gabriel Woolf. *Sir Gareth* Anthony Forwood. *Sir Gawaine* Robert Urquhart. *Green Knight* Niall McGinnis. *Bronwyn* Jill Clifford. *Agravaine* Stephen Vercoe. *Nan* Ann Hanslip. *Simon* Howard Marion Crawford. *Bedivere* John Brooking. *Bishop* Peter Gawthorne. *Steward* Alan Tilvern. *Lambert* John Sherman. *Vivien* Dagmar Wunter [Dana Wynter]. *Brizid* Mary Germaine. *John* Martin Wyldeck. *Green Knight's first squire* Barry McKay. *Green Knight's second squire* Derek Tansley. *Leograuce* Roy Russell. *Enid* Gwendoline Evans. *Dancer* Michel De Lutry. ¶An American production filmed in England, this was the first wide screen feature shot in the U.K. The first film in Perspecta

THE GREAT EVENT THAT
USHERS IN M-G-M's
30ᵀᴴ ANNIVERSARY
JUBILEE!

Soon the World will see M-G-M's
FIRST Production in the magic of

CINEMASCOPE IN COLOR MAGNIFICENCE
Knights Of The Round Table

How fitting that this mighty picture marks
the start of a great industry celebration
"M-G-M's 30ᵀᴴ ANNIVERSARY JUBILEE"!

Ad for Knights of the Round Table.

Sound. This is generally accepted as the first film shot with Panavision anamorphics. A flat version was shot simultaneously. Officially remade as *Sword of Lancelot* (a.k.a. *Lancelot and Guinevere;* Universal, 1963) and *Excalibur* (Orion, 1981) though the same story has been told many times on the screen.

Knyazi Igori (1971). Filmed in Sovscope 70. *Screen authors* I. Glikman and R. Tikhomirov. *Based on the opera by* Aleksandr Porfirevich Borodina. *Director* R. Tikhomirov. *Operator* A. Chirov. *Artists* V. Zachinyaev and A. Fedotov. *Sound operator* Georgi Zlibert. ¶A Lenfilm

production. International distribution Sovexportfilm. Sovcolor. Six-track magnetic stereophonic sound. 110 minutes. Filmed at Lenfilm Studios, Leningrad, R.S.F.S.R. ¶CAST: B. Khmelinitskiy, N. Pshennaya, B. Tokarev, A. Slastin, B. Vataev, I. Moryueva, M. Sidorkin, P. Merkuriev, M. Akhunbaev and M. Ikaev. ¶A Soviet production released in Russia in 1971.

Kogda ozivayut ostrova (1982). Filmed in Sovscope 70. International distribution Sovexportfilm. Sovcolor. Six-track magnetic stereophonic sound. A Soviet production released in Russia in 1982.

Kogda poyut muzchini (1981). Filmed in Multifilm. International distribution Sovexportfilm. Sovcolor. Six-track magnetic stereophonic sound. A Soviet production released in Russia in 1981. This was presented in 70mm polyscreen format.

Komandir schastlivoy "Shuki" *see* **Commander of the Lucky "Pike."**

Komitet 19-ti *see* **Committee of 19.**

Koney na pereprave ne menyayut *see* **One Doesn't Change Horses in Midstream.**

Der Kongress Amuesiert sich *see* **Congress of Love.**

Korolevskaya regata *see* **Royal Regatta.**

Koroli gor i drugie (1971). Filmed in Sovscope 70. *Screen author* B. Dolin *in collaboration with* L. Belokurova and M. Vtstukhnovskogo. *Director* B. Dolin. *Operator* Z. Ezov. *Artist* M. Galkin. *Composer* A. Muravlev. *Sound operator* V. Kutuzov. ¶A Tsentrnaufilm production. International distribution Sovexportfilm. Sovcolor. Six-track magnetic stereophonic sound. 97 minutes. Filmed at Tsentrnaufilm Studios, Moscow, R.S.F.S.R. ¶CAST: O. Zakov, V. Dorofeev, A. Kochetkov and N. Kryukov. ¶A Soviet production released in Russia in 1971.

Koroli maneza (1970). Filmed in Sovscope 70. *Screen authors* Yu. Kazakova, Yu. Chulyukin and I. Gostev. *Based on the story "Teddi" by* Yu. Kazakova. *Director* Yu. Chulyukin. *Operators* M. Ardabievskiy, V. Belokopiton and K. Brovin. *Artist* B. Chebotarev. *Composer* A. Lepin. *Sound operator* A. Shargorodskiy. ¶A Mosfilm prouction. International distribution Sovexportfilm. Sovcolor. Six-track magnetic stereophonic sound. 92 minutes. Filmed at Mosfilm Studios, Moscow, R.S.F.S.R. ¶cast: I. Kudrayavtsev, V. Pitsek, Z. Abert and A. Kashperov. ¶A Soviet production released in Russia in 1970.

Kosmicheskiy splav (1964). Filmed in Sovscope 70. *Screen author* A. Perventsev. *Director and producer* T. Levchuk. *Operator* V. Voytenko. *Artists* A. Bobrovnikov and G. Zukovskiy. *Sound operators* A. Gruzov and F. Rikov. ¶A Kievskaya kinostudiya im. A.P. Dovzenko production. International distribution Sovexportfilm. Sovcolor. Six-track magnetic stereophonic sound. 123 minutes. Filmed at Kievskaya kinostudiya im. A.P. Dovzenko, Kiev, Ukrainian S.S.R. ¶CAST: A. Khanov, V. Vinogradov, A. Maksimov, N. Veselovskaya, N. Rizov, M. Sidorkin, V. Safonov, G. Mikhaylov, V. Polishuk, A. Tolstih, A. Movchan, N. Kryukov, V. Emeliyanov, K. Bartashevich. ¶A Soviet production released in Russia in 1964.

Krakatoa *see* **Krakatoa East of Java.**

Krakatoa East of Java (May 14, 1969). Filmed in Todd-AO and Super Panavision 70. Presented in 70mm Super Cinerama. *Producers* William R. Forman and Philip Yordan. *Director* Bernard L. Kowalski. *Writers* Clifford Newton Gould and Bernard Gordon. *Coproducer* Lester A. Sansom. *Director of photography* Manuel Berenguer. *Production designer and special effects sequences director* Eugene Lourie. *Film editors* Maurice Rootes, Warren Low, Walter Hanneman and Derek Parson. *Sound editors* Kenneth Heeley-Ray and Kurt Herrnfeld. *Special effects* Alex C. Weldon. *Music* Frank DeVol. *Songs* "Teacher, Teacher," "I'm an Old Fashioned Girl" and "Java Girl" *music and lyrics* Mack David. *Production supervisor* Gregorio Sacristan. *Titles and montage* Pacific Title & Art Studio, *designer* Don Record. *Production managers* Jose Manuel M. Herrero and Irving Lerner. *Assistant director* Jose Maria Ochoa. *Script supervisors* Eva del Castillo and Lew Gerard. *Costume design* Laure de Zarate. *Wardrobe* Charles Simminger. *Makeup artist* Julian Ruiz. *Special effects assistant* Basilio Cortijo. *Set decorations* Antonio Mateos. *Property master* Julian Mateos. *Still photography* Antonio Luengo. *Second unit director* Frank L. Kowalski. *Second unit photography* John Cabrera. *Underwater photography* Egil S. Woxholt. *Camera operators* Eduardo Noe and Cezare Allione. *Sound recordists* Wallace H. Milner and Gordon K. McCallum. *Dialog coach* John Kirby. *Assistant cameramen* Luis Pena and Jose Martinez. *Assistant cameraman, second unit* Jose Mateos. *Art directors* Julio Molina, Luis Espinosa and Saverio de Eugenio.

Krakatoa East of Java. *Rossano Brazzi and Sal Mineo are being photographed with a Mitchell Todd-AO camera. The crew shown are probably designer and special effects director Eugene Lourie, cameraman John Cabrera, and behind the camera, focus puller Jose Mateos. The director is holding a pole used to push the gondola and give motion to a static scene. The background is a natural sky and not a blue screen for traveling matte work. Long shots of the balloon were done with a very large miniature. Matte printing was avoided whenever possible.*

Hairdressing Antonio Lopez. *Casting director* Lillian Kelly. *Chief grip* Julian Fernandez. *Gaffer* Vicente Acitores. *Sketch artist* Manolo Mampaso. *Construction manager* Francisco Prosper. *Assistant to Eugene Lourie* Fernando Gonzales. *Unit manager* Giorgio Oddi. *Miniature construction* Henri Assola. *Helicopter pilot* Claude. *Tidal wave photography* Jack Willoughby. ¶A Cinerama, Inc. presentation. A Security Pictures, Inc.–Cinerama, Inc.–American Broadcasting Companies, Inc. production. From American Broadcasting Companies, Inc. Released by Cinerama Releasing Corporation. Color by Fotofilm. Prints by Technicolor. Westrex six-track magnetic stereophonic sound. 143 minutes including overture, intermission and exit music. Filmed at Estudios Sevilla and Samuel Bronston Studios, Madrid and Studio Cinecitta, Rome, and on location in Gijon, Denia, Mallorca, Puerto Soller, Marjorca, Spain, Java, Hawaii and on the Mediterranean Sea. ¶CAST: *Ship's Capt.*

Chris Hanson Maximilian Schell. *Laura Travis* Diane Baker. *Harry Connerly* Brian Keith. *Charley Adams* Barbara Werle. *Giovanni Borghese* Rossano Brazzi. *Douglas Rigby* John Leyton. *Danzig* J.D. Cannon. *Toshi* Jacqui Chan. *Ship's Mate Jacobs* Marc Lawrence. *Leoncavallo Borghese* Sal Mineo. *Kiki* Victoria Young Keith. *Convict guard* Robert Hall. *Midori* Midori Arimoto. *Harbor Master Henley* Niall MacGinnis. *Sumi* Sumi Hari. *Second Mate Kuan* Joseph Hann. *Ship's Helmsman Jan* Alan Hoskins. *Bazooki sailor* Geoffrey Holder. *Peter Travis* Peter Kowalski. *Ship's wireless operator* Eugene Lourie. *With* John Clark, Leoncito Cayetano, Peter Graves, Mike Brendel, Jerry Radlowski, Larry Hawkins, Max Slaten, Jose Jaspe, Martin Diaz and David Aller. ¶Working title was *Krakatoa*. A very loose remake of *Fair Wind to Java* (Republic Pictures, 1953). William R. Forman replaced Philip Yordan as producer and Security Pictures withdrew from the production after completion of most or all special effects scenes. With the involvement of Cinerama and ABC a new screenplay was written. Lester A. Sansom was screen-billed as associate producer but was credited as coproducer on the unit list and "official credits" issued by Cinerama. The running time sans overture, intermission and exit music was 127 minutes. Various sources also give the length as 135 and 131 minutes but this includes either or both the overture and exit music times. Reedited to 101 minutes for 35mm general release and 16mm nontheatrical prints. Retitled *Volcano* and restored to 127 minutes for television though some prints bear the original title. Also reissued as *Volcano* in Europe in the mid-seventies, in a Sensurround-type system called Feelarama.

Krakh (1969). Filmed in Sovscope 70. *Screen authors* V. Ardamatskiy, Z. Smirnov and V. Chebotarev. *Director* V. Chebotarev. *Operator* Yu. Gantman. *Artist* E. Serganov. *Composer* A. Muravlev. *Sound operator* O. Upenik. ¶A Mosfilm production. International distribution Sovexportfilm. 225 minutes plus intermission. Filmed at Mosfilm Studios, Moscow, R.S.F.S.R. ¶CAST: Yu. Yakovlev, V. Samoylov, A. Falikovich, E. Kopelyan, E. Matveev, A. Evdokimova, V. Pokrovskiy, A. Karapetyan, G. Voropaev, L. Kuravlev, A. Shirvindt, L. Zolotukhin, V. Safonov, V. Tatosov and L. Gluzskiy. ¶A Soviet production released in Russia in 1969 in two parts running 98 minutes and 127 minutes.

Krasnaya palatka *see* **The Red Tent.**

Krasnie dipkurieri *see* **The Red Diplomatic Couriers.**

Krasnie kolokola *see* **Red Bells.**

Krepostnaya aktrisa (1963). Filmed in Sovscope 70. *Screen author* Z. Zakharov. *Libretto* E. Gerkena. *Based on the operetta "Kholopka" by* N. Strelinikova. *Director and producer* R. Tikhomirov. *Chief operator* E. Shapiro. *Chief artist* I. Vuskovich. *Composer* N. Strelinikova. *Chief sound operator* Georgi Elibert. ¶A Lenfilm production. International distribution Sovexportfilm. Sovcolor. Six-track magnetic stereophonic sound. 100 minutes. Filmed at Lenfilm Studios, Lenin-

grad, R.S.F.S.R. ¶CAST: T. Semina, D. Smirnov, G. Miatsakanova, S. Filippov, S. Yurskiy, M. Polbentseva, E. Leonov, G. Pogdanova-Chesnokova and E. Lemke. ¶A Soviet production released in Russia in 1963.

Krislallen *see* **Cristallisation.**

Krushenie imperii (1971). Filmed in Sovscope 70. *Screen authors* M. Bleyman and N. Kovarskiy. *Director* V. Korsh-Sablin. *Codirector* N. Kalinin. *Operator* I. Remishevskiy. *Artist* Yu. Alibitskiy. *Composer* V. Cherednichenko. *Sound operator* K. Bakk. ¶A Belarusifilm production. International distribution Sovexportfilm. Sovcolor. Six-track magnetic stereophonic sound. 123 minutes. Filmed at Belarusifilm Studios, Minsk, Belorussian S.S.R. ¶CAST: N. Eremenko, Z. Kirienko, E. Samoylov, A. Soloviev, T. Konovalova, A. Vertogradov, V. Tarasov, V. Stazelichik, S. Karnovich-Valua, K. Kulakov, V. Makhov, D. Masanov, A. Gribov, N. Kryufkov, F. Zynas, P. Pankov, B. Klyuev, F. Nikitin, M. Volkov, V. Balashov and M. Vasiliev. ¶A Soviet production released in Russia in 1971.

Krutoe pole (1980). Filmed in Sovscope 70. *Screen authors* L. Saakov and A. Timm. *Director* L. Saakov. *Operator* V. Vladimirov. *Artist* P. Kiselev. *Composer* V. Levashov. *Sound operator* I. Urvantsev. ¶A Mosfilm production. International distribution Sovexportfilm. Sovcolor. Six-track magnetic stereophonic sound. 89 minutes. Filmed at Mosfilm Studios, Moscow, R.S.F.S.R. ¶CAST: D. Franiko, N. Lebedev, O. Azeeva, A. Khryakov, A. Grachev, E. Shutov, N. Menishikov, P. Lyudeshkin, V. Ananiina and A. Savostiyanov. ¶A Soviet production released in Russia in 1980.

La Fayette *see* **Lafayette.**

Lady and the Tramp (July 1955). Filmed in CinemaScope. *Producer* Walt Disney. *Associate producer* Erdman Penner. *Directors* Hamilton Lukse, Clyde Geronimi and Wilfred Jackson. *Story* Erdman Penner, Joe Rinaldi, Ralph Wright and Donald Da Gradi. *Based on an original story by* Ward Greene. *Directing animators* Milt Kahl, Franklin Thomas, Oliver

Lady and the Tramp *was the first animated feature in anamorphic format, but the first cartoon in 'scope was* Toot, Whistle, Plunk and Boom, *released by Disney in November 1953.*

Johnston, Jr., John Lounsbery, Wolfgang Reitherman, Eric Larson, Hal King and Les Clark. *Animators* George Nichols, Hal Ambro, Ken O'Brien, Jerry Hathcock, Erick Cleworth, Marvin Woodward, Ed Aardal, John Sibley, Harvey Toombs, Cliff Nordberg, Don Lusk, George Kreisl, Hugh Fraser, John Freeman, Jack Campbell and Bob Carson. *Backgrounds* Claude Coats, Dick Anthony, Ralph Hulett, Albert Dempster, Thelma Witmer, Eyvind Earle, Jimi Trout, Ray Huffine and Brice Mack. *Layout* Ken Anderson, Tom Codrick, Al Zinnen, A. Kendall O'Connor, Hugh Hennesy, Lance Nolley, Jacques Rupp, McLaren Stewart, Don Griffith, Thor Putnam, Collin Campbell, Victor Nabouch, Bill Bosche and Joe Hale. *Effects animation* George Rowley and Dan McManus. *Music score* Oliver Wallace. *Orchestrations* Edward H. Plumb and Sidney Fine. *Songs* "He's a Tramp," "La La Lu," "Siamese Cat Song," "Peace on Earth" and "Bella Notte" Sonny Burke and Peggy Lee. *Vocal arrangements* John Rarig. *Film editor* Donald Halliday. *Sound director* C.O. Slyfield. *Sound recording* Harold J. Steck and Robert O. Cook.

Music editor Evelyn Kennedy. *Special processes* Ub Iwerks and Art Cruickshank. ¶A Walt Disney production. Released by Buena Vista Distribution Company. Technicolor. RCA Photophone recording. Four-track MagOptical stereophonic sound. 75 minutes. Filmed at Walt Disney Studios. ¶VOICE CHARACTERIZATIONS: *Darling, Peg, Si and Am* Peggy Lee. *Lady* Barbara Luddy. *Tramp* Larry Roberts. *Jock, Bull and Dachsie* Bill Thompson. *Trusty* Bill Baucon. *Beaver* Stan Freberg. *Aunt Sarah* Verna Felton. *Boris* Alan Reed. *Tony* George Givot. *Toughy and Professor* Dallas McKennon. *Jim Dear* Lee Millar. *Singers* The Mello Men. ¶The first animated feature filmed in anamorphic format. A spherical version was shot simultaneously. Reissued in December 1986 in Dolby Stereo.

Lafayette (April 10, 1963). Filmed in Super Technirama 70. *Producer* Maurice Jacquin. *Director* Jean Dreville. *Screenplay* Suzanne Arduini, Jacques Sigurd, Maurice Jacquin, Jean-Bernard Luc, Francois Ponthier and Jean Dreville. *Dialog* Jean-Bernard Luc. *English subtitles* John Hunter, Norbert Terry and Robert

Braum. *Associate producer* Hugo Benedek. *Directors of photography* Claude Renoir and Robert Hubert. *Set designer and decorator* Maurice Colasson. *Editor* Rene Le Henaff. *Music* Steve Laurent and Pierre Duclos. *Sound* Norbert Gernolle. *Assistant director* Louis A. Pascal. *Costumes* Jacqueline Guyot, Francoise Tournafond and Leon Zay. *Special effects* William Warrington. ¶A Copernic Films-Cosmos Film production. Released by Maco Film Corp. Technicolor. Westrex six-track magnetic stereophonic sound. 110 minutes. Filmed on location in Yugoslavia. ¶CAST: *Marie Joseph du Motier, Marquis de Lafayette* Michel Le Royer. *Gen. Cornwallis* Jack Hawkins. *Benjamin Franklin* Orson Welles. *Gen. George Washington* Howard St. John. *Bancroft* Vittorio De Sica. *Silas Deans* Edmund Purdom. *Adrienne de Lafayette* Pascale Audret. *Duc d'Ayen* Jacques Castelot. *Le Boursier* Folco Lulli. *Baron Kalb* Wolfgang Preiss. *Marie Antoinette* Liselotte Pulver. *King Louis XVI* Albert Remy. *Vergennes* Georges Riviere. *Duchesse d'Ayen* Renee Saint-Cyr. *Comtesse de Simiane* Rosanna Schiaffino. *Segur* Henri Amilien. *Monsieur* Gilles Brissac. *La Bergerie* Roger Bontemps. *Maurepas* Jean-Roger Caussimon. *Aglae* Sylvie Coste. *Gen. Philip* Christian Melsen. *Abbe de Cour* Claude Naudes. *Mauroy* Roland Rodier. *Lauzun* Rene Rozan. *With* Henri Tisot, Lois Bolton, Jean Degrave, Jean-Jacques Delbo, Michel Galabru, Jean Lanier and Anthony Stuart. ¶Released in French with English subtitles and in an English-language version. A French and Italian coproduction released in France in February 1962 by UFA-Comico as *La Fayette* running 158 minutes plus intermission; released in Italy in November 1962 as *Lafayette (Una spada per due bandiere)* running 115 minutes. Optically converted to three-panel Super Cinerama and released in parts of Europe by Cinerama.

Lafayette (Una spada per due bandiere) *see* **Lafayette.**

Lana Turner *see* **More Milk Evette.**

Land of Promise (1975). Filmed in 70mm. *Director and script* Andrezj Wajda. *Based on the novel by* Wladyslaw Stanislaw Reymont. *Camera* Witold Sobocinski, Edward Klosinski and Waclaw Dybowski. *Settings* Tadeusz Kosarewicz. *Music* Wojiech Kilar. ¶An X Film Unit production. International distribution Film Polski. Eastman Color. Six-track magnetic stereophonic sound. 165 minutes. ¶CAST: *Karol Borowiecki* Daniel Ollbrychski. *Moryc Welt* Wojciech Pozoniak. *Maks Baum* Andrej Seweryn. *Anka* Anna Nehrebecka. *Karol's father* Tadeusz Bialoszozynski. *Mada Mueller* Bozena Dykiel. *Mueller* Franciszek Pieczka. *Mrs. Mueller* Danuta Wodynska. *Wilhem Mueller* Marian Glinka. *Bucholc* Andrzej Szalawski. *Mrs. Bucholc* Jadwiga Andrzejesska. *Lucy* Kalina Jedrusik. ¶A Polish production released in Poland in Spring 1975 as *Ziemia obiecana* running 178 minutes. This is listed for the record as the only Polish film we are aware of released in 70mm though there may have been others. It is likely this was a blow up from 35mm as Film Polski publicity material only stated 70mm and did not credit a photographic process. It is of interest to note that Eastman Color was used instead of Sovcolor.

The Lash (January 1, 1931). Filmed in Vitascope. *Producer and director* Frank Lloyd. *Adaptation and dialog* Bradley King. *Story* Lanier Bartlett and Virginia Stivers Bartlett. *Photographer* Ernest Haller. *Film editor* Harold Young. *Recording supervisor* Nathan Levinson. *Recording engineer* Oliver S. Garretson. ¶A First National picture. Released by Warner Bros. Pictures. Western Electric Movietone recording. 79 minutes. Filmed at First National Studios. ¶CAST: *Francisco Delfino* Richard Barthelmess. *Rosita Garcia* Mary Astor. *Peter Harkness* Fred Kohler. *Dolores Delfino* Marian Nixon. *David Howard* James Rennie. *Don Marino Delfino* Robert Edeson. *Juan* Arthur Stone. *Lupe* Barbara Bedford. *Concha* Mathilde Comont. *Judge Travers* Erville Alderson. ¶Working title was *Adios*. Filmed simultaneously in regular 35mm.

The Last Storming *see* **Liberation.**

(James Clavell's) The Last Valley (February 1971). Filmed in Todd-AO. *Executive producer* Martin Baum. *Screen writer, producer and director* James Clavell. *Based on the novel by* J.B. Pick. *Director of photography* John Wilcox. *Music composer and conductor* John

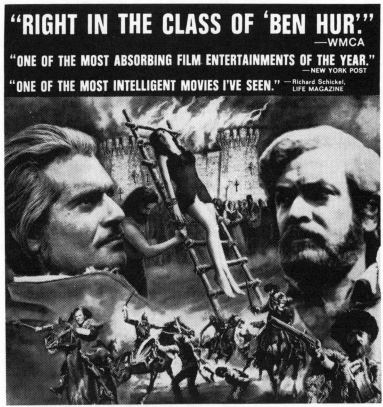

"RIGHT IN THE CLASS OF 'BEN HUR.'"
—WMCA

"ONE OF THE MOST ABSORBING FILM ENTERTAINMENTS OF THE YEAR."
—NEW YORK POST

"ONE OF THE MOST INTELLIGENT MOVIES I'VE SEEN." —Richard Schickel,
LIFE MAGAZINE

the last valley

ABC Pictures Corp. presents James Clavell's
"The Last Valley"
starring Michael Caine   Omar Sharif
Florinda Bolkan   Nigel Davenport   Per Oscarsson
co-starring Arthur O'Connell   Madeline Hinde ~Yorgo Voyagis   Miguel Alejandro   Christian Roberts
Music by John Barry   Executive Producer Martin Baum
Written for the Screen, Produced and Directed by James Clavell   A Season Production
Original Soundtrack Recording Available on ABC/Dunhill Records and Tapes   A Subsidiary Of The American Broadcasting Companies, Inc.
Color Filmed in TODD-AO   Distributed by Cinerama Releasing Corporation   GP   ALL AGES ADMITTED Parental Guidance Suggested

Cinerama's last epic show, but not given the giant curved screen treatment.

Barry. *Editor* John Bloom. *Associate producer* Robert Porter. *Second unit cameraman* Norman Warwick. *Art director* Peter Mullins. *Costume designer* Yvonne Blake. *Sound recordist* Bob Peck. *Dubbing mixer* Bob Jones. *Assistant editor* Lesley Walker. *Dubbing editor* Chris Greenham. *Assistant director* William P. Cartlidge. *Second assistant director* Brian Cook. *Austrian assistant director* Wolfgang Glattes. *Visual effects* Wally Veevers. *Special assistant and production illustrator* Maurice Zuberano. *Production manager* Marguerte Green. *Location managers* Terence Churcher and Wolfram Kohtz. *Austrian unit manager* Kent McPherson. *Construction manager* John Paterson. *Camera operator* Paul Wilson. *Second unit operator* Eric Besche. *Continuity* Pamela Carlton. *Unit publicist* Alan Arnold. *Casting director* Maude Spector. *Wardrobe* Jim Smith. *Makeup* Wally Schneiderman and Alberto de Rossi. *Hairdressing* Eileen Warwick. *Special effects* Pat Moore. *Stunt arranger* John Sullivan. *Production secretary*

Midge Warnes. *Stills* John Jay. *Special stills* Sergio Strizzi. *Assistant art directors* Ted Clements and Roy Smith. *Gaffer* Len Crowe. *Lighting* Lee Electric Ltd. *Titles* Trickfilm London. ¶An ABC Pictures Corp. presentation. A Season-Seamaster production. A James Clavell film. From the American Broadcasting Companies, Inc. Released by Cinerama Releasing Corporation. Eastman Color. Westrex six-track magnetic stereophonic sound. 129 minutes. Filmed on location in the Austrian Alps. MPAA rating: GP. ¶CAST: *Captain* Michael Caine. *Vogel* Omar Sharif. *Erica* Florinda Bolkan. *Gruber* Nigel Davenport. *Father Sebastian* Per Oscarsson. *Herr Hoffman* Arthur O'Connell. *Inge Hoffman* Madeline Hinde. *Pirelli* Yorgo Voyagis. *Julio* Miguel Alejandro. *Andreos* Christian Roberts. *Graf* Ian Hogg. *Hansen* Michael Gothard. *Korski* Brian Blessed. *Vornez* George Innes. *Frau Hoffman* Irene Prador. *Matthias* Vladek Sheybal. *Geddes* John Hallam. *Schultz* Andrew McCulloch. *Eskesen* Jack Shepherd. *Czerski* Leon Lissek. *Svensen* Chris Chittell. *Tzarus* Kurt Christian. *Sernen* Mark Edwards. *Peasant girl* Michaela. *Garnak* Larry Taylor. *Helga* Claudia Butenuth. *Zollner* Paul Challon. *Tub* Tony Vogel. *Rethman* Patrick Westwood. *Corg* Frazer Hines. *Gnarled peasant* Edward Underdown. *Nansen* Seyton Pooley. *Little girl* Holly du Marrek. *Claus* Ralph Arliss. *Pastori* Dave Crowley. *Stoffel* Mike Douglas. *Yuri* Richard Graydon. *Norseman* Terry Richards. *Kass* Joe Powell. *Rape girl* Lisa Jager. *Stuntmen* John Morris, Terry Plummer and Joe Powell. ¶Officially the last film made for, but not exhibited in 70mm Super Cinerama. See *The Great Waltz.*

The Last Victim (1976). Filmed in Sovscope 70. *Screen authors* Vladimir Zuev and Pyotr Todorovskiy. *Based on the play "Poslednyaya zertva" by* Aleksandr N. Ostrovskogo. *Director* Pyotr Todorovskiy. *Operator* Leonid Kalashinkov. *Artist* Gennady Myasnikov. *Composer* Isaak Shvarts. *Sound operator* V. Kurganskiy. *Romantic dialog* B. Okudzavi. ¶A Mosfilm production. International distribution Sovexportfilm. Sovcolor. Six-track magnetic stereophonic sound. 99 minutes. Filmed at Mosfilm Studios, Moscow, R.S.F.S.R. ¶cast: *Yulia Tugina* Margarita Volodina. *Vadim Dulchin* Oleg

Strizenov. *Flor Fedulich Pribytkov* Mikhail Gluzskiy. *Lavr Mironovich* Leonid Kuravlev. *With* Vladimir Kenigson, O. Naumeko, V. Filippov, L. Pirieva, M. Vinogradova, P. Vinnik and L. Savchenko. ¶A Soviet production released in Russia in 1976 as *Poslednyaya zertva.*

Lautare (1973). Filmed in Sovscope 70. *Screen author and director* Emile Lotyanu. *Operators* Vitali Kalashnikov and V. Adoliskiy. *Artist* Georgev Dimitrich. *Composer* Evgeni Doga. *Sound operators* A. Buruyanz and E. Reyttsh. ¶A Moldova-film production. International distribution Sovexportfilm. Sovcolor. Six-track magnetic stereophonic sound. 175 minutes plus intermission. Filmed at Moldova-film Studios, Kishinev, Moldavian S.S.R. ¶CAST: *Toma Alistar* Sergei Lunkevich. *Toma as a young man* Ekhenya Roliko. *Lyanka* Olga Kimpyanu. *With* Dimitru Khzbzshesku, Galina Vodyanitskaya, A. Yashchenku, V. Musayan, Kh. Berdaga, L. Iorga and N. Fagurel. ¶A Soviet production released in Russia in 1973 as *Lautari* in two parts running 82 minutes and 93 minutes.

Lautari *see* **Lautare.**

The Law of the Antarctic (1963). Filmed in Sovscope 70. *Screen authors* Bogdan Chaily and Sergei Alekseev. *Director and producer* Timofei Levchuk. *Chief operator* Suren Shchakhbazyan. *Artist* A. Bobrovnikov. *Composer* G. Zukovskiy. *Sound operators* A. Gruzov and Yu. Rikov. ¶A Kievskaya kinostudiya im. A.P. Dovzenko production. International distribution Sovexportfilm. Sovcolor. Six-track magnetic stereophonic sound. 98 minutes. Filmed at Kievskaya kinostudiya im. A.P. Dovzenko, Kiev, Ukrainian S.S.R. and on location. ¶CAST: Vsevolod Safonov, Radier Muratov, Gurgen Tonunts, Nikolai Kryukov, A. Movchan, P. Morozenko, V. Volchik, V. Kolokolitsev, Kh. Kryukov, V. Breznev, P. Varandi, R. Dombran and A. Motorniy. ¶A Soviet production released in Russia in May 1963 as *Zakon Antarktidi.*

Lawrence of Arabia (December 16, 1962). Filmed in Super Panavision 70. *Producer* Sam Spiegel. *Director* David Lean. *Screenplay* Robert Bolt, Michael Wilson and Beverley Cross. *Based on "Seven*

Pillars of Wisdom," "Revolt in the Desert," "The Essential T.E. Lawrence" (with preface by David Garnett), *"Secret Dispatches from Arabia," "Crusader Castles," "Men in Print: Essays in Literary Criticism," "The Diary of T.E. Lawrence," "La bibliotheque ideale: T.E. Lawrence," "The Home Letters of T.E. Lawrence and His Brothers," "Selected Letters of T.E. Lawrence"* (edited by David Garnett), *"The Selected Letters of T.E. Lawrence"* (edited by Irving Howe) and *"The Mint"* by Thomas Edward Lawrence; *"With Lawrence in Arabia"* by Lowell Thomas; *"Lawrence and the Arabs"* and chapter 28 of *"Goodbye to All That"* by Robert Graves; *"T.E. Lawrence and His Biographers, Robert Graves and Liddell Hart"; "Lawrence of Arabia"* by Richard Aldington; *"T.E. Lawrence in Arabia and After"* by Basil Liddell Hart; *"Heroes of the Empty View"* by James Aldridge; *"The Desert and the Stars"* by Flora Armitage; *"T.E. Lawrence: By His Friends"* and *"Letters to T.E. Lawrence* edited by A.W. Lawrence; *"Lawrence of Arabia"* by Anthony Nutting; *"Lawrence of Arabia"* by Alistair MacLean; *"Lawrence of Arabia"* by Robert Payne; and *"Private Shaw and Public Şhaw"* by Stanley Weintraub. *Music composer* Maurice Jarre. *Orchestrations* Gerard Schurmann. *Players* The London Philharmonic Orchestra. *Conductor* Sir Adrian Boult. *Director of photography* Frederick A. Young. *Production designer* John Box. *Art director* John Stoll. *Costume designer* Phyllis Dalton. *Editor* Anne V. Coates. *Sound editor* Winston Ryder. *Second unit direction* Andre Smagghe, Noel Howard and Andre de Toth. *Second unit photography* Skeets Kelly, Nicholas Roeg and Peter Newbrook. *Production manager* John Palmer. *Location managers* Douglas Twiddy and Eva Monley. *Casting director* Maude Spector. *Set dresser* Dario Simoni. *Wardrobe* John Wilson Apperson. *Assistant art directors* Roy Rossotti, George Richardson, Terence Marsh and Anthony Rimmington. *Property master* Eddie Fowlie. *Chief electrician* Archie Dansie. *Camera operator* Ernest Day. *Assistant director* Roy Stevens. *Continuity* Barbara Cole. *Sound recording* Paddy Cunningham. *Sound dubbing* John Cox. *Makeup* Charles Parker. *Hairdressing* A.G. Scott. *Construction manager* Peter Dukelow. *Construction assistant* Fred Bennett.

Special effects Cliff Richardson and Wally Veevers. *Music coordinator* Morris W. Stoloff. *Associate editor* Norman Savage. *Footsteps* Beryl Mortimer. *Stills photographers* Mark Kaufman and Ken Danvers. *Production accountant* David White. *Unit publicist* John R. Woolfenden. *Research* Marie Budberg. *Catering* The Location Caterers Ltd. *Sketch artist* Charles Bishop. *Draughtsman* John Graysmark. *Sound* Shepperton Studios. ¶A Sam Spiegel-David Lean production. A Horizon Pictures (G.B.) Ltd. film. Released by Columbia Pictures. Technicolor. RCA six-track magnetic stereophonic sound. 221 minutes including overture and intermission. Filmed at Shepperton Studios, Middlesex, England, and on location in Jebel Tubeiq and Wadi Rhumm, Jordan, Sevilla and Aquaba, Spain, and Morocco. ¶CAST: *Thomas Edward Lawrence* Peter O'Toole. *Prince Feisal* Alec Guinness. *Sheikh Auda Abu Tayi* Anthony Quinn. *Gen. Sir Edmund Allenby* Jack Hawkins. *Turkish bey* Jose Ferrer. *Col. Harry Brighton* Anthony Quayle. *Mr. Dryden* Claude Rains. *Jackson Bentley* Arthur Kennedy. *Gasim* I.S. Johar. *Majid* Gamil Ratib. *Tafas* Zia Mohyeddin. *Farraj* Michel Ray. *Daud* John Dimech. *Gen. Murray* Donald Wolfit. *Sherif Ali Ibn el Kharish* Omar Sharif. *Medical officer* Howard Marion Crawford. *Club secretary* Jack Gwillin. *R.A.M.C. colonel* Hugh Miller. *Cpl. Jenkins* Norman Rossington. *Elder Martin* John Ruddock. *Allenby's aide* Kenneth Fortescue. *Regimental sergeant-major* Stuart Sanders. *Turk sergeant* Fernando Sancho. *Reciter* Henry Oscar. *Train wreck stunt* Emilio Noriega. *With* M. Cher Kaoui, Mohammed Habachi and members of the Jordanian Desert Patrol and the Royal Moroccan Army Camel Corps. ¶A British production released in England in November 1962 running 222 minutes with a BBFC A certificate. Originally announced as an Alexander Korda production to be directed by John Ford. Rereleased running 204 minutes which is the only version now available.

Lebedinoe ozero *see* **Swan Lake.**

Legend of Love (1984). Filmed in Sovscope 70. *Screen authors* Ulmas Umarbekov and Latif Fayziev *in collaboration with* Dhavad Sidki and Umesh Mehra. *Directors* Lafit Fayziev and

Umesh Mehra. *Operators* Davron Abdullaev and Abu Rashid Panu. *Artists* Sadriddin Ziyamukhamedov and Baburao Poddaro. *Composers* Vladimir Milov and Inni Malik. *Sound operators* Erkin Kayumov and Bramanand Sharma. ¶A Uzbekfilm-Eagle Films production in collaboration with Sovinfilm. International distribution Sovexportfilm. Sovcolor. Six-track magnetic stereophonic sound. 141 minutes plus intermission. Filmed at Uzbekfilm Studios, Tashkent, Uzbek S.S.R. and on location in India. ¶CAST: Sunny Doel, Punam Dhillon, Nabi Rakhimov, Shammi Kapur, Zinnat Aman, Zakir Mukhamedzanov, T. Oganesyan, Isamat Ergashev, Frunzik Mkrtchyan, Pran, G. Dzamilova, Rakesh Bedi and Tanuja. ¶A Soviet and Indian coproduction released in Russia in 1984 as *Legenda o lyubvi* in two parts running 77 minutes and 64 minutes.

The Legend of Princess Olga (1984). Filmed in Sovscope 70. *Screen author and director* Yuri Ilienko. *Operator* Vilen Kalyuta. *Artists* Vasill Beskrovniy and Valery Safronov. *Composer* Evgeny Stankevich. *Sound operator* V. Bryunchugin. *Still photo* Leonid Kritenko. ¶A Kievskaya kinostudiya im. A.P. Dovzenko production. International distribution Sovexportfilm. Sovcolor. Six-track magnetic stereophonic sound. 169 minutes plus intermission. Filmed at Kievskaya kinostudiya im. A.P. Dovzenko, Kiev, Ukrainian S.S.R. and on location at Mount Baldy. ¶CAST: *Princess Olga* Lyudmila Efimenko. *Vladimir* Vanya Ivanov. *With* Les Serdyuk, K. Stepankov, Ivan Mikolaychuk, Ivan Gavrilyuk, D. Mirgorodskiy, Nikolai Olyalin, S. Romashko, G. Morozyuk, Yu. Dubrovin, L. Obolenskiy and I. Savkin. ¶A Soviet production released in Russia in 1984 as *Legenda o knyagine Olige* in two parts running 84 minutes and 85 minutes.

The Legend of Tile (1977). Filmed in Sovscope 70. *Screen authors and directors* Aleksandr Alov and Vladimir Naumov. *Based on the novel "Legenda o Tile" by* Sh. de Kostera. *Operator* Valentin Zeleznyakov. *Artists* Alexei Parkhomenko and Evgeni Chernyaev. *Composer* Nikolai Karetnikov. *Sound operator* R. Kazaryan. ¶A Mosfilm production. International distribution Sovexportfilm. Sovcolor. Six-track magnetic stereophonic sound.

Filmed at Mosfilm Studios, Moscow, R.S.F.S.R. ¶CAST: *Tile* Lembit Ulifsak. *Nele* Natalia Belokhvostikova. *Lamme* Evgeni Leonov. *Katlina* Alla Demidova. *With* Mikhail Uliyanov, Larissa Malevannaya, Anatoly Solonitsin, Innokenty Smoktunovskiy, Vladimir Dvorshetsky, Igor Ledogorov, E. Evstigneev, V. Zakharchenko, O. Vidov and Yu. Budraytis. ¶A Soviet production released in Russia in 1977 as *Legenda o Tile* in two parts: *Pepel klassa* running 155 minutes plus intermission (part one: 81 minutes, part two: 74 minutes) and *Da zdravstvuyut nishchie!* running 157 minutes plus intermission (part one: 76 minutes, part two: 81 minutes). A version edited from both parts was also released. The novel has been filmed several times in Europe.

Legenda o knyagine Olige *see* **The Legend of Princess Olga.**

Legenda o lyubvi *see* **Legend of Love.**

Legenda o Tile *see* **The Legend of Tile.**

Leningrad (1971). Filmed in Sovscope 70. International distribution Sovexportfilm. Sovcolor. Six-track magnetic stereophonic sound. A Soviet production released in Russia in 1971.

The Leningrad Metronome *see* **Blockade.**

Leningradskiy metronom *see* **Blockade.**

Lesnaya pesnya, Mavka (1982). Filmed in Sovscope 70. *Screen author, director and operator* Yu. Ilienko. *Based on the play "Lesnaya pesnya" by* L. Ukrainki. *Artist* A. Manontov. *Composer* E. Stankevich. *Sound operator* A. Kovtun. ¶A Kievskaya kinostudiya im. A.P. Dovzenko production. International distribution Sovexportfilm. Sovcolor. Six-track magnetic stereophonic sound. 104 minutes. Filmed at Kievskaya kinostudiya im. A.P. Dovzenko, Kiev, Ukrainian S.S.R. ¶CAST: L. Efimenko, V. Kremnev, M. Bulgakova, I. Mikolaychuk, L. Lobza, B. Khmelinitskiy, N. Shatskaya and S. Sergeeva. ¶A Soviet production released in Russia in 1982.

Let's Go (1985). Filmed in Showscan. Produced and released by Showscan Film

Corporation. Eastman Color. Six-track magnetic Dolby Stereo. 15 minutes. Originally made for EXPO in Tsukuba, Japan.

Liberation (1970). Filmed in Sovscope 70. *Screen authors* Yuri Bondarev, Oschar Kurganov and Yuri Nikolayevitch. *Director* Yuri Nikolayevitch. *Producer for DEFA* Kurt Lichterfeld. *Producer for Dino De Laurentiis Cinematografica* Dino De Laurentiis. *Operator* Igor Slabnevich. *Artist* Aleksandr Myagkov. *Composer* Yuri Levitin. *Sound operators* E. Kashchkevich, Yuri Mikhailov and E. Indelina. *Assistant director* Yuli Kun. *Script editor* Grigori Maryamov. *Chief consultant* Gen. Sergei Shtemenko. *Consultants* Marshal Georgi Zkhukev, Konev and Moskalenek. *Historical consultant* Col. Wiezleban. ¶A Mosfilm production in association with DEFA, PRFZF and Dino De Laurentiis Cinematografica S.p.A. International distribution Sovexportfilm. Sovcolor. Six-track magnetic stereophonic sound. Filmed at Mosfilm Studios, Moscow, R.S.F.S.R., and on location in Vilnius, Lithuanian S.S.R. ¶CAST: *Zoya* Larisa Golubkina. *Tsvestaiyey* Nikolai Olyalia. *Marshal Georgi Zhukev* Mikhail Ulyanov. *Joseph V. Stalin* Bukhuti Zakariadze. *Col. Stauffenberg* Alfred Struve. *Gen. Rokossovskiy* Vladlen Davidov. *Gen. Berling* Tadeusz Schmidt. *Orlov* Boris Zaidenberg. *Yartsev* Mikhail Nozkhkin. *Marshal Vassilevskiy* Evgeni Burenkov. *Gen. Vatutin* Sergei Kharchenko. *Benito Mussolini* Ivo Garrani. *Adolf Hitler* Fritz Dits. *With* Sergei Nikonenko, Vladimir Samoilov, Florin Piersic, Barbara Briliska, Daniel Olidrikhskiy, V. Shukshin, V. Strzelichik, V. Wieland, Hardy Kruger, A. Waller, I. Klose, G. Steiger, G. Hennsberg, S. Weiss, Hanio Hasse, N. Gize, A. Struve, E. Strecher, V. Sanaev, Yu. Kamorniy, Valeri Nosik, Ya, Znglert, V. Avdyushchkin, I. Ozerob, M. Uliyanov, Yu. Legkov, Yu. Durov, V. Glinskiy, N. Rushchkovskiy, S. Yasikevich, Z. Tide, Kh. Keyn, A. Shturm, V. Vilants, V. Zamanskiy, N. Ribnikov, V. Karen, K. Protasov and P. Strum. ¶A Soviet production released in Russia during 1970 and 1971 as *Osvobozdenie* in five parts: *Ognennaya duga (The Flaming Bulge)* (1970) running 117 minutes; *Provib (The Breakthrough)* (1970) running 113 minutes; *Napravlenie glavnogo udara (Main Thrust)* (1970) running 163 minutes plus intermission (part one: 74 minutes; part two: 89 minutes); *Battle for Berlin* (1971) running 81 minutes; and *The Last Storming* (1971) running 75 minutes. The last two parts, for which the actual Soviet titles weren't provided, were made in collaboration with East German, Polish and Italian production companies.

The Life and Death of Ferdinand Luce (1977). Filmed in Sovscope 70. *Screen author* Yulian Semenov. *Director* Anatoly Bobrovskiy. *Operator* Nikolai Olonovskiy. *Artist* Leonid Pertsev. *Composer* Isaak Shvarts. *Sound operator* L. Bulgakov. *Song words* B. Okudzavi. ¶A Mosfilm production. International distribution Sovexportfilm. Sovcolor. Six-track magnetic stereophonic sound. 281 minutes. Filmed at Mosfilm Studios, Moscow, R.S.F.S.R. ¶CAST: *Prosecutor* Pavel Pankov. *With* Vsevolod Safonov, Donates Banionis, Nikolai Gritsenko, Igor Ledogorov, Yuozas Budraytis, Zeva Kivi, Ekaterina Vasilieva, Suimenkul Chokmorov, E. Evstigneev, B. Ivanov, E. Khanaeva, O. Basilashvili, V. Shuligin, M. Pogorzeliskiy, V. Livanov, A. Poposhin, A. Kalyagin and R. Kurkina. ¶A Soviet production released in Russia in 1977 as *Zizni i smerti Ferdinanda Lyusa* in four parts running 70 minutes, 74 minutes, 69 minutes and 68 minutes.

The Light Fantastic *see* **Brainstorm.**

Lights of New York (July 6, 1928). Recorded in Western Electric Vitaphone. *Director* Bryan Foy. *Adaptation and dialog* F. Hugh Herbert and Murray Roth. *Story* Charles L. Gaskill. *Photographer* Edwin B. DuPar. *Film editor* Jack Killifer. *Recording engineer* Col. Nathan Levinson. *Sound engineer* George R. Groves. *Makeup artist* Perc Westmore. *Technical director* R. Lewis Geib. ¶Produced and released by Warner Bros. Pictures. 59 minutes. Filmed at Warner Bros. Studios. ¶CAST: *Kitty Lewis* Helene Costello. *Eddie Morgan* Cullen Landis. *Molly Thompson* Gladys Brockwell. *Gene* Eugene Pallette. *Sam* Tom Dugan. *Police Chief Collins* Tom McGuire. *Mrs. Morgan* Mary Carr. *Hawk Miller* Wheeler Oakman. *Detective Crosby* Robert Elliott. *Tommy* Guy Dennery. *Jake Jackson* Walter Percival. *Dan Dickson* Jere

Delaney. ¶The first all-talking feature film which, befitting the times, was also released in a silent version. *The Jazz Singer* is generally credited as the first "talker," but it was actually a silent film with limited ad lib dialog during live music recording and cannot be considered a true sound feature in the accepted sense.

Lika-Chekhova lyubovi *see* **Lika-Chekhov's Love.**

Lika-Chekhov's Love (1971). Filmed in Sovscope 70. *Screen author* Leonid Malyugin. *Director* Sergei Yutkevich. *Operator* Naum Ardashnikov. *Composer* Rodion Shchedrin. ¶A Mosfilm–Telsia Film production. International distribution Sovexportfilm. Sovcolor. Six-track magnetic stereophonic sound. 86 minutes. Filmed at Mosfilm Studios, Moscow, R.S.F.S.R. ¶CAST: Marina Vlady, Nikolai Griniko, Ilya Savvina and Yuri Yakovlev. ¶A Soviet and French coproduction released in Russia in 1971 as *Lika-Chekhova lyubovi.*

Living Planet (1979). Filmed in IMAX. *Executive producer* Francis Thompson. *Producer and director* Dennis Earl Moore. *Photographers* Laszlo George and Burleigh Wartes. *Production manager* Richard Gelfand. ¶A Francis Thompson, Inc. production. Sponsored by S.C. Johnson & Son, Inc. (Johnson Wax). Released by Dennis Earl Moore Productions. Eastman Color. Six-track magnetic stereophonic sound. 30 minutes. Filmed around the world. Originally made for the National Air and Space Museum in Washington, D.C.

Lofty Title (1973). Filmed in Sovscope 70. *Screen authors* Yuly Dunskiy and Valeri Frid. *Based on the opera "Ya-Shapovalov T.P."* *Director* Evgeni Karelov. *Operator* Anatoli Petritskiy. *Artists* Valeri Filippov and Vladimir Filippov. *Composer* Evgeni Ptichkin. *Sound operator* I. Urvantsev. *Song text* E. Karelova. ¶A Mosfilm production. International distribution Sovexportfilm. Sovcolor. Six-track magnetic stereophonic sound. 124 minutes. Filmed at Mosfilm Studios, Moscow, R.S.F.S.R. ¶CAST: *Shapovalov* Evgeni Matveev. *Tzhovrebov* Armen Dzigarkhanyan. *Cmdr. Gaidabura* Dmitri Franiko. *Alexei* Semyon Morozov. *With* Valentina Malyavina, Nina Popova, Boris Tokarev,

Tatyana Nazarova, Valeri Nosik, Boris Yurchenko, N. Sergeev, V. Kashpur, E. Burenkov, Yu. Kuzimenkov, E. Steblov, V. Basov, V. Pavlov, Yu. Gusev, A. Soloviev, O. Shobev and D. Lizak. ¶A Soviet production released in Russia in 1973 as *Visokoe zvanie.* Reedited and also released in Russia in 1973 in two parts: *Ya-Shapovalov T.P. (I, Shapovalov T.P.)* running 98 minutes and *Radi Zkhizni na zemle (For the Sake of Life on Earth)* running 92 minutes.

The Long Flight *see* **John Ford's Cheyenne Autumn.**

The Long Ships (June 24, 1964). Filmed in Super Technirama 70. *Producer* Irving Allen. *Director* Jack Cardiff. *Screenplay* Berkely Mather and Beverley Cross. *Based on the novel "Rode Orm" by* Frans Bengtsson. *Director of photography* Christopher Challis. *Second unit director* Cliff Lyons. *Associate producer* Denis O'Dell. *Music composer* Dusan Radic. *Conductor* Borislav Pascan. *Art directors* Zoran Zorcic, William Constable, Vlastimir Gavrik and John Hoesli. *Costume designers* Anthony Mendleson and David Ffolkes. *Film editor* Geoffrey Foot. *Production managers* David W. Orton and Milenko Stonkovic. *Assistant directors* Bluey Hill and Stevo Petrovic. *Camera operators* Austin Dempster and Ray Parslow. *Continuity* Angela Allen and Eileen Head. *Sound recordists* Paddy Cunningham and Hugh Strain. *Sound editor* Gordon Daniel. *Action sequences* Bob Simmons. *Special effects* Syd Pearson and William Warrington. *Second unit cameraman* Skeets Kelly. *Technical adviser* Erik Kiersgaard. *Matte artist* Ivor Beddoes. *Makeup* Neville Smallwood. *Hairdresser* A.G. Scott. *Wardrobe master* Ronald Beck. *Prolog and main titles* Maurice Binder. *Mosaics* A. Benzon. *Assistant to the producer* Paul Maslansky. ¶An Irving Allen production. A Warwick Film Productions, Ltd.–Avala Film picture. Released by Columbia Pictures. Technicolor. Westrex six-track magnetic stereophonic sound. 125 minutes. Filmed at Studio Cinecitta, Rome and on location in Yugoslavia. ¶CAST: *Rolfe* Richard Widmark. *El Mansuh* Sidney Poitier. *Aminah* Rosanna Schiaffino. *Orm* Russ Tamblyn. *Kork* Oscar Homolka. *Aziz* Lionel Jeffries. *Sven* Edward Judd. *Gerda*

Ad for The Long Ships; *some prints screen-billed Technirama 70, as in this ad, while others simply credited Technirama.*

Beba Loncar. *King Harald* Clifford Evans. *Rhykka* Colin Blakely. *Vahlin* Gordon Jackson. *Olla* David Lodge. *Raschild* Paul Stassino. *Ylva* Jeanne Moody. *Auctioneer* Henry Oscar. ¶A British and Yugoslavian coproduction advertised in Technirama 70mm with some prints screen billing Technirama 70 and other prints simply crediting Technirama. Released in England in 1964 by British Lion–Columbia; released in Yugoslavia in 1964 as *Dugi brodovi*.

Lord Jim (February 25, 1965). Filmed in Super Panavision 70. *Executive producers* Jules Buck and Peter O'Toole. *Producer, screenwriter and director* Richard Brooks. *Based on the novel by* Joseph Conrad. *Production designer* Geoffrey Drake. *Photographer* Frederick A. Young. *Music* Bronislau Kaper. *Conductor* Muir Mathieson. *Adviser in Oriental music* Prof. Mantle Hood, U.C.L.A. *Film editor* Alan Osbiston. *Costume designer* Phyllis Dalton. *Chief makeup* Charles Parker. *Chief hairdresser* Gordon Bond. *Production manager* Rene Dupont. *Assistant director* Roy Stevens. *Camera operator* Ernest Day. *Story editor* Arthur Knight. *Sound recordists* Paddy Cunningham and Bob Jones. *Wardrobe supervision* John Wilson Apperson. *Sound editor* Chris Greenham. *Music editor* Peter Zinner. *Art directors* Bill Hutchinson and Ernest Archer. *Special effects* Cliff Richardson and Wally Veevers. *Property master* Eddie Fowlie. *Second assistant director* Michael Stevenson. *Continuity* Angela Martelli. *Still photographer* Ken Danvers. *Special effects assistant* John Richardson. *Sound supervisor* John Cox. *Studio construction manager* Peter Dukelow. ¶A Richard Brooks film. A Columbia Pictures Corp.–Keep Films, Ltd. production. Released by Columbia Pictures. Technicolor. Westrex six-track magnetic stereophonic sound. 154 minutes plus intermission. Filmed at Shepperton Studios, London, and on location in Kowloon and Aberdeen, Hong Kong, Angkor Wat and Siem Reap, Indochina and in the Gulf of Siam. ¶CAST: *Lord Jim* Peter O'Toole. *Gentleman Brown* James Mason. *Cornelius* Curt Jurgens. *The General* Eli Wallach. *Marlow* Jack Hawkins. *Stein* Paul Lukas. *The Girl* Daliah Lavi. *Schomberg* Akim Tamiroff. *Waris* Ichizo Itami. *Du-Ramin* Tatsuo Saito. *Brierly*

Andrew Keir. *Robinson* Jack MacGowran. *Malay* Eric Young. *Capt. Chester* Noel Purcell. *Captain of S.S. Patna* Walter Gotell. *Moslem leader* Rafik Anwar. *Elder* Marne Maitland. *Doctor* Newton Blick. *Magistrate* A.J. Brown. *French officer* Christian Marquand. *French lieutenant* Serge Reggiani. ¶35mm general release prints ran 143 minutes without an intermission. Restored to 154 minutes for video cassette sales.

Love in Chicago *see* **The Bat Whispers.**

Love in 3-D (March 1974). Filmed in 70mm Triarama. *Producer* Wolf C. Hartwig. *Director* Walter Boos. *Screenplay* Florian Vollmer. *Camera* Klaus Werner. *Music* Sonoton Musikproduktion. *Editor* Herbert Taschner. *Settings* Peter Rothe. *Assistant director* Walter Molitor. *Camera assistant* Klaus Beckhausen. *Production manager* Ludwig Spitaler. *Unit managers* Bernd Bergemann and Dieter Rauh. *Sound* Mandred Kohn. *Costumes* Renate Schutz. *Makeup* Ingeborg Reinhart. *Music publisher* Musik-Verlag Sonoton. *International distribution* Exportfilm Bischoff & Co. GmbH. *3D licensing* Munchener Filtheater-besellschaft. *Optical conversion* Film Effects of Hollywood. *Negative* Eastman Color. ¶A Constantin Film presentation. A Rapid-Film GmbH production. Released by Dimension Pictures, Inc. Technicolor. 85 minutes. Filmed at Rapid-Film Atelier and on location in Munich and Umgebung, West Germany. MPAA rating: X. ¶CAST: *Petra* Ingrid Steeger. *Dagmar* Evelyn Reese [Evelyn Raess]. *Inge* Christine Lindberg. *Manfred* Achim Neumann. *House mistress* Rosl Mayr. *Anita* Dorith Henke. *Udo* Nico Wolferstetter. *Fanni* Dorothea Rau. *Susu* Anik Ellahee. *Heinz* Gerhard Ruhnke. *Italian* Renaldo Talamonti. *Rosy* Elizabeth Volkman. *Lissy* Ulrike Butz. *Otto* Andre Eismann. *Rudi* Konstantin Wecker. *With* Leopold Gemeinwieser. ¶PROGRAM: 1) "Love in Schwabing, Part 1 (Liebe in Schwabing, 1. Teil)." 2) "The Rope Trick (Der seiltrick)." 3) "The Revenge (Die revanche)." 4) "Love in Schwabing, Part 2 (Liebe in Schwabing, 2. Teil)." 5) "The Frightful Experience (Das schreckliche erlebnis)." 6) "Neighbor on the Left (Nachbar zur linken)." 7) "Love in Schwabing, Part 3 (Liebe in Schwabing, 3.

Teil)." ¶A West German production released in West Germany in 1973 by Constantin-Film GmbH as *Liebe in drei dimensionen* in 70mm with four-track magnetic stereophonic sound. Advertised in the U.S. in "3 Dimensional 70mm" even though the side-by-side anamorphic 70mm images were converted to 35mm over-and-under spherical format. The U.S. version was issued with mono sound. Rereleased in the U.S. in 1977 by Monarch Releasing as an Allan Shackleton presentation and advertised in StereoVision 3D.

Lovers' Romance (1974). Filmed in Sovscope 70. *Screen author* Evgeni Grigoriev. *Director* Andrei Mikhalkov-Konchalovskiy. *Operator* Levan Paatashvili. *Artist* Leonid Pertsev. *Composer* Aleksandr Gradskogo. *Sound operator* I. Zelentsova. ¶A Mosfilm production. International distribution Sovexportfilm. Sovcolor. Six-track magnetic stereophonic sound. 172 minutes plus intermission. Filmed at Mosfilm Studios, Moscow, R.S.F.S.R. ¶CAST: *Tanya* Elena Koreneva. *Sergei* Evgeni Kindinov. *Tanya's mother* Iya Savvina. *Trumpeter* Innokenti Smoktunovskiy. *Sergei's brother* Vladimir Konkin. *Sergei's wife* Irina Kupchenko. *With* E. Solodova, A. Zbruev, R. Gromadskiy, N. Griniko and A. Samoylov. ¶A Soviet production released in Russia in 1974 as *Romans o vlyublennikh* in two parts running 86 minutes each.

Lunar Rainbow *see* **Moon Rainbow.**

Lunnaya raduga *see* **Moon Rainbow.**

The Luzhsky Defense Line *see* **Blockade.**

Luzskiy *see* **Blockade.**

Lyubiti cheloveka *see* **For Love of Man.**

Lyubovi Yarovaya (1971). Filmed in Sovscope 70. *Screen author* A. Vitoli. *Based on the play by* K. Treneva. *Director* V. Fetin. *Operator* E. Shapiro. *Artist* I. Vuskovich. *Composer* V. Soloviev-Sedoy. *Sound operator* Georgi Elibert. ¶A Mosfilm production. International distribution Sovexportfilm. Sovcolor. Six-track magnetic stereophonic sound. 128 minutes. Filmed at Mosfilm Studios, Moscow, R.S.F.S.R. ¶CAST: Lyudmila Chursina, V. Lanovoy, R. Nifontova, R. Shukshin,

K. Lavrov, A. Papanov, N. Alisova, R. Kenison, A. Gribov, I. Makarova, I. Dmitriev, M. Ladigin, N. Fedosova, A. Kozevnikov, B. Noikov and V. Matveev. ¶A Soviet production released in Russia in 1971.

Lyubovi zemnaya *see* **Earthly Love.**

Lyudi na Nile (1972). Filmed in Sovscope 70. *Screen authors* Kh. Figurovskiy, A.R. Sharkun and Yu. Shakhin. *Director* Yu. Shakhin. *Operators* A. Shelenkov and I. Chen. *Artists* E. Svidetelev and R.A. Megid. *Composer* A. Khachaturyan. *Sound operator* S. Minervin. ¶A Mosfilm–Kayra-film production. International distribution Sovexportfilm. Sovcolor. Six-track magnetic stereophonic sound. 123 minutes. Filmed at Mosfilm Studios, Moscow, R.S.F.S.R. and on location. ¶CAST: I. Vladimirov, V. Ivashov, Yu. Kamorniy, V. Kutsenko, S. Zgun, S. Zulifikar, M. Salem, A. Khamdts, A. M. Barrak and Seyf Zlidin. ¶A Soviet production released in Russia in 1972.

Lyudi v okeane *see* **People in the Ocean.**

Machekha (1973). Filmed in Sovscope 70. *Screen author* Z. Smirnov. *Based on the story by* M. Khalfinoy. *Director* O. Bondarev. *Operator* I. Chernikh. *Artists* N. Usachev and S. Portnoy. *Composer* G. Ponomarenko. *Sound operator* E. Indlina. ¶A Mosfilm production. International distribution Sovexportfilm. Sovcolor. Six-track magnetic stereophonic sound. 112 minutes. Filmed at Mosfilm Studios, Moscow, R.S.F.S.R. ¶CAST: T. Doronina, L. Nevedomskiy, N. Fedosova, V. Samoylov, L. Kostereva, S. Daleriy and T. Sovchi. ¶A Soviet production released in Russia in 1973.

Mackenna's Gold (May 10, 1969). Filmed in Super Panavision 70. *Producers* Carl Foreman and Dimitri Tiomkin. *Director* J. Lee Thompson. *Screenplay* Carl Foreman. *Based on the novel by* Will Henry. *Director of photography* Joseph MacDonald. *Production designer* Geoffrey Drake. *Music composer and conductor* Quincy Jones. *Art directors* Geoffrey Drake and Cary Odell. *Film editor* Bill Lenny. *Set decorator* Alfred E. Spencer. *Assistant director* David Salven.

Production manager Ralph Black. *Hair styles* Virginia Jones. *Wardrobe design* Norma Koch. *Orchestrations* Leo Shuken, Jack Hayes and Hal Mooney. *Second unit photography* Harold Wellman. *Additional photography* John Mackey, Donald C. Glouner, Farciot Edouart and Richard Moore. *Second unit director* Tom Shaw. *Stunt coordinator* Buzz Henry. *Sound supervisor* Derek Frye. *Unit sound recorder* William Randall, Jr. *Stereophonic dubbing* Bob Jones at Shepperton Studios and John Blunt at Cine Tele Sound. *Associate film editors* John Link, Jr., Raymond Poulton and Donald Deacon. *First assistant film editor* Lois Gray. *Special visual effects* Geoffrey Drake; John Mackey and Bob Cuff at Abacus Productions, Ltd.; Willis Cook and Lawrence W. Butler at Butler-Glouner, Inc.; and Brian Johncock [Johnson]. *Sound editor* Jeanne Henderson. *Assistant sound editor* Peter Bond. *Continuity* Marvin Weldon and John Dutton. *Song "Old Turkey Buzzard": music* Quincy Jones; *lyrics* Freddie Douglass; *singer* Jose Feliciano. ¶An Open Road Films, Ltd. presentation. A Carl Foreman production. A Highroad Productions, Inc. picture. Released by Columbia Pictures. Technicolor. Westrex six-track magnetic stereophonic sound. 129 minutes plus overture, intermission and exit music. Filmed at Columbia Studios and Paramount Studios, Hollywood and Shepperton Studios, London and on location in Grand Pass, Oregon, Canyon de Chelly, Arizona, Kanab, Monument Valley and Bryce, Utah, Palmdale, California and along the Colorado River. With cooperation of United States Dept. of the Interior, National Park Service and Bureau of Land Management. ¶CAST: *Marshal Mackenna* Gregory Peck. *Colorado* Omar Sharif. *Sgt. Tibbs* Telly Savalas. *Inga* Camilla Sparv. *Sanchez* Keenan Wynn. *Hesh-ke* Julie Newmar. *Hachita* Ted Cassidy. *Hadleyburg newspaper editor* Lee J. Cobb. *Hadleyburg preacher* Raymond Massey. *Hadleyburg storekeeper* Burgess Meredith. *Older Englishman* Anthony Quayle. *Old Adams* Edward G. Robinson. *Ben Baker* Eli Wallach. *Prairie Dog* Eduardo Ciannelli. *Avila* Dick Peabody. *Besh* Rudy Diaz. *Monkey* Robert Phillips. *The Pima squaw* Shelley Morrison. *Young Englishman* J. Robert Porter. *Old Adams' boy* John Garfield, Jr. *Laguna* Pepe Callahan. *Old Apache woman* Madeleine Taylor Holmes. *Cavalry lieutenant* Duke Hobbie. *Old man* Trevor Bradette. *Narrator* Victor Jory. ¶Filmed for 70mm Super Cinerama presentation but shown only in standard wide gauge format.

Madame (February 13, 1963). Filmed in Super Technirama 70. *Executive producers* Luciano Perugia and Carlo Ponti. *Producer* Maleno Malenotti. *Director* Christian-Jaque. *Screenplay* Henri Jeanson, Ennio de Concini, Christian-Jaque, Franco Solinas and Jean Ferry. *Based on the novel "Madame sans-gene" by* Emile Moreau and Victorien Sardou. *Director of photography* Roberto Gerardi. *Music* Angelo Francesco Lavagnino. *Film editors* Jacques Desagneau and Eraldo da Roma. *Set designers* Jean d'Eaubonne and Mario Rappini. *Costumes* Marcel Escoffier and Itala Scandariato. *Sound engineer* Ennio Sensi. *Production manager* Nello Meniconi. *Assistant directors* Raymond Villette and Maurizio Lucci. ¶A Joseph E. Levine presentation. A Cine-Alliance-GE.SI. Cinematografica-CC Champion Cinematografica, S.p.A.–Agata Film production. Released by Embassy Pictures. Technicolor. Westrex six-track magnetic stereophonic sound. 104 minutes. Filmed at Studio Tirrenia, Rome and on location in Caserta, Italy and Spain. ¶CAST: *Catherine Hubscher* Sophia Loren. *Lefebvre* Robert Hossein. *Napoleon Bonaparte* Julien Bertheau. *Elisa* Marina Berti. *Jerome* Carlo Giuffre. *Heloise* Gabriella Pallotta. *Caroline* Annalia Gade. *Pauline* Laura Valenzuela. *Roquet* Gianrico Tedeschi. *Fouche* Renaud Mary. *With* Celina Cely. ¶An Italian, French and Spanish coproduction released in Europe as *Madame sans-gene*. Advertised in Technirama 70mm. Released in Italy in December 1961 running 105 minutes; released in France in May 1963 running 97 minutes; and released in Spain in April 1962 running time undetermined. Previously filmed in Denmark in 1910, in France in 1911, in the U.S. in 1925 and in France in 1941. Sophia Loren replaced Gina Lollobrigida in the lead.

Madame sans-gene *see* **Madame.**

Magic Egg (1984). Filmed in OMNIMAX. *Producer and director* Eddie Garrick. *OMNIMAX computer graphic research developer* Dr. Nelson Max. ¶A Garrick

Films production for ACM SIGGRAPH in cooperation with Science Museum of Minnesota. Sponsored by Control Data Corporation, Gray Research, Inc. and DICOMED Corporation. Eastman Color. Six-track magnetic stereophonic sound. 15 minutes. This film consists entirely of computer-generated animation.

Magic Journeys (October 1, 1982). Filmed in Kodak-Disney 3D. *Executive producer* Randy Bright. *Producer, writer and director* Murray Lerner. *Director of photography* Paul Ryan. *Music and lyrics* Richard M. Sherman and Robert B. Sherman. *Film editor* Randy Roberts. *Special photographic effects* Art Cruickshank, Eric Brevig and Peter Anderson. *Executive production manager* Don Henderson. *Production manager* John Romeyn. *Production designer* Rick Carter. *Animation coordinator* John Scheele. *Computer animation* Information International, Inc. *Hand animation* Chris Casady. *Orchestration and additional music* Richard Clemens. *Editorial video transfers* Bill Hogan at Ruxton, Ltd. *Postproduction supervisor* Ray DeLeuw. *Supervising rerecording mixer* Shawn Murphy. *Rerecording mixers* Andy Bass and Richard Portman. *Supervising sound engineer* Nelson Meacham. *First assistant cameraman* Steve Slocomb. *Underwater photography and camera housing* Jordan Klein and Peter Romano for Mako Products. *Still photographer* Stan McClain. *Gaffer* Tim Griffith. *Key grip* John Black. *Special equipment* Howard Pearson and Howard Patterson. *Camera helicopter pilot* Rick Holly. *3D technology* Steve Hines, Murray Lerner, Dave Inglish, Don Iwerks, Ernest McNabb and Bob Otto. *Hasselblad photographic lenses* Zeiss. *Film stock* Eastman Kodak. ¶An MFL Productions, Inc. film for Eastman Kodak Company and Walt Disney Productions. Technicolor. Digital magnetic Dolby Stereo. 16 minutes. Filmed at Laird International Studios and Walt Disney Studios and on location in Florida and Sierra Mountains, Malibu Beach and Disneyland, Pasadena, California. ¶CAST: The Bob Yerkes Circus. ¶The first American film in dual 70mm widescreen 3D. Produced specially for the Magic Eye Theatre in Eastman Kodak's Journey Into Imagination Pavilion in the Future World section of Walt Disney World's Epcot Center, Orlando, Florida.

Magic Mirror *see* **The Enchanted Mirror.**

Magirama (1956). Filmed in Magirama. *Producer* Abel Gance. *Direction, Screenplay and editing* Abel Gance and Nelly Kaplan. *Music* Henri Verdum, Michel Magne and Claude Debussy. *Commentators* Abel Gance and Rene Vatier. ¶A French production released in France on December 19, 1956. Magirama was Gance's old Triptych format. This consisted of excerpts from *J'accuse* (1937, made by Gance), *Napoleon* (q.v.), *Begone Dull Care* (made by Canadian Norman McLaren), *Aupres de ma blonde* (q.v., featuring Michel Bouquet),*Chateaux de nuages* (q.v.) and *Une fete foraine* (q.v.) reedited for triscreen presentation. This may have been shown in Cinerama, converted to 'scope, and given a wide release.

Main Thrust *see* **Liberation.**

Man Belongs to the Earth (1974). Filmed in IMAX. *Producers* Roman Kroitor and Graeme Ferguson. *Director and photographer* Graeme Ferguson. *Filmed by* Imax Systems Corporation. ¶A Paramount Pictures Corporation production. Released by United States Department of Commerce. Eastman Color. Six-track magnetic stereophonic sound. 23 minutes. Filmed in the Western U.S.A. ¶cast: Chief Dan George. ¶Originally made for the U.S. Pavilion at Spokane's Expo 74.

The Man in the Hat (1982). Filmed in Sovscope 70. *Screen author* Viktoria Tokareva. *Director* Leonid Kuinikhidze. *Operator* Igor Slabnevich. *Artist* Viktor Petrov. *Composers* Gennady Podeliskiy and O. Nutsenko. *Choreographer* I. Beliskiy. *Songs* L. Derbeneva. *Sound operator* V. Alekseeva. ¶A Mosfilm production. International distribution Sovexportfilm. Sovcolor. Six-track magnetic stereophonic sound. 115 minutes. Filmed at Mosfilm Studios, Moscow, R.S.F.S.R. ¶CAST: *Mila* Lyudmila Savelieva. *Dmitri Denisov* Oleg Yankovskiy. *Director* Igor Kvasha. *Dmitri's ex-wife's husband* Anatoly Solonitsin. *Young dancer* Natalia Trubnikova. *Provincial girl* Galina Mikeladze. *With* O. Vardasheva, S. Farada, T. Akulova, O. Barnet and I. Miroshnichenko. ¶A Soviet production released in Russia in 1982 as *Shlyapa*.

La marca del hombre lobo *see* **Frankenstein's Bloody Terror.**

Marine (1928). Filmed in Triptych. *Producer and director* Abel Gance. *Photography* Jules Kruger. *Editors* Abel Gance and Marguerite Beauge. ¶A Societe Generale de Films production. 11 minutes. A French production released in France on February 10, 1928. It consisted of a montage of seascapes originally shot for *Napoleon*.

Mark of the Devil (April 1972). Filmed in Hi-Fi Stereo 70mm. *Producer* Adrain Hoven. *Director* Michael Armstrong. *Original story and screenplay* Sergio Casstner and Percy Parker. *Music* Michael Holm. *Photography* Ernst M. Kalinke. *Assistant cameramen* Joachim Gitt and Michael Georg. *Art director* Max Melin. *Decorator* Walter Karsth. *Costumes* Barbara Grupp. *Makeup* Gunther Kulier and Alena Heidankova. *Film editor* Siegrun Jager. *Sound* Hans-Dieter Schman. *Production manager* Gerhard Motel. *Production assistant* Gerhard Cepe. *Unit manager* Heinz Scheloks. *World distribution* Atlas International. ¶A Kroger Babb presentation. A Hi-Fi Stereo 70 KG (Munich) production. Released by Hallmark Releasing through American International Pictures. Eastman Color. 90 minutes. Filmed in West Germany. MPAA rating: R. ¶CAST: *Lord Cumberland* Herbert Lom. *Vanessa* Olivera Vuco. *Baron Christian von Mery* Udo Kier. *Chief executioner* Herbert Fux. *Albino* Reggie Nalder. *With* Michael Maien, Ingeborg Schoener, Johannes Buzalski, Gaby Fuchs, Gunter Clements, Doris von Danwitz, Dorothea Carrera, Marlies Petersen, Rob Gerry and Adrian Hoven. ¶A West German production released in West Germany in 1971 in 70mm and six-track magnetic stereophonic sound as *Hexen bis aufs blut gequalt* (a.k.a. *Brenn, hexe, brenn*) running 95 minutes. Advertised in the U.S. as being "Rated V for Violence" with theaters handing out "barfbags" and "vomit-sacks." Apparently shown in the U.S. in 35mm 'scope with mono sound only. Sequel was *Mark of the Devil Part 2 (Hexen: geschandet und su tode gequalt)* (Hallmark, 1975).

Matveeva radosti *see* **Matvey's Joy.**

Matvey's Joy (1986). Filmed in Sovscope 70. *Screen authors* Irina Poplavskaya and V. Soloviev. *Based on the story "Matveeva radosti"* by B. Shergina. *Director* Irina Poplavaskaya. *Operator* Vladimir Papyan. *Artists* Anatoli Kuznetsev and Pavel Safonov. *Composer* K. Volkov. *Sound operator* S. Urusov. ¶A Mosfilm production. International distribution Sovexportfilm. Sovcolor. Six-track magnetic stereophonic sound. 126 minutes. Filmed at Mosfilm Studios, Moscow, R.S.F.S.R. ¶CAST: *Matveev* Boris Galkin. *Tekton* Regimantas G. Adomaytis. *Maria* Natalia Egorova. *With* N. Trofimov, V. Kuivun, M. Bulgakova, G. Frolov, V. Kurkov, A. Latenas, S. Pavlov, I. Danilov, V. Kryuchkov and M. Brilkin. ¶A Soviet production released in Russia in 1986 as *Matveeva radosti.*

Mediterranean Holiday (March 5, 1964). Filmed in Superpanorama 70. Presented in Wonderama and 70mm Super Cinerma. *Producer* Georg M. Reuther. *Directors* Herman Leitner and Rudolf Nussgruber. *Screenplay* Gerd Nickstadt, Arthur Elliott and Hans Dieter Bove. *Narration writer* William Lovelock. *Associate producers* Claus Hardt and Juan C. Hutchison. *Photography* Siegfried Hold, Heinz Holscher, Toni Braun, Klaus Konig and Bernhard Stebich. *Aerial photography* Heinrich Schafer and Heinz Holscher. *Hollywood prolog* Harold J. Dennis, Harold McKenzie and Edward P. Campbell. *Music composer and director* Riz Ortolani. *Editors* Harold J. Dennis, Harold McKenzie and Edward P. Campbell in Hollywood and Karl Aulitzky. *Sound* Jean Neny at LTC, Paris. *Production supervisor* Rudolf J. Tranicek. *Assistant to the producer and directors* Don Jose. *Production managers* Richard Oehlers and Peter Homfeld. *Stills* Bob Klebig. *Sound* Hans Joachim Richter and Hans von Hoessein. *Technical equipment* Arnold & Richter. *Music recording* Bavaria Tonstudio. *Symphony orchestra* Kurt Graunke. *Stereophonic recording* LTC, Paris. "Wherever You May Go," "Have Faith" and "Sing Sagapo" *lyrics* George David Weiss, *music* Riz Ortolani, *singer* Katyna Ranieri. *Burl Ives' songs from the Decca Album "Down to the Sea in Ships" by courtesy of* Decca Records. *Assistance* governments of Egypt, France, Greece, Lebanon, Portugal, Sweden, Spain, Turkey, Yugoslavia and Monaco and commander of U.S. 6th Fleet and commanding officer and crew of *U.S.S. Shangri-La.* ¶A Walter Reade-Sterling presentation. An MCS-Film K.G.-Rudolf

Ad for Mediterranean Holiday.

J. Tranicek production. Released by Continental Distributing, Inc. Eastman Color. Prints by Technicolor. Westrex six-track magnetic stereophonic sound. 158 minutes plus overture, intermission and exit music. ¶CAST: *Host and narrator* Burl Ives. *Officers and men of Flying Clipper* Capt. Skoglund, Florian Bauer, Michael Hornung, Gunther Metz, Christoph Gerhard, Udo Janson, Erich Moritz and Jurgen Richter. *Willy Kubler's chimpanzee* "Mr. Charley." ¶A West German production released in West Germany in December 1962 as *Flying Clipper — Traumreise Unter Weissen Segeln* running 154 minutes. Presumably the first feature in Superpanorama 70 which was also known as MCS 70 and Cinevision 70. The screen credits read *in "MCS 70" modern cinema*

systems. The Hollywood prolog with Burl Ives was probably shot in Todd-AO. 35mm version advertised in CinemaScope.

Meksika v ogne *see* **Red Bells.**

La Merveilleuse vie de Jeanne d'Arc (1929). Filmed in Hypergonar. *Director* Marco de Gastyne. ¶This French production supposedly used 'scope for the battle scenes only. It is often cited as the first anamorphic feature release, but it actually was predated by *Pour construire un feu* (q.v.) in 1927.

Meteli (1964). Filmed in Sovscope 70. *Screen author, director and producer* V. Basov. *Based on the story "Meteli" by* A.C. Pushkina. *Operators* S. Vronskiy and E. Kumanikov. *Composer* G. Sviridon. *Sound operators* G. Korenblyum and A. Ryabov. ¶A Mosfilm production. International distribution Sovexportfilm. Sovcolor. Six-track magnetic stereophonic sound. 80 minutes. Filmed at Mosfilm Studios, Moscow, R.S.F.S.R. ¶CAST: V. Titova, G. Martinyuk, O. Vidov, M. Pastukhova, S. Popov, V. Marenkov, N. Burlyaev, S. Plotnikov and N. Vilivovskaya. ¶A Soviet production released in Russia in 1964.

Mexico in Flames *see* **Red Bells.**

Mi, russkiy narod (1965). Filmed in Sovscope 70. *Screen authors* S. Vishnevedraya, A. Mariyamov and V. Stroeva. *Based on the novel by* Vs. Vishnevskogo. *Director and producer* V. Stroeva. *Chief operators* A. Zgina and V. Dombrovskiy. *Chief artists* N. Usachev and Yu. Kladtsenko. *Composer* R. Ledenev. *Sound operators* Ya. Kharon and V. Belyarov. ¶A Mosfilm production. International distribution Sovexportfilm. Sovcolor. Six-track magnetic stereophonic sound. 194 minutes plus intermission. Filmed at Mosfilm Studios, Moscow, R.S.F.S.R. ¶cast: D. Smirnov, Nikolai Griniko, I. Savkin, V. Gaft, G. Nekrasov, V. Treshchalov, N. Pogodin, A. Orlov, F. Gladkov, A. Shalyapin and Kh. Trifonov. ¶A Soviet production released in Russia in 1965 in two parts running 93 minutes and 101 minutes.

Millie Goes to Budapest *see* **The Golden Head.**

Millie Goes to Budapest and Who Is Millie? *see* **The Golden Head.**

Mimino (1978). Filmed in Sovscope 70. *Screen authors* Revaz Gabriadze, Viktoria Tokareva and Georgi Daneliya. *Director* Georgi Daneliya. *Operator* Anatoly Petratskiy. *Artists* Boris Nemechek and Z. Nemechek. *Composer* Georgi Kancheli. *Sound operator* E. Fedorov. *Verses* P. Gruzinskogo, E. Evtushenko and R. Rozdestvenskogo. ¶A Mosfilm production. International distribution Sovexportfilm. Sovcolor. Six-track magnetic stereophonic sound. 120 minutes. Filmed at Mosfilm Studios, Moscow, R.S.F.S.R. ¶CAST: *Valiko* Vakhtang Kikabidze. *Rubik* Frumzik Mkrtchyan. *With* Elena

Proklova, Evgeni Leonov, K. Daushvili, R. Mikhaberidze, Z. Sakhvadze, M. Kukushkina-Dyuzeva, R. Morcheladze and A. Gomiashvili. ¶A Soviet production released in Russia in 1978.

Mr. McKinley's Flight (1976). Filmed in Sovscope 70. *Screen author* Leonid Lesnov. *Director* Mikhail Shveytser. *Operator* Dilshat Fatkhulin. *Artist* Levan Shengeltsya. *Composer* Isaak Shvarts. *Sound operators* V. Shchedrina and E. Bazanov. *Song text* V. Visotskiy. ¶A Mosfilm production. International distribution Sovexportfilm. Sovcolor. Six-track magnetic stereophonic sound. 202 minutes plus intermission. Filmed at Mosfilm Studios, Moscow, R.S.F.S.R. ¶CAST: *Mr. McKinley* Donates Banionis. *Mrs. Shalway* Angelina Stepanova. *Streetwalker* Alla Demidova. *Singer* Vladimir Visotskiy. *Sam Boulder* Boris Babochkin. *With* Ekhanna Bolotova, A. Vokach, Tatiana Lavrova, I. Kashintsev, Leonid Kuravlev and V. Sergachev. ¶A Soviet production released in Russia in 1976 as *Begstvo mistera Mak-Kinli.*

Mkhitar *see* **The Star of Hope.**

Mnogo shuma iz nichego (1973). Filmed in Sovscope 70. *Screen author and director* S. Samsonov. *Operators* M. Bits and E. Guslinskiy. *Artists* Aleksandr Boym and S. Voronkov. *Composer* I. Egikov. *Verses* Yu. Morits. *Sound operators* G. Korenblyum and A. Erukhimovich. ¶A Mosfilm production. International distribution Sovexportfilm. Sovcolor. Six-track magnetic stereophonic sound. 102 minutes. Filmed at Mosfilm Studios, Moscow, R.S.F.S.R. ¶CAST: G. Loginova, K. Raykin, T. Vedeneeva, L. Trushkin, B. Ivanov, A. Samoylov, V. Korenev, A. Dobronravov, P. Pavlenko, Z. Garin, V. Doveyko and M. Logvinov. ¶A Soviet production released in Russia in 1973.

Molodie *see* **The Newlyweds.**

Moon Rainbow (1983). Filmed in Sovscope 70. *Screen authors* Valentin Ezov and Andrei Ermash. *Based on the novel "Lunnaya raduga" by* Sergei Pavlova. *Director* Andrei Ermash. *Operator* Naum Ardashnikov. *Artist* Vladimir Aronin. *Composer* Eduard Artemiev. *Sound operator* L. Bulgakov. *Chief trick operator*

Boris Travkin. *Consultant* Vladimir Shatalov. *Still Photo* Vladimir Murashko. ¶A Goskino presentation. A Mosfilm production. International distribution Sovexportfilm. Sovcolor. Six-track magnetic stereophonic sound. 90 minutes. Filmed at Mosfilm Studios, Moscow, R.S.F.S.R. ¶CAST: Vladimir Gostyukhin, Igor Starigin, Vassily Livanov, Yuri Solomin, Georgi Taratorkin, Natalia Sayko, Grazkhina Baykshtite, Vladimir Kenigson, Aleksandr Porokhovshchiko, Gediminas Girdvaynis, Boris Ivanov and Leonid Nevedomakiy. ¶A Soviet production released in Russia in 1983 as *Lunnaya raduga*. U.S. distribution is unconfirmed. Some sources list this as *Lunar Rainbow* but the title given by Sovexportfilm is as above.

More Milk Evette (February 8, 1966). Presented in 16mm Dual Screen. *Producer, director and photographer* Andy Warhol. *Writer* Ronald Tavel. *Music* The Velvet Underground. *Production assistant* Paul Morrissey. ¶An Andy Warhol production. Released by Film-Makers' Cooperative. Eastman Color. Optical sound. 70 minutes. Filmed in New York City. ¶CAST: *Mother* Mario Montez. *With* Paul Caruso, Richard Schmidt and Larry Kent. ¶This was probably shown in split screen as a gimmick only. It was not filmed with special equipment and most likely was shown as a single-screen item outside its initial screenings. Most of the picture is in black-and-white, with color sections. Also known as *Lana Turner* and *More Milk Yvette*.

More Milk Yvette *see* **More Milk Evette.**

More v ogne *see* **The Sea in Flames.**

Moskva pervomayskaya (1964). Filmed in Sovscope 70. International distribution Sovexportfilm. Sovcolor. Six-track magnetic stereophonic sound. A Soviet production released in Russia in 1964.

The Most Charming and Attractive (1985). Filmed in Sovscope 70. *Screen authors* Anatoly Zyramdzan and Gerald Bezanov. *Director* Gerald Bezanov. *Operator* Valentin Tizanov. *Artist* Evgeny Vinitskiy. *Composer* Vladimir Rubashevskiy. *Sound operator* L. Bulgakov. *Song text* V. Shlenskogo. ¶A Mosfilm

production. International distribution Sovexportfilm. Sovcolor. Six-track magnetic stereophonic sound. 88 minutes. Filmed at Mosfilm Studios, Moscow, R.S.F.S.R. ¶CAST: *Nadya Klyueva* Irina Muravieva. *Susanna* Tatiana Vasilieva. *Smirnov* Aleksandr Abdulov. *Diatlov* Leonid Kuravlev. *Priakhin* Mikhail Kokshenov. *With* Lyudmila Ivanova, Larisa Udovichenko, Aleksandr Shirvindt, Vladimir Nosik, L. Perfilov and L. Sokolova. ¶A Soviet production released in 1985 as *Samaya obayatelinaya i udivitelinaya.*

Mothers and Daughters (1975). Filmed in Sovscope 70. *Screen author* Aleksandr Volodin. *Director* Sergei Gerasimov. *Operator* Vladimir Rapopport. *Artist* P. Pashkevich. *Composer* S. Viacheslav Chekin. *Sound operator* N. Ozornoy. ¶A kinostudiya im. M. Gorikogo production. International distribution Sovexportfilm. Sovcolor. Six-track magnetic stereophonic sound. 101 minutes. Filmed at kinostudiya im. M. Gorikogo, Gorki, R.S.F.S.R. ¶CAST: *Elena Alexeievna* Tamara Makarova. *Olga Vasilev* Lubov Palekhina. *Vadim Antonovich* Innokenty Smoktunovskiy. *Piotr Vorobiov* Sergei Gerasimov. *Ania Vasilev* Svetlana Smekhnova. *Galia Vasilev* Larisa Udovichenko. *Rezo* Zurab Kipshidze. ¶A Soviet production released in Russia in 1974 as *Dochki-materi.*

Mournful Unconcern (1987). Filmed in Sovscope 70. *Screen author* Yuri Arabov. *Based on the play "Heartbreak House" by* George Bernard Shaw. *Director* Aleksandr Sokurov. *Operator* Sergei Yurisditsky. *Artist* Elena Amshinskaya. *Sound operator* Vladimir Persov. ¶A Lenfilm production. International distribution Sovexportfilm. Sovcolor. Six-track magnetic stereophonic sound. 97 minutes. Filmed at Lenfilm Studios, Leningrad, R.S.F.S.R. ¶CAST: *Capt. Shotover* Ramaz Chkhikvadze. *Ariadna* Alla Osipenko. *Gessiona* Tatyana Egorova. *Hector* Dmitriy Bryantsev. *Ellie's father* Vladimir Zamansky. *Ellie* Viktoria Amitova. *Mangan* Ilya Rybin. *Dr. Knife* Vadim Zkhuk. *With* Irina Sokolova, Andrei Reshetin and Yuri Sergeev. ¶A Soviet production released in Russia in 1987 as *Skorbnoye beschuvstviye.* Judging from the synopsis this film has nothing to do with Shaw's original play.

Moy laskoviy i nezniy zveri *see* **The Shooting Party.**

Moya Moldova (1982). Filmed in Sovscope 70. International distribution Sovexportfilm. Sovcolor. Six-track magnetic stereophonic sound. A Soviet production released in Russia in 1982. A film with the same title was released in 1984 and is presumed to be an upgrading of this one.

Moya Moldova (1984). Filmed in Sovscope 70. International distribution Sovexportfilm. Sovcolor. Six-track magnetic stereophonic sound. A Soviet production released in Russia in 1984. We presume this is an upgrading of the 1982 film of the same title.

Moya Moskva (1970). Filmed in Sovscope 70. International distribution Sovexportfilm. Sovcolor. Six-track magnetic stereophonic sound. A Soviet production released in Russia in 1970.

Moya Poltava (1974). Filmed in Sovscope 70. International distribution Sovexportfilm. Sovcolor. Six-track magnetic stereophonic sound. A Soviet production released in Russia in 1974.

La muraglia cinese *see* **Behind the Great Wall.**

(Meredith Willson's) The Music Man (June 19, 1962). Filmed in Super Technirama 70. *Producer and director* Morton DaCosta. *Screenplay* Marion Hargrove. *Based on the play with book by* Meredith Willson and Franklin Lacey; *and music and lyrics by* Meredith Willson; *as produced on the stage by* Kermit Bloomgarden *with* Herbert Greene *in association with* Frank Productions Inc. *Director of photography* Robert Burks. *Music and lyrics* Meredith Willson. *Music supervisor and conductor* Ray Heindorf. *Vocal arrangements* Charles Henderson. *Orchestrations* Ray Heindorf, Frank Comstock and Gus Levene. *Choreography* Onna White. *Film editor* William H. Ziegler. *Costume designer* Dorothy Jeakins. *Art director* Paul Groesse. *Set decorator* George James Hopkins. *Makeup supervisor* Gordon Bau. *Supervising hair stylist* Jean Burt Reilly. *Shirley Jones' hair styles* Myrl Stoltz. *Sound supervisor* George R. Groves. *Sound* M.A. Merrick

and Dolph Thomas. *Assistant choreographer* Tom Panko. *Production supervisor* Joel Freeman. *Assistant director* Russell Llewellyn. *Unit publicist* Carl Combs. *Casting* Hoyt Bowers. *Music publisher* Frank Music Corp. ¶A Morton DaCosta production. Released by Warner Bros. Pictures. Technicolor. RCA six-track magnetic stereophonic sound. 151 minutes. Filmed at Warner Bros. Studios. ¶CAST: *Prof. Harold Hill* Robert Preston. *Marian Paroo* Shirley Jones. *Marcellus Washburn* Buddy Hackett. *Eulalie MacKenzie Shinn* Hermione Gingold. *Mayor Shinn* Paul Ford. *Ewart Dunlop* Al Shea. *Oliver Hix* Wayne Ward. *Jacey Squires* Vern Reed. *Olin Britt* Bill Spangenberg. *Mrs. Paroo* Pert Kelton. *Tommy Djilas* Timmy Everett. *Zaneeta Shinn* Susan Luckey. *Winthrop Paroo* Ronny Howard. *Charlie Cowell* Harry Hickox. *Constable Locke* Charles Lane. *Mrs. Squires* Mary Wickes. *Amaryllis* Monique Vermont. *Norbert Smith* Ronnie Dapo. *Avis Grubb* Jesslyn Fax. *Gracie Shinn* Patty Lee Hilka. *Dewey* Garry Potter. *Harley MacCauley* J. Delos Jewkes. *Harry Joseph* Ray Kellogg. *Lester Lonergan* William Fawcett. *Oscar Jackson* Rance Howard. *Gilbert Hawthorne* Roy Dean. *Chet Glanville* David Swain. *Herbert Malthouse* Arthur Mills. *Duncan Shyball* Rand Barker. *Jessie Shyball* Jeannine Burnier. *Amy Dakin* Shirley Claire. *Truthful Smith* Natalie Core. *Dolly Higgins* Therese Lyon. *Lila O'Brink* Penelope Martin. *Feril Hawkes* Barbara Pepper. *Stella Jackson* Anne Loos. *Ada Nutting* Peggy Wynne. *Undertaker* Hank Worden. *Farmer* Milton Parsons. *Farmer's wife* Natalie Masters. *Townswomen* Peggy Mondo, Sarah Seegar, Adnia Rice and Maudie Prickett. *Townsman* Percy Helton. *Salesmen* Casey Adams and Charles Perchesky. ¶Advertised in "Hi Hi Fi Stereo Sound." Al Shea, Wayne Ward, Vern Reed and Bill Spangenberg were screen billed under their barbershop quartet name, The Buffalo Bills.

Mutiny on the Bounty (November 8, 1962). Filmed in Ultra Panavision 70. *Producer* Aaron Rosenberg. *Directors* Lewis Milestone and Carol Reed. *Directors of certain scenes* George Seaton, Billy Wilder and Fred Zinneman. *Screenplay* Charles Lederer, Eric Ambler, William L. Driscoll, Borden Chase, John Gay and Ben

Hecht. *Based on the books "Mutiny on the Bounty," "Men Against the Sea" and "Pitcairn's Island" by* Charles Nordhoff and James Norman Hall. *Music* Bronislau Kaper. *Orchestra conductor* Robert Armbruster. *Director of photography* Robert L. Surtees. *Additional photography* Harold E. Wellman. *Art direction* George W. Davis and Joseph McMillan Johnson. *Special effects* Glenn E. Robinson. *Special visual effects* A. Arnold Gillespie, Lee LeBlanc and Robert R. Hoag. *Set decoration* Henry Grace and Hugh Hunt. *Film editor* John McSweeney, Jr. *Marine and second unit direction* James C. Havens, Andrew Marton and Richard Thorpe. *Assistant director* Ridgeway Callow. *Color consultant* Charles K. Hagedon. *Costume designer* Moss Mabry. *Hair styles* Mary K. Keats. *Makeup creator* William Tuttle. *Recording supervisor* Franklin Milton. *Rerecording* William Steinkamp. *Choreographer* Hamil Petroff. *Technical advisers* Capt. Donald MacIntyre, Bengt Danielson, Aurora Natua and Leo Langomazino. *Unit production manager* Rudy Rosenberg. *Second assistant director* Major Roup. *Production assistant* Alan Callow. *Camera operator* Conrad Hall. *Assistant cameramen* Bruce Surtees and Charles Termini. *Stunt coordinator* Larry Duran. *Associate film editor* Thomas J. McCarthy. *Sound editor* Milo Lory. *Music editor* William Saracino. *Still photographer* Eric Carpenter. *Location liaison* Nick Rutgers. *Property master and ship's rigger* Olof Olsson. *Miniature rigger* Jonathan Haze. *Unit publicist* Morgan Hudgins. *Ship construction* Smith & Rhuland Shipyard. *Block maker* Alfred Dauphinee. *Sail maker* Charlie Hebb. *Ship's captain* Ellsworth Coggins. *Song "Follow Me": music* Bronislau Kaper; *lyrics* Paul Francis Webster. *Titles* Pacific Title & Art Studio. *Opticals* MGM Laboratories. ¶An Aaron Rosenberg production. An Arcola Pictures Corp. film. Released by Metro-Goldwyn-Mayer. Technicolor. Westrex six-track magnetic stereophonic sound. 185 minutes plus overture, intermission and exit music. Filmed at MGM Studios and on location in Tahiti, Bora Bora and Pitcairn's Island. ¶CAST: *First Ofr. Fletcher Christian* Marlon Brando. *Capt. William Bligh* Trevor Howard. *John Mills* Richard Harris. *Alexander Smith* Hugh Griffith. *William Brown* Richard Haydn.

Maimiti Tarita [Taritatumi Teriipaia]. *Mathew Quintal* Percy Herbert. *Edward Birkett* Gordon Jackson. *William McCoy* Noel Purcell. *John Williams* Duncan Lamont. *Michael Byrne* Chips Rafferty. *Samuel Mack* Ashley Cowan. *John Fryer* Eddie Byrne. *Edward Young* Tom Seely. *Minarii* Frank Silvera. *James Morrison* Keith McConnell. *Tahitians* Rahera Tuia, Ruita Salmon, Nathalie Tehahe, Tematai Tevaearai, Odile Hinano Paofai, Teretiaiti Maifano, Virau Tepii, Maeva Maitihe, Louise Tefaafana, Tinorua Vaitahe, Adrien Mahitete, Tufariu Haamoeura, Leo Langamazino, Aurora Natua, Bengt Danielson, Marabayshi, Tefaaoro, Faatiarau, Ahuroa, Teriitemihau, Manitearo, Agnes, Marie and Emily. *Chief Hitihiti* Matahiarii Tama. *Sailors* Wayne DeWar and Larry Duran. *Court martial judge* Henry Daniell. *Graves* Ben Wright. *Staines* Torin Thatcher. ¶Prerelease publicity credited Camera 65. Lewis Milestone replaced Carol Reed as director. Reedited to 179 minutes plus overture, intermission and exit music by removing the prolog and epilog. Other versions: *The Mutiny of the Bounty* (Crick & Jones, 1916), *In the Wake of the Bounty* (Expeditionary Films, 1933), *Mutiny on the Bounty* (MGM, 1935) and *The Bounty* (Orion, 1984).

My Fair Lady (October 21, 1964). Filmed in Super Panavision 70. *Producer* Jack L. Warner. *Director* George Cukor. *Screenplay* Alan Jay Lerner. *Based on the play with book and lyrics by* Alan Jay Lerner; *and music by* Frederick Loewe; *as produced on the stage by* Herman Levin; *from the play "Pygmalion" by* George Bernard Shaw. *Director of photography* Harry Stradling. *Costumes, scenery and production designer* Cecil Beaton. *Art director and second unit director* Gene Allen. *Film editor* William H. Ziegler. *Sound supervision* George R. Groves. *Sound* Francis J. Schied and Murray Spivack. *Lyrics* Alan Jay Lerner. *Music and additional music* Frederick Loewe. *Music supervisor and conductor* Andre Previn. *Vocal arrangements* Robert Tucker. *Orchestrations* Alexander Courage, Robert Franklyn and Albert Woodbury. *Choreography* Hermes Pan. *Unit manager* Sergei Petschnikoff. *Set decorator* George James Hopkins. *Makeup supervisor* Gordon Bau. *Supervising hair stylist* Jean Burt Reilly. *Assistant director*

David Hall. *Camera operator* Harry Stradling, Jr. *Second unit photography* Robert L. Surtees. *Phonetics adviser* Dr. Peter Ladefoged, U.C.L.A. *Ascot adviser* Wilfrid Hyde-White. *Dialog supervisor* Susan Seton. *Wardrobe* Joe Wiatt, Eleanor Abbey, Norma Brown, Geoffrey Allen, Bob Richards, Anne Laune and Betty Huff. *Costume design coordinator* Gerda Roberson. *Milliner* Leah Barnes. *Audrey Hepburn's makeup artist* Frank McCoy. *Special photographic effects* Linwood G. Dunn and Film Effects of Hollywood. *Assistant art director* Stanley Fleicher. *Production illustrator* Ed Graves. *Unit publicists* Max Bercutt, Carl Combs and Mort Lichter. *Still photographers* Bob Willoughby and Mel Traxel. *Gaffer* Frank Flanagan. *Casting* Hoyt Bowers. ¶A Warner Bros.-First National picture. Released by Warner Bros. Pictures. Technicolor. RCA six-track magnetic stereophonic sound. 170 minutes plus intermission and exit music. Filmed at Warner Bros. Studios. ¶CAST: *Eliza Doolittle* Audrey Hepburn. *Prof. Henry Higgins* Rex Harrison. *Alfred P. Doolittle* Stanley Holloway. *Col. Pickering* Wilfrid Hyde-White. *Mrs. Higgins* Gladys Cooper. *Freddie Eynsford-Hill* Jeremy Brett. *Zoltan Karpathy* Theodore Bikel. *Mrs. Pearce* Mona Washbourne. *Mrs. Eynsford-Hill* Isobel Elsom. *Higgins' butler* John Holland. *Jamie* John Alderson. *Harry* John McLiam. *Queen of Transylvania* Baroness Veronica de Goldschmidt-Rothschild. *Ad lib at ball* Betty Blythe. *Lady Boxington* Moyna Macgill. *Doolittle's dance partner* Barbara Pepper. *Cockney with pipe* Marjorie Bennett. *Landlady* Miriam Schiller. *Fat woman at pub* Ayllene Gibbons. *Man at Ascot and ball* Grady Sutton. *Guest at ball* Maj. Sam Harris. *Bystander who warns Eliza* Walter Burke. *Man at coffee stand* Owen Mc-Giveney. *George* Jack Greening. *Algernon* Ron Whelan. *First maid* Dinah Anne Rogers. *Second maid* Lois Battle. *Parlor maid* Jacqueline Squire. *Cook* Gwen Watts. *Fantasy king* Charles Fredericks. *Lady ambassador* Lillian Kemble-Cooper. *Prince Gregor* Henry Daniell. *Footmen at ball* Ben Wright, Roy Dean, Tom Cound and William Beckley. *Greek ambassador* Oscar Beregi. *Prince* Buddy Bryan. *Mrs. Higgins' maid* Jennifer Crier. *Mrs. Hopkins* Olive Reeves-Smith. *Costermongers* Ben Wrigley, Clive Halliday, Richard

Peel, Eric Heath and James O'Hara. *Elegant bystanders* Kendrick Huxham and Frank Baker. *Cockney bystander* Queenie Leonard. *Hoxton man* Laurie Main. *Selsey man* Maurice Dallimore. *Male member* Jack Raine. *Elegant daughter* Britannia Beatey. *Grand lady* Beatrice Greenough. *Bystander* Hilda Plowright. *Jugglers* Eugene Hoffman and Kai Farrelli. *Cockneys* Raymond Foster, Joe Evans, Marie Busch, Mary Alexander, William Linkie, Henry Sweetman, Andrew Brown, Samuel Holmes, Thomas Dick, William Taylor, James Wood, Goldie Kleban, Elizabeth Aimers, Joy Tierney, Lenore Miller, Donna Day, Corinne Ross, Phyllis Kennedy and Davie Robel. *Flower girls* Iris Briston and Alma Lawton. *Toffs* Gigi Michel, Sandy Steffens, Sandy Edmundson, Marlene Marrow, Carol Merrill, Sue Bronson and Lea Genovese. *Ascot spectators* Orville Sherman, Harvey Dunn, Barbara Morrison, Natalie Core, Helen Albrecht and Diana Bourbon. *Ascot gavotte* Colin Campbell. *Ascot ad libs* Marjorie Hawtrey, Paulle Clark and Allison Daniell. *Ambassador* Alan Napier. *Cabbie* Geoffrey Steele. *Bit man* Pat O'Moore. *Policeman* Victor Rogers. *Bartender* Michael St. Clair. *Leaning man* Brendon Dillon. *Church ad libs* Elzada Wilson, Jeanne Carson, Buddy Shea, Jack Goldie, Sid Marion, Stanley Fraser, George Pelling, Colin Kenny, La Wana Backer, Monika Henried, Anne Dore, Pauline Drake, Shirley Melline, Wendy Russell, Meg Brown, Clyde Howdy, Nicholas Wolcuff, Martin Eric, John Mitchum and Phyllis Kennedy. *Dancer* Nick Navarro. *Audrey Hepburn's vocals* Marni Nixon. *Jeremy Brett's vocals* Bill Shirley. ¶Originally announced as a Super Cinerama presentation. Cecil Beaton's screen credit was contractual. He had nothing to do with the sets, but actually designed the costumes, makeup and hair. The screen billing was rendered as Beaton's stage credit had been.

My Strange Uncle (November 20, 1981). Filmed in IMAX. *Executive producer and director* George Englund. *Producer* Michael Greenburg. *Director of photography* Gayne Rescher. *Film editor* Gary Griffin. ¶Produced by George Englund Productions. Released by Quest Management. Eastman Color. Six-track magnetic stereophonic sound. 32 minutes. Filmed in

New Zealand. ¶CAST: Cloris Leachman, John Considine and Bruce McLaren. ¶This was not the first dramatic film in MAX as claimed by some.

My Tender and Gentle Beast see **The Shooting Party.**

The Mysterious House of Dr. C. see **Dr. Coppelius.**

Na podvodnikh skuterakh (1964). Filmed in Kinopanorama 70. International distribution Sovexportfilm. Sovcolor. Nine-track magnetic Kinopanorama Sound. A Soviet production released in Russia in 1964.

Na samom bolishom stadione (1966). Filmed in Kinopanorama 70. International distribution Sovexportfilm. Sovcolor. Nine-track magnetic Kinopanorama Sound. A Soviet production released in Russia in 1966.

Na ves zolota (1984). Filmed in Sovscope 70. *Screen author* A. Slavuta-Loguinenko. *Director* E. Sherstobitov. *Operators* M. Cherniy and A. Cherniy. *Artist* V. Novakov. *Composer* M. Boyko. *Sound operator* A. Chernoochenko. ¶A Kievskaya kinostudiya im. A.P. Dovzenko production. International distribution Sovexportfilm. Sovcolor. Six-track magnetic stereophonic sound. 80 minutes. Filmed at Kievskaya kinostudiya im. A.P. Dovzenko, Kiev, Ukrainian S.S.R. ¶CAST: R. Khomyatov. I. Gavrilyuk, N. Krashoyarskaya, A. Podubinskiy, A. Yurchenko, N. Gavrilov, N. Volchek, I. Borodin, V. Stepanenko, A. Nishchenkin and N. Oleynik. ¶A Soviet production released in Russia in 1984.

Nabat see **Duma o Kovpake.**

Nachni snachala (1986). Filmed in Sovscope 70. *Screen authors* A. Borodyanoskiy and A. Stefanovich. *Director* A. Stefanovich. *Operator* V. Klimov. *Artist* Z. Drobitskiy. *Composer* V. Ladigina. *Sound operator* V. Babushkin. *Music and song text* A. Makarevicha. ¶A Mosfilm production. International distribution Sovexportfilm. Sovcolor. Six-track mag-

netic stereophonic sound. 71 minutes. Filmed at Mosfilm Studios, Moscow, R.S.F.S.R. ¶CAST: A. Makarevich, M. Polteva, I. Sklyar, A. Yakovleva, Rolan Bikov, S. Nemolyaeva, A. Mouernyuk, D. Yuzovskiy, I. Agafonov and V. Spesivtsev. ¶A Soviet production released in Russia in 1986.

Napoleon (February 17, 1929). Filmed in Triptych. *Producer, writer, director and editor* Abel Gance. *Associate director* Henry Krauss. *Second unit director and editor* Wladimir Viacheslav Tourjansky. *Chief cameraman* Jules Kruger. *Brienne and Corsica principal cameraman* Jean-Pierre Mundviller. *Principal cameramen* Leonce-Henry Burel, Roger Hubert, Lucas and Emile Pierre. *Triptych technician and cameraman* Paul Briquet. *Second unit chief cameraman* Roger Hubert. *Cameramen* Fedor Bourgassoff, Eyvinge* and Monniot. *Assistant directors* Henri Andreani, Pierre Danis-Voogd, Anatole Litvak, Mario Nalpas, Jean Epstein, Germaine Dulac, Blaise Cendrara and Joseph Ermolieff. *Editorial associates* Marguerite Beauge and Henrietta Pinson. *Designer* Alexandre Benois. *Chief art director* Pierre Schild [Schildknecht]. *Art direction* Lochakoff, Jacouty, Meinhardt and Pimenoff. *Chief grip* Simon Feldman. *Studio manager* Michel Feldman. *Casting director* Louis Osmont. *Financial administration* Edouard de Bersaucourt and Noe Bloch. *Production managers* Louis Osmont, William Delafontaine and Simon Schiffrin. *Corsica production manager* Pierre Bonardi. *Unit managers* Constantin Geftman, Hoden, Komerovsky, Georges Lampin, Metchikoff, Pauly, Pironet, Rufly and Michel Scripnikoff. *Production assistant* Pavlov. *Script girl and Abel Gance's secretary* Simone Surdieux. *Negative cutting* Henriette Pinson. *Matte artist* W. Percy Day. *Director of storm sequence photographic effects* Edward Scholl. *Storm sequence miniature cameraman* Eugen Schufftan. *Special effects cameraman* Guy Wilky. *Projection* Bonin. *Nurse* Marthe Melinot. *Triptych design* Abel Gance. *Triptych construction* Andre Debrie. *Chief engineer for Andre Debrie* Maurice Daloted. *Stills* Desboutins, Gedovius and Lipnitzki. *Makeup*

The French have a habit of listing only last names in credits. We have listed here as many full names as we could possibly track down.

Wladimir Kwanine and Boris de Fast. *Prop master and caterer* Pironet. *Military liaison at Toulon* Gen. Vincent. *Special effects* Simon Feldman and Lemirt. *Armorer* Lemirt. *Arms supplier* Mauger. *Pyrotechnics supplier* Ruggieri. *Wigs* Pontet-Vivant. *Technical director for Les Films Abel Gance* Leonce-Henry Burel. *Electricians* Albinet, Doublon and Graza. *Costumes* Charmy, Sauvageau, Mme. Augris and Mme. Neminsky. *Gina Mane's costumes designer* Jeanne Lanvin. *Costumes supplier* Muelle et Souplet. *Footwear supplier* Galvin. *Trainees* Jean (Juan) Arroy, Jean Mitry and Sacher Purnal. *Production services* Westi Company. *Production representative for Westi Company* Dr. Rudolph Becker. *Societe Generale des Films board of directors* Alexander d'Arbeloff (original president), Henri de Çazotte (president), le Duc d'Ayen, Charles Pathe, le Comte H. de Bearn, le Comte J. de Breteuil, E. Karmann, C. Lemoine, J. Grinieff and de la Roziere. *Production cooperation* Duchesse d'Ayen, Princesse Edmond de Polignac, Comtesse Charles de Polignac, S. Guggehheim, Comte de Chevigne, Comte Jean de Polignac, Duc de Gramont, Baron Paul de Thoisy, Baron Foy, la Caze, Marcus Loew, Arthur Loew, Leon Gaumont, Rubin, E. Costil, Ludwig Lawrence, Dr. Brausback, Rudolph Becker, Paul Brunet, Antonio Mosco, Luchaire, Georges d'Esparbes, Elie Faure, Pierre Roche, Rene Delange, N. Bloch, Andre Debrie, Michel Feldman, H. Niepce and Frederix. *U.S. version: Producer* Harry Rapf. *Film editor* Frank Hull. *Titles* Lotta Woods. *Recording director* Douglas Shearer. ¶A Les Films Abel Gance production for Societe Generale des Films in association with Pathe Consortium, Paris, Consortium Wengeroff-Stinnes (Westi Company), Berlin, Vilaseca y Ledesma, Spain, Kanturek, Prague, Wilton, Voorburg and Svensk Filmindustri, Stockholm. Released by Metro-Goldwyn-Mayer. Western Electric Movietone recording. 8 reels. Filmed at Studio Billancourt and Studio Cinefrance Film and on location in Briancon, Toulon, La Garde, Plaine, de la Crau and de Sorena, France, and Ajaccio, Grandval and Iles Sanguinaires, Corsica. ¶CAST: *Napoleon Bonaparte* Albert Dieudonne. *Maximilien Robespierre* Edmond van Daele. *Danton* Alexandre Koubitzky.

Marat de Sade Antonin Artaud. *Violine Fleuri* Annabella (Power). *Louis de Saint-Just* Abel Gance. *Charlotte Corday* Marguerite Gance. *Napoleon as a boy* Wladimir Roudenko. *Briancon master* Rene Jeanne. *Tristan Fleuri* Nicolas Koline. *Gen. Lazare Hoche* Pierre Batcheff. *Pozzo di Borgo* Acho Chakatouny. *Antonio Salicetti* Philippe Heriat. *Freron* Daniel Mendaille. *Gen. Dugommier and Collot d'Herbois* Alexandre Bernard. *Gen. Andre Massena* Philippe Rolla. *Camille Desmoulins* Robert Vidalin. *Francois Talma* Roger Blum. *Fouquier-Tinville* Paul Amiot. *La Fayette* Boudreau. *Joseph Bonaparte* Georges Lampin. *J.-J. Rousseau* Alberty. *Capt. Desaix* Robert de Ansorena. *King Louis XVI* Louis Sance. *Gen. O'Hara* Jack Rye. *Jean-Jean* Armand Bernard. *Monge* Albert Bras. *Vicomte de Beauharnais* Georges Cahuzac. *Josephe Fouche* Guy Faviere. *Rouget de Lisle* Harry-Krimer. *Capt. Joachim Murat* Genica Missirio. *Lucien Bonaparte* Sylvio Caviccia. *Couthon* Viguier. *Andre Chenier* Vonelly. *La Bussiere* Jean d'Yd. *Josephine de Beauharnais* Gina Manes. *Marie-Antoinette* Suzanne Bianchetti. *La Marseillaise* Maryse Damia. *Elisa Bonaparte* Yvette Dieudonne. *Pauline Bonaparte* Simone Genevois. *Mme. Recamier* Suzy Vernon. *Theresa Cabarrus Tallien* Andree Standard. *Lucile Desmoulins* Francine Mussey. *Mlle. Lenormant* Carrie Carvalho. *L'Oeil-Vert* Boris Fastovich-Kovanko [Boris de Fast]. *Augustin Robespierre-le-jeune* Daniel Burret. *Capt. August Marmont* Pierre de Canolle. *Marcellin Fleuri* Serge Freddy-Karll. *Laetitia Bonaparte* Eugenie Buffet. *Santo-Ricci* Henri Baudin. *Pasquale Paoli* Maurice Schutz. *Adm. Lord Samuel Hood* W. Percy Day. *Gen. Carteaux* Leon Courtois. *Thomas Gasparin and Ricord* Caillard. *Col. Muiron* Pierre Danis. *Gen. du Teil* Dacheux. *Sgt. Andoche Junot* Jean Henry. *Moustache* Henry Krauss. *Jean Lambert Tallien* Jean Gaudray. *Gen. Scherer* Mathillon. *Hortense de Beauharnais* Janine Pen. *Caroline Bonaparte* Pierette Lugan. *Capt. le Marois* Robert Guilbert. *George Washington* Ernest Maupin. *Calmelet* Blin. *Gen. Menou* Bonvallet. *Jerome Bonaparte* Roger Chantal. *Cordeliers* M. Peres, Pierre Ferval, Edmond Greville, Michel Zahar and de Bourgival. *Gen. Henriot* Angeli. *Beaumarchais* Beaulieu. *Cromwell* Benedict.

Guillotin and Lomon Beuve. *Capt. Suchet* Jean Demercay. *Laurent-Basse* Engeldorff. *Carnot* Fleury. *Corsican Shepherd* Felix Guglielmi. *Archer* Joe Hamman. *Member of Bonaparte Family* Haziza. *Eugene de Beauharnais* Georges Henin. *Montesquiou* Jacquinet. *Dutheil* Georges Leclercq. *Fabre d'Englantine* Raphael Lievin. *Herault de Sechelles* Lomon. *Voltaire* Martin. *Augereau* Metchikoff. *Staff officer* Laurent Morlas. *Louis Bonaparte.* Fernand Rauzena. *Diderot* Regnier. *Faviere* Joachim Renez. *Brissot* Emilien Richaud. *Peccaduc* Roblin. *David* Saint-Allier. *Volontaire de l'Ardeche* Andre Scherer. *Benjamin Franklin* Vaslin. *Phelipeaux* Vidal. *Boissy d'Anglas and staff officer* Raoul Villiers. *Mme. Danton* Florence Dalma. *Mme. Marat* Noelle Mato. *Mme. Elisabeth* Georgette Sorelle. *Louise* Gely Talma. *Mme. Royale* Thomassin. *Sans-Culotte at Toulon* Jean Arroy. *Convention members* Floquet and Robert Arnoux. *Soldiers* Andre Cerf and Francis. *Photo doubles and stuntmen* Pierre de Canolle, Engeldorff and Robert Guilbert. *With* Wells, Medus, Jean Mitry, Jean Dreville, Maggy Pironet, Sylvie Gana and Chabez. ¶Credits for currently available U.S. version: *Executive producer* Francis Ford Coppola. *Production supervisors* Robert A. Harris and Steven Feltes. *Reconstructor* Kevin Brownlow. *Music composer, arranger and conductor* Carmine Coppola. *Performers* The Milan Philharmonic Orchestra. *Organ soloist* Dennis James. *Postproduction facilities* Gomillion Studios, Inc. *Music mixer* Don MacDougall. *Music editor* Douglas Lackey. *Recordist* Brad Sherman. *Engineer* Keith Klawither. *Recording director in Milan* Mike Berniker. *Recording mixer in Milan* Paolo Bocchi. *Assistant recording mixer in Milan* Alfred di Muro. *Rerecording mixer in Milan* Don Pulse. *Milan rerecording facilities* Studio Regson. *Music producers* Carmine Coppola and Mike Berniker. *Music publisher* Coppola Music Company. *Color injection optical negative* Cinema Services, Inc. and John E. Allen, Inc. *Tinting supervisor* Peter Williamson. *70mm Triptych optical negative* Zoetrope Images, Inc. *Optical cameraman* Jim McCoy. *Assistant optical cameraman* Rusty Geller. *Polyvision alignment consultant* Christopher Reyna. *Credits photography* The Title Works. *Subtitles photography* Frameline Productions, London and Stuart Lacock. *Negative cutting* Mike Fraser Associates, London. *Restoration laboratory* Henderson's Laboratories, South London. *Timer* John Ling. *Financial assistance* The National Film Archive, London with the cooperation of members of The International Federation of Film Archives and The British Film Institute. ¶A Francis Ford Coppola presentation. From Zoetrope Studios. Released by Image Archives, Inc. through Universal Pictures. 70mm. Tinted. Four-track magnetic Dolby Stereo. 235 minutes plus intermission. ¶The current U.S. version contains mistranslated titles and some sequences and shots out of order. A considerably more complete and accurate reconstruction exists in England but Francis Ford Coppola refuses to allow its screening in the states for obvious reasons. No fewer than 21 versions of *Napoleon* have been exhibited. Gance was constantly altering the film, reshooting, reworking and rereleasing it in various forms. One edition in 1935 had stereophonic Perspective Sonore. The film has been shown in various formats with the three panels as individual frames and on the same frame. When first released in the U.S. the Triptych footage was retained, regardless of what the *Napoleon* authorities claim. The three-panel scenes appeared reduced on one frame and garnered complaints from theatermen and patrons who saw nothing epic or spectacular about three tiny images on the screen. In effect the Triptych sequences did not expand three times over the regular footage but shrank to one-third their size (as they do on the TV version). The so-called "Coppola Version" was originally exhibited in the U.S. as a roadshow with Carmine Coppola touring and conducting the local city's orchestra. The film had been transferred to 70mm and during the Triptych scenes the frame was reduced in height considerably. A 35mm anamorphic version was also produced and released along with the 70mm edition in January 1981 with Coppola's music in Dolby Stereo. Other release dates over the years and for different versions include: Paris premiere on April 7, 1927; May 8, 1927; October 11, 1927; November 1927; March 1928; June 28, 1928; January 1929; 1935 (with new scenes and in Perspective Sound); mid-1950s (conflicting information but possibly in anamorphic format);

1970; 1979; and 1982. Different musical scores have been used over the years, and some of the composers (or arrangers) were Arthur Honegger, Werner Heymann, Henri Verdum and Carl Davis (at least two versions). *Napoleon* is definitely not the ultimate silent movie. It takes far too long to show what in the end is a very few scenes. The Triptych scenes were originally misaligned and no attempt has been made to correct that glaring fault. The music on the U.S. version is poor and the lack of sound effects dulls the imagery. It is no better than any large scale Hollywood film from the same period, though more visually arresting due to the three-panel and multipanel (Polyvision, as it was called) shots. The video cassette edition, on which the three panels appear extremely small, is especially uninteresting.

Napravlenie glavnogo udara *see* **Liberation.**

Natasha Rostova *see* **(Leo Tolstoy's) War and Peace.**

Nebo so mnoy (1975). Filmed in Sovscope 70. *Screen authors* O. Stukalov, T. Kozevnikova and M. Popovich. *Director* V. Lonskoy. *Operator* I. Chernikh. *Artist* B. Nemchek. *Composer* G. Firtich. *Sound operator* L. Voskalchuk. ¶A Mosfilm production. International distribution Sovexportfilm. Sovcolor. Six-track magnetic stereophonic sound. 97 minutes. Filmed at Mosfilm Studios, Moscow, R.S.F.S.R. ¶CAST: I. Ledogorov, L. Luzina, V. Zamanskiy, N. Bondarchuk, Z. Kirienko, U. Liedidz, Yu. Dudko and V. Zemlyanikin. ¶A Soviet production released in Russia in 1975.

Nevolinikts svobodi *see* **Yemelyan Pugachov.**

New Magic (1984). Filmed in Showscan. *Producer* Peter Beale. *Director and writer* Douglas Trumbull. *Cinematographer* James R. Dickson. *Special effects supervisor* Eric Allard. *Magic consultant* Ricky Jay. *Special electrical properties* Kenneth Strickfaden. *Special miniature photography* Pete Slagle. ¶A Showscan Corporation production for Showpiz Pizza Place, a Division of Brock Hotel Corporation. Metrocolor. Six-track magnetic Dolby Stereo. 22 minutes. Filmed at Laird

International Studios. ¶CAST: *Jeremy* Gerrit Graham. *Mr. Kellar* Christopher Lee. ¶The first Showscan film.

New Orleans Frolic *see* **Happy Days.**

The Newlyweds (1971). Filmed in Sovscope 70. *Screen author* Aleksandr Chervinskiy. *Based on the novel "Rassudite nas, lyudi" by* Aleksandr Andreyev. *Director* Nikolai Moskalenko. *Operator* Nikolai Olonovskiy. *Artist* N. Meshkova. *Composer* Mark Fradkin. *Sound operator* T. Batalova. *Song text* E. Dolmatovskogo. ¶A Mosfilm production. International distribution Sovexportfilm. Sovcolor. Six-track magnetic stereophonic sound. 115 minutes. Filmed at Mosfilm Studios, Moscow, R.S.F.S.R. ¶CAST: *Alexei Nikolayev* Evgeni Kindinov. *Zkhenya* Lyubov Nefedova. *Darya Vassilyevna* Nonna Mordyukova. *Arkadi* Vladimir Tikhonov. *With* Tatyana Pelittser, Alla Larionova, Z. Goroshchenya, N. Pshennaya, A. Glazirin, Armen Dzigarkhanyan, M. Kokshenov, N. Sergienko, G. Kozlov and V. Nevinniy. ¶A Soviet production released in Russia in 1971 as *Molodie.*

Neylon 100% (1974). Filmed in Sovscope 70. *Screen authors* S. Shatrov and V. Basov. *Based on the story "Neylonovaya shubka" by* S. Shatrova. *Director* V. Basov. *Operator* I. Slabnevich. *Artist* A. Parkhomenko. *Composer* M. Vaynberg. *Sound operator* E. Fedorov. *Song text* R. Sefa. ¶A Mosfilm production. International distribution Sovexportfilm. Sovcolor. Six-track magnetic stereophonic sound. 108 minutes. Filmed at Mosfilm Studios, Moscow, R.S.F.S.R. ¶CAST: V. Basov, V. Titova, N. Agalova, M. Pogorzeliskiy, M. Drozdovskaya, E. Vesnik, E. Evstigneev, L. Kuravlev, R. Markova, V. Ztush, L. Kanevskiy, N. Krachkovskaya, M. Pugovkin, M. Krepkogorskaya, A. Karapetyan, B. Novikov, Yu. Belov, T. Sovchi, S. Kharitonova and Yu. Volintsev. ¶A Soviet production released in Russia in 1974.

Neytralinie vodi (1969). Filmed in Sovscope 70. *Screen authors* V. Vendelovskiy and V. Soloviev. *Director* V. Berenshteyn. *Operators* M. Kirillov and A. Kirillov. *Artist* A. Dikhtyar. *Composer* K. Molchanov. *Sound operator* S. Gurin. ¶A kinostudiya im. M. Gorikogo production. International distribution Sovexportfilm. Sovcolor. Six-track magnetic stereophonic sound. 104 minutes. Filmed at kinostudiya im. M. Gorikogo, Gorki, R.S.F.S.R. ¶CAST: K. Lavrov, A. Ushakov, V. Chetverikov, M. Yanushkevich, A. Panikin, N. Popova, A. Pilyus and V. Samoylov. ¶A Soviet production released in Russia in 1969.

Nezabivaemoe *see* **The Unforgettable.**

Niagara Falls (1926). Filmed in Natural Vision. *Producers* George K. Spoor and P. John Berggren. ¶Produced and released by Natural Vision Pictures. Color. This travelog short was a demonstration of the wide gauge film process in color. While information is extremely sketchy it would appear the color was a tint and/or toning technique. It would be highly unlikely that an actual photographic color process was used.

Niagara Falls (February 13, 1930). Filmed in Grandeur. *Executive producer* William Fox. *Producer* Winfield R. Sheehan. ¶A William Fox presentation. A Grandeur Scenic. Produced and released by Fox Film Corporation. Western Electric Movietone recording. 1 reel. Released with *Happy Days.*

Niagara: Miracles, Myths & Magic (1987). Filmed in IMAX. *Producer* Nick Gray. *Writer and creator* Kieth Merrill. *Music* Bill Conti. *Stills* Brett Cardinell. ¶A Heno-Hinum production. Released by Cinema Group Venture. Eastman Color. Six-track magnetic stereophonic sound. 35 minutes. A Canadian production.

Niagara Wonders (May 1987). Filmed in Showscan. Produced and released by Showscan Film Corporation. Eastman Color. Six-track magnetic Dolby Stereo. 23 minutes. Originally made for the Centennial Theater, Niagara Falls, New York.

Night of Dreams (1986). Filmed in Showscan. Produced and released by Showscan Film Corporation. Eastman Color. Six-track magnetic Dolby Stereo. A short subject.

Night Passage (August 1957). Filmed in Technirama. *Producer* Aaron Rosenberg. *Directors* James Neilson and Anthony Mann. *Screenplay* Borden Chase. *Based on the novel by* Norman A. Fox. *Music composer and conductor* Dimitri Tiomkin. *Director of photography* William Daniels. *Film editor* Sherman Todd. *Art direction* Alexander Golitzen and Robert Clatworthy. *Set decoration* Russell A. Gausman and Oliver Emert. *Costumes* Bill Thomas. *Makeup* Bud Westmore. *Sound* Leslie I. Carey and Frank H. Wilkinson. *Special photography* Clifford Stine. *Assistant director* Marshall Green. *Technicolor color consultant* William Fritzsche. *Second unit director* James C. Havens. *Choreography* Kenny Williams. *Music supervision* Joseph Gershenson. *Songs "You Can't Get Far Without the Railroad" and "Follow the River": music* Dimitri Tiomkin; *lyrics* Ned Washington; *singer* James Stewart. ¶A Universal-International picture. Released by Universal Pictures Company. Technicolor. Westrex recording system. 90 minutes. Filmed at Universal City Studios and on location in Northern California. ¶CAST: *Grant McLaine* James Stewart. *Lee "The Utica Kid" McLaine* Audie Murphy. *Whitey Harbin* Dan Duryea. *Charlotte "Charley" Drew* Diane Foster. *Verna Kimball* Elaine Stewart. *Joey Adams* Brandon de Wilde. *Ben Kimball* Jay C. Flippen. *Will Renner* Herbert Anderson. *Concho* Robert J. Wilke. *Jeff Kurth* Hugh Beaumont. *Shotgun* Jack Elam. *Howdy Sladen* Tommy Cook. *Clarence Feeney* Paul Fix. *Miss Vittles* Olive Carey. *Tim Riley* James Flavin. *Jubilee* Donald Curtis. *Mrs. Feeney* Ellen Corby. *Latigo* John Day [Daheim]. *O'Brien* Kenny Williams. *Trinidad* Frank Chase. Pick Gannon Harold Goodwin. *Shannon* Harold (Tommy) Hart. *Dusty* Jack C. Williams. *Torgenson* Boyd Stockman. *Poche* Henry Wills. *Roan* Charles (Chuck) Roberson. *Click* Willard Willingham. *Rosa* Polly Burson. *Linda* Patsy Novak. *Leary* Ted Mapes. *Barney* William "Bill" Phipps. *Pete* Ben Welden. ¶The first film in Technirama. Neilson replaced Mann as director. This may have been released with four-track MagOptical or Perspecta stereophonic sound.

Nights of Farewell (1966). Filmed in 70mm. *Realizer* Jean Dreville. *Scenario* Paul Andreota and Alexandre Galitch. *Director of the photography* Michel

Kelber. *Montage* Claude Nicole. ¶An Alkam-CICC-Cocinor-Lenfilm production. Sovcolor and Eastman Color. Six-track magnetic stereophonic sound. 97 minutes. Filmed in the R.S.F.S.R. and France. ¶CAST: *Petipas* Gilles Segal. *Macha* Nathalie Velitchko. *Minkh* Jacques Ferriere. *Highness* Nikolas Tcherkossov. *Sister* Sabine Lods. ¶A French and Soviet coproduction released in France in November 1966 by Cocinor as *La nuit des adieux.* Photographic process is unknown and may be a blowup from 35mm anamorphic or spherical. If actually shot in 70mm then Sovscope 70, Superpanorama 70 or Super Technirama 70 (or possibly a combination of them) was utilized. This film was not included in the material suplied by Sovexportfilm and may have been exhibited only in France in 70mm. The fact it wasn't noted in the Russian data also strongly implies it was a blowup for French domestic release, but it is included here for the record.

Niya: Artifical Person *see* **To the Stars by Hard Ways.**

Niyya — iskusstvenniy chelobek *see* **To the Stars by Hard Ways.**

No Return (1974). Filmed in Sovscope 70. *Screen author and director* Alexei Saltikov. *Based on the story "Vozvrata net" by* Anatoli Kalinina. *Operator* Boris Brozovskiy. *Artist* V. Kislikh. *Composer* A. Zshpay. *Sound operator* R. Berz. ¶A Mosfilm production. International distribution Sovexportfilm. Sovcolor. Six-track magnetic stereophonic sound. 124 minutes. Filmed at Mosfilm Studios, Moscow, R.S.F.S.R ¶CAST: *Antonina Kashirina* Nonna Mordyukova. *Anastasiya* Tatyana Samoylova. *Nikitin* Vladislav Dvorzetskiy. *Irina* Olga Prokhorova. *Irina's husband* Nikolai Eremenko. *With* Alexei Batalov, Boris Kudryavtsev, N. Menishikova and V. Bekeric. ¶A Soviet production released in Russia in 1974 as *Vozvrata net.*

Nomads of the Deep (1979). Filmed in IMAX. *Producer* David Keighley. *Director* John Stoneman. *Underwater photography* Chuck Nicklin and John Stoneman. *Surface photography* David Douglas. ¶A Mako Films, Ltd. production. Released by Imax Systems Corporation. Eastman Color. Six-track magnetic stereophonic sound. 20 minutes. Originally made for Ontario Place.

North of Superior (1971). Filmed in IMAX. *Writer, producer, director and photographer* Graeme Ferguson. *Associate producers* Robert Kerr, Roman Kroiter and William Shaw. *Sound recording* Brian Avery. *Production manager* David Hughes. *Assistant cameraman* Ronald Lautore. *Editor* Toni Trow. *Sound editor* Tony Lower. *Assistant editors* Robin Botting and Betty Ferguson. *"Ojibwa Country" composer and performer* Bill Houston. *Musical score* Zalman Yanovsky. *Music recording* Chris Kene at Eastern Sound Co., Ltd. *Stereo rerecording* John Aldred at Film House Toronto. *Laboratory and titles* MGM Laboratory, Inc. *Musicians* Maribeth Solomon, Leonard Solomon, Mickey Erbe, David Brown, Jack Franchman and Brian Leonard. ¶A Multiscreen Corporation, Ltd. production. Released by Imax Systems Corporation. Eastman Color. Six-track magnetic stereophonic sound. 18 minutes. Filmed in Northern Ontario, Canada. ¶This Canadian production was the second IMAX film and is generally believed to be the most widely viewed movie from that country. Originally produced for Ontario Place.

Novie priklyucheniya neulovimikh (1969). Filmed in Sovscope 70. *Screen authors* Z. Keosayan and A. Makarov. *Director* Z. Keosayan. *Operator* F. Dobronravov. *Artist* V. Golikov. *Composer* Ya. Frenkeli. *Sound operator* A. Vanetsian. ¶A Mosfilm production. International distribution Sovexportfilm. Sovcolor. Six-track magnetic stereophonic sound. 92 minutes. Filmed at Mosfilm Studios, Moscow, R.S.F.S.R. ¶CAST: M. Metelkin, V. Vasiliev, V. Kosikh, V. Kurdyukova, Armen Dzigarkhanyan, B. Sichkin, A. Tolbuzin, E. Kopelyan, I. Pereverzev, E. Vesnik, S. Filippov, S. Kramarov and K. Sorokin. ¶A Soviet production released in Russia in 1969.

O tekh, kogo pomnyu i lyudlyu *see* **About Those I Remember and Love.**

Ocean (1977). Filmed in OMNIMAX. *Producer and director* Graeme Ferguson. *Underwater photography* Mal Wolfe.

Surface photography Graeme Ferguson and Averill Townsend. ¶Released by Imax Systems Corporation. Eastman Color. Six-track magnetic stereophonic sound. 25 minutes. Filmed at Catalina Island, California and Oregon. Originally made for San Diego's Reuben H. Fleet Space Theater.

October *see* **Red Bells.**

Odinnadtsat nadezkhd *see* **Eleven Hopefuls.**

Odinochnoe plavanie *see* **Detached Mission.**

Ognennaya duga *see* **Liberation.**

Oklahoma! (October 13, 1955). Filmed in Todd-AO. *Executive producers* Richard Rodgers and Oscar Hammerstein II. *Producer* Arthur Hornblow, Jr. *Director* Fred Zinnemann. *Screenplay* Sonya Levien and William Ludwig. *Based on the play with book and lyrics by* Oscar Hammerstein II *and music by* Richard Rodgers, *as produced on the stage by* The Theatre Guild, Inc., *from the play "Green Grow the Lilacs" by* Lynn Riggs. *Music* Richard Rodgers. *Lyrics* Oscar Hammerstein II. *Music supervisor and conductor* Jack Blackton. *Background music arranger and supervisor* Adolph Deutsch. *Director of photography* Robert L. Surtees. *Todd-AO technician* Schuyler A. Sanford. *Production executive* Barney Briskin. *Orchestrations* Robert Russell Bennett. *Dances stager* Agnes de Mille. *Costumes* Orry-Kelly and Motley. *Production designer* Oliver Smith. *Art director* Joseph Wright. *Set decorator* Keogh Gleason. *Supervising film editor* Gene Ruggiero. *Film editor* George Boemler. *Sound editor* Milo Lory. *Music editor* Ralph Ives. *Sound recording supervisor* Fred Hynes. *Sound recorder* Joseph I. Kane. *Rerecording* Metro-Goldwyn-Mayer Studios and Todd-AO. *Music coordinator* Richard Helfer. *Color consultant* Elvord Eisenman. *Camera operator* Robert Moreno. *Second unit cameraman* Floyd Crosby. *Still photographer* Schuyler Crail. *Assistant director* Arthur Black, Jr. *Production aide* John Emerson. *Men's wardrobe* Frank C. Beetson. *Women's wardrobe* Ann Peck. *Makeup* Ben Lane and Ben Nye, Sr. *Hair stylist* Anna Malin. *Production publicist*

H. Thomas Wood. *Negative* Eastman Color. *Todd-AO developers* American Optical Company and Magna Theatre Corporation. ¶A Rodgers and Hammerstein Pictures, Inc. production. Released by Magna Theatre Corporation. Color by Consolidated Film Industries. Westrex six-track magnetic Orthosonic Sound. 148 minutes plus intermission. Filmed at Metro-Goldwyn-Mayer Studios and on location in Nogales, Arizona. ¶CAST: *Curly* Gordon MacRae. *Ado Annie* Gloria Grahame. *Will Parker* Gene Nelson. *Aunt Eller* Charlotte Greenwood. *Laurey* Shirley Jones. *Ali Hakim* Eddie Albert. *Carnes* James Whitmore. *Jud Fry* Rod Steiger. *Gertie* Barbara Lawrence. *Skidmore* Jay C. Flippen. *Marshal* Roy Barcroft. *Dream Curly* James Mitchell. *Dream Laurey* Bambi Lynn. *Dancers* James Mitchell, Bambi Lynn, Jennie Workman, Kelly Brown, Marc Platt, Lizanne Truex, Virginia Bosler, Evelyn Taylor and Jane Fischer. *Cowboy at train depot* Ben Johnson. ¶Filmed simultaneously in CinemaScope. Consolidated Film Industries in New Jersey processed and release-printed all original 70mm prints which were mixed using Westrex equipment. However the screen credits on all 70mm and 35mm prints billed Technicolor (which did do the 70mm release prints made after 1955 as well as all the 35mm prints) and Western Electric Movietone recording. Exactly why is anybody's guess. Released in 35mm by RKO Radio Pictures running 140 minutes. Rereleased by 20th Century-Fox in Todd-AO and CinemaScope. Reissued again by The Samuel Goldwyn Company, Inc., in Todd-AO and advertised in 70mm CinemaScope *(sic!)*. The 35mm prints did not have the overture, intermission or exit music. Additionally the main titles were changed (dropping a couple of the credits) and opening music altered considerably. Since the film was shot in two different formats, staging of some scenes is variable from version to version.

Old Seterhand *see* **Shatterhand.**

Old Shatterhand *see* **Shatterhand.**

Ombre bianche *see* **The Savage Innocents.**

On the Wing (June 19, 1986). Filmed in IMAX and OMNIMAX. *Producers, writers*

The Aero Vironment team prepares the artificial pterodactyl for launching in On the Wing. *Director Bayley Silleck rides the camera boom with the WILCAM IW5 IMAX camera. (Photo by Martyn Cowley.)*

and directors Francis Thompson and Bayley Silleck. *Based on an idea by* Walter Boyne. *Photographers* Burleigh Wartes and Leonidas Zourdoumis. *Special effects supervisor* Peter Parks. *Stills* Martyn Cowley. *Musical score* Richard Einhorn. ¶A Francis Thompson, Inc. production. Sponsored by Smithsonian Institution and S.C. Johnson & Son, Inc. (Johnson Wax). Released by Imax Systems Corporation. Eastman Color. Six-track magnetic stereophonic sound. 33 minutes. ¶CAST: Dr. Paul MacCready and the AeroVironment team. *Narrator* F. Murray Abraham. ¶A Canadian production originally made for the Smithsonian Institution's Samuel P. Langley IMAX Theater at the National Air and Space Museum in Washington, D.C.

One Doesn't Change Horses in Midstream (1981). Filmed in Sovscope 70. *Screen authors* Naum Melinikov, Aleksandr Misharin and Gavriil Egiazarov. *Director* Gavriil Egiazarov. *Operator* Elizbar Karavaev. *Artist* Valery Filippov. *Composer* Dokhn Ter-Tatevosyan. *Sound operator* V. Kurganskiy. *Song text* I. Shaferana. ¶A Mosfilm production. International distribution Sovexportfilm. Sovcolor. Six-track magnetic stereophonic sound. 179 minutes plus intermission. Filmed at Mosfilm Studios, Moscow and on location in Naberezhniye Chelny, R.S.F.S.R. ¶CAST: *Borisov* Leonid Markov. *With* Vladimir Samoylov,

Natalia Andreychenko, Boris Ivanov, Gennady Korolikov, Armen Dzigarkhanyan, Yuri Vasiliev, V. Sedov, A. Smolyakov, G. Poliskikh and Sofia Pavlova. ¶A Soviet production released in Russia in 1981 as *Koney na pereprave ne menyayut* in two parts running 94 minutes and 85 minutes. See *Rasskaz o film "Koney na pereprave ne menyayut.*

One More Night of Sheherezade (1985). Filmed in Sovscope 70. *Screen author* Valeri Karen. *Based on stories from "1001 Nights" and a story by* V. Gauffa. *Director* Takhir Sabirov. *Operator* Vladimir Klimov. *Artist* Vladimir Ptitsin. *Composer* Gennady Aleksandrov. *Sound operator* S. Bogdanov. ¶A Tadzikfilm production. International distribution Sovexportfilm. Sovcolor. Six-track magnetic stereophonic sound. 100 minutes. Filmed at Tadzikfilm Studios, Dushanbe, Tadzhik S.S.R. ¶CAST: Elena Tonunts, Abel Ali-Hadad, Larisa Belozurova, Sharif Kabulov, Burkhon Rodzabov, Tamata Yanutseva, Galib Ismailov, D. Umarov, S. Dtskambaev and Takhir Sabirov. ¶A Soviet production released in Russia in 1985 as *I eshche odna nochi Sheherezadi*
. . . .

Oni srazalisi za rodiny *see* **They Fought for Their Motherland.**

Oni zivut ryadom *see* **They Live Close By.**

Onkel Tom's hutte *see* **Uncle Tom's Cabin.**

Only You (1972). Filmed in Sovscope 70. *Screen authors* Vladimir Massa and Evgeni Sherstobitov. *Based on the operetta "Belaya akatsuya" by* Isaak Dunaevskogo. *Director* Evgeni Sherstobitov. *Choreographer and producer* Boris Komenkoviy. *Operator* M. Cherniy. *Artist* P. Slabinskiy. *Sound operator* N. Trakhtenberg. *Composer* B. Klup. ¶A Kievskaya kinostudiya im. A.P. Dovzenko production. International distribution Sovexportfilm. Sovcolor. Six-track magnetic stereophonic sound. 89 minutes. Filmed at Kievskaya kinostudiya im. A.P. Dovzenko, Kiev, Ukrainian S.S.R. ¶CAST: *Tonya* Irina Borisova. *Maxim Chaika* Nikolai Soloviov. *Larisa* Galina Stetsenko. *Yakov Nakonechnikov* Spartak Mishulin. *With* S. Sibelv, F. Pantyushin, N. Gavrilov, G. Nekhaevskaya, A. Milyutin and A. Gay. ¶A Soviet production released in Russia in 1972 as *Toliko ti.*

Ontario/Summertide (1976). Filmed in IMAX. *Producer and director* David Mackay. *Photographer* Miklos Lente. ¶Released by Imax Systems Corporation. Eastman Color. Six-track sterephonic sound. 21 minutes. Filmed in Ontario, Canada. This Canadian production was originally made for Ontario Place.

Opasnie povoroti (1961). Filmed in Kinopanorama. International distribution Sovexportfilm. Sovcolor. Nine-track magnetic Kinopanorama Sound. A Soviet production released in Russia in 1961.

Operation Spark *see* **Blockade.**

Operatsiya Iskra *see* **Blockade.**

The Optimistic Tragedy (February 22, 1964). Filmed in Sovscope 70. *Screen authors* Sofiya Vishhevetskaya and Samson Samsonov. *Based on the play "Optimisticheskaya tragediya" by* Vsevolod Vitaliyevich Vishnevskogo. *Director and producer* Samson Samsonov. *Story editor* N. Glagoleva. *Chief operator* Vladimir Monakhov. *Operators* I. Bogdanov and V. Zakharchuk. *Assistant operators* E. Borkman and E. Shvedov. *Artists* I. Novoderzkin and Sergey Voronkov. *Editor* A. Kamagorova. *Composer* Vasiliy Dekhterev. *Song text* M. Matousovskiy. *Conductor* V. Dudarova. *Sound operator* Grigoriy Korenblyum. *Assistant directors* Lyutsiya Okhrimenko, M. Koldobskaya and N. Solovyov. *Manager of production* A. Yablochkin. *Costumier* V. Perepvolov. *Makeup* S. Kalinin. *Special effects* I. Felitsyn and Klimenko. *Military consultants* N. Molotkov, N. Smirnov, N. Oslikovskiy and S. Kornilov. *Sculptor* L. Berlin. ¶A Mosfilm production. International distribution Sovexportfilm. Released by Artkino Pictures. 121 minutes. Filmed at Mosfilm Studios, Moscow and on location in Kiev and on the Black Sea, R.S.F.S.R. ¶CAST: *Commissar* Margarita Volodina. *Vozhak* Boris Andreev. *Aleksey* Vyacheslav Tikhonov. *Siplyy* Vsevolod Sanaev. *Vaynonen* Orko Berninen. *Bering* Vsevolod Safonov. *Boatswain* I. Zevago. *Ryaboy* V. Netrebin. *Old sailor* Grigoriy Mikhaylov. *Ship's doctor* P. Sobolevskiy. *Vozhachok* Erast Garin. *First officer* Oleg Strizenov. *Second officer* Gleb Strizenov. *Leaders* A. Glazirin and V. Belokhvestik. *Tattooed sailor* I. Vankov. *Woman in black* V. Nedobrovo-Buzkhinskaya. *Tall sailor* V. Shulgin. *With* I. Bychkov, I. Bondar, V. Grave, V. Demidovskiy, V. Zabavin, E. Zosimov, Yuri Kireyev, L. Knyazev, N. Kendratyev, P. Kononykhin, A. Mulyukhin, V. Novikov, D. Orlovskiy, V. Prikhodko, A. Sakhnovskiy, S. Savashenko, V. Skuridin, A. Stroyev and N. Khryashchikov. ¶A Soviet production released in Russia in June 1963 as *Optimisticheskaya tragediya* in 70mm, Sovcolor and six-track magnetic stereophonic sound running 121 minutes. Later optically converted to Kinopanorama and nine-track magnetic stereophonic sound. Released in the U.S. in black-and-white 35mm only.

Optimisticheskaya tragediya *see* **The Optimistic Tragedy.**

Oslinaya shkura (1982). Filmed in Sovscope 70. *Screen author* M. Volipin. *Based on the story by* Sh. Perro. *Director* N. Kozeverova. *Operator* Z. Rozovskiy. *Artists* M. Azizyan and V. Kostin. *Composer* M. Vaynberg. *Sound operator* S. Shumyacher. ¶A Mosfilm production. International distribution Sovexportfilm. Sovcolor. Six-track magnetic stereophonic sound. 106 minutes. Filmed at Mosfilm Studios, Moscow, R.S.F.S.R. ¶CAST:

R. Ztush, S. Nemolyaeva, V. Novikova, A. Galibin, Z. Gerdt, V. Panina, T. Pelittser, N. Karachentsov, L. Makarova, S. Parshin, B. Arakelov, A. Domashov, S. Filippov and M. Barabanova. ¶A Soviet production released in Russia in 1982.

Osobo vaznoe zadanie *see* **Special Assignment.**

Osvobozdenie *see* **Liberation.**

Ot zari do zari *see* **From Dawn to Dusk.**

Our Debts (1977). Filmed in Sovscope 70. *Screen author* Eduard Volodarskiy. *Director* Boris Yashin. *Operator* Dilshat Fatkhulin. *Artist* Leonid Platov. *Composer* Boris Chayovskiy. *Sound operator* V. Belyarov. ¶A Mosfilm production. International distribution Sovexportfilm. Sovcolor. Six-track magnetic stereophonic sound. 89 minutes. Filmed at Mosfilm Studios, Moscow, R.S.F.S.R. ¶CAST: *Ivan Krutov* Leonid Markov. *With* Lyudmila Zaytseva, Lydia Fedosevva-Shukshina, N. Andreychenko, N. Penikov, Sergei Nikonenko, P. Bolinikh, V. Grachev, E. Ivanichev, F. Odinokov, V. Pavlov, V. Plotnikov and O. Tsarikov. ¶A Soviet production released in Russia in 1977 as *Dolgi nashi.*

Outer and Inner Space (February 8, 1966). Presented in 16mm Dual Screen. *Producer, director and photographer* Andy Warhol. ¶An Andy Warhol production. Released by Film-Makers' Cooperative. 70 minutes. Optical sound. Filmed in New York City. ¶CAST: *Young woman* Edie Sedgwick. ¶As originally presented the first section, approximately half of the film, was shown in dual screen projection, though the last half apparently was exhibited only on one screen. After the initial New York playdate it probably was projected as a single screen item. It does not seem to have been shot with the intention of simultaneous projection; this was probably done as a gimmick.

Panorama Blue (February 1974). Filmed in 70mm Super Panoramascope. *Executive producer* Richard S. Ellman. *Producer and director* Alan Roberts. *Screenplay and music* Steve Michaels. *Director of photography* Bob Brownell. *Film editor* James Walters. *Associate producers* Donald Alvin, Thomas Shelton, Bernard Ellman and Stephen B. Ginsberg. *Costumes* Leigh Mitchell. *Set decorator* Don Mulderick. *Sound* Phil Brandon. ¶Produced and released by Ellman Film Enterprises. Eastman Color. Four-track magnetic stereophonic sound. 85 minutes. Filmed in Southern California. Self-imposed rating: X. ¶CAST: *Host* Richard S. Ellman. *With* Carona Faoro, Stephen Nave, Sue Moses, Dennis Zlamal, Rene Bond, Sandy Dempsey, John Paul Jones, Ric Loots, Linda York, John Holmes, Rick Cassidy, Uschi Digard, Bob Silvani, Dristi Fletcher, Charlotte Ruse, Bob Taylor, Reg Bartram, Melody Dillberg, Jenni Such, Lizzy Koske, Ruth Robinson, Sidney Jollivette, John Cole, Randolph Hardesty, Ron Lawrence, Kristin Schwarzer, Duane Paulsen, Rick West, Mary Ann Whitney, William Margold, Con Covert, Johna Lee, Liz Wolfe, Robert De Chatelenne, Cyndee Summers and Roberto Rogisini. ¶While this softcore skinflick was advertised "in 70mm Super Panoramascope and Four-Track Stereophonic Sound" (why not six-track?), it is very questionable whether it actually was photographed in 70mm. It definitely was in 35mm 'scope and four-track magnetic stereo. The beginning was a takeoff on the beginning of *This Is Cinerama* with black-and-white 1.33 × 1 footage expanding to full wide screen, color and stereo sound. (The rollercoaster scene was a sexual encounter done in front of a transparency.) Some flat footage was 'scoped to match the new material. It is included here for the record, being one of those oddities that certainly won't be documented anywhere else.

Parallel 50 (1987). Filmed in IMAX. *Executive producer* Roman Kroitor. *Line producer* Jack Clements. *Coproducer* Sally Dundas. *Directors* Norma Bailey, John Paskievich, Derek Mazur, Richard Condie, Kim Johnston, Brion Whitford and Gail Singer. *Production manager* Connie Bortnick. *Director of photography* Ian Elkin. *Sound recordist* Leon Johnson. *Camera assistant* Linda Danchak. *Key grip* Owen Smith. *Editing assistant* Toni Trow Myers. ¶A Parallel 50 (a subsidiary of Imax Systems Corporation) production. Released by Imax Systems Corporation. Eastman Color. Six-track magnetic stereophonic sound. Filmed in

Shooting with the IMAX camera, on location in Churchill, Manitoba, Canada, for Parallel 50.

Canada. A Canadian production originally made for Winnipeg's Portage Place IMAX Theatre.

Patton (February 4, 1970). Filmed in Dimension 150. *Executive producer* Darryl F. Zanuck. *Associate executive producer* Elmo Williams. *Producer* Frank McCarthy. *Director* Franklin J. Schaffner. *Screen story and screeplay* Francis Ford Coppola, James R. Webb and Edmund H. North. *Newsreel narrative* Franklin J. Schaffner. *Based on factual material from "Patton: Ordeal and Triumph" by* Ladislas Farago *and "A Soldier's Story" by* Omar N. Bradley. *Senior military adviser* General of the Army Omar N. Bradley, U.S.A. *Music* Jerry Goldsmith. *Director of photography* Fred J. Koenekamp. *Art direction* Urie McCleary and Gil Parrando. *Set decoration* Antonio Mateos and Pierre-Louis Thevenet. *Special photographic effects* L.B. Abbott. *Makeup supervision* Daniel Striepeke. *Creative makeup design* John Chambers. *Makeup artists* Del Acevedo and Jose Sanchez. *Action coordinator* Joe Canutt. *Film editor* Hugh S. Fowler. *Unit production managers* Francisco Alonzo Day, Eduardo G. Maroto and Tadeo Villalba. *Assistant directors* Eli Dunn and Jose Lopez Rodero. *Second unit cameramen* Clifford Stine and Cecilio Paniaqua. *Orchestration* Arthur Morton. *Mechanical effects* Alex C. Weldon. *Associate producer* Frank Caffey. *Technical advisers* Gen. Paul D. Harkins, U.S.A. Retd. and Col. Grover S. Johns, Jr.,

U.S.A. Retd. *Second unit directors* D. Michael Moore and Bill Hickman. *Sound supervision* James B. Corcoran. *Sound production* Don Bassman. *Sound rerecording* Douglas O. Williams, Murray Spivack and Theodore Soderberg. *Process consultants* Richard Vetter and Carl Williams. *Titles* Pacific Title & Art Studio. *Supervising sound editor* Don Hall, Jr. *Sound editor* Raymond V. Bomba. *Supervising music editor* Leonard Engel. *Gaffer* Gene Stout. *Key grip* Glenn Harris. *Camera operators* Bill Norton and Riccardo Navarreto. *Assistant cameramen* Charles G. Arnold, Emilio Calori and Mike Benson. *Lighting equipment* Mole-Richardson Company. *Executive in charge of production* Richard D. Zanuck. *Casting* Michael McLean. *Special photography* Clifford Stine. *Optical photography* Art Cruickshank. *Spanish military adviser* Lt. Col. Luis Martin de Pozuelo. *Script consultant* Kitty Buhler Bradley. ¶A Frank McCarthy–Franklin J. Schaffner production. Released by 20th Century–Fox. Color by Fotofilm and De Luxe. Prints by De Luxe. Westrex six-track magnetic stereophonic sound. 171 minutes plus intermission. Filmed at Estudios Sevilla, Madrid and on location in Southern California; Almeria, Madrid, Segovia, Rio Frio and Pamplona, Spain; Knutsford, England; Marrakech, Morocco; Crete; and Greece. MPAA rating: M. ¶CAST: *Gen. George S. Patton, Jr.* George C. Scott. *Gen. Omar N. Bradley* Karl Malden. *Field Marshal Sir Bernard Law Montgomery* Michael Bates. *Maj. Gen. Walter Bedell*

Smith Edward Binns. *Col. Gaston Bell* Lawrence Dobkin. *Maj. Gen. Lucian K. Truscott* John Doucette. *Sgt. William George Meeks* James Edwards. *Lt. Col. Henry Davenport* Frank Latimer. *Col. Gen. Alfred Jodl* Richard Muench. *Capt. Richard N. Jenson* Morgan Paull. *Capt. Oskar Steiger* Siegfried Rauch. *Lt. Col. Charles R. Codman* Paul Stevens. *Brig. Gen. Hobart Carver* Michael Strong. *Field Marshal Erwin Rommel* Karl Michael Vogler. *Capt. Chester B. Hansen* Stephen Young. *Willy the dog* Abraxas Aaran. *Col. John Welkin* Peter Barkworth. *Air Vice Marshal Sir Arthur Coningham* John Barrie. *Lt. Gen. Harry Buford* David Bauer. *Pfc slapped by Patton* Tim Considine. *Moroccan minister* Albert Dumortier. *Air Chief Marshal Sir Arthur Tedder* Gerald Flood. *Gen. Sir Harold Alexander* Jack Gwillim. *Clergyman* David Healy. *Patton's driver* Bill Hickman. *War correspondent* Sandy Kevin. *Bradley's driver* Carey Loftin. *British briefing officer* Alan MacNaughton. *Third Army chaplain* Lionel Murton. *Tank captain* Clint Ritchie. *Maj. Gen. Francis de Guingand* Douglas Wilmer. *First Lt. Alexander Stiller* Patrick J. Zurica. *Fox Movietone News narrator* Lowell Thomas. ¶The title was shortened from *Patton: Salute to a Rebel* just as the first roadshow engagements were beginning and many of the first ads carried that longer monicker. Released in England as *Patton: Lust for Glory*. Working title: *Patton—Blood & Guts*. Sequel was *The Last Days of Patton* (CBS-TV, 1986) also featuring George C. Scott in the lead.

Patton—Blood & Guts *see* **Patton.**

Patton: Lust for Glory *see* **Patton.**

Patton: Salute to a Rebel *see* **Patton.**

People in the Ocean (1980). Filmed in Sovscope 70. *Screen authors* Eduard Volodarskiy and Pavel Chukhary. *Director* Pavel Chukhary. *Operators* Mikhail Ardabievskiy and Vladimir Shevtsik. *Artist* Anatoly Kuznestova. *Composer* A. Grech. ¶A Mosfilm production. International distribution Sovexportfilm. Sovcolor. Six-track magnetic stereophonic sound. 97 minutes. Filmed at Mosfilm Studios, Moscow, R.S.F.S.R. ¶CAST: Vadim Spiridonov, Boris Smorchkov, Boris Galkin, Svetlana

Toma, Larissa Udovichenko, Vladimir Zamanskiy, O. Li, T. Yakovleva, A. Sun, A. Khuazeni, A. Kim, N. Lin, S. Tsigali, V. Berezustkaya and V. Uraliskiy. ¶A Soviet production released in Russia in 1980 as *Lyudi v okeane.*

The People of the Sun *see* **El pueblo del sol.**

Per aspera ad astra *see* **To the Stars by Hard Ways.**

Pervaya konnaya *see* **The First Cavalry Army.**

Pervie starti (1981). Filmed in Sovscope 70. International distribution Sovexportfilm. Sovcolor. Six-track magnetic stereophonic sound. A Soviet production released in Russia in 1981.

The Pharaoh's Woman (May 1961). Filmed in Techniscope High Fidelity Wide Screen. *Executive producer* Victor Tourjansky. *Producer* Giorgio Venturini. *Directors* Giorgio Rivalta and Wenceslav Tourjansky. *Screenplay* Ugo Liberatore, Remigio del Grosso, Virgilio Tosi and Massimo Vitalo. *Story* Virgilio Tosi and Massimo Vitalo. *Director of photography* Pier Ludovico Pavoni. *Film editor* Antonietta Zita. *Music* Giovanni Fusco. *Art director* Arrigo Equini. *Costumes* Giancarlo Bartolini Salimbeni. *Production manager* Gianpaolo Bigazzi. *Choreography* Adriano Vitale. *Technical adviser for battle scenes* Giorgio Rivalta. *Technical adviser in Egypt* Charles Lifshitz. *Negative* Eastman Color. ¶A Victor Tourjansky production. A Vic Films-Faro Film coproduction. Released by Universal-International. Technicolor. Optical sound. 88 minutes. Filmed in Rome and on location in Egypt. ¶CAST: *Prince Sabaku* John Drew Barrymore. *Akis* Linda Cristal. *Prince Ramsisu* Armando Francioli. *Court Physician Amosi* Pierre Brice. *Mareth* Lilly Lembo. *With* Guido Celano, Ugo Sasso, Andreina Rossi, Nerio Bernardi, Nando Angelini, Nadia Brivio, Enzo Fiermonte, Fedele Gentile, Nino Marchetti, Anna Placido, Wilma Sempetery and Anita Todesco. ¶The first film in Techniscope which was screen-billed as above. An Italian production released in Italy in December 1960 as *La donna dei Faraoini* running 100 minutes.

Picture Holland (1986). Filmed in OMNIMAX. *Producers* Alewijn Dekker and Gerard J. Raucamp. *Director* John Armstrong. *Photographer* Anton von Munster. ¶A Carillonproducers, Amsterdam production. Sponsored by Nederlandse Aardolic Maatschappij, a subsidiary of Shell and Esso. Released by Omniversum. Eastman Color. Six-track magnetic stereophonic sound. 15 minutes. A Dutch production originally made for Omniversum, The Hague.

Pier Bezyukhov *see* **Leo Tolstoy's War and Peace.**

The Pink Panther (March 18, 1964). Filmed in Super Technirama 70. *Executive producer* Walter Mirisch. *Producer* Martin Jurow. *Director* Blake Edwards. *Screenplay* Blake Edwards and Maurice Richlin. *Music* Henry Mancini. *Director of photography* Philip Lathrop. *Claudia Cardinale and Capucine's principal wardrobe* Yves St. Laurent. *Art director* Fernando Carrere. *Set decorators* Reg Allen, Jack Stevens and Arrigho Breschi. *Makeup* Euclide Santoli and Michele Tremarchi. *Hairdressing* Amalia Paoletti. *Film editor* Ralph E. Winters. *Assistant film editors* Marshall M. Borden and David B. Zinnemann. *Sound* Alexander Sash Fisher. *Music editor* Richard Carruth. *Sound effects editor* Gilbert D. Marchant. *Special effects* Lee Zavitz. *Production supervisors* Guy Luongo and Jack McEdward. *Assistant director* Ottavio Oppo. *Script supervisor* Betty Abbott. *Dialog coach* James Lanphier. *Wardrobe consultant* William Ware Theiss. *Wardrobe supervisor* Analisa Nasali Rocca. *Main title* DePatie-Freleng Enterprises, Inc. *Associate producer* Richard Crockett. *Production executives* Marvin Mirisch and Harold Mirisch. *Camera operator* Cliff King *Assistant cameraman* Richard H. Kline. *Still photographer* Sherman Clark. *Boom operator* William Hamilton. *Choreography* Hermes Pan. *Song "It Had Better Be Tonight (Meglio Stasera)" music* Henry Mancini, *English lyrics* Johnny Mercer, *Italian lyrics* Franco Migliacci, *singer* Fran Jeffries, *tenor sax solos* Plas Johnson. ¶A Mirisch Company, Inc. presentation. A Blake Edwards production. A Mirisch–G-E Productions picture. Released by United Artists. Technicolor. Westrex six-track magnetic stereophonic sound. 113 minutes. Filmed at Studio Cinecitta, Rome, on location in Italy and the Swiss Alps and completed at Samuel Goldwyn Studios. ¶CAST: *Sir Charles Litton* David Niven. *Insp. Jacques Clouseau* Peter Sellers. *George Litton* Robert Wagner. *Simone Clouseau* Capucine. *Angela Dunning* Brenda de Banzie. *Tucker* Colin Gordon. *Defense attorney* John LeMesurier. *Saloud* James Lanphier. *Artoff* Guy Thomajon. *Novelist* Michael Trubshawe. *Greek shipowner* Riccardo Billi. *Hollywood starlet* Meri Wells. *Photographer* Martin Miller. *Greek cousin* Fran Jeffries. *Princess Dala* Claudia Cardinale. ¶Screen credits bill Technirama, while pressbook credits say Super Technirama 70. Home video version has original descrete stereo sound. First in the long-running series that includes *A Shot in the Dark* (United Artists, 1964), *Inspector Clouseau* (United Artists, 1968), *Return of the Pink Panther* (United Artist, 1975), *The Pink Panther Strikes Again* (United Artists, 1976), *Revenge of the Pink Panther* (MGM/UA, 1982) and *Curse of the Pink Panther* (MGM/UA, 1983). There have been many cartoons made for theatrical and television release with the Pink Panther (and sons) and Insp. Clouseau characters.

Plastic Inevitables (Velvet Underground) *see* **The Velvet Underground and Nico.**

Po yuznomy beregu Krima (1978). Filmed in Sovscope 70. International distribution Sovsportfilm. Sovcolor. Six-track magnetic stereophonic sound. A Soviet production released in Russia in 1978.

Pochtoviy roman (1970). Filmed in Sovscope 70. *Screen author* Daniil Khrabrovitskiy. *Director* Evgeny Matveev. *Operator* V. Ilienko. *Artist* V. Miguliko. *Composers* M. Fradkin and R. Bunin. *Sound operator* L. Bachi. ¶A Kievskaya kinostudiya im. A.P. Dovzenko production. International distribution Sovexportfilm. Sovcolor. Six-track magnetic stereophonic sound. 173 minutes plus intermission. Filmed at Kievskaya kinostudiya im. A.P. Dovzenko, Kiev, Ukrainian S.S.R. ¶CAST: Yu. Kayurov, A. Falikovich, A. Parra, S. Korkoshko, Evgeny Matveev, A. Gashnskiy, A. Maksimova, G. Tonunts, N. Grabbe, Yu. Lavrov, G. Yudin, P. Vinnik and S. Nagornaya. ¶A Soviet production released in Russia in 1970 in two parts running 88 and 85 minutes.

Poem of a Sea (1958). Filmed in Todd-AO. *Screen author* Aleksandr P. Dovzenko. *Director and producer* Yulia Solntseva. *Operators* Gavriil Yegiazarov and G. Pcholkin. *Artists* Aleksandr Borisov and I. Plastinkin. *Composer* Gavriil Popov. *Sound operator* V. Lagutin. ¶A Kievskaya kinostudiya im. A.P. Dovzenko production for Mosfilm. International distribution Sovexportfilm. Sovcolor. Six-track magnetic stereophonic sound. 92 minutes. Filmed at Kievskaya kinostudiya im. A.P. Dovzenko, Kiev, Ukrainian S.S.R. ¶CAST: *Gen. Fedorchenko* Boris Livanov. *Writer* M. Romanov. *Aristarkhov* M. Tsaryov. *Sava Zarudny* Boris Andreyev. *Maria Kravchyna* V. Volodymyrova. *Maxim Fedorenko* G. Kovrov. *Ivan Kravchyna* Evkhen Bondarenko. *Katrina* Zinaida Kirienko. *Ivan Khurenko* L. Parkhomenko. *Olesya* N. Naum. *Kholyk* T. Tarabarinov. *Kobzar* Ivan Kozlovsky. *Antonina* M. Vital. *Grekov* E. Agurov. *Valya* A. Konchakova. *Shiyan* E. Gurov. *Kovzkh* K. Marinchenko. *Basansky* V. Vitrishchak. *Alchevsky* F. Tregub. *With* Yuriy Timoshenko, P. Nyatko, S. Bobrov, S. Bubnov, N. Bugay, V. Khubenko, L. Kadrov, L. Kalyuzkhna, M. Kovaleva, A. Krotova, O. Petrenko, Kh. Pluzkhnyk, N. Sazonova, A. Timontayev, Sasha Sokolov and Yura Chugunov. ¶A Soviet production released in Russia on November 4, 1958, as *Poema o morye*. It is unknown if a Mitchell Todd-AO camera was employed or if the Soviets only used the name. Their 70mm system is identical to Todd-AO.

Poem of Wings (1980). Filmed in Sovscope 70. *Screen authors* Anatoli Zakharov and Daniil Khrabrovitskiy. *Director* Daniil Khrabrovitskiy. *Operator* Naum Ardashnikov. *Artist* David Vinitskiy *Composer* Roman Ledenev. *Sound operator* B. Vengerovskiy. ¶A Mosfilm-ICAIC-DEFA-Gomon International production. International distribution Sovexportfilm. Sovcolor. Six-track magnetic stereophonic sound. 204 minutes plus intermission. Filmed at Mosfilm Studios, Moscow, R.S.F.S.R. ¶CAST: *Andrei Tupolev* Vladimir Strzelichik. *Igor Sikorsky* Yuri Yakovlev. *Nikolay Zkhukovsky* Nikolai Annenkov. *Yulia Tupolev* Ada Rogovtseva. *Sergei Rakhaminov* Oleg Efremov. *Aircraft industry official* Pyotr Veliyaminov. *With* Yuri Kayurov, Anatoli Azo, Igor Ledogorov, Z. Romanov, Igor Vasiliev, G. Etsifantsev and V. Dolgorukov. ¶A Soviet, Cuban, East German and French coproduction released in Russia in 1980 as *Poema o kriliyakh* in two parts running 91 minutes and 113 minutes.

Poema o kriliyakh *see* **Poem of Wings.**

Poema o morye *see* **Poem of a Sea.**

Pokhishchenie veka (1982). Filmed in Sovscope 70. *Screen author* V. Bakhnov. *Director* V. Makarov. *Operator* Yu. Malinovskiy. *Artists* O. Aradyshkin and A. Vaginev. *Composer* B. Saveliev. *Sound operator* V. Duritsin. *Song text* M. Plyatskovskogo. ¶A kinostudiya im. M. Gorikogo production. International distribution Sovexportfilm. Sovcolor. Six-track magnetic stereophonic sound. 85 minutes. Filmed at kinostudiya im. M. Gorikogo, Gorki, R.S.F.S.R. ¶CAST: A. Nikiforov, E. Menishov, M. Dyuzeva, E. Kuznetsova, D. Abashidze, G. Lordkipanidze, A. Loriya, Yu. Sarantsev, R. Rudin and Yu. Chekulaev. ¶A Soviet production released in Russia in 1982.

Porgy and Bess (June 25, 1959). Filmed in Todd-AO. *Producer* Samuel Goldwyn. *Director* Otto Preminger. *Screenplay* Richard Nash. *Based on the play with book by* Dubose Heyward; *lyrics by* Dubose Hayward and Ira Gershwin; *and music by* George Gershwin; *as produced on the stage by* The Theatre Guild; *from the play "Porgy" by* Dubose *and* Dorothy Heyward; *and the novel "Porgy" by* Dubose Heyward. *Director of photography* Leon Shamroy. *Production designer* Oliver Smith. *Art directors* Serge Krizman and Joseph Wright. *Set decorator* Howard Bristol. *Film editor* Daniel Mandell. *Sound supervisors* Gordon E. Sawyer and Fred Hynes. *Music* George Gershwin. *Lyrics* Dubose Heyward and Ira Gershwin. *Musical director* Andre Previn. *Associate musical director* Ken Darby. *Choreography* Hermes Pan. *Costume designer* Irene Sharaff. *Dialog coach* Max Slater. *Assistant director* Paul Helmick. *Production manager* Doc Herman. *Music editor* Richard Carruth. *Sound editor* Don Hall, Jr. *Music recorders* Murray Spivack and Vinton

Vernon. *Rerecording* Samuel Goldwyn Studios and Todd-AO. *Todd-AO consultant* Schuyler A Sanford. *Camera operator* Irving Rosenberg. *Assistant cameramen* Lee "Red" Crawford. *Makeup* Frank McCoy and Layne "Shotgun" Britton. *Hair stylist* Joan St. Oegger. *Orchestrations* Alexander Courage, Conrad Salinger, Robert Franklyn and Albert Woodbury. ¶A Samuel Goldwyn production. Released by Columbia Pictures. Technicolor. Westrex six-track magnetic stereophonic sound. 146 minutes including intermission. Filmed at Samuel Goldwyn Studios. ¶CAST: *Porgy* Sidney Poitier. *Bess* Dorothy Dandridge. *Sportin' Life* Sammy Davis, Jr. *Maria* Pearl Bailey. *Crown* Brock Peters. *Jake* Leslie Scott. *Clara* Diahann Carroll. *Serena* Ruth Attaway. *Peter* Clarence Muse. *Annie* Everdinne Wilson. *Robbins* Joel Fluellen. *Mingo* Earl Jackson. *Nelson* Moses LaMarr. *Lily* Margaret Hairston. *Jim* Ivan Dixon. *Scipio* Antoine Durousseau. *Strawberry Woman* Helen Thigpen. *Elderly man* Vince Townsend, Jr. *Lawyer Frazier* Roy Glenn. *Undertaker* William Walker. *Detective* Claude Akins. *Coroner* Maurice Manson. *Bit woman* Nichelle Nichols. *Sidney Poitier's vocals* Robert McFerrin. *Dorothy Dandridge's vocals* Adele Addison. *Diahann Carroll's vocals* Loulie Jean Norman Price. *Ruth Attaway's vocals* Inez Matthews. ¶Not filmed simultaneously in CinemaScope. The Gershwin estate has filed legal action to prevent future exhibition of this film.

Portrait of Jennie (December 30, 1948). Presented in Cycloramic Screen and Cyclophonic Sound. *Producer* David O. Selznick. *Associate producer* David Hampstead. *Director* William Dieterle. *Screenplay* Paul Osborn, Peter Berneis and David O. Selznick. *Prolog* Ben Hecht. *Adaptation* Leonardo Bercovici. *Based on the novel by* Robert Nathan. *Directors of photography* Joseph August, Paul L. Eagler and Lee Garmes. *Sound and technical director* James G. Stewart. *Music composer and director* Dimitri Tiomkin. *Based on the themes "The Maid with the Flaxen Hair," "Arabesque One and Two," "Clouds" and "Prelude to the Afternoon of a Faun" by* Claude Debussy. *Supervising film editor* William Morgan. *Film editor* Hal C. Kern, Sr. *Associate film editor* Gerald Wilson. *Sound editor*

Charles L. Freeman. *Recorder* Don McKay. *Mixer* Fred Hynes. *Special effects* Paul L. Eagler, Joseph McMillan Johnson, Clarence W.D. Slifer and Russell Shearman. *Production designer* Joseph McMillan Johnson. *Associate production designer* Joseph B. Platt. *Set decoration* Claude Carpenter. *Costume designer* Lucinda Ballard. *Assistant costume designer* Anna Hill Johnstone. *Makeup* Mel Berns. *Hair stylist* Larry Germain. *Production executive* Daniel O'Shea. *Staff executive* Don Downs. *Production manager* W. Argyle Nelson, Sr. *Unit manager* Clem Beauchamp. *Assistant director* Arthur Fellows. *Scenario assistant* Lydia Schiller. *Production assistant* Peter Scoppa. *Casting* Ruth Burch. *"Jennie's Song," music and lyrics by* Bernard Hermann. *Publicity* Paul MacNamara. *Portrait painter* Robert Brackman. *Camera operator* Arthur E. Arling. *Story editor* Margaret McDonnell. ¶A David O. Selznick Productions, Inc. presentation. A Selznick Studio production. A Vanguard Films, Inc. picture. Released by Selznick Releasing Organization. Technicolor and green tinted sequence. Western Electric Mirrophonic Recording. 86 minutes. Filmed at The Selznick Studio and on location in New York City and Boston, Massachusetts. ¶CAST: *Eben Adams* Joseph Cotten. *Miss Spinney* Ethel Barrymore. *Matthews* Cecil Kellaway. *Jennie Appleton* Jennifer Jones. *Mrs. Jekes* Florence Bates. *Mrs. Bunce* Esther Somers. *Gus O'Toole* David Wayne. *Mr. Moore* Albert Sharpe. *Policeman* John Farrell. *Old doorman* Felix Bressart. *Clara Morgan* Maude Simmons. *Mother Mary of Mercy* Lillian Gish. *Capt. Caleb Cobb* Clem Bevans. *Old mariner* Robert Dudley. *Eke* Henry Hull. *Teenager* Ann Francis. ¶This first U.S. film presented on the giant screen (using Magnascope) with surround sound. This special presentation was employed only for the storm sequence which was tinted green. The last scene and end titles were in Technicolor. Eagler and Garmes took over as DPs after August died of a heart attack while on location in New York.

Poruchiti generalu Nesterovu (1985). Filmed in Sovscope 70. *Screen author* A. Bondarev. *Director* B. Galkin. *Operator* V. Fridkin. *Artist* R. Nagaev. *Composer* K. Volkov. *Sound operator* S. Urusov. ¶A Mosfilm production. International distribution Sovexportfilm. Sovcolor. Six-track magnetic stereophonic sound. 97 minutes. Filmed at Mosfilm Studios, Moscow, R.S.F.S.R. ¶CAST: V. Sedov, V. Tarasov, I. Okhlupin, B. Tokarev, S. Tormakhova, L. Gladunko, O. Golubitskiy, S. Zigunov, V. Filippov, N. Krachkovskaya, A. Soloviev and V. Frolov. ¶A Soviet production released in Russia in 1985.

Poslednyaya okhota (1980). Filmed in Sovscope 70. *Screen author* A. Makarov. *Director* I. Sheshukov. *Operator* V. Biryulin. *Artist* E. Gukov. *Composer* V. Bibergan. *Sound operators* Z. Vanints and L. Shumyacher. ¶A Lenfilm production. International distribution Sovexportfilm. Sovcolor. Six-track magnetic stereophonic sound. 101 minutes. Filmed at Lenfilm Studios, Leningrad, R.S.F.S.R. ¶CAST: Yu. Bogatirev, O. Borisov, Nikolai Griniko, M. Munzuk, M. Likhukh, B. Vampilov, A. Masyulis, A. Oorzak, B. Bayshenaliev, A. Kuular, N. Ribnikov, I. Bortnik and V. Bukin. ¶A Soviet production released in Russia in 1980.

Poslednyaya zertva *see* **The Last Victim.**

Potseluy Chaniti (1974). Filmed in Sovscope 70. *Screen authors* E. Shatunovskiy and E. Sherstobitov. *Based on the operetta by* Yu. Milyutina and E. Shatunovskogo. *Director* E. Sherstobitov. *Operator* M. Cherniy. *Artist* I. Yutsevich. *Ballet-master* I. Vitebskiy. *Composer* M. Boyko. *Sound operator* L. Vachi. ¶International distribution Sovexportfilm. Sovcolor. Six-track magnetic sterephonic sound. ¶CAST: L. Eremina, A. Evdokimova, N. Drozzina, B. Diyachenko, F. Pantyushchin, V. Doroshenko, A. Gorelik, S. Mishulin, G. Gavrilov and O. Volin. ¶A Soviet production released in Russia in 1974.

Pour construire un feu (1927). Filmed in Hypergonar. *Director* Claude Autant-Lara. ¶This French feature is the first full length anamorphic release. Sources disagree whether the entire show was in 'scope or if only selected scenes employed the process. While it was made in 1927 it may not have actually been exhibited, at least in anamorphic format, until 1929.

Povesti plamennikh let *see* **The Story of Flaming Years.**

Pravo na lyubovi (1978). Filmed in Sovscope 70. *Screen authors* V. Likov and A. Slesarenko. *Director and music and song text* A. Slesarenko. *Operator* A. Pishchikov. *Artist* A. Bobrovnikov. *Sound operator* A. Kovtun. ¶A Kievskaya kinostudiya im. A.P. Dovzenko production. International distribution Sovexportfilm. Sovcolor. Six-track magnetic stereophonic sound. 111 minutes. Filmed at Kievskaya kinostudiya im. A.P. Dovzenko, Kiev, Ukrainian S.S.R. ¶CAST: A. Poddubinskiy, I. Shevchuk, B. Stupka, K. Stepankov, V. Belokhvostik, F. Panasenko, D. Kayka, L. Slesarenko, B. Boldirevskiy and L. Alfimova. ¶A Soviet production released in Russia in 1978.

Predislovie v bitve (1982). Filmed in Sovscope 70. *Screen authors* V. Faradzev and A. Slavumskiy. *Director* N. Stambula. *Operator* S. Taraskin. *Artist* P. Safonov. *Composer* A. Zshpay. *Sound operator* V. Karasev. ¶A Mosfilm production. International distribution Sovexportfilm. Sovcolor. Six-track magnetic stereophonic sound. 122 minutes. Filmed at Mosfilm Studios, Moscow, R.S.F.S.R. ¶CAST: R. Antsans, A. Zbruev, N. Kochegarov, I. Saverskaya, B. Andreev, Yu. Gusev, N. Burov, Yu. Grebenshchikov, N. Smorchkov, Yu. Martinov and D. Orlovskiy. ¶A Soviet production released in Russia in 1982.

Prikhodi svobodnim (1985). Filmed in Sovscope 70. *Screen author* S. Sheripov. *Director* Yu. Mastyuzin. *Operator* A. Mass. *Artist* K. Zagorskiy. *Composer* A. Zurbin. *Sound operator* A. Drozdov. ¶A kinostudiya im. M. Gorikogo production. International distribution Sovexportfilm. Sovcolor. Six-track magnetic stereophonic sound. 90 minutes. Filmed at kinostudiya im. M. Gorikogo, Gorki, R.S.F.S.R. ¶CAST: D. Zolotukhin, E. Bondarchuk, A. Denisov, M. Tsitskiev, N. Olyalin, A. Fatyushin, B. Kikabidze, V. Dvorzetskiy, D. Omaev, V. Kenigson, I. Krasko, A. Karapetyan, I. Budkevich and V. Eremichev. ¶A Soviet production released in Russia in 1985.

Prishla i govoruy *see* **I Am Here Talking to You.**

Pristupiti k likvidatsii (1984). Filmed in Sovscope 70. *Screen author* Z. Khrutskiy. *Director* B. Grigoriev. *Operators* P. Kataev and A. Ribkin. *Artist* B. Dulenkov. *Composer* G. Dmitriev. *Sound operator* D. Bogolepov. ¶A kinostudiya im. M. Gorikogo production. International distribution Sovexportfilm. Sovcolor. Six-track magnetic stereophonic sound. 134 minutes plus intermission. Filmed at kinostudiya im. M. Gorikogo, Gorki, R.S.F.S.R. ¶CAST: O. Strizenov, M. Zigalov, V. Lanovoy, V. Voytyuk, G. Yumatov, N. Butirtseva, A. Filippenko, O. Sirina and V. Shuligin. ¶A Soviet production released in Russia in 1984 in two parts each running 67 minutes.

Privalov's Millions (1973). Filmed in Sovscope 70. *Screen authors* Igor Bolgarin and Viktor Smirnov. *Based on the novel "Privalovskie millioni" by* Dmitri N. Mamina-Sibiryaka. *Director* Yapopolk Lapshin. *Operator* Igor Lukshin. *Artist* Yuri Istratov. *Composer* Yuli Levitin. *Sound operator* M. Tomilova. ¶A Sverdlovskaya kinostudiya production. International distribution Sovexportfilm. Sovcolor. Six-track magnetic stereophonic sound. 209 minutes plus intermission. Filmed at Sverdlovskaya kinostudiya, Sverdlovsk, R.S.F.S.R. ¶CAST: *Sergei Privalov* Leonid Kulagin. *Zosya Lyakhovskaya* Lyudmila Chursina. *Polovodov* Vladislav Strzelichik. *Antonina* Lyudmila Khityaeva. *Lyakhovski* Andrei Fayt. *Veryovkin* Yuri Puzirev. *With* G. Shtsireli, N. Kolofidin, L. Sokolova, G. Kindinova, A. Demiyanenko, L. Shagalova, Evgeni Evstigneev, V. Chekmarev, S. Chekan, Yu. Leonidov, A. Kubatskiy, V. Marenko, I. Golovin, O. Melinikov, P. Fedoseev, M. Butorina, V. Sharikina and I. Yasulovich. ¶A Soviet production released in Russia as *Privalovskie millioni* in two parts running 107 minutes and 102 minutes.

Privalovskie millioni *see* **Privalov's Millions.**

Prizvanie (1971). Filmed in Sovscope 70. International distribution Sovexportfilm. Sovcolor. Six-track magnetic stereophonic sound. A Soviet production released in Russia in 1971.

Proshchanie s Peterburgom *see* **A Fare-**well to St. Petersburg.

Prosheay *see* **Nights of Farewell.**

Provib *see* **Liberation.**

El pueblo del sol (1983). Filmed in OMNIMAX. *Director* Alberto Isaac. ¶An Auditec Tijuana S.A. production. Released by Centro Cultural Tijuana, Tijuana, Mexico. Eastman Color. Six-track magnetic stereophonic sound. 25 minutes. A Mexican production. The title translates as *The People of the Sun.*

The Pulkovo Meridan *see* **Blockade.**

Pulkovskiy meridian *see* **Blockade.**

Queen of the Gypsies (April 1979). Filmed in Sovscope 70. *Screen author and director* Emil Latyanu. *Based on the story "Makar Chudra" by* Maxim Gorokogo. *Operator* Sergei Vronskiy. *Artist* Felix Yasyukevich. *Composer* Evgeny Doga. *Choreographer* N. Andreychenko. *Sound operator* M. Bronshteyn. ¶A Mosfilm production. Released by Sovexportfilm. Sovcolor. 106 minutes. Filmed at Mosfilm Studios, Moscow, R.S.F.S.R. ¶CAST: *Loiko Zobar* Grigory Grigoriu. *Radda* Svetlana Toma. *Makar Chudra* Boris Mulaev. *Rusalina* Nelly Volshaninova. *With* Sergei Finiti, Pavel Andreychenko, Ion S. Shkurya, Elena Sadovskaya, Borislav Brondukov, L. Chernaya, V. Gavrilov and M. Shishkov. ¶A Soviet production released in Russia in 1976 as *Tabor ukhdit v nebo* in 70mm and six-track magnetic stereophonic sound running 126 minutes. The U.S. version was in 35mm only. The international title is given as *The Gypsy Camp Goes Skyward.*

Racers (1973). Filmed in Sovscope 70. *Screen authors* Yuri Olishanskiy, Nina Rudneva and Igor Maslennikov. *Director* Igor Maslennikov. *Operator* Vladimir Vasiliev. *Artist* Vladimir Gasilov. *Composer* Vladimir Dashkevich. *Sound operator* A. Zvereva. ¶A Lenfilm production. International distribution Sovexportfilm. Sovcolor. Six-track magnetic stereophonic sound. 101 minutes. Filmed at Lenfilm Studios, Leningrad, R.S.F.S.R. ¶CAST: Oleg Yankovskiy, Evgeni Leonov, Larisa Luzina, Yu. Ivin, Armen Dzigarkhanyan, L. Merzin and N.

Ferapontov. ¶A Soviet production released in Russia in 1973 as *Gonshchiki.*

Radi zhizni na zemle *see* **Lofty Title.**

Raintree County (October 4, 1957). Filmed in Camera 65. *Executive producer* Dore Schary. *Producer* Davis Lewis. *Director* Edward Dmytryk. *Associate producer and screenplay* Millard Kaufman. *Based on the novel by* Ross Lockridge. *Director of photography* Robert L. Surtees. *Music* Johnny Green. *Art directors* William A. Horning and Urie McCleary. *Set decorations* Edwin B. Willis and Hugh Hunt. *Costumes* Walter Plunkett. *Recording supervisor* Dr. Wesley C. Miller. *Supervising film editor* Margaret Booth. *Film editor* John D. Dunning. *Editorial consultant* Sidney Franklin. *Sound editor* Milo Lory. *Music editor* Earl Gates. *Music adaptation* Alexander Courage, Sidney Cutner, Robert Franklyn, Conrad Salinger and Albert Sendrey. *Orchestrations* Albert Sendrey, Robert Franklyn, Arthur Morton and Albert Woodbury. *Unit production manager* Edward Woehler. *Assistant director* Ridgeway Callow. *Dialog coach* Marguerite Lampkin. *Makeup creator* William Tuttle. *Hair styles* Sydney Guilaroff and Mary K. Keats. *Sound recording* Fred McAlphin, William Steinkamp and Franklin E. Milton. *Sound consultant* Douglas Shearer. *Special effects* A. Arnold Gillespie and Warren Newcombe. *Color consultant* Charles K. Hagedon. *Songs "Never Till Now" and "Raintree County" music* Johnny Green, *lyrics* Paul Francis Webster. *"Raintree County" singer* Nat King Cole. *Cooperation* Baltimore & Ohio Railroad Company and Tennessee State Game & Fish Commission. *Photographic lenses* Panavision. ¶A Loew's, Inc. production. Released by Metro-Goldwyn-Mayer. Technicolor. Westrex six-track magnetic stereophonic sound. 168 minutes plus intermission. Filmed at MGM Studios and on location in Danville, Kentucky, Natchez and Port Gibson, Mississippi and Reelfoot Lake, Tiptonville, Tennessee. ¶CAST: *John Wickliff Shawnessy* Montgomery Clift. *Susanna Drake* Elizabeth Taylor. *Nell Gaither* Eva Marie Saint. *Prof. Jerusalem Webster Stiles* Nigel Patrick. *Orville "Flash" Perkins* Lee Marvin. *Garwood B. Jones* Rod Taylor. *Ellen Shawnessy* Agnes

Moorehead. *T.D. Shawnessy* Walter Abel. *Barbara Drake* Jarma Lewis. *Bobby Drake* Tom Drake. *Ezra Gray* Rhys Williams. *Niles Foster* Russell Collins. *Confederate soldier* DeForrest Kelley. *Lydia Gray* Myrna Hansen. *Jake* Oliver Blake. *Cousin Sam* John Eldredge. *Soona* Isabelle Cooley. *Parthenia* Ruth Attaway. *Miss Roman* Eileene Stevens. *Bessie* Rosalind Hayes. *Tom Conway* Don Burnett. *Nat Franklin* Michael Dugan. *Jesse Gardner* Ralph Vitti [Michael Dante]. *Starter* Phil Chambers. *Veteran with gun* James Griffith. *Granpa Peters* Burt Mustin. *Mme. Gaubert* Dorothy Granger. *Blind man* Owen McGiveney. *Party guest* Charles Watts. *Federal lieutenant* Stacey Harris. *Jim Shawnessy at age 2 ½* Donald Losby. *Jim Shawnessy at age 4* Mickey Maga. *Blackface pantomimist* Robert Foulk. *Photographer* Jack Daly. *Old colored man* Bill Walker. *Bearded soldier* Gardner McKay. *First spectator* William Challee. *Second spectator* Frank Kreig. *Spectators* Joe Brown, Nesdon Booth and Robert Forrest. *First girl* Janet Lake. *Second girl* Luana Lee. *Third girl* Judi Jordan. *Fourth girl* Phyllis Douglas. *Fifth girl* Sue George. *Woman* Josephine Cummins. *Man* Mil Patrick. ¶Released in 35mm in four-track MagOptical stereophonic sound and Perspecta Stereophonic Sound. Some battle footage was converted to Super Cinerama and incorporated into *How the West Was Won.* Stock footage has been utilized in *The Plainsman* (Universal, 1966) and several other features and television shows.

Rasskaz o film "Koney na pereprave ne menyayut" (1981). Filmed in Sovscope 70. A Mosfilm production. International distribution Sovexportfilm. Sovcolor. Six-track magnetic stereophonic sound. Filmed at Mosfilm Studios, Moscow, R.S.F.S.R. A Soviet production released in Russia in 1981. This is a documentary on the making of *One Doesn't Change Horses in Midstream* (q.v.).

Razgovor s tovarishchem Leninim (1969). Filmed in Sovscope 70. International distribution Sovexportfilm. Sovcolor. Six-track magnetic stereophonic sound. A Soviet production released in Russia in 1969.

Red Bells (1982). Filmed in Sovscope 70. *Screen authors* Sergei Bondarchuk, A. Saguzra and Valentin Ezov *in collabora-*

tion with Ricardo Garibai and Carlos Ortis. *Based on the books "Insurgent Mexico" and "Ten Days That Shook the World"* by John Reed. *Director* Sergei Bondarchuk. *Operator* Vadim Yusov. *Artist* L. Shengeltsya. *Composer* Gorges Eras Sviridov. *Sound operator* Yuri Mikhaylov. *Still photo* Vladimir Uvarov. *World sales* Manley Productions, Inc. ¶A Mosfilm–Conacite dos production in collaboration with Vides Internazionale, S.p.A., RAI Radiotelevisione Italiana and Cinefin. International distribution Sovexportfilm. Sovcolor. Six-track magnetic stereophonic sound. 343 minutes. Filmed at Mosfilm Studios, Moscow, R.S.F.S.R. and on location in Tlaskala, Mexico, Italy and the R.S.F.S.R. ¶CAST: *John Reed* Franco Nero. *Mabel Dodge* Ursula Andress. *Louise Bryant* Sydne Rome. *Albert Ris Williams* Pyotr Vorobyov. *Pancho Villa* Heraclio Zapeda. *With* Blanca Guerra, Jorge Luke, B. Geppa, S. Harkin, A. Duarte, A. Ustyuzaninov, B. Stupka, A. Sayko, I. Skobtseva, V. Sedov, G. Kolchinskiy and U. Elizondo. ¶A Soviet, Mexican and Italian coproduction. Working title was *John Reed.* Released in Russia in 1982 as *Krasnie kolokola* in two parts: *Meksika v ogne (Mexico in Flames)* running 168 minutes plus intermission (part one: 85 minutes, part two: 83 minutes) and *Ya videl rozdenie novogo mira (I Saw the Birth of a New World;* a.k.a. *Ten Days That Shook the World* and *October*) running 174 minutes plus intermission (part one: 84 minutes, part two: 90 minutes). Interestingly the dialog was in English and Spanish with Russian subtitles. The British *Reds* (Paramount, 1981), based on the same source material, was a tremendous success in the U.S. and effectively killed any chance *Red Bells* had for American distribution.

The Red Diplomatic Couriers (1978). Filmed in Sovscope 70. *Screen authors* Eduard Volodarskiy and Anatoly Prelovskiy. *Director* Villen Novak. *Operator* Vadim Avloshenko. *Artist* Georgi Yudin. *Composer* Aleksandr Zatsepin. *Sound operator* Z. Goncharenko. *Verses* V. Lugovskogo and I. Selivinskogo. ¶An Odesskaya kinostudiya production. International distribution Sovexportfilm. Sovcolor. Six-track magnetic stereophonic sound. 99 minutes. Filmed at Odesskaya kinostudiya, Odessa, Ukrainian S.S.R.

¶CAST: *Vasil Pereguda* Mikhail Matveev. *Aurin* Igor Starigin. *Lena* Natalia Vavilova. *Georgi Chicherin* Boris Rizukhin. *With* Leonid Nevedomskiy, D. Kozlov, Ernsht Romanov, Yuri Mazuga, Vladimir Vikhrov, Kh. Lieshinish, B. Saburov and V. Doroshenko. ¶A Soviet production released in Russia in 1978 as *Krasnie dipkurieri.*

The Red Tent (August 1971). Filmed in Sovscope 70. *Producer* Franco Cristaldi. *Screen authors* Ennio de Concini, Richards Adams, Robert Bolt and Mikhail K. Kalatozov. *Director* Mikhail K. Kalatozov. *Operator* Leonid Kalashnikov. *Art director* Giancarlo Bartolini. *Artist* David Vinnitskiy. *Music (international version)* Ennio Morricone. *Composer (Soviet version)* A. Zatsepin. *Sound operators* Viktor Babushkin and L. Bulgakov. *Sound engineers (international version)* David Hawkins, Tonino Cacciuottolo and David Hildyard. *Sound editor (English language version)* Alex Neiman. *Mixing (international version)* Fausto Ancillai. *Editor (English language version)* Peter Zinner. *Decorators* Franco d'Andria and Yuri Ekonomzev. *Costumes* Natalia Meshkova. *Makeup* Max Alautdinov and Antonio Mecacci. *Hairdresser* Luciano Vito. *Associate producer* Fernando Ghia. *Production executive* Paul Maslansky. *Production managers* Vittorio Musi Glori and Vladimir Maron. *Assistant directors* Marina Lebesheva, Valeri Sirovski and Marina Voloris. ¶A Vides Cinematografica–Mosfilm production. A Franco Cristaldi film. Released by Paramount Pictures. Sovcolor. Prints (international version) Technicolor. 121 minutes. Filmed at Studio Vides Film and Studio De Laurentiis Cinematografica S.p.A., Rome and Mosfilm Studios, Moscow, R.S.F.S.R. and on location in the R.S.F.S.R., Estonian S.S.R., and Greenland. MPAA rating: G. ¶CAST: *Gen. Umberto Nobile* Peter Finch. *Roald Amundsen* Sean Connery. *Valeria* Claudia Cardinale. *Lundborg* Hardy Kruger. *Finn Malmgren* Eduard Martsevich. *Chuknovskiy* Nikita Mikhalkov. *Capt. Zappi* Luigi Vannucchi. *Biagi* Mario Adorf. *Mariano* Donatas Banionis. *Samoilovich* Grigori Gay. *Romana* Massimo Girotti. *Troiani* Yuri Solomin. *Cecioni* Otar Koberidze. *Viglieri* Boris Khmelinitskiy. *Kolka* Nicolai Ivanov. *Behovnek* Yuri Vizbov. *With* T.

Archvadze, V. Sirovskiy, V. Smirnov and O. Mokshantsev. ¶An Italian and Soviet coproduction released in Italy in 1969 as *La tenda rosse* running 121 minutes and released in Russia in 1970 as *Krasnaya palatka* in 70mm and six-track magnetic stereophonic sound running 195 minutes plus intermission (part one: 95 minutes, part two: 100 minutes). Purchased for U.S. distribution in 1969 but withheld for two years before being released to modest box office results. Here is the perfect example of difficulties arising when attempting to ascertain credits and cast on international coproductions. The above data were culled from three sources: the American billing, the Italian billing and the Soviet billing. Very often they did not match, not only in assigned positions but in spelling of names. (Sean Connery appeared as Sh. Konnori on the Soviet titles, for example.) All names have been given here by the correct spelling in the country of origin of the individuals and thus will not necessarily match those on any print the reader might view. The Italians list the film as being produced by them, in association with the Soviets, while the Soviets reverse the situation. Of interest: The Italian credits carry the notation (when translated into English) that the film is an Italian production "under Italian law." This probably was due to their tax structure. The Italians credited de Concini and Adams for the screenplay while the Soviets listed de Concini, Bolt and Kalatozov. In an interview Adams stated Bolt worked on the project but declined a credit. Perhaps so, but the Soviets gave him one. It has also been published that the Soviet edition was over four hours in length, but their actual running time is noted above. The Soviet cast list was longer, so it is possible some of the Russian actors did not appear in the international version. It is also of special interest that the international edition was in 35mm spherical with a 1.66×1 hard matte and not anamorphic, at least in the U.S. This can be presumed to indicate that only the Soviet version was in 70mm and that it was a blowup from 35mm spherical. The Soviets, by the way, use a standard 1.37×1 aspect ratio on their nonanamorphic 35mm films.

The Renault Dauphin (1962). Filmed in Super Cinerama. Produced and released by Renault, Paris. Technicolor. Seven-track magnetic Cinerama Sound. 3 minutes. Filmed in France. This French theatrical commercial promoted the new Dauphin "motor car" and was released in Europe in 1962 for exhibition with *How the West Was Won*. In London it was shown before the beginning of Act II of the feature, which must have been an awkward intrusion to say the least.

Retsept ee molodosti *see* **The Secret of Her Youth.**

Return from Orbit (1984). Filmed in Sovscope 70. *Screen author* Evgeni Mestyatsev. *Director* Aleksandr O. Surin. *Operator* Sergei Stasenko. *Artists* Sergei Brzestovskiy and Vitaly Lazarev. *Composer* Z. Artemiev. *Sound operator* V. Lukash. ¶A Kievskaya kinostudiya im. A.P. Dovzenko production. International distribution Sovexportfilm. Sovcolor. Six-track magnetic stereophonic sound. 89 minutes. Filmed at Kievskaya kinostudiya im. A.P. Dovzenko, Kiev, Ukrainian S.S.R. ¶CAST: *Cosmonaut Kuznetsov* Yuozas Budraytis. *Flight Eng. Mukhin* Vitaly Solomin. *Girlfriend* Tamara Akulova. *With* A. Porokhovshchikov, I. Vasiliev, V. Yurchenko and M. Chigarev. ¶A Soviet production released in Russia in 1984 as *Vozvrashchenie s orbiti.*

River Journey (1984). Filmed in IMAX. *Executive producer* Robert Verrall. *Producer* Andy Thomson. *Conceiver and director* John N. Smith. ¶A National Film Board of Canada production. Released by Imax Systems Corporation. Eastman Color. Six-track magnetic stereophonic sound. 15 minutes. Filmed in Canada. A Canadian production originally made for the Canadian Pavilion at the 1984 Louisiana World Exposition in New Orleans.

The Robe (September 17, 1953). Filmed in CinemaScope. *Producer* Frank Ross. *Director* Henry Koster. *Screenplay* Philip Dunne. *Adaptation* Gina Kaus. *Based on the novel by* Lloyd C. Douglas. *Music* Alfred Newman. *Director of photography* Leon Shamroy. *Art direction* Lyle R. Wheeler and George W. Davis. *Set decorations* Walter M. Scott and Paul S. Fox. *Wardrobe direction* Charles LeMaire. *Costume designer* Emile Santiago. *Film editors* Maria Morra and Barbara

McLean. *Sound* Bernard Freericks, Roger Heman, Carlton W. Faulkner, and Murray Spivak. *Technicolor color consultant* Leonard Doss. *Orchestration* Edward B. Powell. *Makeup* Ben Nye. *Special photographic effects* Fred Sersen, Ray Kellogg, L.B. Abbott, James B. Gordon and Emil Kosa, Jr. *Vocal direction* Ken Darby. *Music editor* George Adams. *Production supervisor* Sid Rogell. *Assistant directors* Tom Connors, Jr. and Donald C. Klune. *Camera operator* Irving Rosenberg. *Assistant cameramen* Lee "Red" Crawford and Harvey Slocum. *Negative* Eastman Kodak. ¶Produced and released by 20th Century–Fox. Technicolor. Western Electric Movietone recording. Four-track MagOptical stereophonic sound. 135 minutes plus intermission. Filmed at 20th Century–Fox Studios. ¶CAST: *Marcellus Gallio* Richard Burton. *Diana* Jean Simmons. *Demetrius* Victor Mature. *Peter* Michael Rennie. *Caligula* Jay Robinson. *Justus* Dean Jagger. *Senator Gallio* Torin Thatcher. *Pontius Pilate* Richard Boone. *Miriam* Betta St. John. *Paulus* Jeff Morrow. *Emperor Tiberius* Ernest Thesiger. *Junia* Dawn Adams. *Abidor* Leon Askin. *Quintus* Frank Pulaski. *Marcipor* David Leonard. *Judas Iscariot* Michael Ansara. *Jonathan* Nicholas Koster. *Dodinius* Francis Pierlot. *Marius* Thomas Browne Henry. *Sarpedon* Anthony Eustrel. *Lucia* Pamela Robinson. *The Voice of Jesus Christ* Cameron Mitchell. *First ship's captain* Ford Rainey. *Second ship's captain* Sam Gilmer. *Woman* Mae Marsh. *Rebecca* Helen Beverly. *Tiro* Jay Novello. *David* Harry Shearer. *Nathan* Emmett Lynn. *Cornelia* Sally Corner. *Julia* Rosalind Ivan. *Lucius* Peter Reynolds. *Specialty dancer* Virginia Lee. *Shalum* Leo Curley. *Slave girl* Gloria Saunders. *Twin slave girls* Joan and Jean Corbett. *Caleb* Percy Helton. *Chamberlain* Roy Gordon. *Gracchus* George E. Stone. *Cleander* Ben Astar. *Auctioneer* Marc Snow. *Slave* George Keymas. ¶The first American film released in Cinema-Scope. Filmed simultaneously in regular 35mm. Sequel was *Demetrius and the Gladiators* (20th Century–Fox, 1954).

Rollercoaster (June 1986). Filmed in Showscan. Presented in Dynamic Motion. Produced and released by Showscan Film Corporation in collaboration with Intamin Corporation, Inc., Establishment. Eastman Color. Six-track magnetic Dolby Stereo. Approximately 3 minutes. An American and Liechtensteinian coproduction made for showing in a Dynamic Motion Theater, in which the seats move in sync with action on the screen to give the audience the feeling of participating in the filmed action.

Rollercoaster Ride (1926). Filmed in Natural Vision. *Producers* George K. Spoor and P. John Berggren. ¶Produced and released by Natural Vision Pictures. This short was a demonstration of the wide film process. Interestingly, it would be duplicated in *This Is Cinerama*. It was not stereoscopic even though publicized as three-dimensional.

Romans o vlyublennikh *see* **Lovers' Romance.**

Royal Regatta (1967). Filmed in Sovscope 70. *Screen authors* Boris Vasiliev, Semyon Listov and Kiriil Rapoport. *Director* Yun Chulyukin. *Operators* Pyotr Satunovskiy and German Shatrov. *Artist* Dmitri Vinitskiy. *Composer* Mikhail Ziv. *Sound operators* Vasili Leshchev and Georgi Morozov. ¶A Mosfilm production. International distribution Sovexportfilm. Sovcolor. Six-track magnetic stereophonic sound. 91 minutes. Filmed at Mosfilm Studios, Moscow, R.S.F.S.R. ¶CAST: *Vasya* Valentin Smirnitskaya. *Alyonka* Natalya Kustinskaya. *Sportsmen* Leonid Brusin and Felix Sergeev. *Clerk* Aleksandr Gruzinskiy. *Coach* Georgi Kulakov. *General* Aleksandr Khanov. *With* Aleksandr Potapov, V. Zakharov, G. Bolibok, Aleksandr Martishkin, Ionas Yurashas and O. Mokshantsev. ¶A Soviet production released in Russia in 1967 as *Korolevskaya regata.*

Rozigrish *see* **A Bit of Fooling.**

Run for the Sun (July 30, 1956). Filmed in SuperScope 235. *Executive producers* Robert Waterfield and Jane Russell. *Producer* Harry Tatelman. *Director* Roy Boulting. *Screenplay* Dudley Nichols and Roy Boulting. *Based on the story* "The Most Dangerous Game" *by* Richard Connell. *Director of photography* Joseph La Shelle. *Music* Frederick Steiner. *Film editor* Fred Knudtson. *Art director* Alfred Ybarra. *Assistant directors* Edward Killy and Robert Stillman. *Songs* "Taco" *and*

Ad for Run for the Sun, *the first film in* SuperScope 235.

"Triste Ranchero": music Frederick Steiner; *lyrics* Nestor Amaral. *Negative* Eastman Kodak. ¶A Russ-Field Corp. production. Released by United Artists. Technicolor. RCA Photophone recording. 98 minutes. Filmed in Mexico. ¶CAST: *Mike Latimer* Richard Widmark. *Browne* Trevor Howard. *Katy Anders* Jane Greer. *Van Anders* Peter Van Eyck. *Jan* Carlos Henning. *Fernandez* Juan Garcia. *Hotel proprietress* Margarito de Luna. *Pedro* Jose Chavez Trowe. *Paco* Guillermo Talles. *Waiter* Guillermo Bravo Sosa. *Paco's wife* Enedina Diaz de Leon. ¶The first film in *Super*Scope 235.

Russian Field (1972). Filmed in Sovscope 70. *Screen author* Mikhail Alekseev. *Director* Nikolai Moskalenko. *Operator* Yuri Gantman. *Composer* Aleksandr Flyarkovskiy. *Artist* N. Meshkova. *Sound operator* T. Batalova. *Song text* L. Derbeneva. ¶A Mosfilm production. International distribution Sovexportfilm. Sovcolor. Six-track magnetic stereophonic sound. 113 minutes. Filmed at Mosfilm Studios, Moscow, R.S.F.S.R. ¶CAST: *Fedosyallgryumova* Nonna Mordyukova. *With* Inna Makarova, Zoya Fedorova, Lyudmila Khityaeva, Leonid Markov, Sergei Plotnikov, Vladimir Tikhonov, Vyacheslav Nevinniy, L. Malinovskaya, N. Maslova, L. Gladunko, Yu. Blashuk and A. Soloviev. ¶A Soviet production released in Russia in 1972 as *Russkoe pole.*

Russkoe pole *see* **Russian Field.**

Rustam and Sukhrab (1973). Filmed in Sovscope 70. *Screen author* Grigori Koltunov. *Based on the poem "Shakh-Namekh" by* Abulcasim Firdousi. *Director* Boris Kilyagarov. *Operator* Dovlatyan Khudonazarov. *Artist* I. Abdusalamov. *Composer* Arif Melinov. *Sound operator* L. Voskalichuk. ¶A Tadzikfilm production. International distribution Sovexportfilm. Sovcolor. Six-track magnetic stereophonic sound. 97 minutes. Filmed at Tadzikfilm Studios, Dushanbe, Tadzhik S.S.R. ¶CAST: *Rustam* Bimbulat Vataev. *Shakh Kavus* Otar Koberidze. *Tulad* Makhmud Vakhidov. *Takhmina* Svetlana Norbaeva. *With* Kh. Gakoev, S. Isaeva, G. Zavkibekov, A. Khodzaev, A. Rakhimov, M. Rafikov, G. Tokhadze and R. Khamraev. ¶A Soviet production released in Russia in 1973 as *Rustam i*

Sukhrab. This is a sequel to *Skaz pro Rustam (Tale of Rustam)* (Tadzikfilm, 1972).

Rustam i Sukhrab *see* **Rustam and Sukhrab.**

Ruz iznachalnaya *see* **Ancient Russia.**

Ryan's Daughter (November 9, 1970). Filmed in Super Panavision 70. *Producer* Anthony Havelock-Allan. *Director* David Lean. *Writer* Robert Bolt. *Director of photography* Frederick A. Young. *Original music composer and conductor* Maurice Jarre. *Editor* Norman Savage. *Associate producer* Roy Stevens. *Second unit directors* Roy Stevens and Charles Frend. *Second unit cameramen* Denys Coop and Bob Huke. *Production designer* Stephen Grimes. *Art director* Roy Walker. *Set dresser* Josie MacAvin. *Costume designer* Jocelyn Rickards. *Special effects* Robert A. MacDonald, Sr. *First assistant director* Pedro Vidal. *Second assistant director* Michael Stevenson. *Production manager* Douglas Twiddy. *Locations and properties* Eddie Fowlie. *Makeup* Charles Parker. *Hairdresser* A.G. Scott. *Sound recordist* John Bramall. *Music recordist* Eric Tomlinson. *Dubbing mixer* Gordon K. McCallum. *Sound editors* Winston Ryder and Ernie Grimsdale. *Music editor* Robin Clarke. *Assistant art director* Derek Irvine. *Chief electricians* Bernie Prentice and Roy Rodhouse. *Construction manager* Peter Dukelow. *Production liaison* Col. William O'Kelley. *Camera operator* Ernest Day. *Continuity* Phyllis Crocker. *Master of horse* George Mossman. *Unit publicist* Ralph Cooper. ¶A Faraway Productions, A.G. picture. A David Lean film. Released by Metro-Goldwyn-Mayer. Metrocolor. Westrex six-track magnetic stereophonic sound. 206 minutes including intermission. Filmed on location in Dingle, County Kerry and Coumeenoole Cove, Dunquin, Eire. ¶CAST: *Rosy Ryan Shaughnessy* Sarah Miles. *Charles Shaughnessy* Robert Mitchum. *Father Collins* Trevor Howard. *Maj. Randolph Doryan* Christopher Jones. *Michael* John Mills. *Tom Ryan* Leo McKern. *Tim O'Leary* Barry Foster. *McCardle* Archie O'Sullivan. *Mrs. McCardle* Marie Kean. *Moureen* Evin Crowley. *Corporal* Barry Jackson. *Driver* Douglas Sheldon. *Paddy*

Philip O'Flynn. *Bernard* Ed O'Callaghan. *Captain* Gerald Sim. *Lanky private* Des Keogh. *O'Keefe* Niall Toiban. *Moureen's beau* Donal Meligan. *Constable O'Connor* Brian O'Higgins. *Joseph* Niall O'Brien. *Peter* Owen O'Sullivan. *Sean* Emmet Bergin. *Storekeeper* May Cluskey. *Old woman* Annie Dalton. *Policeman* Pat Layde. ¶35mm general release prints ran 176 minutes without an intermission.

S O N (1964). Filmed in Sovscope 70. *Screen author* L. Pavlichko. *Director and producer* V. Denisenko. *Chief operator* M. Cherniy. *Art director* N. Reznik. *Composer* A. Bilash. *Sound operators* R. Maksimtsov and A. Chernoochenko. ¶A Kievskaya kinostudiya im. A.P. Dovzenko production. International distribution Sovexportfilm. Sovcolor. Six-track magnetic stereophonic sound. 122 minutes. Filmed at Kievskaya kinostudiya im. A.P. Dovzenko, Kiev, Ukrainian S.S.R. ¶CAST: I. Mikolaychuk, Yura Leontiev, L. Milyutenko, N. Naum, M. Derzavin, I. Konovalenko and V. Goncharov. ¶A Soviet production released in Russia in 1964.

SSSR s otkritim serddem (1961). Filmed in Kinopanorama. A Tsentrnauchfilm production. International distribution Sovexportfilm. Sovcolor. Nine-track magnetic Kinopanorama Sound. A Soviet production released in Russia in 1961. Excerpts later incorporated into *Cinerama's Russian Adventure.*

Il sacco di Roma (1923). Filmed in Panoramico Alberini. *Director* Enrico Guazzoni. ¶This Italian production is considered the first wide screen feature. It employed a 70mm format identical to that used today and developed in 1914 by Filoteo Alberini for one sequence only.

Sacred Site (1986). Filmed in OMNIMAX. *Director and photographer* Ron Fricke. *Music* Michael Stearns. ¶A Canticle Films, Ltd. production. Released by Reuben H. Fleet Space Theater. Eastman Color. Six-track magnetic stereophonic sound. 7 minutes. Filmed at Ayers Rock, Australia. ¶Originally made for San Diego's Reuben H. Fleet Space Theater.

Samaya obayatelinaya i udivitelinaya *see* **The Most Charming and Attractive.**

Samiy zarkiy mesyats *see* **The Hottest Month.**

Santa Fe Trail (December 16, 1940). Presented in Vitasound. *Executive producer* Hal B. Wallis. *Associate producer* Robert Fellows. *Director* Michael Curtiz. *Original screenplay* Robert Buckner. *Music* Max Steiner. *Director of photography* Sol Polito. *Dialog director* Jo Graham. *Film editor* George Amy. *Art director* John Hughes. *Sound* Robert B. Lee, George R. Groves and Nathan Levinson. *Costumes* Milo Anderson. *Makeup artist* Perc Westmore. *Special effects* Byron Haskin and Hans F. Koenekamp. *Orchestrations* Hugo Friedhofer. *Assistant director* Jack Sullivan. *In charge of production* Jack L. Warner. *Musical director* Leo F. Forbstein. *Songs* Al Dubin, Will Grosz, Edwina Coolidge, M.K. Jerome and Jack Scholl. *Camera operator* Al Greene. *Assistant cameraman* Frank Evans. ¶A Warner Bros.-First National picture. Released by Warner Bros. Pictures. RCA Photophone recording. 110 minutes. Filmed at Warner Bros. Studios and on location in Southern California. ¶CAST: *Lt. J.E.B. Stuart* Errol Flynn. *Kit Carson Halliday* Olivia de Havilland. *John Brown* Raymond Massey. *Lt. George Armstrong Custer* Ronald Reagan. *Tex Bell* Alan Hale, Sr. *Lt. Bob Halliday* William Lundigan. *Rader* Van Heflin. *Jason Brown* Gene Reynolds. *Cyrus Halliday* Henry O'Neill. *Windy Brody* Guinn "Big Boy" Williams. *Oliver Brown* Alan Baxter. *Martin* John Litel. *Lt. Robert E. Lee* Moroni Olsen. *Lt. Phil Sheridan* David Bruce. *Barber Doyle* Hobart Cavanaugh. *Maj. Sumner* Charles D. Brown. *Kitzmiller* Joseph Sawyer. *Lt. James Longstreet* Frank Wilcox. *Townley* Ward Bond. *Shoubel Morgan* Russell Simpson. *Gentry* Charles Middleton. *Jefferson Davis* Erville Alderson. *Conductor* Spencer Charters. *Charlotte* Suzanne Carnahan [Susan Peters]. *Lt. George Pickett* William Marshall. *Lt. John Hood* George Haywood. *Weiner* Wilfred Lucas. *J. Boyce Russell* Russell Hicks. *Sampson* Napolean Simpson. *Engineers* Roy Barcroft and Frank Mayo. *Adjutant* Lane Chandler. *Military doctor* Richard Kipling. *Agitators* Nestor Paiva and Trevor

Bardette. *Man* Eddy Waller. *Negro man* Clinton Rosemond. *Telegrapher* Creighton Hale. *Preacher* Rev. Neal Dodd. *Sheriff* Addison Richards. *Lieutenant* Emmett Vogan. *Negro women* Libby Taylor, Bernice Pilot, and Mildred Glover. *Farmer's wife* Grace Stafford. *Farmer* Louis Jean Heydt. *Guards* Edmund Cobb, Edward Peil, Sr., Edward Hearn, and Eddy Chandler. *Dispatch rider* Victor Kilian. ¶The first film in Vitasound.

The Savage Innocents (February 15, 1961). Filmed in Super Technirama 70. *Producer* Maleno Malenotti. *Coproducer* Joseph Janni. *Director and screenplay* Nicholas Ray. *Adaptation* Hans Ruesch and Franco Solinas. *Based on the novel "Top of the World" by* Hans Ruesch. *Directors of photography* Aldo Tonti and Peter Hennessy. *Music* Angelo Francesco Lavagnino. *Conductor* Muir Mathieson. *Editors* Ralph Kemplen and Eraldo Da Roma. *Second unit director* Baccis Bandini. *Second unit photography* Riccardo Pallottini and Patrick Carey. *Sound recordist* Geoff Daniels. *Sound editor* Winston Ryder. *Production managers* Douglas Pierce and Bianca Lattuada. *Assistant directors* Tom Pevsner and Jacques Giraldeau. *Arctic consultant* Douglas Wilkinson. *Art directors* Don Ashton and Dario Cecchi. *Costume designer* Vittorio Nino Novarese. *Makeup* Geoffrey Rodway. *Camera operator* Allan Bryce. *Assistant operator* Luciano Tonti. *"Iceberg" writers and performers* The Four Saints. *Song "Sexy Rock": music* Angelo Francesco Lavagnino; *lyrics* Panzeri; *performer* Colin Hicks. ¶A Magic Film–Playart–Gray Films–Societe Nouvelle Pathe Cinema–Joseph Janni Productions, Ltd. production in association with Paramount Pictures Corp. Released by Paramount Pictures. Technicolor. Westrex six-track magnetic stereophonic sound. 110 minutes. Filmed at Pinewood Studios, London, and Studio Cinecitta, Rome and on location in Churchill, Manitoba, Canada and Greenland. ¶CAST: *Inuk* Anthony Quinn. *Asiak* Yoko Tani. *First Canadian trooper* Peter O'Toole. *Second Canadian trooper* Carlo Guistini. *Powtee* Marie Yang. *Missionary* Marco Guglielmi. *Imina* Kaida Horiuchi. *Itti* Lee Montague. *Anarvik* Andy Ho. *Hiko* Anna May Wong. *Iulik* Yvonne Shima. *Kidok* Anthony Chin. *Trading post*

proprietor Francis De Wolff. *Undik* Michael Chow. *Airplane pilot* Ed Devereaux. ¶Reedited to 89 minutes after initial engagements. Peter O'Toole was looped by Robert Rietty [Roberto Rietti]. A British, French, Italian and American coproduction released in England in July 1960 running 107 minutes, released in France in September 1960 as *Les dents du diable* running 90 minutes and released in Italy in March 1960 as *Ombre bianche* running 110 minutes.

(Hugo Fregonese's) Savage Pampas (July 1967). Filmed in Superpanorama 70. *Executive producer* Samuel Bronston. *Producer* Jaime Prades. *Director* Hugo Fregonese. *Screenplay* Hugo Fregonese and John Melson. *Based on the novel "Pampa barbara" by* Homero Manzi and Ulises Petit de Murat. *Director of photography* Manuel Berenguer. *Decorators* Gil Parrondo and Angel Canizares. *Accessories* Roberto Carpio. *Editor* Juan Serra. *Music* Waldo de los Rios. *Choreography* Alberto Masulli. *Sound editor* Alfonso Carvajal. *Assistant directors* Julio Sempere and Antonio (Tony) Tarruella. *Production manager* Ramon Plana. *Costumes* Marian Ribas. *Makeup* Juan Farsac. *Hairdresser* Antonio Lopez. *Special effects* Pablo Perez. *Script supervisor* Eva del Castillo. *Second unit operator* Andres Berenguer. *Laboratory* Fotofilm Madrid, S.A. ¶A Jaime Prades presentation. A Jaime Prades Producciones Cinematografica, S.A.–Dasa Films, S.A.–Samuel Bronston International, Inc. production. Released by Comet Film Distributors. Eastman Color. Westrex recording system. 97 minutes. Filmed at Samuel Bronston Studios, Madrid, and on location in Las Matas, Spain. ¶CAST: *Capt. Martin* Robert Taylor. *Padron* Ron Randell. *Sgt. Barril* Marc Lawrence. *Padre Carreras* Ty Hardin. *Rucu* Rosenda Monteros. *Lt. Del Rio* Angel del Pozo. *El Gato* Charles Fawcett. *Petizo* Enrique Avila. *Luis* Jose Jaspa. *Chicha* Julio Pena. *Mimi* Laya Raki. *Carmen* Laura Granados. *Gen. Chavez* Jose Nieto. *Santiago* Mario Lozano. *Alfonso* Milo Quesada. *Pepe* Hector Quiroga. *Isidro* Juan Carlos Galvan. *Vigo* Lucia Prado. *Priest* Barta Barri. *Magnolia* Pastora Ruiz. *Carlos* Sancho Gracia. *Old man* Georges Riguad. *Lucy* Isabel Pisano. *With* Ingrid Oatenschlager and Wallie Ellie. ¶A Spanish, Argentinean

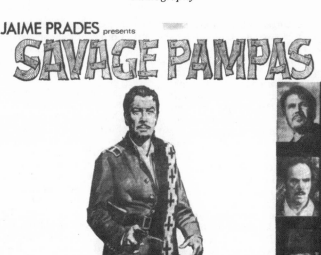

JAIME PRADES presents

SAVAGE PAMPAS

JAIME PRADES presents HUGO FREGONESE'S

SAVAGE PAMPAS

STARRING
ROBERT TAYLOR • RON RANDELL • MARC LAWRENCE
TY HARDIN AND ROSENDA MONTEROS ANGEL DEL POZO
FELA ROQUE • ENRIQUE AVILA • LAYA RAKI • LAURA GRANADOS • JULIO PEÑA
CHARLES FAWCETT • LUCIA PRADO • JOSE NIETO • JOSE MARIA CAFARELL
DIRECTED BY HUGO FREGONESE PRODUCED BY JAIME PRADES
SUPERPANORAMA 70 m/m MCS • Color by EASTMANCOLOR • STEREOPHONIC SOUND

This is one Samuel Bronston epic that did not get roadshow treatment in the U.S. Bronston didn't even take a screen credit or advertising billing. He was deliberately promoting the career of one of his executives, Jaime Prades. "MCS" after 70 m/m (sic) refers to Superpanorama's owners, Modern Cinema System [MCS-Film].

and American coproduction. Released in Spain in April 1966 as *Pampa salvaje* in 70mm and six-track magnetic stereophonic sound running 112 minutes. Apparently released in the U.S. only in 35mm 'scope with mono sound. A remake of Fregonese's 1945 Argentinean feature *Pampa barbara*.

Scent of Mystery (January 12, 1960). Filmed in Todd-70. Presented in Smell-O-Vision. *Executive producer* Elizabeth Taylor. *Producer* Michael Todd, Jr. *Director* Jack Cardiff. *Screenplay* William Roos. *Additional situations* Gerald Kersh. *Story* Kelley Roos. *Director of photography* John von Kotze. *Music composer* Mario Nascimbene. *Theme* Mario Nascimbene and Jordan Ramin. *Additional music* Jordan Ramin and Harold Adamson. *Music conductor* Franco Ferrara. *Music supervisor*

Jack Saunders. *Singer* Eddie Fisher. *Film editor* James E. Newcom. *Associate producer* Ned (Herbert) Mann. *Production supervisor and art director* Vincent Korda. *Sound* Joseph I. Kane and Fred Hynes. *Sound system* Todd-AO. *Assistant director* Piero Mussetta. *Second unit photography* John Drake. *Special effects* Cliff Richardson. *Wardrobe* Charles Simminger. *Makeup* Neville Smallwood. *Set decorator* Dario Simoni. *Production manager* Lee Katz. *Osmologist inventor* Prof. Hans Laube. *Osmological development* Scentovision, Inc. *Cameras* Mitchell Camera Corporation. *Process lenses* Panavision. *Negative* Eastman Kodak. *Processing* Fotofilm, Barcelona. *Prints* Technicolor. ¶A Michael Todd, Jr. presentation. Produced and released by The Michael Todd Company, Inc. New Todd Color Process. Westrex recording system. Magnetic Belock 8-Channel Sound. 125 minutes plus intermission. Filmed on location in Granada, Cordoba, Sevilla, Madreidos, Guadix, Malaga, Gilbralfaro, Ronda and Pamplona, Spain. ¶CAST: *Oliver "Lucky" Larker* Denholm Elliott. *Smiley* Peter Lorre. *Decoy Sally Kennedy* Beverly Bentley. *Baron Saradin* Paul Lukas. *Johnny Gin* Liam Redmond. *Tommy Kennedy* Leo McKern. *Richard Fleming* Peter Arne. *Winifred Jordan* Diana Dors. *Margharita Kennedy* Mary Laura Wood. *Lorry operator* Jean Olaguivel. *Pepi* Maurice Marsac. *Miss Leonard* Judith Furse. *Constance (Connie) Walker* Billie Miller. *British aviator* Michael Trubshawe. *Real Sally Kennedy* Elizabeth Taylor. ¶Reedited to 102 minutes, optically converted to three-panel Super Cinerama by Film Effects of Hollywood and rereleased in 1961 as *Holiday in Spain* sans the Smell-O-Vision system. Released in Europe in 70mm Super Cinerama as *Holiday in Spain* sans Smell-O-Vision. An extremely poor quality video version under the original title and running only 73 minutes appeared in December 1986 from a dubious company calling itself Smell-o-Vision (sic). This tape copy, obviously made by videographing from a projected and very badly faded print, has deplorable monophonic sound apparently culled by placing a microphone at the center of the screen. It is available with scratch-and-sniff "Smell-o-Vision" cards boasting 24 scents, some of which are not actually in the film, and which are not always on the card in order of their screen appearance. The use of the card is noted by rather obstructive numbers in the lower right hand of the screen.

Scheherazade (May 12, 1965). Filmed in Superpanorama 70. *Executive producers* Jose G. Maesso and Robert Haggiag. *Producers* Michel Safra and Serge Silberman. *Directors* Pierre Gaspard-Huit and Jacques Bourdon. *Screenplay* Marc-Gilbert Sauvajon, Pierre Gaspard-Huit and Jose G. Maesso. *Dialog* Marc-Gilbert Sauvajon. *Second unit director* Jacques Bourdon. *Directors of photography* Christian Matras and Andre Domage. *Set designers* Georges Wakhevitch and Francisco Canet. *Costumes* Georges Wakhevitch. *Sound engineer* Antoine Petitjean. *Music* Andre Hossein. *Film editor* Louisette Hautecour. *Production manager* Henri Baum. *Choreography* Janine Charrat. *Processing* Laboratoires Francais. *World sales* Speva Film-Cine Alliance. ¶A Michel Safra-Serge Silberman presentation. A Speva Film–Cine Alliance–Filmsonor–Dear Film Produzioni–Tecisa, S.A. production. Released by Shawn International, Inc. Eastman Color. Westrex recording system. 115 minutes. Filmed in France and Spain. ¶CAST: *Princess Scheherazade* Anna Karina. *Renaud de Villecroix* Gerard Barray. *Haroun-al-Raschid* Antonio Vilar. *Shinrin* Marilu Tolo. *Grand Vizier Zaccar* Jorge Mistral. *Barmak* Fausto Tozzi. *Didier* Giuliano Gemma. *Thierry* Gil Vidal. *Anira* Joelle Latour. *With* Fernando Rey and Jose Manuel Martin. ¶A French, Spanish and Italian coproduction released in Europe in 70mm and six-track magnetic stereophonic sound. Apparently released in the U.S. in 35mm 'scope with mono sound only. Released in France in May 1963 as *Scheherazade* running 124 minutes; released in Spain in June 1963 running time undetermined; and released in Italy in September 1963 as *La schiava di Bagdad* running 105 minutes.

La Schiava di Bagdad *see* **Scheherazade.**

The Sea in Flames (1972). Filmed in Sovscope 70. *Screen authors* Leon Saakov and Nikolai Figurovskiy. *Director* Leon Saakov. *Operator* Anatol Petritskiy. *Composer* Veniamin Basner. *Artist* S. Volkov. *Sound operators* V. Popov and

An international trade ad in which the title is given as on the French version and not the more common Scheherazade as on the English language edition.

V. Shchedrina. *Song text* M. Matusovskiy. ¶A Mosfilm production. International distribution Sovexportfilm. Sovcolor. Six-track magnetic stereophonic sound. 182 minutes plus intermission. Filmed at Mosfilm Studios, Moscow, R.S.F.S.R. ¶CAST: Nikolai Griniko, Vladimir Kashpur, Yuri Solomin, G. Antonenko, R. Yankovskiy, V. Platov, K. Tirtov, D. Shcherbakov, S. Dyakhnitskiy, A. Grachev, N. Ivanov, O. Kornich, O. Ostroumova, G. Krasheninnikov, D. Franiko, G. Baysak, N. Richagova, N. Marufov, V. Safonov, N. Eremenko, N. Alekseev, K. Luchko and M. Uliyanov. ¶A Soviet production released in Russia in 1972 as *More v ogne* in two parts, running 110 minutes and 72 minutes.

The Sea Nymph *see* **September Storm.**

Search for Paradise (September 25, 1957). Filmed in Cinerama. *Executive producer for Stanley Warner Cinerama Corporation* S.H. Fabian. *Producer* Lowell Thomas. *Director* Otto Lang. *Scenario and narration* Prosper Buranelli, Lowell Thomas and Otto Lang. *Based on an idea by* Lowell Thomas. *Music composer and conductor* Dimitri Tiomkin. *"Search for Paradise," "Happy Land of Hunza," "Shalimar"* and *"Kashmir Street Song" lyrics* Ned Washington and Lowell Thomas. *Singer* Robert Merrill. *Cinerama Symphony Orchestra recorded at* Carnegie Hall, New York City. *Vocals* Norman Luboff and Choir. *Piano solos* Ray Turner. *Carillonic bells instruments* Schulmerich Carillons, Inc. *Aerial sequences supervisor* Paul Mantz. *Aerial sequences with the cooperation of* United States Air Force. *River sequences supervisors* Bus and Don Hatch. *Director of photography* Harry Squire. *Cameramen* Jack Priestley and Fred Fordham. *Supervising editor* Harvey Manger. *Film editor* Lovel S. Ellis. *Music editor* Richard C. Harris. *Sound editors* Walter Hanneman and Paul Davis. *Sound* Fred Bosch, Richard Vorisek, Ray Sharples and Avery Lockner. *Paintings* Fred Sersen and Mario Larrinaga. *Title paintings* Milton Bellin. *Public relations* Jacob Y. Brodsky. *Production staff* Edward R. Evans, Gustavo Quinterio, Peter Passas, Michael

G. Zingale and Kenneth Snavely. *Advance arrangements* E. Thomas Gilliard, Col. Mohammed Ata Ullah, Stephen Bradley and Bok Reitzel. *Production supervisor for Stanley Warner Cinerama Corporation* Nat Lapkin, first vice president. *Assistant to Mr. Lapkin* Arthur M. Rosen. *Cinerama technicians* Peter Gibbons and Walter Gibbons-Fly. *Sound system* Reeves Sound Studios. *Negative* Eastman Color. ¶A Lowell Thomas production. Released by Stanley Warner Cinerama Corporation. Technicolor. Six-track magnetic Cinerama Sound. 104 minutes plus overture, intermission and exit music. Filmed in Ceylon, Hunza, Indus, Kashmir and Nepal and at United States Air Force Air Proving Ground, Eglin Air Force Base, Florida. ¶CAST: *Host and narrator* Lowell Thomas. *Maj.* Steve Shaw Christopher Young. *Sgt.* Jim Parker James S. Parker. *Themselves* Col. Mohammed Ata Ullah, Gov. Kiani of Pakistan, Prince Mohammed Ayasch Khan, Crown Prince Chazanfar, Ghazi-e-Millat, Col. Mir Mohammed Jemal Kahn, Rana of Hunza and her children, Bus Hatch, Don Hatch, King Mahendra, Queen Ratna Devi, Mrs. Robert Low Bacon, Dr. Charles W. Mayo, Lord Chamberlain, Earl of Scarborough, Chinese Deputy Premier Ulanfu, Indian Vice President Sravapalli Rahhakrishnan, Bhutan Prince Druk Gyalpo Jigme Wanchuk and Sik Crown Prince. ¶Sequences were later incorporated into *The Best of Cinerama.*

Seasons (1987). Filmed in OMNIMAX. *Executive producers* Mike Day, George Casey and Paul Novros. *Producer and director* Ben Shedd. *Director of photography* David Douglas. *"The Four Seasons" composer* Antonio Vivaldi. *Saint Paul Chamber Orchestra conductor* Pinchas Zukerman. ¶A Graphic Films Corporation production. Released by Science Museum of Minnesota. Eastman Color. Six-track magnetic stereophonic sound. 32 minutes. Originally made for the Science Museum of Minnesota.

The Secret of Her Youth (1984). Filmed in Sovscope 70. *Screen author* Aleksandr Adabashian. *Based on the play "Sredstvo Makropulosa" by* K. Chapeka. *Director* Evgeny Ginzburg. *Operator* Genry Abramyan. *Artist* Yuri Kladienko. *Composer* Georgi Garanyan. *Choreographer*

Valentin Manokin. *Verses* Yu. Ryashentseva. *Sound operator* L. Benevoliskaya. ¶A Mosfilm production. International distribution Sovexportfilm. Sovcolor. Six-track magnetic stereophonic sound. 115 minutes. Filmed at Mosfilm Studios, Moscow, R.S.F.S.R. ¶CAST: *Emily Marty* Lyudmilla Gurchenko. *Prus* Oleg Borisov. *Hauk-Schendorf* Armen Dzigarkhanyan. *Kolensty* Anatoly Romashin. *With* Aleksandr Abdulov, Sergei Shakurov, Elena Stephanova, A. Kalmikov, S. Dityatev and L. Sabitova. ¶A Soviet production released in Russia in 1984 as *Retsept ee molodosti.*

The Secret of St. Jur (1982). Filmed in Sovscope 70. *Screen authors* Valerian Pidpaliy and V. Dobrichev. *Director* Valerian Pidpaliy. *Operators* A. Pishchikov and S. Lisetskiy. *Artist* M. Rakovskiy. *Composer* G. Lyashenko. *Sound operator* R. Krupenina. ¶A Kievskaya kinostudiya im. A.P. Dovzenko production. International distribution Sovexportfilm. Sovcolor. Six-track magnetic stereophonic sound. 99 minutes. Filmed at Kievskaya kinostudiya im. A.P. Dovzenko, Kiev, Ukrainian S.S.R. ¶CAST: A. Kharitonov, V. Talashko, E. Dedova, V. Sherbakov, S. Polezaev, B. Stupka, A. Gay, F. Strigun, E. Chekan and I. Nayduk. ¶A Soviet production released in Russia in 1982 as *Tayni Svyatogo Yura.*

Sekret uspekha *see* **Bolshoi Ballet 67.**

Semi stikhiy (1985). Filmed in Sovscope 70. *Screen authors* V. Shcherbakov and G. Ivanov. *Based on the novel by* V. Shcherbakova. *Operator* A. Yatsinevichyus. *Artist* V. Pasternak. *Composer* Z. Artemiev. *Sound operator* B. Koreshkov. ¶A kinostudiya im. M. Gorikogo production. International distribution Sovexportfilm. Sovcolor. Six-track magnetic stereophonic sound. 96 minutes. Filmed at kinostudiya im. M. Gorikogo, Gorki, R.S.F.S.R. ¶CAST: A Dunovska, I. Starigin, I. Alferova, U. Nerenbergs, A. Filippenko, B. Khimichev, and L. Virolaynen. ¶A Soviet production released in Russia in 1985.

Semiya Ivanovikh (1975). Filmed in Sovscope 70. *Screen author* Yu. Nagibin. *Director* A. Saltikov. *Operator* V. Boganov. *Artist* S. Volkov. *Composer* A.

Zshpay. *Sound operator* V. Shmelikin. ¶A Mosfilm production. International distribution Sovexportfilm. Sovcolor. Six-track magnetic stereophonic sound. 123 minutes. Filmed at Mosfilm Studios, Moscow, R.S.F.S.R. ¶CAST: N. Mordyukova, N. Ribnikov, O. Prokhorova, N. Eremenko-Mladshiy, A. Khvilya, A. Larionova, O. Vidov, G. Tonunts, A. Krichenkov, F. Odinokov, B. Kudryavtsev, S. Bubnov and E. Shutov. ¶A Soviet production released in Russia in 1975.

The Sensorium (1986). Presented in Widescreen 3D, Scent-a-Vision and Multiple Track Discrete Sound. *Executive producer* Gary Goddard. *Producers* Steve Schklair and Keith Melton. *Director* Keith Melton. *Director of photography* Steve Schklair. *3D technical adviser* Stan Loth. *Art director* Arlene Alen. *First assistant cameraman* Vance Piper. *Special photographic effects* Sean Phillips. *Gaffer* Chris Morley. *Equipment* Wally Mills and Cinemills. ¶An Infinity Filmworks production for Landmark Entertainment. ArriVision. Color by Consolidated Film Industries. Sixteen-track magnetic stereophonic sound. Filmed on location in California. This short was made for exhibition at Six Flags Corporation's amusement parks. It is the only film to our knowledge to incorporate all the elements of film technology: color, stereoscopics, widescreen, scents, surround sound and body motion (via Bodysonic Seats).

September Storm (September 9, 1960). Filmed in Natural Vision 3-Dimension and *Super*Scope 235. Presented in Stereo-Vision and CinemaScope. *Producer* Edward L. Alperson. *Director* Byron Haskin. *Screenplay* W.R. Burnett. *Story* Steve Fisher. *Director of photography* Jorge Stahl, Jr. *Music* Edward L. Alperson, Jr. *Music director* Raoul Kraushaar. *Editorial supervision* Otto Ludwig. *Film editor* Alberto Valenzuela. *Underwater director* Paul Stader. *Underwater photography* Lamar Boren. *Production designer* Boris Leven. *Special effects* John R. Cosgrove. *Optical research* Ray Mercer & Company. *Underwater equipment* Healthways. *Wardrobe supplier* Jantzen. *Preproduction 3D consultant* Lothrop B. Worth. *3D consultants and cameramen* Leonard J. South and Richard Johnson. *Production supervisor* Alberto F. Giles.

Production manager and first Assistant director Clarence Eurist. *Unit manager and second assistant director* James Cranston. *Executive production secretary* Nettie S. Cohn. *Assistant to the producer* Edward L. Alperson, Jr. *Script supervisor* Jose Luis Ortega. *Makeup artist* Rosa Guerrero. *Hair stylist* Pina Lozada. *Songs* "Be Bye You" and "Passing By" *music* Edward L. Alperson, Jr., *lyrics* Jerry Winn. ¶An Edward L. Alperson presentation. An Alco Pictures Corporation production. Released by 20th Century-Fox. Color by Fotofilm. Prints by De Luxe. 99 minutes. Filmed on location in Majorca, Spain. ¶CAST: *Anne Traymore* Joanne Dru. *Joe Balfour* Mark Stevens. *Ernie Williams* Robert Strauss. *Manuel del Rio Montoya* Asher Dawn. *Rene le Cleric* Pierre Kerien. *Yvette* Claude Ivry. *Girl* Vera Valmont. *Rivera* G. Ariel. *Montserrat* Adam Genette. *Flamenco dancers* Charito y Ernesto. ¶The only 3D feature released in dual anamorphic format. Working titles were *The Sea Nymph* and *The Girl in the Red Bikini.*

Sestra muzikanta (1972). Filmed in Sovscope 70. *Screen author* A. Aleksin. *Directors* P. Khomskie and I. Khomskie. *Operator* M. Suslov. *Artist* Boris Blank. *Music* M. Kazlaeva. *Song text* R. Rozdestenskogo. *Balletmaster* G. Mayorov. *Sound operator* V. Sharun. ¶A Mosfilm production. International distribution Sovexportfilm. Sovcolor. Six-track magnetic stereophonic sound. 90 minutes. Filmed at Mosfilm Studios, Moscow, R.S.F.S.R. ¶CAST: I. Popova, S. Smekhnova, A. Vdovin, V. Shishkin, N. Vorobieva, S. Shevkunenko, N. Agapova and E. Menishov. ¶A Soviet production released in Russia in 1972.

Seven Wonders of the World (April 10, 1956). Filmed in Cinerama. *Producer* Lowell Thomas. *Directors* Tay Garnett, Paul Mantz, Andrew Marton, Ted Tetzlaff, Walter Thompson, John Farrow and William P. Lipscomb. *Based on an idea by* Lowell Thomas. *Scenario and narration contributions* Prosper Buranelli and William P. Lipscomb. *Music* Emil Newman, David Raksin and Jerome Moross. *Additional music* Lionel Newman and Sol Kaplan. *Music consultant* Monsignor William T. Green. *Cinerama Symphony Orchestra conductor* Emil Newman.

Japanese dance creator Tetsuzo Shirai. *Choral group* Apollo Club of Minneapolis, *conductor* William McPhail. *Carillonic Bells instruments* Schulmeric Carillons, Inc. *Photography* Harry Squire and Gayne Rescher. *Aerial photography* Gayne Rescher. *Editors* Harvey Manger and Jack Murray. *Music editors* Lovel S. Ellis and Richard C. Harris. *Sound editor* Monty Pearce. *Sound* Richard J. Pietschmann, Jr., Richard Vorisek, Fred Bosch and Avery Lockner. *Production staff* Edward R. Evans, Arnold Granan, Robert Herndon, Edward Hyland, Gus Leonidas, Matthew Loscalzo, Eileen McCollum, George Muller, Gustavo "Gus" Quinterio, Philip Reilly, John Sola and William Terry. *Paintings* Mario Larrinaga. *Cinerama stereophonic sound system* Cinerama Laboratories, Oyster Bay, Long Island, I.A.T.S.E. *Advance arrangements* Lowell Thomas, Jr., Maynard Malcolm Miller, Robert W. Heussler and Eileen Salama. *Advice and cooperation* Gen. Merian C. Cooper. *Associate producer* Maynard Malcolm Miller. *Assistant directors* Emmett Emerson, Henry Hartman and Andre Smagghe. *Assistant cameramen* John S. "Jack" Priestley, Bert Eason and Fred Fordham. *Still photography* Edwin W. Sippel and Maria La Yacona. *Cinerama technician* Peter Gibbons. *Grips* Michael Mahoney, Coleman Thomas Conroy, Jr. and James R. Morrison. *Electrician* John Wallace, Jr. *Pilots* Capt. Page W. "Willie" Smith, Paul Mantz and Lowell Thomas. *Copilots* Frank Schwelle, Arthur G.W. "Art" La Shelle and John Bateman. *Flight navigators* Frank Schwelle, R.C. Olson and Edwin W. Sippel. *Flight engineer* James Courtland "Cort" Johnston. *Production accountant* Ralph M. Leo. *Script girl* Gloria Tetzlaff. ¶A Lowell Thomas production. Released by Stanley Warner Cinerama Corporation. Technicolor. Seven-track magnetic Cinerama Sound. 128 minutes including overture, intermission and exit music. Filmed in the United States (Pawling, New York City and Niagara Falls, New York; Hoover Dam, Nevada; Grand Canyon National Park, Arizona; Texas; and Los Angeles, Sequoia National Park and Yosemite National Park, California), India (Benares, Agra, Darjeeling, New Delhi and Bangalore), Thailand (Bangkok), Cambodia (Angkor Wat), Hong Kong, Japan (Fujiyama and Tokyo), Hawaii, Argentina (Iguassu and Angel Falls), Brazil (Rio de Janeiro and Recife), French West Africa (Daker and Timbuktu), Southern Rhodesia (Wankie), Belgian Congo (Usumbura and Gangala-Na-Bodio), Tanganyika, Kenya (Nairobi), Uganda (Victoria Nile), Ruanda-Urundi (Kabgaye), Sudan, Yemen (Rub-al Khadi, Aden and Shibam), Saudi Arabia (Riyadh, Dhahran and Wadi Beihan), Iraq (Baghdad), Israel (Jerusalem, Nazareth, Dead Sea and Sea of Galilee), Jordan (Jericho, Bethlehem, Jordan River and Mount of Temptation), Egypt (Cairo, Gizeh and Mount Sinai), Greece (Athens, Mount Olympus and Acropolis), Turkey (Istanbul), Italy (Rome, Naples, Castel Gandolfo, Pisa, Mount Vesuvius) and England (London). ¶CAST: *Host and narrator* Lowell Thomas. *Themselves* King Mwami, Butera, Sherif Hussein, Giovanni, Maria and Pope Pius XII. ¶Excerpts later incorporated into *The Best of Cinerama.* Lowell Thomas wrote a book on the filmmakers' adventures called *Seven Wonders of the World* (Hanover House, 1956).

Shaka *see* **Buddha.**

Shans (1984). Filmed in Sovscope 70. *Screen authors* K. Bulichev and A. Mayorov. *Director* A. Mayorov. *Operator* G. Belenikiy. *Artist* P. Safonov. *Composer* A. Ribnikov. *Sound operator* E. Urvantseva. ¶A Mosfilm production. International distribution Sovexportfilm. Sovcolor. Six-track magnetic stereophonic sound. 85 minutes. Filmed at Mosfilm Studios, Moscow, R.S.F.S.R. ¶CAST: S. Plotnikov, I. Shkurin, M. Kapnist, D. Kambarova, R. Kurkina, V. Izotova, V. Pavlov, M. Menglet, I. Yasulovich, V. Novikova and A. Nikolaev. ¶A Soviet production released in Russia in 1984.

Shatterhand (October 1967). Filmed in Superpanorama 70. *Executive producer* Georg M. Reuther. *Producer* Arthur Brauner. *Director* Hugo Fregonese. *Script* Robert A. Stemmle and Ladislaus Fodor. *Based on characters created by* Dr. Karl Friedrich May. *Chief cameraman* Siegfried Hold. *Music composer and conductor* Riz Ortolani. *Editor* Alfred Srp. *Settings* Otto Pischinger. *Makeup* Raimund Stangl. *Cameraman* Richard Reuven Rimmel. *Production managers* Manfred Korytoroski and Manfred Dolle. *Assistant director* Hertha Friedl. *World sales* Omnia Film Export GmbH. ¶A Don Kaye Associates presentation. A CCC Filmkunst–Avala Film–Criterion Film–Serena Film production. From Walter Manley Enterprises, Inc. Released by Goldstone Film Enterprises. Eastman Color. 89 minutes. Filmed on location in Yugoslavia. ¶CAST: *Old Shatterhand* Lex Barker. *Chief Winnetou* Pierre Brice. *Paloma* Daliah Lavi. *Capt. Bradley* Guy Madison. *Sam Hawkins* Ralf Wolter. *Bush* Gustavo Rojo. *Dixon* Rik Battaglia. *Rosemary* Killi Mattern. *Tujunga* Alain Tissier. *Gen Taylor* Charles Fawcett. *Sheriff Brandon* Nikola Popovic. *Joe Barker* Mirko Ellis. *Timpe* Bill Ramsey. *Tom* Burschi Putzgruber. *Bit* James Burk. ¶Released in the U.S. in 35mm only and advertised in CinemaScope. Released in Europe in 70mm with six-track magnetic stereophonic sound. A West German, Yugoslavian, French and Italian coproduction. Released in West Germany in 1964 as *Old Shatterhand* running 122 minutes; released in Yugoslavia in 1965 as *Old Seterhand* running 117 minutes; released in France in 1965 as *Les cavaliers rogues* running 112 minutes; and released in Italy in 1965 as *La battaglia di Fort Apache* running time unknown. Guy Madison was looped by another actor for the English-language version. Part of a long-running series, but the only entry in 70mm, that includes *Apache Gold* (Columbia, 1965), *Treasure of Silver Lake* (Columbia, 1965), *Rampage at Apache Wells* (Columbia, 1966), *Frontier Hellcat* (Columbia, 1966), *Last of the Renegades* (Columbia, 1966), *The Desperado Trail* (Columbia, 1967), *Thunder at the Border* (Columbia, 1967), *Flaming Frontier* (Warner Bros.-Seven Arts, 1968), *Winnetou und Old Shatterhand im Tal der Toten (Winnetou and Old Shatterhand in Death Valley)* (not released in the U.S.; 1968) and *Half-Breed* (Hampton Associates, 1973).

Shellarama (1965). Filmed in Super Technirama 70. Presented in 70mm Super Cinerama. *Producer* Dimitri de Grunwald. *Photography* Stanley Sayer. *Music* Johnny Scott. ¶Produced and released by Shell International Petroleum Company, Ltd. Eastman Color. RCA six-track magnetic stereophonic sound. 14 minutes. Filmed in England, Iran and Nigeria. ¶This British theatrical commercial was released in England in May 1965 and was shown with *Battle of the Bulge*. It was eventually released internationally and supposedly exhibited in the U.S. though probably not in 70mm Super Cinerama. Prints were distributed in 70mm, 35mm (anamorphic with four-track magnetic stereo, anamorphic with mono optical sound and 1.66×1 spherical with mono optical sound) and 16mm (1.66×1 spherical with optical sound). It was reissued as *Push Button Go*. 70mm prints are still available for booking from Shell in London.

Shin No Shikotei *see* **The Great Wall.**

Shiroka strana moya rodnaya (1969). Filmed in Sovscope 70. International distribution Sovexportfilm. Sovcolor. Six-track magnetic stereophonic sound. A Soviet production released in Russia in 1969.

Shlyapa *see* **The Man in the Hat.**

The Shooting Party (September 1981). Filmed in Sovscope 70. *Screen author and director* Emil Lotyanu. *Based on the novel "Moy laskoviy i nezniy zveri" by* Anton Chekov. *Operator* Anatoly Petritskiy. *Artist* Boris Blank. *Composer* Evgeni Doga. *Sound operator* V. Kurganskiy. *Editor* Leonid Knayzevoy. ¶A Joseph Papp presentation in association with FDM Foundation for the Arts. A Mosfilm-Inter-Aliyans-Film production. Released by Corinth Films by arrangement with Sovexportfilm. Sovcolor. 105 minutes. Filmed at Mosfilm Studios, Moscow, R.S.F.S.R. ¶CAST: *Olga Skvortsova* Galina Belyaeva. *Sergia Kamysheve* Oleg Yankovskiy. *Count Alexei Karneyva* Kirill Lavrov. *Peter Urbenin* Leonid Markov. *Polychrony Kalidis* Grigory Grigoriu. *Tina* Sveltana Toma. *With* V. Simchich, O. Fedorov and A. Zvenigorodskiy. ¶A Soviet production released in Russia in 1978 as *Moy laskoviy i nezniy zveri* in 70mm and six-track magnetic stereophonic sound running 136 minutes. The international title was given in English as both *The Shooting Party* and *My Tender and Gentle Beast*. The U.S. version was in 35mm only.

Ad for Shatterhand.

The Shore (1984). Filmed in Sovscope 70. *Screen authors* Yuri Bondarev, Aleksandr Alov and Vladimir Naumov. *Based on the novel "Bereg" by* Yuri Bondareva. *Directors* Aleksandr Alov and Vladimir Naumov. *Operator* Valentin Zeleznyakov. *Artists* Evgeni Chernyaev and Vladimir Kirs. *Composer* Aleksandr Goldstein. *Sound operator* B. Vengerovskiy. ¶A Mosfilm production in collaboration with Alliance Filmprod--uktion and FRG Television. International distribution Sovexportfilm. Sovcolor. Six-track magnetic stereophonic sound. 175 minutes plus intermission. Filmed at Mosfilm Studios, Moscow, R.S.F.S.R. and on location in Hamburg, West Germany. ¶CAST: *Emma Herbert* Natalia Belokhvostikova. *Vadim Nikitin* Boris Shcherbakov. *Sgt. Mezkhenin* Vladimir Gostyukhin. *Lt. Knyazkhko* Valery Storozik. *Lt. Granaturov* Mikhail Golubovich. *With* Bernhard Wikki, Vladimir Zamanskiy, A. Gusev, Armen Dzigarkhanyan, Kornelia Boye, Bruno Ditrin, Natasha Naymova, Albina Matveeva, Georgy Sklyanskiy, Kostya Kozlov, Mikhail Bychkov and Andrei Stankovich. ¶A Soviet and West German coproduction released in Russia in 1984 as *Bereg* in two parts running 87 minutes and 88 minutes.

The Shores of Hope (1967). Filmed in Sovscope 70. *Screen author* Aleksandr Levada. *Director and producer* Nikolay Vinfgranovskiy. *Operator* Yuri Tkachenko. *Artist* V. Novakov. *Composer* V. Guba. *Sound operators* L. Vachi and G. Matus. ¶A Kievskaya kinostudiya im. A.P. Dovzenko production. International distribution Sovexportfilm. Sovcolor. Six-track magnetic stereophonic sound. 74

minutes. Filmed at Kievskaya kinostudiya im. A.P. Dovzenko, Kiev, Ukrainian S.S.R. ¶CAST: *Markarov* Yuri Leonidov. *Prof. Sherwood* Boris Bibikov. *Maj. Greasly* Afanasi Kochetkov. *Vaslav* Nikolay Vinfgranovskiy. *Linda* Ausma Kantane. *Mary* Elsa Radzinya. *Vandenburg* Vladimir Zelidin. With K. Yakubov. ¶A Soviet production released in Russia in 1967 as *Bereg nadezdi.*

Shyrokr strana moya rodnaya... *see* **Great Is My Country.**

The Siberiad (November 1979). Filmed in Sovscope 70. *Screen authors* Valentin Ezov and Andrei Mikhalkov-Konchalovskiy. *Director* Andrei Mikhalkov-Konchalovskiy. *Operator* Levan Paatashvili. *Artists* Nikolai Dvigubskiy and Aleksandr Adabashian. *Composer* Eduard Artemiev. *Editor* Valentina Koulaguine. *Costumier* Nathalia Litchmanova. *Sound operator* V. Bobrovskiy. ¶A Mosfilm production. Released by International Film Exchange and Satra Film Corporation by arrangement with Sovexportfilm. Sovcolor. Six-track magnetic stereophonic sound. 210 minutes plus intermission. Filmed at Mosfilm Studios, Moscow and on location in Siberia, R.S.F.S.R. ¶CAST: *Yaya Solomin* Lyudmila Gurchenko. *Nikolai Ustiuzkhanin* Vitaly Solomin. *Alexei Ustinuzkhanin* Nikita Mikhalkov. *Afanassi Ustinuzkhanin* Vladimir Samoilov. *Erofei Solomin* Evgeni Perov. *Spiridon Solomin* Sergei Shakurov. *Anastassia* Nathalia Andreychenko. *Filipp Solomin* Igor Okhupin. *Rodion Klimentov* Mikhail Kononov. *Eternal old man* Pavel Kadochnikov. *Ermolai* Nikolai Skorobogatov. *Taya as a youth* Elena Koreneva. *Alexei as a youth* Evgeni Leonov-Gladishev. *Tofik Rustamov* Ruslan Mikaberidze. *Fedor Nikolayevich* Vsevold Larionov. *Guryev* Konstantin Grieoryev. With Micha Baboukov, Tavaslava Khlapova, Maxime Munzuk, Alioche Tiorkine, Volodia Levitan, E. Petrov, L. Pleshakov and A. Potapov. ¶A Soviet production released in Russia in 1979 as *Sibiriada* in two parts running 136 minutes plus intermission (part one: 70 minutes, part two: 66 minutes) and 139 minutes plus intermission (times for two parts unknown). Rereleased in the U.S. in September 1982 as *Siberiad* by IFEX Films (International

Film Exchange) running 190 minutes plus intermission. The U.S. version(s) may have been in 35mm only; sources conflict.

The Siberian Woman (1973). Filmed in Sovscope 70. *Screen author* Afanasi Salinckiy. *Director* Alexei Saltikov. *Operators* Gennadi Tsekaviy and Viktor Yakushev. *Composer* Andrei Eshpay. *Artist* S. Volkov. *Sound operator* A. Kosobokov. *Song text* M. Nozkina. ¶A Mosfilm production. International distribution Sovexportfilm. Sovcolor. Six-track magnetic stereophonic sound. 172 minutes plus intermission. Filmed at Mosfilm Studios, Moscow, R.S.F.S.R. ¶CAST: *Maria Odintsova* Valeria Zaklunnaya. *Dobrotin* Evgeni Matveev. With Rimma Markova, Sofia Pilyavskaya, Olga Prokhorova, R. Gromadskiy, P. Chernov, V. Sedov, V. Moroz, A. Potapov, S. Bubnov, F. Odinokov, A. Eliseev and S. Kurilov. ¶A Soviet production released in Russia in 1973 as *Sibiryachka* in two parts running 89 minutes and 83 minutes.

Sibiriada *see* **The Siberiad.**

Sibiryachka *see* **The Siberian Woman.**

Silent Sky (1977). Filmed in IMAX. *Producers and directors* David Mackay, Laszlo George and Douglas Murray. *Photographer* Laszlo George. ¶Released by Imax Systems Corporation. Eastman Color. Six-track magnetic stereophonic sound. 30 minutes. Filmed in California. ¶CAST: *Pilot* Oscar Boesch. ¶A Canadian production originally made for Ontario Place.

Sinoviya *see* **The Sources.**

Sinyaya ptitsa *see* **The Blue Bird.**

Skaz pro to, kak tsari Petr arapa zenil *see* **The Story of How Tsar Peter Married Off His Blackamoor.**

Skazka o tsare Saltane *see* **The Tale of Tzar Saltan.**

Skorbnove beschuvstviye *see* **Mournful Unconcern.**

Skorosti (1983). Filmed in Sovscope 70. *Screen author* M. Zvereva. *Director* D. Svetozarov. *Operator* S. Astakhov. *Artist*

Yu. Pugach. *Composers* A. Makarevich, A. Kutikov and L. Zaytsev. *Sound operators* L. Gavrichenko and L. Shumyager. ¶A Lenfilm production. International distribution Sovexportfilm. Sovcolor. Six-track magnetic stereophonic sound. 74 minutes. Filmed at Lenfilm Studios, Leningrad, R.S.F.S.R. ¶CAST: A. Batalov, D. Kharatiyan, M. Talivik, V. Shilovskiy, A. Stepanova and B. Puladze. ¶A Soviet production released in Russia in 1983.

Sky Over Holland (1967). Filmed in Super-panorama 70. *Producer and director* John Ferno. *Writer* Simon Koster. *Camera* Robert Gaffney. *Music* Robert Heppener. *Associate producer* Douwes Fernhout. ¶A Ferno production for The Netherlands. Released by Seneca International. Technicolor. Six-track magnetic stereophonic sound. 17 minutes. Filmed in the Netherlands. A Dutch short subject which received a 1967 Academy Award nomination for Best Live Action Short Subject. Rereleased in June 1968 by Warner Bros.-Seven Arts. Originally made for EXPO 67. One source claims Robert Gaffney was also involved as producer and director. The above credits are from the Warner Bros. files.

Skyward (1985). Filmed in IMAX. *Producers* Roman Kroitor and Susumu Sakane. *Director* Stephen Low. *Photographer* Leon Zourdoumis. ¶A Skyward Film Productions, Ltd. picture. Released by Imax Systems Corporation. Eastman Color. Six-track magnetic stereophonic sound. 24 minutes. Filmed at Suncoast Seabird Sanctuary, St. Petersburg, Florida. ¶CAST: Ralph Heath. ¶A Canadian and Japanese coproduction originally made for the Suntory Pavilion at the 1985 International Exposition in Tsukuba, Japan.

Sladkaya zenshchina *see* **Sweet Woman.**

Sleeping Beauty (February 1959). Filmed in Super Technirama 70. *Producer* Walt Disney. *Production supervisor* Ken Peterson. *Supervising director* Clyde Geronimi. *Sequence directors* Eric Larson, Wolfgang Reitherman and Les Clark. *Directing animators* Milt Kahl, Franklin Thomas, Marc Davis, Oliver Johnston, Jr. and John Lounsbery. *Story adaptation* Erdman Penner. *Based on the story by*

Charles Perrault. *Additional story* Joe Rinaldi, Winston Hibler, Bill Peet, Ted Sears, Ralph Wright and Milt Banta. *Production design* Donald Da Gradi and Ken Anderson. *Backgrounds* Frank Armitage, Thelma Witmer, Albert Dempster, Walt Peregoy, Bill Layne, Ralph Hulett, Dick Anthony, Fil Mottola, Richard H. Thomas and Anthony Rizzo. *Layout* McLaren Stewart, Tom Codrick, Don Griffith, Erni Nordli, Basil Davidovich, Victor Haboush, Joe Hale, Homer Jonas, Jack Huber and Ray Aragon. *Color styling* Eyvind Earle. *Character styling* Tom Oreb. *Character animation* Hal King, Hal Ambro, Don Lusk, Blaine Gibson, John Sibley, Bob Carson, Ken Hultgren, Harvey Toombs, Fred Kopietz, George Nicholas, Bob Youngquist, Eric Cleworth, Henry Tanous, John Kennedy and Ken O'Brien. *Effects animation* Dan MacManus, Joshua Meador, Jack Boyd, Jack Buckley and Dorse Lanpher. *Music adaptation* George Bruns. "*Sleeping Beauty Ballet*" Peter Ilyich Tchaikovsky. *Choral arrangements* John Rarig. *Film editors* Roy M. Brewer, Jr. and Donald Halliday. *Sound supervision* Robert O. Cook. *Music editor* Evelyn Kennedy. *Special processes* Ub Iwerks and Eustace Lycett. *Optical photography* Art Cruickshank. *Optical coordinator* Robert Broughton. "*Once Upon a Dream*" *music and lyrics* Sammy Fain and Jack Lawrence. "*Hail the Princess Aurora*" and "*The Sleeping Beauty Song*" *music and lyrics* Tom Adair and George Bruns. "*I Wonder*" *music and lyrics* Winston Hibler, Ted Sears and George Bruns. "*The Skump Song*" *music and lyrics* Tom Adair, Erdman Penner and George Bruns. *Photographic lenses* Panavision Inc. ¶A Walt Disney production. Released by Buena Vista Distribution Co. Technicolor. RCA six-track magnetic stereophonic sound. 75 minutes. Filmed at Walt Disney Studios. ¶VOICE CHARACTERIZATIONS *Princess Aurora* Mary Costa. *Prince Phillip* Bill Shirley. *Maleficent* Eleanor Audley. *Flora* Verna Felton. *Fauna* Barbara Jo Allen [Vera Vague]. *Merryweather* Barbara Luddy. *King Stefan* Taylor Holmes. *King Hubert* Bill Thompson. *Goons* Candy Candido. ¶LIVE ACTION MODELS *Princess Aurora* Helene Stanley. *Prince Phillip* Ed Kemmer. *Maleficent* Jane Fowler. ¶The first animated film in 70mm. Advertised in Technirama

70. Shown with the CinemaScope short *Grand Canyon* which was not blown up to 70mm as generally supposed.

The Sleeping Beauty (May 4, 1966). Filmed in Kinopanorama 70. *Screen authors* Konstantin Sergeev and Iosif Shapiro. *Based on "La belle au bois dormant" by* Charles Perrault *and "Spyashchaya krasavitsa" by* P.I. Chaykovskogo. *Directors and producers* Apollinariy Dudko and Konstantin Sergeev. *Chief operator* Anatoly Nazarov. *Artists* T. Vacilikovskaya and V. Ulitko. *Set* Ye. Yakuba. *Music* P.I. Chaykovskogo. *Conductors* B. Khaykin and V. Gamaliya. *Players* Kirov State Academic Theatre Orchestra. *Choreographer* Konstantin Sergeev *based on original choreography by* Marius Petipa. *Sound operator* A. Bekker. *Assistant director* A. Sokolov. *Special effects* N. Pokoptsev and M. Krotkin. *Prints* Technicolor. ¶A J. Jay Frankel-E. Douglas Netter presentation. A Lenfilm production. Released by Royal Films International [Columbia Pictures] by arrangement with Sovexportfilm. Sovcolor. Six-track magnetic stereophonic sound. 90 minutes. Filmed at Lenfilm Studios, Leningrad, R.S.F.S.R. ¶CAST: *Princess Aurora* Alla Sizova. *Prince Desire* Yuriy Soloviev. *Wicked fairy* Natalya Dudinskaya. *Lilac fairy* Irina Bazenova. *King* Vsevolod Ukhev. *Queen* O. Zabotkina. *Princess Florina* Natalya Makarova. *Blue bird* Valeriy Panov. *Master of ceremonies* V. Ryazanov. *Tenderness* E. Minchenok. *Playfulness* I. Korneyeva. *Generosity* L. Kovalyova. *Courage* K. Fedicheva. *Lightheartedness* N. Sakhnovskaya. *White pussy* G. Kekisheva. *Puss in boots* S. Kuznetsov. *With* Sergey Vykulov, Kirov State Academic Theatre Corps de Ballet and students of Vaganova Dancing School. ¶A Soviet production released in Russia in 1964 as *Spyashchaya krasavitsa* running 108 minutes. According to one source the U.S. 35mm prints were advertised in Techniscope but no newspaper ad was located to substantiate the claim. This may have been shown in the U.S. in 35mm only.

Slovo dlya zashchiti *see* **Witness for the Defense.**

Sluchay v kvadrate 36-80 *see* **An Icci-**

dent in Map Grid 36-80.

Snow Job (1974). Filmed in IMAX. *Producer and director* Graeme Ferguson. *Writer* Don Harron. *Photographer* Henri Fiks. ¶Produced and released by Imax Systems Corporation. Eastman Color. Six-track magnetic stereophonic sound. 17 minutes. Filmed in Canada. ¶CAST: *School principal* Barbara Hamilton. *Bus driver* Eric House. ¶A Canadian production originally made for Ontario Place. This was the first dramatic (storytelling) IMAX film and was a slapstick comedy.

Soldati svobodi *see* **Soldiers of Freedom.**

A Soldier's Play *see* **A Soldier's Plaything.**

A Soldier's Plaything (November 1, 1930). Filmed in Vitascope. *Director* Michael Curtiz. *Adaptation* Percy Vekroff. *Dialog* Arthur Caesar. *Story* Vina Delmar. *Photographer* J.O. Taylor. *Film editor* Jack Killifer. *Recording engineer* Col. Nathan Levinson. *Sound engineers* Clifford A. Ruberg and George R. Groves. *Makeup artist* Perc Westmore. ¶A Warner Bros.-First National picture. Released by Warner Bros. Pictures. Western Electric Movietone recording. 57 minutes. Filmed at Warner Bros.-First National Studios. ¶CAST: *Georgie* Ben Lyon. *Tim* Harry Landon. *Gretchen Rittner* Lotti Loder. *Hank* Fred Kohler, Sr. *Capt. Plover* Noah Beery, Sr. *Grandfather Rittner* Jean Hersholt. *Herman* Otto Matieson. *Cpl. Brown* Lee Moran. *Lola* Marie Astaire. *Dave* Frank Campeau. ¶Working title was *Come Easy*. Released in England as *A Soldier's Play*. Filmed simultaneously in 35mm and released in that format in May 1931 running 71 minutes. This may have played in only one theater in Vitascope or possibly not at all. One source says the sound system was Vitaphone.

Soldiers of Freedom (1977). Filmed in Sovscope 70. *Screen authors* Yuri Ozerov, Oscar Kurganov, Dimitr Metodiev, Atanas Semerdziev, Zbignev Zaluskiy, Petro Szlkudyanu and Boguslav Khneupeka. *Director* Yuri Ozerov. *Chief operator* Igor Slabnevich. *Chief artists* Aleksandr Myagkov and Tatiana Lapshina. *Composer* Yuri Levitin. *Sound* *operator* E. Indlina. ¶A Mosfilm production in collaboration with Mafilm, DEFA, Barrandov, Koliba, Za Ugrakbu Film, PRF EF and Bukuresti. International distribution Sovexportfilm. Sovcolor. Six-track magnetic stereophonic sound. 518 minutes. Filmed at Mosfilm Studios, Moscow, R.S.F.S.R. and on location in Most, Banska-Bystrica and Prague, Czechoslovakia and Warsaw and Lublin, Poland. ¶CAST: *Marshal Rokossovskiy* Vladlen Davydov. *With* Stepan Getsov, Bogush Pastorek, Horst Proysker, Yakov Tripoliskiy, Lubomir Kabakchiev, Tadeush Lomnitskiy, P. Popandov, N. Uzunov, G. Radanev, H. Shramm, N. Eremenko-starshiy, B. Stutska, Ivan Lyubeznov, Ivan Misgirik, Viktor Avdyushko, Evgeny Burenkov, Evgeny Matveev, Mikhail Uliyanov, Vasily Lanovoy, N. Rushkovskiy, N. Manokhin, Naum Shopov, Ladislav Khudik, Fritz Litz, Kristiana Mikolaevska, Boris Belov and Stanislav Mikyulski. ¶A Soviet, Hungarian, East German, Czechoslovakian, Bulgarian and Rumanian coproduction released in Russia in 1977 as *Soldati svobodi* in four parts running 114 minutes, 138 minutes, 131 minutes and 135 minutes.

Soldiers on the March (1977). Filmed in Sovscope 70. *Screen authors* Boris Vasiliev and Kiriil Rapoport. *Director* Leonid Bikov. *Operator* Vladimir Voytenko. *Artist* Georgi Prokopets. *Composer* G. Dmitriev. *Sound operator* N. Avramenko. *Songs* B. Okudzavi and V. Levashova. ¶A Kievskaya kinostudiya im. A.P. Dovzenko production. International distribution Sovexportfilm. Sovcolor. Six-track magnetic stereophonic sound. 87 minutes. Filmed at Kievskaya kinostudiya im. A.P. Dovzenko, Kiev, Ukrainian S.S.R. ¶CAST: *Sgt. Sviatkin* Leonid Bikov. *Lt. Col. Konstantin Sviatkin* Leonid Bakshttsev. *Anna Suslin* Evgenia Uralova. *Lt. Suslin* Vladimir Konkin. *Saiko* Ivan Gavrilyuk. *Kimka* Elena Shanina. *Khabarbekov* Atabek Ganiev. *Glebov* Nikolai Sektimenko. *Koderidze* Vano Yantbelidze. *With* Natalia Naum, M. Ezepov, Nikolai Griniko, V. Miroshinchenko and A. Yunusova. ¶A Soviet production released in Russia in 1977 as *Ati-bati shli soldati.*

Solomon and Sheba (December 24, 1959). Filmed in Super Technirama 70. *Executive producer* Edward Small. *Producer* Ted Richmond. *Director* King Vidor. *Screenplay* Anthony Veiller, Paul Dudley and George Bruce. *Story* Crane Wilbur. *Second unit director* Noel Howard. *Director of photography* Frederick A. Young. *Second unit photography* John Von Kotze. *Art direction* Richard Day and Alfred Sweeney, Jr. *Coordinator of design* Ralph Jester. *Music composer and conductor* Mario Nascimbene. *Choreography* Jaroslav Berger. *Assistant directors* Piero Mussetta and Pepe Lopez. *Film editor* John Ludwig. *Gina Lollobrigida's costumes* Emilio Schuberth. *Wardrobe coordinator* Eric Seelig. *Wardrobe mistress* Pearl Miller. *Orgy sequence production* Hamilton Keener. *Orgy sequence technical adviser* Granville Heathway. *Production manager* Richard F. McWhorter. *Special effects* Alex C. Weldon. *Sound recordists* David Hildyard and Fred C. Hughesdon. *Makeup* John O'Gorman, Tom Lee and Tom Tuttle. *Hair stylist* Ann Box. *Technical advisers for cavalry sequences* Augustin Medina and Kenneth Lee. *Military adviser* Maj. Martin de Pozuelo, Chief Staff Officer, Spanish Army. *Property master* Robert Goodstein. *Continuity girl* Elaine Schreyeck. *Camera operator* Paul Wilson. *Sound editor* Aubrey Lewis. *Optical effects* Wally Veevers. ¶An Edward Small presentation. A King Vidor production. A Theme Pictures S.A. (London) Film. Released by United Artists. Technicolor. Westrex six-track magnetic stereophonic sound. 139 minutes. Filmed in Spain. ¶CAST: *King Solomon* Yul Brynner. *Queen Magda* Gina Lollobrigida. *Adonijah* George Sanders. *Abishag* Marisa Pavan. *Pharaoh* David Farrar. *Joab* John Crawford. *King David* Finlay Currie. *Hezrai* Laurence Naismith. *Ahab* Jose Nieto. *Sittar* Alejandro Rey. *Baltor* Harry Andrews. *Zadok* Julio Pena. *Nathan* William Devlin. *Bathsheba* Maruchi Fresno. *Egyptian general* Felix de Pomes. *Takyan* Jean Anderson. *Josiah* Jack Gwillim. ¶A British production. Credits on some prints read "Super Technirama 70, a product of Technicolor." Production began with Tyrone Power playing Solomon but he died before completion of principal photography. Yul Brynner was hired to replace him, the script was rewritten and almost all major scenes were reshot. Power does appear in long shots and in some action scenes.

Song o' My Heart (March 11, 1930). Filmed in Grandeur. *Executive producer* William Fox. *Producer* Winfield Sheehan. *Director* Frank Borzage. *Continuity* Sonya Levien. *Adaptation and dialog* Tom Berry. *Story* J.J. McCarthy. *Grandeur photographer* J.O. Taylor. *35mm photographers* Chester Lyons and Al Brick. *Art director* Harry Oliver. *Film editor* Margaret V. Clancey. *Chief sound engineer* Edmund H. Hansen. *Recording engineer* George P. Costello. *Assistant director* Lew Borzage. *Costumes* Sophie Wachner. *Songs: "I Feel You Near Me," "A Pair of Blue Eyes" and "Song o' My Heart" music and lyrics by* Charles Glover, William Kernell and James Hanley; *"Paddy, Me Lad" music and lyrics by* Albert Hay Malotte; *"The Rose of Tralee," "A Fair Story by the Fireside," "Just for a Day" and "Kitty My Love" music and lyrics by* Charles Glover and C. Mordaunt Spencer; *"Then You'll Remember Me" music and lyrics by* Alfred Burns and William Michael Balfe; *"Little Boy Blue" music and lyrics by* Ethelbert Niven; *"I Hear You Calling Me" music and lyrics by* Harold Herford and Charles Marshall; *"Loughi sereni e cari" and "Ireland, Mother Ireland"* traditional. *Singer* John McCormack. ¶A William Fox presentation. Produced and released by Fox Film Corp. Western Electric Movietone recording. 85 minutes. Filmed at Fox Studios and on location in Ireland. ¶CAST: *Sean O'Carolan* John McCormack. *Mary O'Brien* Alice Joyce. *Eileen O'Brien* Maureen O'Sullivan. *Tad O'Brien* Tommy Clifford. *Peter Conlon* J.M. Kerrigan. *Fergus O'Donnell* John Garrick. *Vincent Glennon* Edwin Schneider. *Joe Rafferty* J. Farrell MacDonald. *Mona* Effie Ellsler. *Elizabeth* Emily Fitzroy. *Guido* Andres de Segurola. *Fullerton* Edward Martindel. ¶Filmed simultaneously in regular 35mm.

Song of Norway (November 4, 1970). Filmed in Super Panavision 70. Presented in 70mm Super Cinerama. *Producers* Andrew and Virginia Stone. *Director and screen story and screenplay* Andrew L. Stone. *Based on the play with book by* Milton Lazarus; *and music and lyrics (based on the works of* Edvard Grieg*) by* Robert Wright and George Forrest; *as produced on the stage and directed by* Edwin Lester; *from a play by* Homer Curran. *Music and lyrics* Robert Wright and

George Forrest. *Director of photography* Davis Boulton. *Editor* Virginia Lively Stone. *Choreographer* Lee Theodore. *Musical supervisor, orchestrator and conductor* Roland Shaw. *Piano concerto: players* The London Symphony Orchestra; *conductor* Oivin Fjeldstad; *piano soloists* John Odgen and Brenda Lucas; *violin soloist* Manoug Parikian. *Assistant director* John O'Connor. *Second unit director* Yakima Canutt. *Art director* William Albert Havemeyer *Costume designers* David Walker and Fiorella Mariani. *Camera operators* Stan Mestel and Kelvin Pike. *Second unit cameramen* Terry Gould and Ken Cameron. *Assistant editor* Peter Halsey. *Sound recordist* John Purchese. *Second assistant directors* Bill Graf and Paul Cowan. *Danish coordinator and second unit assistant director* Lief Jul. *Choreography assistants* Avind Harum and Larry Oaks. *Key grip* Tony Gridlin. *Makeup* Kay Freeborn. *Hairdressers* Jan Dorman and Mary Bredin. *Wardrobe* Dora and Ralph Lloyd. *Chief electricians* Svend Bregenborg and Thomas Holeway. *Production supervisor* John Benson. *Production managers* Peter Crowhurst and Ted Wallis. *Second unit production manager* Fred Slark. *Casting directors* Leslie Pettit and Rebecca Howard. *Props* Jan Mathias. *Animation* Kinney-Wolf. *Animation based on characters of* Theodor Kittelsen. *Second unit camera assistant* Mike Matthews. *Music recording* Anvil Films Ltd. *Rerecording* Lyle Burdridge at Metro-Goldwyn-Mayer Inc. *Boom operators* Tony Cripps and Svein Ellefsen. *Stunt coordinator* Joe Yrigoyen. *Special photographic effects* Linwood G. Dunn, Film Effects of Hollywood and David Stanley Horsley. *Made with the cooperation of the following museums* Old Town, Aarhus, Denmark; Funen Village, Odense, Denmark; Old Bergen, Bergen, Norway; De Sandvigeke Semlinger, Lillehammer, Norway; Transportation Museum, Hammer, Norway and Folk Museum, Oslo, Norway. ¶An ABC Pictures Corp. presentation. An Andrew and Virginia Stone production. From the American Broadcasting Companies Inc. Released by Cinerama Releasing Corp. Color by De Luxe. Westrex six-track stereophonic sound. 142 minutes plus intermission. Filmed on location in Norway, Denmark, England and Italy. ¶CAST: *Edvard Grieg* Toralv

Maurstad. *Nina Hagerup Grieg* Florence Henderson. *Therese Berg* Christina Schollin. *Rikard Nordraak* Frank Porretta. *Bjornsterne Bjornson* Harry Secombe. *Berg* Robert Morley. *Krogstad* Edward G. Robinson. *Mrs. Bjornson* Elizabeth Larner. *Engstrand* Oscar Homolka. *Henrik Ibsen* Frederick Jaeger. *Franz Lizst* Henry Gilbert. *Hans Christian Andersen* Richard Wordsworth. *George Nordraak* Bernard Archard. *Aunt Aline* Susan Richards Chitty. *Hagerup* John Barrie. *Mrs. Hagerup* Wenke Foss. *Gade* Ronald Adam. *Magdalene Thoresen* Aline Towne. *Irate woman* Nan Munro. *Berg's butler* James Hayter. *Carl Helsted* Erik Chitty. *Capt. Hansen* Carl Rigg. *Violinist Manoug Parikian.* *First councilman* Richard Vernon. *Second councilman* Ernest Clark. *Bjornson's secretary* Eli Lindtner. *Freddie* Avind Harum. *Doctor* Rolf Berntzen. *Mrs. Schmidt* Tordis Maurstad. *Chevalier* Charles Lloyd Pack. *Winding* Robert Rietty [Roberto Rietti]. *Liszt's friends* Rosalind Speight and Ros Drinkwater. *Receptionist* Tracey Crisp. *Rome butler* Cyril Renison. *Girl's mother* Ilse Tromm. *Male dancers* Jeffrey Taylor, Peter Salmon, Roy Jones, Gordon Coster, Paddy McIntyre, Barrie Wilkinson, Robert Lupone and Stephen Reinhardt. *Female dancers* Jane Darling, Barbara Von Der Heyde, Hermione Farthingale, Jennie Walton, Michele Hardy, Susan Claire, Denise O'Brien and Janie Kells. ¶The 35mm general release and 16mm and Super 8 nontheatrical versions ran approximately 118 minutes. When first on television it was only in the shorter edition but is now available full length. For some inconceivable reason this is often referred to as a sequel to *The Sound of Music.*

Sons *see* **The Sources.**

(Rodgers and Hammerstein's) The Sound of Music (March 2, 1965). Filmed in Todd-AO and Superpanorama 70. *Producer and director* Robert Wise. *Screenplay* Ernest Lehman. *Based on the play with book by* Howard Lindsay and Russell Crouse, *lyrics by* Oscar Hammerstein II *and music by* Richard Rodgers *as produced on the stage by* Leland Hayward, Richard Halliday, Richard Rodgers and Oscar Hammerstein II, *from the book "The Story of the Trapp Family Singers" by* Maria Trapp, *with the partial use of ideas by* Georg Hurdalek. *Associate producer* Saul Chaplin. *Music and additional words and music ("I Have Confidence in Me" and "Something Good")* Richard Rodgers. *Lyrics* Oscar Hammerstein II. *Music supervisor, arranger and conductor* Irwin Kostal. *Production designer* Boris Leven. *Director of photography* Ted McCord. *Choreography* Marc Breaux and Dee Dee Wood Breaux. *Puppeteers* Bil and Cora Baird. *Second unit supervision and continuity sketches* Maurice Zuberano. *Vocal supervision* Robert Tucker. *Film editor* William Reynolds. *Additional photography* Paul Beeson. *Sound* Murray Spivack, Bernard Freericks, Douglas O. Williams and Eugene Grossman. *Unit production manager* Saul Wurtzel. *Assistant director* Ridgeway Callow. *Dialog coach* Pamela Danova. *Music editor* Robert Mayer. *Set decorations* Walter M. Scott and Ruby Levitt. *Special photographic effects* L.B. Abbott and Emil Kosa, Jr. *Sound recording supervisors* Fred Hynes and James Corcoran. *Makeup* Ben Nye. *Hair styles* Margaret Donovan. *Todd-AO developers* American Optical Company and Magna Theatre Corporation. *Superpanorama 70 camera* Modern Cinema System-Film. *Unit publicist* Howard Liebling. *Camera operator* Paul Lockwood. *Assistant art director* Harry Kemm. *Art illustrator* Leon Harris. *Assistant film editor* Larry Allen. *Recorder* William Buffinger. *Second assistant director* Richard Lang. *Production assistant* Alan Callow. *Script supervisor* Betty Levin. *Men's wardrobe* Richard James. *Women's wardrobe* Josephine Brown. *Julie Andrews' makeup* Willard Buell. *Hairdresser* Ray Foreman. *Still photographer* James Mitchell. *Gaffer* Jack Brown. *Key grip* Walter Fitchman. *Property master* Ed Jones. *Rerecording* Todd-AO and 20th Century–Fox Studios. *Titles* Pacific Title & Art Studio. ¶A Robert Wise production. An Argyle Enterprises, Inc. picture. Released by 20th Century–Fox. Color by De Luxe. Westrex six-track magnetic stereophonic sound. 174 minutes plus intermission. Filmed at 20th Century–Fox Studios and on location in Salzburg and Salzkammergut, Austria. ¶CAST: *Maria Augusta Kutschera* Julie Andrews. *Capt. Gaylord von Trapp* Christopher Plummer. *Baroness Elsa Schraeder* Eleanor Parker. *Max Detweiler* Richard Haydn. *Mother Abbess* Peggy Wood. *Liesl von Trapp* Charmian Carr. *Louisa von Trapp* Heather Menzies.

Friedrich von Trapp Nicholas Hammond. *Kurt von Trapp* Duane Chase. *Brigitta von Trapp* Angela Cartwright. *Marta von Trapp* Debbie Turner. *Gretl von Trapp* Kym Karath. *Sister Margaretta* Anna Lee. *Sister Berthe* Portia Nelson. *Herr Zeller* Ben Wright. *Rolf* Daniel Truhitte. *Frau Schmidt* Norma Varden. *Franz* Gil Stuart. *Sister Sophia* Marni Nixon. *Sister Bernice* Evadne Baker. *Baroness Ebberfeld* Doris Lloyd. *Ball guest* Maria Trapp. *Christopher Plummer's vocals* Bill Lee. *Peggy Wood's vocals* Margaret McKay. *Puppets* The Bil Baird Marionettes. ¶Only the aerial shots were done in Superpanorama 70. This is a remake of *Die Trapp-familie* (West German, 1956) which was reedited with its sequel *Die Trapp-familie in Amerika* (1958) and released in the U.S. by 20th Century–Fox as *The Trapp Family* (1961).

The Sources (1974). Filmed in Sovscope 70. *Screen authors* Grigory Koltunov and Nikolai Rozkov. *Based on the novel "Istoki" by* G. Konovalova. *Director* Ivan Lukinskiy. *Operator* Vadim Korniliev. *Artist* Semen Velednitskiy. *Composer* Anatoli Lepin. *Sound operator* A. Izbutskiy. ¶A kinostudiya im. M. Gorikogo production. International distribution Sovexportfilm. Sovcolor. Six-track magnetic stereophonic sound. 187 minutes plus intermission. Filmed at kinostudiya im. M. Gorikogo, Gorki, R.S.F.S.R. ¶CAST: *Denis Stepanovich Krupnov* Ivan Lapikov. *Matver Krupnov* Vladislav Strzelichik. *Yuri Krupnov* Nikolai Olyalin. *Yulia* Alina Pokrovskaya. *Lyuba Krupnov* Aleksandra Klimova. *Konstantin Krupnov* Gennadi Chulkov. *Solntsev* Viktor Khokhryakov. *Savva Krupnov* Georgi Epifantsev. *With* Gennadi Sayfulin, L. Belokoni and E. Kindinov. ¶A Soviet production released in Russia in 1974 as *Istoki* in two parts: *Bratiya (Brothers)* running 98 minutes and *Sinoviya (Sons)* running 89 minutes.

South Pacific (March 1958). Filmed in Todd-AO. *Executive producers* Richard Rodgers, Oscar Hammerstein II and George P. Skouras. *Producer* Buddy Adler. *Director* Joshua Logan. *Screenplay* Paul Osborn. *Based on the play with book and lyrics by* Oscar Hammerstein II; *and music by* Richard Rodgers; *as produced on the stage by* Richard Rodgers, Oscar Hammerstein II, Joshua Logan and

Leland Hayward; *and directed by* Joshua Logan; *from the book "Tales of the South Pacific" by* James A. Michener. *Music* Richard Rodgers. *Lyrics* Oscar Hammerstein II. *Director of photography* Leon Shamroy. *Music supervisor and conductor* Alfred Newman. *Associate music supervisor* Ken Darby. *Art direction* Lyle Reynolds Wheeler and John De Cuir, Sr. *Set decoration* Walter M. Scott and Paul S. Fox. *Boar's tooth ceremonial dance number choreographer* Leroy Prinz. *Costume designer* Dorothy Jeakins. *Makeup* Ben Nye. *Hair styles* Helen Turpin. *Orchestrations* Edward B. Powell, Pete King, Bernard Mayers and Robert Russell Bennett. *Assistant director* Ben Kadish. *Production associate* William Reynolds. *Special photographic effects* L.B. Abbott. *Sound recording supervisor* Fred Hynes. *Sound recorder* Joseph I. Kane. *Music recorder* Murray Spivack. *Todd-AO camera and film consultant* Schuyler A. Sanford. *Technicolor color consultant* Leonard Doss. *Film editor* Robert Simpson. *Music editors* George Adams and Robert Mayer. *Wardrobe managers* Reeder Boss and Norma Brown. *Wardrobe assistants* Mickey Sherrard and Dale Henderson. *Makeup artists* Allan Snyder and Willard "Bill" Buell. *Body makeup* Bunny Gardel. *Hairdressers* Marie Walter and Buddy King. *Second assistant directors* Morris Harmell and Michael Salamunovich. *Dialog coach* Joseph Curtis. *Script clerk* Marshall J. Wolins. *Unit production manager* Eric G. Stacey. *Production researchers* Frances Richardson and Katherine Lambert. *Production publicist* Sonia Wolfson. *Camera operator* Paul Lockwood. *Assistant cameraman* Lee "Red" Crawford. *Second assistant cameramen* Al Baalas, William (Bill) Cronjager, William (Bill) Jurgenson, Al Baerthlein and Arthur Gerstle. *Camera assistant (mechanic)* William (Bill) Schneider. *Art directors' assistant* Rodger Maus. *Art directors' illustrator* Dale Hennesy. *Continuity artist* Ed Graves. *Matte artist* Emil Kosa, Jr. *Set specifications* George Dudley. *Construction coordinator* Walter Ledgerwood. *Construction foreman* Loren Woods. *Plasterers* James Stephens and Robert Thompson. *Painters* Harvey Jackson and John Lowess. *Landscapers* George Novak, Peter Rea and Joe Fisher. *Draperymen* James Cane and Charles Long. *Prop master* Ed Jones.

Propmen Robert McLaughlin and Wayne Smothers. *Propmakers* Paul Skelton and Walter de Hart. *Leadman* Sid Greenwood. *Assistant sound recorder* Jack Rizey. *Boomman* Orik Barrett. *Cableman* Jack Woltz. *Playback operator* Harold Bavaird. *Todd-AO sound consultant* Newt Woltz. *Production portraits photographers* Frank Powolny and Derujinsky. *Production stills photographer* James Mitchell. *Studio stills photographer* Gaston Longet. *Key grip* Leo McCreary. *Grip best boy* Frank McCardle. *Grips* Delmar Blair, Richard Cameron, Eric Ericson, Walter Fitchman, Frank Gilley, W.A. Machado, John Murray, Al Parker and Fred Richter. *Gaffer* Fred Hall. *Best boy* Bob Henderson. *Juicers* Jack Brown, Leo Davis, Sam Fisher, Ted Husserl, Grover Jones, Fred Kuhnau and Charles Rosebrook. *Generatormen* Hank Vadare and Bob Smith. *Studio manager* Sid Rogell. *Process lenses* Panavision, Inc. *Todd-AO developers* American Optical Company and Magna Theatre Corporation. *Sound system* Todd-AO. *Negative* Eastman Kodak. *Production assistance* Department of Defense, Navy Department, U.S. Pacific Fleet and Fleet Marine Force, Pacific. *Miniatures and second unit: Director* Ray Kellogg. *Cameraman* Stanley Cortez. *Camera operators* Al Lebovitz and Ken Williams. *Assistant cameraman* Hugh Crawford. *Second assistant cameraman* Bert Kershner. *Camera mechanic* Grover Laube. *Effectsman* Bill Middlemas. *Propmaker* Don Nobles. *Painter* Joe Krutak. *Landscaper* Fred Lutz. *Grip* Lou Pazzelli. *Electrician* Clyde Taylor. ¶A Rodgers & Hammerstein presentation. A Magna Theatre Corporation-South Pacific Enterprises, Inc. production. Released by Magna Pictures. Technicolor. Westrex six-track magnetic stereophonic sound. 171 minutes including overture, intermission and exit music. Filmed at 20th Century–Fox Studios and on location in Kauai, Hawaii. ¶CAST: *Emile de Becque* Rossano Brazzi. *Ens. Nellie Forbush* Mitzi Gaynor. *Lt. Joseph Cable* John Kerr. *Luther "Big Dealer" Billis* Ray Walston. *Bloody Mary* Juanita Hall. *Liat* France Nuyen. *Capt. J.M. Brackett* Russ Brown. *Professor* Jack Mullaney. *Stewpot* Ken Clark. *Cmdr. Harbison* Floyd Simmons. *Ngana de Becque* Candace Lee. *Jerome de Becque* Warren Haieh. *Lt. Buzz Adams* Tom

Laughlin. *Henry* Francis Kahele. *Boar's tooth ceremonial dance chief* Archie Savage. *Subchief* Galvan De Leon. *First communications man* Robert Jacobs. *Second communications man* John Gabriel. *Co-pilot* Richard Harrison. *Navigator* Ron Ely. *Seabee dancer* Steve Wiland. *Adm. Kester* Richard Cutting. *U.S. commander* Joe Bailey. *Fighter pilots* Buck Class and Richard Kiser. *Pilots in hospital* Linc Foster, Doug McClure and Stephen Ferry. *Nurses on Nurses' Beach* Jean Baker, Diane Reid, Phyllis Butcher, Dian Goodman, Diane DuBois, Anna James, Karen Gallant, Joyce Kramer, Barbara Cole, Mary Bishop, May Fewell, Beverly Johnson, Jane Lucas, Janet Hanrahan, Helene Patridge, Barbara Kesser, Marlene Lizzio, Muffet Webb, Mary Jo Flanders and Debbie Wilcox. *Nurses in Thanksgiving Show* Faye Antaky, Donna Pouget, Dorothy Abbott, Pat Volasko, Jan Haller, Beverly Adland, Bonnie Lene, Jonnie Paris, Diane Myles, Barbara Donaldson, Ila McAvoy, Joanne Jones, Lorri Thomas, Darlene Engle, Kay Tapscott, Evelyn Ford, Betty Bunch and Sue Logan. *Sailors and seabees* Dan Wallace, Karl Heyer, Jim DeCloss, Mike Vincent, James Stacey, Donald Mundell, Alvin Arnold, Mark Pinkston, Gene Bergman, Velton Parker, John Chasey, Lee Thomas, Carl Esser, Joseph Schlichter, Jim Canley, Richard Smith, Murray Gaby, Robert Nielson, William Glisson, Hadley Gray, George Hooper, John Caler, Charles Joyner, Morris Harnell, Donald Lane, Donald Nobles and Tom Moore, Michael Salamunovich and Tom Logan. *Marines and sailors in Thanksgiving Show* Durwood Bloomgren, Charles Lunard, Tex Brodus, Joe Paz, Bob Calder, Ed Searless, Ray Damron and Clark Lee. *Boar's tooth ceremonial dance:* *Whipman* Bob Destine; *Birdmen* Sidney Hurston and Leroy Hamilton; *Ashmen* James Truitt, Clyde Webb and Steve Pappich; *Firetenders* Victor Upshaw, Nat Bush, Garland Thompson and Ralph Weaver. *Baruas* James Field, William Washington, Marco Lopez, Charles Carter, Alex Young, Ray Mendez, George Hill, Richard Domasin, James Malcolm, Maaka Nua, Johnny Morgan, Tonu Nua, Jack Williams, Selu Nua, Andrew Robinson and Niki Nua. *Blue boys* Kirk Boone, Walter Davis, Wesley Gale, Don Marshall, Clarence Landry, David Walker,

IN TODD-AO

Ad for South Pacific.

Andrew Isaacs, Harold Walker, Walter Smith and Charles Mohr. *Drummers and musicians* George Davis, Santiago Mos, Kenneth Walker, Gregory Christmas, Bill Ornelles, Gary Christmas, Freddy Baker, Gene Fontaine, James Green, Charles R. Rogers and Don Martin. *Polynesian women* Anita Dano, Ann Darris, Yvonne De Lavallade, Joan Fontaine, Lemmana Guerin, Paulette Easley, Telu Mansfield, Claire Alcantara, Vicki Orozco, Misaye Meyer, Bobbi Cote and Mimi Dillard. *Missionaries* Dorothy and James A. Michener. *Rossano Brazzi's vocals* Giorgio Tozzi. *John Kerr's vocals* Bill Lee. *Juanita Hall's vocals* Muriel Smith. ¶Released by Magna Pictures in 35mm running 150 minutes plus overture, intermission and exit music. Rereleased in 70mm and 35mm by Twentieth Century–Fox with prints by De Luxe and reissued again by The Samuel Goldwyn Company in 70mm with prints by Technicolor. The difference in the 70mm and 35mm versions seems to be in minor cuts throughout the film and not in the elimination of musical material or any complete scene. While this carried the *Produced in Todd-AO* credit on the 70mm version, the 35mm prints bore only the *Process Lenses by Panavision* billing. Insomuch as this was actually shot with Panavision lenses, it technically was photographed in Super Panavision 70 and not Todd-AO. Todd-AO Corporation did provide the Mitchell cameras and master the soundtrack, though.

South Seas Adventure *see* **Cinerama South Seas Adventure.**

Space Angels *see* **To the Stars by Hard Ways.**

Space Library (1980). Filmed in OMNI-MAX. *Producer and director* Les Novros. ¶Produced and released by Graphic Films Corp. Eastman Color. Six-track magnetic stereophonic sound. Thirty films of about one minute each, made for showing with other OMNIMAX films individually or as one 30-minute film.

The Sparkling World (1984). Filmed in Sovscope 70. *Screen author and director* Bulat Mansurov. *Based on the novel and Krasnaya magazine serial "Blistayushchiy mir" by* Alexander Greene [Aleksandr Grina]. *Operator* Nikolai Vasilikov. *Artists* David Vinnitskiy and Sergei Voronkov *Composer* Aleksandr Lunacharskiy. *Sound operator* E. Fedorov. ¶A Mosfilm production. International distribution Sovexportfilm. Sovcolor. Six-track magnetic stereophonic sound. 114 minutes. Filmed at Mosfilm Studios, Moscow and on location in Klaipeda, R.S.F.S.R. ¶CAST: *Drude* Tiit Khyarm. *Runa* Ilza Liepa. *Tavi* Yulle Tudre. *With* Pavel Kadochnikov, Lev Prigun, A. Vokach, L. Polokhov, Gleb Strizenov and Yuri Katin-Yartsev. ¶A Soviet production released in Russia in 1984 as *Blistayushchiy mir.*

Spartacus (October 7, 1960). Filmed in Super Technirama 70. *Executive producer* Kirk Douglas. *Producer* Edward Lewis. *Directors* Stanley Kubrick and Anthony Mann. *Screenplay* Dalton Trumbo. *Based on the novel by* Howard Fast. *In charge of production* Edward Muhl. *Director of photography* Russell Metty. *Music composer and conductor* Alex North. *Production designer* Alexander Golitzen. *Art director* Eric Orbom. *Set decorations* Russell A. Gausman and Julia Heron. *Main titles and design consultant* Saul Bass. *Sound* Waldon O. Watson, Joseph Lapis, Murray Spivack and Ronald Pierce. *Production aide and unit publicist* Stan Margulies. *Historical and technical adviser* Vittorio Nino Novarese. *Additional and special photography* Clifford Stine. *Wardrobe* Peruzzi, Rome. *Jean Simmon's costumes* William Thomas. *Costumes* J. Arlington Valles. *Film editor*

Robert Lawrence. *Assistants to the film editor* Robert Schulte and Fred A. Chulak. *Makeup* Bud Westmore and Steve Clensos. *Music editor* Arnold Schwarzwald. *Hair stylist* Larry Germain. *Unit production manager* Norman Deming. *Assistant director* Marshall Green. *Second unit directors* Yakima Canutt and Irving Lerner. *Music supervision* Joseph Gershenson. *Additional film editors* William A. Horning and Irving Lerner. *Sound editor* Louis B. Moss. *Matte artists* Peter Ellenshaw and Albert J. Whitlock. *Second assistant directors* Foster Phinney, James Welch, Joseph Kenny and Charles Scott. *Production illustrator* Tom Van Sant. *Camera operator* Edwin L. Pyle. *Color technicians* Ledger Haddow and George Dye. *Still photographers* Rollie Lane, William Read Woodfield, Jack Geraghty and Dick Miller. *Titles* National Screen Service. *Lenses* Panavision. ¶A Bryna Productions, Inc. presentation. A Kirk Douglas production. A Universal-International picture. Released by Universal Pictures Co. Technicolor. Westrex six-track magnetic stereophonic sound. 196 minutes plus intermission. Filmed at Universal City Studios and on location in Thousand Oaks, San Simeon and Death Valley, California and Guadalajara, Colmenar, Viejo, Alcazarde Hernandez, Navacerrada, Taracena and Iriepal, Spain. ¶CAST: *Spartacus* Kirk Douglas. *Marcus Licinius Crassus* Laurence Olivier. *Antoninus* Tony Curtis. *Varinia* Jean Simmons. *Gracchus* Charles Laughton. *Lentulus Batiatus* Peter Ustinov. *Julius Caesar* John Gavin. *Helena Glabrus* Nina Foch. *Tigranes* Herbert Lom. *Crixus* John Ireland. *Gladrus* John Dall. *Marcellus* Charles McGraw. *Claudia Marius* Joanna Barnes. *Draba* Woody Strode. *David* Harold J. Stone. *Ramon* Peter Brocco. *Gannicus* Paul Lambert. *Captain of the guard* Robert J. Wilke. *Dionysius* Nicholas Dennis. *Caius* John Hoyt. *Laelius* Frederick Worlock. *Symmachus* Dayton Lummis. *Crone* Lili Valenty. *Julia* Jill Jarmyn. *Slave girls* Jo Summers, Autumn Russell, Kay Stewart, Lynda Lee Williams and Louise Vincent. *Otho* James Griffith. *Marius* Joe Haworth. *Trainers* Dale Van Sickel and Marvin Croux. *Metallius* Vinton Hayworth. *Herald* Carleton Young. *Beggar woman* Hallene Hill. *Fimbria* Paul Burns. *Garrison officer* Leonard Penn. *Middle aged slave* Edwin Parker. *Slaves* Harry Harvey, Jr., Harold Goodwin and Chuck Roberson. *Slave leaders* Saul Gorss, Charles Horvath and Gilbert Perkins. *Gladiators* Bob Morgan, Reg Parton, Tom Steele, Jack Perkins, Aaron Saxon and Wally Rose. *Ad libs* Ken Terrell and Boyd "Red" Morgan. *Guards* Richard (Dick) Crockett, Harvey Parry, Carey Loftin, Rod Normond and Larry Perron. *Pirates* Bob Burns, Seaman Glass, George Robotham and Stubby Kruger. *Soldiers* Jerry Brown, Chuck Courtney, Russ Saunders, Valley Keene, Tap Canutt, Joe Canutt, Chuck Hayward, Buff Brady, Cliff Lyons, Rube Schaffer, Wayne "Buddy" Van Horn and Brad Harris. *Legionnaires* Ted de Corsia, Arthur Batanides and Robert Stevenson. *Major domo* Terence De Marney. *Senator* Paul Kruger. *Little girl* Judy Erwin. *Capua guard* John Daheim. *Petitioner* Anthony Jochim. *Roman general* Otho Malde. *Man* Louis Zeto. *Narrator* Victor Perrin. ¶Kubrick replaced Mann as director. Considerably reedited for 1969 rerelease in 35mm when it was advertised in Panavision. The supporting cast looks like a Who's Who of Hollywood stuntmen. Sequel: *The Slave* (a.k.a. *Son of Spartacus*) (MGM, 1963).

Special Assignment (1981). Filmed in Sovscope 70. *Screen authors* Boris Dobrodeev and Pyotr Pepogrebskiy. *Director* Evgeny Matveev. *Operator* Igor Chernikh. *Artists* Semyon Valyushok and G. Koshelev. *Composer* Evgeny Ptichkin. *Sound operator* I. Mayorov. *Song text* R. Rozdestvenskogo. ¶A Mosfilm production. International distribution Sovexportfilm. Sovcolor. Six-track magnetic stereophonic sound. 173 minutes plus intermission. Filmed at Mosfilm Studios, Moscow and on location at Voronezh, R.S.F.S.R. ¶CAST: Evgeny Matveev, Valeria Zaklunnaya, Aleksandr Parra, Lyudmila Gurchenko, Vladimir Samoylov, Nikolai Kryuchkov, Petr Chernov, Georgy Yukhtin, E. Lazarev, Evgeny Kindinov, R. Khomyatov and L. Borisov. ¶A Soviet production released in Russia in 1981 as *Osobo vaznoe zadanie* in two parts running 86 minutes and 87 minutes.

Speed (1984). Filmed in IMAX. *Producer, director and photographer* Greg MacGillivray. ¶A MacGillivray Freeman Films production. Released by MacGillivray Freeman Films Distribution Company.

Eastman Color. Six-track magnetic Dolby Stereo. 33 minutes. Originally made for Six Flags AutoWorld, Flint, Michigan.

Spyashchaya krasavitsa *see* **The Sleeping Beauty.**

Standing Up Country (1973). Filmed in IMAX. *Producer, writer and director* Roger Tilton. *Photographer* Barry O. Gordon. *Aerial supervision* Frank Tallman. *Aerial sequences* Tallmantz Aviation. ¶A Roger Tilton Films, Inc. production. Eastman Color. Six-track magnetic stereophonic sound. 22 minutes. Filmed in Colorado, Utah, Arizona and New Mexico. A Canadian production.

Star! (October 22, 1968). Filmed in Todd-AO. *Executive producer* Robert Wise. *Producer* Saul Chaplin. *Director* Robert Wise. *Writer* William Fairchild. *Dances and musical numbers stager* Michael Kidd. *Production designer* Boris Leven. *Director of photography* Ernest Laszlo. *Costume designer* Donald Brooks. *Music supervisor and conductor* Lennie Hayton. *Dance music composer* Jay Thompson. *Production associate and illustrator* Maurice Zuberano. *Film editor* William Reynolds. *Sound supervision* James P. Corcoran. *Sound* Murray Spivack, Douglas O. Williams and Bernard Freericks. *Set decorations* Walter M. Scott and Howard Bristol. *Assistant director* Ridgeway Callow. *Dance assistant* Shelah Hackett. *Unit production manager* Saul Wurtzel. *Music editor* Robert Tracy. *Special photographic effects* L.B. Abbott, Art Cruickshank and Emil Kosa, Jr. *Hair styles for Julie Andrews* Hal Saunders. *Makeup* Willard Buell and William Turner. *Wardrobe* Ed Wynigear and Adele Balkan. *Property master* Dennis Parrish. *Research and story editor* Max Lamb. *Unit publicist* Howard Newman. *Jewelry* Cartier, Inc. *Wigs* Cal-East, Inc. *Furs* Somper Furs. *Songs* "Star!" Sammy Cahn and James Van Heusen; "In My Garden of Joy" Saul Chaplin; "Down at the Old Bull and Bush" H. Von Tilzer, H. Sterling, L. Hunting and P. Krone; "Piccadilly" Paul Morande, Walter Williams and Bruce Seiver; "Oh, It's a Lovely War" J.P. Long and Maurice Scott; "Forbidden Fruit," "Parisian Pierrot," "Someday I'll Find You" and "Has Anyone Seen Our Ship" Noel Coward; "'N' Everything"

Buddy G. De Silva, Gus Kahn and Al Jolson; "Burlington Bertie from Bow" William Hargreaves; "Limehouse Blues" Philip Brahm and Douglas Furber; "Someone to Watch Over Me," "Dear Little Boy" and "Do, Do, Do" George Gershwin and Ira Gershwin; "The Physician" Cole Porter; "My Ship" and "Jenny" Kurt Weill and Ira Gershwin. *Todd-AO developers* American Optical Co. and Magna Theatre Corp. ¶A Robert Wise Productions film. Released by 20th Century–Fox. Color by De Luxe. Westrex six-track magnetic stereophonic sound. 174 minutes plus intermission. Filmed at 20th Century–Fox Studios and on location in New York City, Cape Cod, London and the French Riviera. ¶CAST: *Gertrude Lawrence* Julie Andrews. *Richard Aldrich* Richard Crenna. *Sir Anthony Spencer* Robert Reed. *Arthur Lawrence* Bruce Forsyth. *Rose* Beryl Reid. *Jack Roper* John Collin. *Andre Charlot* Alan Oppenheimer. *David Holtzman* Richard Karlan. *Billie Carleton* Lynley Laurence. *Jack Buchanan* Garret Lewis. *Jeannie Banks* Elizabeth St. Clair. *Pamela Lawrence* Jenny Agutter. *Ben Mitchell* Anthony Eisley. *Alexander Woollcott* Jock Livingston. *Dan* J. Pat O'Malley. *Bert* Harvey Jason. *Jerry Paul* Damian London. *Cesare* Richard Angarola. *Dorothy* Matilda Calnan. *Lord Chamberlain* Lester Matthews. *Assistant to Lord Chamberlain* Bernard Fox. *Bankruptcy judge* Murray Matheson. *Hyde Park speaker* Robin Hughes. *Eph* Jeannette Landis. *Molly* Dinah Ann Rogers. *Mavis* Barbara Sandland. *Moo* Ellen Plasschaert. *Beryl* Ann Hubbell. *Hostess* Anna Lee. *Gertrude's "Limehouse Blues" dance partner* Don Crichton. *Newsreel narrator* Peter Church. *Stage manager* Jan Gernat. *Cartier salesman* Conrad Bain. ¶Reedited to 120 minutes and rereleased in 35mm (advertised in Cinema-Scope) with mono sound as *Those Were the Happy Times*.

The Star of Hope (1979). Filmed in Sovscope 70. *Screen author* Konstantin Isaev. *Based on the novel "Mkhitir Sparapet" by* Sero Khanzaryana. *Director* Edmond Keosayan. *Operator* Mikhail Ardabievskiy. *Artists* Sergei Andrikyan and Anatoly Plastinkin. *Composer* Edgar Oganesyan. *Sound operator* Z. Vanunts. ¶A Mosfilm–Armenian-film production. International distribution Sovexportfilm.

Sovcolor. Six-track magnetic stereophonic sound. 199 minutes plus intermission. Filmed at Mosfilm Studios, Moscow, R.S.F.S.R. and on location in Armenia, Armenian S.S.R. ¶CAST: *Mkhitar* Armen Dzigarkhanyan. *Satenik* Laura Gevorkanyan. *Prince Barkhudar* Kote Daushvili. *Movses* Sos Sarkisyan. *With* Zdisher Magalashvili, Khoren Abramyan, Alla Tumanyan, R. Mkrtchyan, A. Gasparyan and Lusine Oganesian. ¶A Soviet production released in Russia in 1979 as *Zvezda nadezdi* in two parts: *David-Bek* running 96 minutes and *Mkhitar* running 103 minutes. Previously filmed as *David-Bek*.

The Stewardesses. Filmed in StereoVision. Presented in StereoVision 70. *Executive producer* Louis K. Sher. *Producer* Allan Silliphant. *Writer and director* Alf Silliman, Jr. [Allan Silliphant]. *Director of stereo-cinematography* Christopher Bell [Chris J. Condon]. *Music* Jaime Mendoza Nava. *Film editor* C. Fray. *Art director* Victor Silliphant. *Assistant cameraman* Daniel L. Symmes. *Sound* James Nava. *Sound transfers* Romness Recording. *Rerecording* Metro-Goldwyn-Mayer Studios. *Makeup* William J. Condos [William Condon]. *StereoVision technology* Magnavision, Inc. [Chris J. Condon and Allan Silliphant]. *Processing* Movielab. *35mm prints* Cinereel. *70mm prints* De Luxe. ¶A Louis K. Sher presentation. A Magnavision, Inc. production. Released by Sherpix, Inc. Eastman Color. RCA Photophone recording. 85 minutes. Filmed in Hollywood and Hawaii. ¶CAST: *Samantha* Christina Hart. *Colin Wintrop* Michael Garrett. *Jo* Angelique De Moline. *Horney Annie* Donna Stanley. *Tina* Paula Erickson. *Kathy* Kathy Ferrick. *Wendy* Jane Wass. *Karen* Patricia Fein. *Cindy* Beth Shields. *Ursella* Monica Gayle. *Capt. Masters* William Basil. *Cappy* Jerry Litvinoff. *Charles* Robert Keller. *Soldier* Andy Roth. *Pilot* John Barcado. *Loren Hatcher* Gordon White. *Steve White* Barry Schoenborn. *Stewardesses* Alicia Taggart, Linda Francis, Cindy Hopkins, Barbara Caron, Lynn Harris, Candy Stekes, Brenda Morrison, Mindy Baker, Phyllis Stangel, Ann Reynolds, Nancy O'Gorman, Karen Sherman, Nancy Ison and Babbette Cartier. ¶The first U.S. film photographed in single strip side-by-side 3D and blown up to 70mm. Interest-

ingly, the 70mm version had mono sound and was in 1.33 × 1 aspect ratio.

Storm *see* **Atmos.**

The Story of Flaming Years (1961). Filmed in Todd-AO. *Screen author* Aleksandr P. Dovzenko. *Director and producer* Yulia Solntseva. *Executive producers* L. Basov, L. Kanareykina and I. Soluyanov. *Operators* Fyodor Provorov and Alexei Temerin. *Artist* Aleksandr Borisov. *Composer* Gavriil Popov. *Costumiers* S. Bykhovskaya and G. Epishin. *Special effects* Mikhail Semyonov and B. Travkin. *Sound operators* Yakov Kharon and I. Urvantsev. *Second unit operator* V. Minayev. *Consultant* Gen. M. Popov. *Editors* K. Moskvina, A. Bramova and I. Rostovtsev. *Makeup* I. Chechenin. ¶A Kievskaya kinostudiya im. A.P. Dovzenko-Mosfilm production. International distribution Sovexportfilm. Sovcolor. Six-track magnetic stereophonic sound. 107 minutes. ¶CAST: *Gen. Glazunov* Boris Andreev. *Ryasny* Sergei Lukiyanov. *Bohdanovskiy* Vasili Merkuriev. *Ivan Onlyuk* Nykola Vinfgranovskiy. *Ulyana* Svetlana Zgun. *Maj. Velychko* M. Mayorov. *Maria* Zinaida Kirienko. *Von Brenner* B. Bibikov. *Schroeder* V. Akuraters. *Gribovsky* V. Zeldin. *Mandryka* B. Novikov. *Roman Klunny* Evkhen Bonderenko. *Semen Klunny* A. Romanenko. *Antonia* A. Bogdanova. *Demid* S. Petrov. *Tatyana* V. Kapustina. *Olena Stupak* M. Bulgakova. *With* V. Vitrishchak, P. Vynnyk, V. Gulyaev, Olena Maksymova, L. Parkhomenko, A. Pokrovsky, N. Sazonova, V. Seleznev, A. Khovansky, E. Shutov, G. Yukhtin and L. Lobov. ¶A Soviet production released on February 23, 1961, as *Povesti plamennikh let*. Whether a Mitchell Todd-AO camera was employed or if the Soviets only utilized the trade name is unclear. The Sovscope 70 system was identical to Todd-AO. This was later optically converted to Kinopanorama and nine-track magnetic stereophonic sound.

The Story of How Tsar Peter Married Off His Blackamoor (1976). Filmed in Sovscope 70. *Screen authors* Yuli Dunskiy, Valeri Frid and Aleksandr Mitta. *Director* Aleksandr Mitta. *Operator* Valery Shuvalov. *Artists* Igor Lemeshev and Georgi Koshelev. *Composer* Alfred

Shnitke. *Sound operator* Trakhtenberg. *Song text* R. Szf. ¶A Mosfilm production. International distribution Sovexportfilm. Sovcolor. Six-track magnetic stereophonic sound. 126 minutes. Filmed at Mosfilm Studios, Moscow, R.S.F.S.R. ¶CAST: *Ibrahim Hannibal* Vladimir Visotskiy. *Tsar Peter I* Alexei Peterenko. *Natasha* Irina Mazurkevich. *Filka* Valery Zolotukhin. *Procurator-General Yaguzkhinsky* Oleg Tabakov. *Gavrila Rtishchev* Ivan Rizov. *With* Mikhail Kokshenov, E. Mitta, S. Morozov, Mikhail Gluzskiy and Lyudmila Chursina. ¶A Soviet production released in Russia in 1976 as *Skaz pro to, kak tsari Petr arapa zenil.*

Strana moya (1968). Filmed in Sovscope 70. International distribution Sovexportfilm. Sovcolor. Six-track magnetic stereophonic sound. A Soviet production released in Russia in 1968.

Strategic Air Command (April 1955). Filmed and presented in VistaVision Motion Picture High Fidelity. *Producer* Samuel J. Briskin. *Director* Anthony Mann. *Screenplay* Valentine Davies and Beirne Lay, Jr. *Story* Beirne Lay, Jr. *Music score* Victor Young. *Director of photography* William H. Daniels. *Editor* Eda Warren. *Art direction* Hal Pereira and Earl Hedrick. *Set decoration* Sam Comer and Frank R. McKelvey. *Costumes* Edith Head. *Wardrobe supervision* Frank Richardson. *Makeup supervision* Wally Westmore. *Hair stylist* Nellie Manley. *Sound supervision* Loren L. Ryder. *Sound recording* Harry Lindgren, Gene Garvin and George Dutton. *Supervising sound editor* Tommy Middleton. *Technicolor color consultant* Richard Mueller. *Special photographic effects* John P. Fulton. *Optical photography* Paul K. Lerpae. *Process photography* Farciot Edouart. *Aerial supervision* Paul Mantz. *Aerial photography* Thomas Tutwiler. *Production manager* Frank Caffey. *Assistant director* John Coonan. *Technical adviser* Col. L.O.F. Lassiter, U.S.A.F. *"The Air Force Takes Command": music* Victor Young, *lyrics* Ned Washington and Major Tommy Thompson, Jr. *Negative* Eastman Kodak. ¶Produced and released by Paramount Pictures. Technicolor. Western Electric Movietone recording. Perspecta Stereophonic Sound. 114 minutes. Filmed at Paramount Studios and on location at U.S. SAC installations. ¶CAST: *Lt. Col. Robert "Dutch" Holland* James Stewart. *Sally Holland* June Allyson. *Gen. Ennis C. Hawkes* Frank Lovejoy. *Lt. Col. Rocky Samford* Barry Sullivan. *Capt. Ike Knowland* Alex Nicol. *Gen. Joe Espy* Bruce Bennett. *Tom Doyle* Jay C. Flippen. *Maj. Gen. Rusty Castle* James Millican. *Rev. Thorne* James Bell. *Mrs. Thorne* Rosemary De Camp. *Aircraft commander* Richard Shannon. *Capt. Symington* John R. McKee. *Sgt. Bible* Henry Morgan. *Major patrol commander* Don Haggerty. *Radio operator* Glenn Denning. *Colonel* Anthony Warde. *Air clerk offering cigars* Strother Martin. *Baby's nurse* Helen Brown. *Forecaster* William Hudson. *Capt. Brown* David Vaile. *Capt. Johnson* Vernon Rich. *Duty officer* Harlan Warde. *Air Force captain* Robert House Peters, Jr. *Controller lieutenant* Henry Richard Lupino. *Okinawa controller* William August Pullen. *Technical sergeant* Stephen E. Wyman. *Reporter* Max Power. ¶Dedicated to the Strategic Air Command and the young men of America. This was the first film released in VistaVision horizontal format according to Paramount. *White Christmas* was also shown horizontal but apparently limited to "experimental" engagements in Los Angeles.

Sud sumasshedshikh *see* **The Trial of Madmen.**

Sudiba *see* **Destiny.**

Suvenir (1977). Filmed in Sovscope 70. International distribution Sovexportfilm. Sovcolor. Six-track magnetic stereophonic sound. A Soviet production released in Russia in 1977.

Svadiba v Malinovke *see* **Wedding in Malinovke.**

Swan Lake (1968). Filmed in Sovscope 70. *Screen authors* I. Glikman, Apollinariy Dudko and Konstantin Sergeev. *Based on the ballet "Lebedinoe ozero" by* P.I. Chaykovskogo. *Directors* Apollinariy Dudko and Konstantin Sergeev. *Operator* Anatoly Nazarov. *Artists* V. Volin and B. Bikov. *Sound operator* V. Yakovlev. *Choreographers* L. Ivanova and Konstantin Sergeev *based on original choreography by* Marius Petipa. ¶A Lenfilm production. International distribution Sovexportfilm. Sovcolor. Six-track magnetic stereophonic sound. 103 minutes. Filmed at Lenfilm Studios, Leningrad, R.S.F.S.R. ¶CAST: *Odette/Odile* Elena Evteeva. *Sigfried* Dokhn Markovskiy. *Rothbart* Makhmud Zsambaev. *Jester* Valeri Panov. *Sigfried's mother* A. Kabarova. *Tutor* V. Ryazanov. *With* Artists of Kirov Opera and Ballet. ¶A Soviet production released in Russia in 1968 as *Lebedinoe ozero*.

Sweet Woman (1977). Filmed in Sovscope 70. *Screen author* Irina Velvmbovskaya. *Director* Vladimir Fettin. *Operators* Vladimir Kovzeli and Semyon Ivanov. *Artist* Vasily Zachinyaev. *Composer* Vassily Soloviev-Sedoy. *Sound operator* G. Korkhovoy. *Song text* G. Gorbovskogo. ¶A Lenfilm production. International distribution Sovexportfilm. Sovcolor. Six-track magnetic stereophonic sound. 98 minutes. Filmed at Lenfilm Studios, Leningrad, R.S.F.S.R. ¶CAST: *Anna Dobrokholova* Natalia Gundareva. *Tikhon Sokolov* Oleg Yankovskiy. *Nikolai* Pyotr Veliyaminov. *Larik Shubkin* Georgi Korolichuk. *With* S. Karpinskaya, Rimma Markova, N. Alisova and F. Nikitin. ¶A Soviet production released in Russia in 1977 as *Sladkaya zenshchina*.

Tabor ukhdit v nebo *see* **Queen of the Gypsies.**

Take-off (1980). Filmed in Sovscope 70. *Screen author* Oleg Osetinskiy. *Director* Savva Kulish. *Operator* Vladimir Klimov. *Artist* Vladimir Aronin. *Composer* Oleg Karavaychuk. *Sound operator* V. Mazurov. *Technical advisers* Prof. Arkady Ksomodemyansky and Aleksey Kostin. *Makeup* Mikhail Chikireva. *Assistant director* Galina Chikireva. *Costumier* Tatiana Vadetskaya. *Script consultant* Sergei Bondarchuk. ¶A Mosfilm production. International distribution Sovexportfilm. Sovcolor. Six-track magnetic stereophonic sound. 175 minutes plus intermission. Filmed at Mosfilm Studios, Moscow, R.S.F.S.R. ¶CAST: *Tsiolkovsky* Evgeny Evtushenko. *Tsiolkovsky's wife* Larissa Kadochnikova. *Panin* Albert Filozov. *Tsiolkovsky's daughter* Elena Finogeeva. *Tsiolkovsky's son* Kiriil Arduzov. *Tailor* Vadim Aleksandrov. *Landlord* Vladimir

Zrenberg. *Priest* Ion Unguryanu. *With* Georgi Burkov, V. Sedov, Olga Barnet and Sergei Nasibov. ¶A Soviet production released in Russia in 1980 as *Vzlet* in two parts running 86 minutes and 89 minutes.

The Tale of Old Whiff (January 8, 1960). Filmed in Todd-70. Presented in Smell-O-Vision. *Director* Alan Zaslove. *Story* John Hubley. *Sound recording supervisor* Fred Hynes. *Sound system* Todd-AO. *Osmologist* Prof. Hans Laube. *Osmological development* Scentovision, Inc. ¶A Michael Todd, Jr. presentation. Released by The Michael Todd Company, Inc. Technicolor. Magnetic Belock 8-Channel Sound. ¶VOICE CHARACTERIZATION: *Insp. Dribble* Bert Lahr. ¶This cartoon was shown with *Scent of Mystery* and utilized fifteen smells. It is the only cartoon to our knowledge issued with an aroma effect but it was not the first 70mm animation film as claimed by some.

The Tale of Tzar Saltan (1967). Filmed in Sovscope 70. *Screen author and director* Aleksandr Ptushko. *Based on the story "Skazka o tsare Saltane" by* Aleksandr S. Pushkina. *Operators* Igor Geleyn and Valentin Zakharov. *Artists* Anatoly Kuznetsov and Konstantin Khodataev. *Composer* Gavriil Popov. *Sound operator* Maria Blyakhina. ¶A Mosfilm production. International distribution Sovexportfilm. Six-track magnetic stereophonic sound. 108 minutes. Filmed at Mosfilm Studios, Moscow, R.S.F.S.R. ¶CAST: *Tsar Saltan* Vladimir Andreev. *Tsaritsa* Larisa Golubkina. *Guidon* Oleg Vidov. *Gossip* Olga Vikland. *Weaver* Vera Ivleva. *Cook* Nina Velyaeva. *Official* Viktor Kolpakov. *Chamberlain* Yuri Chekulaev. *With* K. Ryabinkina, S. Martinson, V. Nosik, G. Shpigeli and E. Maykhrovskiy. ¶A Soviet production released in Russia in 1967 as *Skazka o tsare Saltane*.

Taming of the Flame (1972). Filmed in Sovscope 70. *Screen author and director* Daniil Khrabrovitskiy. *Operator* Sergei Vronskiy. *Artist* Yu. Kladchenko. *Composer* Andrei Petrov. *Sound operators* Yu. Rabinovich and R. Berz. ¶A Mosfilm production. International distribution Sovexportfilm. Sovcolor. Six-track magnetic stereophonic sound. 166 minutes. Filmed at Mosfilm Studios, Moscow, R.S.F.S.R. ¶CAST: *Bashkirtsev* Kiriil

Lavrov. *Natasha* Ada Rogovtseva. *Lorgunov* Andrei Popov. *Ognev* Igor Gorbachev. *Golovin* Igor Vladimirov. *Tsiolkovski* Innokenti Smoktunovskiy. *With* Z. Gerdt, S. Korkoshko, I. Petrovskiy and P. Shelokhonov. ¶A Soviet production released in Russia in 1972 as *Ukroshchenie ognya.*

The Taste of Bread (1979). Filmed in Sovscope 70. *Screen authors* Aleksandr Lapshin, Alexei Sakharov, Rudolf Tyurin and Valentina Chernikh. *Director* Alexei Sakharov. *Operator* Dilshat Fatkhulin. *Artist* Aleksandr Tolkachev. *Composer* Yuri Levitin. *Sound operators* Yu. Mikhaylov and V. Shchedrina. ¶A Mosfilm–Kazakfilm production. International distribution Sovexportfilm. Sovcolor. Six-track magnetic stereophonic sound. Part one: 191 minutes plus intermission; Part two: 192 minutes plus intermission. Filmed at Mosfilm Studios, Moscow, R.S.F.S.R. and on location in Alma-Ata, Kazakh S.S.R. ¶CAST: *Stepan Sechkin* Sergei Shakurov. *With* Valery Rizakov, Ernest Romanov, Nikolai Eremenko, Idris Nogaybaev, Natalia Arinbasarova, Anatoly Azo, Asanaly Ashimov, Nurzkhuman Ihtimbaev, Evgeny Burenkov, Leonid Diachkov, Lubov Polekhina and Ivan Ageyev. ¶A Soviet production released in Russia in 1979 as *Vkus khleba* in two parts: 1) *Khleb nash nasushchniy* and *Khleb i zemlya;* and 2) *Khleb i lyudi* and *Khleb Otechestva.*

Taste of Immortality (1983). Filmed in Sovscope 70. *Screen author and director* Alexei Saltikov. *Based on the stories "Ubiti pod Moskvoy" and "Krik" by* Konstantin Vorobieva. *Operators* Aleksandr Garibyan and A. Mass. *Artist* Vladimir Pasternak. *Composer* Andrei Eshpay. *Sound operator* A. Neyman. ¶A kinostudiya im. M. Gorikogo production. International distribution Sovexportfilm. Sovcolor. Six-track magnetic stereophonic sound. 76 minutes. Filmed at kinostudiya im. M. Gorikogo, Gorki, R.S.F.S.R. ¶CAST: Andrei Aleshin, Dmitri Matveev, Aleksandr Kazakov, Darya Mikhaylova, Boris Shcherbakov, O. Shtefanko, L. Zolotukhin and A. Novikov. ¶A Soviet production released in Russia in 1983 as *Zkzamen na bessmertie.*

A Tavern on Pyatnitskaya Street (1978). Filmed in Sovscope 70. *Screen author*

Nikolay Leonov. *Director* Aleksandr Fayntsimmer. *Operators* Sergey Vronskiy and Vsevold Simakov. *Artist* Vadim Kislikh. *Composer* Andrei Eshpay. *Sound operator* M. Bronshteyn. ¶A Mosfilm production. International distribution Sovexportfilm. Sovcolor. Six-track magnetic stereophonic sound. 90 minutes. Filmed at Mosfilm Studios, Moscow, R.S.F.S.R. ¶CAST: *Klimov* Gennadi Korolikov. *Seriy (Gray)* Konstantin Grigoriev. *Panin* Viktor Perevalov. *Pashka* Aleksandr Golibin. *Lavro* Lev Prigun. *With* Tamara Semina, Gleb Strizenov, Nikolai Eremehko-mladshiy, Malina Dyuzeva, L. Eremina, G. Strizenov, Yuri Nazarov, Igor Vasiliev, Yu. Volkov, A. Panikin, V. Druznikov, V. Prikhodiko, Yu. Potemkin and V. Kosikh. ¶A Soviet production released in Russia in 1978 as *Traktir na Pyatnitskoy.*

Tayfun *see* **The Battle of Moscow.**

Tayna "Chernikh drozdov" (1984). Filmed in Sovscope 70. *Screen authors* V. Kolodyaznaya and E. Smirnova. *Based on the novel "Karman, polniy rzi" by* A. Kristi. *Director* V. Derbenev. *Operator* N. Nemolyaev. *Artist* D. Vinitskiy. *Composer* V. Babushkin. *Sound operator* R. Sobinov. ¶A Mosfilm production. International distribution Sovexportfilm. Sovcolor. Six-track magnetic stereophonic sound. 97 minutes. Filmed at Mosfilm Studios, Moscow, R.S.F.S.R. ¶CAST: I. Zver, V. Sedov, V. Sanaev, L. Polishuk, Yu. Belyaev, E. Sanaeva, A. Kharitonov, N. Danilova, E. Ivochkina, Z. Radzinya, A. Pyatkov, A. Chernova, I. Mazurkevich, B. Novikov, T. Nosova, V. Zelidin and S. Nemolyaeva. ¶A Soviet production released in Russia in 1984.

Tayni Svyatogo Yura *see* **The Secret of St. Jur.**

Tchaikovsky (January 1972). Filmed in Sovscope 70. *Screen authors* Budimir Metalinikov, Yuri Nagibin and Igor Talankin. *Producer and music arranger, composer and conductor* Dimitri Tiomkin. *Director* Igor Talankin. *Operator* Margarita Pilikhina. *Music* P.I. Chaykovskiy. *Performers* Bolshoi Orchestra and Leningrad Philharmonic. *Artists* A. Borisov and Yu. Rabinovich and V. Shmelikin. ¶A Dimitri Tiomkin presentation. A Mosfilm production. International distribution Sovexportfilm. Released by Artkino Pictures. Sovcolor. Six-track magnetic stereophonic sound. 150 minutes plus intermission. Filmed at Mosfilm Studios, Moscow, R.S.F.S.R. ¶CAST: *P.I. Chaykovskiy* Innokenti Smoktunovskiy. *With* Vladimir Strzelchik, E. Leonov, Antonina Shuranova, Maya Plisetskaya, Sergei Gerasimov, Alla Demidova, Evgeni Evstigneev, L. Yudina, K. Lavrov and B. Freyndlikh. *Narrator* Laurence Harvey. ¶A Soviet production released in Russia in 1970 as *Chaykovskiy* in two parts running 96 minutes and 100 minutes. There is much confusion regarding this project. The Russians claim it was solely their production with prior U.S. distribution agreement with Warner Bros., and that Dimitri Tiomkin was the American representative during shooting. But indications are that Warners had at least some production money involved. In any event that company was not involved in the U.S. release in any way, and trade paper reports state they withdrew from the project completely, either getting their money back or taking the loss if they did indeed have funds tied into the project. Tiomkin may have tried to distribute the film himself in December 1971, but Artkino, the Soviet-owned, U.S.-based distributor, was handling bookings in January 1972. Most Russian material ignored Tiomkin, and he was not included in the credits supplied by Sovexportfilm, but at least one piece of Artkino press material listed him as director! Artkino also listed the title of the film as *Tschaikovsky*. Since the British-made *The Music Lovers* (also available in 70mm), covering the same story material, was released about the same time, *Tchaikovsky* went nowhere in the U.S.

Techet Volga *see* **The Volga Flows On.**

Tegeran-43 *see* **Teheran, 43.**

Teheran, 43 (1981). Filmed in Sovscope 70. *Screen authors* Aleksandr Alov, Vladimir Naumov and Mikhail Shatrov. *Directors* Aleksandr Alov and Vladimir Naumov. *Operator* Valentin Zeleznyakov. *Artists* Evgeny Chernyaev and Vladimir Kirs. *Composers* George Garvarents and Moisei Vainberg. *Sound operator* P. Kazaryan. *Song text and performer*

Charles Aznavour. ¶A Mosfilm-Pro Dis Film A.G.-Mediteranne Cinema production. An Aleksandr Alov-Vladimir Naumov film. International distribution Sovexportfilm. Sovcolor. Six-track magnetic stereophonic sound. 190 minutes plus intermission. Filmed at Mosfilm Studios, Moscow, R.S.F.S.R. and on location in the Middle East. ¶CAST: *Interpol Insp. Foche* Alain Delon. *Maria and Natalie Luny* Natalia Belokhvostikova. *Andre (Andrei Borodin)* Igor Kostolevskiy. *Max Richard* Armen Dzigarkhanyan. *Scherner ("Hangman")* Albert Filozov. *Roger Legrain* Curt [Curd] Jurgens. *Denis Pevl* Georges Geret. *Gerard Simon* Gleb Strizenov. *With* Fosh, Nikolai Griniko, B. Puladze, Claude Jade and V. Sanaev. ¶A Soviet, Swiss and French coproduction released in Russia in 1981 as *Tegeran-43* in two parts running 96 minutes and 94 minutes. The international version was in Dolby Stereo. Despite the year of production and the title this has nothing to do with the Americans held captive by the outlaw government of Iran from 1979 to 1981. The story is set in 1943.

Ten Days That Shook the World *see* **Red Bells.**

Le tenda rosse *see* **The Red Tent.**

Then Came Bumbo (1985). Filmed in Sovscope 70. *Screen authors* Yu. Dunskiy and V. Frid. *Based on the story "I vot prishel Bumbo ..." by* A. Kuprina. *Director* Nadezkhda Kosheverova. *Operator* Z. Rozovskiy. *Artist* M. Azizyan. *Composer* M. Vaynberg. *Sound operators* B. Livshits and S. Shumyauer. ¶A Lenfilm production. International distribution Sovexportfilm. Sovcolor. Six-track magnetic stereophonic sound. 78 minutes. Filmed at Lenfilm Studios, Leningrad, R.S.F.S.R. ¶CAST: O. Basilashvili, V. Zolotukhin, T. Pelittser, S. Nemolyaeva, Z. Gerdt, A. Pankratov, Cherniy, N. Shinakova, S. Filippov, S. Parshin, G. Shtilv and S. Karpinskaya. ¶A Soviet production released in Russia in 1985 as *I vot prishel Bumbo....*

They Fought for Their Motherland (1975). Filmed in Sovscope 70. *Screen authors* Mikhail A. Sholokhova and Sergey Bondarchuk. *Based on the novel "Oni srazalisi za rodiny" by* Mikhail A. Sholokhova.

Director Sergey Bondarchuk. *Operator* Vadim Yusov. *Artist* Felix Yasyukeviy. *Composer* Viacheslav Ovchinnikov. *Sound operator* F. Mikhaylov. ¶A Mosfilm production. International distribution Sovexportfilm. Sovcolor. Six-track magnetic stereophonic sound. 201 minutes plus intermission. Filmed at Mosfilm Studios, Moscow, R.S.F.S.R. ¶CAST: *Lopakhin* Vasily Shukshin. *Zviagintsev* Sergey Bondarchuk. *Streltson* Viacheslav Tikhonov. *Nekrassov* Yuri Nikulin. *Poprischenko* Ivan Lapikov. *Sasha Kopitovsky* Georgi Burkov. *Akim Borzikn* Alexey Vanin. *Natalia Stepanovna* Nonna Mordyukova. *Piotr Lisichenko* Evgeny N. Shutiko. *With* Lidia Fedoseeva, Irina Skobtseva, N. Gubenko, A. Rostotskiy, N. Volkov, E. Samoylov, I. Smoktunovskiy, A. Stepanova, T. Bozok, D. Ilichenko, A. Vanin, G. Safronov and A. Pereverzev. ¶A Soviet production released in Russia in 1975 as *Oni srazalisi za rodiny* in two parts, 104 and 97 minutes.

They Live Close By (1968). Filmed in Sovscope 70. *Screen author* Vera Ketlinskaya. *Director* Georgi Roshali. *Operators* L. Kosmatov and A. Simonov. *Artists* I. Plastinkin and M. Karyakin. *Composer* Dokhn Ter-Tatevosyan. *Sound operator* L. Trakhtenberg. ¶A Mosfilm production. International distribution Sovexportfilm. Sovcolor. Six-track magnetic stereophonic sound. 132 minutes. Filmed at Mosfilm Studios, Moscow, R.S.F.S.R. ¶CAST: *Prof. Kalitin* Fyodor Nikitin. *Nadyezhda Pavlovna* Rufina Nifontova. *Igor Kalitin* Igor Kvasha. *Tata* Tamara Semina. *Vasin* Aleksandr Borisov. *Danilov* Evgeni Evstigneev. *Semyon Efimovich* Vladimir Kenigson. *Korablyov* Pyotr Glebov. *Luzgin* Vsevolod Shestakov. *Tolya* Igor Pushkarev. *Inga* Viktoria Fedorova. *Lotoshnikov* Rogvold Sukhoverko. ¶A Soviet production released in Russia in 1968 as *Oni zivut ryadom*.

13-y film Leonida Gaydaya (1978). Filmed in Sovscope 70. International distribution Sovexportfilm. Sovcolor. Six-track magnetic stereophonic sound. A Soviet production released in Russia in 1978.

34-y skoriy *see* **Express on Fire.**

This Is Cinerama (September 30, 1952). Filmed in Cinerama. *Executive producers* Lowell Thomas, Michael Todd and Louis B. Mayer. *Producers* Merian C. Cooper and Robert L. Bendick. *European sequences and rollercoaster sequence supervisors* Michael Todd and Michael Todd, Jr. *Prolog supervisor* Walter Thompson. *America the Beautiful supervisor* Fred Rickey. *Pilot* Paul Mantz. *Additional sequences supervisors* Merian C. Cooper and Michael Todd. *Production executive* Louis B. Mayer. *Associate producer* Michael Todd. *Musical director* Louis Forbes. *Cameraman* Harry Squire. *Assistant cameraman* Jack Priestley. *Camera technician* Coleman Thomas Conroy, Jr. *Grip* Marty Philbin. *Sound* Richard J. Pietschmann, Jr. *Sound assistant* Fred Bosch. *Film editor* Bill Henry. *Paintings* Mario Larrinaga and Willis H. O'Brien. *Sound effects* Reeves Sound Studios. *Music* Cinerama Philharmonic Orchestra, Salt Lake City Tabernacle Choir, Vienna Philharmonic, Vienna Boys Choir and Long Island Choral Society. *Business manager* Frank Smith. *Cinerama research and development* Fred Waller, Hazard E. Reeves, Walter Hicks, Wentworth Fling, Karl Vogel, Dr. Ernest Hare, Fred Koppler, Michael Chitty, Ernest Franck, Norman Prisament, Otto Popelka, Emil Neroda, Richard Vorisek, Ed Schmidt, Richard J. Pietschmann, Jr., C. Robert Fine, Larry Davee, Lyman Wiggins, S.J. (Joe) Begun and Col. Richard Ranger. *Cinerama Sound* Reeves Soundcraft Corporation. *Projectors* Century Projection Corporation. *Advertising* Peter Schaeffer and McCann-Erickson. *Publicist* Lynn Farnol. "American the Beautiful" music and lyrics Katharine Lee Bates and Samuel A. Ward. *Film* Eastman Kodak Company. ¶A Lowell Thomas-Merian C. Cooper presentation. A Lowell Thomas Company production. Released by Cinerama Productions Corporation. Technicolor. Six-track magnetic Cinerama Sound. 120 minutes plus intermission. Filmed in New York City and Niagara Falls, New York, Cypress Gardens, Florida and across the United States and in Scotland, Austria (Salzberg), Spain and Italy (Venice and La Scala Opera, Milan). ¶CAST: *Host and narrator* Lowell Thomas. ¶Portions later incorporated into *The Best of Cinerama*. Rereleased in 1971 by Cinerama Releasing Corporation and Film Effects of Hollywood who did the optical conversion to 70mm Super Cinerama. The preprint material had deteriorated considerably and there was much miscoloring between panels as well as some misalignment. It should be noted that there never was an actual title on release prints, and advertising for the first two years of release referred to the film simply as *Cinerama*. However it was copyrighted under the above title, is generally known as such and was advertised under the above when reissued in the late fifties.

The Thorny Way to the Stars *see* **To the Stars by Hard Ways.**

Those Magnificent Men in Their Flying Machines or How I Flew from London to Paris in 25 Hours and 11 Minutes (June 16, 1965). Filmed in Todd-AO. *Executive producer* Darryl F. Zanuck. *Associate executive producer* Elmo Williams. *Producer* Stan Margulies. *Associate producer* Jack Davies. *Director* Ken Annakin. *Writers* Jack Davies and Ken Annakin. *Music composer and conductor* Ron Goodwin. *Production designer* Tom Morahan. *Director of photography* Christopher Challis. *Costume designer* Osbert Lancaster. *Second unit director* Don Sharp. *Film editor* Gordon Stone. *Sound* John Mitchell and Gordon K. McCallum. *Unit managers* Colin Brewer and Pat Clayton. *Assistant director* Clive Reed. *Set dresser* Arthur Taksen. *Special effects* Richard Parker and Ron Ballanger. *Makeup* William T. Partleton and Stuart Freeborn. *Hairdressers* Barbara Ritchie and Biddy Chrystal. *Title designer* Ronald Searle. *Animation* Ralph Axness. *Title execution* National Screen Service Ltd. *Technical adviser* Air Com. Allen H. Wheeler. *Production supervisor* Denis Holt. *Casting director* Stuart Lyons. *Camera operator* Dudley Lovell. *Dubbing editor* Jonathan Bates *Second unit cameraman* Skeets Kelly. *Second unit assistant director* Jake Wright. *Associate art director* Jim Morahan. *Associate costume designer* Dinah Greet. *Continuity* Joy Mercer. *Blue screen technician* Dennis Bartlett. *Unit publicist* Howard Liebling. *Antique aircraft* Shillaleagh Productions. *Aircraft coordinators* Burch Williams and Cedric Francis. *Aircraft builders* Peter Hillwood and Douglas Bianchi. ¶A Stan Margulies-Ken Annakin production. A 20th Century–Fox Productions Ltd. picture. Released by 20th Century–Fox. Color by De Luxe. RCA six-track magnetic stereophonic sound. 132 minutes plus intermission. Filmed at Pinewood Studios, London and on location in Dover, Booker Air Field and Buckinghamshire, England. ¶CAST: *Orvil Newton* Stuart Whitman. *Patricia Rawnsley* Sarah Miles. *Richard Mays* James Fox. *Count Emilio Ponticelli* Alberto Sordi. *Lord Rawnsley* Robert Morley. *Col. Manfred von Holstein* Gert Frobe [Froebe]. *Pierre Dubois* Jean-Pierre Cassel. *Brigitte, Ingrid, Marlene, Francoise, Claudia, Yvette and Betty* Irina Demick. *Courtney* Eric Sykes. *Sir Percy Ware-Armitage* Terry-Thomas. *Man Through the Ages* Red Skelton. *Fire Chief Perkins* Benny Hill. *Yamamoto* Yujiro Ishihara. *Mother Superior* Flora Robson. *Capt. Rumpelstrosse* Karl Michael Vogler. *George Gruber* Sam Wanamaker. *French postman* Eric Barker. *Col. Willie* Fred Emery. *McDougal* Gordon Jackson. *Jean* Davy Kaye. *French painter* John Le Mesurier. *Lt. Parsons* Jeremy Lloyd. *Sophia Ponticelli* Zena Marshall. *British airline hostess* Millicent Martin. *Italian mayor* Eric Pohlman. *Old Mill Cafe waitress* Marjorie Rhodes. *Assistant fire chief* Norman Rossington. *Tremayne Gascoyne* William Rushton. *Third fireman* Graham Stark. *Old Mill Cafe photographer* Jimmy Thompson. *Niven* Michael Trubshawe. *Harry Popperwell* Tony Hancock. *Second fireman* Gerald Campion. *Trawler skipper* Maurice Denham. *British postman* Robin Chapman. *R.A.C. officer* Ronnie Stevens. *Continental journalist* Steve Plytas. *French official* Fredy Mayne. *American journalist* Bill Nagy. *Muriel* Cicely Courtneidge. *Spectator* Arthur Collins. *Patricia's dog* Addo Miles. *Dog in aeroplane* Baxter Annakin. *Stunts* Joan Hughes and Ken Buckle. *Narrator* James Robertson-Justice. ¶A British production released in England on June 3, 1965, with a BBFC U certificate. 35mm general release and 16mm nontheatrical prints ran 132 minutes without an intermission. Advertised in CinemaScope and Todd-AO/CinemaScope *(sic!)* in 35mm. A sequel of sorts was *Those Daring Young Men in Their Jaunty Jalopies* (or *Monte Carlo or Bust*) (Paramount, 1969).

Those Were the Happy Times *see* **Star!**

The Three Fat Men (1967). Filmed in Sovscope 70. *Screen authors* Alexey Batalov and Mikhail Olishevskiy. *Based on the* *story "Tri tolstyaka" by* Yun Oleshi. *Directors* Alexey Batalov and Iosif Shapiro. *Operator* Suren Shakhbazyan. *Artists* Boris Manevich and Isofi Kaplan. *Composer* Nikolay Sidelinikov. *Sound operator* Boris Antonov.* ¶A Lenfilm production. International distribution Sovexportfilm. Sovcolor. Six-track magnetic stereophonic sound. 114 minutes. Filmed at Lenfilm Studios, Leningrad, R.S.F.S.R. ¶CAST: *Suok* Lina Braknite. *Tutli* Petya A. Artemiev. *Tubil* Alexey Batalov. *Gaspar* Valentin Nikulin. *August* Aleksandr Orlov. *Ganimed* Rina Zelenaya. *Three fat men* Sergei Kulagin, Evgeni Morgunov and Boris Khristoforov. *With* R. Filippov, P. Luspekaev, N. Karnaukhov, N. Valiyano, B. Ardov and V. Sergachev. ¶A Soviet production released in Russia in 1967 as *Tri tolstyaka.*

The Thrill of Todd-AO (October 11, 1955). Filmed in Todd-AO. *Producer and director* Michael Todd. *Director of photography* Robert L. Surtees. *Sound recording supervisor* Fred Hynes. *Film editor* Gene Ruggiero. *Negative* Eastman Color. *Sound system* Todd-AO. *Todd-AO developers* American Optical Company and Magna Theatre Corporation. ¶A Michael Todd Company, Inc. production. Released by Magna Theatre Corporation. Color by Consolidated Film Industries. Westrex six-track magnetic Orthosonic Sound. This short was released with *Oklahoma!* and demonstrated the qualities of the Todd-AO system.

Thrillarama Adventure (August 9, 1956). Filmed in Thrillarama. *Producers and directors* Albert H. Reynolds and Dowlen Russell. *Technical production and photography* Raphael G. Wolff Studios, Inc. ¶Produced by Thrillarama Productions. Released by Thrillarama, Inc. Eastman Color. Four-track magnetic stereophonic sound. 96 minutes plus intermission. Filmed on location in Texas and Weeki Wachee Springs, Florida. It is unclear which sound system was used. It may have been interlocked or sound-on-film.

Tiger Child (Summer 1970). Filmed in IMAX. *Producers* Roman Kroitor and Kiichi Ichikawa. *Writer and director* Donald Brittan. *Director of photography* Georges Dufaux. *Director of film sound* Edward T. Haley. *Music composer* Toshiro Mayuzumi. *Business manager* Paul Salzman. *Camera engineers* Jan Jacobson and Pierre Abelos. ¶A Multiscreen Corporation, Ltd. production for Fuji Group. Metrocolor. Six-track magnetic stereophonic sound. The first IMAX film originally shown in the Fuji Group Pavilion at Expo '70.

To Fly (1976). Filmed in IMAX. *Executive producer* Byron McKinney. *Producers, directors and photographers* Greg MacGillivray and Jim Freeman. *Writer* Francis Thompson. *Narration writer* Tom McGrath. *Music* Bernardo Segall. *Associate producer, production manager, costumer and special effects supervisor* Jeff Blyth. *First assistant cameraman* Philip Schwartz. *Aerial camera mounts* Tyler Camera Systems. *Tyler Camera Systems technician* Larry Barton. *First production assistant* Barbara Smith. *Second camera assistant and production assistant* Cindy Huston. *Grip* Rae Troutman. *Gaffer* Pat Gilluly. *Assistant grip* Brad Ohlund. *Pilot* Frank Tallman. *Helicopter pilots* George Nolan, Chuck Phillips and Adrian Brooks. *Unit secretary and accountant* Elizabeth Howell. *Laser special effects* Jim Palmer. *Optical supervisors* Jim Liles at MGM and Dennis E. Moore. *Editing supervisor* Alexander Hammid. *Rerecording* The Burbank Studios. *Music mixer* Danny Wallin. *Music editor* Richard McCurdy. *Sound effects editor* Sam Shaw. *Special assistant for space sequence* Dennis Root. *Music mix adviser* Paul Martin. *Storyboard developer* John Divers. *Sound mixers* Ray West and Jack Woltz. *Smithsonian Institution representatives* Mike Collins, Mel Zisfein, Von del Chamberlain and Gene Knight. *Conoco representatives* Rud Lawrence and Tony Sheldon-Moir. ¶A Francis Thompson, Inc. production. Sponsored by the Smithsonian Institution and Conoco, Inc., a DuPont company. Released by Lawrence Associates, New York City. Eastman Color. Six-track magnetic stereophonic sound. 27 minutes. Filmed throughout the U.S. ¶CAST: Peter Walker. ¶Originally made for the National Air and Space Museum in Washington, D.C. Sequel was *Flyers* (q.v.).

To the Moon and Beyond (1974). Filmed in Dynavision. Presented in Cinerama 360. *Writer, producer and director* Les Novros. *Based on writings by* Loren Eisley. *Optical printing* Film Effects of

Hollywood. ¶A Graphic Films Corporation production. Eastman Color. Six-track magnetic stereophonic sound. 33 minutes. Originally made for San Diego's Reuben H. Fleet Space Theater. Optically converted from double frame 70mm Dynavision format to OMNIMAX and re-released in that system as *Cosmos.*

To the Stars by Hard Ways (November 1982). Filmed in Sovscope 70. *Screen authors* Kir Bulichev and Richard Viktorov. *Director* Richard Viktorov. *Operator* Aleksandr Ribin. *Artist* Konstantini Zagorskiy. *Composer* Alexei Ribnikov. *Sound operator* Koreshov. ¶A kinostudiya im. M. Gorikogo production. Released by International Film Exchange by arrangement with Sovexportfilm. Sovcolor. 148 minutes plus intermission. Filmed at kinostudiya im. M. Gorikogo, Gorki, R.S.F.S.R. ¶CAST: *Niya* Elena Metelkina. *Stepan* Vadim Ledogorov. *With* Nadezkhda Sementsova, Aleksandr Lazarev, Aleksandr Mikhaylov, Uldis Lieldidz, Vatslav Dvorzetskiy, Elena Fadeeva, Boris Shcherbakov, Igor Ledogorou, Gleb Strizenov, Igor Yasulovich, Vladimir Fedorov, Nikolai Timofeyev, Evgeny Karelskikh, Lyudmila Nilskaya, Svetlana Radchenko and Valeri Nosik. ¶A Soviet production released in Russia in 1981 as *Cherz ternii k zvezdam* in 70mm and six-track magnetic stereophonic sound in two parts: *Niyya—iskusstvenniy chelobek (Niya: Artifical Person)* running 101 minutes and *Angeli kosmosa (Space Angels)* running 87 minutes. Working title was *Per aspera ad astra.* Originally announced for international distribution as *Trough Harsh to the Stars.* One source says the actual title on the U.S. version was *The Thorny Way to the Stars.* Sources disagree on whether this was shown in the U.S. in 70mm or 35mm only.

Toliko ti *see* **Only You.**

Tommy (March 1975). Recorded in Dolby Stereo and Quintophonic Sound. *Executive producers* Beryl Vertue and Christopher Stamp. *Producers* Robert Stigwood and Ken Russell. *Director and screenplay* Ken Russell. *Based on the rock opera by* The Who. *Associate producer* Harry Benn. *Directors of photography* Dick Bush and Ronnie Taylor. *Art director* John Clark. *Sets designer* Paul Dufficey. *Film editor* Stuart Baird. *Pro-*

duction manager John Comfort. *Costume designer* Shirley Russell. *Music director, music synthesizer programmer and songs* "Underture," "Captain Walker Didn't Come Home," "It's a Boy," "'51 Is Going to be a Good Year," "What About the Boy?," "The Amazing Journey," "Christmas," "The Acid Queen," "Do You Think It's All Right?," "Sparks," "Pinball Wizard," "Today It Rained Champagne," "There's a Doctor," "Go to the Mirror (The Specialist)," "Tommy, Can You Hear Me?," "Smash the Mirror," "I'm Free," "Miracle Cure," "Extra, Extra," "Sensation," "Sally Simpson," "Welcome," "Deceived," "We're Not Gonna Take It," "See Me, Feel Me" and "Listening to You" Pete Townshend. *Songs* "Eyesight of the Blind" Sonny Boy Williams; "Fiddle About" and "Cousin Kevin" John Entwistle; *and* "Tommy's Holiday Camp" Keith Moon. *Music editor* Terry Rawlings. *Music recordist* Ron Nevison at Rampart Studios. *Camera operator* Eddie Collins. *Assistant director* Jonathan Benson. *Continuity* Kay Mander. *Sound recordist* Ian Bruce. *Dubbing mixer* Bill Rowe at EMI-MGM Studios. *Rerecording* Todd-AO. *Wardrobe supervisor* Richard Pointing. *Chief makeup artists* George Blackler and Peter Robb-King. *Chief hairdresser* Joyce James. *Location managers* Lee Bolon and Ricky Green. *Choreographer* Gillian Gregory. *Set dresser* Ian Whittaker. *Special effects* Effects Associates, Nobby Clarke, Colin Chivers and Camera Effects, Ltd. *Special material photographer* Robin Lehman. *Unit publicist* Brian Doyle. *Still photography* Graham Attwood. *Lighting contractors* Lee Electrics (Lighting), Ltd. *Second assistant director* Gary White. *Quintophonic Sound developers* John Mosley and Quinta Enterprises, Inc. *Music producer* Kit Lambert. *Theater organist* Gerald Shaw. *Organ arranger* Martyn Ford. *Prop buyer* Bryn Siddall. *Propmaster* Harry Newman. *Propmen* Ron Lewis and Andy Andrews. *Assistant art director* Terry Ackland-Snow. *Flyers* Ken Messenger and Dave Raymond. *Construction manager* Jack Carter. *Sculptor* Christopher Hobbs. *Focus puller* Malcolm Vinson. *Gaffer* Bob Bremner. *Cooperation* Birdman Sports Promotions, Ltd., Bill Churbishley, The Bluebell Railway Preservation Society, The National Trust-Lakes District and

City of Portsmouth. *Negative* Eastman Color. ¶A Robert Stigwood presentation. A Robert Stigwood Organisation, Ltd. production. A film by Ken Russell. Released by Columbia Pictures. Color by Rank Film Laboratories, Ltd. Prints in Metrocolor. 110 minutes. Filmed at Lee International Studios and on location in England. MPAA rating: PG. ¶CAST: *Nora Walker Hobbs* Ann-Margret. *Frank Hobbs* Oliver Reed. *Tommy Walker* Roger Daltrey. *Pinball Wizard* Elton John. *Preacher* Eric Clapton. *Uncle Ernie* Keith Moon. *Specialist* Jack Nicholson. *Group Capt. Walker* Robert Powell. *Cousin Kevin* Paul Nicholas. *Acid Queen* Tina Turner. *Young Tommy* Barry Winch. *Priest* Arthur Brown. *Sally Simpson* Victoria Russell. *Rev. Simpson* Ben Aris. *Mrs. Simpson* Mary Holland. *First nurse* Jennifer Baker. *Second nurse* Susan Baker. *Acid Queen's handmaidens* Juliet King and Gillian King. *Third nurse* Imogen Claire. *Themselves* The Who [Pete Townshend, Roger Daltrey, John Entwistle and Keith Moon]. *Rock musician* Gary Rich. *Black Angels president* Dick Allen. *Bovver boy* Eddie Stacey. *Musicians* Elton John, Eric Clapton, Keith Moon, John Entwistle, Ronnie Wood, Kenny Jones, Nicky Hopkins, Chris Stainton, Fuzzy Samuels, Caleb Quaye, Mick Ralphs, Graham Deakin, Phil Chen, Alan Ross, Richard Bailey, Dave Clinton, Tony Newman, Mike Kelly, Dee Murray, Nigel Olsson, Ray Cooper, Davey Johnstone, Geoff Daley, Bob Efford, Ronnie Ross and Howie Casey. *Vocal chorus* Liza Strike, Simon Townshend, Mylon Le Fevre, Billy Nichols, Jeff Roden, Margo Newman, Gillian McIntosh, Vicki Brown, Kit Trevor, Helen Shappell, Paul Gurvitz and Alison Dowling. *Narrator* Pete Townshend. ¶A British production released in England in 1974 running 108 minutes. This film has been released in more sound formats than any other feature: 70mm with six-track magnetic stereo, 35mm with Quintophonic (Mag-Optical five track), 35mm with four-track MagOptical stereo, 35mm with Dolby Stereo two-track optical and 35mm with standard optical mono. While Quintophonic Sound had no effect on the industry as itself it did lead to the installation of Dolby noise reduction and decoding units in theaters and thus opened up the market for Dolby Stereo that would

have otherwise remained closed, at least until *Star Wars* and *Close Encounters of the Third Kind* in 1977.

Tomorrow in Space (1982). Filmed in OMNIMAX. *Writer, producer and director* Les Novros. ¶A Graphic Films Corporation production. Released by San Diego Hall of Science. Eastman Color. Six-track magnetic stereophonic sound. 33 minutes. Originally made for San Diego's Reuben H. Fleet Space Theater.

Tour of the Universe (May 1986). Filmed in Showscan. Presented in Dynamic Motion. Produced and released by Showscan Film Corporation. Eastman Color. Six-track magnetic Dolby Stereo. 9 minutes. Originally made for the CN Tower in Toronto, Canada. This was shown with a simulator of a space shuttle flight to give the audience the impression of participating in the filmed action.

Tovarishch Sibiri (1975). Filmed in Sovscope 70. International distribution Sovexportfilm. Sovcolor. Six-track magnetic stereophonic sound. A Soviet production released in Russia in 1975.

Traktir na Pyatnitskoy *see* **A Tavern on Pyatnitskaya Street.**

Transitions (May 2, 1986). Filmed in IMAX 3D. *Directors* Colin Low and Tony Ianzelo. *Based on a storyboard by* Colin Low. *Director of photography and stereoscopy* Ernest McNabb. *IMAX 3D development* National Film Board of Canada and Imax Systems Corporation. ¶Produced for CN and released by National Film Board of Canada. Eastman Color. Six-track magnetic stereophonic sound. 21 minutes. A Canadian production originally made for the Canadian Pavilion at Vancouver's EXPO 86. The first, and so far only, IMAX film in full color polarized, dual projection 3D.

Trevoznoe voskresenie *see* **Fateful Sunday.**

Tri tolstyaka *see* **The Three Fat Men.**

The Trial of Madmen (1962). Filmed in Sovscope 70. *Screen author and director* G. Roshali. *Chief operator* L. Kosmatov. *Chief artist* I. Shpineli. *Composer* M. Vaynberg. *Sound operator* L. Trakhtenberg. ¶A Mosfilm production. International distribution Sovexportfilm. Sovcolor. Six-track magnetic stereophonic sound. 122 minutes. Filmed at Mosfilm Studios, Moscow, R.S.F.S.R. ¶CAST: V. Livanov, I. Skobtseva, V. Khokhryakov, V. Belokurov, M. Kozakov, A. Shengelaya, N. Burlyaev and L. Sukharevskaya. ¶A Soviet production released in Russia in 1962 as *Sud sumasshedshikh*. Later optically converted to Kinopanorama and nine-track magnetic stereophonic sound.

The Trials of Oscar Wilde. Filmed in Super Technirama 70. *Executive producers* Irving Allen and Albert R. Broccoli. *Producer* Harold Huth. *Director and screenplay* Ken Hughes. *Based on the book "Trials of Oscar Wilde" by* Montgomery Hyde; *and the play "The Stringed Lute" by* John Fernald. *Director of photography* Ted Moore. *Art directors* Ken Adam and William Constable. *Music composer and conductor* Ron Goodwin. *Editor* Geoffrey Foot. *Sound recordist* Norman Coggs. ¶An Irving Allen-Albert R. Broccoli production. A Warwick Film Productions, Ltd. picture in association with Viceroy Films, Ltd. Released by Kingsley International. Technicolor. Westrex six-track magnetic stereophonic sound. 123 minutes. Filmed in England. ¶CAST: *Oscar Wilde* Peter Finch. *Constance Wilde* Yvonne Mitchell. *Sir Edward Carson* James Mason. *Lord Alfred Douglas* John Fraser. *Sir Edward Clarke* Nigel Patrick. *Marquis of Queensberry* Lionel Jeffries. *Lady Wilde* Sonia Dresdel. *Ada Leverson* Maxine Audley. *Alfred Wood* James Booth. *Robbie Ross* Emrys Jones. *Charles Humphries* Lloyd Lamble. *Frank Harris* Paul Rogers. *Arthur* Ian Fleming. *Prince of Wales* Laurence Naismith. *Lily Langtry* Naomi Chance. *Lady Queensberry* Cicely Paget-Bowman. *Auctioneer* Meredith Edwards. *Clerks* Anthony Newlands and Robert Perceval. *Charles Gill* Michael Goodliffe. *Willy Wilde* Liam Gaffney. *Lord Ashford* William Kendall. *Lord Sonning* Ronald Cardew. *Lord Percy Douglas* Derek Aylward. *Inspector* Cambell Singer. *Justice Collins* A.J. Brown. *Justice Wills* David Ensor. *Landlady* Gladys Henson. *Cafe Royal manager* John Welsh. ¶A British production released in England in May 1960 by Eros. Retitled *The Green Carnation* for some U.S. 35mm playdates. Reissued as *The Man with the Green Carnation*.

Tron (July 1982). Filmed in Super Panavision 70. *Executive producer* Ron Miller. *Producer* Donald Kushner. *Director and screenplay* Steven Lisberger. *Story* Steven Lisberger and Bonnie MacBird. *Associate producer* Harrison Ellenshaw. *Director of photography* Bruce Logan. *Production designer* Dean Edward Mitzner. *Film editor* Jeff Gourson. *Music and music synthesizer performance and processing* Wendy Carlos. *Conceptual artists (electronic world)* Syd Mead, Jean "Moebius" Giraud and Peter Lloyd. *Music and sound design supervisor* Michael Fremer. *Music performers* Los Angeles Orchestra, *conductor* Richard Bowden and The London Philharmonic Orchestra, *conductor* Douglas Gamley. *Orchestrations* Jorge Calandrelli. *Unit production manager* Ralph Sariego. *First assistant director* Lorin B. Salob. *Second assistant director* Lisa Marmon. *Costume designers* Elois Jenssen and Rosanna Norton. *"Only Solutions" and "1990's Theme" writers and performers* Journey. *Sound effects design and synthesis* Frank Serafine at Serafine FX Studios. *Sound department supervisor* Bob Hathaway. *Supervising sound editor* Gordon Ecker, Jr. at wallaWorks. *Sound effects editors* Anthony Milch, Randy Kelley, Marvin Walowitz and Vince Melandri. *Production sound mixer* Jim Larue. *Scoring recordist* John Mosley. *Rerecording mixers* Michael Minkler, Bob Minkler and Lee Minkler. *"MCP" voice processing* Champ Davenport and Jack Manning at Synthefex. *Assistant to the composer* Annemarie Franklin. *Postproduction facilities* Lion's Gate Sound. *Executive in charge of production* Thomas L. Wilhite. *Studio production manager* Ted Schilz. *Art directors* John B. Mansbridge and Al Roelofs. *Set decorator* Roger Shook. *Script supervisor* Edle Bakke. *Casting* Pam Polifroni. *Electronic conceptual design* Jean "Moebius" Giraud and Richard Taylor. *Costume supervisor* Jack Sandeen. *Men's costumes* Lorry Richter. *Women's costumes* Nedra Rosemond-Watt. *Makeup supervisor* Robert J. Schiffer. *Makeup* Gary Liddiard. *Hair stylist* Joy Zapata. *Mechanical special effects* R.J. Spetter. *Production storyboards* Bill Kroyer, Jerry W. Rees, John Norton and Andy Gaskill. *Preproduction concepts* John Norton, Roger Allers, Chris Lane and Peter Mueller. *Assistant editors* Walter Kekking and Baylis Glascock. *Negative cutting* Ed

Capuano. *Dialog editing* Stan Gilbert, Robert Bradshaw and Bill Shenberg. *Foley editor* Mike Wilhoit. *Music layout* Jeffrey Gussman. *Special record coordination* Michael Dilbeck. *Assistant sound editors* Bob Newlan and John M. Lowry. *Camera operators* Ron Vargas, Greg Heschong and Rexford Metz. *First assistant camera operators* Horace Jordan, Mike Weldon, Lynn Tomes and James Anderson. *Second assistant camera operator* Mario Zamala. *Draftsmen* Bob Stahler, Bob Beall, John Dail, Eugene Harris and Antoinette Gordon. *Propmaster* Wilbur Russell. *Production painter* Shelley Phillips. *Grip supervisor* Owen Crompton. *Key grip* Stan Reed. *Second grip* Ron Peebles. *Electrician supervisor* Herbert Hughes. *Gaffer* Roger Redel. *Best boy* Bernie Bayless. *Stunt coordinator* Richard E. Butler, Jr. *Special thanks to* Anicam, Atari Corp., Apple Computer, Inc., Mountain Hardware Corp., Crown International, Goodyear Rubber and Tire Corp., Pacific Telephone, Federal Screw Works, Electro Voice, Inc., Eastern Acoustical Works, Apt Holman Corp., Fairlight Corp., E. Rotberg, Morgan Renard, Daimon Webster, BTX Corp., Audio and Design Recording, Inc., Delta Labs, Inc., Syntauri Corp., L. Basset, Charles Haas, Jetcopters, Inc., Lexicon, Inc., Olympia, U.S.A., After Image, Inc., Gary Demos, John Whitney, Jr., The Burbank Studios/Video, Hal and Alan Landaker, Sam Schatz-Disc Co-Ordinator, Entertainment Effects Group, Music Technology, Inc., Cinema Air, Advanced Music Systems and R.H. and A.H.K. Associates. *Visual Effects Unit: Visual effects concepts* Steven Lisberger. *Visual effects supervisors* Richard Taylor and Harrison Ellenshaw. *Effects technical supervisor* John Scheele. *Scene coordinators* Deena Burkett, Michael Gibson, John Grower, Peter Blinn, Don Butlon, Clint Colver, Linda D. Stokes, Craig Newman, Jim Keating and Kerry Colonna. *Assistant scene coordinators* Jacqui Hooks, Cynthia Rush, Laura Leiben, Lynda Ellenshaw, Scott Russo, James Valentine, Dana Duff, Ron Rae, Shelley Hinton, Paul La Mori and Denise Wethington. *Background design* Peter Lloyd. *Background composite supervisor* Marta Russell. *Background painting supervisor* Jesse Silver. *Background artists* Christopher D. Andrews, Gary Conklin, Larry Grossman, Corey Harris, Tiaw Kratter, Peter Mueller, Donald Towns and Thomas Woodington. *Background composite assistants* Catherine Eby, John Bates, Sandra Harper and Lorraine Schweizer. *Background technical inker* Carolyn Bates. *Background plate photography* Dave Iwerks, Bernie Gagliano and Gene Larmon. *Background plate processing* Tom's Chroma Lab. *Effects animation supervisor* Lee Dyer. *Effects animation* John Van Vliet, John Norton, Barry Cook, Michael Wolf, Chris Casady, Gail Finkeldsi and Darrell Rooney. *Assistant effects animators* Allen Blyth, Ed Coffey, Eric Durst, Peter Gullerud, Maria Ramocki, Ron Stangl, Dave Stephan, Maureen Trueblood, John Tucker, Dennis Edwards, Vicki Banks and Byron Werner. *Airbrush supervisor* Greg Battes. *Airbrushers* Andy Atkins, William Arance and James Walter Shaw. *Effects ink and paint supervisor* Auril Pebley. *Inkers* May Kong, Lillian Fitts, Christina Caspary, Bonny Nardini, Janette Downs and Maria Luisa Alvarez. *Lab coordinator* Robert C. Hummel III. *Color timer* Martin Welsh. *Camera schedule coordinators* Valerie Hagenbush and Christopher Keith. *Film looping* Eileen Kuramoto. *Photographic process lab supervisors* Art Cruickshank and Peter Anderson. *Photo-rotoscope supervisors* Ron Osenbaugh, Frank Amador, Gayl Kelm, Roger Rinati, and Dave Scott. *Photo-rotoscope coordinator* Marian Guder. *Opticals* Bob Broughton. *Matte production supervisor* Arnie Wong. *Matte production* Lynn Singer and Jan Browning at Animation Camera Services. *International cel coordination* Raulette Woods, Julian Pena, Paul Hernandez and Peter Aries. *Sample art supervisor* Stephanie Burt. *Inking and painting* Ann Marie Sorenson, Cathy Crum, Ronnie Prinz, Alison Dicecio, Lisa Adams, Flavia Mitman, Priscilla Alvarez and Elaine Robinson. *Effects unit managers* David V. Lester and Stephen McEveety. *Secretaries to Mr. Lisberger* Anna-Lisa Nilsson and Margaret Flook. *Production assistants* Debra DeVito Jackson, Wendy Williams, Denise Olivo, Michael G. Craig, Mical Morrish and Michael Schilz. *Mechanical designs and conversions* Don Iwerks, Bob Otto, Don Porterfield and Mechanical Concepts. *Computer systems and software development* Dave Inglish, Mark

Kimball, Dave Barnett, Marty Prager, Bill Tondreau and Cinetron, Inc. *Effects transportation* Katy Johnson and Dyke Johnson. *Lithographic production* G2 Graphic Service, Inc. *Production ink and paint matting* Cuckoo's Nest Productions, Taipei, Taiwan. *Animation compositing camera supervisor* Jim Pickel. *Animation compositing camera* Don Baker, Glenn Campbell, Neil Viker, John Aardal, Dana Ross, Brandy Whittington, Annie McEveety, Kiernan Mulgrew, Dick Kendall, Douglas Eby, George Epperson and Paul Wainess. *Additional animation compositing cameras* All Electric Cameraworks, Praxis Filmworks, Cruse and Co., Pacific Art and Title, Movie Magic, Van der Veer Photo Effects and Robert Abel and Associates. *Computer Generated Images Unit: Computer effects supervisor* Richard Taylor. *Computer image choreography* Bill Kroyer and Jerry W. Rees. *Magi Synthavision: Technology concepts* Dr. Philip Mittleman. *Scene creation concepts* Larry Elin Popielinski. *Scene programmers* Nancy Hunter Campi and Christian Wedge. *Synthavision technologists* Dr. Martin G. Cohen, Dr. Herbert Steinberg, Dr. Eugene Troubelzkoy and Kenneth Perlin. *Synthavision production* John Beach and Tom Bisogno. *Information International, Inc.: Scene programmers* Craig W. Reynolds, William Dungan, Jr., Larry Malone, Jeremy Schwartz and Mal McMillan. *Object digitizing* Art Durinski. *Computer production coordination* Lyn Wilkinson. *Transition to electronic world and main title* Robert Abel and Associates. *Design supervisor* Kenny Mirman. *Systems programmers* Frank Vitz, Bill Kovacs, Richard Bailey and Tim McGovern. *Systems supervisor* Robert Abel. *Camera* Patric Kenly and Kris Gregg. *"Tron" formation and the "Bit"* Digital Effects, Inc. *Systems supervisor* Judson Rosebush. *Computer production supervisor* Jeffrey Kleiser. *Computer animators* Donald Leich and Gene Miller. ¶A Walt Disney Productions presentation. A Lisberger/Kushner production. Released by Buena Vista Distribution Co. Technicolor. Six-track magnetic Dolby Stereo. 96 minutes. Filmed at Walt Disney Studios and on location at Lawrence Livermore Lab, Livermore, California. MPAA rating: PG. ¶CAST: *Kevin Flynn and Clu* Jeff Bridges. *Alan Bradley and Tron* Bruce Boxleitner. *Ed*

Dillinger and Sark David Warner. *Lora and Yori* Cindy Morgan. *Dr. Walter Gibbs and Dumont* Barnard Hughes. *Ram* Dan Shor. *Crom* Peter Jurasik. *Peter and Sark's lieutenant* Tony Stephano. *First warrior* Craig Chudy. *Second warrior* Vince Dearick. *Expert disc warrior* Sam Schatz. *Head guard* Jackson Bostwick. *Factory guard* Dave Cass. *First guard* Gerald Berns. *Second guard* Bob Neill. *Third guard* Ted White. *Fourth guard* Mark Stewart. *Fifth guard* Michael Sax. *Sixth guard* Tony Brubaker. *Tank commander* Charles Picerni. *First tank gunner* Pierre Vuilleumier. *Second tank gunner* Erik Cord. *First conscript and video game cowboy* Loyd Catlett. *Second conscript* Michael J. Dudikoff II. *Video game player* Richard Bruce Friedman. *Boys in arcade* Rick Feck and John Kenworthy. *Stunts* Al Jones, Bill Burton, Glenn Wilder, Bennie E. Dobbins, Rita Egleston, Hank Hooker, Donna Garrett, Gary Epper, James Winburn, Gary Jensen, Walter Scott, Larry Holt, Ross Reynolds and James Deeth. ¶There is much confusion regarding this film and unfortunately Technicolor did not clear it up. The opening and closing sequences were shot in Super Panavision 70, but according to trade paper reports the electronic world sequences were shot in either or both VistaVision and Super Technirama 70. It is possible, even likely, that the 70mm footage was reduced to 35mm anamorphic and the electronic world footage, whatever actual format(s) it was, was edited with it, and then the whole show blown back up to 70mm. It is also possible the whole film was produced in Super Panavision 70.

Trough Harsh to the Stars *see* **To the Stars by Hard Ways.**

Tschaikovsky *see* **Tchaikovsky.**

Tsena bistrikh sekund (1972). Filmed in Sovscope 70. *Screen authors* Z. Smirnov, V. Chebotarev and A. Yusin. *Director* V. Chebotarev. *Operator* Yu. Gantman. *Artist* N. Usachev. *Composer* A. Flyarkovskiy. *Sound operator* V. Zorin. ¶A Mosfilm production. International distribution Sovexportfilm. Sovcolor. Six-track magnetic stereophonic sound. 114 minutes. Filmed at Mosfilm Studios, Moscow, R.S.F.S.R. ¶CAST: V. Malyavina, A. Belyavskiy, E. Ryabinkina, L. Aleshnikova, V. Gusev, V. Samoylov, G. Yudin,

V. Abramov and V. Tikhkhe. ¶A Soviet production released in Russia in 1972.

Tumannosti Andromedi *see* **Andromeda Nebula.**

2001: A Space Odyssey (April 2, 1968). Filmed in Super Panavision 70 and Todd-AO. Presented in 70mm Super Cinerama. *Producer and director* Stanley Kubrick. *Screenplay* Stanley Kubrick and Arthur C. Clarke. *Based on the story "The Sentinel" by* Arthur C. Clarke. *Special photographic effects designer and director* Stanley Kubrick. *Special photographic effects supervisors* Wally Veevers, Douglas Trumbull, Con Pederson, Tom Howard, Wally Gentleman, Les Bowie and Charles Staffell. *Production designers* Tony Masters, Harry Lange and Ernest Archer. *Film editor* Ray Lovejoy. *Wardrobe* Hardy Amies. *Director of photography* Geoffrey Unsworth. *Additional photography* John Alcott and Mike Wilson. *"Gayane Ballet Suite" music* Aram Khatchaturian; *performers* The Leningrad Philharmonic Orchestra; *conductor* Gennadi Rozhdestvensky; *courtesy* Deutsche Grammophon. *"Atmospheres" music* Gyory Ligeti; *performers* The Southwest German Radio Orchestra; *·conductor* Ernest Bour. *"Lux Aeterna" music* Gyorgy Ligeti; *performers* The Stuttgart State Orchestra; *conductor* Clytus Gottwald. *"Requiem" music* Gyorgy Ligeti; *performers* The Bavarian Radio Orchestra; *conductor* Francis Travis. *"The Blue Danube" music* Johann Strauss; *performers* The Berlin Philharmonic Orchestra; *conductor* Herbert von Karajan; *courtesy* Deutsche Grammophon. *"Thus Spoke Zarathustra" music* Richard Strauss; *performers* The Berlin Philharmonic Orchestra; *conductor* Karl Bohm. *Associate producer and production supervisor* Victor Lyndon. *First assistant director* Derek Cracknell. *Special photographic effects unit* Colin J. Cantwell, Bryan Loftus, Frederick Martin, Bruce Logan, David Osborne, John Jack Malick, Brian Johncock [Johnson], James R. Dickson, John Dykstra, Zoran Persic, Roy Naisbitt, John Rose, Roger Dicken and Richard Yuricich. *Camera operator* Kelvin Pike. *Art director* John Hoesli. *Sound editor* Winston Ryder. *Makeup* Stuart Freeborn, Graham Freeborn, Kay Freeborn and Colin Arthur. *Editorial assistant* David De Wilde. *Sound supervisor* Anthony W. Watkins. *Sound mixer* H.L. Bird. *Chief dubbing mixer* J.B. Smith. *Scientific consultant* Frederick I. Ordway III. *Production managers* Victor Lyndon and Robert Watts. *Focus puller* Peter MacDonald. *Still photographer* Keith Hamshere. *Sound assistant* Robin Gregory. *Hairdresser* Carol Beckett. *Set dresser* Robert Cartwright. *Draughtsman* John Graysmark. *Production assistant* Ivor Powell. *Publicity supervisor* Dan S. Terrell. *Assistant to the producer and unit publicist* Roger Caras. *Legal representative* Louis Blau. *Postproduction coordinator* Merle Chamberlin. *Music editor* Frank J. Urioste. *Publicity artist* Robert McCall. *Color timer* Harry V. Jones. *Production cooperation and assistance* Aerojet-General Corporation; Aeronautical Chart and Information Center; Aerospace Medical Division, Wright-Patterson Air Force Base; U.S.A.F. School of Aerospace Medicine, Department of the Air Force; Air Force Cambridge Research Laboratories; Analytical Laboratories Ltd.; U.S. Army Map Service; U.S. Army Natick Laboratories; Barnes Engineering Company; Bell Telephone Laboratories Inc.; Bendix Field Engineering Corporation; Boeing Company, Aero-Space Division; Chrysler Corporation; Computer Control Company; U.S. Department of Defense; Douglas Aircraft Company; Elliott Automation Ltd.; Gen. Dr. Don Flickinger, M.D., U.S.A.F. Retd.; Institute for Advanced Study, School of Mathematics, Princeton; Flight Research Center, National Aeronautics and Space Administration; General Atomic, Division General Dynamics Corporation; General Dynamics-Convair; General Electric Company, Missile and Space Division; Goddard Space Flight Center; Grumman Aircraft Engineering Corporation; Harbor General Hospital, Dr. A.T.K. Crockett, M.D., Chief of Urology; Hawker Siddeley Dynamics Ltd.; Honeywell Inc.; Illinois Institute of Technology, Research Institute; International Business Machines; International Business Machines (U.K.) Ltd.; Jet Propulsion Laboratory, California Institute of Technology; Langley Research Center; Lear Siegler Inc.; Food Technology Research, Libby, McNeil and Libby; Lick Observatory; Ling-Temco-Vought Inc.; Lowell Observatory; Lunar and Planetary

Laboratory, University of Arizona; Manned Spacecraft Center, National Aeronautics and Space Administration; George C. Marshall Space Flight Center, National Aeronautics and Space Administration; Martin Company; Minnesota Mining & Manufacturing Company; Mt. Wilson & Palomar Observatories, California Institute of Technology; National Aeronautics and Space Administration Headquarters; National Aeronautics and Space Council; National Institute of Medical Research; U.S. Naval Observatory; Office of Naval Research, Branch Office, U.S. Embassy, London; New York University College of Medicine; North American Aviation Inc., Space and Information Systems Division; Eliot Noyes & Associates; State of Oregon, Department of Geology & Mineral Information; Paris Match; Philco Corporation; Royal Greenwich Observatory; Societe de Prospection Electrique Schlumberger; Smithsonian Astrophysical Observatory; Soviet Embassy, London; United Kingdom Atomic Energy Authority; University of London; University of Manchester, Department of Astronomy; University of Minnesota, School of Physics; Vickers Ltd., Medical Division; U.S. Weather Bureau and Whirlpool Corporation, Systems Division. ¶A Stanley Kubrick film. A Metro-Goldwyn-Mayer production. A Polaris Productions, Inc. picture. Made by Hawk Films, Ltd. Released by Metro-Goldwyn-Mayer. Technicolor and Metrocolor. Westrex six-track magnetic stereophonic sound. 142 minutes plus intermission. Filmed at MGM British Studios Ltd., Borehamwood and Shepperton Studios, Middlesex, England. ¶CAST: *Mission Cmdr. David Bowman* Keir Dullea. *Astronaut Frank Poole* Gary Lockwood. *Dr. Heywood Floyd* William Sylvester. *The moonwatcher* Daniel Richter. *Smyslov* Leonard Rossiter. *Elena* Margaret Tyzack. *Halvosen* Robert Beatty. *Michaels* Sean Sullivan. *H.A.L. 9000 voice characterization* Douglas Rain. *Mission controller* Frank Miller. *Stewardesses* Edwina Carroll and Penny Brahms. *Poole's father* Alan Gifford. *Photographer* Burnell Tucker. *First technician* John Swindell. *Second technician* John Clifford. *Floyd's daughter* Vivian Kubrick. *Interviewer* Martin Amor. *Astronaut* John Ashley. *With* Bill Weston, Mike Lovell, Edward Bishop, Ann Gillis, Heather Downham, Glenn Beck, Jimmy Bell, David Charkham, Simon Davis, Jonathan Daw, Peter Delmar, Terry Duggan, David Fleetwood, Danny Grover, Brian Hawley, David Hines, Tony Jackson, John Jordan, Scott MacKee, Lawrence Marchant, Darryl Paes, Joe Refalo, Andy Wallace, Bob Wilyman and Richard Wood; *Standins* John Francis, Eddie Milburn, Gerry Judge, Brian Chutter, Tom Sheppard and Robin Dawson-Whisker. ¶An American and British co-production. Premiered at 161 minutes plus intermission but reedited after bad audience response. Working titles were *Journey Beyond the Stars* and *Space Odyssey.* Douglas Rain replaced Martin Balsam as the computer voice. Sequel was *2010* (MGM/UA Entertainment Co., 1984).

Two Versions of a Collision (1985). Filmed in Sovscope 70. *Screen authors* Vadim Avloshenko and Yuri Gavrilov. *Director* Villen Novak. *Operator* Vadim Avloshenko. *Artist* Mikhail Bezchastnov. *Composers* Ivar Vigner and Aleksandr Griva. *Sound operator* V. Bogdanovskiy. ¶An Odesskaya kinostudiya production. International distribution Sovexportfilm. Sovcolor. Six-track magnetic stereophonic sound. 96 minutes. Filmed at Odesskaya kinostudiya, Odessa, Ukrainian S.S.R. ¶CAST: *Ekaterina Kravchenko* Ekhanna Prokhorenko. *Eugene Bogart* Igor Gorbachev. *With* Nikolai Olyalin, Oleg Kulikovich, Dmitri Shcheglov, A. Litsitis, E. Kondulaynen, L. Zolotukhin, K. Mauaradze and Yu. Kaminskiy. ¶A Soviet production released in Russia in 1985 as *Dve versii odnogo stolknoveniya.* The story takes place in New York City.

Typhoon *see* **The Battle of Moscow.**

Uchenik lekarya *see* **The Doctor's Apprentice.**

Udivitelinaya okhota (1962). Filmed in Kinopanorama. A Tsentrnauchfilm production. International distribution Sovexportfilm. Sovcolor. Nine-track magnetic Kinopanorama Sound. 78 minutes. A Soviet production released in Russia in 1962. Excerpts later incorporated into *Cinerama's Russian Adventure.*

The Ukraine in Flames *see* The Unforgettable.

Ukroshchenie ognya *see* Taming of the Flame.

Un, deux, trois, quatre *see* Black Tights.

Uncle Tom's Cabin (January 1, 1969). Filmed in Superpanorama 70. *Executive producer* Arthur Brauner. *Producer* Aldo von Pinelli. *Director* Geza Radvanyi. *Screenplay* Geza Radvanyi and Fred Denger. *Based on the novel "Uncle Tom's Cabin or Life Among the Lowly" by* Harriet Beecher Stowe. *Camera* Heinz Holscher. *Music* Peter Thomas. *Additional music: "Old Man River"* Jerome Kern; *"Sword Dance"* Aram Khatchaturian. *Editor* Victor Palfi. *Settings* Willi Schatz. *Costumes* Herbert Ploberger. *Production manager* Georg M. Reuther. *Sound* Michele Neny. *World distribution* Hans Schubert Wertvertrieb. *Supervisor of U.S. version* Kroger Babb. *Editor of U.S. version* Will Williams. ¶A Melodie Film–CCC Filmkunst–Avala Film–S.I.P.R.P.–Debora Film production. Released by Kroger Babb & Associates. Eastman Color. Four-track MagOptical stereophonic sound. 118 minutes. Filmed in Yugoslavia. ¶CAST: *Uncle Tom* John Kitzmiller. *Saint-Claire* O.W. Fischer. *Simon Legree* Herbert Lom. *Mrs. Saint-Claire* Eleonora Rossi-Draga. *Little Eva Saint-Claire* Gertraud Mittermayr. *Harriet* Mylene Demongeot. *Dinah* Juliette Greco. *Cassy* Olive Moorefield. *Eliza* Catana Cayetano. *Topsy* Rhet Kirby. *Mr. Shelby* Charles Fawcett. *George Shelby* Thomas Fritsch. *Virginia* Bibi Jelinek. *Napoleon* Aziz Saad. *Andy* Harry Tamekloe. *Sambo* George Goodman. *Harris* Harold Bradley. *Aunt Ophelia* Erika von Thellmann. *Uncle Tom's Mama* Dorothee Ellison. *Dolph* Felix White. *Mrs. Shelby* Vilma Degischer. *Bit man* Claudio Gore. *Singer* Ertha Kitt. *Dubbed voices for U.S. version* Ella Fitzgerald and Jeffrey Hunter. ¶Released in the U.S. in 35mm only with stereo sound and advertised in CinemaScope. A French, Italian, West German and Yugoslavian coproduction released in Europe in 70mm with six-track magnetic stereophonic sound. Released in France in September 1965 as *La case de l'Oncle Tom* running 125 minutes; released in Italy in 1965 as *Cento dollari d'Odio;* released in West Germany in April 1965 by Nora as *Onkel Tom's Hutte* running 170 minutes plus intermission and released in Yugoslavia in 1965 as *Cica Tomina koliba.* The original U.S. release had been aimed at black audiences by exploiting the sexual and violent aspects of slavery, but this was carried to further extremes when a special edition was released in March 1977 by Independent-International Pictures Corp. Al Adamson directed several insert scenes, with Prentiss Moulden as Napoleon and Mary Ann Jenson as Melissa, that caused the reissue to garner an R rating from the MPAA. Publicity was on the "hate whitey" level and no effort was made to play any but hardcore blaxploitation houses. Filmed several times, most recently in 1987.

The Velvet Underground and Nico (February 8, 1966). Presented in 16mm Dual Screen. *Producer and director* Andy Warhol. *Photographers* Andy Warhol and Barbara Rubin. *Music* The Velvet Underground and Nico. ¶An Andy Warhol production. Released by Film-Makers' Cooperative. 70 minutes. Filmed in New York City. ¶CAST: *Electronic rock musicians* The Velvet Underground and Nico. ¶This was part of a multi-media presentation that was variously known as *The Exploding Plastic Inevitable* and *Plastic Inevitables (Velvet Underground).* As a gimmick, part or all of the film was shown split screen, but it most likely was not filmed with that in mind.

The Unforgettable (October 1969). Filmed in Sovscope 70. *Screen author, director and producer* Yulia Solntseva. *Based on the story "The Ukraine in Flames" by* Aleksandr P. Dovzenko. *Operator* Dilshat Fatkhulin. *Special effects* Nikolai Renkov. *Composer* Alexei Muraviev. *Artist* Nikolay Usachev. *Sound operator* Yu. Rabinovich. ¶A Kievskaya kinostudya im. A.P. Dovzenko production for Mosfilm. Released by Sovexportfilm. Sovcolor. 118 minutes. ¶CAST: *Petro Chaban* Evgeni Bondarenko. *Tatyana Chaban* Zinaida Dekhtyareva. *Olesya* Irina Korotkova. *Vasil* Yuri Fisenko. *Maxim Zabroda* Sergey Plotnikov. *Ivan Chaban* Georgi Taratorkin. *Khristya* Svetlana Kuzimina. *Ludwig Kraus* Yanis Melderis. *Ernst Kraus* Valentine Skulme. ¶A Soviet production released in Russia in 1968 as *Nezabivaemoe* in 70mm and six-track

magnetic stereophonic sound running 120
minutes. Some sequences were in black
and white. This is a reworking of Dovzenko's purposed project that the Soviet
government had not allowed that filmmaker to produce but eventually let his
widow (Solntseva) make with considerable modification. The U.S. version was in
35mm only.

V Antarktiku za kitami (1961). Filmed in
Kinopanorama. International distribution
Sovexportfilm. Sovcolor. Nine-track
magnetic Kinopanorama Sound. A Soviet
production released in Russia in 1961.
Probably made by Tsentrnauchfilm. Some
footage was excerpted in *Cinerama's Russian Adventure*.

V Bolgariyu zimoy (1981). Filmed in Sovscope 70. International distribution Sovexportfilm. Sovcolor. Six-track magnetic
stereophonic sound. A Soviet production
released in Russia in 1981.

V mire tantsa (1962). Filmed in Sovscope
70. *Screen authors* S. Vladimiskiy, K.
Petrichenko, A. Shengediya, F. Mustafaev, R. Tikhomirov, Makhmud Eshmbaev and L. Yakobson. *Directors* R.
Tikhomirov and F. Mustafaev. *Chief
operator* K. Petrichenko. *Chief artist* L.
Shengeliya. *Chief balletmaster* L. Yakobson. *Composers* G. Firtich and N.
Shvarts. *Sound operator* Yu. Mikhaylov. ¶A Mosfilm production. International distribution Sovexportfilm. Sovcolor. Six-track magnetic stereophonic
sound. 68 minutes. Filmed at Mosfilm
Studios, Moscow, R.S.F.S.R. ¶CAST:
Performer Makhmud Eshmbaev. ¶A
Soviet production released in Russia in
1962.

V nebe toliko devushki (1968). Filmed in
Sovscope 70. International distribution
Sovexportfilm. Sovcolor. Six-track magnetic stereophonic sound. A Soviet production released in Russia in 1968.

Vechev nakanune Ivana Kupala (1968).
Filmed in Sovscope 70. *Screen author and
director* Yu. Ilienko. *Based on the story
"Vechev nakanune Ivana Kupala" by* N.V.
Gogolya. *Operator* V. Ilienko. *Artists* P.
Maksimenko and V. Novakov. *Composer*
L. Grabovskiy. *Sound operator* L. Vachi.
¶A Kievskaya kinostudiya im. A.P. Dov-
zenko production. International distribu-

tion Sovexportfilm. Sovcolor. Six-track
magnetic stereophonic sound. 88 minutes.
Filmed at Kievskaya kinostudiya im. A.P.
Dovzenko, Kiev, Ukrainian S.S.R. ¶CAST:
L. Kadochnikova, B. Khmelinitskiy, E.
Fridman, D. Franiko, K. Ershov, D.
Yanover, D. Mikosha, M. Ilienko, B.
Brondukov, V. Panchenko, M. Silis and
S. Sergienko. ¶A Soviet production re-
leased in Russia in 1968.

Velet ("Aeroport") (1965). Filmed in Sov-
scope 70. *Screen author* A. Salukvidze.
Director N. Mchedlidze. *Operator* G.
Chubabriya. *Artist* D. Nodiya. *Composer*
N. Mamzashvili. ¶A Gruziya-film pro-
duction. International distribution Sovex-
portfilm. Sovcolor. Six-track magnetic
stereophonic sound. 17 minutes. Filmed at
Gruziya-film Studios, Tbilisi, Georgian
S.S.R. ¶CAST: Shakro, Dzordzadze, T.
Archvadze and N. Kilosanidze. ¶A
Soviet production released in Russia in
1965. Filmed in 1963.

Vera Cruz (December 1954). Filmed in
*Super*Scope. *Executive producers* Harold
Hecht and Burt Lancaster. *Producer*
James Hill. *Director* Robert Aldrich.
Screenplay Roland Kibbee and James R.
Webb. *Story* Borden Chase. *Director of
photography* Ernest Laszlo. *Music* Hugo
Friedhofer. *Orchestration* Hugo Fried-
hofer and Raul Lavista. *Conductor* Raul
Lavista. *Editorial supervisor* Alan Cros-
land, Jr. *Sound* Manuel Topete Blake and
Galdino Samperio. *Costume designer*
Norma Koch. *Production designer* Alfred
Ybarra. *Production manager* Nate H. Ed-
wards. *Assistant director* Jack R. Berne.
Special effects Russell Shearman. *Makeup*
Robert J. Schiffer. *Hair stylist* Margaret
Donovan. *Sound effects and music editor*
Robert Carlisle. *Unit publicist* Walter
Seltzer. *Executive assistant to the pro-
ducer* Bernard Smith. *Production super-
visor* Rudy Rosenberg. *Choreography*
Archie Savage. *Title song: music* Hugo
Friedhofer; *lyrics* Sammy Cahn; *singer*
Tony Martin. ¶A Harold Hecht presen-
tation. A Hecht-Lancaster Productions–
Flora Productions picture. Released by
United Artists. Technicolor. RCA Photo-
phone recording. 94 minutes. Filmed at
Estudios Churubusco, Mexico City and
on location in Cuernavaca, Mexico.
¶CAST: *Col. Benjamin Trane* Gary
Cooper. *Joe Erin* Burt Lancaster.

Countess Marie Duvarre Denise Darcel. *Marquis de Labordere* Cesar Romero. *Nina* Sarita Montiel. *Emperor Maximilian* George Macready. *Donnegan* Ernest Borgnine. *Capt. Danette* Henry Brandon. *Pittsburgh* Charles Buchinsky [Bronson]. *Gen. Aguilar Romeriz* Morris Ankrum. *Little Bit* James McCallion. *Charlie* Jack Lambert. *Tex* Jack Elam. *Abilene* James Seay. *Ballard* Archie Savage. *Reno* Charles Horvath. *Pedro* Juan Garcia. ¶The first film released in *Super*Scope. The title song was cut before release but did appear on the soundtrack record.

Veroy i pravdoy *see* **With Fidelity and Truth.**

Vey, veterok! *see* **Blow, Breeze!**

Vibor tseli (1976). Filmed in Sovscope 70. *Screen authors* D. Granin and I. Talankin. *Director* I. Talankin. *Operator* N. Ardashnikov. *Artists* T. Lapshina and A. Myatkov. *Composer* A. Shnitke. *Sound operators* G. Korenblyum, S. Litvinov and V. Bobrovskiy. ¶A Mosfilm production. International distribution Sovexportfilm. Sovcolor. Six-track magnetic stereophonic sound. 16 reels. Filmed at Mosfilm Studios, Moscow, R.S.F.S.R. ¶CAST: Sergei Bondarchuk, G. Ezenov, N. Volkov, I. Skobtseva, N. Burlyaev, A. Pokrovskaya, S. Desnitskiy, V. Koretskiy, I. Soloviev, S. Yurskiy, M. Uliyanov, A. Basnlashvili, I. Smoktunovskiy, Kh. Shulitse, Ya. Tritsoliskiy and Alla Demidova. ¶A Soviet production released in Russia in 1976 in two parts: *Iskushenie* running 76 minutes and *Vibor tseli* running 8 reels.

Vishneviy omut (1981). Filmed in Sovscope 70. *Screen authors* M. Alekseev and L. Golovnya. *Based on the novel by* M. Alekseeva. *Director* L. Golovnya. *Operator* O. Martinov. *Artists* P. Safonov and V. Zenkov. *Composer* N. Sidelinikov. *Sound operator* E. Indlina. ¶A Mosfilm production. International distribution Sovexportfilm. Sovcolor. Six-track magnetic stereophonic sound. 170 minutes plus intermission. Filmed at Mosfilm Studios, Moscow, R.S.F.S.R. ¶CAST: V. Barinov, T. Nikitina, L. Polekhina, A. Vanin, V. Shakalo, L. Borisov, V. Brileev, V. Morozov, M. Sizova and S. Grishchenko. ¶A Soviet production

released in Russia in 1981 in two parts running 84 minutes and 86 minutes.

Visokiy pereval (1982). Filmed in Sovscope 70. *Screen author and director* V. Denisenko. *Operator* N. Kulikhitskiy. *Chief artist* A. Mamontov. *Art directors* V. Beskrovniy and A. Bobrovnikov. *Composer* A. Skorik. *Sound operator* Yu. Lavrinenko. ¶A Kievskaya kinostudiya im. A.P. Dovzenko production. International distribution Sovexportfilm. Sovcolor. Six-track magnetic stereophonic sound. 173 minutes plus intermission. Filmed at Kievskaya kinostudiya im. A.P. Dovzenko, Kiev, Ukrainian S.S.R. ¶cast: Natalia Naum, K. Stepankov, L. Boedan, T. Denisenko, A. Denisenko, A. Barchuk, V. Chubarev, L. Yanovskiy, K. Gubenko and N. Oleyink. ¶A Soviet production released in Russia in 1982 in two parts running 88 minutes and 85 minutes.

Visokoe zvanie *see* **Lofty Title.**

Viva Baja (1975). Filmed in OMNIMAX. *Writer, producer and director* Roger Tilton. *Photographer* J. Barry Herron. ¶Produced and released by San Diego Hall of Science. Eastman Color. Six-track magnetic stereophonic sound. 11 minutes. Filmed in Baja California, Mexico. Originally made for San Diego's Reuben H. Fleet Space Theater.

Viy (1967). Filmed in Sovscope 70. *Screen authors* Aleksandr Ptushko, Konstantin Ershov and Georgi Kropachev. *Based on the story by* Nikolay V. Gogolya. *Directors* Konstantin Ershov and Georgi Kropachev. *Operators* Fyodor Provorov and Viktor Pishchalinikov. *Artist* Nikolay Markin. *Composer* Karen Khachaturyan. *Sound operators* Evgeni Kashkevich and Irina Stulova. ¶A Mosfilm production. International distribution Sovexportfilm. Sovcolor. Six-track magnetic stereophonic sound. 77 minutes. Filmed at Mosfilm Studios, Moscow, R.S.F.S.R. ¶CAST: *Khoma* Leonid Kuravlev. *Landowner's daughter* Natalya Varley. *Cossack lieutenant* Alexey Glazirin. *Lavtukh* Stepan Shkurat. *With* V. Zakharchenko and V. Salinikov. ¶A Soviet production released in Russia in 1967.

Vizit vezlivosti *see* **A Courtesy Call.**

Vkus khleba *see* **The Taste of Bread.**

Vladivostok, god 1918 (1982). Filmed in Sovscope 70. *Screen author* P. Demidov. *Director* Z. Gavrilov. *Operator* I. Zarafiyan. *Artists* S. Serebrenikov and E. Shtapenko. *Composer* V. Basner. *Sound operator* D. Bogolepov. *Song text* M. Matusovskogo. ¶A kinostudiya im. M. Gorikogo production. International distribution Sovexportfilm. Sovcolor. Six-track magnetic stereophonic sound. 97 minutes. Filmed at kinostudiya im. M. Gorikogo, Gorki, R.S.F.S.R. ¶CAST: V. Bochkarev, M. Levtova, M. Zigalov, O. Naumenko, A. Rostotskiy, A. Martinov, A. Lazarev, A. Vokach, I. Dmitriev and B. Beyshenaliev. ¶A Soviet production released in Russia in 1982.

Volcano (1973). Filmed in IMAX. *Producer, director and photographer* Christopher Chapman. ¶Released by Imax Systems Corporation. Eastman Color. Six-track magnetic stereophonic sound. 7 minutes. Filmed on Haimaey Island, Ireland. A Canadian production originally made for Ontario Place.

The Volga Flows On (1963). Filmed in Kinopanorama. *Screen authors* V. Ieyuov and Yakov Segel. *Director* Yakov Segel. *Operators* Inna Zarafyan and Bentsion Monastyrsky. *Editor* H. Blinov. ¶A kinostudiya im. M. Gorikogo production. International distribution Sovexportfilm. Sovcolor. Nine-track magnetic Kinopanorama Sound. 80 minutes. Filmed at kinostudiya im. M. Gorikogo, Gorki, R.S.F.S.R. and on the Volga River. ¶CAST: *Stephan* Nikolai Sergeev. *Alexei* Valentina Telegina. *Natasha* Georgi Ypifantsev. *Nastia* N. Gkhoydrakava. ¶A Soviet production released in Russia in 1963 as *Techet Volga.* Generally known as *Volga, Volga.* The first dramatic feature in Kinopanorama.

Volga, Volga *see* **The Volga Flows On.**

Volshebnoe ozero (1979). Filmed in Sovscope 70. International distribution Sovexportfilm. Sovcolor. Six-track magnetic stereophonic sound. A Soviet production released in Russia in 1979.

Volshevnoye zerkalo *see* **The Enchanted Mirror.**

Volya, kroviyu omitaya *see* **Yemelyan Pugachov.**

Vooruzen i ocheni opacen *see* **Armed and Dangerous.**

Voyage to the Outer Planets (1973). Filmed in Dynavision. Presented in IMAX. *Executive producer* Preston M. Fleet. *Director of planetarium media* Michael Sullivan. *Producers* Lester Novros and George Casey. *Writer and director and models* Colin Cantwell. *Planetarium programming* Joseph S. Harrington, George Marchyshyn, John P. Mulligan and Gregg A. Paris. *Music* Paul Novros. *Artwork* Don Moore. *Camera* James Connor. *Special effects cameraman* John Dykstra. *Optical printing and Dynavision technology* Film Effects of Hollywood. *Camera* Todd-AO. *Sound* Glen Glenn Sound. ¶A Show Sphere, Inc. production. Made by Graphic Films Corporation. Released by San Diego Hall of Science. Eastman Color. Six-track magnetic stereophonic sound. 28 minutes. ¶CAST: *Narrator* Gene McGarr. ¶Originally made for the Rueben H. Fleet Space Theater at San Diego Hall of Science. Photographed in double frame 70mm and blown up to IMAX format.

Voyna i mir *see* **Leo Tolstoy's War and Peace.**

Vozdukhoplavateli *see* **Aeronaut.**

Vozimite nas s soboy, turisti (1967). Filmed in Roundframe. International distribution Sovexportfilm. Sovcolor. Six-track magnetic stereophonic sound. A Soviet production released in Russia in 1967. Presented in 70mm onto a spherical (hemispheric) screen.

Vozvrashchenie s orbiti *see* **Return from Orbit.**

Vozvrashchenie "Svyatogo Luki" (1971). Filmed in Sovscope 70. *Screen authors* V. Kuznetsov and B. Shustrov. *Director* A. Bobrovskiy. *Operator* R. Veseler. *Artists* S. Volyushok and S. Menyalishchikov. *Composer* Isaak Shvarts. *Sound operator* V. Kostelitsev. ¶A Mosfilm production. International distribution Sovexportfilm. Sovcolor. Six-track magnetic stereophonic sound. 119 minutes. Filmed at

Mosfilm Studios, Moscow, R.S.F.S.R. ¶CAST: V. Sanaev, V. Dvorzetskiy, A. Basilashvili, E. Vasilieva, N. Richagova, V. Rizakov, V. Smirnov, V. Belyakov, P. Butkevich and D. Masanov. ¶A Soviet production released in Russia in 1971.

Vozvrata net *see* **No Return.**

Vsadnik bez golovi *see* **The Headless Horsemen.**

Vse reshaet mgnovenie (1979). Filmed in Sovscope 70. *Screen authors* V. Ezov, A. Salutskiy and V. Sadovskiy. *Director* V. Sadovskiy. *Operator* V. Karasev. *Artist* B. Burmistrov. *Composer* A. Zurbin. *Sound operator* T. Silaev. *Song text* R. Rozdestvenskogo. ¶A Mosfilm production. International distribution Sovexportfilm. Sovcolor. Six-track magnetic stereophonic sound. 124 minutes. Filmed at Mosfilm Studios, Moscow, R.S.F.S.R. ¶CAST: G. Belyaeva, O. Ageeva, B. Zaydenberg, N. Fateeva, A. Abdulov, A. Demiyanenko, A. Papanov, N. Ozerov and A. Danilov. ¶A Soviet production released in Russia in 1979.

Vzlet *see* **Take-off.**

(Leo Tolstoy's) War and Peace (April 28, 1968). Filmed in Sovscope 70. *Screen authors* Sergei Bondarchuk and Vasily Soloviev. *Based on the novel "Yoyna i mir" by* Count Leo Nikolayevich Tolstogo. *Director and producer* Sergei Bondarchuk. *Chief operator* Anatoly Petritskiy. *Operator* Dmitri Korzhikhin. *Second operator* A. Zenyan. *Special effects operator* G. Aizenberg. *Assistant operator* V. Chemendryakov. *Artists* Mikhail Bogdanov and Gennady Myasnikov. *Composer* Vyacheslav Ovchinnikov conducting Moscow Symphony Orchestra's All-Union Radio and T.V. Chorus and Orchestra. *Sound operators* Yuri Mikhaylov and I. Urvantsev. *Assistant directors* Anatoly Golovanov, Anatoly Chemodurov, Adiba Shir-Akhmedova, A. Aleshin and A. Petrov. *Editors* Tatiana Likhacheva and E. Suraiskaya. *Special effects at Schongraben and Austerlitz* Aleksandr Shelenkov and Chen-Yu-Lan. *Sound recording* Vladimir Mikhaylov. *Editors' assistants* E. Mikhailova and G. Kolodnaya. *Chief manager of production* Viktor Tsirgiladze. *Managers of produc-*

tion Nikolai Ivanov and G. Meyrovitch. *Still photo* Vladimir Uvarov. *Advisers* Gen. of the Army V. Kurasov, Gen. of the Army M. Popov, Lt. Gen. N. Oslikovsky, Col. M. Lyushkovsky, Col. V. Glinka, Col. A. Lubimov and Col. E. Kurbatova. *Costumier* Mikhail Chikovany. *Assistant artists* A. Dikhtyar, S. Valyushek and S. Menyalshchikov. *Pyrotechnician* Vladimir Likhachev. *Uniforms* V. Vavra and N. Buzina. *Makeup* Mikhail Chikirev, T. Gaidukova and T. Kovryagina. *Choreographer* V. Burmeister. *Special effects artists* F. Krasnyi and M. Semenov. *Artists' assistants* Y. Oreshkin and E. Malikov. *Set* G. Koshelev and V. Uvarov. *Director's assistants* V. Dostal, V. Nikolskaya, N. Aparin, V. Badaev and G. Babitcheva. *English language version* Titan Productions, Inc., New York City, *in cooperation with* Sergei Bondarchuk. *Executive producer* Walter Reade, Jr. *Dialog adaptation and direction* Lee Kressel. *Narration writer* Andrew Witwer. *Postproduction supervisor* Winston Sharples, Jr. *Supervising editor* Sidney Katz. *Lip sync editor* Rite, Inc. *Lip sync editor* Eli Haviv. *Assistant lip sync editors* Emil Haviv, Louis Giacchetto, Isobel Burger and William Riss. *Sound mix* Fine Recording, Inc. *Title and introduction creator* Elinor Bunin. *Project coordinator* Andrew L. Sager. *Technical liaison* Alex Goitein. *Publicist* Harold Stern. *Color* Movielab, Inc. *70mm prints* De Luxe. ¶A Walter Reade Organization–Satra Corporation presentation by arrangement with Sovexportfilm. A Mosfilm production. Released by Continental Distributing. Sovcolor. Six-track magnetic stereophonic sound. 373 minutes plus three intermissions. (Part one 195 minutes plus intermission and part two 178 minutes plus intermission with a break between parts.) Filmed at Mosfilm Studios, Moscow and on location in Smolensk, Volokolamsk and Boguslavskiy, R.S.F.S.R. ¶CAST: *Natasha Rostov* Lyudmila Savelieva. *Pierre Bezuhov* Sergei Bondarchuk. *Andrei Bolkonsky* Vyacheslav Tikhonov. *Count Rostov* Viktor Stanitsin. *Countess Rostov* Khira Ivanov-Golovko. *Nikolai Rostov* Oleg Tabakov. *Petya Rostov* Nikolai Kodin and Seryozha Yermilov. *Sonya* Irina Gubanova. *Prince Nikolai Bolkonsky* Anatoly Ktorov. *Princess Maria Bolkonsky* Antonia Shuranova. *Princess Liza Bolkonsky* Anastasia Vertinskaya. *Prince*

Vasily Kuragin Boris Smirnov. *Helene Kuragin* Irina Skobtseva. *Anatole Kuragin* Vasily Lanovoy. *Dolohov* Oleg Efremov. *Count Bezuhov* N. Tolkachev. *Maria Ahrosimova* Elena Tyapkina. *Princess Anna Drubetskoy* K. Polivikova. *Drubetskoy* Eduard Martsevich. *Anna Scherer* Angelina Stepanova and Demma Firsova. *Julie Karagina* G. Kravchenko. *Kutuzov* Boris Zakhaya. *Tushin* Nikolai Trofimov. *Bagration* Giuli Chokhonelidze. *Uncle Mikhail Nikanori* Aleksandr Borisov. *Denisov* Nikolai Ribnikov. *Emperor Aleksandr I* V. Murganov. *Emperor Napoleon Bonaparte* Vladislav Strzelichik. *Emperor Francis II* V. Safronov. *Gen. Mac* N. Bubnov. *Shinshin* I. Soloviev. *Nesvitsky* Y. Chekulaev. *Timokhin* P. Savin. *Officer* A. Smirnov. *Regiment commander* V. Vadaev. *N. Kolushka* A. Semin. *Benningsen* G. Sommer. *Woltzogen* Y. Grantinsh. *Klauzewitz* D. Eizentals. *Davout* B. Molchanov. *Morel* J. Miller. *Capt. Ramballe* Yahn-Klod-Balar. *Tikhon Shcherbati* S. Chekan. *Loriston* D. Polyakov. *Narrator* Norman Rose. ¶A Soviet production released in Russia in 1966 and 1967 as *Voyna i mir* in four parts: *Andrey Bolkonskiy* (1966) running 16 reels with an intermission, *Natasha Rostova* (1966) running 12 reels, *1819 god* (1967) running 10 reels and *Pier Bezyukhov* (1967) running 10 reels. The total running time for all four parts was 480 minutes. M. Khrabrov appears in the cast list supplied by Sovexportfilm but does not appear in the list for the English-language version and is presumed to have been edited from the shorter U.S. edition.

Water and Man (1985). Filmed in OMNIMAX. *Producer* Christian Ferlet. *Director and filmer* Pierre Willemin. ¶Produced by Via Productions. Released by Lawrence Associates, New York City. Eastman Color. Six-track magnetic stereophonic sound. 40 minutes. A French production originally made for La Geode, Paris.

We Are Born of Stars (1985). Filmed in IMAX 3D and OMNIMAX 3D. *Writer and coproducer* Roman Kroitor. *Computer animation* Dr. Nelso Max of Lawrence Livermore National Laboratory, Dr. Koichi Omura of Osaka University and Colin Low of National Film Board of Canada. ¶Produced and released by Imax Systems Corporation: Eastman Color. Six-track magnetic stereophonic sound. 11 minutes. A Canadian production originally for the Fujitsu Pavilion at the 1985 International Exposition in Tsukuba, Japan. The film was made up entirely of computer generated animation and was in duo-color anaglyph stereoscope, not dual projector, polarized 3D.

We Will Rock You (1984). Filmed in MobileVision. *Producer and director* Saul Swimmer. *Director of photography* Dick Brooks. *Optical conversion* Film Effects International. *Conversion supervisor* Don Weed. ¶Produced and released by MobileVision Technology, Inc. Eastman Color. Eight-track magnetic stereophonic sound. Filmed in Montreal. ¶CAST: *Rock performers* Queen. ¶The only film as of this writing in MobileVision. Exhibited in large auditoriums as if it were a live concert.

Wedding in Malinovke (1967). Filmed in Sovscope 70. *Screen author* Leonid Yukhvid. *Based on the musical comedy "Svadiba v Malinovke" by* Boris Aleksandrova. *Director* Andrey Tutishkin. *Operator* Vacheslav Fasmovich. *Artist* Semyon Malkin. *Music* Boris Aleksandrova. *Sound operator* Georgi Elibert. ¶A Lenfilm production. International distribution Sovexportfilm. Sovcolor. Six-track magnetic stereophonic sound. 118 minutes. Filmed at Lenfilm Studios, Leningrad, R.S.F.S.R. ¶CAST: *Nazar* Vladimir Samoylov. *Sofia* Lyudmila Alfimova. *Yarinko* Valentina Lisenko. *Nechipor* Evgeni Lebedev. *Gapusya* Zoya Fedorova. *Yashka* Mikhail Pugovkin. *Andreyka* Gkheli Sisoev. *With* A. Abrinosov, G. Abrikosov, M. Vodyanoy, N. Slichenko, T. Nosova, Z. Ptreyvac and A. Smirnov. ¶A Soviet production released in Russia in 1967 as *Svadiba v Malinovke*.

West Side Story (October 18, 1961). Filmed in Super Panavision 70. *Executive producer* Walter Mirisch. *Producer* Robert Wise. *Directors* Robert Wise and Jerome Robbins. *Screenplay* Ernest Lehman. *Based on the play with the book by* Arthur Laurents; *lyrics by* Stephen Sondheim; *and music by* Leonard Bernstein; *as conceived for the stage, directed and choreographed by* Jerome Robbins; *and produced by* Robert E. Griffith and Harold Prince; *from the play "Romeo and*

Juliet" by William Shakespeare. *Music* Leonard Bernstein. *Lyrics* Stephen Sondheim. *Music conductor* Johnny Green. *Associate producer and music supervisor* Saul Chaplin. *Choreography* Jerome Robbins. *Director of photography* Daniel L. Fapp. *Assistant director* Robert E. Relvea. *Costume designer* Irene Sharaff. *Assistant choreographers* Howard Jeffrey, Margaret Banks, Tommy Abbott and Tony Mordente. *Special photographic effects and title photography* Linwood G. Dunn, Film Effects of Hollywood, Cecil Love and Don Weed. *Titles and visual consultant* Saul Bass. *Production designer* Boris Leven. *Set decorator* Victor A. Gangelin. *Script supervisor* Stanley Scheuer. *Makeup* Emile La Vigne. *Hair stylist* Alice Monte. *Film editor* Thomas Sanford. *Assistant editor* Marshall M. Borden. *Production executives* Marvin Mirisch, Harold Mirisch, Eliot Hyman and Ray Stark. *Production manager* Allen K. Wood. *Second assistant director* Jerome M. Siegel. *Music assistant* Betty Walberg. *Orchestrations* Sid Ramin and Irwin Kostel. *Vocal coach* Robert Tucker. *Solo musicians* Al Viola, Red Mitchell, Jack Dumont, Shelly Manne and Pete Candoli. *Music editor* Richard Carruth. *Sound editor* Gilbert D. Marchant. *Sound supervisors* Gordon E. Sawyer and Fred Hynes. *Sound* Murray Spivack, Fred Lau and Vinton Vernon. *Re-recording* Samuel Goldwyn Studios and Todd-AO. *Wardrobe* Bert Hendrickson. *Property* Sam Gordon. *Construction supervisor* William Maldonado. *Casting* Stalmaster-Lister Co. *Title sequence camera operator* John Finger. *Title sequence dolly grip* Louis Kulsey. *Production illustrators* Maurice Zuberano and Leon Harris. *Negative* Eastman Color. ¶A Mirisch Pictures Inc. presentation in association with Seven Arts Productions Inc. A Beta production. A B&P Enterprises picture. A Robert Wise film. Technicolor. Westrex six-track magnetic stereophonic sound. 155 minutes. Filmed at Samuel Goldwyn Studios and on location in New York City. ¶CAST: *Maria* Natalie Wood. *Tony* Richard Beymer. *Riff* Russ Tamblyn. *Anita* Rita Moreno. *Bernardo* George Chakaris. *Ice* Tucker Smith. *Action* Tony Mordente. *Baby John* Eliot Feld. *A-Rab* David Winters. *Snowboy* Burt Michaels. *Joyboy* Robert Banas. *Big Deal* Anthony "Scooter" Teague. *Gee-Tar* Tony Abbott.

Mouthpiece Harvey Hohnecker. *Tiger* David Bean. *Anybodys* Sue Oakes. *Graziella* Gina Trikonis. *Velma* Carole D'Andrea. *Chino* Joe De Vega. *Pepe* Jay Norman. *Indio* Gus Trikonis. *Luis* Robert Thompson. *Rocco* Larry Roquemore. *Loco* Jaime Rogers. *Juano* Eddie Verso. *Chile* Andre Tayir. *Toro* Nick Covvacevich. *Del Campo* Rudy Del Campo. *Rosalia* Suzie Kaye. *Consuelo* Yvonne Othon. *Francisca* Joanne Miya. *Lt. Schrank* Simon Oakland. *Ofr. Krupke* Bill Bramley. *Doc* Ned Glass. *Gladhand* John Astin. *Mme. Lucia* Penny Santon. *Natalie Wood's vocals* Marni Nixon. *Richard Beymer's vocals* Jimmy Bryant. *Rita Moreno's vocals* Betty Wand. ¶Advertising and screen billing credited Panavision 70. The filmmakers wanted the show run continuously without an intermission, and no announcement title card was included on the released prints; however, a musical buildup and fade out was set at reel's end midway through the story for those houses that wanted to have a break. Jerome Robbins left the production after doing the "Prologue," "In America," "I Feel Pretty" and "Cool" sequences.

The Whiskey Trail *see* **The Hallelujah Trail.**

Whispers *see* **The Bat Whispers.**

White Bim the Black Ear (1977). Filmed in Sovscope 70. *Screen author and director* Stanislav Rostotskiy. *Based on the opera "Beliy Bim Chernoe Ukho" by* Gavriil N. Troepolvskogo. *Operator* Viacheslav Shumskiy. *Artist* Sergei Serebrenikov. *Composer* Andrei Petrov. *Sound operator* I. Starokanov. ¶A Tsentraliniy studiya detskikh yunosheskikh filmov im. M. Gorikogo production. International distribution Sovexportfilm. Sovcolor. Six-track magnetic stereophonic sound. 182 minutes plus intermission. Filmed at Tsentraliniy studiya detskikh i yunosheskikh filmov im. M. Gorikogo, Moscow, R.S.F.S.R. ¶CAST: *Ivan Ivanovich* Viacheslav Tikhanov. *With* Valentina Vladimirova, M. Dadiko, I. Rizov, Irina Shevchuk, M. Zimin, G. Kochkazarov, R. Manukovskaya, L. Sokolova, V. Leonov, V. Sergienko, A. Ribnikova, V. Vorobiev, I. Zevago, B. Zakharova and F. Korchagin. ¶A Soviet production released in Russia in 1977 as *Beliy Bim Chernoe Ukho* in two parts running 95 and 87 minutes.

THRU
UA

MIRISCH PICTURES PRESENTS

"WEST SIDE STORY"
A ROBERT WISE
PRODUCTION

STARRING NATALIE WOOD

RICHARD BEYMER
RUSS TAMBLYN
RITA MORENO
GEORGE CHAKIRIS

DIRECTED BY ROBERT WISE AND JEROME ROBBINS
SCREENPLAY BY ERNEST LEHMAN ASSOCIATE PRODUCER
SAUL CHAPLIN CHOREOGRAPHY BY JEROME ROBBINS
MUSIC BY LEONARD BERNSTEIN

LYRICS BY STEPHEN SONDHEIM BASED UPON THE STAGE PLAY
PRODUCED BY ROBERT E. GRIFFITH AND HAROLD S. PRINCE
BOOK BY ARTHUR LAURENTS PLAY CONCEIVED, DIRECTED AND
CHOREOGRAPHED BY JEROME ROBBINS FILM PRODUCTION
DESIGNED BY BORIS LEVEN MUSIC CONDUCTED BY JOHNNY GREEN
FILMED IN PANAVISION®70 / TECHNICOLOR®
PRESENTED BY MIRISCH PICTURES, INC.
IN ASSOCIATION WITH SEVEN ARTS PRODUCTIONS, INC.

(Irving Berlin's) White Christmas. Filmed in VistaVision Motion Picture High Fidelity. *Producer* Robert Emmett Dolan. *Director* Michael Curtiz. *Writers for the screen* Norman Krasna, Norman Panama and Melvin Frank. *Based on the screenplay "Holiday Inn" by* Claude Binyon *as adapted by* Elmer Rice *from an original idea by* Irving Berlin. *Lyrics and music* Irving Berlin. *Music direction and vocal arrangements* Joseph J. Lilley. *Orchestral arrangements* Nathan Van Cleave. *Music associate* Troy Sanders. *Dances and musical numbers stager* Robert Alton. *Director of photography* Loyal C. Griggs. *Technicolor color consultant* Richard Mueller. *Art direction* Hal Periera and Roland Anderson. *Editor* Frank Bracht. *Special photographic effects* John P. Fulton. *Process photography* Farciot Edouart. *Set decoration* Sam Comer and Grace Gregory. *Costumes* Edith Head. *Makeup supervision* Wally Westmore. *Assistant director* John Coonan. *Sound recording* Hugo Grenzbach, John Cope and George Dutton. *Still photographer* Jack Koffman. *Optical photography* Paul K. Lerpae. *Matte artist* Jan Domela. *Wardrobe supervision* Frank Richardson. *Hair stylist* Nellie Manley. *Sound supervisor* Loren L. Ryder. *Supervising sound editor* Tommy Middleton. *Production manager* Frank Caffey. *Negative* Eastman Kodak. ¶Produced and released by Paramount Pictures. Technicolor. Western Electric Movietone recording. Perspecta Stereophonic Sound. 120 minutes. Filmed at Paramount Studios. ¶CAST: *Bob Wallace* Bing Crosby. *Phil Davis* Danny Kaye. *Betty* Rosemary Clooney. *Judy* Vera Ellen. *Gen. Waverly* Dean Jagger. *Emma* Mary Wickes. *Joe* John Brascia. *Susan* Anne Whitfield. *Adjutant* Richard Shannon. *General's guest* Grady Sutton. *Landlord* Sig Ruman. *Albert* Robert Crosson. *Novello* Herb Vigran. *Assistant stage manager* Dick Keene. *Ed Harrison* Johnny Grant. *Gen. Carlton* Gavin Gordon. *Maitre d'* Marcel de la Brosse. *Sheriff* James Parnell. *Conductor* Percy Helton. *Fat lady* Elizabeth Holmes. *Doris* Barry Chase. *Stationmaster* I. Stanford Jolley. *Specialty*

dancer George Chakiris. *With* Mike P. Donovan, Glen Carlyle, Lorraine Crawford, Joan Bayley, Lester Clark, Ernest Flatt and Bea Allen. ¶The first film in VistaVision. Released in anamorphic with a 1.5 × 1 compression and a 2 × 1 aspect ratio and presented in *Super*Scope, in regular 35mm for 1.85 × 1 wide screen cropping and in lazy 8 horizontal format for 1.85 × 1 wide screen cropping. This was not issued in magnetic stereo sound as believed by many. It was issued only with stereo optical sound using the Perspecta directional system. Current TV syndicated and home videocassette versions have been remixed in stereo by Chase Productions and do not have the original Perspecta soundtrack. A remake of *Holiday Inn* (Paramount, 1942), which also starred Bing Crosby.

Wicked, Wicked (April 1973). Filmed in Duo-Vision. *Executive producer* William T. Orr. *Producer, writer and director* Richard L. Bare. *Music* Philip Springer. *Organ music player* Ladd Thomas. *Director of photography* Frederick Gately. *Art director* Walter McKeegan. *Film editor* John F. Schreyer. *Set decorator* Charles R. Pierce. *Property master* Bob Anderson. *Unit production manager and assistant director* Donald C. Klune. *Second assistant director* Ronald J. Mertinez. *Electronic music effects consultant* Jim Cooper. *Sound* Jerry Jost and Hal Watkins. *Costume supervisor* Barbara Siebert. *Makeup* Paul Stanhope. *Hair stylist* Judy Alexander. *Script supervisor* Cleo M. Anton. *"Wicked, Wicked" and "I'll Be Myself"* music Philip Springer, *lyrics* Irwin Levine. ¶A Richard L. Bare-William T. Orr production. A United National Pictures, Inc. film. Released by Metro-Goldwyn-Mayer. Metrocolor. Westrex recording system. 95 minutes. Filmed on location at Hotel del Coronado, San Diego, California. MPAA rating: PG. ¶CAST: *Rick Stewart* David Bailey. *Lisa James* Tiffany Bolling. *Jason Grant* Randolph Roberts. *Sgt. Ramsey* Scott Brady. *Hank Lassiter* Edd Byrnes. *Dolores Hamilton* Diane McBain. *Hotel*

Opposite: *Since Panavision 70 had been renamed Super Panavision 70 over a year and a half before, it is something of a mystery why it was given the older trade name here. When the film was reissued in 1969, "70" was removed from the ads.*

manager Roger Bowen. *Lenore Karadyne* Madeleine Sherwood. *Genny* Indira Danks. *Hotel engineer* Arthur O'Connell. *Bill Broderick* Jack Knight. *Housekeeper* Patsy Garrett. *Day desk clerk* Robert Nichols. *Owen Williams* Kirk Bates. *Organist* Maryesther Denver. ¶The only dual screen feature released by a major distributor. The release prints were anamorphic 2.35 × 1 with the frame split in the middle. Each half showed a different scene. Occasionally a single, full 'scope shot would be used to bridge story sections. This was unwatchable in any theater not using the full 2.35 × 1 ratio, and since very few cinemas were so equipped it must have looked very strange indeed to the vast majority of individuals who saw it.

(Louis de Rochemont's) Windjammer (April 10, 1958). Filmed in Cinemiracle. *Executive producer for National Theatres* Elmer C. Rhodes, President. *Producer* Louis de Rochemont. *Associate producers* Louis de Rochemont III, Borden Mace, Thomas Orchard and Lothar Wolff. *Directors* Louis de Rochemont III and Bill Colleran. *Story* Louis de Rochemont III. *Story consultants* Capt. Alan Villiers and James L. Shute. *Musical score* Morton Gould. *Conductor of the Cinemiracle Symphony Orchestra* Jack Shaindin. *Directors of photography* Gayne Rescher and Joseph Brun. *Camera operator* Coleman Thomas Conroy, Jr. *Camera assistant* Fred Montague. *Camera technician* Bob Gaffney. *Special New York photography* Weegee. *Prolog (35mm) photography* Finn Bergan and Aasmund Revold. *Film editor* Peter Ratkevich. *Assistant film editors* Richard Sears, Vito Doino and Jerry Klein. *Sound effects editor* Frederick G. White. *Director of sound* Richard J. Pietschmann, Jr. *Sound engineers* Robert A. Sherwood, James O. Porter and Eugene W. Wood. *Assistant to the directors* George Vosburgh. *Titles* Philip Stapp. *Ship's scribe* Erik Bye. *Production controller* Martin Maloney. *General business manager* John J. Wingerter. *Production staff* William H. Terry, James A. Petrie, Michael A. Roemer, Ronald Hobin, Ivan Jacobsen, Costa de Sala, Jean Pages and Curtis W. Davis. *Chief grip* Michael Mahoney. *Second grip* Kenneth Fundus. *Grips* Asbjorn and Arian Fredriksen. *Chief electrician* Frank Rutledge. *Electricians* Egil Tressalt, Billy Ward, Bobby Meyerhoff, Willy Meyerhoff and Richard Falk. *Generator operator* Harvey Genkins. *Unit publicist* James W. Hardiman. *Still photographers* Ormond Gigli, Finn Bergan, Aasmund Revold, Donald Christie, Raul Perestrello, Fred Fischer, Sam Rosenberg and Tex Brewer. *Cinemiracle development* National Theatres Amusement Co. *Director of research and development* Russell H. McCullough. *Electronic lens system development* Smith-Dietrich Corp. *Electronic lens system designer* P. Stanley Smith. *Consultant for Smith-Dietrich Corp.* George Wilbur Moffitt. *Director of technical film services* Richard C. Babish. *Projection research engineers* Ray Melling and Mack G. Lunt. *Projection design engineers* Stefan Jan Biskup and Carl G. Moeller. *Cameras* Mitchell Camera Corp. *Production equipment* Camera Equipment Co. *Technical consultant* Capt. Alan Villiers, S.S. *Mayflower II*. *Technical advisers* Cmdr. Antoine W. Venn, Jr., U.S.N.; Lt. Glenn M. Brewer, U.S.N.; Alf Bjercke, Oslo; Egil Tressalt, Oslo; Capt. Knut Hansen, S.S. *Danmark* and Capt. Paul Heggerstrom, S.S. *Sorlandet*. *Songs:* "Marianne" Terry Gilkyson; "Kari Waits for Me," "The Sea Is Green," "Everybody Loves Saturday Night," "The Village of New York," "Sweet Sugar Cane," "Don't Hurry-Worry Me" and "Life on the Ocean Wave" Terry Gilkyson and The Easy Riders [Richard Dehr and Frank Miller]. "Piano Concerto in A Minor" Edvard Grieg, *performers* Sven Erik Libaek and The Boston Pops Orchestra, *conductor* Arthur Fielder. "Song of the Birds" *cello soloist* Pablo Casals, *violinist* Alexander Schneider, *pianist* Mieczyslaw Horszowski. *Film* Eastman Kodak Co. ¶A Louis de Rochemont Cinemiracle Productions, Inc. picture from National Theatres, Inc. Released by NTA Pictures, Inc. Color by Dubray-Howell. RCA Stereo Hi-Fi 7-Track Cinemiracle Sound. 142 minutes including overture, intermission and exit music. Filmed in Oslo, Norway, Funchal, Madeira (Portugal), San Juan, Puerto Rico, Willemstad, Curacao (Netherlands Antilles), Port-of-Spain, Trinidad (Venezuela), New York City, Portsmouth, New Hampshire and on the Atlantic Ocean aboard the S.S. *Christian Radish*. ¶CAST: *Captain* Yngvar Kjelstrup. *First officer* Nils Arnsten. *Second officer* Oscar Strønen. *Third officer*

First
SOUND
then
COLOR
and now

DUO-VISION

Jack Warner who brought the first all talking picture to the screen says,

"DUO-VISION MAKES FOR EXCITING ENTERTAINMENT AS DID THE INTRODUCTION OF SOUND AND COLOR."

WICKED, WICKED
TWICE THE TENSION! TWICE THE TERROR!

Starring DAVID BAILEY · TIFFANY BOLLING · RANDY ROBERTS

Executive Producer WILLIAM T. ORR · Written, Produced

and Directed by RICHARD L. BARE

METROCOLOR MGM

PG | PARENTAL GUIDANCE SUGGESTED
Some material may not be suitable for pre-teenagers

Why is Jack L. Warner quoted in this ad? Because William T. Orr was his son-in-law. This art work is pretty much representative of what the actual film looked like, except the screen image was 2.35×1 and not 2×1 as in this ad.

Semund Remøy. *Chief engineer* Nils Hermansen. *Doctor* Gunnulv Hauge. *Sergeant* Harmvild Landstad. *First bosun* Asbjørn Espenak. *Second bosun* Arian Fredriksen. *Motorman* Arne Andersen. *Steward* Sverre Solheim. *First cook* Eric Sanbach. *Second cook* Knut Iverson. *Sailmaker* Sigurd Borgen. *First assistant bosun* Gunnar Haugsvaer. *Second assistant bosun* Trygve Bendiksen. *Third assistant bosun* Lasse Kolstad. *Cadets* Harald Tusberg, Sven Erik Libaek, Kaare Terland, Jon Reistad, Frode Ringheim and Per Johnsen. *Other cadets* Bjørn Sanbech, Tor Markussen, Leiv Fornes, Bjørn Amvik, Reider Kjelstrup, Arild Kristoffersen, Frithjof Thoresen, Johan Egeland, Geir Ivar Nustad, Jørgen Lanes, Olav Knudsen, Tormod Tofteland, Tor Fossnes, Fred Hegerstrøm, Otto Snildal, Carl Robert Pihl, Tor Rue, Harry Guttersrud, Per Antonsen, Edvard Hokland, Svein Aske, Peer Dahl, Hans Tandberg, Egil Sandnes, Jan Christiansen, Jan Høyberg, Kjell Holm, Even Børresen, Jan Halversen, Audun Heggertveit, Ola Maerk, Per Kirkaune, Kjell Kristensen, Bjørn Owren, Stein Petterson, Tor-Arne Strømmen, Thormond Saglien, Thor Dalelv and Tore Bilet. *In Oslo* Capt. Aksel Molvig, Capt. Rudolf Heistand, members of the Eastern Norwegian Schoolship Association, officers and men of the Royal Norwegian Navy aboard the K.N.M. *Garm* and The Royal Norwegian Yacht Club. *In Maderia* staff and orchestra of the Hotel Savoy, Delegacao de Turismo da Madeira (Basto Machado, Vasco Mendes, Joao Periera), Mrs. Cary Garton, Senhor Toni Nunes, Mountain Shepherds Band and Dancers, The Camacha Dancers, The Folkloric Dancers, Gov. and Mrs. Luis Munoz-Marin, Pablo Casals, Alexander Schneider, Mieczyslaw Horszowski. *In St. Thomas* Blue Manta Underwater Swimming Club (Dr. Dean Clyde, leader). *In Trinidad* The Boys Town Steel Band, The Silvertones Steel Band, Peter Rapsey's Ocean Extravaganza Group, Mayor Louis Rotant of Port-of-Spain, Royal Norwegian Consul Mathias J. Oeren, Mighty Skipper, Mighty Viper, Lord Superior, Al Thomas, The March of Dimes Singing Sextet, The Limbo Dance Group (featuring Henry "Junio" Trim), Port-of-Spain Police Brass Band and Mounted Officers. *In Curacao* Folk Dance Group of Peter Stuyvesant School (featuring Marian Tulleners and Goutje Kanbier), Pastor Siem, Norwegian Seamen's Home (P.J. Evertsz, James Leander). *In Copenhagen* Tivoli Gardens (Henning Soage, Inge Bock), Tivoli Boys Royal Guard and Band (Capt. O.E. Qvist, director), Jorn Tunbo. *In New York City* Wilbur de Paris, Sydney de Paris, Omar Simson, Lee Blair, Arthur Fielder and the Boston "Pops" Orchestra. *Personnel and ships of the United States Navy* R. Adm. Joseph C. Daniels, Commander, Destroyer Force, Atlantic Fleet; Submarine Squadron Twelve (Capt. W.F. Schlech, Jr., commanding; Cmdr. A.F. Betzel); Underwater Swimmers School, Key West, Florida (Lt. Cmdr. J.C. Roe, commanding; Lt. (j.g.) H.A. Jones, J.R. Hazelwood, R.W. Shouse); officers and men of U.S.S. *Odax* (SS 484) (Lt. Cmdr. E. Barrett, commanding); officers and men of U.S.S. *Thornback* (SS 418) (Lt. Cmdr. O.J. Bryant, commanding); officers and men of U.S.S. *Chivo* (SS 341) (Lt. Cmdr. W.D. Dietricksen, commanding); officers and men of U.S.S. *Bushnell* (AS 15) (Capt. J.B. Hess, commanding); Cmdr. Russell Crenshaw, commanding officer of U.S.S. *Forrest Sherman* (DD 931); Underwater Demolitian Team Twenty-One (Cmdr. Frank B. Kaine, commanding; William O'Brien, George Ball); officers and men of U.S.S. *Willis A. Lee* (DL 4); officers and men of U.S.S. *Manley* (DD 940); officers and men of U.S.S. *Gyatt* (DDG 712); officers and men of U.S.S. *Stribling* (DD 867); officers and men of U.S.S. *Becuna* (SS 426); Operation "Springboard" Task Force 81.3 headed by U.S.S. *Valley Forge* (CVS 45). ¶Presented in Cinerama in some theatres. Copyright registration lists the running time as 113 minutes, but this is an error. It would be 131 minutes not including intermission.

With Death on Your Back *see* **Con la morte alla spalle.**

With Fidelity and Truth (1980). Filmed in Sovscope 70. *Screen author* Aleksandr Chervinskiy. *Director* Andrei Smirnov. *Operators* Igor Bek and V. Osherov. *Artist* Aleksandr Boym and Aleksandr Makarov. *Composer* Nikolai Karetnikov. *Sound operator* Ya. Pototskiy. ¶A

Mosfilm production. International distribution Sovexportfilm. Sovcolor. Six-track magnetic stereophonic sound. 176 minutes plus intermission. Filmed at Mosfilm Studios, Moscow, R.S.F.S.R. ¶CAST: *Vladislav Minchenko* Aleksandr Kalyagin. *Ivan Kvashnin* Sergei Plotnikov. *Sergei Kryakin* Sergei Shakurov. *Klava* Elena Proklova. *With* Nonna Mordyukova, Leonid Markov, Evgeni Leonov, Lev Durov, Valentina Talizina, Kira Golovko and I. Bortink. ¶A Soviet production released in Russia in 1980 as *Veroy i pravdoy* in two parts running 91 minutes and 85 minutes.

Witness for the Defense (1977). Filmed in Sovscope 70. *Screen author* Aleksandr Mindadze. *Director* Vadim Abdrashitov. *Operator* Anatoly Zabolotskiy. *Artist* Ippolit Novoderezkin. *Composer* V. Martinov. *Sound operator* R. Margacheva. ¶A Mosfilm production. International distribution Sovexportfilm. Sovcolor. Six-track magnetic stereophonic sound. 98 minutes. Filmed at Mosfilm Studios, Moscow, R.S.F.S.R. ¶CAST: *Valya* Marina Neylova. *Irina* Galina Yatskina. *Fediayev* Stanislav Lyubshin. *Ruslan* Oleg Yankovskiy. *With* V. Shuligin, E. Kebal, A. Grachev, Z. Izotov, V. Berezutskaya, V. Kupriyanov and A. Alekseev. ¶A Soviet production released in Russia in 1977 as *Slovo dlya zashchiti.*

The Wonderful World of the Brothers Grimm (August 7, 1962). Filmed in Super Cinerama. *Producer* George Pal. *Director* Henry Levin. *Fairy tales director* George Pal. *Screenplay* David P. Harmon, Charles Beaumont and William Roberts. *Screen story* David P. Harmon. *Based on the book "Die Bruder Grimm" by* Dr. Hermann Gerstner. *Music score* Leigh Harline *conducting the* MGM Symphony Orchestra. *Words and music for the songs* "Ah-oom," "Christmas Land," "Dee-Are-A-Gee-O-En (Dragon)" *and* "The Dancing Princess" *and the themes* "The Wonderful World of the Brothers Grimm," "Above the Stars" *and* "Gypsy Fire" Bob Merrill. *Director of photography* Paul C. Vogel. *Art direction* George W. Davis and Edward Carfagno. *Set decoration* Henry Grace and Richard Pefferle. *Color consultant* Charles K. Hagedon. *Special*

visual effects Gene Warren, Wah Chang, Tim Barr, Robert R. Hoag, James Danforth, David Pal, Don Sahlin and Pete Kleinow. *Film editor* Walter Thompson. *Assistant director* Al Jennings. *Costumes* Mary Wills. *Choreography* Alex Romero. *Recording supervisor* Franklin Milton. *Makeup creator* William Tuttle. *Hair styles* Sydney Guilaroff and Mary Keats. *Production supervisor for Cinerama, Inc.* Coleman Thomas Conroy, Jr. *Assistant to the producer* Gae Griffith. *European production coordinator* Robert R. Snody. MGM *sound consultant* Douglas Shearer. *Cinerama sound consultants* Fred Bosch and Ray Sharples. *Rerecording* William Steinkamp. *Cinerama camera engineers* Pete Gibbons and Erik Rondum. *Song "The Singing Bone" music* Bob Merrill; *words* Charles Beaumont. *Vocal arrangements* Robert Armbruster. *Zither soloist* Ruth Welcome. ¶A Metro-Goldwyn-Mayer, Inc.–Cinerama, Inc. presentation. A George Pal production. A Gallen Films, S.A. picture. Technicolor. Westrex recording system. Seven-track magnetic Cinerama Sound. 135 minutes plus overture, intermission and exit music. Filmed at MGM Studios and Bavaria Atelier and on location in Rothenburg ob der Tauber, Dinkelsbuehl, Neuschwanstein, the Rhine River Valley and the Black Forest, Bavaria, West Germany. ¶CAST: *Wilhelm Grimm* Laurence Harvey. *Jacob Grimm* Karl Boehm. *Dorothea Grimm* Claire Bloom. *Stossel* Walter Slezak. *Greta Heinrich* Barbara Eden. *The Duke* Oscar Homolka. *The story teller* Martita Hunt. *Gruber* Ian Wolfe. *Miss Bettenhausen* Betty Garde. *Frau Von Dittersdorf* Cheerio Meredith. *Freidrich Grimm* Bryan Russell. *Pauline Grimm* Tammy Marihugh. *Priest* Walter Rilla. *Choir* The Regensburg Domspatzen Choir. **The Dancing Princess:** *Dancing princess* Yvette Mimieux. *Woodsman* Russ Tamblyn. *King* Jim Backus. *Gypsy* Beulah Bondi. *Prime minister* Clint Sundberg. *Court jester* Billy Barty. **The Cobbler and the Elves:** *Cobbler* Laurence Harvey. *Burgomaster* Walter Brooke. *Ballerina* Sandra Gale Bettin. *Huntsman* Robert Foulk. *Elves* The Puppetoons. **The Singing Bone:** *Ludwig* Terry-Thomas. *Hans* Buddy Hackett. *King* Otto Krueger. *Shepherd* Robert Crawford, Jr. *Spokesman* Sydney Smith. **The Dream:** *tom thumb* Russ Tamblyn. *Rumpelstiltskin*

Ad for The Wonderful World of the Brothers Grimm, *advertised as the first dramatic film in Cinerama.*

Arnold Stang. *Giant* Peter Whitney. *Snow White* True Ellison. *Cinderella* Pamela Beaird. *Hansel* Stanley Fafara. *Gretel* Diana Driscoll. *Little Red Riding Hood* Ruthie Robinson. ¶Advertised as the first dramatic film in Cinerama. Converted to spherical 70mm and anamorphic 35mm formats. 35mm general release and 16mm nontheatrical prints ran 129 minutes

without an overture, intermission or exit music. Interestingly, the 35mm general release trailer contained clips of the cut footage.

Woodstock (March 26, 1970). Filmed in Multi-Screen. *Producer* Bob Maurice. *Director* Michael Wadleigh. *Assistant directors* Martin Scorsese and Thelma

Schoonmaker. *Supervising editors* Michael Wadleigh, Thelma Schoonmaker and Martin Scorsese. *Production head and associate producer* Dale Bell. *Principal photography* Michael Wadleigh, David Meyers, Richard Pearce, Donald Lenzer and Al Wertheimer. *Additional photography* Michael Margetts, Ed Lynch, Richard Chew, Charles Levey, Ted Churchill, Fred Underhill, Robert Danneman and Stan Warnow. *Production managers* Sonya Polonsky and Lewis Teague. *Assistant to the director, still photographer and sound and music editor* Larry Johnson. *Documentary unit coordinator* John Bindor. *Performance location sound* Bill Hanley, Hanley Sound. *Performance sound coordinator* Eric Blackstead. *Performance sound mixer* Ed Kramer. *Performance sound engineer* Dan Turbeville. *Documentary soundmen* Larry Johnson, Charles Groesbeck, Malcolm Hart, Joe Louw, Bruce Perkman and Charles Pitt. *Music scoring mixer* Daniel Wallin. *Postproduction sound supervisor* George R. Groves. *Postproduction sound* Warner Bros. Sound Department. *Location liaison* Bill Hilliker. *Editors* Robert Alverez, Yeu Bun-Yee, Bettina Kugel Hirsh, Jere Huggins, Muffie Meyer and Stan Warnow. *Editing sync* Mirra Bank, Ed Cariati, Ted Duffield, Barney Edmonds, Lana Jokel, Bill Lipsky, Janet Loratano, Susan Steinberg, Anita Thatcher and Winston Tucker. *Editing assistants* Jim Stark, Angela Kirby Miriam Eger and Phyllis Altenhaus. *Sound assistants* Charles Ciriglano, Ed George and Al Zayat. *Production executive* Michael Bell. *Production liaison* Alice Marks. *Location production assistant* Fern McBride. *Unit publicist* Rhona Kane. *Electricians* Martin Andrews and Bobby Vee. *Original 16mm processing and printing* J&D Labs, New York. *Opticals* Cinema Research Corporation. *"Woodstock"* by Joni Mitchell. *"Long Time Gone"* by David Crosby. *"Wooden Ships"* by David Crosby and Stephen Stills. *"Suite: Judy Blue Eyes"* by Stephen Stills; *performers* Crosby, Stills, Nash & Young. *"Going Up in the Country"* by Alan Wilson; *performers* Canned Heat. *"Handsome Johnny"* by Richie Havens and Louis Goussett; *performer* Richie Havens. *"Freedom" (adapted from "Sometimes I Feel Like a Motherless Child") performer* Richie Havens. *"Joe*

Hill" by Earl Robinson and Alfred Hayes; *performer* Joan Baez. *"We're Not Going to Take It"* by Peter Townshend. *"Summertime Blues"* by Jerry Capehart and Eddie Cochran; *performers* The Who. *"At the Hop"* by A. Siger, J. Medora and P. White; *performers* Sha-Na-Na. *"Rock & Soul Music"* by Joe McDonald, Barry Melton, Chicken Hirsch, Bruce Barthol and David Cohen. *"The 'Fish' Cheer"* and *"I-Feel-Like-I'm-Fixin'-to-Die Rag"* by Joe McDonald; *performers* Country Joe & the Fish. *"With a Little Help from My Friends"* by John Lennon and Paul McCartney; *performer* Joe Cocker. *"Coming into Los Angeles"* writer and performer Arlo Guthrie. *"I'm Goin' Home"* by Alvin Lee; *performers* Ten Years After. *"Younger Generation"* writer and performer John Sebastian. *"Soul Sacrifice"* by Carlos Santana, Gregg Rolie, Jose Areas, Mike Carabello, David Brown and Michael Schrieve; *performers* Santana. *"Dance to the Music," "Music Lover"* and *"I Want to Take You Higher"* by Sylvester Stewart; *performers* Sly and the Family Stone. *"Star-Spangled Banner"* and *"Purple Haze" performer* Jimmi Hendrix. ¶A Wadleigh-Maurice, Ltd. production. A Michael Wadleigh film. Released by Warner Bros. Technicolor. RCA four-track MagOptical stereophonic sound. 184 minutes plus intermission. MPAA rating: R. ¶CAST: *Appearing as themselves* Joan Baez, Joe Cocker, Country Joe & the Fish, Crosby, Stills, Nash & Young, Arlo Guthrie, Richie Havens, Jimi Hendrix, Santana, John Sebastian, Sha-Na-Na, Sly and the Family Stone, Ten Years After, The Who and 500,000 others including the residents of Woodstock, New York. ¶The first of the rockumentaries, usually shot in 16mm, which were printed in multi image and released in anamorphic format. *More American Graffiti* (Universal, 1979) parodied the format.

World by Night No.2 (July 1962). Filmed in Super Technirama 70. *Producer* Francesco Mazzi. *Director* Gianni Proia. *Script* Carlo Laurenti. *Music* Piero Piccioni. ¶A Julia Film production. Released by Warner Bros. Pictures. Technicolor. 118 minutes. ¶This Italian documentary was a sequel to *World by Night* (Warner Bros., 1961) and was filmed in cabarets around the world. It was released in Europe in 70mm and six-track magnetic stereophonic sound but appears to have been shown in the U.S. in 35mm anamorphic only. It received extremely limited U.S. distribution.

World Coaster (1981). Filmed in OMNIMAX. *Technical director* Yasvo A. Hara. ¶A Daiei Motion Picture Company, Ltd. presentation. A Gakken Companny, Ltd. production. Released by Imax Systems Corporation. Eastman Color. Six-track magnetic stereophonic sound. 20 minutes. Filmed in Australia, Pearl Islands, California, the Grand Canyon, New York City, the Alps, Bavaria and Kenya. A Japanese production originally made for the Daiei Pavilion at Portopia Exposition in Kobe, Japan.

Ya — grazdanin Sovetskogo Soyuza *see* **I Am a Citizen of the Soviet Union.**

Ya — Shapovalov T.P. *see* **Lofty Title.**

Ya videl rozdenie novogo mira *see* **Red Bells.**

Yaroslav Dombrovskiy (1976). Filmed in Sovscope 70. *Screen author* Yu. Nagiban. *Director* B. Poremba. *Operators* A. Shelzikov and I. Chon. *Artists* S. Ushakov and E. Skshepiniskiy. *Composer* V. Kilar. *Sound operators* I. Urvantsev, K. Grabovskiy and E. Blyashinskiy. ¶A Mosfilm production in collaboration with Panorama. International distribution Sovexportfilm. Sovcolor. Six-track magnetic stereophonic sound. 140 minutes plus intermission. Filmed at Mosfilm Studios, Moscow, R.S.F.S.R. ¶CAST: Z. Malyanovich, M. Pototska, A. Kalyagin, V. Avdyushko, V. Ivashov, S. Novinskiy, S. Shmidt, Yu. Novak, L. Lionet, F. Metr, A. Dimiters, T. Engelv, T. Borovskiy, E. Kopelyan, L. Luzina, M. Kozakov, K. Lenyu, N. Smorchkov and V. Pogorelitsev. ¶A Soviet production released in Russia in 1976 in two parts running 78 minutes and 62 minutes.

Yaroslav Mudriy *see* **Yaroslav the Wise.**

Yaroslav the Wise (1982). Filmed in Sovscope 70. *Screen authors* Pavlo Zagrebeliniy, Mikhail Veprinskiy and Grigori Kokhan. *Director* Grigori Kokhan. *Operator* Felix Gilevich. *Artists* Viktor Zilko and Larissa Zilko. *Composer* Evgeni Stankevich. *Sound operator* V. Sulimov. *Still photo* Aleksandr Bronstein. ¶A Kievskaya kinostudiya im. A.P. Dovzenko-Mosfilm production. International distribution Sovexportfilm. Sovcolor. Six-track magnetic stereophonic sound. 187 minutes plus intermission. Filmed at Kievskaya kinostudiya im. A.P. Dovzenko, Kiev, Ukrainian S.S.R. ¶CAST: *Grand Prince Yaroslav* Yuri Muravitskiy. *Yaroslav's wife* Lyudmila Smorodina. *Lyubava* Tatiana Kondryreva. *Prince Vladimir* Pyotr Veliyaminov. *Prince Stepankov* Konstantin Stepankov. *Nikon* Nikolai Griniko. *Gov. Tverdislav* Leonid Filatov. *With* O. Drach, N. Beliy, N. Babenko, O. Belyavskaya, V. Dvorzetskiy and B. Vataev. ¶A Soviet production released in Russia in 1982 as *Varoslav Mudriy* in two parts running 89 minutes and 98 minutes.

Yarosti (1966). Filmed in Sovscope 70. *Screen authors* E. Onoprienko and A. Satskiy. *Based on the story "Veter" by* B. Lavreneva. *Director and producer* N. Iliinskiy. *Operators* V. Voytenko and A. Pishchkov. *Artist* I. Yutsevich. *Composer* K. Dominchen. *Sound operator* G. Parahnikov. ¶A Kievskaya kinostudiya im. A.P. Dovzenko production. International distribution Sovexportfilm. Sovcolor. Six-track magnetic stereophonic sound. 95 minutes. Filmed at Kievskaya kinostudiya im. A.P. Dovzenko, Kiev, Ukrainian S.S.R. ¶CAST: Evgeny Matveev, V. Mityukov, M. Volodina, A. Glazirin, I. Pereverzev, G. Poloka, A. Ivanov, A. Gay and A. Gorbov. ¶A Soviet production released in Russia in 1966.

Yemelyan Pugachov (1979). Filmed in Sovscope 70. *Screen author* Eduard Volodarskiy. *Director* Alexei Saltikov. *Operator* Igor Chernikh. *Artist* Stalen Volkov. *Composer* Andrei Eshpay. *Sound operator* A. Kosodokov. ¶A Mosfilm production. International distribution Sovexportfilm. Sovcolor. Six-track magnetic stereophonic sound. 197 minutes plus intermission. Filmed at Mosfilm Studios, Moscow and on location in Moscow, Leningrad, Pereyaslavl-Zalessky, Urals, Western Siberia, Belorussia and Eastern Steppes, R.S.F.S.R. ¶CAST: *Emeliyan Pugachev* Evgeny

Matveev. *Stepan Fedulov* Pyotr Glebov. *Katherine II* Via Artmane. *Sofia Pugachev* Tamara Semina. *With* Olga Prokhorova, Grigori Grigoriy, Boris Kulikov, Boris Kudryavtsev, Yuri Ilyanov, Inagam Adylov, Boris Plotnikov, Igor Gorbachov, Anatoly Azo, Yuri Volkov, Viktor Pavlov and F. Odinokov. ¶A Soviet production released in Russia in 1979 as *Emeliyan Pugachev* in two parts: *Nevolinikts svobodi* running 111 minutes and *Volya, kroviyu omitaya* running 86 minutes.

You're in the Army Now (July 18, 1929). Filmed in Magnifilm. *Executive producer* Adolph Zukor. *Director* Joseph Stanley. *Deviser and stager* Jack Partington. *Based on the sketch by* Johnny Burke. ¶An Adolph Zukor presentation. A Paramount Publix Corporation production. Released by Paramount Pictures. Western Electric Movietone recording. 2 reels. ¶CAST: Johnny Burke (?). ¶Filmed simultaneously in 35mm framed for cropping to 1.85×1 for Magnascope wide screen projection. Released in 35mm on October 10, 1930. Until now this film has been the source of much confusion. No studio files seem to exist on this short or on Magnifilm, and the only known frames from the film are of a ship at anchor. This has led all previous writers and researchers to believe — with some justification! — that the title must have been *We're in the Navy,* actually an earlier Paramount feature which was exhibited in Magnascope. The only known contemporary article on the film didn't even mention the title or subject but concerned itself solely the Magnifilm process.

Zabudite slovo smerti *see* **Forget the Word Death.**

Zacharovannaya Desna *see* **The Enchanted Desna.**

Zakhar Berkut (1972). Filmed in Sovscope 70. *Screen author* D. Pavlichko. *Based on the story by* Ivan Franko. *Director* Leonid Osika. *Operator* V. Kvas. *Artist* Georgi Yakutovich. *Composer* V. Guba. *Sound operator* A. Chernoochenko. ¶A Kievskaya kinostudiya im. A.P. Dovzhenko production. International distribution Sovexportfilm. Sovcolor. Six-track magnetic stereophonic sound. 122 minutes.

Filmed at Kievskaya kinostudiya im. A.P. Dovzenko, Kiev, Ukrainian S.S.R. ¶CAST: *Zakhar Berkut* Vassili Simchich. *Tugar Vovk* Konstantin Stepankov. *Lyubomir* Ivan Mikolaichuk. *Maxim* Ivan Gavrilyuk. *Miroslava* Antonia Leftiy. *With* B. Brondukov, B. Beyshenaliev, I. Mikolaychuk, F. Panasenko, E. Prokofiev, V. Razstalinoy and V. Shakalo. ¶A Soviet production released in Russia in 1972.

Zakon Antarktidi *see* **The Law of the Antarctic.**

Zaloznik (1984). Filmed in Sovscope 70. *Screen authors* V. Maksimenkov and L. Makhkamov. *Director* Yu. Yusupov. *Operator* R. Mukhamedzanov. *Composer* G. Aleksandrov. *Sound operator* F. Makhmudov. ¶A Tadzikfilm production. International distribution Sovexportfilm. Sovcolor. Six-track magnetic stereophonic sound. 77 minutes. Filmed at Tadzikfilm Studios, Dushanbe, Tadzhik S.S.R. ¶CAST: K. Butaev, B. Akramov, M. Makhmadov, I. Ergeshev, R. Sagdullaev, Yu. Yusupov, Z. Zarobekova, D. Khamraev, S. Sattarov and R. Urazaev. ¶A Soviet production released in Russia in 1984.

Zalp "Avrori" (1965). Filmed in Sovscope 70. *Screen authors* B. Lavrenev and Yu. Vishinskiy. *Director and producer* Yu. Vishinskiy. *Chief operator* A. Nazarov. *Chief artist* S. Malkin and N. Suvorov. *Composer* V. Soloviev-Sedoy. *Sound operator* T. Silaev. ¶A Lenfilm production. International distribution Sovexportfilm. Sovcolor. Six-track magnetic stereophonic sound. 89 minutes. Filmed at Lenfilm Studios, Leningrad, R.S.F.S.R. ¶CAST: M. Kuznetsov, V. Tatosov, Yu. Balmusov, S. Yakovlev, I. Zabludovskiy, I. Kondratieva, K. Lavrov, Z. Kirienko, B. Freyndlikh, G. Gay, P. Luspekaev and I. Dmitrnev. ¶A Soviet production released in Russia in 1965.

Zarkoe leto v Kabule *see* **A Hot Summer in Kabul.**

Zdesi, na moey zemle (1980). Filmed in Sovscope 70. *Screen author* B. Privalov. *Directors* V. Dostali and A. Chemodurov. *Operators* Yu. Avdeev and V. Fridkin. *Artist* K. Forostenko. *Composer* Evgeni Doga. *Sound operator* Yu. Mikhaylov.

Songs E. Evtushenko. ¶A Mosfilm production. International distribution Sovexportfilm. Sovcolor. Six-track magnetic stereophonic sound. 106 minutes. Filmed at Mosfilm Studios, Moscow, R.S.F.S.R. ¶CAST: V. Sedov, V. Zaklunnaya, V. Gorallo, G. Dunts, S. Gronskiy, N. Volkov, I. Lapikov, M. Kokshenov, V. Vladimirova, N. Timofeev and N. Shutiko. ¶A Soviet production released in Russia in 1980.

Zdravstvuy, Sochi! (1977). Filmed in Sovscope 70. International distribution Sovexportfilm. Sovcolor. Six-track magnetic stereophonic sound. A Soviet production released in Russia in 1977.

Zelezniy potok *see* **The Iron Flood.**

Zerebenok v yablokakh (1981). Filmed in Sovscope 70. International distribution Sovexportfilm. Sovcolor. Six-track magnetic stereophonic sound. A Soviet production released in Russia in 1981.

Ziemia obiecana *see* **Land of Promise.**

Zil otvazniy kapitan (1985). Filmed in Sovscope 70. *Screen author* S. Karmalita. *Director* R. Fruntov. *Operator* O. Martinov. *Artist* V. Zenkov. *Composer* M. Ziv. *Sound operator* N. Kropotov. ¶A Mosfilm production. International distribution Sovexportfilm. Sovcolor. Six-track magnetic stereophonic sound. 116 minutes. Filmed at Mosfilm Studios, Moscow, R.S.F.S.R. ¶CAST: A. Kulyamin, M. Sergeecheva, I. Yasulovich, A. Gusev, Yu. Duvakhov, V. Petrenko, K. Luchko, V. Druznikov, P. Lyubeshkin, S. Konovalova, A. Yanvarev, Vladimir Nosik and B. Puladze. ¶A Soviet production released in Russia in 1985.

Zimnie ztyutsi (1963). Filmed in Kinopanorama. International distribution Sovexportfilm. Sovcolor. Nine-track magnetic Kinopanorama Sound. A Soviet production released in Russia in 1963.

Zizni i smerti Ferdinanda Lyusa *see* **The Life and Death of Ferdinand Luce.**

Zkipaz *see* **The Crew.**

Zkzamen na bessmertie *see* **Taste of Immortality.**

Znetsi (1979). Filmed in Sovscope 70. *Screen author and director* V. Denisenko. *Operator* N. Kulichinskiy. *Artist* P. Maksimenko. *Composer* V. Guba. *Sound operator* G. Parakhnikov. ¶A Kievskaya kinostudiya im. A.P. Dovzenko production. International distribution Sovexportfilm. Sovcolor. Six-track magnetic stereophonic sound. 122 minutes. Filmed at Kievskaya kinostudiya im. A.P. Dovzenko, Kiev, Ukrainian S.S.R. ¶CAST: A. Rudakov, T. Platenko, N. Andreychenko, Natalia Naum, M. Krinitsina, I. Tarapata, A. Khostikoev, B. Benyuk and N. Gebdovskaya. ¶A Soviet production released in Russia in 1979.

Zolotye vorota *see* **The Golden Gate.**

Zskadron gusar letuchikh *see* **The Flying Hussar Squadron.**

Zulu (June 17, 1964). Filmed in Super Technirama 70. *Producers* Stanley Baker and Cyril Endfield. *Director* Cyril Endfield. *Screenplay* John Prebble and Cyril Endfield. *Story* John Prebble. *Director of photography* Stephen Dade. *Original music composer and conductor* John Barry. *Editor* John Jympson. *Associate producer* Basil Keys. *Second unit director* Bob Porter. *Sound recordists* Claude Hitchcock and Jack R. Smith. *Sound editor* Rusty Coppleman. *Assistant editor* Jennifer Thompson. *Art director* Ernest Archer. *Wardrobe supervisor* Arthur Newman. *Makeup creator* Charles Parker. *Stunt director* John Sullivan. *Production manager* John D. Merriman. *Assistant director* Bert Batt. *Continuity* Muirne Mathieson. *Production consultant* Douglas Rankin. *Camera operator* Dudley Lovell. *Construction manager* Dick Frift. *Main title designers* National Screen Service, Ltd. ¶A Joseph E. Levine presentation. A Stanley Baker-Cyril Endfield production. A Diamond Films, Ltd. picture. Released by Embassy Pictures. Technicolor. Westrex six-track magnetic stereophonic sound. 138 minutes. Filmed on location in Tugola River Valley and Natal National Park, South Africa. ¶CAST: *Lt. John Chard, R.E.* Stanley Baker. *Rev. Otto Witt* Jack Hawkins. *Margaretta Witt* Ulla Jacobsson. *Pvt. Henry Hook* James Booth. *Lt. Gonville Bromhead* Michael Caine. *Colour Sgt. Bourne* Nigel Green. *Pvt. Owen*

Ivo Emmanuel. *Sgt.* *Maxwell* Paul Daneman. *Cpl.* *Allen* Glynn Edwards. *Pvt.* *Thomas* Neil McCarthy. *Pvt.* *Hitch* David Kernan. *Pvt.* *Cole* Gary Bond. *Pvt.* *612 Williams* Peter Gill. *Lance corporal* Tom Gerard. *Surgeon Reynolds* Patrick Magee. *Pvt.* *593 Jones* Richard Davis. *Pvt.* *716 Jones* Denys Graham. *Gunner Howarth* Dafydd Havard. *Cpl.* *Schiess* Dickie Owen. *Hughes* Larry Taylor. *Sgt. Windridge* Joe Powell. *Stephenson* John Sullivan. *Sick man* Harvey Hall. *Adendorff* Gert van den Bergh. *Commissary Dalton* Dennis Folbigge. *Company cook* Kerry Jordan. *Bugler* Ronald Hill. *Cetewayo* Chief Buthelezi. *Jacob* Jacob Tshabalala. *Red Garters* Ephraim Mohele. *Dance leader* Simon Burton. *Prolog narrator* Richard Burton. ¶A British production released in England in January 1964 running 135 minutes with a BBFC U certificate. Regardless of what various sources claim, Richard Burton's commentary did appear on British prints. Cyril Endfield also cowrote the prequel *Zulu Dawn* (American Cinema, 1980).

Zuravli v nebe (1978). Filmed in Sovscope 70. *Screen author* V. Merezko. *Director* S. Samsonov. *Operator* E. Guslinskiy. *Artists* S. Voronkov, V. Kostrin and L. Zbruev. *Sound operator* O. Uienik. *Music and compositions* V. Levashova, D. Tukhmanova and A. Zatsepina. ¶A Mosfilm production. International distribution Sovexportfilm. Sovcolor. Six-track magnetic stereophonic sound. 91 minutes. Filmed at Mosfilm Studios, Moscow, R.S.F.S.R. ¶CAST: A. Demiyanenko, S. Ziaditdinov, L. Zaytseva, L. Akhedzakova, V. Pavlov, I. Rizkov, N. Skorobogatov, S. Suborova, L. Arinina and N.

Grabbe. ¶A Soviet production released in Russia in 1978.

Zvezda nadezdi *see* **The Star of Hope.**

Zvezda zkrana (1974). Filmed in Sovscope 70. *Screen authors* B. Ratser, V. Konstantin and V. Gorikker. *Based on the operetta* "*Net menya schastlivee*" *by* A. Eshtsaya. *Music* A. Eshpay. *Director* V. Gorikker. *Operator* V. Bazilev. *Artist* B. Komyakov. *Sound operator* B. Golev. ¶A Kievskaya kinostudiya im. M. Gorikogo production. International distribution Sovexportfilm. Sovcolor. Six-track magnetic stereophonic sound. 90 minutes. Filmed at kinostudiya im. M. Gorikogo, Gorki, R.S.F.S.R. ¶CAST: V. Smelkova, V. Vasilieva, M. Pugovkin, G. Mnatsakanova, N. Merzlikin, A. Lazarev, Yu. Puzirev, V. Iliichev, G. Bogdanova-Chesnokova and S. Kramarov. ¶A Soviet production released in Russia in 1974.

Zvezdi ne gashut (1971). Filmed in Sovscope 70. *Screen authors* I. Guseynov and A. Ibragimov. *Director* A. Ibragimov. *Operator* A. Temerin. *Artist* E. Chernyaev. *Composer* A. Melikov. *Sound operator* V. Belyarov. *Song text* O. Gadzikasimova and F. Gadzi. ¶A Mosfilm production. International distribution Sovexportfilm. Sovcolor. Six-track magnetic stereophonic sound. 130 minutes. Filmed at Mosfilm Studios, Moscow, R.S.F.S.R. ¶CAST: V. Samoylov, E. Samoylov, V. Vinogradov, T. Archvadze, B. Mulaev, N. Samushiya, A. Askerova, T. Voloshina, Z. Veliev, O. Khabalov, I. Osmanli, A. Iskenderov, N. Samoylova, S. Sokolovskiy and A. Ibragimov. ¶A Soviet production released in Russia in 1971.

Afterword

This book is a history of certain film technologies. Like all history books, it is full of memories.

We remember Lowell Thomas spreading his arms and announcing "This is Cinerama!" and the curtains opening, and opening, and opening up to expose the gigantic panoramic screen . . . we remember six tracks of cannon fire booming at the Alamo . . . planes flying overhead in the South Pacific . . . ducking pounding hoofs of stampeding buffalo when the West was being won . . . Rex Harrison walking, talking and singing across the screen to his fair lady . . . . If you were there, we hope this book has helped you remember those wonderful things and many more. If you weren't there, then perhaps in some way this book will have helped you to understand the majesty, the magic and the thrills that once were a part of motion pictures.

Linwood G. Dunn on the miniature set for It's a Mad, Mad, Mad, Mad World *with the "new single-lens Super Cinerama" camera, actually an Ultra Panavision 70 unit.*

Index

This index does not include page references for the Filmography, as those titles are in alphabetical order and thus easily located. Film titles in this index are given in *italics;* process names are in **boldface.**

H

CEDAR CREST COLLEGE LIBRARY

3 1543 50153 1018

778.53 C312w

Carr, R

Wide s

778.53 C312w

Carr, Robert E.

Wide screen movies

**Cressman Library
Cedar Crest College**
Allentown, Pa. 18104

DEMCO